Noble Power i. _
from the Reformation to the Revolution

Why do the wicked live on, growing old and increasing in power?

They see their children established around them, their offspring before their eyes.

Their homes are safe and free from fear; the rod of God is not upon them.

Their bulls never fail to breed; their cows calve and do not miscarry.

They send forth their children as a flock; their little ones dance about.

They sing to the music of the tambourine and harp; they make merry to the sound of the flute.

They spend their years in prosperity and go down to the grave in peace.

Job 21:7–13 (New International Version)

Jesus answered, 'You would have no power over me if it were not given to you from above.'

John 19:11 (New International Version)

Noble Power in Scotland
from the Reformation to the Revolution

Keith M. Brown

EDINBURGH
University Press

To Jenny Wormald

© Keith M. Brown, 2011, 2013

First published in 2011 by
Edinburgh University Press Ltd
22 George Square, Edinburgh EH8 9LF
www.euppublishing.com

This paperback edition 2013

Typeset in Ehrhardt by
Norman Tilley Graphics Ltd, Northampton
and printed and bound in Great Britain by
CPI Group (UK) Ltd, Croydon CR0 4YY

A CIP record for this book is available from the
British Library

ISBN 978 0 7486 1298 7 (hardback)
ISBN 978 0 7486 6466 5 (paperback)
ISBN 978 0 7486 2823 0 (webready PDF)
ISBN 978 0 7486 8119 8 (epub)
ISBN 978 0 7486 8120 4 (Amazon ebook)

The right of Keith M. Brown
to be identified as author of this work
has been asserted in accordance with
the Copyright, Designs and Patents Act 1988.

Published with the support of the Edinburgh
University Scholarly Publishing Initiatives Fund.

Contents

Tables

Acknowledgements

This volume is a companion to an earlier work, *Noble Society in Scotland. Wealth, Family and Culture from Reformation to Revolution* (Edinburgh, 2000), that I planned to finish long ago. A shift in the emphasis of my career into university management and the need to concentrate on the *Records of the Parliaments of Scotland* with the accompanying volumes of *The Scottish Parliament* brought about what is a very long delay in publication. I am enormously grateful to Edinburgh University Press for their patience when many other publishers might have given up. Whether this longer period of gestation has improved the eventual output is for others to decide, but it has certainly seen a continuous flow of research on early modern European nobilities that affirms their tenacious hold on power.

Thank you to Dr David Adamson, who conducted some of the preliminary research for Chapter 5; to Professor Steve Murdoch and Dr Alan MacDonald, who read and commented on a number of the chapters; and to Professor Hamish Scott and Dr Jenny Wormald, who did likewise for the entire volume. Along with other colleagues with whom I have talked and argued over the years they have all forced me to think again and again about the core issue of political power and how it was exercised in early modern Scotland. My interest in the political role of Scotland's noble families was ignited by Jenny Wormald's inspirational teaching at the University of Glasgow when I was a junior honours undergraduate in 1977–8. The influence of her ideas on my own thinking is ongoing and this book is dedicated to her.

Much of the research for this book was carried out in the University Library at St Andrews, in the National Library of Scotland and the National Archives of Scotland, and I am grateful to the staff in each of these institutions for their expertise and helpfulness. The map was drawn by the Reprographic Services at the University of St Andrews and made use of information provided by Ian Morrison in P. G. B. McNeill and H. L. McQueen (eds), *Atlas of Scottish History to 1707* (Scottish Medievalists, Edinburgh, 1996), 15.

Finally, thank you to my wife, Janice, who alone knows the true cost and who can be forgiven for wishing a plague on all their houses.

Glossary

assythment	a mutually agreed level of compensation between parties, often as part of a wider settlement of a feud
baron	tenant-in-chief and lowest rank of the nobility
barony	a legal jurisdiction and franchise of court powers granted to a landlord by the crown, the lowest level of the Scottish legal system
buannachan	professional soldier serving Highland chiefs
convention of estates	assembly of estates summoned by the king with less formal powers than parliament
court of session	college of justice, highest civil law court
feu-ferm (feuing)	practice of land tenure which boomed from the early sixteenth century, whereby tenants made an annual payment for their land (feu or feu-duty), increasingly of money rather than goods
fine	clan elite
general assembly	highest court of the Church of Scotland
kirk session	lowest level of court in Protestant Church of Scotland
laird	a landed proprietor, possibly of baronial status
lords of erection	peerages created by parliament from former abbatial estates
master of	courtesy title accorded to eldest sons of peers
new extent	a measure of land valuation for the purposes of taxation that was introduced in 1474 to replace the old extent which dated from the thirteenth century
regality	legal jurisdiction granted by the crown to substantial landlords, which included exemption from royal intervention in judicial matters, saving the four pleas of the crown (murder, treason, arson, rape)
repledge	legal process of recalling a case from the jurisdiction of one court to that of another

teinds	tithes: tenth of the produce of the lands of a church parish, nominally for the upkeep of the local church and clergy
thane	Anglo-Saxon term denoting either landed status or a jurisdictional office similar to sheriff; introduced to Scotland by twelfth century at least
tutor	legal guardian of a minor and executor of their affairs
wapenschaw	weaponshow or muster conducted principally under the authority of the sheriff
warden	one of three Border officers appointed to govern a march

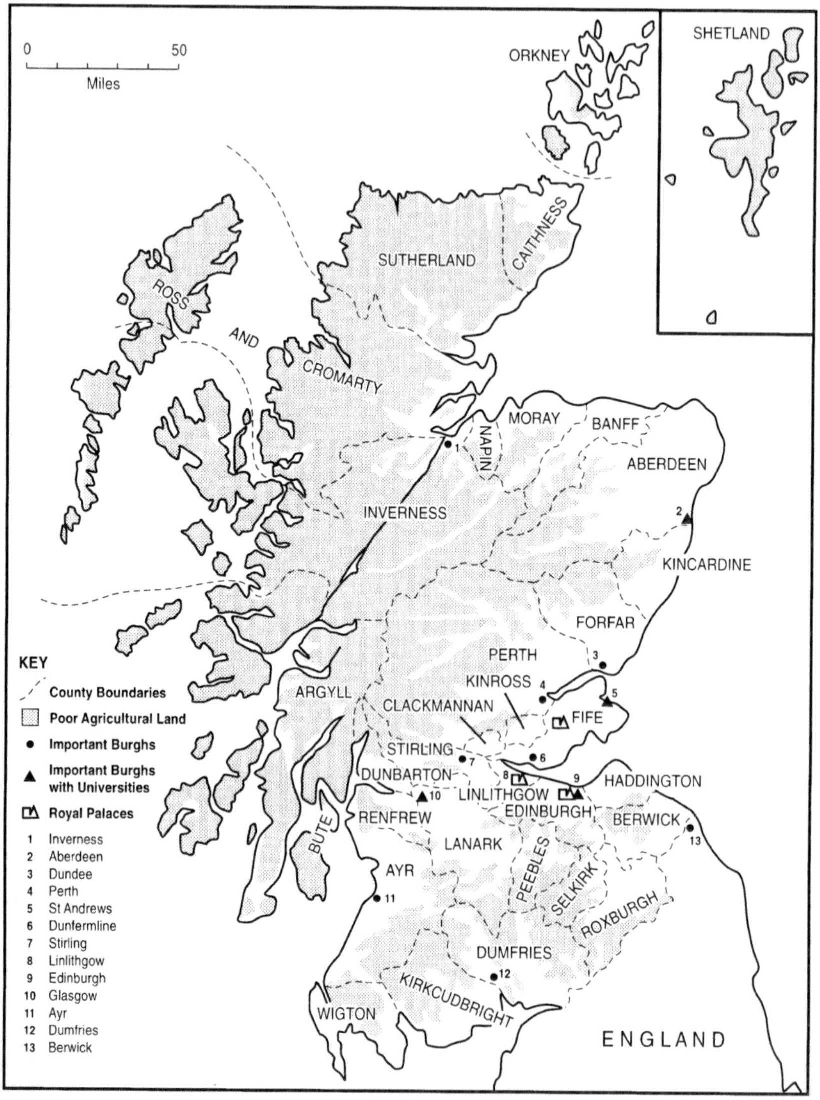
0
50
Miles
ORKNEY
SHETLAND
SUTHERLAND
CAITHNESS
ROSS
AND
CROMARTY
MORAY
BANFF
NAIRN
ABERDEEN
INVERNESS
KINCARDINE
FORFAR
PERTH
KINROSS
ARGYLL
CLACKMANNAN
FIFE
STIRLING
DUNBARTON
HADDINGTON
LINLITHGOW
EDINBURGH
RENFREW
BERWICK
BUTE
LANARK
AYR
PEEBLES
SELKIRK
ROXBURGH
DUMFRIES
KIRKCUDBRIGHT
WIGTON
ENGLAND
KEY
County Boundaries
Poor Agricultural Land
Important Burghs
Important Burghs with Universities
Royal Palaces
1 Inverness
2 Aberdeen
3 Dundee
4 Perth
5 St Andrews
6 Dunfermline
7 Stirling
8 Linlithgow
9 Edinburgh
10 Glasgow
11 Ayr
12 Dumfries
13 Berwick

Scotland *c.* **1600.** The shaded areas represent medium- and poor-quality land. Based upon P. G. B. McNeill and H. L. MacQueen (eds), *Atlas of Scottish History to 1707* (Scottish Medievalists, 1996), 15 (Ian Morrison).

CHAPTER I

Noble Power and Politics, 1560–1603

Power can be measured in many different ways and political power is usually an outward expression of deeper forms of power embedded in society. Like nobilities elsewhere in early modern Europe, the Scottish nobility's predominance rested on economic, familial and cultural forms of power, which in the latter half of the sixteenth century and the early decades of the seventeenth century faced unprecedented challenges from inflation, massive shifts in land ownership, rising population, educational reform and religious revolution. The response of the nobility was to adapt, initiating the entrepreneurial exploitation of their estates, optimising the deployment of their family members, embracing the new learning and engaging with confessional issues. Consequently, while individual noble houses were ruined, noble society shifted and changed but remained intact, rooted in the deep soil of enormous landed wealth, strong family bonds and a pervasive cultural dominance.[1] In this volume the focus is on political power and the functions or roles through which nobles exercised that power. In understanding how nobles acquired, maintained and expressed their power as chiefs, lords, magistrates, soldiers, governors and courtiers it is possible to appreciate the extent, strengths and vulnerabilities of their political power. The interrelated structures, ideas and relationships that wind their way through all of these roles provided the tools with which nobles manoeuvred to seek advantages and enhance the position of their house and lineage. The threats were constant and enormous, not least from other nobles, and some individuals and some lineages played this highly competitive game better than others. A challenge of a different sort came from a more assertive crown. The European-wide debate over what at one time was seen as a backward-looking, traditional nobility and a forward-looking early modern monarchy has moved on, and the continuity and dynamism of noble power sits alongside a more refined awareness of the limits of royal absolutism.[2] In Scotland, political revolution, deep religious division and widespread feuding formed the political context in which crown–noble relations were renegotiated. But a fundamental and unpredictable reordering of that context was created by the regal union of 1603 when James VI succeeded to the crowns of England and Ireland. This volume suggests that the continuities in noble power during this period were far greater than the changes, and that while the creation of a British imperial monarchy posed a threat to that power, the underlying grip the nobility enjoyed at a local and national level was undisturbed.

An analysis of Scottish politics in 1595 concluded that the power of the king of Scotland 'is concentrated in the nobility of the realm'.[3] In the context of late medieval and early modern European kingdoms this observation is unremarkable, since governments relied extensively on noble power to carry out their activities. Crown and nobility needed one another, and the likes of Venice and a handful of other Italian and Swiss city-states where a noble oligarchy governed without a king were exceptions. In the course of the later sixteenth century the United Provinces constituted itself as a republic, but on the whole Europe continued to be governed by partnerships of kings, or other hereditary rulers, and nobles. The question for even the most aggressive of kings was never one of eradicating their nobles, something that was neither desirable nor possible, but of constructing an acceptable working relationship with them. Strong adult kings aggregated power to themselves, occasionally wiping out great magnate families who represented real or perceived threats to their own pre-eminence. Occasionally, kings were assassinated, either because they were too strong, or because they were weak, and at times the power of the crown in individual kingdoms declined, most commonly during unsuccessful foreign warfare or civil war, weak and incompetent governance, or prolonged royal minorities. Late medieval Scotland experienced all of the above so that the power of the Stewart dynasty waxed and waned. Noble power, consequently, fluctuated, and while the role of 'overmighty magnates' can be exaggerated, there is no doubt that the nobility exercised enormous collective power within the late medieval kingdom.[4]

During the middle decades of the sixteenth century royal authority suffered significant reverses: the early death of James V in 1542, the succession of an infant daughter, Mary, English and French military intervention, the defeat of the Guise regency and Protestant Reformation in 1560 and the overthrow of Mary in 1567 cumulatively eroded the crown's ability to function effectively.[5] Further minority government, civil war, successive rebellions and coups, political upheaval and widespread feuding ensured that the instability continued for another three decades. This was the political context in which up to 1500 noble houses competed for advantage in the localities, while seeking the protection of greater lords. Consequently, those fifty families that by the mid-sixteenth century constituted the higher nobility of peerage houses benefited most, along with a smaller number of the more powerful untitled baronial houses, generally consolidating power in the localities and dominating royal political institutions. This process was most marked in regions distant from the centre of royal power, in the Highlands, the Borders, the northeast and the southwest where a handful of noble houses were dominant. James VI did not begin to redress this imbalance until his emergence as a young ruler in the early 1580s, it was the mid-1590s before the scales tipped in his direction. Even at the regal union in 1603 there was nothing to indicate that his own death would not lead to a reversal of his recent, and modest, achievements. By the time James VI inherited the English throne he had succeeded only in bringing back into balance that relationship of mutual dependence between king and nobles that the political community recognised as necessary in a stable commonweal.[6]

The Reformation of 1560 profoundly affected the course of Scottish history, and in the immediate aftermath religion remained high on the political agenda. Because of their public roles, the religious faith of the nobility, like that of kings, cannot be considered entirely within the realm of the private, or inner, life.[7] Throughout early modern Europe nobles played a crucial role in the success or failure of the Reformation and the subsequent Counter Reformation, while decisions taken by territorial rulers with regard to matters of faith were enormously important in determining the future course of religion in that territory, a principle conceded by the Holy Roman Emperor in the 1555 peace of Augsburg. Even at the level of the lesser magistracy, the individual choice of magnates impacted on the communities over which they had authority. In France, the inability of the crown to enforce its will on the localities allowed nobles to pursue their own religious agendas, leading to a series of civil wars in which rival noble factions became aligned with confessional allegiances.[8] Scotland, too, experienced a phase of civil conflicts between 1558 and 1594 that amounted to intermittent religious warfare, although like the struggle between Catholic and Protestant elsewhere, it was never only about religion.

Unsurprisingly, a period of prolonged civil and religious strife, in which the principal law enforcers in the localities were engaged in conflict, impacted on general levels of law and order. In a feuding society this was especially destructive, removing the restraints that communities needed to ensure that bloodfeud did not cause social disintegration. Political and religious divisions were grafted onto existing local tensions, and disputes over honour, economic resources or killings became entangled with King's Men and Queen's Men or Protestant and Catholic. Noble power was exercised in its most naked and violent form as much to defeat local rivals as it was to support or oppose royal authority, or to promote or defeat a confessional position. The result was a political situation in which the weakening of royal authority, the fracturing of the confessional community and the rampant increase in feuding combined to unleash the more destructive aspects of noble power.

Resistance and Obedience

Late medieval Scotland experienced few successful rebellions, and although individual kings were killed in 1437 and 1488, the reaction of the political community was to condemn the former and cover over the latter in a fiction that the king had been slain accidentally.[9] But in the 1560s the political conservatism that had served the Stewart dynasty well for almost two hundred years was overturned. Scotland experienced successful revolution in 1559–60 and again in 1567–8, as well as a series of palace coups in 1578, 1580, 1582, 1583 and 1585 that attained their objectives of removing the counsellors around the king. There were also failed rebellions or coups in 1562, 1565, 1584, 1587, 1588, 1589, 1591, 1592, 1593, 1594, 1596 and 1600. On the whole, rebellion was a resort undertaken by normally loyal and co-operative lords who had been provoked by the king or his advisers. Nevertheless, it is difficult to avoid concluding that the political culture of the later sixteenth century altered to one in which open defiance of the crown was more likely than in previous decades.

Sixteenth-century historians commonly placed kings and great noble houses at the centre of Scotland's story, underlining their importance in preserving the kingdom's liberties from foreign oppressors and tyrannical rulers. Unusually, in his *History of Greater Britain* (1521) John Mair argued that the kingdom's future was best served by a powerful crown working in cooperation with a stronger order of lesser nobles freed from dependence on the magnates. Although Mair disapproved of royal tyranny, he was unsympathetic to noble houses, like the Black Douglases who had been destroyed by fifteenth-century kings, and he displayed disdain for chivalric virtues, denouncing feuding, and being critical of the connection between land-holding and maintenance. On the other hand, while Hector Boece explicitly warned against rebellion, noble society preferred his more deferential *Scotorum historiae* (1526), and his retelling of successful efforts by individual nobles to restrain royal oppression gained widespread popular currency.[10] Therefore, when the eighth earl of Angus allegedly commented that 'it is good for kings sometimes that their hands bee held', he was drawing on a long-established tradition. Indeed, there was little novelty in the idea that the power of late medieval kings was limited, even if it was grounded more in episodic historical events than in any coherent resistance theory or constitutional understanding.[11] The Reformation, the unstable years of Mary's personal rule and the civil war of 1567–73 sucked the nobility into a dangerous struggle in which personal, family, local and national issues meshed. Thus, when in *c.* 1579 the imprisoned queen reflected on her experiences of Scottish politics, she commented that 'most commonly the spirits of that country were fickle, and that the policy was turned and evil governed rather by surnames than otherwise, which bred factions and inconveniences in every estate'.[12] Certainly, it is possible to interpret the civil war as a conflict among noble houses. George Buchanan's black propaganda against the Hamiltons in 1570, 'Ane admonitioun to the trew lordis', conveys a sense of dynastic politics, of Hamiltons and Stewarts vying for control over the kingdom. At worst, this civil dissension might be interpreted as family bloodfeuds in which the public good was subordinated to private interests. This is a view of the Marian civil war that sir James Melville of Halhill put into the mouth of the regent Mar, who argued that 'nother King nor Quen was in any of ther myndis, bot only pouffit be ther awen parcialites of ambition, gredines, and vengeance'. By April 1570, following the murder of the regent Moray, the duke of Chatelherault suggested that the conflict was spreading, with factions composed of 'not only the persons of the nobility, but descending from them to the gentlemen and commons universally in the "haile liegis"'. Here was the anarchic chasm into which a divided nobility might fall, but it was one that Chatelherault had fostered, Moray being killed by the duke's client. It is a reminder that for the higher nobility political instability was not desirable. When sir William Kirkcaldy of Grange expressed the wish that Elizabeth I would bring the conflict to an end by securing a 'union of this nobility', he too was reflecting a view that the war was being waged by rival noble lineages.[13] It is tempting to view this decline into a series of interlinked local wars as evidence of Scotland's relative political immaturity, a product of the kingdom's weak institutions, over-mighty warlords and violent culture. But comparisons with late medieval and later sixteenth-century France reveal there the same spiral into civil war and bloodfeud driven on by political ideology, religion and the ambitions of rival noble houses who saw in rebellion and warfare an opportunity for reward and advancement.[14]

In 1571, William Maitland, younger of Lethington, anticipated the practical and ideological difficulties facing the adult James VI who 'shall find no kingdom at all apt for rule, but in place therof a confused chaos and a country divided into 200 or 300 kingdoms resembling Shane O'Neil's whereof every one will be a king in his own bounds'. Lethington's astute predictions were echoed elsewhere. Two decades later, the equally conservative Halhill thought the reverence due to the prince 'is mekle decayed in this contre'. He conceded that there had always been a tension between kings and nobility; what he described as 'the auld emulation that hes lested betwen the Kingis of Scotland and ther nobilite'. Halhill identified throughout history a numerous, wealthy nobility made powerful by the social structures of kinship and lordship, and determined to withstand absolute power either indirectly, or by open and forceful resistance. Facing the nobility was a poor crown, lacking the means to pay for soldiers, plagued by long minorities between reigns, and yet with aspirations 'to command absolutely as *soverain monarque*'.[15]

Other observers were even more critical. A report compiled in *c.* 1580 for the English government identified an over-powerful nobility as the root cause of an unstable polity, so dominating society that the entire community 'follow the lords quarrels either among themselves or against the Prince, wherby the Prince and commonwealth is ever waving like a boat on the sea tossed to and fro *vento nobilitatis et vulgi fluctibus*'. To a Tudor official like lord Burghley it was surprising that the Scottish nobility 'ar not acqueynted with absolut government of ther King but rather ar them selves in a sort absolut'. Elizabeth I's lord treasurer misunderstood the informal nature of power in Scotland, but he was not entirely wrong: the mid-sixteenth century did see a tipping of the scales of power towards the localities and the private, hereditary powers of a nobility 'so linked by blood or allied one with another … there is no possibility that he [= the king] dare deal with his nobility as he would and should'. Hence the persistent attempts by Elizabeth I to employ nobles as instruments of English foreign policy. Nor was the road back for the crown an easy one, and in June 1593, in the aftermath of the Spanish blanks affair, an English diplomat commented, 'This state has slidden so deeply into confusion that the King's power does not suffice to recover it. Few noblemen seek to relieve, but many of them practise to exchange or else overthrow it.' A decade after beginning his personal rule, James VI was still labouring with the legacy of religious and political revolution, and it was commonly said in public that the people 'had neither luck nor grace since the King was first born, nor better to be looked for as long as he lived'. Even in 1600 an English agent reported that, such was the level of discontent, 'if any should take upon them, the country I fear would all back them against this government'.[16]

In James VI's defence, no previous Stewart king had to overcome such forbidding obstacles. One significant change from the late medieval period was the shift in political language as religious upheaval proved to be the midwife to a new and dangerous vocabulary of resistance. In the late 1550s, John Knox deployed the idea of an inferior magistracy to urge the nobility to fulfil a prior calling to God above those obligations owed to the king, warning that failure to act decisively might lead to a loss of political control to others who were willing to answer God's call. It was a challenge to which the Protestant lords responded, and in December 1557 the Lords of the Congregation signalled their preparedness to 'apply our whole power, substance and our verray lyves, to manteane, sett forward, and establish the most blessed word of God and his Congregation'. Two years later, in a letter to the regent Guise, the Protestant nobility intimated that opposition to the crown was a matter of conscience. Human institutions that acted contrary to God's divine purposes in fulfilment of that covenant entered into between God and the elect were to be overthrown. Those bands made by the Protestant lords in 1559 placed loyalty to religion above obedience to the crown, and the Lords of the Congregation declared that the duty of the nobility was 'to brydle the fury and raige of wicked men, wer it of Princes or Emperouris'. This line of thinking culminated in October 1559 when an assembly of Protestant lords met to discuss the practical problem of what to do about the regent Guise. The third lord Ruthven opened a debate in which the preacher, John Willock, argued that since Guise was guilty of failing to provide justice to the people, or to defend the subjects against foreign conquest, and since she denied their right to hear God's Word preached freely, 'the borne Counsallouris, Nobilitie, and Baronis of the realme' could legitimately deprive her of authority. This was a seminar in revolutionary theory and it was followed by revolutionary action as Mary was removed from office by an act of suspension, authority being transferred to a godly council of nobles. Subsequently, the prophetic, revolutionary rhetoric was toned down to avoid any hint of popular insurrection, or of acting outside the law, while every effort was made to have the Reformation approved by parliament. Yet while the *First book of discipline* (1560) underlined the necessity of recognising and submitting to lawful authority, the Protestant nobility and clergy ominously agreed that a prince might be compelled to live within the law.[17]

Throughout Mary's personal reign of 1561–7 she aroused considerable noble opposition, although much of the criticism took the form of traditional complaints about 'bad counsel' by frustrated and jealous rivals. The first earl of Moray accused Mary of being influenced by David Rizzio to the point that she 'misregaurded the advyse of her nobilitie'. At Rizzio's murder in March 1566, the third lord Ruthven supposedly lectured the queen on the need to follow the advice of the nobility, warning her of the calamities that had overtaken kings who ignored such counsel. It was a persistent and not entirely unjustifiable accusation made against Mary that she refused to listen to her nobles 'contrar the ancient custoum'. Nevertheless, the rebel propaganda of June 1567 exaggerated the queen's alleged plan to encompass the 'overthraw and distruction of the nobilitie and haill state of this common weill'.[18] The uprising against Mary in 1567 went beyond the removal of a tyrannical adviser, the fourth earl of Bothwell, leading to the queen's imprisonment and enforced abdication by a more radical faction of the rebels. In parallel with developments among French Huguenots in the 1560s, Scottish Protestants embraced a theory of resistance, and it was George Buchanan who provided the justification. Buchanan updated Boece's history, and embedded within his *De jure regni apud Scotos* (unpublished until 1579) theories of elective kingship, contractual government and resistance based on humanist thinking and natural law that placed on the nobility the function of regulating relations between the prince and his subjects. Although the estates played a crucial role in formally approving the overthrow of royal authority in 1560, 1567 and 1582, Buchanan gave no explicit emphasis to parliament, or any other institutional mechanism by which this regulation of the crown might be effected, but left the political initiative to a publicly-spirited nobility. National history was wedded to the idea of an ancient constitution in which the nobles acted as arbiters on behalf of the community when faced with tyrannical kings. Even more than Boece, Buchanan constructed in his *Rerum Scoticarum historia* (1582) a world akin to republican Rome through which ran Livian themes of civic virtue. Here a constitutional monarchy shared power with the nobility, the *primores*, who guaranteed freedom from tyranny.[19] It was on this issue that the civil war was primarily fought.

Resistance ideas continued to appeal to some nobles beyond the civil war, surfacing as justification for seizure of the young king by a faction opposed to the courtiers at the Ruthven raid in August 1582. That deed was welcomed by the general assembly of the church and approved by a convention of estates in October. But faced with an adult, male and Protestant king who wished to free himself from restraints, such revolutionary rhetoric had a diminishing appeal and nobles found recourse in an older language of resistance that focused on bad counsel. The first duke of Lennox was accused of plotting against the Protestant religion, perverting the law and constitution, and endeavouring the 'wreck of the nobility' who, it was claimed, were excluded from court and prevented from offering counsel to the king. Lennox and his ally, the earl of Arran, were presented as ruthless upstarts who desired 'not onlie to be equals, but superiors to the ancient nobilitie' and who were bent on 'ascribing to his Majestie the odious title of an absolut power'. John Colville, the most likely author of the *Historie and life of king James the sext*, saw the fall of the first duke of Lennox in terms of the nobility acting to redress the political balance, but he questioned the motives of the Ruthven lords, perceiving the nobility's historic role to be as 'extraordinar correctors of Prences enormiteis in Scotland, rather for advancement of thair awin particulers than for any gude zeale that thay bure to the commonweill'.[20]

Allegations of evil counsel continued to be at the heart of the opposition to chancellor Arran following his return to power in 1583, the failed coup of April 1584 being justified as an attempt to remove morally corrupt and seditious men of low birth who aimed at the 'ruine of the greatest number of the ancient nobilitie of this realme'. The aggrieved nobles issued proclamations from exile, claiming to be acting 'according to the ancient lawes of Scotland, used when kings are misgoverned by evil counsell'. Yet the parameters within which rebellion could be articulated were narrowing as James VI came of age. The proclamation justifying the successful actions of the rebel lords in November 1585 referred only to the threat posed to the king, the nobility and the commonweal by evil counsel. The triumphant rebels ritually threw themselves at the king's feet, craving mercy, and while James called them traitors and their actions treasonable, he had no option but to pardon them and appoint them to office. In fact, the rebellion was settled by force of arms, and the king was forcefully deprived of his servants and compelled to accept into his government men he distrusted. In spite of the absence of resistance ideology there was no disguising the fact that 'the laughfull Prence [was] depryvit from his auctorite', a humiliation that James VI did not forget.[21] Yet in the context of a discussion about a provocative sermon by John Craig questioning the king's authority, the 'godly' eighth earl of Angus refused to embrace the quasi-republican version of civic responsibility urged on him by his secretary, David Hume of Godscroft, saying only that while it was right for the nobility to pursue their own particulars, the king could not be forced on public matters. Angus was vulnerable to the accusation that having overthrown the 'wicked men' about the king, the subsequent failure to deliver the presbyterian agenda in parliament made his actions appear self-interested. In rejecting this point, Angus insisted that in spite of the recent actions 'profitably and necessarily practised (divers times before) in this Kingdome', it was essential that 'every thing be rightly done'. He recognised the king's aspiration to be free to make his own decisions, and advocated the winning of the king's favour and agreement as long as it was done with 'commune consent', a reference perhaps to parliament. He conceded, however, that this approach was likely to be undermined by factional behaviour.[22]

The issue of evil counsel, especially when deployed in support of the nobility as the guarantors of political liberties, remained at the heart of factional politics. Part of the propaganda of the 1589 Brig o' Dee rebels was that the faction around chancellor Thirlestane intended 'to suppresse and roote out the ancient [n]obilitie', but few believed it, and the general reluctance to oppose the king ensured the collapse of the rebellion. Although led by a powerful coalition of lords, the lesser barons and lairds 'consideddering that his Majestie wes in propper persone upone the feildis, and the lordis quarrell to be sa frivole aganis theare awin native prince, they skayled [scaled = dispersed] ane and ane, and past away'.[23] The threat to the nobility was raised again following the king's visit to Denmark in 1589–90, when a number of disgruntled lords expressed the view that James VI should govern with his nobility 'and not by private persons hated, nor by order of Denmark, against the ancient rights and privileges of the nobility'. The ninth earl of Errol complained that Thirlestane was undermining the nobility, drawing on the mythology of the 1482 rebellion against James III as a source of inspiration:

> Whereupon he [Errol] and others were mynded to give him [Thirlestane] the like reward that was given to Coquharan, who serving under King James the third and offending generallie all the noblemen was sodainelie taken by the Erle of Angusse and others and hanged.

Similarly, a bond of c. 1590 claiming to speak for the nobility alleged that the Protestant religion was being subverted by men 'of base degree and small linage' who had acquired unwarranted influence, offices and dignities during the king's minority. Mutual support was offered to anyone who removed or killed these evil councillors.[24]

The fifth earl of Bothwell sought to align himself with this narrative of noble outrage in his feud with John Maitland of Thirlestane. Exploiting the unpopularity of the king and his officers in the aftermath of the murder of the second earl of Moray in February 1592, Bothwell's open letter to the clergy deployed radical resistance ideas, aligning his own cause with an imagined attack on the church, while highlighting the tyrannous nature of a government presided over by the chancellor. In his February 1593 apologia, Bothwell returned to the fabricated theme of Thirlestane as an evil counsellor, as one of a faction 'following the insolent inclination of all who are suddenly from base estate promoted to high places'. When Bothwell did carry out a successful palace coup in July 1593, he played out the expected ritual submission to the king, but James VI would not be reconciled to the earl who soon found himself a fugitive. In a letter to the presbytery of Edinburgh on 7 September 1594, Bothwell appealed to an imagined past when kings were disciplined by their nobles, and, like Errol, he advocated the need 'to put in practice the lovable custom of our progenitors at Lauder' when the nobles allegedly hanged James III's favourites. But since Bothwell was now in league with the Catholic earls his cause was thoroughly discredited.[25]

Underlying the unease about opposing an adult king was an understanding, acquired in the study of history, that even the greatest of noble families was subject to sudden collapse or prolonged decay.[26] Hence, men thought carefully about the risks involved in rebellion. In the autumn of 1561, within months of Mary's return from France, the duke of Chatelherault, former governor and premier noble of the kingdom, was worried that he was about to lose control of Dumbarton castle: 'For when ever she have that owte of my handes, I knowe that her mynde towardes me and my house cane not be good.' The duke's sense of his own vulnerability was prescient, and within the year he was publicly humiliated. Similarly, in 1575, lord Robert Stewart, half-uncle to James VI and terror of the northern isles, scurried south to enter ward in Edinburgh castle on the orders of the regent Morton. He suffered two-and-a-half years imprisonment before his political fortunes revived.[27] Such apprehension in the face of royal authority, even when wielded by a woman and the representative of a child monarch, was more common than open defiance because compliant obedience made sense given the ease with which even the greatest of noble houses could be broken. In 1562, the fourth earl of Huntly rebelled against Mary, but in spite of being 'the wisest, richest and man of greatest power in Scotland', Huntly was unable to mobilise sufficient support to overcome a royal army. At the battle of Corrichie on 28 October he was defeated, his once great power 'overthrowne with little adoe'. Similarly, the Hamilton family dominated mid-sixteenth-century Scotland, but in the spring of 1579 the kindred was swept aside by a coalition of their enemies. Two years later the Douglases came under attack from the crown. Arguably the earls of Argyll were uniquely able to withstand royal power because of the combination of geographical remoteness and numbers of followers, although even the fifth earl, described as a 'semi-sovereign prince', could not be confident of mounting a successful rebellion.[28]

One explanation for the crown's success in disposing of noble rebellions lies in the inherent conservatism of the majority of the political community, a conservatism expressed in sir Richard Maitland of Lethington's poem 'Aganis treasoun'. After all, in 1559–60 the rebellion against Mary of Guise widened its support by diluting the revolutionary propaganda, while the civil war that followed Mary's imprisonment was possible because a majority of nobles disapproved of her enforced abdication.[29] In his *Historie or chronicle of the hous of Seytoun*, written in *c.* 1559, Lethington encouraged the fifth lord Seton to 'be trew loyall and obedient to thy Princess, and authoritie of this thy native cuntrie'. The houses of Seton and Lethington were consistently committed to such orthodox ideas, and elsewhere Lethington advised his son 'Attour all thingis ay to thy Prince be trew'. The younger Lethington, at whom this advice was aimed, claimed that Mary's abdication was never the intention of those who faced her at Carberry Hill on 15 June 1567. In a satirical letter of 1570, written by Lethington's younger brother, Thomas Maitland, it was the regent Moray who was portrayed as the tyrant. The younger Lethington returned to John Mair's theme of an over-powerful nobility tyrannising over the localities, arguing that during royal minorities the nobility became over-powerful and factional. In the spring of 1572, he and sir William Kirkcaldy of Grange argued that history repeatedly indicated that during a minority the nobility established 'a tyranny over soche as dwell neare thame, not being equall to thame in powre, so that for the most part in every schyre ther is, as it wer, on, two, or a plurality of Kings'. The drift into lawlessness was especially dangerous since 'the inimity contracted particularly betwene two persons doth reache immediatly to the whole kyndreds, which is the more pernicious by reason of the greate clans and nombres of people which depend on the greatmen'. Here was a point to which James VI would return twenty-five years later. There was, therefore, a constituency within noble society that agreed with Alexander Gordon, bishop of Galloway, who, in a sermon on 17 June 1571, at the height of the civil war, preached that 'no inferiour subject hath power to deprive or depose their lawfull magistrat'.[30]

The predominance of conservative ideas acted as a limitation on the ability of nobles to muster popular support, a point observed by the fifth earl of Argyll and lord James Stewart when they admitted to sir James Croft in the summer of 1559 'how difficult it is to persuade a multitude to revolt of established authority'. That reluctance by cautious and self-interested dependants to follow lords in arms against the king, or his representative, ensured that most rebellions failed. As with Huntly's rebellion in 1562, the first earl of Moray's rebellion in the summer of 1565 collapsed because, in spite of the backing from powerful lords, 'the cuntrie people slipt from them, and left them but weaklie accompanied'. During the civil war, the fifth lord Hume, a Marian loyalist, discovered this to his cost when 'fynding that his friends had for the most pairt left him and syded with the King's partie', he had to take refuge with the garrison in Edinburgh castle in the company of a couple of servants. Throughout the war, the loyalty of dependants was often divided. While the fifth earl of Glencairn fought against the queen at Langside in 1568, six of his Cunningham lairds helped garrison Dumbarton castle for Mary. Magnates could not assume that clients would follow their political leadership, and both sides exploited the fear of lesser men that their lords could not protect them. When in 1569 a convention discussed the terms to be offered to rebels, the regent Moray made the distinction between the fifth earl of Huntly's servants, who would be comprehended within his submission, and his political dependants who had to make their own peace with the king.[31]

It is conceivable that the experience of war, remembered by one commentator as a time when 'gude policie and law, justice and equitie was bureit', encouraged a desire for greater stability and conservatism.[32] Halhill believed that 'God abhorris all sic subiectis as hypocritically under pretext of religion, tak occasion to rebell against ther natyf princes, for ambition, gredynes or any warldly respect'. This minor nobleman and courtier's orthodox view, that 'Subiectis suld displaice nane fra ther office' no matter the provocation, was typical of the political conservatism that coalesced around the young James VI after decades of disorder. He advocated the conventional idea that 'Gud obedience is the office of subiectis; for they suld esteam the estait of a maiestrat com down from God'.[33] Hence, the reluctance of lesser men to follow lords in what were often perceived as self-interested ventures such as the abortive Stirling coup in April 1584 when the barons of the Lothians and Fife ignored the appeals of the rebel lords, rallying instead to the king. In 1589, the sixth earl of Huntly's forces melted away when faced by the king, many of the barons of the north only having joined him under a false commission, while only six barons accompanied the fifth earl of Bothwell's first attempted coup at Holyrood on 27 December 1592.[34] Taking up arms against the king, or his officials, was not done lightly, and loyalty to lords was granted conditionally. Hence, the overwhelming majority of bonds of manrent and maintenance and bonds of friendship carried a reservation of allegiance to the king, a testament to the massive reservoir of loyalty to the crown in noble society.[35]

There was another persuasive factor in encouraging prudence: for unsuccessful rebels the cost of failure could be high. One anonymous contemporary adopted a conventional approach to the question of rebellion, seeing in the fates of rebels the just deserts of their treasons:

> As we ar gevin to understand be all historeis, that it is our dewtie of all degreis to obey and be reverent to heigher powers; be the contrare, I find few or nayne, that hes rebellit aganis thair laughfull princes or governors, bot they have bene chastesit in sik sort that thay escapit not unpuneist.[36]

Here was a message that kings and their servants reinforced, not least through a broad definition of treason. Laws regarding treason varied throughout Europe. In England the main changes from the late medieval period was the crown's increasing willingness to apply existing laws, resulting, for example, in the savagery with which the Tudor government crushed the northern rebellion of 1569.[37] The general forfeiture of 1314 indicates the extremes to which the Scottish parliament might go in exacting punishment, but in terms of defining treason there was little beyond the vague wording of *Regiam majestatem*, an early fourteenth-century text, until the 1424 Act provided a statement of parliament's austere view on forfeiture. As the earl of Arran observed to John Knox in 1562, 'It is treassone to conceall treassone', and 'the unreasonable law of Scotland' allowed the crown to forfeit the heritage and goods of the criminal and those of his wife, even if she was innocent. The threat of permanent seizure of entailed property undermined those proprietary rights enshrined in feudal law, but while there was no legal mechanism for heirs to reclaim lost lands, it was common for rebels or their families to be pardoned and restored to their lands and titles. Some tinkering to better administer the process occurred in 1540, 1579, 1584, 1593, while in 1587 parliament added to the list of treasonable crimes at the same time as threatening the pains of treason to anyone who made an accusation of treason that could not be substantiated. In 1540, parliament insisted that the names of forfeited families should be recorded in order to preserve the memory of their treason, a practice implemented in sir David Lindsay's armorial two years later.[38]

Yet James VI thought forfeiture should be deployed sparingly in cases of 'odious crimes', and noble society shared his conservatism, hence, an English commentator's puzzlement in 1589 that 'a riot in England has a greater fine than high treason here', which is more a comment on Tudor brutality than Stewart mercy.[39] In a typical example of the king's leniency, following the eighth lord Maxwell's second rebellion in the spring of 1588, 'great instance and solsitation' was made on his behalf by friends, and after a short imprisonment Maxwell was released.[40] Following the 1589 rebellion the sixth earl of Huntly adroitly declared his innocence and unwillingness to contradict the king into whose will he entered, refusing to defend himself in court. By contrast, the eleventh earl of Crawford and the fifth earl of Bothwell refuted the charges, but were found guilty by an assize of their peers. James VI suspended judgment, but in July 1591 when Bothwell again defied the king, Huntly was formally forgiven and enlisted in the campaign against the rebellious earl whose forfeiture was now invoked.[41] At the parliament held in July 1593 the crown's plans to forfeit the Catholic earls were thrown into confusion when the king's lawyers disputed the legality of parliament proceeding with their forfeiture, and James VI expressed the view that parliament must 'be ruled in trials by fact'. The prosecution was stopped because the king did not want parliament to initiate political trials, but by the summer of 1594 circumstances had changed and James VI's wanted to forfeit the Catholic earls. Other nobles argued that the case had not been proven in court, and within the lords of the articles there was debate with four of the lords voting against the forfeiture. With most of the higher nobility not appearing to vote or abstaining, the forfeitures were passed by majority votes, largely due to the burgh commissioners.[42]

The difficulty in destroying a noble house was noted by English diplomats, one of whom expressed exasperation at the treatment of the Catholic earls in 1595: 'think not as I wrote long ago that so great a house can here be wrecked'. Common sense usually dictated compromise. The debate within the regent Moray's council in 1569 over the issue of pardoning the fifth earl of Argyll and the fifth earl of Huntly indicates a pragmatic realisation that these men were too powerful to be left outside a lasting political settlement. A persuasive argument in favour of this approach was that 'in civil wars nothing was so much to be looked unto as the weakening and dissolving of factions, which is the most easily wrought, when the prince reserves to himself the power of pardon and punishment'. Thus, in 1583 the Ruthven lords debated accepting remissions since this might imply a recognition of guilt to be exploited by their enemies at a later date. In fact, what amounted to the manipulation of temporary forfeiture by the crown was not untypical.[43] Restorations reflected changing political circumstances, or the recognition by the crown that enforcement was counterproductive. For example, the parliament of December 1585 passed an act for the restitution of a long list of forfeited nobles who now dominated the government.[44] As sir Thomas Hope of Craighall's early seventeenth-century list of forfeitures demonstrates, most cases resulted in some or all of the lands being restored to the family, or even to the individual himself, and the forfeiture being reduced. Where restorations did take place, there had to be no question of lingering doubt. The earldom of Sutherland was forfeited by parliament in 1563, but when the queen needed political support a technicality was discovered that allowed parliament to make a restoration *in integrum*, as though it had never taken place, rather than *ex gratia*, thus, having no effect on the rights and privileges of the Sutherland creations. Similarly, in reducing the fourth earl of Huntly's forfeiture, parliament declared that the 'memorie name dignitie honor and armez' of the late earl were to be restored as they were before his forfeiture.[45] The consequences for a noble house that was forfeited, however, could be catastrophic. As a result of the 1600 Gowrie conspiracy, the third earl of Gowrie and his brother were killed, the remainder of the family were persecuted and driven into exile or hiding, all the estates were seized and the name of Ruthven was outlawed.[46]

While the language used in pursuit of traitors was chilling, Halhill pointed out the near impossibility of executing nobles because of the bloodfeud that would follow, and an English observer made the same point after the capture of Huntly in 1589, writing that other nobles were unwilling to press for his punishment, being 'afrayde to toche him in blud'. In 1595, James VI complained that 'in other countries the councillors were the instruments that punished traitors, bute here everyone strives who may do most for them'.[47] This reluctance to shed blood does not mean that the crown was toothless, and the occasional show of butchery was deployed to underline the dreadful nature of treason. In 1562, John Gordon, a younger son of the fourth earl of Huntly, was hastily beheaded in Aberdeen following the battle of Corrichie, being 'pitifully mangled by an unskilful executioner'.[48] The former regent Morton was the first peer to be executed since 1516, being beheaded in June 1581 by the Maiden, a primitive guillotine. Morton thought the nobility would never condemn a man of his rank since it would be 'an ill precedent and preparative against themselves', but there was little doubt about the outcome of his trial, and Morton was convicted of involvement in the assassination in 1567 of the king's father, lord Darnley. He was scornful of the justice of his trial, wryly observing that 'there was nothing sought for but my life however it had bene'.[49] In a few instances the corpses of traitors were punished. The body of the fourth earl of Huntly was laid in a casket and brought before parliament in February 1563, four months after his death. On 28 August 1600, the court of justiciary sat in judgment on the bodies of the dead third earl of Gowrie and his brother, declaring that their corpses 'be hangit, quarterit, and drawin, in presens of the haill peopill'. Their severed heads were stuck on spikes above Edinburgh tollbooth 'ther to stand till the wind blow them offe', and Gowrie's head was still visible to travellers in 1636.[50] Although condemned nobles occasionally used scaffold confessions to affirm their guilt, the justice of their fate and the authority of the crown, there is little evidence for this in Scotland. At the trial of the first earl of Gowrie on 3 May 1584, he repeatedly demonstrated his contempt for the court, while on the scaffold he denied all the charges of which he had been convicted, criticising his enemies at court and advising his audience 'not to depend or put their confidence in kings or princes'.[51]

Reformation and Counter Reformation

Many factors ensured a Protestant triumph in Scotland in 1560. The inadequacy of the church hierarchy, the international context, the geographic spread of Protestantism, the power and commitment of individual nobles and a range of contingent issues were each important ingredients in that success.[52] Such was the political significance of the religious inclinations and commitment of the nobility that intelligence gatherers regularly compiled lists of Protestant and Catholic nobles in the decades after the Reformation. One Catholic commentator made the point in c. 1595 that the nobility could lead their vassals regardless of their own religious convictions because they were 'under the control of their lords and faithful to them'.[53] Of course, this equation was not always true, and in time different confessional allegiances between lord and man threatened to dissolve traditional loyalties. Never-theless, the practical necessity of relying on the power of the nobility was recognised by John Knox in his 1558 *Appelation to the nobility and estates in Scotland*, a manifesto urging the lesser magistrates to act since God had invested them with authority to overthrow the tyrannical government of the Roman Catholic Church and the regency of Mary of Guise. In flattering the nobility, Knox was recognising a political reality while constructing an ideology for shaping noble power to a godly purpose. John Calvin made the observation that magistrates were 'the most sacred and by far the most honourable of all stations in mortal life', but while Calvin had in mind some-thing like the magistracy of ancient Rome, or perhaps the French *noblesse de robe*, Knox had to adapt the language of civic Protestantism to an audience of hereditary territorial nobles. When he described the nobility as 'counsel-lours to their King, fathers of his peiple and defenders and meanteiners of his Kirk' he was writing as much out of need and hope as conviction.[54] This regard for the status quo continued to inform Knox's heirs, who compiled the *Second book of discipline* (1578) affirming that 'It is proper to kings, princes and magistrates to be callit lordis and dominatouris over thair subjectis quhom thay governe civile'. Religious leaders were frustrated by the caution and self-interest of individual nobles, and they railed against their spiritual and moral failings, reminding them that noble power was ulti-mately derived from their role as divinely approved magistrates, not from blood and lineage. But even the most radical of preachers did not question the hierarchic structures of their society.[55]

In the decades immediately before and after 1560, religious commitment among the higher nobility was rarely single-minded and was usually com-plicated, or even compromised, by political issues.[56] Nevertheless, the Protestant lords risked much in rebelling against Francis II and Mary, and there is no reason to doubt that religious conviction formed part of their calculations. At the time of the Chaseabout raid in 1565, the fifth earl of Argyll and his supporters claimed their rebellion was 'advansing of the glorie of God and the commoun welth' even if others saw it as an attempted coup by a disappointed faction of nobles.[57] At the core of the Protestant leadership was a group of predominantly young lords who were converted in the 1550s, or even earlier, men like the fourth earl of Glencairn, the fourth and fifth earls of Argyll, the fourth earl of Morton, the sixth lord Erskine, lord James Stewart and John Erskine of Dun who all wrote assuring John Knox of their steadfast support in 1557.[58] The geographic distribution of these Protestant nobles was widespread, but there were concentrations in regions like Angus, Ayrshire, Argyllshire and east Lothian. Possibly the strongest Protestant community was that of north and central Ayrshire, which provided crucial support in 1559–60 and where in 1562 over seventy local barons and burgesses signed a band pledging in the presence of Christ to 'manteane and assist the preaching of his holy Evangell'.[59]

At the Reformation parliament of August 1560, the fifth lord Lindsay spoke in support of the new Calvinist 'Confession of Faith', commenting 'nowe that it hathe pleased God to lett me see thys daye wher so maynie nobles and other have allowed so worthie a work, I will say with Simon, *Nunc dimittis*'. But the Protestant Reformation was only beginning, and the influence that the nobility wielded over Scotland's religious future did not end with the military victory of the Lords of the Congregation and their English allies in July 1560. The Reformation parliament was dominated by Protestant lords who flooded it with friends and dependants to ensure that the religious and diplomatic revolution would not lose momentum. The fourth earl of Glencairn attended parliament in the company of his eldest son and another nine kinsmen and dependants. Others, like the fourth earl Marischal, who was attended by a coterie of kinsmen, took the pragmatic view that since the Roman Catholic bishops failed to defend the church he had no option other than to support the Protestant legislative proposals.[60]

The religious revolution of the 1560s was the result of a partnership between magnates and ministers that produced remarkable agreement on doctrine and church government. It is apparent in the behaviour of evangelical nobles who participated in the iconoclastic destruction of 1561, severely damaging Paisley abbey by fire, and dismantling the greater part of the abbeys at Failford, Kilwinning and Crossraguel in Ayrshire.[61] Protestant lords sat in the general assembly as elders, and the new church directed appeals for the moral reformation of society to the noble dominated estates, petitioning about sabbath observance and sexual behaviour in 1563 and 1565. The general assembly sought noble expertise and authority in developing policy, as in 1563 when the fourth earl Marischal, the fifth lord Lindsay and William Maitland of Lethington were appointed by the general assembly to revise *The first book of discipline*. Two years later, the fifth earl of Argyll and the fourth earl of Glencairn, along with 'a great company of Lords, Barons and others' met with the clergy to consider the perceived threat to the church from the queen and her Catholic friends.[62]

That ideal of a partnership between magistrates and clergy survived into the following decade when nobles were involved in the editorial production of *The second book of discipline*, which in its discussion of 'the Office of Ane Christian Magistrat' envisaged a partnership committed to the building of a Christian commonweal. In 1586, James Melville expressed the hope that 'the Christian magistrat ought to have a care of religioun, and maters perteaning to the kirk, and employ his authoritie and power to the wealefare and good estat therof'. Such an obligation did not go without reward for Melville sought to reinforce the authority of the godly nobleman who 'is the minister and lieutenant of God, who has receaved the sword, cheeflie, to that effect'.[63] Protestant commentators and historians reinforced this image of the godly magistrate by fashioning a typology from the raw materials of inspiring lives, such as the first earl of Moray, the 'good regent' in whom

Christ's image 'did so cleerly shyne in that personage, that the devill, and the wicked to whom he is prince, could not abide it'. Others like the fifth earl of Argyll, the eighth lord Glamis and John Erskine of Dun were lauded by the clergy as fine exemplars of the Protestant nobleman.[64]

Yet there was tension between nobles and clergy. For many of the former the presence of a Catholic queen created subtle problems of loyalty, obedience and self-interest. In observing the behaviour of those Protestants who sought the queen's favour, Robert Campbell of Kingzeancleughe suggested to the second lord Ochiltree that he would soon have his zeal dampened 'when the holie water of the court sall be sprinkled upon you'. Knox, too, identified tensions, such as in June 1564 when the Protestant nobility attended the general assembly 'sum for assistance of the mynisteris, and sum to accuse thame', while Walter Lundie of that Ilk noted that some courtiers and privy councillors were putting distance between themselves and the rest of the 'bretherin'. A year later, that division became so pronounced that the general assembly sent a deputation to lobby these lukewarm lords. Nevertheless, nobles commonly attended the general assembly until the mid-1570s when attendance began to lapse.[65] At a local level, nobles enjoyed enormous ecclesiastical patronage, bringing political and financial advantages which they refused to surrender in order to fund the church's radical ambitions. Protestant nobles censored those aspects of the *First book of discipline* that were unpalatable at the convention held in January 1561, and clerical claims for additional funding were dismissed in the following year with the remark that 'Thair ar many Lordis have not so much to spend.' The church's financial proposals continued to be blocked over succeeding decades.[66]

While Knox's disregard for hierarchy may be exaggerated, and many of his pronouncements arose from his prophetic role within an orthodox tradition, the blunt assertion to Mary that it was his business 'to informe them [the nobles] of their duetie' was interpreted by some as provocative. He was not alone in being so direct, and even sympathetic nobles bridled at the licence some ministers sought, viewing it as subversive. It was said of the regent Morton that 'he could not suffer Christ to raigne freelie', and in 1574, he was outraged by the publication of John Davidson's book, *The dialogue betwixt the clerk and the courteour*, attacking the financial depletion of the church. The regent was equally irritated by the refusal of the lesser nobility of Kyle to withdraw their support for the combative academic.[67] Furthermore, the Protestant emphasis on the Word of God raised to a higher level of authority a source that lay outside the honour society. As early as 1558, Knox warned the nobility that they received 'honour, tribute and homage at Goddis Commandiment, not be reasson of your birth and progene ... but be reassoun of your office and dewtie'. In pursuit of the need to reform society as a whole *The second book of discipline* was uncompromising on the reciprocal relationship between civil and ecclesiastical authority, stating that just as ministers were subject to the former in civil matters, 'swa aucht the persone of the magistrat be subject to the kirk spirituallie and in ecclesias-tical government'. Here was a point of tension as the evangelical clergy endeavoured to refashion the nobility into godly magistrates. The danger for the clergy lay in provoking a reaction such as in July 1584 when John Craig's sermon on Psalm 82 provoked chancellor Arran to warn Craig that he had 'exceeded the bounds of his text', and he threatened 'to bring him and his fellows to another pass ere long'. Two years later, Patrick Adamson, archbishop of St Andrews, gave conservative fears a voice, claiming in his *Appellation* that the presbyterian clergy were trying to exclude the magis-tracy from decision-making within the church altogether.[68] Furthermore, some nobles were unwelcome as partners in the building of God's kingdom, and the church's insistence that authority be wielded only by those nobles 'knowin to be plainne and true professours of the Evangell' was at odds with the hereditary exercise of authority. While the church was urging nobles to exercise power in its defence, strengthening the right to resist the crown, in shifting the emphasis of the grounds of noble authority it allowed lesser men the same right to disown ungodly lords.[69]

The revolutionary impetus that carried forward Reformation in 1560, deposed Mary in 1567 and won a civil war in 1573 began to run out of steam in the 1580s when faced with a young Protestant king whose discomfort with militant Protestantism was increasingly apparent. The Ruthven raid of August 1582 was a triumph for the religious radicals, and the exiled John Durie returned to Edinburgh on 4 September to be greeted by a jubilant crowd, while the general assembly delivered a ringing endorsement of the raid. It declared that the coup leaders had 'done good and acceptable service to God, their naturall and bound duetie to their soverane, and shewed their carefull affectioun to their countrie'. In spite of its efforts to acquire political legitimacy, however, the new government failed to build a sufficient base of support outside a small party of evangelical lords. The subscription crisis of 1584–5 further underlined the political weakness of the militant clergy.[70] Leadership passed to a younger generation of men, the most im-portant of whom was Morton's nephew, the 'gud, godlie, wyse and stout' eighth earl of Angus. Unfortunately for the presbyterian clergy their champion died in 1588, aged only thirty-three, depriving them of the one magnate who might have shielded them from the king a decade later. Yet even Angus was criticised for failing to drive home the radical agenda after the 1585 coup. He recognised the complaint of the ministers, but argued that he could not compel the king since 'to save an honest man against his will, is commonly regarded with slender thanks'. Following Angus's death, James Melville admitted ruefully that 'I kent him nocht of the nobilitie in Scotland that I could communicat my mynd with anent publict effears, let be haiff a delling with in action'. The English government, too, found it increasingly difficult to exercise effective financial clientage over discontended – or 'well affected' – Protestant nobles as it had done throughout the 1540s to 1580s.[71]

This rift between religious radicals and the nobility would not be healed for half a century. In the early 1580s, the second earl of Mar was a young idealist who participated in the Ruthven raid, he shared exile in England with the Melvilles and remained close to ministers like Robert Bruce, but after 1585 Mar sought to cultivate his relationship with the king. Angus observed that Mar was now 'loathe to involve himself of new, where it can anie wise be eschewed', and when Protestant activists took to the streets in Edinburgh in 1596, Mar ignored appeals to join them.[72] Disappointment and frustration greeted every effort to find another godly magistrate in the mould of the iconic Moray or Angus. The fifth earl of Bothwell's cynical attempt to fashion himself into a Protestant champion was destroyed by an astonishing alliance with the Catholic earls in 1594, while the first lord Thirlestane's reputation as 'a guid christian and lovar of Chrysts servants' was cultivated for pragmatic reasons.[73]

By the mid-1590s, therefore, support among the higher nobility for radical Protestantism had dissipated. Yet while there was growing impatience with the church's desire to impose ecclesiastical discipline on nobles, support for the mainstream reformed church was not in decline. A picture of an increasingly rooted Protestant establishment can be pieced together from the commissions issued by the privy council on 6 March 1589 to local nobles entrusted with suppressing Catholicism.[74] Many Protestant nobles were committed deeply to the defence of their faith, men like the fifth earl of Morton, a Reformation veteran, who was prepared to stand up for the ministers before the king in 1592, or the seventh lord Lindsay, who led a deputation from the burgh of Edinburgh to the palace of Holyrood on 9 January 1593 to demand action against the papist lords. More worrying for the clergy was the impatient attitude among younger courtier nobles like the second duke of Lennox, whose reaction to one of John Davidson's sermons in December 1592 was to threaten to kill him for traducing the memory of the duke's father.[75] Fear of Catholic rebellion maintained a degree of solidarity, but even in the midst of the crisis, Lennox, Mar and the master of Glamis urged caution and stressed the need to obey the king. By the middle of the 1590s James VI's political ideas had matured into a determined opposition to the Buchananite ideology associated with presbyterian ministers and their lay sympathisers. As the king told a deputation on 9 January 1593, times had changed since the Reformation, and most of the higher nobility agreed with him.[76]

The more anxious the radical ministers grew, the more they offended noble sensibilities. Many nobles were outraged by attacks from the pulpit such as that on 2 June 1592 by Walter Balcalquhall who 'charged the king and nobilitie with great negligence of their dueteis', an outburst that took place in the context of the political crisis that saw the king concede the 'golden act' to the presbyterians. The growing clamour from the church against feuding added to the sense that ministers were interfering in noble affairs and eroding the deference due to nobles. The Edinburgh minister, Robert Bruce, publicly attacked the 'great men of this country', accusing them of 'burning and scalding, slaying and murdering, and using all kinds of oppression, and raging so as there were not a king in Israel'. In 1594, his colleague, John Davidson, warned that the nobility could no longer be counted on to further the Reformation. In a blistering sermon based on the prophet Jeremiah he rounded on the king, the queen and the nobles as 'ather young or corrupt, plagues both to themselves and to the land'. Amidst a growing clamour of religious revival and excitement, the March 1596 general assembly agreed on 'the true and right taiking up of the sinnes of our princes and magistrats, superiour and inferiour, and on the sound meanes to deale with them duetifullie and faithfullie, without all flatterie, for their true amendiment'.[77] When a Protestant insurrection broke out in Edinburgh on 17 December 1596, largely in response to an imagined Catholic plot, the seventh lord Lindsay and the eighth lord Forbes lent their weight and events might have unfolded differently had others joined them. A disappointed Robert Bruce later conceded that while some 'godlie barons and other gentle men' were prepared to defend the church's interests, 'they laike a cheefe noble man' to lead them. Consequently, the attempted coup floundered, and the protest contributed significantly to the decline in the general assembly's influence with the king and among the nobility. Archibald Douglas made the cynical observation in May 1597 that 'never a nobleman will countenance the ministry, such excepted as has private quarrels to debate that will be contented for some time to receive their assistance for palliation of their proper designs'.[78] The aftermath of the 1600 Gowrie conspiracy, in which one of the leading Protestant nobles was killed by the king's entourage, saw no nobles prepared to support Bruce in his demands for clarification of the king's version of events, providing final evidence of the collapse of militant Protestantism among the nobility.[79]

The appeal that militant Protestantism held for the nobilities of Europe was waning, especially from c. 1570 when the tide began to turn in favour of a revived Roman Catholicism. As the possibility of Protestant triumph receded it was replaced by a bunkered determination to preserve what had been achieved. With their strong continental connections, Scots were sensitive to these developments, hence, the beginnings of military involvement in Flanders from 1572. Protestants were concerned about the threat posed by the Catholic powers in the form of foreign invasion or sponsored rebellion, hence, William Douglas of Lochleven wrote to his wife from La Rochelle in August 1585, expressing fears for the French Huguenots under Henry III who was working with the papacy 'to exterminat the word of God out of this cuntrey and all partis of Europe'.[80] Lochleven's worries about rampant Catholicism were all the more threatening given the fragility of Protestantism at home. The defence of Roman Catholicism in 1559–60 was inept, and in the absence of episcopal leadership Catholic nobles were left floundering in parliament, resorting to the fourth earl of Atholl's limp comment that 'We will beleeve ... as our fathers beleeved'.[81] Yet it was decades before some parishes received their first Protestant minister, many localities contained significant recusant communities and even in Edinburgh the majority of the population remained sympathetic to the Catholic faith until the 1570s. Within these divided communities neighbours were content to co-exist in spite of the pronouncements from king, parliament and church. Besides, post-Tridentine Catholicism proved to be more difficult to brush aside. In contrast to the Catholics of the mid-sixteenth century, in 1610 the imprisoned ninth earl of Errol's determination to commit suicide rather than conform convinced archbishop Spottiswoode of the sincerity of his Catholic faith. Between Atholl's bewilderment and Errol's conviction was a range of belief that kept Catholicism alive in Scotland, and periodically frightened the Protestant establishment.[82]

The best opportunity for the restoration of Catholicism was during Mary's personal reign of 1561–7. The fourth earl of Huntly boasted in September 1561 that 'if the Queen commanded him, he would set up the Mass in three shires', but his motives were uncertain, and lord James Stewart commented dismissively that 'it was past his power'. Apart from a brief attempt in 1565 to free herself from her Protestant councillors, Mary never offered Catholics the unambiguous leadership they needed, Rome failed to show much interest and the Catholic lords were too entangled in their own local agendas.[83] Meanwhile, individual nobles made their peace with the new church. Ayrshire is commonly identified as a centre of Protestant activity even before the Reformation, but in the 1560s the third earl of Eglinton and the fourth earl of Cassillis remained Catholic, and it was the latter who ensured that the mass was celebrated publicly at Maybole at Easter 1563. Cassillis converted to Protestantism in 1566, the reason being his marriage to Margaret Lyon, sister to the eighth lord Glamis, who persuaded him to embrace the Protestant cause.[84] Such behaviour was repeated elsewhere, and by the time Rome had awoken to the situation in Scotland, Protestantism had put down roots.

Short of a major foreign invasion, Counter Reformation was unlikely after Mary's abdication in 1567, and even less likely by the end of the civil war in 1573. English military intervention in 1560 and again in 1573 demonstrated the extent to which Elizabeth I was prepared to protect a Protestant settlement. Of course, some Catholic nobles remained loyal. The fifth lord Seton stood by the regent Guise in 1559–60, he never gave up hoping that the Protestant Reformation might be overturned, and a decade later he sheltered English jesuits and other Catholics.[85] But it was the arrival in Scotland of the French Guise agent, Esmé Stewart, that was the catalyst to opening up new contacts with Counter Reformation forces on the Continent. Walter Balcanquhall's attack on Stewart in a public sermon in

December 1580 was the opening shot in a long, bitter campaign to keep Catholics out of James VI's government. Even a formal declaration on 2 December 1581 by Esmé Stewart, now duke of Lennox, assuring the church and community of his Protestant faith, failed to convince critics and he was driven from the country within the year. It was a tactic repeated against other suspected Catholics throughout the 1580s and 1590s.[86]

The 1580s saw an intensification of diplomatic activity as James VI's advisers looked for a way to struggle free of English clientage without losing Elizabeth I's goodwill, leading to greater Spanish diplomatic and covert activity in Scotland, activity that the king appeared to encourage in order to put pressure on England. Mary's execution in February 1587 raised support for a pro-Spanish and Catholic agenda. The establishment of a Scottish jesuit college at Douai in 1581 and the first mission to Scotland in 1584 resulted in a number of Catholic converts among the higher nobility, including the sixth earl of Huntly, the eighth lord Maxwell and lord Claud Hamilton, intensifying Protestant fears and inspiring over-optimism among Catholic agents.[87] How much of a threat to the Protestant church these men represented is difficult to estimate. Huntly simulated conformity while provoking occasional controversy, such as in December 1583 when his servants demonstrated their contempt for the general fast proclaimed by eating bread on the streets of Edinburgh. It was not until 1586 that he established relations with Spain, and it was the summer of 1588 before his Catholicism became overtly political.[88] It was reported of the eighth lord Maxwell in 1585 that there were jesuits in his house, that mass was said daily and that he was in receipt of French crowns. Maxwell possibly aimed at a *de facto* toleration and avoided direct confrontation with the king until 1587–8, when he was goaded into premature rebellion and forced into exile in Spain where he sought aid for an invasion of Scotland. Following the failure of the Spanish armada in 1588, Maxwell cut his ties with political Catholicism and put his efforts into regaining royal favour and restoring his house's fortunes.[89]

Nevertheless, while English intelligence reports exaggerated the Catholic menace, the picture they painted was not wholly inaccurate. A memo of January 1593, prepared as the Spanish blanks affair was unfolding, estimated that the Catholic peers included eight earls and ten lords, around a third of the peerage. At the core of this group was the now rebellious Huntly and his neighbour, the ninth earl of Errol, but many Catholic nobles had no interest in political activity.[90] The geographic distribution of Catholicism lends support to the idea of a regional division in the kingdom with the northeast having a high concentration of Catholics, but even within localities there was diversity. The seventy-one northeastern barons and burgh magistrates who signed a band for the defence of the Protestant religion at Aberdeen on 30 April 1589 are matched by a similar number of landed men who were required to find caution for their behaviour at the time of the Brig o' Dee rebellion.[91] An equally fragmented picture can be found in the burghs. In Edinburgh the Catholic nobility pushed at the limits of what was acceptable, and as late as 1596 a number of them held secret masses in the city, while four years later the first marquis of Huntly held mass in his Edinburgh house. Even in that most orthodox of Protestant towns, Perth, a number of Catholics met in secret in 1604 to participate in the mass.[92]

The king's mild treatment of the 1589 rebels failed to satisfy the more aggressively Protestant lords, the church or Elizabeth I, and a campaign was waged to pressure the king into punishing his Catholic nobles. James VI, however, had no desire to be forced into dependence on one faction, or to be seen as an English client, and refused to act. Even the public outrage that followed the murder by Huntly of the second earl of Moray on 7 February 1592 failed to persuade James to change his policy.[93] English interception of correspondence – the Spanish blanks dating from the winter of 1588–9 – between Huntly, Errol and Spain created a panic in London and Edinburgh. Yet the documentation collected by the English privy council indicates that the Catholic nobility sensed that their opportunity had passed with the failure of the Spanish armada. A number of the Catholic nobility in Renfrewshire even signed a bond on 1 January 1593 pledging to serve queen Elizabeth, to maintain the Protestant religion and to remain loyal to the king. But the church and its supporters, along with Elizabeth I's government and Huntly's personal enemies, continued to lobby hard for James VI to take decisive action, resulting in parliament making an unconvincing demand in June 1593 for the enforcement of religious conformity, which was followed by a show of military strength by the king in the northeast.[94]

Possibly the Catholic earls knew the hopelessness of their situation, seeking only 'to blaw at ane bleind coill [= dead coal]', and in a letter of 11 October 1593 they made a case for religious toleration, claiming to 'crave no liberty in public use of any other religion than is possessed in this realm, but only that no compulsion be used to men's conscience'. Further concessions were not forthcoming, formal forfeiture followed in March 1594, and in spite of unexpected success at the battle of Glenlivet on 3 October 1594 there was never any question of the Catholic earls negotiating satisfactory terms without external military intervention.[95] There may be grounds for seeing these rebellions as partly the results of Protestant provocation, and certainly this argument was the stock-in-trade of the Catholic lords, hence, Huntly's legalistic protestation of loyalty to the king 'aganis whome he wald never cum, albeit in a just caus'. Even when Huntly returned illegally from exile in the summer of 1596 he made light of his treasons – 'my offens war never sua great' he wrote to the king. Nevertheless, James VI lacked the means, or the will, to destroy these men, and the impressive following of northern nobles that Huntly and Errol brought with them when they made their entrance into Edinburgh in December 1597 underlined the deep-rooted nature of their power.[96] But trapped between their own conservative rhetoric and a king who did not want to be rescued from his Protestant advisers, Catholics had nowhere to go.

Some attempt was made to turn the defeat of 1594 into an inspirational story, and the jesuit priest, Alexander Macquair, wrote *Vera narratio ingentis miraculi et plenae victoriae* with this in mind. Protestant militants sustained the myth, and as late as 1596 it was reported that the Catholic earls were preparing to receive Spanish troops. When James VI was quizzed about the Catholic earls in 1599, however, he told the English ambassador that the unhelpful attitude of Philip II's government during their exile had cured them of any notions that the Spanish would intervene.[97] He was right, especially as the brief flirtation with Counter Reformation politics had seen a succession of Catholic nobles brought close to ruin. As an exile in 1596 Errol wrote to the king trying to convince him that the blame for his misfortunes lay with 'that over gryt fervor and onnecessar rigor of the ministrie (qua, disdainfullie rejecting all reasonable conditiouns, will force mennis consciencis, nocht as yet persuadit, till imbrace thair opiniouns in matteris of religioune)'. This Catholic apologetic was not without foundation, and two years earlier Andrew Melville told the king:

> it is a mater of great weight to overthrow the estat of three so great men. I grant it is so: yitt it is a greater mater to overthrow and expell out of the countrie three farre greater; to witt, true religioun, the quietnesse of the commoun weale, and the king's prosperous estat.[98]

While the more militant clergy did not fully get their way, the sustained pressure on Catholic nobles took its toll. Following the failure of the Spanish armada in 1588, it was reported that the fifth lord Herries, another jesuit convert, 'is lyk to becum ane guid Protestant outwardlie'. For many Catholics the most realistic option was to become a *politique*, a state of mind cultivated at queen Mary's court in the 1560s, by Lennox in the early 1580s, Maxwell at the end of the decade and, after 1594, by almost all Catholic nobles.[99] This outward conformity under a king who refused to look into men's consciences was the best settlement the Catholic community could expect. A report written by an informed Catholic in *c.* 1595 on the possibility of Scotland becoming Catholic was pessimistic:

> Many nobles who were thought to be Catholic in private, and also attend the sermons and religious exercises of the heretics, whence by the true Catholics they are commonly called lukewarm and in a word not only will they never take arms against the King, but depend upon his absolute will.

Nobles remained in contact with Madrid through agents and jesuits like colonel Robert Semple, William Crichton and Robert Bruce and a network of exiles and agents, but the best hope for the Catholic cause did not lie in militant plotting. Instead, the king's toleration of Catholic nobles followed by the careful missionary work of jesuits like James Gordon under the protection of his nephew, Huntly, offered a route to survival.[100] This was the policy the latter adopted on his return from exile in 1596 and he stuck with it over the next forty years.

For those Catholic and Protestant nobles to whom faith mattered the question of rendering obedience to Caesar or to God presented a dilemma. Knox and the early reformers stripped away the idea that an individual could be absolved from responsibility to God by blind obedience to the authority of the prince.[101] Among Catholics, political action continued into the 1590s, but with little chance of success, and thereafter a persistent determination to preserve the faith took its place. For the more radical Protestants, outbursts of religious enthusiasm, usually sparked off by a sense of the church in danger, continued to attract noble as well as popular support at a national and local level until the end of the sixteenth century. Episodes like the 1593 'Band anent the religioun' recaptured something of the spirit of the bands of the Lords of the Congregation in 1558 and 1559, there were echoes of the 1562 'Ayrshire band' in the 1596 St Andrews presbytery covenant, and the failed insurrection of December 1596 in Edinburgh was a conscious attempt to recreate something of the spirit of 1559-60.[102] But religion did not always inspire action, and might equally encourage a form of providential fatalism. During his English exile, in February 1566, the first earl of Moray counselled his wife to 'prayse God for all that he sendis for it is he only that gevis and takis and it is he only that may and will restoyr agayne'. The murder of a political ally, the tragic loss of a child, the burning down of a house were all met with the same stoicism for, as the deposed regent Morton concluded in the spring of 1578 when considering his political options, 'We mon thank God quhatsumevir it pleasis him to send'.[103]

Bloodfeud

If rebellion was the most extreme manifestation of noble power being deployed against the king, feuding was a more common and daily indicator of the limitations of royal authority.[104] James VI was mistaken in asserting that feuds were peculiar to Scotland and that 'their barbarous name is unknowen to anie other nation', but the king was not alone in suggesting there was something unusually violent about Scottish society. A Spanish diplomat commented disapprovingly that 'mortal feud' was a Scottish phenomenon in which men 'entertain terrible bands and refuse all quarter to each other'. Roger Aston, an Englishman serving in the king's chamber, commented in 1595 that 'Men here for revenge of their particulars will bring in the devil ere their cause perish'.[105] Yet forms of feuding were commonplace throughout much of late medieval and early modern Europe, including Italy, Germany, France, England and Ireland. The feud had a long history within the context of medieval constitutionalism, as a recognised rule-governed process by which nobles defended their rights, as well as being a product of the normal routine of the martial culture of the nobility. The contagious increase in private warfare and duelling in France following the collapse of effective royal government from 1560 suggests that feuding might be exacerbated in any early modern society where civil war and the erosion of central authority occurred. In Ireland, too, it was the impact of warfare on an already militarised society that exacerbated violent conflict.[106] Therefore, while the extent to which a high level of private violence was the norm in a feuding society remains debatable, it does appear that anthropological studies of feud have unduly influenced historical analysis of more hierarchic and martial societies by emphasising the peace in the feud.[107]

The political, economic and social conditions of the mid- and later sixteenth century exacerbated local and national tensions, creating a context of instability and violence in which there was a proliferation of local disputes. Even allowing for problems in reporting and in the nature of the sources, there was a marked escalation of feuding throughout the 1570s, 1580s and 1590s that began to decline significantly only from the second decade of the seventeenth century.[108] This connection between political instability and social disorder did not go un-noticed, and when writing about the Marian civil war half a century later, sir Robert Gordon of Gordonstoun observed that:

> The commounwealth of Scotland wes now in a combustion, not able, by reasone of ther civill discords in the south, to remedie the insolencies which were committed in the remotest pairts of the kingdome, wherby they escaped unpunished.[109]

There was something unusually combustible in a society where even as the regent Morton was sitting in Holyrood Palace in March 1576 two of his own servants were cut down in the Canongate by Andrew Stewart, master of Ochiltree. Similarly, the shooting dead of chancellor Glamis on the High Street of Edinburgh on 17 March 1578 is evidence of major political disorder. Neither of these feuds was resolved until the following century. It is unsurprising, therefore, that to an English visitor in 1591 the kingdom appeared to be torn apart by vicious feuds about which an unpopular and incompetent king did nothing.[110]

Yet such incidents must be located within the social and cultural norms of a feuding society that legitimately resolved disputes by gradations of violence, ranging from personal insults and threats to attacks on property, assaults, the targeting of individuals and full-scale local warfare. Social organisation, kinship and lordship, aligned with an ideology of personal and group honour in an armed community amounted to a recipe for frequent and, indeed, necessary acts of violence.[111] James VI captured the nobility's engagement with feuding in *Basilikon doron* (1599), commenting that:

for anie displeasure, that they [the nobility] apprehend to be done unto them
by their neighbour, to take up a plaine feide against him; and (without respect
to God, King, or common-weale) to bang it out bravely, hee and all his kinne,
against him and all his.

The king's view, articulated at a time when the political community was
beginning to address the problem, was that bloodfeud amounted to illegitimate private warfare conducted without regard for civil society or royal
authority. Halhill, a royal courtier, placed the nobility at the centre of
feuding:

the way taking of the lyf of a nobleman or barroun, bredis ane hundreth
ennemys ma or les, according to the gretnes of the clan or surname; of the
quhilk nomber some will ly at the wait to be revengit, albeit lang efter, when
they se ther turn.

That idea that feuds were essentially private wars between noble families
that endured over time was widely shared. John Leslie, the exiled bishop
of Ross, wrote in his *Historie of Scotland* that 'Gret families they feid, and
that perpetuallie', while the rivalry of the Ayrshire earls of Eglinton and
Glencairn was such that 'Betwix the freynds of thais twa housis, there hes
bene of a lang tyme sa great emulation and invy, not without effusioun of
blude on ather part'. In 1590, chancellor Thirlestane saw the escalation of
feuding 'which hes set the whole north in twoe partes, having taken armes
on both sydes', in terms of a dispute between the earls of Huntly and
Moray.[12] Some 365 feuds have been identified for the period 1573–1625,
most of them in the period up to *c.* 1610, but the uneven nature of the
sources means that this figure is conservative. Feuds involved all ranks of
people, including tenant farmers or burgesses who were acting out their own
quarrels, but feuding was an overwhelmingly noble-led preoccupation with
something like 90 per cent of feuds involving the landed elite.[13] This is
unsurprising since the business of disputes and their settlement was among
the most important responsibilities of lordship. A lesser baron like John
Grant of Freuchie was drawn into an almost constant round of feuds with
his neighbours, or was involved in efforts to mediate in the feuds of those
same neighbours.[14]

Feud, therefore, was an integral part of the political culture of the
nobility. On the occasion of ending a feud between the houses of Sutherland
and Caithness, one Gordon baron told a Sinclair rival that 'from their
infancies they had been bred in jarrs and contentions, the one against the
other'. Among the neighbouring Highlanders this passion for revenge was
most extreme, and Gordonstoun related that 'neither have they regaird to
persone, tyme, aige, nor cause; and ar generallie so addicted that way ... that
therein they surpasse all people whatsoever'. When discussing feud among
the Borders kindreds, Leslie commented that any killing demanded to be

revenged 'quhairof ryses deidlie feid, nocht of ane in ane, or few bot of thame ilk ane and als, quha ar of that familie stock or tribe how ignorant sa evir thay be of the injurie'. As in France, where violence was most extreme in more geographically remote regions like the Haute Auvergne, feuding on the Borders and in the Highlands was particularly ferocious.[115] Yet these Highland and Border clans did not inhabit a world apart from Lowland lords, and two-thirds of all identified feuds took place in the Lowlands. Even on the streets of Edinburgh there were appalling incidents of murder and large-scale conflicts, such as on 24 November 1567 when there was 'ane gret combat' between the Bruces of Airth and the Wemyss family, while in January 1595 rival parties engaged in a vicious battle on the streets 'with gunnis and swordis in great nomber'. Towns feuded with one another, their landed neighbours or different factions within a burgh might feud with one another. The key Border town of Jedburgh was a source of friction and occasional bloodshed between rival branches of the Kers, the Rutherfords and the Turnbulls throughout the later sixteenth century. In 1590, the provost, William Ker of Ancram, was murdered by his rival, sir Robert Ker, younger of Cessford who got away with the killing because he had crown backing.[116] Feuds that have been investigated in detail in Aberdeenshire, Angus, Ayrshire, Dumfriesshire and Islay reveal forms of violence by nobles and their followers that ranged from the sporadic to the endemic.[117] Noble society was pervaded by a culture of violence in which 'blood cryeth', mothers distributed silver bullets to kinsmen entrusted with the business of revenge, bloody shirts were carried in procession in the hope of arousing sympathy, graphically gruesome pictures of murdered men were paraded in procession to work up a desire for revenge, corpses of slain victims were left unburied for years while the kindred sought vengeance, acts of exaggerated brutality were committed against the corpses of enemies, and bodies were cut into pieces in deliberate desecration of the dead.[118]

Leslie's view that feuding families 'persekuted and persuet the hail stok and familie … sa this deidlie faid was nevir put in the buke of oblivione' represents a common exaggeration, or misunderstanding, but it is not difficult to see why feuds can appear indiscriminate and eternal. Unfortunately, one of the difficulties in measuring the lengths of feuds is that while a feud settlement was a formal ritual legally recorded, there was no legal definition of enmity as occurred in much of medieval Europe, or any equivalent means of announcing the commencement of a feud as there was in Poland where the *opdowiedz* intimated the declaration of private war.[119] It is difficult to know what temporal framework chancellor Dunfermline had in mind when in 1607 he described the Cunningham–Montgomery feud as 'the auldest fead hes bene of thame all', having its origins in 'mony bloodis of great antiquitie betuix these houssis'. Close investigation suggests that the feud's immediate origins lay in the quarrel over the commendatorship of Kilwinning abbey in the 1570s, but there is evidence that these two houses had been feuding on and off since the fourteenth century.[120] This revised picture of intermittent bloodfeuds between neighbouring families was recognised by Gordonstoun, who observed 'Neir nyghbours ar seldome frie from jarres and quarralls'. In discussing the relations of his own house of Sutherland with that of Caithness, he warned that even when peace had been agreed between feuding families 'a lytle mater will kendle a hid spark of malice bred and rooted of long in boith your harts'.[121] There are many examples of families keeping alive the fires of hatred over decades. The feud that broke out as a consequence of the regent Morton's treatment of the master of Ochiltree in the mid-1570s led the latter's brother to take a leading role in bringing about Morton's fall and execution in 1581, to the murder of the former chancellor Arran in 1596, and the shooting dead of the first lord Torthorwald on the streets of Edinburgh in 1608.[122] In the archive of the earls of Wigton is a bundle of 147 documents, the last dated 1623, all relating to a feud between the lords Fleming and the Tweedies of Drumelzier that had its origins in the killing of the second lord Fleming in 1524. Nevertheless, while the feuds of great lords generally endured longer, the majority of feuds appear to have lasted only a few years, suggesting that most disputes could be resolved quickly by negotiation.[123]

The origins of feuds lay largely in disputes over honour and over land and its resources, although it is difficult to separate the tangible from the intangible. One explanation for the growing number of the latter feuds in the later sixteenth century lies in the instability of the land market caused by the availability of large swathes of former ecclesiastical estates and the unsettling effect of inflation and feuing on rents. Against a background of unstable government and inadequate confidence in the legal process the result was a scramble by lords for land and for the men to hold it for them; hence, Lethington's attack on what he saw as unscrupulous land lust in his poem 'Aganis covetyce'.[124] It was precisely because issues of landownership were dangerously inflammatory in a feuding society that formal perambulations by community leaders were so important in establishing boundaries.[125] A new problem that afflicted the landed community after the Reformation was the tension between the rights of the new secular superiors and their tenants over their right to collect teinds (= tithes), with the former often resorting to force. Such occasions sparked off incidents that could lead to feuds, a fear that was in the minds of the privy council in August 1573 when it tried to prevent a repetition of the 'grit blude shed deidlie feid and utheris inconvenientis' arising from a quarrel between the followers of the fourth lord Ruthven and Robert Bruce of Clackmannan over teinds. The bloodfeud between the fifth earl of Bothwell and the Humes began in 1586 with a dispute over the possession of the teinds of Coldingham.[126] Old-fashioned military aggression aimed at territorial expansion was most likely to occur in the Highlands where clans often lived on land that their chiefs did not hold by royal charter. It was the determination of many chiefs to align *oighreachd*, their individual heritage, with *duthchas*, the collective inheritance of the entire clan, that resulted in feuding. Such an inherently unstable situation was exacerbated by the crown's determination to exploit the absence of charters to squeeze greater financial returns from the Highlands. One of the most successful expansionist houses in sixteenth-century Scotland was that of Argyll, which moved westward into Kintyre and Islay, north into Nairnshire and eastward into Angus utilising a combination of marriage, ecclesiastical patronage, settlement and violence.[127] Further explanations for the prevalence of feuding lie in a cult of personal and family honour that was taken to extremes by men like the fifth earl of Bothwell whose 'carriage is suche, and haith so embrued himself with bloode, as he is hated almost on everie on'.[128] Undoubtedly, some families gloried in their violent reputation, such as the Gordons of Gight who engaged in bloody deeds over several generations and a number of the male members of the family met with violent deaths.[129] Many of these acts of violence were committed by armed young men under the authority of lords who had not outgrown the exaggerated and socially expected assertiveness of adolescence. Hence, the kinsmen and friends of the ninth lord Maxwell excused his many crimes in the early 1600s on the grounds that he had acted simply 'upoun some foolische and young consait'.[130]

Bloodfeud, therefore, lay at the heart of noble politics, determining local alliances and animosities that in turn shaped the creation and dissolution of faction at a national level and at court.[131] When in 1562 William Maitland, younger of Lethington, was instrumental in bringing home to Scotland the fourth earl of Lennox he knew the effect this would have on his relations with the Hamilton kindred, observing 'This day have I tacken the deadlie haitrent of all the Hamyltonis within Scotland, and have done unto thame no less displeasur than that I had cutted thair throttis.' The shifting allegiances of the Marian civil war reflected the manoeuvring of feuding nobles against a background of royal dynastic politics and religious division. The regent Moray's assassination by the Hamiltons in 1570 and the execution of John Hamilton, archbishop of St Andrews, in revenge a year later were actions within the narrative of a family feud, not only a civil war.[132] The bitter legacy of the war was expressed in further feuding. The fall and execution of Morton in 1580–1 was in large part revenge on the part of the Stewart kindred for the murder of lord Darnley.[133] At times the politics of feud would overwhelm every other consideration, as was increasingly the case in the later 1580s and early 1590s when the court was a dangerous place full of armed and edgy men. A sense of the insecurity surrounding the fifth earl of Bothwell in the summer of 1588 is conveyed in the comment by one onlooker that 'My lord Bodwell wes set round about with mirrouris, because he wald nocht that ony sald secure him'. In the aftermath of the 1589 rebellion, one commentator drew attention to the nature of political violence in Scotland where it was 'the accustomable fassyon of this contry, [and] specyally emonge the best sort, to styk or sh[oot] with a pece or pistoll such one as the Chaunce[lour] if he gave them cause of offence, and not to raise an army to charge and molest the whole r[ealm]'.[134] And even when no violence was intended, the simmering menace that gangs of armed men posed to one another was everywhere prevalent. On the afternoon of 21 June 1593, lord Hamilton and the young seventh earl of Argyll met near the cross in the Canongate with their men. Relations between these two lords were relatively harmonious, but:

> the straitness of the street gave no room for the troops to pass easily, so that the foremost, 'romblinge' together, strove for the gate, and pistols on both sides were 'bended' and sundry swords were drawn in such sudden rage that it was strange that they should so part in sunder.

Fortunately, bloodshed was avoided, but the incident set Edinburgh and the court on edge for the next few days and Hamilton sent for another fifty harquebusiers to increase his personal security.[135]

While European nobilities of the late medieval and early modern eras cultivated a martial ethos that thrived on assertive behaviour constituting rites of social definition, nobles had little to gain from anarchy and much to lose given the financial cost of war.[136] Of course, in any society it is easy to be misled by sensationalised narratives of violent behaviour. Crown officials and the church increasingly waged a concerted campaign against the private violence of the feud that resulted in a rhetoric that talked up the problem. In 1596 the general assembly condemned the 'flood of bloodscheds for eluding of lawes', believing that Scotland was in the midst of a social breakdown. This view was widely shared by clergy, whether they be dissident presbyterians or bishops.[137] The crown, too, had much to gain from reducing private violence and being seen to reduce it. The first lord Binning's peroration to a convention of the nobility in 1617 on the merits of king James's rule, and his graphically painted picture of the barbarism of life during his majesty's earlier years, is a masterful piece of propaganda that exaggerated the extent of the problem in order to draw attention to the king's achievements. But by the 1590s voices from within noble society recognised that feuding had attained unacceptable levels of violence and that something must be done to address the worst aspects of bloodfeud. As crown authority recovered in the context of the more stable political environment of the later 1590s, the political community utilised the mechanisms of the feud to encourage peace and dispute resolution. Hence, the careful declaration by a convention of estates in 1598 that 'all feidis ar ane of thir thrie natures namelie that thair is ather na slauchter upoun nather syde or slauchter upoun ane syde onlie or ells slauchter upoun bath sydis', which avoided outright condemnation, but was part of a growing campaign to reduce violence.[138] Nevertheless, when James VI inherited the English crown in 1603 and departed for London most of the major feuds remained unresolved, bloody incidents continued to occur, and should the political situation deteriorate the ideology and weapons of bloodfeud remained poised to tip the kingdom back into violent chaos.

Conclusion

The Stewart dynasty repeatedly demonstrated that it could eliminate its domestic rivals, and the lesson about the threat from over-mighty magnates was understood by contemporaries. Godscroft argued that the house of Douglas was destroyed in the fifteenth century by a combination of the jealousy of mean men and the fear of kings:

> I knaw it is a Maxime in policie, and plausible to manie; That Princes sould not suffer over great subjects in their Dominions, thogh it be sure without great subjects, never great services.

Yet, he pointed out, the exercise of undoing great men could plunge a kingdom into turmoil, besides which those newly raised mean men might in time become as great a threat to future kings as those cut down.[139] In James VI's Scotland there was no noble house with the raw power of the Albany Stewarts or the Black Douglases, and even the steady accumulation of land and men by the houses of Argyll and Huntly did not amount to the emergence of similar territorial domains. Of course, nobles did engage politically with kings who expected it of them, and it was an obligation laid on them by the lineage, while as individuals they experienced self-discovery in the fulfilment of their ambitions within the public arena. This restlessness was noted in the career of the fourth earl of Lennox, unable to remain in retirement in England where 'he levit in honor, wealth, and ease ... Bot as warldlie men ar for the maist part addictit to temporall pomp and glorie, and hes na respect to the instabilitie of estaitis, sa was he.'[140] Besides, medieval and early modern nobles did not constantly plot to weaken or depose kings, and like any governing elite hoped for stability. Some nobles lived quiet, unadventurous lives, men like the sixth lord Lovat who 'resolved to stay at home and looke to his owne affairs and medle as litle as possible with the publict'.[141] Nor were kings necessarily confrontational, and it is tempting to make too much of the French agent's report in 1584 that the youthful James VI told him that the nobility had grown too powerful over the previous forty years, boasting that it was his intention to subdue them piece by piece.[142] Undoubtedly, the nobility had grown more powerful since the death of James V in 1542, but all the king had in mind was a return to something like the level of authority enjoyed by his grandfather. Mary and James VI cultivated relations with as wide as possible a range of nobles, maintaining the kind of personal contact that was possible in a small kingdom and, on the whole, James VI was 'of a mercifull mynd, and greatly inclynit towardis all the nobilite, intending to won all ther hartis be his awen discret behavour'. His idealised vision of the relationship he wanted with his nobility was vividly expressed in the peace banquet he threw at his palace of Holyrood on 15 May 1587.[143] A sensible king knew that the exercise of royal authority rested on his relationship with these men, and much of the discussion in the following chapters addresses the nature of that relationship. Ten years later, following the infamous anti-Catholic riot of December 1596, the Edinburgh crowd was overawed in the king's name by the military power of loyal nobles deploying their men to seize control of the city gates and to master the streets.[144]

This chapter has focused on the tensions within the political community, on those fissures that broke apart the consensus that made government possible. Ideas about resistance, implacable religious divisions and a legacy of weak government and civil war that fed the worst attributes of a feuding society all threatened to make the kingdom ungovernable. But this introductory discussion has highlighted the nobility's ambivalence towards resistance as James VI came of age, an increasing disenchantment with religious politics and a growing unease at the escalation of feuding. The power of individual nobles, and even factions of nobles, could be broken by the crown when it exploited the natural conservatism of noble society and deployed the power of other nobles in its cause. Of course, Mary's reign ended in 1567 in enforced abdication, while James VI required years to overcome the vortex of rebellions, factionalism and bloodfeuds. But after 1594 even the most militant of Catholic lords realised that rebellion served no useful purpose; in 1596 the Protestant nobility refused to countenance politically militant action by religious radicals. In the last few years of his Scottish reign prior to 1603 James VI acquired the political initiative of his kingdom, although this is often exaggerated and it is unhelpful to read too much into the fall of individual noble houses like that of Bothwell and Gowrie. The defeat of the rebellions of the 1590s did not signal the final phase in a long, drawn out struggle between crown and nobility, and there was no seismic shift of power into the hands of the king before 1603.[145] More important than anything that occurred in Scottish politics, James VI's removal to England in 1603 changed forever the political landscape of Scotland, altering in the process the relationship between crown and nobility.

CHAPTER 2

Chiefs

Noble families with their extended networks of kinsmen and their historical lineage formed a series of complex relationships constituting a deep-rooted and pervasive form of cultural power presided over by heads of houses or, in Scotland, chiefs. The task of unravelling those bonds and identifying the meanings of those intersections between people from whom we are separated by centuries and by the vicissitudes of documentary survival is difficult, and the subtle nuances of family organisation, the extent of kinship relations, changing inheritance strategies and forms of ancestral memory are easily misunderstood. Identifying a man's kin varied in European history with time, place and status in society, and the search to uncover the lineage and kindred of early modern Scottish nobles is helped and, occasionally, obscured by a comparative methodology.[1] Even within Scotland it might be argued that there were differences in the importance attached to kinship in the mid-sixteenth century or the mid-seventeenth century, between the Gaelic speaking Highland world and the Scots speaking Lowland society, and between great lords and minor lairds.

Nevertheless, medieval scholars appear to have reached some agreement on the broad trend in the history of noble families, recognising that even before *c.* 1000 family relationships were relatively fluid and kinship obligations were problematic, and that thereafter there was a shift from larger, bilateral descent groups of kinsmen towards patrilineal and more restricted groups. The pace of change varied greatly from one region to another, with frontier societies like Leon and Castile being slower to adapt. Scotland, too, changed slowly, particularly in those parts of the Highlands less exposed to Anglo-Norman customs.[2] It has been suggested that the next significant transformation took place in the course of the seventeenth century when the predominance of ties within the nuclear family pushed aside commitments to the patrilineal kindred. Some historians, particularly in England, have criticised the evidence for the existence at any time in the early modern and even medieval periods, of large, extended kindreds, arguing for an ego-centred and bilateral idea of kinship that focused on the nuclear family.[3] Yet it is not difficult to demonstrate that the early modern understanding of family embraced at least co-resident relations and household servants as well as, possibly, non-resident kin. The debate has now shifted towards

recognising the survival of bilateral kin groups, especially in regions
influenced by Germanic settlement. To some extent the argument has been
unduly influenced by a concentration on the size of households, a form of
evidence that may say little about the nature of kinship relations. While the
ego-centred nuclear family may be a more appropriate model for understanding kinship rather than one that is exclusively ancestor-centred,
historians need to recognise a range of natural, legal and spiritual relationships, alongside obligations of varying importance and intensity within an
informal, extended bilateral kindred – a structural domain – often, but not
necessarily, living in complex households. Consequently, mere genealogical
information in and of itself is of little value in defining a kindred, or in
understanding the obligations that kinship carried. Qualitative evidence is
necessary to convert a crude genealogical map into a dynamic relational
network.[4]

Kindred and Lineage

Despite the importance of kinship in exercising power in medieval and early
modern Scottish politics and society being widely recognised, historians
have been hesitant to analyse kinship closely. The extent to which these
groupings headed by noble chiefs can be reconstructed from the available
evidence is uncertain given our lack of knowledge about fundamentals
such as what dyadic ties mattered, or what social roles were expected and
delivered by people standing in a particular relationship to one another. It is
too easy to make assumptions about the social function of familiar words,
about the meanings different societies gave to roles such as father, wife, son,
sister, uncle or cousin, and historians need to be sensitive to the social and
cultural context in which biological links existed. What, for example, were
the different obligations and responsibilities that bound a man to a paternal
uncle, a maternal aunt's son, a sister's husband, a younger brother or a
daughter's husband? Such information is difficult to excavate from surviving sources, and there remains the likelihood that each family deployed
a variety of understanding of kinship and its obligations depending upon
circumstances.[5] Even more inaccessible is the meaning conveyed in
genealogical information linking men to a common ancestor who died
hundreds of years in the past. Nevertheless, it appears that in the course of
the twelfth century Scottish nobles adopted the emphasis on lineage that
evolved in France with its emphasis on heraldry, patronymic names and
a family discourse that described its genealogical past. By the fifteenth
century, kinship was becoming increasingly agnatic, possibly in response
to the weakening of central authority, while in the Highlands and Borders
there was an even greater recourse to clanship and kinship as a mean of
countering instability.[6]

The range of relationships that existed between husbands and wives, or parents and children within what might be conceived of as the nuclear noble family in Scotland is well documented. Indeed, from the evidence presented in discussing these relationships it appears that something like a nuclear family centred on the individual and with bonds both to paternal and maternal kin was the norm.[7] An egocentric nuclear family model of kinship, however, is inadequate to explain the role kindreds played in sixteenth-century politics, and there remains the issue of the relative importance attached to the wider range of bilateral kinsmen. For example, there is significant evidence to suggest that women played an important role in creating kinship networks, but was it true that agnatic relationships were stronger and more enduring that those traced through women? Sir John Maxwell of Pollok appears to have believed so when in *c.* 1584 he observed that 'consangnite of bloud is nar and kyndlear nor affinite'.[8] But here, too, there is a problem in unpacking what Pollok meant by these terms. Late medieval Scots law and canon law did give emphasis to heirs of a man's body over the right of collateral kin and illegitimate children, and the lingering idea that consanguinity was established by the father's semen, believed to be a product of blood, persisted.[9] One obvious manifestation of this emphasis placed on male descent, and on the hierarchic authority of the head of the lineage, is the huge number of early modern entail settlements in which the over-riding concern was to resist the random impact of biology and guarantee male succession and the survival of the kindred surname. On 21 February 1598, George Ross of Balnagowan signed an entail that regu-lated the succession of his estates to his male heirs, failing which he and the twelfth earl of Sutherland nominated six men each to sit in judgement and decide on an heir-male bearing the name of Ross. Sir Robert Gordon of Gordonstoun related that his father, the eleventh earl of Sutherland, made a tail and entail of his earldom and entire estate to the heirs male of his own body, which failing, to the house of Huntly 'least the earldome of Souther-land should, by a daughter, fall from the surname of Gordoun to some other familie'. Parliamentary ratifications commonly stipulated the inheritance rights of male heirs 'bearing the surname' of the grantee.[10]

That emphasis on the surname offers a route into identifying kinship, although it is one that must be approached with caution. In a letter of 1588, George Dundas of that Ilk instructed his eldest son, then in France, 'As for your awin name fallow it furth as ye do and change it nocht'. Although the spelling of surnames was not standardised, and some surnames like Mackay had a considerable number of variations in English and Gaelic, the name was a powerful means of creating group solidarity. At the heart of the corporate identity of the kindred was the surname, that common designation more potent even than armorial distinctions. Godscroft began his narrative of the house of Douglas with the proud lines:

> So manie, so good, as of Douglases hes beine,
> Of one surname, war never in Scotland seine.

Surnames even became an indicator of character, so that the Frasers of Lovat were 'a surname esteemed honest and very hardy'. In 1600, following the Ruthven conspiracy, parliament abolished the surname altogether, requiring people to change their name. Two years later, the privy council proclaimed that even those members of the family who obeyed this law were not free to attend court, and that they had been mistaken in thinking that 'changeing of thair surenames, did utterlie translait thame sa fer frome being ony langer of that race'.[11] The surname was not entirely unproblematic in terms of kinship, however, and men who shared the same surname might not be kinsmen at all; for example, it was not uncommon for men to take the surname of their lord. Wives, meanwhile, continued to use their own surnames.

Lineage provided men with a genealogical map with which they could find their kinsmen, the men who constituted the living kindred and who, increasingly, shared its surname, and it provided lords with a means of strengthening the loyalty of their men. When in 1575, John Melville of Raith compiled his ancestry he accounted for the five previous generations of his family, tracing it back to a founder in the early fifteenth century 'howbeit the hous was mekyll alder of a lang time'. He knew little of these male ancestors, other than their names, their marriages and the fact that his father and great-great-grandfather had been knighted, while the women were ignored as were the networks that linked him to his other cognatic ancestors.[12] Nevertheless, this historical information provided the laird of Raith with a body of kinsmen descended from a common ancestor with whom he shared mutual obligations, or at least with whom he might share mutual obligations if that descent corporation was reinforced by political, social and ideological bonds. The advantage of this emphasis on male lineage is perhaps most apparent when the immediate kin was predominantly female or few in number. Gilbert Kennedy, fourth earl of Cassillis, known in his day as 'the king of Carrick', can be situated in an egocentric bilateral kinship model that suggests he was a man with few kin. A snapshot of his relatives around the time of his death in 1576 shows that his only close kinsmen were two infant sons and one younger brother. His nearest kinswomen were his wife, Margaret Lyon, the sister of the eighth lord Glamis, who was chancellor at the time, his sister Jean who was married to lord Robert Stewart, the unruly bastard son of James V whose estates were on the distant isles of Orkney and Shetland, and another sister, Katherine, whose husband was sir Patrick Vaus of Barnbarroch, a minor nobleman and court of session judge. This onion model fixed at a particular point in time portrays Cassillis as a man with few agnatic kinsmen and, therefore, as likely to be politically vulnerable. Yet 'sondry lordes and gentlemen' were descended from sir

Gilbert Kennedy of Dunure who died shortly after 1408, and as many as a dozen or so cadet houses of Kennedy owed allegiance and recognised Cassillis as chief of their kindred.[13] Similarly, Walter Scott of Buccleuch was chief of a large, Border kindred, but on the basis of a similar egocentric snapshot of his bilateral kin in *c.* 1600 he had no close agnatic ties other than his young son, and neither he, his father, his grandfather, nor his great-grandfather had any brothers. Buccleuch had a wide range of affinal relations through his own daughters, his mother, sisters and aunts, some of whom proved to be useful allies, but these men did not constitute his political following in the same way as the numerous Scott lairds.[14] The function of kinship as the basic building block of society was especially recognised in the Gaelic world of Ireland and Scotland, and the genealogical memory of Gaelic culture has proved relatively reliable even if modern scholarship has raised doubts about the composition of the clan and the precise structure of the clan system. It is clear that there were differences between clans in terms of formation and structure, and that few clans were bound together by people sharing a common kinship. Instead, one dominant kindred absorbed smaller kindreds, as occurred in the case of the Grants, or even formed fairly loose associations of different kindreds, as in the case of the Clan Chattan.[15] Perhaps the most meaningful way to understand the Scottish kindred or clan is as a number of houses connected by patrilineal lineages with shared agnates, identified by their common surname, and stratified by a chief who had to work at cultivating those bonds to ensure they endured into the next generation. At any point in time that chief's particular kinship relationships, his egocentric kindred, mapped onto the descent model, or family tree, providing a range of qualitatively different options that might be deployed to strengthen the larger kindred group. It is a picture not unlike that uncovered in sixteenth-century Germany where there was an explicit understanding of the distinction between the *geschlecht*, the lineage, and the *freundschaft*, the bilateral extended kin group.[16]

Throughout Europe the later medieval period saw a growing interest by noble families in constructing a collective and individual identity by manipulating history and genealogy. A key to this process was memory, posing questions for historians about how people remembered their ancestors, who shared in that remembrance, who shaped the memories and about what was forgotten, deliberately or by negligence.[17] The ways in which the lineage was imagined and articulated embraced a number of forms from a social memory that emphasised lineal ascent to a common ancestor, a generational memory in which prominence was given to distinguished ancestors, often men who acquired and passed on titles and designations, and an ethnic memory that looked back, for example, to a Norman or British origin. Obviously, there were variations on how lineage was conceived. The Neapolitan clans of southern Italy were constituted by those families who could trace a real descent from a common ancestor, while

Polish clans, or *herby*, were formed by associations of nobles around a
common coat of arms and generally dated from the twelfth century.[18] As in
much of Europe, Scottish noble houses of this period were enthusiastic in
compiling genealogical information that mixed history with myth. Many
dated their origins to the eleventh or twelfth centuries, but kindreds also had
ethnic origin myths commonly claiming descent from an eponymous
founder hailing from the early medieval or ancient world. The Duffs, for
example, claimed ancestry from the ninth-century Macduff of Fife,
allegedly a descendant of Darius the Mede. Others had more historically
rooted memories such as the Murrays who believed that their Flemish
founder, Freskin, had arrived in Scotland with David I in the twelfth
century. The Campbells encouraged a number of different origin myths,
drawing on traditions that might broadly be categorised as Anglo–Norman,
Irish and British depending on what most suited their audience. Highland
chiefs generally manipulated imagined genealogies to connect themselves
not only to ancient Irish ancestors, but also to Gaelic and Norse forebears.
Genealogy was the major tool in fashioning and aiding that collective
memory, providing historians with the basic principles for organising time,
and it is unsurprising that those writers who recorded the narratives of noble
houses followed in this tradition, transforming oral memories into written
texts.[19] Of course, there were other related forms of memorialisation. The
classic family tree was developed in the fifteenth century, shifting from an
earlier descent model to one in which a founding ancestor was illustrated
either in the roots or the trunk of a tree with generations of descendants
settled throughout the sprouting branches: heraldry acted as an aid to
memory; the dead had a role to play in their visible reconstruction in tomb
memorialisation; and the idea that noble houses had exotic continental
ancestry and kindred was maintained in decorative genealogical representa-
tions such as adorned the painted ceilings in castles and country houses.[20]

Nevertheless, noble society was aware that such claims might be spurious.
In 1580, a member of the fallen Hamilton kindred vented his frustration
at the attacks on the family by the Protestant clergy, wondering if 'the
Hamiltones was the eldest surname in Scotland, seeing the ministers fund
thame to be in the bibill evin from the begyning of Genesis to the end of
Apocalyps'. Two decades earlier, sir Richard Maitland of Lethington
observed that surnames were devised by Malcolm IV in the latter half of the
eleventh century, before which 'thair faderis name was ay thair surename ...
as yit is in thir dayis the use of the Heyland of Scotland'. That knowledge
informed the wider noble community in its use of documentation so that,
for example, in 1590 the fifth lord Sinclair prepared a pedigree of his
house, tracing its origins back to an eleventh-century French ancestor. A
Cunningham genealogist of the early seventeenth century described how the
question of the origins of the family name formed the subject for debate at
the table of the sixth earl of Glencairn, being resolved by looking up 'my

Lord's ancient evidents'.[21] Sir James Balfour of Denmilne, the lord lyon and the crown official charged with heraldic affairs, recognised that surnames had been prevalent among the Romans and Greeks, while the Hebrews had lived in tribes and retained their fathers' names in a manner similar to the Highlands. But he agreed with Lethington's more sceptical analysis, opting for the emergence of surnames in the mid-eleventh century 'which I know seimes somequhat strange to some of my loftie headed countreymen quho lyke the Arcadians, perhaps thinks ther surnames als ancient as the Moone'. Even Denmilne made a few exceptions, such as the Hays and Keiths (who claimed a descent that could be traced back sixteen hundred years to a German tribe serving in Scotland as auxiliaries to the Roman army), and he recognised that some surnames arrived from Hungary with queen Margaret, principally the Crichtons, Maules, Borthwicks and Leslies. But on the whole, Denmilne was dismissive of claims to ancient pedigrees, pointing out that even the royal surname was derived from an office in relatively recent times.[22] A similar scepticism is apparent in the works of sir Thomas Urquhart of Cromarty, who amused himself by constructing a fabulous tongue-in-cheek genealogy in which he appeared as one-hundred-and-fifty-third in line from Adam, the first Urquhart being Nomoster, a fourth century BC son-in-law of the Athenian general, Alcibiades.[23]

Yet while scepticism and humour punctures some of the more absurd claims made about the origins and invented histories of kindreds, genealogical data formed the building blocks for a serious form of history, providing families with a shared, if partially imagined, identity, fulfilling a pedagogical purpose in encouraging virtue, and promoting the glory of the lineage. Godscroft, writing about the Douglases, boasts that in the whole of history no one could discover 'such hereditarie valour in the discent of anie one familie', and that each generation of Douglases 'luiking stil with curious eyes upon the noble deides of his Ancesters, did stryve by a vertuous emulation to surpasse them in their heigest degrie of excellencie'.[24] Among the Gaelic clans of the Highlands the memorialisation and later recording of genealogies was the responsibility of the bards, who held esteemed positions within their culture. The MacDonalds maintained a credible tradition of being descended from a fourth-century high king of Ireland, while the MacLeans left a genealogical record suggesting that their ancestry can be reliably traced back to Old Dubhghall in the eleventh century, and there is a tradition linking this clan with the seventh-century brother of a king of Dál Riata. The historic record for the ancestors of the earls of Argyll can be traced back to the thirteenth-century Gillespic Campbell, but the *Mac Cailein Mór*, the Gaelic name for the Campbell chiefs, had bards who could sing of his descent from a sixth-century British warlord named Arthur or even to Adam himself.[25] Imaginative genealogies allowed nobles to project an international image. Cromarty played with this conceit, claiming that there were Urquharts scattered throughout Europe, but he lacked supporting evidence since 'by the iniquity of time and confusion of languages, their names have been varied, their coat armour altered, and, as new scions, transplanted into another soil, without any reference almost to the stock from whence they sprang'. Occasionally, real connections were established. The Montgomeries of Eglinton believed they were related to the French house of Montmorency, and in 1626, the antiquarian eleventh earl of Angus was delighted to receive letters from an Italian noble who assured the Douglas chief that he was 'your most affectionate and devoted kinsman' on the grounds of a common descent dating from the eighth century.[26]

These traditions and histories were contested, as is evident in the partisan work of Gordonstoun who took his inspiration from Tacitus and described the house of Sutherland as descendants of a noble Germanic tribe that had fearlessly resisted Roman imperialism. By contrast, he seized every opportunity to denigrate the Sinclair house of Caithness and to bastardise the ancestry of the Mackays, whose own traditions claimed descent from the thirteenth-century earls of Ross. Godscroft was more polite in dealing with the claims of other families, conceding that the Murrays and Grahams were ancient families dating from the fifth and first centuries, but he countered this pre-eminence in ancestry by choosing to emphasise ethnicity, pointing out that they were of German and Danish descent. The powerful Gordons, Hamiltons and Campbells were dismissed on the grounds that, unlike the Douglases, 'none of them in their beginning are natural Scottis men, al drawing their extraction from forrane Countries'. Such denigration of rivals took a more violent form in feuds when rival lineages seized on opportunities to separate a rival from their past by destroying their records. Hence, in 1585 the eighth lord Maxwell's deliberate burning of the Johnstone family archive at Lochwood castle.[27]

The European lineage sustained historically rooted memories of their most distinguished members and their deeds, memories that were nurtured by a system of male primogeniture in which land, titles and chieftaincy were passed down to the present.[28] Here legend and history are more difficult to disentangle than in those origin myths that are obviously fantastic. The house of Arbuthnot's ancestor, Hugh le Blond, might have been a real, heroic knight around whom were woven earlier tales about rescuing a queen from the stake and slaying a dragon. Godscroft believed the founder of the Douglases was Sholto, who won royal favour by playing a major part in the defeat of a rebel in 767, although he conceded that it was the mid-eleventh century before a more reliable ancestry could be identified. The ancestral hero of the family, however, was the 'Good' sir James, eighth lord of Douglas, also known as the 'Black Douglas', who played a prominent role in the fourteenth-century war of independence, but who also acquired elements of mythic stature.[29] The purpose of these stories was to reinforce the relationship between a hierarchic system of lordship and the lineage by representing the feudal superior and his ancestors as men of honour and valour, as protectors and defenders of their kinsmen and, therefore, as worthy chiefs of the kindred to whom the rest of the surname had some real or fictional claim of kinship. The founding ancestor of the Hay earls of Errol was thought to have been 'a base country man', but he acquired fame and fortune in *c.* 980 by inspiring the Scots to victory in battle with the Danes in the reign of Kenneth III, a legend preserved in the Hay arms. The Livingstons of Callendar emphasised the exploits of the thirteenth-century sir Andrew de Livingston and his lineal descendants, who were represented in the early seventeenth century by the earls of Linlithgow. The Ogilvy house of Airlie dated from the early fifteenth century, although the Ogilvy kindred was able to identify a longer pedigree to an offshoot of the Umfraville earls of Angus in the twelfth century.[30] In Highland clans the relationship between lordship and chieftaincy was not always clear, and kinship provided a unifying idea, sustained by a commonly recognised ancestry kept alive in the patronymic of the chief and in the memory of the lineage. Chiefs had to work at maintaining the cohesion of the clan, deploying forms of manrent, fictive kinship and military organisation to bind together a range of dependants who were not naturally united by kinship.[31] Kindreds of every size sought to exploit this idea of chieftaincy, so that Francis Stewart, fifth earl of Bothwell, addressed his cousin, James Stewart, king of Scots, as 'my soverane and chief', the king being head of the large Stewart kindred, while James Dunlop of that Ilk, an Ayrshire baron of modest power and wealth, was described as 'cheiffe of his name'. Even courtier noblemen of the early seventeenth century like the first earl of Stirling, a man who began his career as a client of the seventh earl of Argyll and who was perhaps the most British-minded of his contemporaries, indulged in what has the appearance of antiquarian self-fashioning in having himself recognised as chief of the MacAlexander clan. Allegiance to a chief was not unqualified. Gordonstoun advised his nephew to respect the first marquis of Huntly as his chief, but 'if he do not respect you as your place and qualitie, then desist to folow him, bute use him as another nyghbour; for you neid not be in any mans reverence but your princes, of whom you hold immediatlie'.[32]

Affinal Kin

Despite the legal emphasis on agnatic kin, the ways in which noble houses constructed their memories indicate a broader conception of kinship that lords were keen to exploit. If Pictish society ever had been matrilineal, no remnant of it survived into the late medieval period, but men could not ignore the value of their own daughters and female relatives in establishing links with other houses, nor could they fail to take account of the presence of females imported from other kindreds. Active relationships involving female kin did not necessarily imply weak agnatic bonds, and a lineage might be strengthened by exploiting its own women and absorbing others without sacrificing its cohesion or identity.[33] Contemporary family historians concentrated on the narrative of the lineage, particularly that of the principal house, but usually they did not ignore females. In writing his history of the Setons, Lethington believed that his patron, the fifth lord Seton, was interested in the marriage alliances of his ancestors as far back as the early fourteenth century, and in the implications those marriages had for the relationships between the Setons and the descendants of these unions. Similarly, in compiling the genealogical tables of his family, Gordonstoun was interested principally in the Gordon families, but he researched and drew up tables of those other families with which his own house had marital relationships, indicating a view of kinship that was more complex than a strictly agnatic world view might suggest.[34]

The importance of marriage in noble society, therefore, was overwhelming. Nobles – both male and female – married almost without exception, they married relatively young and, if widowed, they were likely to remarry. Marriage was central to the economic and political strategy of noble houses, and it played a role in strengthening ties within kindreds, reinforcing lordship, cementing alliances and settling bloodfeuds. Younger sons were encouraged to marry and were allocated portions of the heritable estate in a legal form that ensured it would in time return to the main branch of the family. But nobles were prepared to compromise on estate consolidation in order to establish cadet houses of their own surname and to widen the range of allies by marriage.[35] Indeed, not to marry was to put at risk the identity of a noble house and even that of the wider kindred. In the 1590s, the constant foreign travel of the sixth lord Sanquhar and his failure to settle down with a wife caused concern among his kinsmen that the 'ancient lordship might not go away to some stranger ... but such as should beare the surname and armes of Crichton'. In due course lord Sanquhar died without a legitimate heir and a disputed succession followed.[36] This determination to preserve the lineage and its surname was evident within the royal family. It was rumoured in 1565 that queen Mary urged her half-brother, the first earl of Moray, to give public support to her marriage to Henry Stewart, lord Darnley, wishing him 'to be so much a Stewart, as to consent to the keeping of the Crown in the family, and the surname, according to their Father's will and desire'. James V was disappointed at Mary's birth following the death of his young sons and at a time when he was seriously ill, commenting of his dynasty 'It came with a lass, and it will pass with a lass.' The dying king's fear was probably a literary invention, but the view expressed would be understood in a patriarchal society, reflecting the opinion of the third century jurist who wrote that 'A woman is the beginning and the end of her family.'[37] Even when biology conspired against a family, depriving it of male heirs, or suitable husbands from within the kindred, the fiction of male descent was preserved through surname substitution, a process authorised by parliament in which a man married an heiress and took her family's surname. When in 1612 sir Alexander Seton inherited the earldom of Eglinton through his mother (a sister of the fourth earl of Eglinton), he was required to change his surname to Montgomery. This was not the first time the ambitious Setons had changed names. The writer of the family history, Lethington, shifted his focus away from those Setons who emigrated north in the early fifteenth century, excusing himself on the grounds that 'thay changeit thair surename [to Gordon], and concernis na mair to my mater'.[38] As far as Lethington was concerned the Gordons had no further part in his narrative about the Seton lineage.

Yet estimates of the power of individual lords usually commented on their marital allies, indicating that in political terms marriage did matter. In the case of the fifth earl of Argyll, his two marriages and his maternal relations provided powerful links with the royal house of Stewart (his first wife was a bastard daughter of James V), the Cunningham earls of Glencairn, the Hamiltons and the Graham earls of Menteith. The earls of Argyll only married daughters of Lowland peers, while the marriages of the sons of cadet houses and of Campbell women were used to strengthen the earl's links with Ireland and other clans in the region. Similar concerns to expand territory, to provide political protection or to end bloodfeuds motivated the marriage strategies of families of lower rank such as the Mackintoshes and Grants. In November 1571, John Grant of Freuchie agreed a marriage between his daughter and the grandson of Alexander Macdonald of Glengarry with the express purpose of protecting the furthermost reaches of Freuchie's territory in western Inverness from depredations by the Clanrannald. In discussing the deployment of the daughters of the house of Sutherland, Gordonstoun counselled:

> above all things marie them to men that have weell to mainteyne them, althogh they be but gentlemen; for if they be maried to your equalls, these noble men will expect that yow will follow them, and make ther benefite of your allyance; but if yow marie your daughters to men of lower degreis then your self, yow shall be sure they and ther issue wilbe followers of yow and your house.[39]

Even in the 1620s, therefore, marriage was about more than wealth, and it brought families into new relationships that had to be reconciled with existing obligations of kindness and lordship. And those relationships could endure for a long time. In August 1570, the second lord Drummond assured Colin Campbell of Glenorchy that 'The auld kyndnes that hes indurit hundreth yeiris sall not faill in my pairt'. Of course, Drummond was exaggerating the importance of a distant marital alliance, as Glenorchy no doubt realised, but the sentiments were real, and both men wanted to believe that their relationship was founded on ancient loyalties.

The genealogical significance of women and the power they represented was recognised in family trees and in heraldry where repeated matriculations allowed new quarterings to be devised, publicly demonstrating recent matrimonial alliances between houses. Women were remembered in family tombs, and at funerals kinship was recognised among the lineal descendants of all eight great-grandparents of the deceased, thus extending beyond the agnatic kindred. In February 1635, the third earl of Mar wrote to sir Colin Campbell of Glenorchy about arrangements for the funeral of his father, reminding Glenorchy that 'you do repre[sen]t one of my aught Branches'.[40] This connection with Glenorchy arose because the late second earl of Mar's great-grandmother's father had been sir Duncan Campbell of Glenorchy who was killed at Flodden in 1513. One hundred-and-twenty-two years later, his great-great grandson was asked to participate in the Mar funeral procession.

The law recognised extended bilateral kinship. The consent of all four branches of a man's kin was a legal requirement in the granting of a letter of slains forgiving an enemy for murder. Typical of such settlements was the letter of slains granted on 24 July 1592 by Patrick Barclay of Tollie and his kinsmen to William Meldrum of Moncoffer and his servants for the murder of his father in Edinburgh three years earlier. The granters included Tollie's mother, his three brothers, two sisters, his paternal uncle and three named friends who all constituted the 'narrest of kyn and maist speciall freyndis' of the murdered man. Forgiveness was granted to Moncoffer, two named kinsmen and 'quhatsomever thair kyn freyndis assistares and partakeris'.[41] The potentially prejudicial role affinal kin might play in court was also understood. In 1631, two worried advocates appeared before the privy council to plead successfully that on the grounds of kinship – Thomas Nicholson claimed that he and the late wife of the first earl of Haddington were 'sister barnes' – they be excused defending the fourth lord Ochiltree who was facing serious political charges arising from a feud with the Hamiltons.[42]

What obligations were placed on kinsmen linked by marriage? Evidence suggests that cognatic kinsmen struck up a range of relationships from business partnerships and political alliances through to lasting friendships. Clearly the tenth earl of Angus enjoyed a good relationship with his brother-in-law, William Forbes of Monymusk, to whom he wrote in 1610 offering to help in a legal dispute, 'seing ye gat bot litle tocher gude with our sister, it was the leist thing we could give yow our kyndnes and gudwill'. When George Elphinstone of Blytheswood came to write his testament, he sought to place his family under the protection of two nobles, his own lord, the master of Elphinstone, and the lord of his wife's family, the master of Eglinton, thus maximising the advantages to be gained from his connections with his own kinsmen and those of his wife. Blytheswood was not only taking out double insurance, he was recognising that his in-laws had a say in the welfare of his children, and, indeed, this was desirable, particularly as the master of Eglinton was a powerful man. It was relatively uncommon for maternal uncles to be named as the tutor to a minor, and in 1585 parliament repeated the 1474 legislation insisting on the appointment of the nearest male agnate as tutor. It was more acceptable for a mother's kinsmen to be named as curators at a later stage in the minority. A wife's father, brothers-in-law, sons-in-law and maternal uncles appear in the prosecution and the settlement of feuds, as well as in more mundane roles such as offering bonds of caution or surety for good behaviour or debt.[43]

The extent to which women's roles as mediators of power relations in the early middle ages were restricted by the greater emphasis on lineage in early modern noble families is debatable, but women were not simply passive points of contact between men. Even in the world of male-dominated genealogies there is evidence from elsewhere that in constructing a mental grid of their kin relations some women took a broader, more inclusive view than did men.[44] On the whole, early modern noble women did not necessarily contract loyalty to their husband's kin, retaining their own surname and with it strong bonds to their own kinsmen. But they often played important roles in cultivating their husband's kindred, exploiting hospitality and other forms of social contact to impress on kinsmen that they were important persons in the broader world of the kindred.[45] The bitter quarrel between the tenth lord Forbes and John Forbes of Pitsligo was especially felt by Alexander, master of Forbes, who had married Pitsligo's daughter in 1618 and who tried to act as a mediator for as long as possible. In February 1624, the master of Forbes told his father he would make one final effort to effect a reconciliation, while his wife sent lord Forbes word that 'come what will come she must and will gladlie take a part wyth y[ou]r Lo[rdshi]p and me for the standing of the house against all the world'. Another insight into the political complexity of these relationships can be seen in the impact upon two kindreds when a marriage broke down. The marriage of the second duke of Lennox and his second wife, Jean Campbell, had irretrievably foundered by December 1609, creating for the duchess's brother, the first lord Loudon, difficulties in finding a means to 'do my sister honour without dishonour to his Lordship in any sort'. The collapse of this marriage did not necessarily mean a breach in the alliance between the heads of these two powerful west of Scotland houses, but it did place a strain on Loudon. Knowledge of what such a fissure might do prompted sir Robert Ker of Ancram in 1629 to pass on to James Johnstone of that Ilk the common-sense advice not to fall out with his father-in-law, sir James Douglas of Drumlanrig, because 'that will make a warre at your owne fyirsyde, for your children are also his'.[46]

Marriage was a means to make peace between warring kindreds. When Gordonstoun wrote to his nephew about the old feud between his own house of Sutherland and that of Caithness he commented that 'out of all question that ancient hereditarie heatred long rooted betuix your two famelies cannot be intirely taken away, nor heartelie reconciled without mariage'. Examples of marriage being used successfully to cement the peace between feuding families can be found, for example, between the Scotts and Kerrs in 1564, or in the settlement of the Huntly–Moray–Argyll feuds in 1607.[47] Yet marriage was a poor means of reconciling feuding parties. It was the political will behind the settlement that ensured peace endured, the marriage itself was a means of affirming what had been agreed and it served as a living tableau of that peace. Where the peace was insecure, marriage was unlikely to overcome a desire to resume hostilities. The 1570 marriage between David Lindsay of Edzell and Helen, only daughter of his chief, the tenth earl of Crawford, was intended 'for confirming the amity, love and tenderness between them'. Unfortunately, the bitter rivalry between the two branches of the kindred continued with bloody consequences for both houses. Ultimately, late medieval and early modern marriage by itself was a fragile bond between noble houses and between kindreds, and it rarely created durable political loyalties.[48] On the whole, strong loyalties to cognatic kin undermined the cohesion of a kindred and it was the confluence of agnatic ties and lordship that made the noble lineage so powerful.[49]

The Dynamics of Kinship

Kinship, therefore, persisted as a powerful societal bond even if it was reinforced and stretched, and it constituted a bond with real implications for the exercise of noble power by chiefs. When David Hume of Godscroft described a political environment in which nobles were 'linked and bound to one another by kindred and alliance', the kinship bonds he had in mind went beyond immediate bilateral relatives to embrace the lineage and its living kindred. This was an intensely localised society with deep tribal loyalties where two warring clans were described as 'two races of people', a world that John Napier of Merchiston conceptualised as divided among the 'kindreds of the earth'. The sixth lord Lovat reputedly said 'there was no earthly thing he put in ballance with his kindred', and was 'wont to say that his men wer his ammunition, his guard, his glory and honor, and few could compeat with them'. In an undated letter of the 1620s, the exiled seventh earl of Argyll asked a friend 'to lett the wourlde know how much I love my hous above all other temporall good'. Gordonstoun used similar language at this time: 'Let a Gordones querrell be your own, so farr as he hath right and equitie on his syde. Preferre your surname (though they be not within degrie defendant) to your neerest allyance.'[50] Here in the language of these lords was an uncompromising, albeit exaggerated, view of the mutual loyalty owed among kinsmen.

The strong bond that existed between kinship and territory served to reinforce the kindred's or clan's sense of identity, and shaped the geopolitical map of the kingdom. Many surnames had their origins in places; thus, the Ogilvies took their name from the lands of Pury Ogilvy in Angus.

As in France, most nobles who did not possess a title were designated by the name of their estate, although the Scots developed a more user-friendly system than the French. Lethington believed that initially surnames were given to landed gentlemen since many of them were derived from place names, while Gordonstoun was of the opinion that 'in auntient tymes countreyes took ther names from the inhabitants'. On this point Denmilne declared that place names obviously pre-dated surnames.[51] Whatever came first, the connection between place and name was strong, and many localities were intimately identified with a particular surname. The eastern march is best understood politically in terms of the families living within that geographic and administrative space: the Humes, Kers, Pringles and other lesser families numbering 307 noble houses of varying status.[52] In the Highlands, charter-based right to land – the *oighreach* – was crucially important, but rival claims founded on customary rights backed up by physical possession – the *duthchas* – often created tension and many of the feuds of the period had at their root the territorial integrity of rival kindred groups. Genealogy was often manipulated as a tool to legitimise that control, descent offering an opportunity to claim a right to tenancy and clanship being a means to extend the power of chiefs. When the seventh earl of Argyll sought to expand his influence into Islay in the early seventeenth century, sir James Macdonald, heir to MacDonald of Dunyveg, swore that 'I will die befoir I see a Campbell possess it'. Here was an extreme point of view, but sir James nearly did die in his vain attempt to halt the expansion of the house of Argyll.[53]

Territory, therefore, was intimately connected to kindreds, hence, in the mid-1560s Carrick was defined by one observer as a geographic space 'Inhabited by therle of Cassills and his frendes'. Intelligence reports compiled for the English government drew attention to the strength of a particular surname in a given locality. Furthermore, most of these reports took as their starting point not the locality itself but the dominant lord of that locality and his surname. This was a world divided into kindreds focused on noble houses and their lords, where one commentator, writing in *c.* 1600 about the feuds of north Ayrshire, summarised the political realities of the locality in terms of families, and, in particular, of the lords who were the chiefs of those families: 'Thair be twa famous housis of antiquitie in the west of Scotland: To wit, Montgomerie of Eglintoun, and Cunynhayme of Kylmawres.' There was little need to explain further. That same sense of the identity of the locality being fused with a particular family is evident in the conceptualisation of Gordonstoun's *History of the house of Sutherland*. In writing about the change of surname in the earldom at the beginning of the sixteenth century, he commented 'we must begin a new government under a new surname'.[54] With the change in name, a chapter closed in the history of Sutherland and its people.

The strength of a kindred was affected by the geographic proximity of its

branches. A relatively minor chief like the Leslie house of Balquhane had
significant influence in Aberdeenshire because 'the haill cuntrey is of thair
surname, kin freindis or assistaris'. But Balquhane had little contact with the
earls of Rothes in Fife, the nominal head of the Leslie kindred, in contrast
to the second lord Lindores, another Fife landowner, who, in spite of his
own status, still referred in 1637 to the sixth earl of Rothes as his chief.[55]
Efforts were made by some lords to draw disparate kin groups together by
bonds. On 3 March 1599, sir John Murray of Tullibardine and seventeen
Murray lairds, including James Murray of Cockpool whose estates were
located far from the main concentration of the kindred, signed a bond of
association recognising that 'we are far dispersed in sundry parts of this
realm far distant from others', and promising mutual defence in lawful
causes and internal arbitration in cases of disagreement. A similar bond was
entered into by the Campbells of Cawdor to retain links with their kinsmen
in Argyll. In a remarkable bond of 8 August 1625, mutual maintenance was
agreed between various members of the Farquarson and Shaw kindreds in
recognition of an oral tradition that the Farquharsons were descended from
the Shaws, having moved north and settled on Speyside centuries earlier.
Therefore, since:

> thir sundrye and divers aiges bygane past memorie of man, baith the saidis
> pairteis hes throche the remotenes and distance of thair dwelling places bein
> ignorant of utheris or of thair freindschipe, sua that the consanguinite betwixt
> them till now hes bein altogether obscure, and seeing the saidis pairteis and
> freindis acknowleges them selffes to be of one blood and to be cum of one
> stock and race, so that of all equitie and conscience, freindschipe and amitie
> sould be keipit and interteinit amngis them.[56]

Government recognised these long-distance relationships. Significantly,
when in 1580 the leading Gordon lairds of the northeast were summoned
to Edinburgh to discuss their feud with the Forbes, John Gordon of Lochinvar, the head of a cadet branch of the Gordons that had separated off from
the main family in the late thirteenth century and were located in the south-
west of the country, was included. Similarly, in 1600 the crown underlined
the fact that the Ayrshire Campbells of Loudon were a 'a branch of the
house of Argyll', being a cadet house established in the early fourteenth
century. Uniquely, the MacDonalds continued to recognise an ongoing
relationship with the Irish earls of Antrim, which was to be mobilised
during the warfare of the 1640s.[57] These examples are unusual, however, and
a degree of territorial integrity was normally essential to the functioning of
a kindred and to the power of its chief.

That power was measured by the size and cohesion of their kinsmen, and
in the intelligence reports gathered for the English government in the later
sixteenth century some nobles were dismissed as unimportant on account of
the fact that there were 'not many of their surname'. In the early 1590s,

the clientele of the second earl of Moray recognised that his lordship was weakened by the fact that so few of his tenants were Stewarts of his own surname. When in 1597 the relatively weak sixth lord Innermeath inherited the earldom of Atholl, he faced enormous problems in holding together that once powerful affinity. The indebtedness of the estates and his own meagre following made it difficult to step into the vacuum created by the ending of the senior Stewart line of earls. In April of that year he wrote to John Ogilvy of Inverquharitie in an attempt to stir up enthusiasm for his lordship within the region, pointing out the historic relationship between the two houses and their 'proximitie of blude' as the basis for a common interest in which 'we ar alse willing and reddie to plesour yow and to do for yow and youris aganis quhatsumevir ye haif adoo wyth, as the Erlis of Athole hes done of befoir, and better gif we may, heirfoir'.[58] This does not conjure up a picture of the great magnate summoning his dependants, but of an insecure earl begging a neighbouring laird to take him seriously, using for an argument an unconvincing appeal to the tenuous kinship connection between the two houses.

The number of kinsmen a nobleman could summon, therefore, was a crucial indicator of political potency. This point was made by an indignant fourth earl of Huntly in March 1560 when he wrote to the French ambassador, accusing him of lying, pointing out that 'we have 100 gentlemen "*de nostre nourriture*", the least of whom is your equal', offering to fight to prove the lie when the ambassador demitted office.[59] It is important to be cautious about the size and cohesiveness of these kindreds, but in broad terms sprawling, powerful noble clans were most likely to be found across Europe in territories such as Scotland where the idea of a nobility of birth was strong, there were large numbers of undifferentiated poor nobles, and in upland and frontier regions where the use of real and socially constructed kinship was intended to maximise the number of men available to chiefs.[60] Political and economic factors were significant in affecting the collective success of the kindred, and it is no great surprise to discover that successful families like the Douglases, Campbells, Gordons and Hamiltons spawned large kindreds over the course of the fifteenth and sixteenth centuries. The patronage available to the houses of Angus, Argyll, Huntly and Arran ensured that cadet houses could be supported by land, and the size of these kindreds in turn made it certain that their chiefs would be recognised as magnates of the first order.[61] A list of January 1566 contains 264 names with the duke of Chatelherault's surname, household and dependants who received a remission from the queen. Another list of *c.* 1570 names 227 men, including over one hundred Hamiltons who formed the core of this powerful interest. In addition to Chatelherault, his sons, and his brother, the heads or heirs of some sixty-five barons are named, an astonishing number of lesser nobles that the Hamilton chief could number among his kinsmen. When in 1579 lords John and Claud Hamilton were driven into exile the privy council denounced, or demanded caution, of 143 Hamiltons, their friends, servants and tenants. In the 1640s the third marquis of Hamilton's immediate affinity amounted to 28 household men, 123 dependants, 50 removable tenants, and 17 retainers, 218 men in all. Even in the 1640s the power that Hamilton could summon from among his own kindred should not be disregarded.[62] The Hamiltons were among the largest kindred, and only a handful of other families could claim so many landed heads of houses among its number. Most kindreds were more modest, like the fifty or so Johnstones, not all landed men, who pledged loyalty to John Johnstone of that Ilk in a bond of January 1579, promising to be answerable for any crimes that might lead to their chief being charged for their actions.[63] A more textured reconstruction of a kindred can be achieved by using such lists and other forms of surviving evidence, such as charters, cautions, assurances, testaments and letters, to construct detailed kinship maps of individuals and of entire kindreds. For example, prior to the final settlement of the Cunningham–Montgomery feud in 1609, summons were directed to the sixth earl of Glencairn and twenty-five of his kindred and friends, a mixture of the heads of cadet houses and others among whom were tenants and servants.[64]

Relatively few bonds of manrent and maintenance were made between men of the same surname, because lords normally had no need to take men into a relationship that conferred the privileges of kinship if they already were kinsmen. Yet such bonds did occur. In October 1566, twenty-six Johnstones pledged themselves and their kinsmen, friends and servants to obey and serve their chief, John Johnstone of that Ilk. In a self-regulating bond of December 1578, the Johnstones comprehended within their kindred all those 'that beris and hes the nayme of Johnnstounis in speciall and in generall quha dependis upon the lard of Johnnstoun'.[65] For the Johnstones, the core of their power was the surname, but here kinship was enlarged to include those dependent upon their chief. In a 1595 bond of manrent granted by sir Alexander Hume of Manderston to the sixth lord Hume, the former stated that 'I am obleist to serve and acknawledge ane noble and potent lord Alexander, Lord Home my verie gude lord and cheiff, as ane member of his house'. Even in the settled context of January 1613, a number of Ogilvy lairds signed a bond recognising sir Walter Ogilvy of Findlater and his heirs as their chief, promising to ride with, assist and accompany him in all his actions concerning the welfare of the house of Findlater. Repeatedly bonds strike this note: lords and their men were reaffirming kinship, or, by the very act of making a bond of this nature, they were becoming like kinsmen. As the fourth earl of Montrose wrote in a letter to his friend and client sir William Livingston of Kilsyth in 1609, 'I look ye will honour the sam as ane Graem, whilk I have found you ever in effecte'.[66]

Gordonstoun advised the thirteenth earl of Sutherland in *c.* 1620 to nurture 'a strict freindschip and inviolable union betuix you and your surname, and mutuallie among them selfs, otherways it may undo you all'. It was the Gordon surname that made the house of Sutherland strong, 'And if they be wise they will endevoir with all ther might to uphold your house, without the which they ar but a handfull, exposed to the hatred and rage of there nighbours'.[67] Kinship, therefore, offered a form of collective security, and its cultivation was taken seriously, but those same bonds could be deployed destructively in feuding. Alexander Arbuthnot, principal of King's College, Aberdeen, reflected ruefully on these obligations in a poem in 1572 during the civil war:

> I luif justice; and wald that everie man
> Had that quhilk richtlie dois to him perteine;
> Yet all my kyn, allya, or my clan,
> In richt or wrang I man alwayis mantene,
> I maun applaud, quhen thai thair matters mene,
> Thoch conscience thairto do not consent,
> Quhat marvel is thoch I murne and lament?

Kinship, therefore, provided one of the foundations for the exercise of a form of noble power that could be seen as destructive even if the organising principle was mutual self-defence. A commitment to aid kinsmen in feuds, either in assisting in the peace process or in the prosecution of violence, was one of the most important tests of kin relationships.[68] Violence between kindreds was commonplace, and while political pressures began to alter the behaviour of lords and men in the early seventeenth century, instances of kinsmen and clansmen being mobilised to deploy force continued into the 1620s and 1630s.[69] Nevertheless, it is important to recognise that the violent prosecution of a bloodfeud was only one option available to nobles, and kinsmen were expected to participate in the business of making peace and in seeking justice. When in 1605 sir David Lindsay of Edzell's comfortable life was shattered by his son's killing of a rival, the counsel from a number of leading lawyers was that he must mobilise his kindred. Edzell was advised to enlist the assistance of his chief, the eleventh earl of Crawford, and other prominent kinsmen and friends to discuss his defence. He should summon:

> the best and perfytest rackoneris of genealogies within ilk shirefdom north and south, to be present in this towne to confer thairupon for decyding of the persones of Inqueist, and to try and gif up in dew tyme be perfyte rollis in weritt the genealogies alsweill of the persewaris as of all the barrounes and utheris quha may be summondit upon your assyse.

Edzell's kinsmen were not urging him to engage in violence, but the kindred was being mobilised by a court of session judge to protect him from the injustices of bloodfeud and legal action.[70]

The influence played by kinship and lineage on broader political behaviour varied across early modern Europe; for example, it was relatively unimportant in Russia, but essentially it provided a basis for meaningful obligations and relationships that shaped politics. Kinship was more stable than brittle patron–client relationships and the political factions that formed around them.[71] When in 1594 a client told lord Hamilton that the Campbells 'ar no freinds to your lordship your hous and name' he was stating one of the well-known and widely recognised fixed points of political life.[72] Among the later sixteenth-century peerage, numbering around fifty houses, the impression can be of a single extended family: thus, it was said that the eighth earl of Angus had a great number of friends, 'his house having beene so eminent of a long time, and there being few of the nobles, but were either descended of it, or tied to it by some consanguinity, affinity, or other relation'. Examples are plentiful: the fourth earl of Atholl counselled his son in April 1579 'to keep friendship and kindness with my Lord Earle of Argyle and that house in respect of the proximitie of blude standand betwix thame and grit friendship continowit betwix us and our forbearis'.[73] Consequently, the fortune of entire surnames, not only the heads of noble houses, was affected by court and local politics. In October 1579, after the fall of the Hamiltons, a proclamation was issued ordering all persons of that name to leave Edinburgh and not to come within six miles of the king, while other kindreds suffered similar persecution under different circumstances. When the Magregors were condemned to death on account of their repeated banditry they were offered a pardon if individuals of the clan appeared penitent before the privy council 'to ressave a new name'.[74] Yet in spite of the risks, kinsmen could be remarkably loyal to all but the least competent or untrustworthy lords. The well-established Gordon cadet houses of Gight, Abergeldie, Coclarchie and Lesmoir demonstrated fierce faithfulness to successive earls of Huntly throughout the turbulent decades after 1560, taking part in feuds and rebellions that cost these families in terms of lives, wealth and forfeitures. They were still dependent on their chief in the 1630s, standing by Huntly over the notorious Frendraught affair.[75]

Chiefs and their kindreds went to great lengths to ensure that potentially destructive internal conflicts were resolved by self-regulation. Bonds of manrent and maintenance were used to reinforce customary obligations as in October 1572 when an exchange of bonds between the third earl of Eglinton and Hugh Montgomery of Giffen included a clause in the latter's manrent relating that Eglinton had initiated a legal action against Giffen on the grounds that he and his predecessors had alienated land without his consent.[76] Where quarrels did break out, mechanisms were negotiated to allow for internal arbitration. In 1578, it was agreed that any dispute among the Johnstone kindred over blood, goods or land would be submitted to 'as amable freindis equalie chosin be the rest and consent of the nayme that hecht Johnnstoun'. In June 1582 the Ker lairds signed a self-regulating bond following a killing within the kindred, and in July 1586, a bond was drawn up by the principal Murray lairds providing for mutual defence and self-regulation 'sua that anis cause shall be all and all shall be aine'. In February 1588 an agreement was made by sir Archibald Stirling of Keir, his friends, kinsmen and surname to voluntarily submit any quarrel they might have to Keir himself and four friends 'maist newtreale to the parteis' in what was intended to prevent litigation or feuding within the kindred.[77] Nevertheless, even strong kindreds did not always display solidarity, a point supported by evidence from France and Ireland where kinship was not weak.[78] In 1592, sir Alexander Bruce of Airth with his family and friends signed an obligation not to assist John Bruce of Auchinbowie and his house against David Sommerville of Plean. Airth wanted nothing to do with his kinsmen's feuds, but relationships within the kindred could deteriorate to the point of creating internal conflict. Sir Thomas Craig of Riccarton observed that 'So far from acting as a protection against discord, community of blood often intensifies the bitterness of family quarrels'. Hence, Gordonstoun's strictures on the absolute necessity of keeping peace within families:

> Heat that man as the pest who would preasse to sowe dissention betuix you and your brethren, for by discord great things do perishe, and by concord small things do become great. Your famelie had ever that good propertie to keip a perpetuall love and freindship among themselfs.

His strong views on this subject grew out of the good relationship that characterised the house of Sutherland, and was informed by the contrasting fortunes of the earls of Caithness whose internal squabbles had been so damaging to the Sinclairs. Gordonstoun drew attention to the Forbes who 'wer at warrs with another, daylie impairing ther owne strenth by ther owne slaughters, and in end wrought ther owne confusion, by preassing to stryve against the Gordouns'.[79]

Kin solidarity could be tested in many ways, especially during the minority of a lord or chief. When the fifth lord Lovat unexpectedly died in 1577, leaving a seven-year-old son, an assembly of the gentlemen of the clan discussed the appointment of a tutor. Rival claims were made by the uncle and brother of the late lord Lovat, and the meeting almost ended in the exchange of blows before narrowly reaching a compromise. Where there were feuds within a kindred every effort was made to bring the warring parties to an accommodation, such as that made in the early 1580s between different branches of the Scott kindred following a number of killings.[80] But as the Scott case exemplifies, kindreds did tear themselves apart in bloody and bitter conflicts, significantly weakening the power of their chiefs. Divisions within the Lindsays dated back to 1537 when the 'wicked master of Crawford' was excluded from succeeding to the earldom of Crawford, provoking a feud with the house of Edzell that claimed the life of the first lord Spynie in 1605, and drove both families close to ruin. The internecine Innes kindred committed a series of bloody murders in the late 1570s

and early 1580s; the usually well-disciplined Campbells came close to dis-
integrating as a clan during the minority of the seventh earl of Argyll when
the tutor of Argyll was assassinated; the MacDonnells of Antrim and
Dunyveg feuded throughout the 1590s, fatally undermining Clan Ian Mor;
the long rivalry between the Ker houses of Cessford and Ancram over the
provostry of Jedburgh led in December 1590 to the murder of William Ker
of Ancram, shot dead on the stairway of an Edinburgh close; and the
Kennedies waged open warfare in south Ayrshire in the early 1600s.[81]

None of these kindreds, or any other caught up in murderous quarrelling,
fragmented entirely, and these exceptions do not support the view advanced
by those late medieval English historians who argue that kindred ties did
not work. Furthermore, the disappearance of kindreds and the decline of
kinship as a political bond is commonly exaggerated, and the differentiated
rate of change from one region to another, the subtle ways in which informal
networks of power remained undisturbed, and the many variables suggested
as an explanation make a simple cause and effect unlikely.[82] What can be
advanced in the Scottish case is that the successful campaign against the
bloodfeud made kinship less crucial to a system of mutual protection, while
the removal of the royal court to London began to change the nature
of political clientage. Yet evidence for lords turning their backs on their
kinsmen in pursuit of more commercially driven goals arises from the
mid-sixteenth century. Lethington repeatedly decried the falling away of
kindness as more material interests took precedence, but his view of the
world was that of an old man who imagined the sun shone brighter when he
was a boy. His cry that 'Sen in this warld, in na degree,/Is kyndnes, nor
fidelitie' was simply not true. The theme is developed further in 'Advyce to
kyndness':

> From nather honour faith nor conscience,
> Nor gratitud done of benevolence,
> Neirness of bluide, nor yet affinitie,
> Can in this warld gar kyndnes keipit be,
> As may be sein be plaine experience.

There is no question that the feuing (the granting of leases heritably over a
very long number of years in return for much higher rentals) of customary
tenures over the course of the sixteenth century displaced many kindly
tenants, but the process of placing estate management on a more commercial basis was retarded by the political instability of the sixteenth century. A
renewed determination on the part of landlords to extract greater revenue
from their estates in the more settled conditions of the early seventeenth
century contributed to a changing pattern in some lord–man relationships,
placing some strain on kinship ties. In 1632, Gordonstoun's younger
brother, sir Alexander Gordon of Navidale, was offended when the
thirteenth earl of Sutherland redeemed lands from him in circumstances

that were financially painful. He drew wider implications from his nephew's behaviour, commenting that 'thair was never any man so onnaturallie delt withall for goode serwice'. Navidale observed that 'I am not the first cadent off ane hous that hes bein put to his shift, albeit the first so ongraitfullie usit'. The anger and bewilderment of this man was not unique for in the end chiefs took decisions that were based on a hard-headed estimation of their own interests. The first earl of Nithsdale, a rapacious and heavily indebted courtier who was chief of the Maxwell kindred, refused to sell sir John Maxwell of Pollok the superiority of his land, preferring instead to find a buyer elsewhere. In 1629, Pollok wrote an indignant letter to his chief:

> I pray your Lordship use me kyndlie, and remember of my service main-tenance done to your Lordship, bothe be my self and my predicessouris, and remember quhat distres I and they hes for your Lordship and your house. Remember, lykewyse, my Lord, that I and myne is Maxwellis, and will be reddie to serve your Lordship heirefter, bot give anie other bwy it, and they pay your Lordship for it, they will think they have no more to doe with your Lordship.

Nithsdale's self-interest is an indication of the commercial motivation among lords that would in due course undermine the kinship ties at the heart of lordship, but in the early seventeenth century the earl's behaviour was regarded as unusual and offensive. Pollok was articulating the com-monly held attitude of the kinship community that as a Maxwell he owed loyalty to Nithsdale that went beyond the obligations of a rent-paying tenant. Here in the emphasis on the primacy of the ancestral blood within the estate community were the foundations on which chiefs built their power and which lords like Nithsdale threatened to undermine.[83]

The church, too, threatened to erode the bonds of kinship. One obvious change that took place after the Reformation was that the connection between the living and the dead of a kindred was loosened because the former no longer prayed, or paid others to pray, for the souls of their ancestors. In other respects the church's impact upon the kindred was indirect, a product of an imperceptible shift in allegiances rather than a direct assault on the ideology of kinship. John Knox's family had been clients of the fourth earl of Bothwell, a fact that explains his relative lack of criticism of this nobleman and his point that 'this is part of the obligation of our Scottish kindness'. But the Reformation added a new complication to the nature of lord–man relationships in that lords and men now had to allow for one another's religion, with some dependants unwilling to follow their chief's choice in matters of faith. This was a gradual process and bonds of personal loyalty continued to cut across religious divisions such that within a lord's affinity there might be both Catholics and Protestants. In 1560, the English ambassador, Thomas Randolph, recognised that new confessional divisions might place strains on lordship, identifying the willingness of the fourth earl of Cassillis to support the Protestants, while admitting that 'his friends are harder to be agreed with than he himself'. Loyalties worked in the opposite direction. When in 1584 the ultra-Protestant eighth earl of Angus was challenged for having Catholic servants he replied that he had little choice but 'to keep such as he found most obedient and faithful to him and his causes'.[84] The church impacted on noble power structures in other ways. In the course of an audience with the king in July 1583, David Fergusson, minister of Dunfermline, said 'I would there were not a surname in Scotland, for they mak all the cummer [= disturbance]', a sentiment with which the young James VI agreed. But there was nothing intrinsically sinful about kinship, and it was the abuse of kinship obligations in the violent pursuit of a feud, or in the avoidance of justice, that drew most criticism. In a sermon in 1589 the outspoken Edinburgh minister, Robert Bruce, warned noblemen that 'no community of name, ally, proximity of blood, or whatever it be, move you to pervert justice, but let every man be answered according to the merit of his cause'. Of course, the idea that a man should turn his back on his family for the sake of the gospel was orthodox Christian teaching, but it took on a new edge in the 1590s in the hands of a clergy who were 'but kinless bodies'. Not everyone subscribed to the more extreme views of these ministers, but within the educated circles of society there was a broader debate about the role of kinship in a civic society, particularly once that society was thrown into closer contact with English political culture. The case against nobles exercising power through kinship was not clear-cut, even among those ministers who saw that power as a defence against imperial monarchy.[85]

At a secular level, too, there was some understanding that while kinship was a basic building block of a society in the early stages of development, the bonds of kinship should mature into the broader social relations of a civic society. Riccarton made this point in *Jus feudale*, arguing that society should expect 'the extention of amicable and social relations beyond the limits of kinship and dependancy', resulting in 'the wider relation of common citizenship'.[86] But there was no initiative on the part of the crown to confront the existence of kindreds, or to weaken the bonds within them. Royal government was too dominated by men steeped in these same values and lacked the will or the resources to attack the role of noblemen as chiefs. Instead, kings encouraged nobles to use their influence in the service of the crown. In January 1606, the earl of Dunbar brought to Edinburgh 'ane very great number of honorabill baronis, and gentilmen of gude rank and wourth, of his kindred and freindschip' in order to pack the assize for the trial of those ministers accused of holding an illegal and treasonable assembly at Aberdeen. Kings had no quarrel with kinship as long as it was deployed in the interests of the crown. Of course, courtier magnates had to work at cultivating their kinsmen, and the failing of the third marquis of Hamilton to raise the Hamiltons in support of Charles I in 1638 was not due to a collapse in kindreds as political forces, but to the combination of ideological differences of opinion and the particular deficiencies of Hamilton as a chief.[87] More broadly, the crown encouraged and exploited the authority of nobles over their kinsmen to impose and maintain order by way of the general band that was extended from the Borders into the Highlands. The 1587 legislation that regularised the practice of making lords responsible for the behaviour of their men specifically recognised the authority of 'chiefs and chieftains of all clans'. In 1594, parliament condemned the 'wicked thieves and rogues of the clans and surnames', and the seventh earl of Argyll was among the first to give his assurance that he would be responsible for 'all the persons of the surname of Campbell' dwelling on his lands. Critics jumped on the implications of a law that made noblemen responsible for the criminal behaviour of men with whom they shared a surname, but over whom they wielded no practical authority. Here was a wedge being driven unintentionally between kinsmen. In 1635, the old first marquis of Huntly tried to evade responsibility for the behaviour of his men, claiming they were 'discendit of ane stok be them selfis, who wes seiking revenge of thair blood, and wold nather be counsallit nor reullit be him', but the privy council disagreed and insisted that he was their chief.[88]

Conclusion

Early modern historians can be too quick to under-rate the enduring importance of kinship relations in local and national politics. Often the assumption that underlies such thinking places kinship in an unnecessary opposition to government when it was noble families and their broader kinship connections that determined the actions of government. In seventeenth-century England there is evidence to suggest that a lineage culture thrived, that local political relationships were largely shaped by kinship and that these bonds and obligations were carried through into the civil war. Indeed, a persuasive case has been made for the survival of the concept of the lineage family in English society into the eighteenth century. Elsewhere longitudinal studies of noble families confirm a similar lasting emphasis on ideas about the lineage and a practical cultivation of kinship ties that extend beyond the nuclear family. It was the bonds of kinship, reinforced by religious cohesion, that ensured the modest success of the Lacger family in southern France generation after generation.[89] It is unlikely, therefore, that the powerful form of kinship that dominated Scottish political life for centuries, and was so pervasive throughout the last decades of the sixteenth century, simply withered away in the few decades before the revolution of 1637. The political history of the later seventeenth century and the eighteenth century suggest otherwise, as court and electoral politics continued to be organised around noble clienteles that had kinship at their core. Nor is it necessary to see the emphasis placed on kinship through the encouragement of family histories and genealogies as a primarily defensive psychological reaction to unwelcome societal change.[90] From *c.* 1610, however, the decline of feuding removed some of the external threat that pushed kinsmen together, at least in the Lowlands. The desire to run estates more profitably and the church's criticism of the abuses of kinship loosened ties, but the crown did not seek to accelerate changes that were barely perceptible at the time and kings continued to deal with noblemen as heads or chiefs of kindreds and clans. When revolution and civil warfare did break out after 1637 the nobility were not slow to harness kinship to their cause just as their fathers and grandfathers had done, and from the conduct of lords and men in the military conflicts of the covenanting era that kinship continued to contribute to the mobilisation and deployment of force.[91] In the northeast, a region that was certainly not Highland in character, or dominated by Gaelic clans, local historians recount the early years of the conflict in the same language as that used of the previous civil war of 1567–73. In narrating the preparations for the Raid on Turriff on 14 February 1639, Patrick Gordon recounted that:

> The Gordounes and some other barrones, with them that favoured the king, was forced to looke to themselfes; for the Forbesses, there old enemies, being a great and numerous familie of brave and valient gentlemen, for the most part, with the Hayes, Keathes, Frasers, Crichtones, and the whole rest of the north, being all Covenanters, drew themselfes to a head, having thre randevoues at Tuuefe, where there came numbers of goodly gentlemen, well horsed, with a confident foot of power.[92]

Arguably the greater part of Scotland's localities saw nobles mobilising their kindreds in a similar manner. It was the covenanting revolution, with its increasingly fractured ideological divisions alongside engagement in a massive military enterprise throughout all three British kingdoms, that ripped apart any vestiges of the Lowland kindred as the basis of a private army. In the Highlands it had the opposite effect, consolidating the clan and its rhetoric of kinship as the basic unit of violent power for another century.

CHAPTER 3

Lords

Late medieval Scottish lordship shared many of the features of lordship found elsewhere in the British Isles where Norman ideas encountered native societies, resulting in a range of solutions from the outright imposition of Norman lordship in England to varieties of adaptation to local conditions elsewhere.[1] The survival of lordship in later sixteenth-century Europe has been interpreted as a sign of societal backwardness and of the weakness of royal government. Underlining such analysis is a tendency to approach lordship as a form of power that was anachronistic, in decline and waiting to be swept aside by the forces of the state, religion and commercialisation. Yet while, for example, Scottish nobles did place their estates on a more commercial footing in the early seventeenth century, this did not inevitably lead to a shift in the political usefulness of those long-established power networks created by lord–man relationships.[2] Of course, there were societal changes, but is it possible that in the desire to dismiss lordship prematurely those features which persisted have been overlooked?

In discussing lordship, a simple vertical model of unproblematic connections between those exercising power and those subject to that power is inadequate in describing a network through which a range of power relationships were mediated. Undoubtedly, lords exercised power over their men, and that power was exercised differently in relation to different kinds of men, but lords had to negotiate with their men at the limits of that power. The societal values that defined good lordship, the nature of service by a range of men and the dynamics of the lord's affinity contributed to the power of individual nobles and to the collective power of the nobility. Why these foundations of noble power were so durable requires further exploration, as do the changes that impacted upon lordship at the beginning of the seventeenth century.

Good Lordship

In March 1584, the dying John Grant of Freuchie consulted his kinsmen on his record as their lord and was presented with a declaration signed by fourteen of his principal followers declaring that they 'findis na falt with our said cheif, his son nor oo [= grandson], in ony proceiding past'.[3] Freuchie's consultation exercise proved to be gratifying, as was intended, but what constituted a good lord? Noble society produced its own guidance and memorials to inspire and instruct nobles that contain elements of wishful thinking and hagiography, but they provide a useful starting point.[4] Sir Richard Maitland of Lethington's mid-sixteenth-century ideal of good lordship was of a faithful Christian and a loyal subject who would:

> keip societe peax and cherite wyth thy nychtbouris, and hurt thame nocht in thair same bodie nor gudis, nor provoik thame nocht to ire; and gif thame no occasioun nor caus of displesour aganis thy self, or ony uther. And Ferdlie, that thow treit thy tenentis and thame that ar in thy cure wyth meiknes and mercy, and lat name of thame do wrang to uther, bot hald thame in gude ordour be justice. Defend thame from oppressioun of thair inimeis: oppres thame nocht thy self be importable service and extorsiounis. Tak thy dewite of thame wyth discretioun; and gif ony of thame, be adventure, fall in poverte, gif thame, len thame, and feist thame of thy geir. Defend wedois and puir orphalingis. Remove nane of thy pure tennentis fra thair posessounis wythout notable probable and intollerable causis.[5]

Here was an ideal of good lordship, inherited from medieval society, and still powerful in the sixteenth century when writers penned sketches of individual lords consistent with this picture. It was said of the fourth earl of Bothwell that 'the cair of the commoun weill appertenit maist till him and the rest of the nobilitie, wha suld be fathers to the same'; the duke of Chatelherault was remembered as 'a prince so debonaire as any uther in all respects, will belovit of all the people of Scotland, and naymelie of the pure'; the second duke of Lennox was 'weill liked for his courtesis, meekness, liberalitie to his servants and followers'.[6] The point is not that these descriptions were accurate, but that writers believed these to be worthy attributes.

The early seventeenth century provides vigorous evidence of societal conformity around ideas of good lordship. In discussing the eighth earl of Angus (d. 1587, but the text is early seventeenth century) as an ideal lord, his secretary, David Hume of Godscroft, related that 'duetie, justice and vertue were the men of his counsell, and the square by which he ruled all his actions'. The sixth lord Lovat was remembered as 'a very good man, generous, free and hospital, much given to charety', fondly remembered for his concern to keep peace and his open hospitality. John Spalding penned a biographical note of the first marquis of Huntly as 'ane gryte spirit' who avoided conflict with his neighbours, disliked litigation and loved peace, quiet and a modest lifestyle. Caution is required since Godscroft and Spalding were writing against a background of discontent with their current lords, and were pointing to these dead nobles as ideal types. Sir Robert Gordon of Gordonstoun, however, was offering practical advice when sketching his portrait of the good lord in *c.* 1620:

Let your kindred and allyes bee welcome alwayes to your table; grace them
with your counteinance, and ever further them in all ther honest actions by
word, liberalitie or industrie; for by that meanes you shall double the bond of
nature.[7]

Whatever was happening to lordship in the early seventeenth century, it is
significant that there was no change in the ideal circulating within noble
society.

An essential requirement expected of nobles was a physical presence
within the lordship community. The first earl of Orkney's reputation on
Shetland was not helped by the fact that he visited the islands only five times
between 1567 and 1593. Narrative accounts of the second earl of Moray
suggest a popular, warlike lord cruelly murdered by his enemies in February
1592, but more objective evidence reveals an absentee, neglectful and incompetent lord.[8] Effective lords continued to reside mostly in their localities, and
one of the crown's problems lay in persuading nobles to leave their estates to
attend parliament, privy council or the royal court. After 1603, a handful
of nobles were absent in London, but the focus of their interests remained
their estates. The correspondence of William Cunningham, lord Kilmaurs,
between 1615 and 1630 was local affairs: the activities of neighbours, a letter
about a horse, the business of the neighbouring burgh court, property
matters, the problems over the minister at Dreghorn, dealings with vassals,
taxation, a quarrel with his father. The exceptions are correspondence with
agents in Edinburgh and one from a kinsman at court in London.[9]

The most obvious physical manifestation of the lord's presence was
the castle or tower house. These buildings, ranging from stark fortresses to
flamboyant country houses, projected a chivalrous image that underlined
the martial nature of lordship and the lord's political and economic dominance of the locality. They served as administrative centres and as places
where patronage and hospitality was dispensed. Great lords built in a grand
style so that they could reside in state and impress royalty with their power;
hence, the huge investment by the earls of Huntly at Strathbogie or the earls
of Atholl at Balvenie. When Huntly rebuilt Strathbogie castle in the early
1600s he did not downscale, but insisted on a great hall 43 ft long, 29 ft wide
and 16 ft high (13.1 × 8.8 × 4.8 m), an appropriate setting in which to display
the theatre of powerful lordship. Even lesser nobles reinforced their lordship
by constructing houses that evoked martial, chivalric values, an example of
which was John Kennedy of Baltersan's refashioning of Baltersan house in
the mid-1580s. In the west march there were scores of castles and different
forms of tower houses built to defend against foreign and domestic enemies,
but also to project power within the locality.[10]

That physical presence was reinforced by a range of relational behaviours. In a letter of 1634, the dying second earl of Mar assured sir Colin
Campbell of Glenorchy that 'my hartt is good and alls willing (albeit not so

able) to serve my freinds as ever I was'. Good lords understood this need to
cultivate service, and followers reminded them of their obligations, for as
one client reminded the sixth earl of Morton in 1629, 'I find he that servis a
guid maister hes not his fie to crave'. Nobles were astute in the psychological manipulation of power within the lord–man relationship, hence,
Gordonstoun's advice to 'Employ your countreymen often with voluntarie
contributions and supports ... not only to hold them in use therof, but also
to stop ther mouthes from seiking any favour at your hands incaise they
refuse you'.[11] Nobles and dependants engaged in the balanced series of
exchanges characteristic of a gift culture. Fynes Moryson observed the
hospitality of noble society in 1598, describing a baronial household where
there were few formal indications of deference or status. The visiting
Englishman noted that Scottish nobles 'living then in factions, used to keepe
many followers, and so consumed their revenew of victuals, living in some
want of money'. This baronial rusticity is evident in the life of Hugh Rose
of Kilravock who maintained a large household until his death in 1643,
leaving behind a reputation as 'provident and frugall, given to hospitalitie,
friends and strangers being kindlie entertained at his house'. In the Highlands the power of chiefs was measured by their generosity in distributing
largesse, but after 1603 even Lowlands nobles continued to cultivate this
aspect of lordship to ensure the loyalty of their dependants, tenants and
servants.[12]

Among the attributes of good lordship was peacemaking. The value
of peacemakers was recognised in April 1615 by the dowager countess of
Winton, who warned her son not to get embroiled in a quarrel, for 'Thair
ar too manye to yoke men to trouble, bot not halfe so cairfull or foirseing
how they sall ridd them out of it agane'. Therefore, lords who could restore
broken relationships without sacrificing justice were respected, but the
dilemma they faced lay in the reputational damage arising from failing to
protect a dependant. The inherent tension in the feud, therefore, was the
need to threaten violence in order to acquire justice and ultimately to restore
peace.[13] Nevertheless, noble society did not thrive on disorder, and lords
made strenuous efforts to anticipate disputes. When the feud between sir
Walter Scott of Branxholm and Walter Kerr of Cessford was pacified in
1564, an agreement was signed providing for arbitration mechanisms to
govern any future controversy. In that same year, in a precautionary move
designed to ensure that Ayrshire politics were not disturbed by the inflam-
ing of old grudges, the fourth earl of Cassillis and Matthew Campbell of
Loudon renewed bonds of manrent and maintenance made by their fathers
twenty years earlier when a feud between their houses had been settled.
Some agreements had greater political significance, such as that made in the
spring of 1569 between the fourth earl of Atholl and the fifth earl of Argyll
regulating a range of regional issues, and impacting on the wider national
struggle between the king's party and the queen's party. In June 1578, the

principal noblemen of north and central Ayrshire responded to a national political crisis by signing a local peace agreement designed to prevent the palace coup at Stirling having local repercussions.[14]

Nobles restrained their followers to prevent disputes escalating into violent feuds. In the summer of 1570 the killing of some of the fourth earl of Atholl's men by dependants of Colin Campbell of Glenorchy led to a flurry of letters between these two lords in the course of which Atholl accepted Glenorchy's apology on condition that the latter demonstrated the incident had arisen from a misunderstanding. When in 1592 a quarrel broke out between the fifth lord Ogilvy's son and David Lindsay of Vane, Ogilvy was determined to pursue mediation, while his wife entered into the attempt to avoid 'deidlie feidis quhair freindship suld be'.[15] Strong personal relations between lords, therefore, were important in maintaining and negotiating peace. When in exile in France in December 1584, the fifth lord Boyd was informed that one of his men had been killed by followers of the sheriff of Ayr, sir Matthew Campbell of Loudon. Boyd refused to over-react, writing home to urge that the matter be handled carefully, pointing out that 'ther hes been lang kyndness betwixt our houses and never slachter befoir', expressing disbelief that Loudon had been behind the incident, and insisting that the affair be settled by arbitration rather than by violence or law. Similarly, in an undated letter the tenth lord Forbes impressed on the fifth earl Marischal his desire to avoid feud by resolving this 'unhappiy accident fallen out betuix your l[ordship's] kynsmen and myn'.[16] In May 1630, in the midst of resolving a dispute, the first marquis of Huntly wrote to the second earl of Mar, asking him to recall 'our auld freindships and kyndnes and allyens', and suggesting that 'fekles particulars suld not cast us sindrie, seing that we ar both cum to that aige that we suld think more of the lyfe to cum nor the schort tyme that nature hes to give us heir'. Mar agreed, suggesting 'itt war a sin in us give we should nott stryve in our tyms to satill all things that may mak the leist scrupill or distrust amongst their quha shall cum efter us'.[17] Even when lords were less inclined to pursue peace there were friends ready to offer counsel. When sir James Johnstone of Dunskellie asked for the tenth earl of Angus's help to avenge a murder, Angus advised Dunskellie to be patient and to 'use no rigour nor hostilitie, ether in bur[n]ing or slaing', for in 'suspending your wreithe and leiffin of all violent reweng' he would reduce tension in the locality and win the king's favour.[18]

Lords had a key role in arbitration because they had the authority to make a settlement endure, and the efficiency and economy of private arbitration was recognised in a mixed system that blended it with adversarial and expensive litigation.[19] The importance of lords performing this role was recognised in a letter of 18 June 1591 from James and Patrick Grahame to sir James Johnstone of that Ilk in which they insisted that they were prepared to negotiate with their father's killers if this would please their lord.[20] The process of mediation might take the form of a formal decreet arbitral by an arbitration committee that often included officers of state and privy councillors, or informally as in 1583 when the first earl of Gowrie set up a meeting with the sixth earl of Argyll to discuss a quarrel between the lairds of Wemyss and Glenorchy. Arbitration skills, therefore, were essential to effective lordship. In May 1568, John Johnstone of that Ilk, acting for himself and 'for his surname of Johnstonis and their servandis', entered into an agreement with a number of other kindreds by which the two sides submitted a quarrel arising from a slaughter to a twelve-man arbitration committee. In some cases the crown encouraged negotiations, as in January 1580 when the privy council brokered a settlement between the Gordons and Forbes that involved 'the maist wyis, and discreit personis, thair principall freindis'.[21]

A minority of bonds of manrent and maintenance recorded that the lord was forgiving an offence. On 27 May 1578, the eighth earl of Angus accepted the manrent of John Kennedy of Blairquhan in compensation for the fact that Blairquhan and his men had mutilated one of Angus's servants. Similarly, in a bond of c. 1579–80 granted to John Johnstone of that Ilk, the Armstrongs admitted their guilt in slaying one of Johnstone's servants, offering to come to Moffat church 'in our lyneng clathes, kneleng upone our kneyes, with our sordes drawne in our handis, and sall delyvar them to you be the hiltis in tokynyng of repentens' along with a compensation package for the dead man's family.[22] On occasion lords swallowed their pride for the good of the wider community. The scene in Irvine in 1561 when the fifth lord Boyd made a humiliating submission to Neil Montgomery of Langshaw in repentance for the murder of the latter's father by the Boyds fourteen years earlier is a powerful image of how far lords were prepared to go in pursuit of peace. Similarly, in October 1606, the first lord Roxburghe offered to make peace with sir Robert Ker of Ancram, sixteen years after Roxburghe had murdered Ancram's father. Both men were London courtiers, but the feud was reconciled in the traditional manner. Roxburghe confessed to 'the unspeikabill greitnes of my grevous offens' agreed to pay 10,000 merks in compensation, and publicly craved forgiveness of Ancram and his family on the tomb of the regent Moray in St Giles kirk when he received his letter of slains and forgiveness.[23]

Unfortunately, peace could not always be sustained. A bewildered Englishman recorded in 1589 that 'in this country thei oft shake handes when thei are inclined to reveng', and that 'the Scottish nature is hardly reconciled', while Gordonstoun advised his lord 'Trust never too much unto a reconciled enemie'.[24] The key issue was trust. Patrick Murray of Ochtertyre was reluctant to accept sir William Douglas of Lochleven's intervention in his quarrel with a kinsman, telling Lochleven that 'as ye call him my freind I wuld god that I never haid knawin him nor nane of his'. In 1587–8 the exile of the eighth lord Maxwell allowed his friends to open up talks with the Johnstones such that 'incredible peax was concludit amany thayme, evin besyd all menis expectatioun'. Without the lord's good will, however, peace would not endure and Maxwell was later killed by the Johnstones. Sir David Lindsay of Edzell was warned in January 1609 to be wary of the twelfth earl of Crawford, 'Albeit the erle tak you be the hand in face of counsale yea and promeis you frindschip, yit I beseik you gaird yourselff, and have na less cair of your persone charge nor now, but rather mair'. A few weeks later Crawford tried to murder Edzell in Edinburgh. Negotiating peace was extraordinarily difficult for as Gordonstoun conceded, 'the smallest circumstances wer sufficient to put all out of frame and temper'.[25] Maintaining the peace was not dependent upon a legally enforceable agreement, and rested on honour and social pressure, but above all on the personal authority and determination of lords.

Unsurprisingly, the crown encouraged lords to use their authority to make peace. In *c.* 1589 John Gordon, younger of Gight, murdered Thomas Fraser of Strachin, and the sixth earl of Huntly was obliged to present Gight for trial. Gight was found guilty, but the king agreed that his execution would serve no purpose and that 'a soume of mony might do more good to the widow of Strachin than John Gight's blood'. The early seventeenth-century privy council continued to favour reconciliation by lords. On 2 August 1610, Archibald Maxwell of Cowhill and William Maxwell of Kirkhouse made peace in the council's presence, embracing one another after which they 'choppit' hands, and similar negotiations were assisted by the privy council in the 1630s.[26] The traditional skills lords needed to arbitrate and reconcile continued to be put to use within localities and with the approval of royal government.

Related to the business of peacekeeping was the power exercised by nobles in protecting their followers and in seeking justice on their behalf. This protection might be exercised in a political context, such as in the aftermath of the battle of Langside in May 1568 when the fourth earl of Glencairn tried to use his influence to shield sir John Maxwell of Pollok from the victorious regent Moray.[27] More commonly, the context was judicial. In December 1578, when Duncan MacFarlane and Duncan MacCoull MacFarlane were arrested on a murder charge, the third lord Drummond intervened to ensure his men would receive a public hearing. Similarly, when in 1577 the second earl of Mar was informed that a client was facing legal action arising from a feud, he resolved to take up 'the mainteinans of my dependeris action for saiftie of his lyf and provyd for his defence at the day of law approchand'. Mar was acting within acceptable limits, and most nobles were careful to remain within the law.[28] Hence, lord Hamilton's letter of March 1587 to sir Patrick Vaus of Barnbarroch, a court of session judge, concerning a servant who was facing trial asked only for assistance 'as ye may of law'. Thomas Craig of Riccarton, a leading jurist, approved of the obligations by which feudal law united lords and men in mutual bonds to protect one another in righteous causes.[29] This duty on the

part of lords to protect their dependants at law was spelled out by Gordonstoun who saw it as a nobleman's responsibility to 'Suffer no stranger to
oppresse your countreymen by lawe, and when they shall happen to be so
troubled, defend them with all your meanes, although it should be to your
loise at that present, for so others will be lother in tyme coming to trouble
and vex your countrey in that kynd'. In the Highlands, where feudal law was
less pervasive, clan chiefs provided protection and justice, obligations for
which they enjoyed hereditary authority, or *duthchas*, invested in them
personally as trustees of the clan.[30]

In a hostile and threatening world where royal government could be
impotent, and the only recourse for vengeance, or justice, was the power of
the local magnate, it was necessary for men to have a lord. In an agreement
of July 1567, Hugh Crawford of Kilbirnie exchanged bonds of manrent and
maintenance with the fifth lord Boyd, who promised that if Kilbirnie
died before his wife, Boyd would defend her and her children 'in all actionis
caussis and debaittis lauchfull and ressonable aganis all persones as said is
during his lyiftyme'. Here the lord's obligation to a good servant's wife
and children continued after Kilbirnie's death. In a 1573 bond of manrent
between John Johnstone of that Ilk and a kinsman, the former promised
protection 'as ane faithfull maister aucht to debait his true servand'. In
return for good service, Johnstone promised to take up his man's case
against predatory neighbours, defend him against overpowering lords, and
pursue his interests in the courts.[31] Some measure of how such influence
might be deployed is caught in the fifth earl of Argyll's letter to Hugh Rose
of Kilravock in September 1560 regarding a dependant, asking that 'ye tholl
nane of your kin nor frendis do to him or that hous ony unkyndnes, for the
quhilk ye sall have our guid mynd and kyndnes efter as ye have ado'. In
another incident Argyll sounded a more threatening note to those who
abused his servants, 'we cann nocht leaff the slachter of our servandis un-
revenget'. The anonymous Kennedy historian expressed exactly this sense
of common identity between lord and man in discussing the attitude of
the fifth earl of Cassillis to any attack, or slight, inflicted on his servants,
relating that 'my lord thocht the samin done to him'.[32] In pursuing justice
for their dependants, nobles reinforced their own authority, creating confidence among followers, and fear, or at least prudence, among rivals.

While lords did not necessarily set out to obstruct justice, injustice could
be the consequence of their behaviour. A note dashed off by the fifth lord
Herries on 4 June 1585 to his neighbour, John Johnstone of Greenhill,
concerning the imprisoned servant of a client is indicative of how lords
might influence the judicial process:

Quhairfor, Johne, I desyr you to lat this pure man to libertie as ye wald I suld
do for you. Utherwayis I will think ye do over lytill for me, and I will haif the
les to do with you in tyme cuming, and seik the nixt remeid. This gentill man

is my freind quhom I man do for, and ye are ane man that I have to do with to, and gif ye lat him nocht to libertie, I can not think you to be my freind.[33]

The question of guilt or innocence was not addressed, Herries wanted his man freed. In 1588, the sixth earl of Huntly was ordered by the king to bring John Gordon of Gight to trial for a killing, but instead the earl 'aunserd that if hee might bring his frinds and forces with him hee would bring the Lairde of Giche to underlaye the law – otherwise not'. On another occasion when Huntly defended a kinsman who had committed slaughter his sole justification was that he 'must be a Gordon when it came to the worst'. In a bond of 1593 a number of Maxwell lairds swore to uphold one another in all causes 'in the law or by the law', counting a quarrel with one as quarrel with them all.[34] Here was the root of societal unease with nobles who believed that the obligations of kinship and lordship over-rode obedience to the king, the law and their religious obligations, encouraging what James VI observed to be a willingness among lords 'to maintaine their servants and dependers in any wrong, although they be not answerable to the lawes (for any body will maintaine his man in a right cause)'.[35]

There were occasions when lords and their followers behaved as though there was no law. In April 1590, lord Hamilton took a liking to one of the fifth earl of Morton's horses, and when Morton's gardener tried to stop him taking it, Hamilton's retainers shot the man dead. The incident highlights the problem created by armed and aggressive men who could count on the protection of powerful lords, hence, the observation that 'Many offenders are countenanced by noblemen, with great contempt of the laws and justice'. James Melville of Halhill articulated the view of the outraged courtier against the 'many gret combersom clannes, sa reddy to concur togither' in order to pursue 'the deffence of any ane of ther name, or to revenge the just execussion of some of them, for mourther, slaughter, thift, or sic uther crymes'. This connection between the determination of lords to protect their dependants, allied to an ideology that sustained feuding and vengeance, made it difficult to address the problem of private violence given that the magistracy, especially in the localities, was largely composed of these same nobles.[36]

The decline in feuding from c. 1610, alongside the increasing effectiveness of royal justice, impacted on the exercise of lordship without removing the need for it. Chancellor Dunfermline, one of the finest Roman jurists in the kingdom, was prepared to help out friends in trouble with the law. With such attitudes permeating government and the law courts it was unsurprising that in the localities there was little change. In 1624, the earls of Annandale and Buccleuch stitched up an out-of-court deal to save the life of Robert Elliot of Redheugh after he attempted to murder Buccleuch. When in 1630 the first earl of Galloway's gardener was killed by servants of John Gordon of Lochinvar, it was Galloway who pursued the case at law on behalf of the dead man's family. In 1634, Patrick Edmonston of Wolmet took up the case of a woman charged with theft so that he 'was drawn to great expense in defending her'.[37] These nobles exercised lordship in defence of friends and dependants, but within the limits of the law.

Bewailing a decline in lordship was a familiar theme among writers and poets. In the mid-sixteenth century, Lethington suggested in his 'Satire on the age' that lordship was crumbling in the face of commercial attitudes in contrast to a time when 'Our fatheris wyse were, and discreit,/Thai had bayth honour, men and meit'. Lethington's poetry is infused with bitterness at debased lordship, his criticism of the magnates being most pronounced in 'Of the warldis ingratitude' where he targets nobles who failed to reward deserving dependants:

> Thocht ye have servit, monye ane yeir,
> Ane lord, on your awin cost and geir;
> And ye be fallin in distress,
> You to releive he will be sueir,
> And count na thing your auld kyndness.[38]

The early seventeenth-century writer, William Lithgow, wrote in a similar vein, mourning the passing of lost ideals:

> They [lords] have no deadly fead, thats gone of late,
> But they're at deadly fead with their own state:
> And care not for Allyes, blood, wives, nor friends,
> Kindred nor bairnes, save their own wasting ends.[39]

In 1615, sir Duncan Campbell of Glenorchy complained that 'thir ar few or none that will serve nowadayes without commodite', and Gordonstoun believed that the world of upright and honourable lords was disappearing in 'these our dayes, wherein integritie lyeth speechles and upright dealling is readie to give up the ghost'.[40] Here is a picture of lords and men who had abandoned one another in pursuit of material gain, but was this anything more than the poetic cliche of a lost golden age?

Evidence always can be found of men discontented with their lords. In 1570, Colin Campbell of Glenorchy complained that the fifth earl of Argyll was failing to protect him from Magregor raids, angrily asserting that his chief's tolerance of these bandits meant that 'I am the sairest handlit baroun in Scotland this day'. The eighth earl of Angus was criticised for a meekness that deprived his followers of opportunities for advancement, one anonymous client writing, 'I blame most his own simplicitie ... seing his authoritie ought to put order to others, where now he is onely a beholder of that which it pleaseth others to doe'. In an undated letter to the second earl of Mar, John Bruce of Auchinbowie demanded that his inattentive lord defend him 'and nocht suffer me to be wrackit or yit schamit'. George Ogilvy told David Lindsay of Edzell in 1587 that since the latter had neither paid nor helped him, therefore, 'I will be the les obleist in servis and guid-will to you'. In similar vein, an irritated sir David Lindsay of Balcarres wrote to the sixth earl of Rothes in 1625, tartly reminding him that 'Benefits amangs men can not run infinitlie, nor be alwayes alyk greatt, speciallie if they flow from one pairtie'. In 1634, a disappointed client complained to the sixth earl of Morton, the lord treasurer, about his pension arrears, complaining that Morton had done nothing to help and that he was likely to 'perish under the climat of your Lordship's heigh dignittie and grand office of estate'.[41] This catalogue of discontent merely documents what could and did go wrong between nobles and their dependants.

It has been argued that throughout much of western Europe, clientage relationships were dissolving between, on the one hand, rich and powerful noblemen with a foot in expensive royal courts and, on the other hand, poor, dependent noblemen rooted in their localities. Yet there is equally strong evidence to indicate a continuity in relationships.[42] In Scotland, the ideal of lordship remained unchallenged, and there is little evidence to suggest significant change in residence, hospitality, peacemaking within the local community or in the protection of dependants.

Service

Riccarton saw no tension between the exercise of good lordship and obligations owed to the king. In his 1603 work, *Jus feudale*, he argued that a vassal 'by his every word and deed ... must shew to his lord, as to a father, all revererence and fidelity'. Recent analysis of the relationships between lords and men in late medieval Scotland emphasises personal bonds and mutual benefits. Written bonds of manrent outline the general features of service, such as defending a lord from harm and warning him of danger, giving good counsel, being ready to 'ride and gang' with him on his lawful affairs, and taking his part in honest and lawful disputes.[43]

One of the most common forms of service was attendance on a lord, perhaps at social events, or to days of law, either local arbitration or at the central law courts. This duty of attendance was not specific. In December 1560, the third earl of Montrose wrote to Thomas Liddell, officer of the barony of Dundaffmuir, instructing him to charge his tenants to obey the orders of his cousin, sir David Graham of Fintry, and to 'ryd and gang' with him whenever he desired it. How frequently lords made these demands on their followers is unknown, although there was an expectation on the part of lords that their men would always be prepared to attend on them.[44] With lesser men, lords could afford to be more imperious so that on 1 January 1590 the fifth earl of Morton ordered his baillies and officers to impose a fine of £10 on every horseman and £5 on every footman who failed to attend on him. But, as Morton's fines suggest, lords did not always get the response they desired. In August 1560, an irritated fifth earl of Argyll wrote to Hugh Rose of Kilravock regarding the latter's excuse for not attending the crucial Reformation parliament, commenting 'it hald bene better ye hald bene heir'. The tenth earl of Angus demonstrated greater annoyance in January 1601 in writing to his baillie, sir John Ogilvie of Inverquharitie, requesting that he accompany the earl before the privy council, adding the caustic postscript, 'I dout nocht bot ze will obey this my requeist, becaus ze come nocht the last I wrait for zow'. Therefore, lords employed a degree of negotiation and persuasion in dealing with more powerful dependants. The latter had their own interests to consider, and when one anxious Campbell laird was summoned to attend the seventh earl of Argyll in 1635 he was reluctant to obey since no expenses were offered, but he knew that if he ignored his lord's request it would be interpreted as a neglect of duty and no further favours would be granted.[45]

Although elements of accountability survived in the Highlands where chiefs were expected to consult the clan *fine*, and the earls of Argyll employed a body that had the appearance of an advisory council, there is little evidence of formal baronial councils of the kind found in late medieval society.[46] Nevertheless, Gordonstoun advised that a wise lord would 'Do nothing of consequense without the advyse and counsell of your speciall freinds'. In July 1567, following Mary's abdication and the crowning of James VI, the fifth earl of Huntly wrote to Hugh Rose of Kilravock that 'I haif to awiss with my freindis, and to haif thair awice and assistance in sic thingis concerning the weill of my hous'. Similarly, when the eleventh earl of Crawford was charged with the killing of the eighth lord Glamis in the spring of 1578 he wrote a circular letter to all his friends and dependants seeking their support as 'it is and hes ever beine the custome in this cuntry in the lyk to caus to crave and requyre the advise of thair freindis'.[47] Lords were advised by close confidantes, such as William Gordon of Gight, iden- tified as the first marquis of Huntly's 'onley prinsepall man' who 'knowes most of the earles mynd of aney man livinge'. Other men, like Robert Murray of Abercairny, performed an honest broker's role in the community, and between 1574 and 1583 the regent Morton, the second earl of Mar, the eighth earl of Errol and the third earl of Montrose all asked for this man's advice.[48] Occasionally the fruits of these discussions are preserved. Follow- ing a meeting with his kinsmen and friends before setting out for London in July 1627, the second earl of Mar was presented with a sixteen-point set of guidelines on how to proceed with his business at court.[49]

Clearly there was an expectation that lords would take heed of counsel. In February 1570, an English diplomat seeking to mediate in the civil war, prevailed on the friends of the fifth lord Hume to persuade him to 'yield to reason' or lose their support. In some cases counsel was uncomfortably blunt, as when the regent Morton demitted office in 1578 and was told by the fifth lord Boyd that he had been a fool to 'presume too much of his own wit, who in a matter of so great moment would not once ask the opinion of his friends'. In 1597, immediately after his return from exile, the Catholic tenth earl of Angus met with his leading clients and advisers, most of whom were Protestants, to discuss how to protect their mutual interests. In return for their assistance the chastened earl promised 'in all his doeings to followe the faythfull and trew advyse of sa many as his best assisters and wysest frends as salbe nominat to him be common consent'. In December 1632 unsolicited advice from a London kinsman warned James Johnstone of that Ilk to be reconciled with his father-in-law and to make 'ane ende rather by mediatione then tryall in lawe, because the events of pleaes are doubtfull'.[50]

Lords who ignored counsel endangered their authority. This was an issue within the house of Argyll over a prolonged period. A 1586 bond of friendship signed by disgruntled Campbell lairds signalled disapproval of the minority government of the seventh earl of Argyll, claiming they had no access to him. They bound themselves to free their chief in order that the whole kindred might 'haif excesse to giff thair opinioun and counsaill' in his affairs. Unfortunately, Argyll remained suspicious of his kinsmen throughout his life, and his later financial problems and Catholic recusancy exacerbated bad relationships within the clan. In a letter of c.1630, one of his followers reflected upon nearly twenty years of frustration at the earl's mismanagement. As far as he was concerned, 'thair be nocht ane mair miserable surname in Scotland', but his greatest gripe was not Argyll's demand for a tax that he was willing to pay 'provyding that I get ane honest kyndlie meiting'. Failure to seek counsel lay at the heart of the problems besetting the house of Argyll throughout the minority and lifetime of the seventh earl, a man so fearful and suspicious of his own kinsmen that 'he uses them not as councellors, but as strangers, for which cause they holde the further from him'.[51]

Nobles sought professional counsel from men of law, for as the fifth earl of Argyll conceded in 1569 'we ar nocht ourself verie expert in the lawis'. As justice grew in complexity, and as more disputes were settled in court rather than by feud or arbitration, the service of a professional lawyer was invaluable. Gordonstoun believed it was necessary for the earls of Sutherland to retain 'the best men of lawe and advocats in Edinbrugh for your counsell' along with a pensioned Edinburgh agent and a local notary in the household. At a local level these notaries were far removed from the influential Edinburgh advocates. In April 1589, John Lennox of Cally entered into an agreement with his notary in which he gave the latter a horse on condition he agreed 'to do the said Johnne Lewenax haill besines efferand to ane notar' for four years, acting as his procurator and advising him on his affairs.[52] The value of employing Edinburgh lawyers is evident in the correspondence between 1627 and 1630 from Craighall to his client, the first earl of Annandale, detailing his dealings on the latter's behalf. As Craighall wrote, 'with your lordschippis preferment standis my fortun upon earth', and he made considerable sums of money working for noble clients.[53] But while litigation between lords was becoming more common, it was considered unnecessary between the dependants of the same lord, and certainly within the kindred. Alexander Lindsay, bishop of Dunkeld was disappointed that John Stewart, younger of Arntullie, initiated litigation against his cousin, pleading with him to seek arbitration 'and not to suffer yourself and your frinds to com to forder faschry and expensas'. In July 1620, John Grant, younger of Freuchie, intercepted dependants on route to a hearing before the privy council and expressed anger that they had chosen to enter into 'sic idle and nochtie actiounes to thair disgraces and thair cheiffis also'. He sent them home after giving them their expenses. Gordonstoun believed that a lord should 'Stryve to keip the inhabitants of your countrey at home from vexing one another with unnecessarie suits in law', advising, 'Hazard rather to receave some loise by the arbitriment of freinds, for he that winneth most at law, loiseth'. If legal action was unavoidable and the case was just, 'spare no charges to obtein the victorie'.[54]

The deep-rooted loyalty of men to their lords was noted by that English enthusiast for all things chivalrous, sir Henry Lee, who in May 1573 asked while observing the siege of Edinburgh castle, 'In what place of the world will kin, friends and servants adventure more for the lords?'. Gordonstoun, who had long experience of French and English society, made a similar point almost half a century later, writing that the Scots were 'by nature, most bent and prone to adventure themselves, their lyffs, and all they have, for their masters and lords, yea beyond all other people'. Godscroft retells a discussion between the eighth earl of Angus and sir George Hume of Wedderburn when the latter said that 'if his Chiefe should turne him out at the foredoore, he would come in againe at the back-doore'. The same regard for *fidelitas* moved a dying John MacDougall of Dunollicht to write to Colin Campbell of Glenorchy on 26 January 1561 asking him to maintain kindness to his kindred in return for their ongoing service to Glenorchy, 'and I leif my maledictioun upoun thame geif thai do nocht my bidding'.[55] Unsurprisingly, nobles placed a high premium on prolonged good service, favouring men like Robert Porterfield of Chapeltown who was granted a charter by the second earl of Mar in 1587 relating that he and his ancestors had given good service to the house of Mar for eight score years. Bonds of manrent and maintenance were often repeated in successive generations, for example, the Cheynes of Essilmont granted their manrent to the earls of Errol on at least four occasions from 1499, creating the impression of a ritualised reinforcement of social relations.[56]

While the debate over *fidelité* in France offers polarised notions of lord–man relationships, it is possible to conceive of loyalty and self-interest operating on a spectrum that varied between different lords and men over time.[57] Therefore, the above discussion about the general faithfulness of dependants to their lords is not invalidated by pointing out that the majority

of bonds of manrent and maintenance were exchanged in response to immediate political circumstances. The fifth lord Boyd's policy throughout
the turbulent 1560s and 1570s was to extend his political control in north
Ayrshire by securing the recognition of his lordship from local barons. The
taking of bonds by the young eighth earl of Angus from Teviotdale lairds
in the mid-1570s was prompted by the regent Morton's promotion of his
nephew as his agent on the Borders. The bonds of manrent granted to the
sixth earl of Huntly in the years after 1585 present a picture of the dynamic
reconstruction of Gordon power following the defeats of the previous two
decades. By the spring of 1589 at least eighteen barons and chiefs scattered
throughout the northeast, the central Highlands and even the western isles,
had given Huntly their manrent. Close study of the Mackintosh and Grant
clans reveals a concern among dependants to negotiate bonds in the context
of particular and changing political pressures that appear to be at odds with
the language of bonds emphasising life-long relationships.[58]

Largely absent from Scotland was the equivalent of those English gentry
warning about the untrustworthiness of the peerage, and it is notable that
most of the men who gave their allegiance to lords were lesser nobles and
men of local significance.[59] Yet tensions did arise between lords and men,
who often took measures to anticipate problems in their relationship. In a
bond of manrent given by William Barclay, fiar of Perstoune, to the third earl
of Eglinton in August 1577, Barclay conceded that any failure on his part
would lead to the nullification of the earl's bond of maintenance following
an investigation by two kinsmen. Problems were more likely where a lord's
wealth and clientage were challenged by one of his followers. In 1572, the
regent Mar's comment that 'thair wes gentlemen of the surname of Hume
that mycht have levit, and levit beside the Lord Hume evin quhen he wes in
gretest authoritie' showed an awareness of such tension. Lords encouraged
instability by poaching one another's men. A list of grievances prepared
in the name of the fifth earl of Atholl against the sixth earl of Huntly in
1587 was principally concerned with demarcation disputes between them.
Among these was one complaint by Atholl that John Menzies of Weem had
deserted him for Huntly 'to my dishonour and contemp'. It was often this
relationship between a great lord and a lesser noble house where the bond
between lord and man was weakest because of a clash of interests, or because
of the absence of tenurial relationship.[60]

Those men who broke with their lords could expect a tough response
because such actions were an affront to a nobleman's honour and to the
public perception of his authority. In 1595, Angus Macdonald of Dunyveg
was forced to go before the seventh earl of Argyll 'and on his knees asked
mercy for his offences committed to his lordship'. Similarly, when the
authority of the fifth earl of Cassillis was challenged by the most important
of the Kennedy cadet families, the resulting feud led to the death in 1600 of
the laird of Bargany and the downfall of his house.[61] But lords were more

interested in preserving their local power than in punishing disloyal followers. Hugh Mackay of Farr was a vassal of the eleventh earl of Sutherland,
but in the vicious feuding of the 1580s he sided with the fifth earl of
Caithness only to be abandoned by the latter when the two earls made peace
in 1588. Farr had no choice but to grovel to his rightful lord who offered
generous terms, choosing to exploit his vassal's debts and to reinforce his
lordship by marrying Farr to his eldest daughter. John Grant of Freuchie
and Lauchlan Mackintosh struggled to free themselves from the sixth earl
of Huntly's lordship in the early 1590s, taking advantage of alternative offers
from the second earl of Moray and the seventh earl of Argyll, only to be
forced into submission militarily. Yet when they showed a penitent desire to
return to the Gordon fold, Huntly was magnanimous, and the two young
lairds agreed 'alwayis to contenew with his lordship, swa lang as thai
keip thair dewtie and faythfull service to his lordship and his houss, but
[= without] defectioun'. In fact, Huntly's relations with both chiefs continued to be dogged by ill-feeling; there was disagreement within these clans
over where to place their allegiance, and it was 1609 before a stable peace was
agreed.[62]

The tone of lord–man relations was relatively informal, thus the
paternalistic atmosphere of the regent Moray's household was established
by the earl who was 'affable to his owne domesticks, and yitt rebooked them
more sharplie than anie other'. The relatively relaxed tone of social relations
might have made it easier to preserve customs like kneeling in the homage
ritual that in France was viewed as humiliating. There was little of the
language of excessive courtesy found in France, and Scottish nobles generally were less insistent on the stiff formality that typified social relations in
England. Hence, that sour Englishman, sir Anthony Weldon, alleged that
the early seventeenth-century Scottish nobility were over-familiar with their
dependants, commenting that 'Thair followers ar thair fellowes'.[63] This is an
exaggeration, but it contains a germ of truth. Gordonstoun argued for a
balance between familiarity and distance in dealing with social inferiors,
recommending that nobles should 'Forbear to be too familiar with the
inhabitants of your countrey, for it breedeth contempt. Let them once
knowe that you ar ther superiour'. Yet he argued that lords should 'be
oppen and affable in giving accesse to every honest persone when they have
ado that they may mak there owne suits to you themselves'. He advised
his nephew to 'Be courteous towards all men, and cheiflie towards your
inferiours, who ar not bound by dewtie to folow you, wherby you shall
insinuat yourself into ther affections'. A case has been made for alleging that
following the regal union 'that English divell, keeping of state' made inroads
into Scotland, but while there are isolated examples like the second marquis
of Huntly who caused disquiet by flaunting affected mannerisms in the
localities, the evidence is slight.[64]

It might be expected that the spread of religious dissent, significant population growth with an attendant increase in masterless men, and the decreasing need for military protection from lords would have eroded deference, but there is little evidence to support this suggestion. In November 1616, sir Alexander Gordon of Navidale, uncle to the young thirteenth earl of Sutherland, was incandescent at the behaviour of his nephew's tenants when they refused to give him extra horses to uplift the teinds.

> I pray God the Erll of Suthirlandis guid turn be never lippinit [= trusted] to manie in this cuntrey, for i think give they sawe his bake at the wall in ane gryt mater they wald stres thame selffis littil to releiff him quhen they maid scruppill in sik ane triffil.

This outburst might reflect irritation at societal change, but it is more likely that lords always struggled to impose their will on reluctant tenants. Certainly, overt challenges to noble authority were rare, but they did occur. In October 1590, William Lockhart admitted in the barony court of Calder that he had pulled the second lord Torpichen's officer from his horse when the man was trying to execute a poinding. In the mid-1620s, James Cunningham of Aiket rescued a servant of lord Kilmaurs who had been sent on royal business to collect taxation, but found himself faced by a hostile crowd whose 'undeutifull deilling' shocked both men.[65] Nobles closed ranks in response to challenges to the hierarchic order. On 27 February 1606, the privy council heard a complaint of assault from David Flesher, a Dundee merchant burgess, against John Scrimgeour, eldest son and heir of the provost and hereditary constable of Dundee, who did not deny the accusation, having been offended by Flesher's repeated refusal to remove his hat. While some privy councillors thought Scrimgeour's actions were unlawful, the tenth earl of Angus expressed the majority view that 'all cairlis [= churls] and inferiour men aucht honour to noblemen, and aucht to be compellit gif they will not do it wilfullie'.[66] A similar sternness was on display when in 1633, Thomas McKie, a burgess of the royal burgh of Wigton, publicly defamed the first earl of Galloway. McKie admitted the charge and offered financial compensation, but the privy council ordered that he be placed in the Wigton stocks, following which he was ordered to confess his fault before the congregation of the parish church.[67] These few incidents do not amount to any significant trend, and serve only to illustrate the confidence with which the nobility addressed isolated challenges to the social hierarchy.

The Affinity

The affinity of a late medieval or early modern lord was composed of 'kin freindis allya parttakaris tennentis servandis and dependaris', with there being some distinctions in the Highlands. All these participants were engaged in interlocking relationships as active agents and not merely as

passive reactors to lordly initiatives.[68] Little distinguished the early modern
affinity from its medieval antecedent, and the detailed anatomisation of the
Dudley or Stanley clienteles of Elizabethan England, or the Anjou or Guise
affinities in France, exposes a variety of dependants drawn from a number
of localities and social backgrounds, each of whom could offer legal, military, financial or some other service.[69] Similarly, the clientele of the first earl
of Orkney reveals a picture of 176 men serving him from the 1560s through
to his death in 1593 in a variety of ways and for different lengths of time,
from the tight-knit 'inner circle' to the menial servants. Here was a household of the loyal and the transient, containing only a handful of landed men
who had followers of their own, indicating Orkney's modest wealth and
power.[70] By contrast, the affinity of the fifth earl of Argyll made him so
powerful that he was impregnable within his own 'country'. That power was
based on a late medieval inheritance that fused Gaelic lordship with the
astute cultivation of court connections. More immediately, it relied on
men, lands and jurisdictions, strategic marriages and a remarkable cohesion
among clan Campbell's cadet houses. To some extent the differences in the
power of these two lords was a product of geography, historical legacy and
circumstances, but it was also due to the personal role of the individual lords.
That last point is relevant even within a single lineage. The skill of the fifth
and sixth earls of Argyll between 1558 and 1584 in dealing with tensions
among their Macdonald and Macleod neighbours contrasts with the weakness of their father, the fourth earl, in the three previous decades and the
absence of a forceful personality during the minority of the seventh earl in
the ten years after 1584.[71] A lord's personal knowledge of his men, therefore,
was crucial. In a letter of 11 June 1606, the dying fifth lord Ogilvy instructed
his grandson to:

> love and respect your friends and followers thairof: and know their natturis
> weil that you may accomodat yourselff thairto. Seeing many of thame hald
> nothing of you but Guidwill and Kyndness, be cheerful in youre countenance
> and readie and honest to thame for it is a gryt tressure that my hous hes, thair
> freindis.

Gordonstoun gave similar advice to his nephew, detailing how to behave
towards each of the neighbouring chiefs and barons that formed the Sutherland affinity in the 1620s.[72]

The typical noble affinity was made up of concentric circles of household
servants, tenants and dependants. As in the Orkney case, not all lords could
count on a significant core of kinsmen, for example, in 1577 it was reported
that the second earl of Mar 'hath very few landed men of their surname, and
get of good power by their friends and alliaunces within that shire'. But this
absence of kinsmen was uncommon, and the 264 persons named in the 1566
remission to the duke of Chatelherault broke down into 138 men who shared
his surname, including the most prominent Hamilton barons or lairds, forty

gentlemen who were dependants, fifty-five tenants on the duke's estates and thirty-one household servants.[73] When sir John Johnstone of that Ilk made peace with his neighbours in the mid-1580s he offered to be bound for the behaviour of 414 named Johnstones, Grahames, Irvines with their kinsmen, tenants and servants, who all recognised his lordship.[74]

Beyond his immediate kin, at the heart of the affinity was the lord's personal household. Here in this intimate environment the loyal and trusted servant was highly valued. When John Auchmowie, an old servant and client wrote to sir John Lindsay of Balcarres that 'ye are my only comfort, hope and trust in this world, except God only', he was only mildly exaggerating their strong bond. Similarly, Hugh Gordon of Balledo, baillie and sheriff depute of Sutherland, was 'all his dayes a faithfull and trustie servant' under four successive earls of Sutherland until his death in March 1612, aged eighty-two. The fourth lord Elphinstone's chamberlain in the barony of Kildrummy was Thomas Esplein, who first entered his service in 1580 at the age of fourteen and remained with him for over fifty years.[75] Yet servants were not always fixed in their employment patterns, being alert to better opportunities. In discussing the activities of Archibald Douglas, his former servant at the time of the Darnley murder, the fourth earl of Morton related that 'Mr Archibald at that time was a depender upon the Erle of Bothwell, making court for himself, rather than a depender of myne'. Nor did nobles always offer long-term employment. When in 1576 the second earl of Mar and his curators appointed Andrew Hagg, burgess of Stirling, as chamberlain over all his lands, he was granted a one-year renewable contract.[76]

Relations between nobles and servants were not always harmonious. Nobles could be ruthless in imposing terms on servants, their paternalism masking an authoritarian relationship. This reality was underlined in 1621 when parliament sought to restrict the freedom of servants to leave their employers during the months between Whitsunday and Martinmas.[77] Disgruntled servants tried to get their own back on masters, engaging in passive obstruction and taking comfort in small vengeful protests. Servants stole, defied their mistresses (male servants disliked obeying women), and vandalised property. Gavin Hamilton served sir Duncan Campbell of Glenorchy as lawyer and secretary for £120 per annum, but in 1608 he resigned, writing angrily to his master about the 'manyfold lichtleis contemptis and dunngingis [= shit] I have recevit of your m[astership]'. He took revenge by tearing up a book of writs, initiated a legal action against Glenorchy and threatened to reveal his secrets. Within the year Hamilton was back in the laird's service, but following his death in 1620 his wife tried to blackmail Glenorchy into paying a pension as the price of her silence. Even more startling was the case of Thomas Crombie, who was dismissed from the service of the first earl of Traquair for stealing from his wine cellar. In January 1638, when Traquair was in London, a resentful Crombie ran amok in Dalkeith palace, then inhabited by the earl's family, severely wounding two servants defending the countess and her children from the enraged man. Crombie was hanged.[78]

Early modern noble households experienced changes in function as well as in the social and cultural significance of their use of space, objects and ritual, but the essentially medieval nature of the household community did not disappear before the covenanting era. The forms of service demanded by nobles varied from that of menials to specialist servants like a chaplain, tutor, secretary, doctor, chef, or huntsman, important officials like the steward or chamberlain, gentlemen attendants, usually kinsmen, and even other barons who waited on their lord. Some of the higher offices provided a lord with useful patronage, although there is no evidence of lords multi-plying offices in order to increase their following.[79] Servants were entrusted with enormous responsibility by their masters. The management of the young third earl of Gowrie's affairs was placed in the hands of trusted friends and servants during his absence on the continent in the mid-1590s, while the fifth earl of Morton relied on Mungo Rig of Carberry as his business manager in the early 1600s. Among the greatest of nobles the service by men of rank in their household was an indicator of wealth and power. An Ayrshire baron like sir Thomas Kennedy of Bargany 'had evir in his houshald xxiiij galland gentilmenne, doubill horsitt, and gallantly clad'. The eighth earl of Angus was served by Robert Douglas of Cavers, hereditary sheriff of Selkirk, in the capacity of 'gentleman of his horses'.[80] Service in a noble household brought rewards ranging from the material pensions and fees, food, clothing, stabling, bedding and miscellaneous gifts to less tangible opportunities to exercise influence and do favours.[81] Gordonstoun urged his nephew to observe and even augment pensions awarded to servants who had given good service to his father or grandfather 'which shall encourage others in tyme coming to hazard themselfs, ther fortones and ther deerest blood in your service'. Generosity was com-mended, but Gordonstoun suggested keeping a written record of gifts so that all could be rewarded in turn, although highly favoured servants should receive their bounty in secret, and he advised the earl to 'Keip rather too few then too many servants'.[82]

Beyond the household was the lord's tenantry. In sixteenth-century Britain and Ireland most land was held under a form of territorial lordship; it was southern England that was exceptional. In Scotland the territorial basis of lordship may have been underestimated due to the emphasis placed on the less tangible aspects of bonds of manrent in which as few as 10 per cent of the hundreds of surviving documents were given to lords in return for land or money. While these bonds got around the complexities created by land tenure, reinforcing tenurial relationships and even drawing into an affinity other landlords who had no tenurial contract with a magnate, the inter-relationship between land, jurisdiction and men remained strong.[83]

As Gordonstoun's early seventeenth-century history of the earldom of

Sutherland indicates, noble houses continued to project an image of themselves as being identified with a geographical location.[84] Riccarton believed
that the feudal bond between lord and vassal was 'so close as to prevail over
the ties of blood however near, and over the obligations of friendship
however sacred'. This is an exaggeration, and by the later sixteenth century
vassalage was a less powerful bond between lords and men than formerly.
Nevertheless, land remained the point of contact that made all other connections possible, and there was a correlation between the size of estates and
the number of men a lord could summon. Hence, the territorial view of the
nobility in intelligence reports compiled for the English government, and
Godscroft's description of the leading magnates of the Marian civil war as
'almost all pettie Princes in their severall Counties and Shires'. Even in the
1630s, Gordonstoun described the house of Sutherland as 'verie strong,
and of great power', due to the fact that the gentlemen of the earldom held
their land of the earl, mostly in ward and relief, while he exercised civil and
criminal authority over all his territories.[85]

Although patrons and clients accrued honour from the exchange of
rewards and gifts, in times of political instability lords were pressured to
strengthen their affinities with land and gifts.[86] During the 1570s, the fifth
lord Boyd and the third earl of Eglinton exchanged bonds of manrent and
maintenance with a string of local men whose service was won in return for
leases of land, quantities of grain and cash payments. Throughout the 1560s,
the first earl of Moray had difficulty creating a territorial base in his newly
acquired estates in the northeast. The troubles of the second earl of Moray
leading up to his murder in 1592 were interwoven with difficulties in establishing lordship, and half a century later the third earl struggled to persuade
his tenants to render him service. The underlying problem for the Moray
earls was the lack of adequate landed wealth.[87] By contrast, the fifth earl of
Argyll lorded over a huge territorial expanse. Argyll understood the need to
retain control over his lands in order to exercise lordship, and when in 1563
the ambitious Colin Campbell of Glenorchy sought the superiority of his
lands, Argyll dismissed the request 'for I beleif that my foirbearis gaiv it not
so lychtly'. Yet even in the Argyll case, the financial devices employed by the
fifth earl to raise political support in the 1560s created problems for his
successors in the 1630s.[88] Changes in feudal superiority altered lordship
relations. Between the 1560s and 1590s, the loyalties of the lairds of Menzies
switched from the fourth earl of Morton to the eighth lord Maxwell, the
sixth earl of Huntly and the fifth earl of Morton as political circumstances
affected landholding and territorial influence. Furthermore, lords could be
ruthless in understanding the value of their tenants, thus, the regent Morton
bluntly advised James Menzies of that Ilk to clear the Magregors from his
land 'because ye ressave nether proffite nor obedience of thame'.[89] But whatever the circumstances, lords could not count on the tenurial connection by
itself to create loyalty. Problems beset William Douglas of Glenbervie when

in 1588 he was catapulted from the status of an obscure Aberdeenshire baron to become ninth earl of Angus. It was observed in the Angus region that 'though he beare this title, [he] hathe no commandemente but that moste of the gentlemen holde theyre landes of hym'.[90]

Towns were not excluded from the lordship of powerful nobles. A range of relationships can be uncovered embracing a tripartite negotiation between the crown, the burgh and the local nobility, in which towns navigated a line between isolated independence and reluctant dependence.[91] Where a town was a burgh of barony, the lord's interest in its welfare and his authority over it was more assured. The latter was visibly evident when the new tollbooth erected in the Canongate in 1591 was decorated with an inscription on the tower to sir Lewis Bellenden of Broughton, the feudal superior of the burgh. In times of insecurity and political instability even royal burghs found it difficult to escape the clutches of neighbouring nobles. During the civil war, lord Robert Stewart forced himself on the royal burgh of Kirkwall as its provost, establishing an exploitative relationship and destroying the burgh's charter chest in order to overturn its privileges. In that same year the royal burgh of Inverkeithing experienced bitter infighting as a faction sought to curb the influence of its *de facto* heritable provost, James Henderson of Fordell, a servant of the regent Moray. At a convention of the estates in July 1569, nine burghs were represented, five of them by noble provosts, an indication of the influence of landed nobles in town affairs.[92]

The ending of the war in 1573 allowed burghs the opportunity to free themselves from unwanted noble dominance, but this was not always desirable. The baillies and council of Dundee wrote to the fifth lord Gray in March 1574 expressing gratitude for his help in a dispute with the burgh of Perth, and promising Gray their faithful services in the future. An English commentator in 1580 was struck by this development, observing that 'the boroughs and burgess towns are wholly at the devotion of some nobleman or other', but sometimes these lords were fulfilling their roles with the connivance of the crown. In 1580, Renfrew astutely gave its bond to the powerful sixth earl of Argyll, who held the office of chancellor, allowing him the right to nominate one baillie and one officer in every election.[93] In Perth, control of the burgh council passed to the Ruthven family in the middle decades of the sixteenth century and the provostship was held by three generations of lords Ruthven. At the time of the Gowrie Conspiracy in 1600, the people of Perth irritated the king by their obdurate support for the doomed Ruthvens 'for they loved the earl, as being their provost, beyond all measure'.[94] These bonds survived in many instances into the seventeenth century. The burgh of Dumfries stood in dependence to the lords of Maxwell, and in spite of efforts by rivals and the crown to break the bond, it was reported in 1621 that 'the towne of Dumfreis cairies their olde respect to the name of Maxwell'.[95] In 1622, the eleventh earl of Angus went to court to defend the rights of 'my burgh' of Kirriemuir against the neighbouring royal burgh of Forfar that had charged it with 'nocht beand fre burgh'. Similarly, the burgh of Musselburgh benefited from the patronage of the earls of Dunfermline. Even Edinburgh cultivated powerful nobles. In April 1625, the provost and baillies of Edinburgh addressed a letter to 'Our veray honorable and guid lord', the young third marquis of Hamilton, seeking to maintain the patronage relationship established by his father.[96]

Burghs were not always content with noble interference. In 1574, the burgesses of Forres complained that sir Alexander Dunbar of Cumnock, the local sheriff, had intruded himself and his friends into the offices of provost and baillies, and was refusing to hold free elections. In 1578, Hugh Campbell of Loudon's election as provost of Ayr along with that of one of his clients, George Jameson, as baillie, sparked complaints that the election had been fraudulent.[97] In the 1580s, Aberdeen was engaged in a struggle to be free from an overbearing provost, Gilbert Menzies of Pitfoddels, a client of the sixth earl of Huntly. By 1590, complaints to the convention of royal burghs painted a picture of the town as 'thrallit to serve ane race of pepill, as it was ane burgh of baronaye'. It was only Huntly's defeat in the rebellion of 1594 that loosened his grip, leading to a more even relationship between the town and a local lord it could never afford to ignore.[98] In 1604, a strong popular movement was organised by agitators among the craft guilds of Dundee to oust the dominant merchant faction on the burgh council led by sir James Scrymgeour of Dudhope, hereditary constable of the burgh and *de facto* hereditary provost.[99] Even in their own burghs of barony lords faced challenges to their authority. In 1625, William Cunningham, lord Kilmaurs, began an investigation into the rights of the burgh of Kilmaurs, especially the right to sell wine, that led him to take legal action against the 'pretended' magistrates and people of the burgh of Kilmaurs when elections for burgh officers were held without his warrant.[100]

It was the dependence of lesser nobles on greater lords that did most to swell the ranks of magnate followings. The men of substance who belonged to the affinities of the feuding Lindsays and Ogilvies were named by the privy council in 1600 in the course of taking surety for their good behaviour. It is an impressive list of lords, knights, lairds and burghs.[101] The more important were the men attached to a lord's retinue the better he projected his power, and there was persistent pressure from earls to have retinues at court of at least twenty-four gentlemen with lords demanding sixteen and barons ten gentlemen. Anything less was unacceptable as the privy council recognised in February 1591 by overturning the low limits previously set by parliament.[102] Sixteenth-century lords were accompanied by much larger retinues, such as when in 1562 the fifth lord Lovat raised around 400 'truely prime, expert men, most of them gentlemens children, the flour of the clan', or the eighty mounted men who accompanied the fifth earl of Atholl to Edinburgh in January 1595, or the 200 footmen and 500 horsemen raised

by the second duke of Lennox to accompany the king to Dumfries in
December 1597.[103] The significance of lordship over lesser barons, or lairds,
lay in this extended manpower. A 1569 remission to John Grant of Freuchie
named forty-six Grants, all tenants of their chief, while the immediate
entourage of William Gordon of Gight in the early 1600s amounted to over
thirty men drawn from his sons, kinsmen, tenants and servants.[104] Both
these barons were dependants of the earls of Huntly. One of the most
remarkable affinities for which there is surviving evidence is that of the
Campbell lairds of Glenorchy, who created a network of dependants among
the small, largely Gaelic-speaking tenants on their Perthshire estates.[105]
The house of Glenorchy was dependent on the earls of Argyll, and those
granting the Glenorchy lairds their bonds of manrent accepted their allegiance to the earl. But personality and close knowledge of the particular
circumstances of the individuals involved was crucial. Gordonstoun took
the view that for the earls of Sutherland to have influence in Strathnaver it
was necessary to win over Uistean Du Mackay of Farr, for 'if you have
Macky you shall hav them; if you want [= lack] him, they can little profit
you'. In Caithness, where the fifth earl of Caithness was a rival, 'If you may
purchase the love of the inhabitants of that country, you shall care the less
for the earl's friendship or favour'.[106]

It was this form of lordship, in which powerful nobles extended their
influence or authority over men who owed them no tenurial obligations,
that annoyed James VI. He attacked what was a voluntary partnership
between nobles, unfairly alleging that the greater lords sought 'to thrall by
oppression, the meaner sort that dwelleth neere them, to their service and
following, although they holde nothing of them'.[107] Likewise, what drew
the attention of contemporary commentators was not the size of the estates
of the greater nobility, or their productivity, but the size of their followings
and the authority they wielded over their men, which 'is so great that they
regard as much or more their patron or nobleman than their Prince'. To
English observers, indoctrinated by Tudor propaganda, the nobility were
'too hard for the prince', their dependants lacking 'regard of the prince, law
or equity'. Certainly, during the early days of James VI's adult reign, royal
officials were wary of tackling noble criminality or rebellion as they were
afraid of the consequences of offending powerful noblemen. Halhill
was critical of this world of localised lordship in which noble affinities
represented threats to the peace and stability of the commonweal. From
his perspective at court, noblemen lorded over:

> many gret cumbersom clannes sa reddy to concur togither, and to rebell for
> the defence of any of ther name, or to avenge the just execusion of some of
> them, for mowther, thift, or sic uther crymes.[108]

The loyalty between lords and men was perceived to threaten the crown
and even civil society, hence, in 1589 a report on the Brig o' Dee rebellion

commented that the barons of the northeast were entirely dependent on the sixth earl of Huntly and 'hes forget their dewtie to thair naturale Prince'. In fact, loyalty had its limits, especially in those relationships between magnates and lesser nobles who had to be persuaded to follow a dangerous political course. Huntly's affinity was powerful, based on extensive territorial control and a large Gordon kindred, but those lairds pressured into recognising the lordship of a man who was a royal lieutenant, sheriff and the king's friend were unlikely to risk all in his service. By 1594, Huntly's headlong rush to embrace Counter Reformation conspiracies had fragmented his support, and many of the barons who had backed him 'lately stooping to him only in fear of his greatness, now frankly offer themselves and their services against him'.[109] The fifth earl of Bothwell gathered an impressive array of supporters in the later 1580s, but he, too, was helped by royal offices, being lord admiral, keeper of Liddesdale and in Lothian 'moste of the inferiors followe the Erle of Bothwell as sherife'. In fact, his support was unstable and far from unconditional. When in April 1589 he allied with the Catholic faction against the English party at court, the more important barons of the region 'refused him of the playn feld, and onles they saw the Kinges warrant they wold enter into no band nor service'. After his disgrace in 1591 it was Bothwell's forceful personality, English support and the complex political circumstances of the time that allowed him to remain a political presence.[110]

Bonds of friendship between lords were another feature of noble politics, and Annas Keith, countess of Argyll, commented in a letter in 1584, 'allayn maid without freindschipe is nathing proffitable'. That point was recognised in *c.* 1566 by Donald Dubh Cameron of Lochiel when writing to Colin Campbell of Glenorchy about their bond of friendship 'quhairthrow gif ye had ocht ado that I suld be reddy with all my mycht tow do your guid service as I sall evir do salang as ye will accept the samin, ye supportand me in lik maner'. Such ideas of friendship were crucial in defining social relations in early modern society, extending from the family to embrace patrons and clients as well as political allies in a range of nuanced relationships. Hence, the nobility was 'linked and bound one to another by kindred or alliance', and in observing these alliances, the English peer, lord Burgh, observed in 1593 that in Scotland 'it is very usual there to make bands of mutual defence and offence'.[111] Yet bonds between powerful nobles were inherently unstable, hence, the perplexed and frustrated tone of reports to the English government as ambassadors and agents tried to keep up with the sudden and unexpected changes in alliances and friendships. All too often these were brittle relationships between proud men seeking advantage through convenient and short-term agreements with rivals. When in January 1632 the thirteenth earl of Sutherland hesitated in choosing between giving up friendship with the laird of Frendraucht, his brother-in-law, and supporting the first marquis of Huntly, his nominal chief who was at feud with Frendraucht, Huntly 'suddantlie answerit then God be with you my Lord, and tunit about his bak'.[112] Nevertheless, here was the point at which noble affinities joined to one another in alliance became politically threatening to the crown, and it was this perceived threat in the mid-fifteenth century that drove James II to attack the eighth earl of Douglas and his allies.

The political circumstances of the latter half of the sixteenth century encouraged lords to cement bonds of kinship and friendship. The bands of the Lords of the Congregation in 1558, 1559 and 1560 were traditional means of indicating commitment to a cause, in this case, religious reform. John Knox recognised noble power, but in November 1559 he cautioned against over-reliance on those who thought that 'This Lord will bring these many hundred spearis: this man hath the credite to perswaid this cuntrey; yf this Erle be ouris, no man in suche a boundis will truble us'. Throughout the following turbulent decade those power blocks that defined the political struggles of the day were delineated in the March 1566 Newcastle bond, the April 1567 Edinburgh bond and the May 1568 Dumbarton bond.[113] After the end of civil war in 1573 no bond of friendship threatened the authority of the crown directly, while many sought to uphold it. The bond of November 1578 between the sixth earl of Argyll and the second earl of Mar was part of a broader political settlement emphasising the shared experience of these two great houses in 'the true service of there soveraigne princes thir many years bygone'. In 1594, the privy council encouraged the nobility of the northeast to sign bands in defence of the Protestant religion against the Catholic earls, while the 1599 bond pledging allegiance to the king in support of his claim to the English throne amounted to an emphatic declaration of loyalty.[114]

Conclusion

Lordship was not a static means of exercising power over land and men, it was instead constantly adjusting to time and place.[115] There may have been periods when more significant shifts took place, and in Scotland one of these changes might be located in the twelfth and thirteenth centuries when Anglo-Norman and native Scottish forms of lordship came together to create something new and distinct. But even this process was prolonged and is not without interpretive problems.[116] Arguably, the next major change in lordship occurred in the late medieval period as territorial earldoms and feudal vassalage allegedly were replaced by a titular peerage, scattered land-holding and personal bonds, but here, too, the process is slow and the degree of change remains open to dispute. Indeed, the entire debate over 'bastard' feudalism hinges on how different historians evaluate the degrees of change when balanced against indicators of continuity.[117] The question of the extent to which Scotland moved along the line from lord–man relations to patron–

client relations in the early modern period, therefore, is situated within a longer continuum. There was an underlying process at work, but the kind of lordship operating in the 1360s was closer to that operating in the 1560s than the latter was to the clientage networks of the 1760s. But the differences between the 1560s and the 1630s were barely recognisable, and it required the upheavals of the following two decades to alter lord–man relationships. Here the pattern is not unlike that in France where the crucial shift did not occur until the reign of Louis XIV following the Fronde, an episode of similar crisis for the nobility as was experienced by Scottish nobles in the collapse of the covenanter government and English conquest.[118]

The debate over the extent to which early modern nobilities ceased to preside over territorially based affinities held together by lordship and migrated to more fluid patronage clienteles remains unresolved. Recent research has pushed back the chronology of that process, particularly when attention is focused away from centres of royal power and when tested by longitudinal studies. It is clear that large noble clienteles survived into the later seventeenth century, even in France where royal absolutism was most pervasive.[119] What the above evidence indicates is remarkably little change in lordship and in lord–man relationships between the later sixteenth century and the decades prior to the outbreak of the covenanting revolution. This is not to argue for social and political stasis. The military dimensions of lordship did recede with the removal of court politics from the pressures that lords could exercise from their localities and with the simultaneous and related decline in feuding.[120] Lords were not slow to see the opportunities this presented to them. In 1562, the fourth earl of Bothwell grumbled that if he could make peace with his enemies 'I wald await upoun the Court with a page and a few servandis, to spair my expensis, whare now I am compelled to keap, for my awin saifty, a number of wicked and unprofitable men, to the utter destructioun of my living that is left'. But it was more than four decades before conditions were such that nobles could dispense with high levels of protection. Lords placed more emphasis on financial management, economising on unnecessary service at the ruinously expensive London court, investing heavily in expensive building programmes, litigation and the consumption of luxuries, which all contributed to a form of estate management more attuned to commercial considerations but one rarely dominated by commercialisation.[121] One measurable change was the rapid decline in the need for bonds of manrent and maintenance. Ultimately bonds were an indication of a troubled society, and in the more peaceful and prosperous conditions of the early seventeenth century the need to reinforce lordship with personal bonds declined. Significantly, when national tensions rose following the signing of the National Covenant, itself a form of bonding, Highland lords resumed their traditions, and in June 1638 the earls of Argyll and Seaforth signed bonds of mutual friendship.[122] Yet there was no wholesale overturning of those traditional relationships that nobles deployed in exercising power locally and that formed a reservoir of power that might still be mobilised nationally, as indeed occurred in 1637–8. What is also absent is any effective intervention from the crown to weaken lordship, and Charles I's revocation, which did seek to weaken lord–man relationships, caused such a backlash throughout all ranks of noble society that it contributed to the collapse of royal government.[123] The disappearance of feuding brought with it some shifts in how nobles exercised power over other men, but it did not mean that they ceased to act as lords.

CHAPTER 4

Magistrates

At a local level, early modern government essentially involved the administration of the law during a period that saw the extension of seigneurial jurisdiction throughout much of Europe. Along with the nobilities of Hungary, Bohemia, Austria, Poland, Brandenburg, Sicily, Naples and the provinces of Holland, Zeeland and Utrecht, the Scottish nobility exercised private justice. Private jurisdiction was less common and less powerful in Sweden, Castile, northern Italy and England, but even in England the veneer of royal authority concealed the reality of huge fiefdoms dominated by a handful of magnate families like the earls of Derby in the northwest of the kingdom. Nevertheless, the division of Scotland into powerful private and hereditary feudal jurisdictions was extreme, even more so than the kingdom of Sicily where the percentage of land subject to feudal jurisdiction was a little over half in the late sixteenth century.[1]

Late medieval Scotland developed a system of courts and law that ultimately derived authority from the crown, creating a pronounced legal culture that should not be underestimated.[2] Another legacy of the late medieval era was that as a consequence of warfare, particularly in the fourteenth century, local government was largely in the hereditary hands of the nobility. The advantages to nobles of controlling local justice were a combination of economic, social and political rights in law that underpinned their authority over the common people who lived under their jurisdiction, prestige along with power that conferred advantages over rival noble houses, and important links to royal government at the centre. As a system of delivering justice and providing local administration there is little reason to question its effectiveness, and it is important to avoid assuming that central justice was fairer or more efficient. Besides, until the later sixteenth century there was no enthusiasm for renegotiating that compact, and any objective observer could see that the crown lacked the opportunity, the means or the sustained will to break up the magnate clienteles that provided local government and maintained order as they did throughout the greater part of Europe. Unwanted and unsubtle interference in that complex balance of relationships risked pulling crown and localities apart and creating political disintegration.[3]

Justice and Injustice

James VI wrote that among his subjects the nobles were 'farre first in great-
nesse and power, either to doe good or evill, as they are inclined', and this
was most true of their role as local magistrates where their power had such
an impact on the lives of the common people.[4] Sir Richard Maitland of
Lethington, a court of session judge, recognised that attitudes towards
justice were tarnished by hypocrisy as people condemned lawlessness while
seeking to find ways to circumscribe the law:

> Quhen ane of thaime susteinis wrang,
> We cry for justice, heid and hang;
> Bot, when our neichbouris we our-gang,
> We labour justice to delay;
> Affectione blindis us sa lang,
> All equitie is put away.

In addressing injustice, Lethington did not escape from the conservatism of
his rank, arguing that it was for nobles to set good examples, since disorder
might lead to anarchy and the overthrow of nobility.[5] Unfortunately, James
VI contributed to the myth that nobles thrived on lawlessness, writing in
Basilikon doron (1599) that:

> The naturall sicknesse that I have perceived this estate subject to in my time,
> hath beene, a fectlesse arrogant conceit of their greatnes and power.

The king perceived this problem to be rooted in noble society where young
men were encouraged to believe that 'their honor stood in committing three
points on iniquitie': the oppression of 'the meaner sort', who were forced
into dependence; the maintenance of their followers even when they were in
the wrong; and private feuding. What is often misunderstood about this
passage is that it did not apply to all nobles, and that it must be read alongside the king's other comments on nobles in maintaining order and in
providing justice. In 1605, James VI observed of the nobility that it was their
duty:

> by thair goode example to teiche thair inferiouris how to live civilie, with
> that dew respect to oure obedyence whiche apperteyneth, and to be by thair
> force and power assisting to oure justice and officiaris of the same in all thingis
> tending to the conservatioun of the peace and observatioun of the law.[6]

This conventional view was widely shared. In 1568, sir William Douglas of
Lochleven made his premature will (he died in 1606) in which an authentic
voice of responsible lordship is heard claiming that 'the gratest cair that I
ever haid wes that justice suld be ministrat amangis my tenants without
parsialitie of ony'. A contemporary historian insisted that king and nobles
shared responsibility for dispensing justice since 'The dewtie of all Prence,

Majistrat, and King, is equallie to do justice to all men, ever having respect to the caus, and not to the persone'. David Hume of Godscroft was of the opinion that only 'a solid and perfect peace established amongst the Nobilitie' was the surest way to keep the peace. Sir Robert Gordon of Gordonstoun, an experienced judge in his family's hereditary courts, believed that a magistrate should 'Execute justice duely without exception of persons or any other circumstance whatsoever'.[7]

At a local level the commitment of nobles to the enforcement of law and the provision of justice was essential.[8] But, of course, the most obvious weakness in a hereditary office was that many office-holders were inadequate. In spite of parliament's injunctions to raise standards among the magistracy, hereditary judges included among their number the average share of the lazy and the incompetent. The personal nature of this justice is illuminated by two ineffective lords: one who was an invalid, the other who was incompetent. William Douglas of Cavers, hereditary sheriff of Roxburgh, was described in April 1586 as 'unable and sua corpolent as he mycht nocht travel'. The privy council's view of the second earl of Atholl in 1607 was scathing, blaming his shortcomings for 'the miserable estate of the countrey', while chancellor Dunfermline dismissed 'the imbecillitie and weaknes of this Earle'.[9] Even the non-residence of a lord could result in a slide into disorder. In the summer of 1599 the absence from the kingdom of the seventh earl of Argyll was seen as a contributory factor to criminality east of Braemar where little could be done without 'the help of sik greitt men as suld putt order to sike matteris'. Absenteeism became a more pressing problem after the regal union, although the privy council anticipated potential disorder, for example, in 1603 the first lord Roxburghe was granted permission to attend court on condition that he guaranteed there was someone 'to haif the chairge of his freyndis in his absence'. In 1608, the privy council noted that law and order on the island of Arran had declined since the second marquis of Hamilton had gone to court. Three years later the council conceded that its decision to ward the Catholic first marquis of Huntly had contributed to an increase in lawlessness in Badenoch and Lochaber, because there was no effective alternative to Huntly lordship.[10]

Much of the pressure for better justice and the establishment of law and order came from the nobility. On 26 September 1579, the privy council listened to a complaint by the second earl of Mar, hereditary sheriff of Stirling, concerning general lawlessness and the problems of seeking redress through the court of session 'quhair the proces is commonlie langsum and the executioun of decreittis sclender, the expenssis commonlie exceiding the principall'. Similarly, in 1589 the ninth earl of Errol complained to the privy council about the 'want of justice', claiming that it was the absence of royal justice that forced men to seek 'privat revenge at thair maist advantage'. Instances of nobles pressurising the crown to take an interest in disorder in their localities continued into the early seventeenth century. In November

1633, the seventh lord Ogilvy notified the privy council of the rise in crime in Glenisla, and was successful in persuading it to order the restitution of better community defence.[11]

Most noblemen took their role as magistrates in royal government and in their own private courts seriously. The regent Morton was remembered as 'wise and able for government, a lover of justice, order and policy', and he took a tough line with fellow magnates who transgressed the law. In September 1573, Morton ordered the fourth earl of Cassillis – the 'king of Carrick' – into ward for repeatedly failing to enforce a decreet.[12] The fifth lord Lovat was idealised in clan memory as a man relentless in the pursuit of criminals. Colin Campbell of Glenorchy was 'ane great justiciar all his tyme' who 'caused execut to the death mony notable lymmaris [= thieves]', and Duncan Campbell of Glenorchy shared his father's commitment to maintaining order, complaining in September 1591 that whenever thieves struck in his locality 'I as Magistrat of this cuntray beris the burdene'.[13] William Maitland, younger of Lethington, wrote in 1562 that 'the magistrat caryeth not the swerd in vayne', and some nobles had ferocious reputations as law enforcers. In that same year, the first earl of Mar drowned twenty-two thieves at Hawick 'for lacke of trees and halters', while in one judicial raid on the Borders the first earl of Moray captured and executed fifty thieves. In 1574, the sixth earl of Argyll made a progress of his lands, holding justice courts, and although 'hemp and tow were scant', the number put to death was estimated at 160 people. Gordonstoun was another enthusiastic justiciar, boasting of tracking and punishing every kind of criminal.[14]

The business of formal justice was time consuming, onerous and not without risk. In 1566, the fourth earl of Bothwell, keeper of Liddesdale, was wounded by a thief ; two wardens of the west march were killed in the line of duty, the eighth lord Maxwell in 1593 and sir John Carmichael of that Ilk in 1600; while in 1611 Alexander Dunbar of Westfield, sheriff of Moray, was murdered. Nor did personal risk entirely disappear in the more peaceful reign of Charles I.[15] The greater part of the burden of office, however, involved the tedious business of holding court. When in May 1577 the eighth lord Maxwell was dismissed as warden of the west march, he was ordered to hand over 'all bukis, scrollis, rollis, indentis, aggrementis, bandis, and uther writtis', a body of documents that required complex and meticulous record-keeping by his officers. Similarly, the records of the tenth earl of Angus's lieutenancy of the marches in 1598–1600 offer an insight into the busy and demanding schedule expected of these men.[16] The expertise of local lords informed the making of crown policy either because many of the greater nobles were councillors or courtiers, or because they were consulted. In January 1579, there was a heated four-day debate before the privy council over how to administer the unruly western march in the course of which local lords and councillors demonstrated an acute awareness of the issues.[17]

While most nobles would have shared Gordonstoun's classical view of law that 'It is better for a commonwealthe to have few lawes weill keipit than to have many good lawes evill executed, and farr worse obeyed', the number of laws and its administration was increasing. Nobles needed to have a better understanding of the growing volume of law and royal proclamations, a point that was brought home to John Lennox of Cally in Kirkcudbright in 1609 when he had to pay £6 as his stent for printing sir John Skene's *Regiam majestatem*. By 1626 the administrative complexities of office were such that sir Patrick Hume of Polwarth wanted professional judges from the court of session to take over the administration of sheriffdoms because his scholarly interests had been interrupted by the 'troublesome office of Sherifschip'.[18]

Of course, not all lords were scrupulous in observing the law, and many nobles upheld their own version of justice while ignoring decreets of the court of session, disobeying instructions from the privy council and physically assaulting royal messengers.[19] The most notorious example of overawing a court occurred in April 1567 when the court of justiciary was ringed with armed men to ensure that the fourth earl of Bothwell was not brought to trial for the murder of king Henry.[20] Nobles were bound by the obligations of lordship to protect their dependants and tenants employed in committing injustices. John Leslie identified a 'peculiar and proper vice' in which dependants and servants engaged in 'seditione and stryfe' at the command of their lords, and another commentator observed that 'Many offenders are countenanced by noblemen, with great contempt of law and justice'. In January 1591 the fifth earl of Bothwell hauled a man from the bar of the court of session in order to protect a client, an action that James VI referred to in a speech in the following June when he alleged that crime was rife because 'all men set themselves more for freendes then for justice and obedience to the lawe'.[21] Other lords abused their judicial authority, so that in 1589 James Conheith complained to the privy council that it was impossible to get justice in Dumfries because his alleged assailant was a 'household man and servand' of the fifth lord Herries, the lord provost. In one of the most flagrant abuses of judicial power in this period, on 20 December 1615 the Gordons exploited their control of the sheriffdom of Aberdeen to carry out the judicial murder of Francis Hay.[22]

A means of avoiding partial justice was to seek exemptions from local jurisdiction, a device that further fragmented local justice, and it was not unknown for lords to allege feud and partiality with this aim in view. The problem was stated in 1595 by an English agent who recognised that 'it will be found a hard thing indeed to subject one great man to another in "feade" with him and that by authority may under colour of justice oppress him'. As late as 1623 James VI was persuaded to grant an exemption to 'those of the surname of Johnston' from the jurisdiction of the Border commissioners, one of whom was the first earl of Nithsdale, because of the alleged malice of the Maxwells, their old enemies.[23] Nor was justice at the centre immune from noble influence. In July 1599, the countess of Atholl wrote to sir David

Lindsay of Edzell, an extraordinary lord of the court of session, complaining that he had been unhelpful to her husband, and suggesting that 'ye follow his lordship in tyme cuming in ane mair effectuiss maneir of freyndschip nor ye haif done afoirtymes gyf ye wiss to haif his Lo[rdship] to do you plesour'. In 1631, Nithsdale's servants escaped punishment for burning down the manse of a local minister when a case against them in the justice court mysteriously collapsed.[24]

Overt criminality by nobles was uncommon, but notorious incidents did occur. The litany of noble thuggery includes the roasting of Allan Stewart, commendator of Crossraguel abbey, by the third earl of Eglinton in August 1571 in an attempt to extort lands from him; the decades of oppression committed by lord Robert Stewart in the islands and waters around Orkney and Shetland; and the many charges laid against the fourth earl of Caithness, a man who 'lived too long for these adjacent cuntries, wher he had been the instrument of civill dissention and shedding of much blood'.[25] Sustaining these nobles in their disorderly activities were relationships with broken men, outlaw gangs protected by their lords, especially in the Highlands where bandits continued to be protected by landlords in the 1630s.[26] Towns were affected by noblemen who indulged in disorder. The fifth lord Ross was accused in 1585 of terrorising the people of Renfrew; in May 1598, the sixth lord Hume burned Lauder tollbooth; and in 1609 the twelfth earl of Crawford and his men beat up people on the streets of Forfar and Dundee.[27] Scottish nobles lacked many of the formal privileges that protected nobles elsewhere from criminal prosecution, but punishment was rare. James VI admitted in 1610 in the course of discussing the second earl of Orkney that 'we haif ever bene moir cairfull to minister phisik for cureing of the disease then onywayes to cutt of the member'. A handful of lesser nobles were punished for their crimes, usually for particularly heinous crimes that shocked noble society. Jean Livingston, daughter of John Livingston of Dunipace, was beheaded for the murder of her husband, John Kincaid of Wariston; Robert Muir of Auchindrain and his son were executed in 1617 for the killing of sir Thomas Kennedy of Culzean in 1602 and a brutal murder which formed part of the cover-up; Robert Erskine and his two sisters were executed in 1614 for poisoning their nephew, John Erskine of Dun, in a plot to acquire his lands. Even the top ranks of the nobility were not immune to the full rigour of the law, but the circumstances were exceptional. The execution in November 1609 of John Stewart, son of the first lord Doune, was for the notorious crime of hamesucken (killing a man in his own home), while the beheading of the ninth lord Maxwell on 21 May 1613 resulted from the dishonourable nature of his offence, that of murdering a rival under trust, along with a persistent record of violence and criminality.[28]

The decline of private violence was accompanied by a rise in litigation driven by broader social and economic changes in society.[29] The longstanding and bloody quarrel between the first marquis of Huntly and the tenth lord Forbes finally became the subject of a decreet by the court of session in 1621.[30] But while the law offered an alternative means of prosecuting a feud, a legal decision did not necessarily restore peace to the community, and litigation was a means of prosecuting a quarrel, not a route to resolving differences. Thus, the Mackenzies preyed on the Glengarry Macdonalds who 'being unexpert and unskilfull in the lawes of the realme' were man-oeuvred into outlawry so that 'the tryb of Clankeinzie become great in these pairts, still incroaching upon ther nighbours, who are unacquented with the lawes of this kingdome'. The first earl of Haddington was an aggressive litigant, inspiring the bitter comment by a rival in 1632 regarding 'the desire he hes of heaping and hatching wealth, [he] thinks it a leassning of the opinion men have of it, if he have left any hole for the law to come in to take away anything from him'.[31] It is mistaken, therefore, to see litigation as a necessary prelude to stability, and challenges in the courts to the possession of land created uncertainty in the community. It might be argued that from the mid-1620s, the crown's attempts to use a royal revocation as the pretext to manipulate the law offered by far the gravest threat to the peace of local society.[32]

In 1608, James VI was annoyed to hear that grants made to two of his servants were being challenged in the court of session by the sixth lord Herries 'upon some olde evident'. In this contest the charter was the crucial weapon, hence, the determination of rivals to destroy one another's charter archive, the digging around for old documents and the searching for copies of lost documents in order to demonstrate entitlement in a society where possession carried great weight at law.[33] The establishment of a register of sasines in 1617 was intended to remove tensions within the landed community that arose from disputed ownership. By declaring that title to land indisputably held by a family for the previous forty years would be recog-nised provided there was no successful challenge before 1630, the crown opened the floodgates for litigation. Legal challenges continued in spite of this enactment; the sixth earl of Glencairn began processes of reduction against a list of neighbouring landowners on the basis of a charter dating from the reign of David II.[34] One of the most remarkable cases of the period involved the dispute between the houses of Elphinstone and Mar over the barony of Kildrummy that began in the 1560s when the first earl of Mar initiated a campaign to gain possession of the lands of the ancient earldom, and was finally resolved in favour of Mar's son in 1626.[35]

The Courts

The principal local officer of the crown in Scotland was the sheriff, and the kingdom was divided into sheriffdoms and stewardships to which parliament might add new ones and divide or annex to existing ones. Essentially, the role of the sheriff was to collect revenue from the crown's feudal casualties, organise military activities in the locality, preside over the sheriff court and execute crown letters and decreets. In the early seventeenth century the business of the office grew and sheriffs increasingly collected taxes, regulated the local economy, enforced religious conformity and were expected to preside over the annual election of shire commissioners to parliament. This was an important and distinguished office that provided a formal contact with the king's government and gave limited advantages in local politics.[36] Nevertheless, much of the business done in sheriff courts was dull and uncontroversial, possibly because many criminal cases were repledged to regality courts, or were processed through justice ayres and the central court of justiciary.[37] A comparison of 200 cases at Forfar sheriff court in 1568–9 and the same number in 1632–3 indicates that debt cases rose from 33 per cent to 45 per cent, cases involving feudal dues fell from 23 per cent to 13 per cent, and service of heirs cases rose slightly from 11 per cent to 14 per cent. In both periods these cases constituted 67 per cent and 72 per cent, respectively of the court's business. Instances of criminal behaviour were few, with only 8 per cent of cases in 1568–9 concerning forms of violence, and that fell to 4 per cent of cases in 1632–3.[38] Similarly, Stirling sheriff court records for 1633–9 underline the court's primary role in the administration of landed society.[39]

What most distinguished Scottish sheriffs from their English counterparts, or even from the provincial governors of France, was that they were in the hereditary hands of the nobility – 'a great public misfortune', according to Thomas Craig of Riccarton. As hereditary offices, sheriffdoms were subject to the usual human frailties such as incompetence, while the occurrence of a minority required the appointment of a sheriff wardator. There were occasions of women exercising authority in the absence of their husbands, as occurred at Stirlingshire c. 1633–4 when the countess of Mar presided over the sheriff court. Shrieval office occasionally changed hands, and might be bought and sold, although crown approval was required. From time to time the office fell to the crown as a consequence of forfeiture, such as in December 1567 when the fifth lord Hume was appointed hereditary sheriff of Berwickshire following the forfeiture of the fourth earl of Bothwell, or when an individual was persuaded to resign his office into the hands of the king.[40]

Nobles commonly did not exercise in person the authority of their office, instead manipulating local patronage to reward servants. The sheriff court was staffed by the sheriff depute, sheriff clerk, clerk depute and procurator fiscal, all usually requiring a trained notary, as well as bailiffs and the dempster, whose job was to pronounce sentence. Sheriffs appointed their deputes, and while royal confirmation was required, it was unusual for the king to withhold that consent. Consequently, it was common for sheriffs to select kinsmen or dependants who 'dois no thing in ony actione persewit afoir thame [the sheriff] but as he commandis thame'. In practice, it was the sheriff depute who was the principal officer of the court, conducting most of its business and receiving a share of the fees and fines paid to the court. On occasion, the ordinary depute would be required to stand aside for a replacement where it was alleged that he was a kinsman of a litigant, but given the texture of relationships in local society this device was employed rarely.[41] A similar level of private patronage operated in other nominally royal offices. On 19 February 1600, the second duke of Lennox issued letters of bailiery to William Cunningham of Caprington as bailie and justiciar in the lands and barony of Tarbolton in Ayrshire for nineteen years, an office held by his family for generations. Caprington, in turn, was granted power to appoint his own clerks, sergeants, dempsters and other officers who were often kinsmen.[42] Naturally, this local patronage was subject to political change. In 1595, John Leslie of Balquhane took advantage of the exile of the sixth earl of Huntly to remove from office by a process of underhand dealing and threatening behaviour the sheriff clerk of Aberdeen, Alexander Fraser, a Huntly appointee who had been confirmed in office by the king since his patron's rebellion.[43]

The most powerful royal office deployed in the localities was the lieutenant, an office that was not hereditary. Usually a lieutenancy was created in response to a crisis, often for a limited duration, their powers were exceptional and they had a quasi-military function, as when in July 1578 the eighth earl of Angus was charged with raising troops and conducting operations against rebels. Lieutenants were entrusted with wide-ranging authority that granted jurisdiction over other royal officers and private jurisdictions within a large geographic area. When the tenth earl of Angus was appointed lieutenant and justiciar in the north in November 1592 he was given authority over nine shires north of the Tay. Because of the enormous extent of these powers, lieutenants were drawn from the top ranks of the nobility, but this did not stop other nobles from protesting against what was perceived as a threatening imbalance within the local community, as occurred in the southwest in 1593 when the eighth lord Maxwell was granted extensive powers as lieutenant. Similarly, when in 1600 the tenth earl of Angus tried to use his commission as lieutenant of the Borders to extend his authority over Kyle and Carrick, the local community protested that he was 'intending thairby to draw thame under a yoke and servitude quhairwith nane of thair predecessouris wer nevir heirtofoir burdynit'. In the face of this clamour the king backed down.[44]

Unsurprisingly, most lieutenancies were granted to deal with difficulties arising in the Borders or Highlands. Of the seventeen commissions of lieutenancy over the Border marches issued to thirteen different men between 1561 and 1599 the great majority were to lords whose power chiefly lay outside the region. All these men were drawn from the highest ranks of the nobility, all were involved in the king's government and all had a presence in adjacent territories.[45] Fewer lieutenancies were granted in the Highlands. After the civil war only the sixth earl of Huntly was appointed lieutenant on an open-ended basis. His lieutenancy of the north was granted in 1586 and terminated in February 1592 following his murder of the second earl of Moray. Subsequent appointments were of a more limited nature, but the men selected continued to be drawn from the highest ranks of the nobility. The second duke of Lennox served as lieutenant of the north from November 1594 to August 1596 with a remit to pacify the region, and also had short-lived lieutenancies over Highland localities in 1598, 1599 (shared with Huntly) and 1601. The seventh earl of Argyll had lieutenancies in July 1594 to suppress rebellion, over the Magregors in 1601, over a number of isles in 1607 and to crush rebels on Kintyre in 1615. After the third earl of Moray's lieutenancy in 1624 the crown saw no need to issue such powerful commissions.[46]

The Borders offered particular opportunities for nobles to serve in powerful royal offices in a politically sensitive region organised for war, parts of which were frequently disorderly and yet in which the king was often present.[47] The offices of wardens of the eastern, middle and western marches along with the keepership of Liddesdale were not hereditary, but were among the most onerous and dangerous in the kingdom, carrying no fee, and there were no royal troops to command. In 1564, a frustrated Walter Ker of Cessford, warden of the middle march, complained that local barons failed to attend his court or recognise his authority. When the fifth earl of Bothwell was offered the keepership of Liddesdale in 1583 he was reluctant to take it 'without greater entertainment than the King is hitherto pleased to bestow therewith'. Yet from the crown's perspective it was essential that the warden exercise strong lordship and be widely connected to supportive kinsmen, hence, the reluctance to appoint less powerful men. On the more peaceful east march, the only occasion between 1560 and 1603 when a member of the Hume kindred was not warden was 1570–3. In the middle march there was a similar dominance by the Kers. In the west march, however, the office changed hands twenty-five times during this period, being exercised by ten different men drawn from the Douglas, Maxwell, Johnstone, Carmichael and Hamilton kindreds.[48]

The late sixteenth-century crown's preference for, and dependence on, nobles to govern the localities is evident in the issuing of special commissions. Some of these commissions arose in the context of crown initiatives aimed at tackling a perceived law and order problem. But, as always, local politics could not be ignored. In July 1582, commissions of justiciary were issued to lords to hold courts in various localities in an effort to make justice available to poor people; other initiatives followed, notably in 1588 to clear the backlog of criminal cases and to enforce the laws against jesuits. The revocation of the July 1582 commissions on 8 September, shortly after the Ruthven raid, points to their political dimension, and sir James Melville of Halhill commented that courtiers and councillors were guilty of 'causing his majetie subscryve sindre hurtfull signatours and commissions'. Hence, the frequent discharges, for example, in 1587, 1594 and 1598. The most common form of commission licensed by the crown was the special commission issued to hereditary office-holders allowing them to extend their authority in pursuit of criminals, a practice that increased in the early seventeenth century. For example, in 1621 the seventh earl of Menteith was granted a commission of justiciary because the king was assured of 'his goode inclinatioun to justice'.[49]

In spite of these crown offices and commissions, overwhelmingly justice was sought in private and hereditary local courts. These jurisdictions were characterised by the absence of a rational structure, or even a strong sense of immemorial custom, changes being made to their size and shape by royal charter.[50] Lords disposed of offices as they did other forms of feudal property, and baronial jurisdiction was bought and sold, with royal permission, or it might be granted to other family members, as in 1629 when the second earl of Mar made over the office of sheriff of Stirling to his eldest son.[51] The confusing texture of local administration is evident in the variety of legal officers. In early seventeenth-century Lanarkshire the sheriffdom was held heritably by the house of Hamilton, there were a number of private jurisdictions, including two large regalities, Hamilton and Glasgow, and three smaller regalities, as well as at least thirty baronies and the two royal burghs of Lanark and Rutherglen. In addition, there were a number of ecclesiastical jurisdictions. As though local administration was not complicated enough, the crown created another level of administration in 1609 with the shire commissions of the peace.[52] It is difficult to argue that Scotland was under-governed.

Disputes over local office were essentially about power, reputation and honour. Such quarrels occurred in England where crown control was relatively effective and where ideas about public authority were widely accepted, often acting as a restraint on the conduct of the parties.[53] Unsurprisingly, the consequences for litigants in Scotland of a feuding culture and the structure of overlapping and contested jurisdiction could be confusing and potentially threatening. In 1568, officials representing the fourth lord Gray, as sheriff of Forfar, and Patrick Learmonth of Dairsie, in his capacity as bailie-principal of the regality of St Andrews, contested which of them was the court of appeal from the barony court of Balgavie of which Dairsie was the lord.[54] Because the exercise of jurisdiction was closely linked to lordship, nobles defended fiercely the rights and privileges of their courts. In 1595, the eleventh earl of Crawford was pursuing at law his claim to the sheriffdom of Forfar, surrendered to the lords Gray in 1488.[55] The explanation for such tenacity is not difficult to understand. When in September 1606, the ninth lord Maxwell and the sixth earl of Morton were

warned not to use the excuse of holding courts in Eskdale as a means 'to
shaw thair powar and forces and to mak a brag and provocatioun ather of
thame aganis utheris', the privy council was describing how nobles exploited
judicial office to project their own authority.[56] The hereditary nature of
justice, and its close connection with local power, inevitably drew neighbouring lords into quarrels, and Halhill observed that the roots of some of
the worst feuds of the early 1590s lay in the fact that 'dyvers of them [nobles]
had maid suttis, and obtenit commissions, with ample preveleges over other
landis, asweill as over ther awen'.[57] Crown interference could create or fuel
these tensions. In 1563, queen Mary's decision to award the disputed
sheriffdom of Fife to the fifth earl of Rothes instead of to the fifth lord Lindsay 'raisit gret seditioun in all fyff' that rumbled on for another ten years.[58]
In the northeast it was difficult to avoid appointing the earl of Huntly to
a lieutenancy, and when in 1592 the office went to the fifth earl of Atholl,
and again when the third earl of Moray was appointed lieutenant in 1624,
enormous resentment was generated among the Gordons that undermined
the authority of the office.[59]

The legal route to contesting the jurisdictional authority of another lord
was to seek a reduction in the court of session, as occurred in 1582 with
the fourth earl of Caithness's extensive commission of justiciary, followed
two years later by parliament issuing a formal annulment. This was neither
the end of legal proceedings nor of the local feud with the Gordons who
brought the action against Caithness.[60] Jurisdictional disputes, therefore,
might easily escalate into bloodfeud. Sometimes the disagreement arose
because the office in which authority resided was contested, as in 1572 when
John Wallace of Craigie heightened tensions in Kyle by intimating that
he would oppose the second lord Ochiltree holding court on the conjunct
fee lands of Craigie's mother, now Ochiltree's wife.[61] More commonly the
problem arose because of the structure of the court system in which overlapping and ill-defined jurisdictions made conflict likely. When in 1574
the eighth lord Maxwell, warden of the west march, summoned the local
nobility and freeholders to a sitting of his warden's court, William Crichton,
tutor to the eighth lord Sanquhar, in whose name he exercised the office of
hereditary sheriff of Dumfries, summoned the sheriff court to sit on the
same days, using the opportunity to give judgments against individuals who
chose to attend the warden's court.[62] Disputes over jurisdiction can be found
between sheriffs and their deputes, and between nobles and their vassals,
while officers with responsibility in more than one court found themselves
at the centre of bitter disputes.[63] Towns, too, became embroiled in these
quarrels with nobles over jurisdiction.[64]

The effect of this competition was the destabilisation of local government. For example, the failure of crown policy in dealing with the
Magregors led the earl of Dunbar to conclude in September 1610 that royal
interests were undermined by 'you quho are Campbells Drummons and

Murrayis by the distrust ane of you hes of the uther'.[65] Although feuding declined from the early 1600s, litigation increased and the same uncooperative behaviour permeated local administration. In 1627, in the midst of a war with France and Spain, the mustering of the feuars and parishioners of the lordship of Coupar in Angus was disrupted by the mutually threatening claims to administer the muster by the first lord Coupar and the seventh lord Ogilvy. In order to avoid an open confrontation as the two lords tried to exert control over the wapenschaws, the privy council ordered the men of the lordship to muster under the authority of the sheriff of Perth.[66] Fortunately, Scotland's defences were not tested by French invasion.

This exercise of jurisdictional authority was at the core of noble identity and power. The tenth earl of Angus held jurisdictions scattered throughout the country, amounting to nine baronial and three regalian jurisdictions across six eastern shires. Where local autonomy was combined with nominally royal offices the degree of regional power was even greater. When in 1585 parliament ratified the fifth earl of Bothwell's infeftments, these included the office of sheriff of Edinburgh, three lordships of Hailes, Crichton and Bothwell, fourteen baronies scattered throughout six shires and the stewartry of Kirkcudbright. The fifth earl of Argyll was described as 'regal within himself'. Until 1628 the earls were hereditary justice-generals, presiding over the court of justiciary in Edinburgh with the right to hold justice ayres throughout the kingdom. Successive earls were appointed lieutenants in the west, they were hereditary sheriffs of Argyll, and held the offices of justiciar in Lorn, Knapdale and Kintyre, chamberlain in Bute, and bailie in Kintyre, Uist and Skye. Their hereditary regalities covered Lorn, Cowal and Over Cowal along with many baronial jurisdictions. These jurisdictions were not only found far from the centre of royal power; sir Lewis Bellenden of Broughton had 2,000 vassals living under his baronial jurisdiction in the Edinburgh suburbs of the Canongate and Leith.[67]

Baronies were the administrative building blocks of the kingdom, being royal creations with their jurisdiction defined in a charter that could be altered only by the king issuing a new charter. The regality of Melrose was granted to the abbey of Melrose in 1358, but the lands and jurisdiction changed hands repeatedly between 1557 and 1621 when a new creation was granted to the first earl of Melrose. Barony courts did not necessarily embrace geographically consolidated territory, being the result of centuries of haphazard land accumulation, and the barony as a unit of land could be broken up. For example, the barony of Rosyth was created by a new charter in 1587 uniting lands in the shires of Fife, Perth and distant Dumfries.[68] Legislation of 1401 required that when earldoms or lordships fell into the hands of the king any constituent baronies would in future be held directly of the crown, and by the mid-sixteenth century few baronies were held of a lord. There continued to be exceptions, for example, the barony of Urie was carved out of the barony of Cowie in 1430 by the seventh lord Hay of Errol, and when William Hay of Urie succeeded to the barony in 1607, he was a dependant of the ninth earl of Errol. Financial problems forced the laird of Urie to sell up and between 1616 and 1630 the earls of Errol reacquired possession of the barony after almost two hundred years.[69]

The extent to which private baronial courts were exempt from royal authority has been exaggerated, and the later sixteenth and seventeenth centuries saw a weakening of the powers of these courts as the court of session intruded, allowing individuals to make advocation to it following a judgment. From the mid-sixteenth century, therefore, there was an increasing tendency for vassals to try to move civil cases from the barony court to the court of session, where professional advocates defended their customary rights against the policies of aggressive landlords. Furthermore, unless regality powers had been granted to a lord, most sixteenth-century barons were subject to the sheriff, or any judge ordinary who held superior jurisdiction over the barony.[70] The unease over the partiality of local courts was a significant issue in seeking to remove cases from the locality. In 1589, George Ross of Balnagowan refused to appear before the sixth earl of Huntly, the sheriff of Inverness, on the grounds that he would not receive a fair trial from a Gordon judge. Balnagowan flattered the central court, arguing that the business was too complex for the sheriff court, and that its resolution required the skills of the best trained lawyers. In August 1617, the privy council transferred the trial of James Forbes of Blacktoun from Aberdeen to Edinburgh because trouble was feared in the burgh where 'the pairtyis and thair freindis who will kythe in that mater ar mony and grite'. By contrast, it was claimed, the parties could expect impartial treatment in Edinburgh where 'the power, freindship, or credite of ony of the pairtyis salbe no hinder, latt, nor impediment to the dew and laughfull course of justice'. Nevertheless, there was an also an increasing desire for better qualified legal advice in the localities. In 1629, a dispute arose between lord Lorne and the inhabitants of the northern isles over the location for holding the court of justiciary. Lorne's opponents argued that no advocates would journey into the isles, thus depriving people of expert counsel, but the king dismissed their claims.[71] Professionalism, however, did not necessarily mean better justice or more civil behaviour, and corruption and abuse within the central courts was a common concern in early modern society.[72]

Most legislation affecting barony courts concerned matters of economic regulation, such as fixing prices or preserving woods. In the 1580s, much of the business of Torphichen regality court was concerned with the settlement of liferents and the organisation of feudal dues and tenancies. The majority of the cases brought before sir William Douglas of Lochleven's barony court of Keillour in Perthshire concerned boundary disputes between the tenants, along with matters related to farming, such as the straying of cattle, or debts, while in the mid-1630s, sir Colin Campbell of

Glenorchy noted the 'ordinarie persuts' outstanding in his courts, largely mundane matters like the regulation of kailyards and wood management.[73]

An important distinction was between barony courts with a limited judicial authority over the vassals of the baron, predominantly in matters relating to the management of the estate, relations between the vassals and the superior and neighbourhood disputes, and those baronies with charters creating them *in liberam baroniam*. The latter remained private franchise courts, but they dispensed public justice, tried a range of civil cases and, since the eleventh century, barony courts had the right to try all crimes except the four pleas of the crown, robbery, rape, murder and arson, and only those with rights of pit and gallows might try capital cases and carry out executions. Those courts without such powers were obliged to hand the suspect over to the sheriff. In 1591, the barony court of Alloway banished John Miller for a violent assault, while on 15 February 1603, John Lennox of Cally's barony court of Cally in Kirkcudbright sentenced a vagabond to be drowned for theft. But crime was not the most significant part of the business of these courts. Only 21 per cent of the cases before Monimail regality court between 1591 and 1639 concerned crime, only three cases in 1609, 1627 and 1639 involved bluidwyte (= cases involving the shedding of blood), and nine cases concerned hurting or wounding, all between 1620 and 1639. Urie barony court regulated community behaviour, endeavouring to deal with neighbourly disputes between tenants, or seeking to prevent drunkenness and swearing, and the court appointed birliemen (or barley-men who were members of a neighbourhood court) to preside over minor neighbourly disputes. The barony court of Alloway was used to protect the interests of the tenants against strangers seeking to settle within its jurisdiction.[74]

Repledging was among the most potent measures available to regality lords in protecting their rights. Lords could repledge cases from the sheriff or justiciary court to their own courts on condition that they found caution to see justice done within a year and a day, a form of caution known as 'culreach'.[75] This power was not necessarily abused and lords exercised it to give protection to vulnerable people. In the summer of 1576, the eighth earl of Angus wrote to his bailie of Kirriemuir regality court about a family who had been evicted from their kindly tenancy. Angus thought this action was 'nocht godlie', telling his bailie to postpone the case, but if it were taken to another court he was to 'repledge thame hame to my courte of regalitie, as ze haif done of befoir'.[76] Nevertheless, repledging exacerbated tensions between rival jurisdictions, and was a crucial issue in local politics. In the spring of 1591 the sheriff depute of Dumfries, Thomas Kirkpatrick of Closeburn, was challenged for arresting a man living within the regality of Morton by his local rival, sir James Douglas of Drumlanrig, bailie of the regality, who saw it as his duty to uphold 'the libertie of the said regalitie'.[77] The crown disliked repledging and persuaded some regality lords not to repledge from royal courts in return for having their own bailie sit alongside the crown officer to judge the case. At a justice ayre in Stirling in the spring of 1624 the bailie of the regality court of Lennox registered his intention to repledge a number of the second duke of Lennox's vassals and tenants. Substantial concessions were offered by privy councillors, but the bailie stuck to the view that he lacked authority to surrender his lord's privileges and successfully insisted on sitting alongside the king's justice in the trial.[78]

As occurred elsewhere in western Europe where lordship was exercised lightly, the reluctance of Scottish lords to bear down too heavily on their tenants resulted in a relatively harmonious community relationship. Lords understood that it was in their interests to cultivate confidence in the justice meted out in their courts to minimise external interference or attempts by locals to go elsewhere. Unsurprisingly, perhaps, there is little evidence from their own records of oppressive behaviour. Sir Colin Campbell of Glenorchy's court provides a few instances of individuals being subjected to corporal punishment, or executed, but this followed trials of persons found guilty of stealing from their neighbours or of committing a murder. The justice was affirmed by the assize in the name of the community even if it was Glenorchy's court. The Monimail regality court passed no death sentence in the forty-eight years that records survive, but it succeeded in enforcing justice through fines and public penance. In one case, dated 19 November 1625, John Melville in Letham failed to appear in court to answer a charge of assault, resulting in a court order to remove himself and his family from the lord's lands and warning other inhabitants of the community not to give them shelter or work. With such an effective demonstration of power it is unsurprising that courts protected the interests of the landlord against tenants who sought to evade their legal responsibilities, or who committed offences, usually of an economic nature, such as damaging the lord's green woods, and the court might be employed to force tenants to undertake improvements. The records of the regality court at Monimail indicate that 43 per cent of its business was concerned with upholding the lord's privileges. In particular, the court was used to insist that the tenants use the lord's mill and fulfil their obligations of carriage, and it imposed fines, arbitrated on questions of tenancies and set the price of ale.[79]

Lords did not have it all their own way, and their own courts could not prevent protest against perceived injustices. In the barony of Urie, the court records for June to November 1604 indicate that John Hay was struggling to maintain authority. Tenants were accused of interfering with the regulating of the mill workings, selling fuel illegally in Stonehaven, there was resistance to paying the multure due to the laird's mill, theft was commonplace, there were quarrels between the tenants over boundaries and some of these disputes ended in violence. The laird's peats were pilfered systematically, his woods were cut, the smith complained that the tenants were not paying him the coal he was due for his services, carriage and labour services were avoided and some tenants were taking their complaints to the sheriff court, or the court of session. By 1622, little had changed and the court recorded the 'great abuse that is enterit in amangs the cowmond people in steilling'. After the ninth earl of Errol's officers assumed control of the barony court in 1623 there was a marked decrease in the number of fines imposed for criminal activities against the lord or for avoiding service.[80]

Barony courts could, therefore, be battlegrounds in which lords, lairds and their officers struggled to assert and maintain power. One factor that weakened the lord's authority was that barony courts had restricted powers of enforcement, having to turn to the sheriffs for letters of horning. Lords were sensitive to attempts by tenants to appeal to external authorities, as in the dispute between sir Robert Melville of Murdocairny and the tenants and feuars of the lands of South Ferry of Portincraig over 'ane pretendit confirmation purchest' by the tenants. The case dragged on between 1591 and 1594 until the privy council found in Murdocairny's favour. In October 1604, John Hay of Urie employed his court to rule that disputes within the barony community should not be taken to the court of session, the sheriff or any other external authority. Of course, lords used the higher courts to force compliance with their own edicts. In 1628, Andrew Cunningham, the eighth lord Yester's chamberlain in the barony of Snaid in Dumfriesshire, pursued a number of awkward tenants before the sheriff. Cunningham had problems with new tenants who lacked deference to their lord, and 'sa fer asse I can persave thay ar lyk supperriour'. One particularly trying vassal refused to recognise Yester's authority, and had 'forbid ony of his tennent to compeir to ony court hald in the barrony bot to himselfe or his baillzeis'. Nor would this man allow these sub-tenants to pay tax, as they had in the past, since he believed that the valuation set for the barony was too high. Cunningham yielded nothing and the case went before the sheriff.[81]

Over the course of the sixteenth century there was a decline in the use of sworn inquisitions in civil cases and instead the principal officer of the court examined witnesses and passed judgment. This development followed the 1540 act of parliament encouraging sheriffs to adopt court of session procedures, and thereafter it spread to regality and barony courts.[82] While the 1540 reforms alongside the evolving role of the court of session contributed to a greater professionalism, it remained important to ensure the smooth working of relationships between the lord, the tenants, the miller, the smith and the brewers of the barony. The barony court required the involvement of the local community, since the free-tenants were summoned at least thrice a year to give 'suit and presence', to serve on the assize, to appear as witnesses, to act as arbiters, to value goods, to fix boundaries or to act in other miscellaneous ways.[83] The barony court of Calder sat three or four times a year throughout the 1580s when it commonly dealt with between twenty and thirty cases, although there were exceptional years like 1586 when it sat eight times and handled fifty-seven cases.[84] The range of regulation laid down by the Campbell lairds of Glenorchy in their barony courts points to a community legislating locally to govern social relationships and a wide range of economic activities associated the management of the land in the interests of both the lord and his tenants.[85] This idea of the community meeting to resolve its problems explains the pressure from below for the court to sit. In 1630, the countess of Nithsdale wrote to her husband's bailie, sir John Maxwell of Pollok, instructing him to hold a court in the barony of Mearns as she had received a complaint from the tenants that meetings of the court had been too irregular.[86] Tenants expected their lord to take an active interest in their affairs, seeing him as an authority figure who would deal fairly with their quarrels.

Regality courts covered around half the country and exercised more extensive powers than ordinary barony courts, and their territorial dimensions were often greater than those of a single barony, commonly being composed of baronies scattered across more than one shire. In 1588, an English agent reporting on a scene in which the fifth earl of Bothwell had spoken roughly to James VI, added 'these Scottish earls account themselves but followers of their King, and presume much upon their regalities'.[87] Lords of regality enjoyed quasi-royal authority within their courts, the crown having devolved on them its sovereign rights, and thus the regality was 'a frie jurisdictione within itself and not subject to the shireffe'. The administrative integrity of the regality was such that it was recognised as a fiscal unit by crown tax collectors. A lord of regality, therefore, was the equivalent of the sheriff in his civil jurisdiction, having the same powers as the justiciar over criminal affairs, including the four pleas of the crown and the right to execute offenders. The one limitation on his authority involved jurisdiction over treason cases. This represented a remarkable degree of private authority that was at the other extreme from England, Normandy or most of the kingdoms of the Spanish monarchy.[88] It was in recognition of the dangers of such autonomy that in 1455 the king and parliament agreed that the former should be limited in his freedom to grant regalian authority without the consent of the estates. The legislation was frequently ignored, and in 1617 this was recognised in a statute that conceded unchallengeable prescriptive rights to any lord who held an heritable right of jurisdiction for forty years.[89] Regality rights could be exercised only over those lands owned by the holder of the regality, and 'it is impossible that any lands haulden of the king immediate can be within a regalitie'. Nevertheless, authority was often devolved. In many crown or ecclesiastical regalities the *de facto* authority was vested in a hereditary bailie, usually a local noble.[90] A stewartry was a forfeited regality, but the only records that survive for this period, those of Kirkcudbright and Menteith, are sparse and reveal little of interest.[91]

In spite of the great powers of regality courts, their business was mundane, and, like baronies, were administered by bailies and their officers, although some lords did exercise personal responsibility. The first lord Melville presided over thirty-eight of the thirty-nine sittings of Monimail regality court between 1591 and 1621. Having acquired the office of steward of the regality of St Andrews in 1606, sir John Lindsay of Balcombie found himself over the next quarter of a century heading a murder inquiry, adjudicating in assault cases, collecting customs, trying cases of theft and investigating infanticide, but most business was more ordinary.[92] Melrose regality court sat on seventy-five occasions between August 1605 and June 1609, with there being few sittings over the winter months, or around the time of the harvest in August or September. The business of the regality court was overwhelmingly concerned with minor breaches of the peace and making judgments in small debt actions between tenants; 21 per cent of the business of Monimail court was concerned with debt. Court records suggest that the unfolding political crisis that gripped the kingdom in 1637 made no impact on local administration or justice. During that year, Falkirk regality court continued to sit in judgment on minor issues of concern to the community as though nothing of note was happening in the world at large.[93]

Reforming the Localities?

Although hereditary jurisdictions had long been entrenched in the hands of noble families, it was known that those powers had been granted by kings. Robert Maule, writing *c.* 1620, argued that an eleventh-century thane was a judge, the term being 'ane Gothique or Danishe word signifiing ane Juge or gever of dome', and that formerly these officers were appointed 'duringe the kingis wil, or at the maist duringe thear lyftyme'.[94] Even nobles shared some unease over the disadvantages of hereditary offices, and in 1567 a parliament presided over by the regent Moray expressed concern about young and incompetent judges, decreeing that when heritable offices fell to the crown they should be retained, 'the samyn nevir tobe disponit heretablie frathyne-furth'. The problem of heritable sheriffdoms was raised three decades later in *Basilikon doron* by James VI, who argued that they were the 'greatest hinderance to the execution of the Lawes in this countrie'. Untroubled by his own hereditary authority, the king argued that 'being in the hands of the great men, [they] do wracke the whole countrie', but while the later 1590s saw some attempt to make sheriffs more accountable, the king knew that his power was limited:

> I know no present remedie, but by taking the sharper account of them in their Offices; using all punishment against the slouthfull, that the Law will permit: and ever as they vaike [= become vacant], for any offences committed by them, dispone them never heritably againe: preassing, with time, to draw it to the laudable custome of England.[95]

During the royal progress to Scotland in 1617, the king attended parliament which discussed the issue of heritable office. Parliament recorded that since his youth the king had wished to see judicial offices disposed to suitably qualified men as occurred in 'well governed states', but had been unwilling to trample on the rights of the heritable office-holders. Therefore, a parliamentary commission was established to investigate how heritable offices might be surrendered to the crown and adequate compensation paid to the owners. Three weeks later the king presided over a debate on the issue at Stirling where Patrick Sands, a former regent of the university of Edinburgh, argued against hereditary offices so effectively that the king turned to the second marquis of Hamilton, heritable sheriff of Lanark, remarking perkily 'James, you see your cause is lost, and all that can be said for it distinctly answered and refuted'.[96] Whatever the merits of the argument, however, the legal obstacles to reform were enormous, and the commission made no progress.

The extent to which the nobility constrained the crown's freedom to manoeuvre is evident in the failure to take greater advantage of the possibilities for reform that were opened up by the Reformation. In 1567, parliament introduced a requirement that all public office-holders, or members of a court, be professing Protestants, but the estates excluded heritable offices. In practice the 1567 legislation was ignored by the crown as it represented a threat to prerogative powers and risked destabilising local politics. Even the Catholic rebels of the late 1580s and early 1590s had their heritable offices restored when their forfeitures were overturned. It was not until 1628 that archbishop Spottiswoode was able to persuade Charles I to exploit antirecusancy laws to promote the crown's policy of acquiring greater control over shrieval offices. In 1629, using the 1609 legislation banning excommunicated persons from possessing their lands, rents and revenues, the privy council required the thirteenth earl of Sutherland to dismiss his depute, sir Alexander Gordon of Netherdene, on account of his recusancy. Much more significantly that year, the first marquis of Huntly's persistent determination to remain Catholic finally resulted in him being forced to resign the sheriffdoms of Inverness and Aberdeen.[97] That singular success serves to highlight the crown's extreme sensitivity to allowing religious issues to restrict its own prerogative or noble property rights.

The Reformation offered another route to address the issue in the large number of temporalities of benefices that after 1560 were in the possession of noble families. After more than a quarter of a century of bickering between crown, church and nobility, in 1587 these lands were annexed to the crown. As part of the settlement it was decided that the rights of heritable bailies and stewards, including the right to repledge cases from sheriff courts, would be unaffected. A compromise was agreed for dealing with cases initiated by the justice general, allowing for the sharing of responsibility and the profits of justice. Once more the crown was not in a position to insist on any significant concessions from the nobility.[98] In 1606, the issue of the ecclesiastical temporalities was again under discussion, being resolved in favour of the nobles whose heritable rights were further entrenched by parliament in the erection of temporal lordships.[99] Charles I's efforts to strengthen royal control over local administration and justice resulted in the 1633 parliament annexing to the crown all ecclesiastical regalities, nullifying the rights of lords of erection to exercise regality authority in jurisdictions formerly held by beneficed persons prior to the act of annexation. In order to gain noble approval for this reform, parliament reserved the rights of heritable bailies and stewards of those regalities and it preserved the regality rights of the bishops.[100]

Given the crown's inability to dislodge nobles from former ecclesiastical jurisdictions, a wholesale alteration of the system of local administration was beyond its means, while the political demands on rulers to reward supporters made it difficult to avoid making hereditable grants. In 1567, Mary granted the first earl of Mar the heritable captaincy of Stirling castle; John Maitland of Thirlestane received the heritable grant of the bailiary of the lordship of Lauderdale at the 1587 parliament; and the earl of Dunbar was granted the heritable captaincy of St Andrews castle in 1606. In spite of his more aggressive policy towards reclaiming crown jurisdictions, Charles I faced the same dilemma, and the heritable powers of the earls of Argyll over Argyll and Tarbet were strengthened by parliament in 1633.[101]

There is little evidence of an appetite to address fundamental issues of justice and its administration prior to the 1598 convention of estates that passed legislation to tackle feuding and the illegal use of firearms. Even the 1587 act establishing regular justice ayres throughout the kingdom was more important in signalling good intentions than in delivering better justice.[102] The disapproval of hereditary office that James VI expressed in *Basilikon doron* may have reflected frustrations circulating within some government circles, and an obvious place to start was with corrupt or negligent sheriffs. In 1597, sheriffs and sheriffs depute in the west were summoned to answer for defects in their tax returns. Two years later, a number of Border sheriffs were charged with failing to enforce laws, and in 1600 one of their number, James Douglas of Cavers, sheriff of Roxburghshire, was summoned to answer regarding his failure to administer tax returns appropriately. In January 1600, a privy council commission was established to investigate how sheriffs might be better assisted by the king's subjects.[103] One issue that concerned sheriffs and other local officials was the arduous, unpopular and increasingly annual administration of collecting taxes. In 1621, parliament agreed that the privy council should negotiate payment with sheriffs who agreed on a 5 per cent fee. Nevertheless, tax gathering remained unpopular with sheriffs, and those appointees who replaced hereditary sheriffs in some shires proved especially weak in persuading landlords to pay up.[104]

Within the privy council vested interests, including chancellor

Dunfermline, lined up on the side of hereditary offices, and it was archbishop Spottiswoode who pressed for sheriffs to resign on a voluntary basis,
hoping to replace them with annual crown appointees. In January 1613,
Spottiswoode encouraged the second duke of Lennox and the second
marquis of Hamilton to surrender their sheriffdoms, but even these
absentee courtiers offered only a conditional and temporary lease of their
jurisdictions. From April 1613 Lennox's sheriffdom of Renfrewshire was
filled by the crown making annual appointments from a pool of local barons,
men like sir John Buchanan of that Ilk, John Colquhoun of Luss and
William Semple of Foulwood.[105] The king possessed powers to discipline
sheriffs, and even to remove them from office for culpable or partial
proceedings, but the legal and political complications were such that the
crown rarely had the confidence to proceed. In March 1616, the king
acquired the sheriffdom of Caithness when the fifth earl of Caithness was
outlawed and the crown exploited the opportunity, appointing in his place
the earl's kinsman, James Sinclair of Murchill.[106] Caithness's persistent
criminal behaviour and his soaring debts made him unusually vulnerable,
with the route the crown had to go down for most other sheriffs being
one of largely unaffordable financial compensation. The crown failed to
prioritise buy-outs and the offers to purchase the sheriffdom of Selkirk
in 1619 from sir John Murray of Philiphaugh for 20,000 merks and
Roxburghshire in 1620 from James Douglas of Cavers for £20,000 were
wildly optimistic. It is not clear if Philiphaugh was paid in full, although
from 1620 the privy council made annual appointments of sheriffs to
Roxburghshire, but by 1633 Cavers had received only 4,000 merks and as
the outstanding sum was never paid he retained his sheriffdom.[107] Consequently, lease arrangements were favoured, and by the 1630s the king was
making annual appointments in seventeen shires, while hereditary lords
continued to exercise authority in thirteen shires.[108]

Finding the means to purchase sheriffdoms was not the only flaw in royal
policy as the crown's dependence on the personal power of individual noble
houses limited the options it had in a locality. In Aberdeenshire the lairds of
Balquhane served as sheriff depute to the earls of Huntly from 1541, but in
the political turmoils of the 1560s and early 1590s they took opposite sides.
During the forfeiture of the fifth earl (1563–7), the minority of the sixth earl
(1576–81) and the latter's forfeiture (1594–7) the barons of Balquhane acted
as sheriff. On this last occasion, John Leslie of Balquhane sought to advance
his own power, appointing kinsmen as deputes, but by 1597 his record of
oppression, feuding and failure to return accounts to the treasurer was such
that the crown was relieved to welcome Huntly back to his sheriffdom. On
this occasion there was no reconciliation, and in 1598 Huntly appointed
John Gordon of Boigs as his sheriff depute.[109] The crown had no effective
means of replacing sheriffs with royal officers from outside the locality,
while selecting lesser men from within the locality was unlikely to deliver

better justice and administration. In early modern society authority was not simply exercised through office, but was projected through the individual holding that office, by their ability to act out an expected role through their appearance, behaviours and words. In itself, noble rank contributed to the process of governance. Unlike England, there is no evidence of men avoiding shrieval office because of its burdens, but there was concern expressed by royal officials over the 'scairstie of personis of rank and qualitie, to discharge the office of schirefship'. When in 1613 the king chose Thomas Kirkpatrick of Closeburn as sheriff of Dumfriesshire, problems were anticipated due to 'the burding of his estate and the straitnes of his creditours'. Following the death in June 1611 of Alexander Dunbar of Westfield, hereditary sheriff of Moray, the office was apprised by an Edinburgh merchant, David Kinloch, 'a person altogether unfit and uncapable of such a charge and burden', and after a prolonged interregnum the sixth lord Lovat was appointed to clear up the mess. In the summer of 1621 the king upset the privy council by selecting William Scott, the goodman of Harden, to be sheriff of Selkirkshire for the coming year, an illiterate and infirm old man in his seventies who did not reside within the sheriffdom.[10] The most significant advance made by the crown was in enforcing the resignation of the Catholic first marquis of Huntly and his son, lord Gordon, from the hereditary sheriffdoms of Aberdeen and Inverness over the summer of 1629. Huntly was a victim of archbishop Spottiswoode's campaign against recusant nobles and of the jealousy of local rivals like the third earl of Moray, who told Charles I that Huntly was 'sic ane gryt man of sic freindschip and power that none culd leive besyd him, except thir shirefschipis war takin fra him and his posteritie'. Unfortunately, the administrative chaos that resulted from the removal of the Gordons exacerbated criminality so that 'the countrie wes cassin louss', and the ineffectual efforts of the less powerful replacement sheriffs underlined that it was Huntly who held the real strings of power in the north.[11]

Problems arose over the patronage of lesser officials in the sheriff courts. The first earl of Home conditionally surrendered the sheriffdom of Berwick in 1616, following which his kinsman, Alexander Home of Renton, was nominated by the king as sheriff of Berwick for the coming year. The king made a separate appointment to the office of sheriff depute for life, offending Renton who threatened to refuse office unless he could appoint his own depute. When the privy council debated the management of lesser court officials, lord Binning sensibly pointed out that if the annually appointed sheriffs were permitted to select their own officers chaos would result since 'thair court boukes sall fall in confusion, and the schyre in disordour, all the members of court being alyke strengers to that which hes bene done in the jugement before thair entrie'. Binning argued for the established practice of appointing the sheriff clerk *ad vitam* from among well-trained lawyers, thus providing a continuity and experience lacking in the 'oft changed schireffis'.

By 1619 the privy council was working towards a system of permanent subordinate officers under those annually appointed sheriffs chosen by the king from a list of shire nominees forwarded by the privy council.[112] Further difficulties were created by the growing involvement in the financially risky business of tax gathering, for example, in Dumbartonshire in 1627 no one was prepared to serve as deputes or clerks.[113]

Faced with the difficulties of dislodging nobles from hereditary sheriff-doms it is unsurprising to discover that it was impossible for the crown to interfere in regalities or other lesser jurisdictions. Even a London-based courtier like the second duke of Lennox was careful of his local interests. When in 1605 he resigned his right to appoint the magistrates of the burgh of Glasgow, the duke required the king and privy council to register that his rights as justiciar and bailie of the regality of Glasgow were unaffected. Gordonstoun explicitly warned the thirteenth earl of Sutherland that while it might be necessary in the future to surrender the sheriffdom, he must never give up his regality, 'For seing all Sutherland (for the most pairt) doth hold of you and your regalitie, you neid not care much for the shirref-schip'.[114] Besides, there was little enthusiasm for reform in a royal court, parliament, privy council or even court of session dominated by men who exercised their own local hereditary authority. Significantly, chancellor Thirlestane's lordship of Musselburgh was exempted from the act of annexation in 1587. When in December 1603 the sixth lord Hume was appointed lieutenant and justiciar of the entire Anglo-Scottish marches, he was instructed by the king not to allow repledging from his jurisdiction. Hume was not prepared to hurt his friends, and informed the fifth earl of Morton that 'I haif overpast all your Lordship's regalities'. Furthermore, the privy council repeatedly backed the authority of regality lords, as in May 1604 when inhabitants of the regality of Spynie tried to wriggle out of their obedience to the first lord Spynie's court.[115] The near impotence of the crown in achieving lasting reform was brought home to the privy council in 1623 when William Douglas of Drumlanrig insisted on repledging cases from the Border commission to his own regality, throwing crown policy into disarray.[116]

Charles I believed that in attacking regality powers he was liberating the lesser nobility, but with many regalities being in the hands of untitled barons or lairds this policy could never drive a wedge between them and the peerage. The king misunderstood local government, besides which he lacked the funds to pay compensation to lords who surrendered their rights. When the teind commission was established in February 1627, one of its remits was to compensate lords for the surrender of their regalities or other heritable offices, excluding baronies. It quickly became apparent that the teind commission, which served for ten years instead of the intended six months, could do nothing to dislodge regality powers, and the king fell back on the policy of cooperating with regality lords who were invited to sit on

justice ayres. As an inducement to persuade nobles to resign their jurisdictions, half-hearted attempts were made at purchasing offices, but these
foundered on the usual lack of money.[117] Only five temporal lords had
enquired about surrendering their rights and titles by the 1 January 1627
deadline. The king wrote to the convention of estates that met in July 1630
asking it to provide taxation to fund the buy-out of heritable office holders.
A tax was voted, but crown priorities lay elsewhere and in the autumn of
1634 the programme was suspended due to financial embarrassment. By
that time agreement had been reached on the surrender of five regalities and
thirteen heritable offices, but the offices were mortgaged back to the holders
until the crown could pay the full sum.[118]

An alternative policy was for the crown to establish a new layer of
dependent local officeholders. The idea of introducing commissioners
of the peace was under discussion from the early 1580s, and parliament
legislated to that effect in 1587. Ineffective commissions were selected that
year and again in 1593, further legislation being required in 1609 before
working commissions could be established. The 420 new commissioners
named in 1610 (excluding those granted to burgh magistrates) embraced a
range of ranks, and included bishops, peers and lairds, the numbers varying
from shire to shire with Orkney having as few as seven commissioners and
Aberdeen twenty-nine. These commissioners of the peace were modelled on
the English justices of the peace, and were appointed by the privy council,
as was the convener of the shire commission. They did not replace the
existing judicial structures, however, and they lacked authority to deal with
hereditary jurisdictions, to block repledging or to try criminal cases, being
restricted to reporting cases to sheriffs. It is clear from the communications
between the privy council and commissioners that what most interested the
former was the fines these new officials might gather. The uncertainty over
their roles required further attempts at refinement in 1611, with the crown's
proposals being so heavily criticised at the 1612 parliament that they were
withdrawn, and a further raft of revisions followed in 1617.[119]

When first introduced to Ireland, Wales and the north of England,
justices of the peace struggled to overcome the entrenched power of local
nobles who had little respect for the new officials.[120] A similar tension was
apparent in Scotland where David Calderwood claimed that commissioners
of the peace offended some nobles who 'thought that this new office
impaired their credite and freindship in the countrie'. In an exchange at
a council meeting in June 1611, archbishop Gledstanes questioned their
legality, criticised them as unnecessary and pointed out that 'the realme had
many hundredth yeares bene weill governed without justices of the peace'.[121]
Locally, the commissioners faced opposition from vested interests, for
example, in 1611 the Selkirkshire commissioners complained to the privy
council about the refusal of the magistrates of the burgh of Selkirk to recognise their authority. A year later, at least nine shires failed to 'mak compt' of

their fines to the crown, and in Edinburgh the record of the commissioners was unimpressive.[122] Less than half the shires had functioning officers in 1625, and Charles I attempted to inject new life into the commissions in a series of failed initiatives in 1628, 1630 and 1634. He expanded the number of commissioners, increasing those for Edinburgh from the twenty established in 1610 to forty-seven in 1634. In December 1633, at least twenty-one localities failed to return lists of candidates for office, and in the following year the sheriffs of fifteen shires, along with three royal bailies and two stewards, failed to send in returns of men eligible to serve as commissioners of the peace. In 1636, the crown highlighted the many localities where justices were neglecting to do their job, failing even to hold quarter sessions. One option was to make greater use of bishops in the hope of stiffening the commissions and extending episcopal authority. The 1634 initiative to appoint bishops to commissions within their own diocese underlined the general disenchantment with these offices, while adding further to dissatisfaction with the bishops who were intruding on lay authority.[123]

While the principal reason for the establishment of the commissions was to prevent feuds arising from minor local disagreements, and the responsibilities and regulations governing their function were potentially far-reaching, the unpopularity of the office grew with the dreary tasks assigned to them. The records for Renfrewshire in 1611–12 show them chiefly concerned with inquests, unemployed women, listing cautions, regulating wages, collating information on servants, craftsmen and their apprentices and adjudicating on breaches of the peace. In the mid-1620s, a new use was found for commissioners in organising the military training of the men of the shire and in implementing the work of the teind commission. The private archives of men like sir John Maxwell of Pollok, commissioner of the peace for Renfrewshire, filled up with papers detailing his growing responsibilities, but unfortunately the business of the commissioners is difficult to identify because of the paucity of official records. Edinburgh's records survive from 1613, but the number of cases are few before 1628 when Charles I attempted to reinvigorate the office. Of the 101 cases recorded between 1613 and 1640, 94 per cent were bonds to keep the peace, and 3 per cent involved incidents of hurting and wounding.[124]

In 1612, the privy council asked parliament to consider what commissioners of the peace might do 'for pacifying the cuntrie incaise of the disobedience or negligence of the heritable officers, or contempt of the powerfull men of the cuntrie', a wholly unreasonable proposition that parliament ignored. Part of the problem arose from the fact that most commissioners of the peace were recruited from within noble society and shared in its values. On 3 November, within days of parliament rising, sir James Crichton of Ruthven, a newly appointed commissioner of the peace for Forfar, turned up at a quarter session at Dundee with eighty armed followers, stormed into the meeting and attacked another of the commissioners, sir David Wood of Craig.[125] Some efforts were made by the crown to exclude the higher nobility from commissions, although the role of sheriffs in drawing up lists from which the privy council made its choice demonstrates that the process could never be removed from local power networks. In a letter of 1625, William Sutherland of Duffus, convener of the commissioners of the peace in Elgin and Forres, referred to a quarter session attended by the barons and gentlemen of the shire, a body from which the peerage were excluded. The privy council appointed the conveners of the commissions, and implemented a half-hearted commitment towards placing this responsibility in the hands of men more answerable to the crown. In 1629, John Wemyss of that Ilk was created lord Wemyss and was relieved of his office as convener of the commissioners of the peace for Fife. But crown policy was inconsistent and pragmatic in the face of the need to staff commissions with men who were sufficiently powerful and wealthy to be effective. For example, between 1633 and 1637 John Lockhart acted in contempt of one of the commissioners of the peace for Stirlingshire, William Justice, minister of Gargunnock. At best, commissioners lacking in personal authority might succeed in making an arrest and handing an accused over to the sheriff or regality lord for trial. In 1634, new commissions were drawn up in which only a handful of localities did not have a member of the peerage serving as a commissioner. Besides, the lairds were unwilling to serve in local government as agents of an unpopular crown, and the relaunch of the commissions in 1630 proved counterproductive as the king was faced with further apathy and obstructionism. Crown patronage was subverted by the traditional exercise of noble power. In 1635, sir Colin Campbell of Glenorchy and sir John Campbell of Lawers asked to be excused from serving on the Perth commission on account of their age. It was these same men, no doubt under orders from lord Lorne, who suggested alternatives, both younger Campbell men, who were accepted by the privy council, satisfying the crown and keeping the Campbell presence on the commission.[126]

Royal government intruded itself into the detailed business of administering the marches in the later 1590s as the international stability arising from the 1586 Anglo-Scottish League brought peace dividends. Initiatives like the imposition of the general band, obliging landlords to take responsibility for the behaviour of those living on their estates, were important, as was direct intervention by the king in the form of judicial raids, but the cooperation of the nobility was vital. It was the tenth earl of Angus's successful lieutenancy of the three marches from 1598 to 1600 that persuaded Border lords to exercise restraint.[127] But it was only after regal union with England that the crown made enduring gains in pacifying the region. Between 1606 and 1611 a form of quasi-military policing under the supervision of the earl of Dunbar terrorised the region into sullen civility. Following Dunbar's death in 1611, a Border commission was established that contained none of the great magnate families, but the exclusion of powerful local lords was unsustainable and by 1618 it was dominated by the leading nobles of the region. The premature abolition of the Border guard for financial reasons in 1621 exposed the hollowness of the crown's claim to have changed the nature of the region, and rising disorder prompted the privy council to summon a conference at Edinburgh in March 1622 attended by a who's who of the Border nobility. A new commission was appointed composed of the earls of Nithsdale, Buccleuch and John Murray of Lochmaben, the first two being the heads of the Maxwell and Scott kindreds, the third an absentee courtier. When Nithsdale and Buccleuch came to nominate their ten deputies, Nithsdale listed six Maxwells, Buccleuch three Scotts along with an Armstrong, an Elliot and a Pringle, all surnames traditionally dependent upon him, while the remaining men were clients and servants. As the privy council told Buccleuch in January 1625, he was in a position 'to use that power and authoritie quhilk is verie weele knowne your Lordship hes for reduceing of these rebells to obedience'. When in 1631 the eleventh earl of Angus took up office he submitted a list of subordinates drawn largely from his own clientele, including his two brothers. Charles I's meddling approach succeeded only in irritating Nithsdale, who complained that James VI had understood the Borders, hence, his faith in powerful nobles prepared to provide services free of charge.[128]

In the Highlands the crown's ability to act independently was even more constrained by geographic inaccessibility and the region's frontier culture.[129] Here the crown's episodic and often unhelpful intervention was driven by a series of local expedients and periodic bursts of energy determined by a series of relationships between the king, courtiers, privy councillors and local nobles. From the crown's perspective, intervention was motivated by a combination of concern at perceived and real law and order issues on that frontier and by a belief that the riches of the Highlands were not being adequately taxed. From 1587 the general band was extended to the region with a view to recruiting local nobles into crown service by obliging all landlords to present before the relevant justice, or his deputes, any person dwelling on their lands at the time of an alleged offence, failing which they would incur a financial penalty. Parliament was providing a legitimate framework within which lordship should operate. The 1597 act requiring nobles to demonstrate title to their lands was especially effective in forcing Highland landlords to negotiate with crown officers, since failure to register with the exchequer could result in losing any right to title. By the 1600s noblemen were denounced regularly by the privy council for failing to bring broken men to justice; for example, in July 1602 the seventh earl of Argyll found himself castigated by the privy council for his failure to keep order among his men.[130] The crown adopted a pragmatic policy towards enforcing the general band, recognising the problems facing landlords especially over the mismatch between landownership and lordship. Hence, in 1613 the crown recognised twenty-one different lords who owned land on which dwelt the small Magregor clan for whom the question of overlordship was impossible to resolve easily. Often crown initiatives had a counterproductive effect, for example, its treatment of Clan Chattan pushed it into closer co-operation and involvement with the clans of the Gaelic west.[31]

Archbishop Spottiswoode was dismissive of the role played by the magnates in the Highlands, commenting in *c.* 1608 that 'nothing was done to any great purpose, the great men of those parts studying only the increase of their own grandeur, and striving whose command should be greatest'. Yet without the cooperation of these noble houses the crown was powerless. This gap between rhetoric and reality was demonstrated by the fruitless colonisation scheme on Lewis that was pursued from 1597. By 1610 the consortium of lesser Fife nobles contracted to carry it out had cut their losses, leaving the crown to fall back on traditional methods. Kenneth Mackenzie of Kintail was encouraged to expand into MacLeod territory, and thus 'doe the tryb of Clankeinzie become great in these part, still incroaching upon ther nighbours who are unacquented with the lawes of the kingdome'. Nor did the 1609 statutes of Iona and the subsequent negotiations with Highland chiefs that dragged on to 1616 represent a breach with the past, being an attempt to harness the authority of clan chiefs to civilise Highland society according to the norms of the Lowlands. In terms of its primary objective, increasing the tax yield of the region, these measures proved to be disappointing. Royal aspirations remained dependent on noble cooperation. In January 1623, the privy council was faced with disorder on the lands of the second marquis of Hamilton in Kintyre where the thieves were emboldened by the fact that he 'makis not his residence in these boundis'. Since the king insisted that Hamilton remain at court, the privy council had no choice other than to strengthen the marquis's officers. Faced with greater threats to law and order, such as the Islay rebellion of 1615, the crown pleaded with the seventh earl of Argyll to intervene. A decade later, among the first commissions granted by Charles I was that of 21 April 1625 to Argyll's son, lord Lorne, to sweep the MacDonald lands of notorious criminals, which he did with his own army of 1,500 men. But crown officers knew how dependent the king was on these nobles, and in April 1629 the first earl of Haddington admitted to a colleague that:

> All our power will be in paper, unles your lordship informe his Majestie how necessare it is that powerfull noblemen and magistrats residing too long at court be sent home to attend and execute their charges, or substitute in their place men willing and able to obey the Counsels commandments for his service.

A similar observation was made to a number of Gordons by the privy

council in 1634 in the context of discussing the first marquis of Huntly as
'the onelie person of power and commandement within the bounds where
they dwell'.[132]

In burghs the nobility retained influence over local office. Control of
burgh offices was often an objective within wider power struggles, as in 1583
when the fifth earl of Rothes replaced the sixth lord Lindsay as provost of
Cupar, reflecting a shift in court politics that impacted on a longstanding
local feud. There was no coherent crown policy to drive nobles out of burgh
politics, and depending upon the occasion, or the shift in faction, king, lords
and burgh magistrates were engaged in a triangular relationship. In 1583,
loyal nobles were deployed as royal agents in towns, the earl of Arran
being appointed provost of Stirling and the eleventh earl of Crawford being
imposed as provost of Dundee. In October 1599, the magistracy and council
of the burgh of Montrose was committed to ward for refusing to elect the
second earl of Mar as provost. Yet in 1590, James VI battled against his own
councillors to prevent sir Robert Ker of Cessford objecting to Jedburgh
electing an alternative to himself as provost. When in October 1608
Edinburgh elected chancellor Dunfermline as its provost, the king forced
the burgh to replace him with sir George Arnott of Birswick, and in the
following year parliament legislated against non-residents holding office in
burghs. In 1635, the dispute between the bishop of Brechin and sir Patrick
Maule of Panmure over the appointment of bailies of the burgh of Brechin
was resolved by a crown commission that allowed them to appoint one each.
What the above reveals is that each case was different and depended on local
circumstances. Some flavour of what is a complex range of motives is
evident in the case of Glasgow's relationship to the house of Lennox. In the
early 1580s the king promoted the first duke of Lennox's power in Glasgow,
by 1605 he was asking the second duke to surrender authority, and in 1637
the fourth duke tried futilely to restore his family's popularity in order to
shore up support for Charles I.[133]

Burghs continued to welcome noble involvement in their affairs even
after parliament legislated in 1609 against nobles holding provostships. In
1619, the burghs of Perth, Linlithgow and Banff were reprimanded for
electing noble provosts, and yet it was another nine years before a faction
within Perth decided to try and overthrow their domineering noble provost.
Finally, in December 1627 the dean of the merchant guild led a protest in
the town, accusing the first viscount Stormont of 'useing thame as slaves and
cotters to sheare his cornes', and trying to have his own arms engraved on
the tollbooth. Stormont drew his dagger and chased the terrified dean, an
incident that led to him being stripped of his office. In an indignant letter of
13 August 1635, the first earl of Traquair denounced a recent tax riot in
Aberdeen that involved burgh magistrates who he accused of tolerating
Gordon outlaws. Traquair wanted the king to make greater use of his
authority to appoint burgh magistrates, but only a few months earlier sir

John Grant of Freuchie told the privy council that the first marquis of Huntly was the only person able to guarantee order in the region.[134]

Conclusion

Within those elites who governed early modern Scotland there was a broad consensus over what constituted justice and injustice. The one issue that pitted rival interpretations of justice against one another was the bloodfeud, but even on this seemingly intractable problem a growing consensus emerged by the end of the 1590s. No one in noble society was advocating a wholly different version of justice, or of how a nobleman should behave in his important role of magistrate. Nobles wanted order and were prepared to work hard at maintaining it in the local courts where the great majority of the cases involved relatively mundane matters that, nevertheless, mattered greatly to the people who lived under the jurisdiction of those courts. Here was one of the key points at which noble power impacted on the lives of the common people. Of course, where their own interests were involved nobles were more likely to be partisan and self-serving, although relatively few lords used the cover of their local offices to engage in persistent criminality. The patchwork of overlapping and largely heritable jurisdictions served to entrench noble power within localities and to create tension between neighbouring noble houses that led to feuding and to litigation. In the background, the crown played the role of a bystander or, at best, a referee with limited powers to intervene even in the affairs of sheriff courts where the king's business was conducted.

It is easy to exaggerate the rate or depth of change that occurred in the government of local society in Scotland in the decades before the Covenanting revolution.[135] Where local studies have been carried out, the evidence suggests that networks of nobles connected by clientage and service to the king and the court remained more important to local government than institutions and administrative structures.[136] This should come as no surprise. Evidence from elsewhere in early modern Europe demonstrates again and again the limitations of royal government at a local level. In seventeenth-century Languedoc, the French crown struggled to impose itself against the cultural values of local society, limited administrative structures, the unavailability of policing agencies, competing jurisdictions and local rivalries. When Louis XIV's government did succeed in penetrating Languedoc society it was through traditional hierarchies and by creating a common culture of shared values and objectives between court and province.[137] Scotland had a long way to go before the crown had anything like the authority over local society that was exercised in France. What was largely absent was the direct relationship between lesser nobles holding crown office in the localities and the king, a relationship that did exist in England. Besides, it was not necessarily the case that even in England dominant noble houses were weakened by an enhancement of royal authority.[138] The same point can be made from the experience of Tuscany where the relationship between centre and locality was mediated by families rather than institutions, where there was an on-going negotiation of power between individuals, and in which the power of local elites was largely reinforced.[139] James VI and Charles I in their different ways tried to instigate reforms that would strengthen the crown's grip over local office, but while the case against hereditary jurisdictions was strong, there was no affordable way forward either politically or financially. The crown lacked the resources, and between the late 1590s and the 1630s little was achieved beyond the conditional control over the selection of a proportion of sheriffdoms and the creation of largely ineffective commissioners of the peace. Heritable noble power remained entrenched at every level of local administration either formally through the ongoing rights of regality lords or informally in the inescapable need to engage leading nobles in the business of governing the localities.

CHAPTER 5

Soldiers

The sixteenth-century French writer, Michel Ey-quem de Montaigne, asserted that 'the proper, sole and essential life for one of the nobility in France is the life of the soldier'. This statement was true for most European nobilities who largely owed their rank and privilege to their origins as knightly warriors, although it is worth observing that the relationship between nobility, chivalry and military function was not constant through-out the middle ages. While few nobilities might be described as a warrior caste by the late medieval era, that military function remained at the heart of noble identity and self-perception. Changes in military technology and battlefield tactics (the concept of a military revolution remains persuasive) challenged aspects of noble pre-eminence in war, but early modern nobles continued to choose the profession of arms as a route to service, their right and expectation to command other soldiers surviving, often at the king's encouragement. War and martial pursuits generally remained essential in the acquisition of honour, and the conditioning for a martial life began in childhood as male kinsmen and servants used honour and shame to incul-cate personal courage and self-discipline, while noble education continued to emphasise military skills and the study of warfare and military history. Newcomers to noble rank often cultivated a martial image to enhance their social acceptability, and the seventeenth century arguably saw a reinvigor-ation of martial ideas among the nobility as escalating warfare stimulated an increase in the military capacity of early modern governments.[1]

Scotland's late medieval nobility conformed to the European norm in their embracing of a martial ethos, their active engagement in warfare and in the pursuits that ensured war preparedness. The prolonged fourteenth-century wars of independence followed by intermittent wars with England into the 1550s required a high level of military preparedness. The frontier societies of the Anglo-Scottish Border and of the Highlands promoted martial cultures and caused difficulties for government that increased the need for military confrontation within the context of domestic politics. Scotland's late medieval kings were expected to be soldiers: Robert I was a great warrior leader; David II was taken prisoner in battle; and James II, James III and James IV were all killed on military campaigns. Likewise, the late medieval nobility were trained as knights and expected to experience

some form of military activity over the course of their lives.[2] If the decline
of Scotland's military prowess was signalled by the cataclysmic defeat by
the English at the battle of Flodden in 1513 and confirmed at the equally
disastrous defeat, again at English hands, at the battle of Pinkie in 1547,
the real scale of that decline was evident in the reliance on French military
intervention in 1523, 1545 and from 1547 to 1560 and on English military
intervention in 1559–60 and intermittently during 1571–3.[3] In contrast to
the greater part of Europe, Scotland was not involved formally at state level
in international war after 1560 and there was no large-scale civil war between
1573 and 1638. This absence of warfare raises questions about the nature
of society and about the extent to which the nobility inhabited a world
dominated by martial values and behaviour. Arguably this issue is at the
core of noble identity, being entangled with the exercise of power over other
men and the projection of that power in architecture, weaponry and in the
deployment of violence. The military weakness of the crown allowed no
opportunity for that martial energy to be harnessed to the service of the
king. But the prevalence of warfare on the continent did impact on Scotland,
creating opportunities for military service that were grasped by nobles who
continued to see in warfare the proper expression of their self image and
their honour. Such was the level of involvement in the major European war
theatres that the experience continued to influence noble society. It is in that
native environment that the military power of the nobility and the sustained
emphasis on martial ideas encountered the ambitions of the crown to defend
the realm and to claim control over the right to exercise legitimate force.

A Martial Nobility?

From the smug safety of the early sixteenth-century academy, John
Mair poured scorn on the nobility's obsession with their warrior identity
alongside their ideas of a nobility of blood, a theme added to by sir David
Lindsay of the Mount, and later developed by the Protestant clergy.[4]
The Renaissance critique of a martial nobility was counterbalanced by the
on-going popularity of chivalric culture conveyed in the likes of Gavin
Douglas's *Palice of Honour* (1501), which eulogised a military ethos and
was republished in Edinburgh in 1579. That idea of a martial nobility was
maintained by later writers like David Hume of Godscroft, who plundered
Scottish history for exemplars such as the 'Good' sir James Douglas
who fought alongside Robert I, or the second earl of Douglas who died
at Otterburn in 1388, hoping to inspire the nobility to martial deeds in
virtuous service to the king. In the early seventeenth century, the European
market in war literature and reporting of events in Germany remained lively,
supplemented by the tales of those men who returned from war theatres.
In Scotland, sir Thomas Kellie dedicated his 1627 manual on military

technique, *Pallas armata or military instructions for the learned*, to the sixth earl of Rothes, a man with no military experience but whose education gave him a broad appreciation of the merits of warfare.[5] Clearly humanist virtues and military values were not incompatible, and in the increasingly professional armies of France, for example, those traditional qualities of courage, magnanimity and liberality were recognised as necessary attributes of leadership. Officers had to master technical skills, but they were expected to possess a moral dimension formed in their education, and nobles commonly were trained in arms. The seeking out of new weapons and the interest in military history and manuals forced noblemen to confront the innovative implications of gunpowder as a levelling technology, and to understand the classical age from which so much military experience was drawn.[6] Scottish nobles shared in that education, participating in wapenschaws (= weapon-shows, i.e. musters), taking part in local competitions like the St Andrews Silver Arrow, and undergoing training in arms. There were no formal schools of defence in the country, but fencing masters like Rocco Bonetti spent time in Scotland in the 1570s and early 1580s, while young Scots travelled to England and France to complete their formation.[7]

At the heart of ideas of nobility in early modern Europe, therefore, was an enduring legacy from the medieval age of the chivalrous knight that survived on the battlefield in the cavalry and elsewhere in equestrian pursuits. Nobles retained their dominant position in mounted warfare in a form adapted to the impact of gunpowder, the strategic importance of siege operations and the brutalising conduct of professional mercenaries. The right of nobles to lead in war continued to be seen as a legitimate privilege, even in the Dutch Republic where a more professional approach to warfare necessarily led to nobles losing out and to the abandonment of chivalric ideals. In this context of increasing professionalisation and further innovations in military organisation and tactics, nobles had to strive to maintain pre-eminence in battlefield command.[8] Young nobles like the third earl of Arran trained for warfare in France in the 1550s before returning in 1560 to participate in the struggle against the professional French troops of the regent Guise in 1560. The episodic domestic violence of the civil war of 1567–73 saw an uneven mix of semi-professional soldiering from effective military leaders like the fourth earl of Morton or sir William Kirkcaldy of Grange. There is evidence of the usual incompetent amateurism in the military exploits of lords like the fat, middle-aged fourth earl of Huntly, who was shaken out of a deep sleep at ten o'clock in the morning to lead his army to defeat and his own death at the battle of Corrichie on 28 October 1562, or the fifth earl of Argyll whose reputation was damaged at the battle of Langside on 13 May 1568 when he 'shew nather curage nor vassalage'. After 1573, the only military experience to be found in Scotland was in rebellions and quasi-policing operations – James VI took part in a number of military campaigns within Scotland – and in the violent pursuit of bloodfeuds.

Hence, the eighth lord Sanquhar's complaint in 1602 that he loathed the country because 'there was no employment for gallant men'.[9] Furthermore, the tournaments that had played such an important role in late medieval court culture disappeared following the death of James V in 1542, and James VI did not encourage a chivalric culture of the kind that flourished under Elizabeth I in England.[10]

Besides, even in war-torn Europe questions were asked about the military role of the nobility in the light of the changes in how armies were raised and wars were conducted, and there is evidence to suggest that while many nobles continued to engage in soldiering, others showed no interest in war. Even in France's intense religious wars as many as half of all nobles never engaged in any military activity.[11] Among the English peerage, involvement in active warfare fell significantly from the end of the 1540s until the mid-1580s when opportunities again arose as a consequence of Elizabeth I's aggressive foreign policy, only to be reined back under James VI and I.[12] That French and English noblemen could be comfortable with an image of themselves that did not require demonstrations of military prowess provides a useful context for evaluating the military experiences of Scottish nobles who inhabited a world increasingly free of warfare. In 1585, around half of Scotland's titled nobles had experienced some form of military service, but that share fell to around a third by the first decade of the seventeenth century. When in the course of preparing to take the field in the autumn of 1562, the first earl of Moray wrote to the laird of Kilravock asking for his support, he pointed out that 'it is the first tyme that I haif bourdenyt you with sic thing, and the lyik not hable oft to occurre'. Even in the troubled middle decades of the sixteenth century, Moray's request for military support was unusual, hence, the apologetic tone of his letter.[13]

Yet that military tradition was not wholly dependent on the kingdom being at war. A political context in which rebellion was not uncommon until the mid-1590s, and where feuding was widespread until the second decade of the seventeenth century encouraged nobles to consider the need to deploy violence and to defend themselves and their followers. Yet in spite of what was often a threatening environment, few Lowland nobles directly employed professional soldiers because of the crippling cost. Even during the Marian civil war of 1567–73 lords were reluctant to engage soldiers in their service. In January 1570, the duke of Chatelherault raised cash among his friends and by wadsetting (= mortgaging) land in order that he might retain paid soldiers, but even this wealthy lord had difficulty keeping 140 horsemen and eighty harquebusiers in the field without French funds. As the regent Lennox explained to Elizabeth I in 1571, 'Wageit force we are not able to sustain on Scottish rents', and home-grown mercenaries attracted better rates of pay on the continent. Furthermore, the retaining of waged soldiers in the Lowlands was frowned on by a nervous government, and before the civil war ended the fifth earl of Glencairn and the third lord Sempill were accused of raising 'wageit men of weare' to settle their differences.[14] Those nobles who did employ professional soldiers usually had access to external funds and they entered into relatively short contracts. The fifth earl of Bothwell levied paid soldiers in 1588 – without royal warrant – in the expectation of an invasion of England; a year later he was said to have 400 hired troops under his command, paying them 50 shillings a month, and following his successful palace coup of July 1593 he hired 1,000 soldiers. Bothwell had access to Spanish and English money, however, and by the 1590s the presence of significant numbers of professional soldiers in the service of individual nobles was highly unusual.[15]

Instead, Lowland nobles looked to their own affinities for military support. Thomas Craig of Riccarton observed that long before the end of the sixteenth century 'the military character of the feudal relation faded', but his observation was true only in a strictly legal sense as nobles continued to exercise lordship over tenants. A contract of July 1560 between the fourth earl of Caithness and Magnus Halcro of Brught stipulated that the latter would support the earl's ambitions should he 'invaid the cuntre of Orknay in persecutione of his auld ennymeis'. In April 1570, the duke of Chatelherault summoned his men 'bayth on fuit and horse that will do for him ... arrayit with jak and speir' on two days' notice and provisioned for eight days' service. Widespread feuding and repeated rebellions kept nobles in a state of quasi-military preparedness so that, for example, at short notice in 1583 the earls of Crawford and Montrose raised mounted companies of 200 and 300 mounted men, respectively. But while military obligations to late medieval lords were spelled out in contracts and charters, only occasional examples survive in this later period. In a charter of October 1578 the Berwickshire laird, John Swinton of that Ilk, made provision of an eight husbandland for his younger son, Alexander, on condition that at royal musters or any lawful hostings he would attend his elder brother, or his heirs, at the latter's expense. In the grain producing northeast, landlords were alert to the dangers posed by neighbouring Highland clans. The fourth earl Marischal set military tacks in the 1570s, for example, the lease setting the lands of Ackergill to John Keith and his sons for three years in 1575 specified that 'Na Sinclair, Clangun, nor of Makkyes kin na clan be resauvit or enterit in any of the said nobil Lordis lands', and that the tower of Ackergill should be maintained. Similarly, the eleventh earl of Sutherland, who 'did alwayes manteyn a cursarie and runing guard, to preserve the cuntrey from such unlooked-for invasions', infeft John Thomasson and his clan in lands in June 1587 in return for their promise to answer the earl's summons for military aid.[16] By the later sixteenth century few charters appear to have been concerned with specific military obligations in contrast to the general agreement to 'ride and gang' that appears in bonds of manrent, and bonds significantly declined in number from the first decade of the seventeenth century.[17]

Gaelic society in Ireland and Scotland encouraged a particularly strong martial ethos, and throughout the western seaboard the retaining of professional soldiers, the gallowglass, or *buannachan* was nurtured by lords within the affinity. These feared and easily recognisable soldiers had a significant impact on the course of the Elizabethan military campaigns in Ireland.[18] An analysis of the military potential of the island chiefs in 1593 is impressive. On Lewis the Macleods could muster 700 gallowglass, while the smaller Macleod clan on Harris could raise a further 140 men. On Skye the various competing clans were able to field over 2,000 men, Mull 900 men, Islay 800 men and the smaller islands correspondingly smaller numbers amounting to a total of some 6,000 professional gallowglass.[19]

Arguably the most powerful independent military force in Britain or Ireland was commanded by the Campbell earls of Argyll, whose military capacity might usefully be compared with the great magnate houses of France. In the 1560s the fifth earl possessed castles, a fleet, artillery, commanded 1,500 professional gallowglass, and allegedly could levy 12,000 to 15,000 thousand armed men 'whereof his neighbours were afraid'. The house of Argyll was prepared to use that military power against neighbours like Lauchlan MacLean of Duart, who complained in May 1579 of an attack in Glen Loyne by sixty of the earl's soldiers 'bodin in feir of weir, with bowis, dorlochis, haberschonis, and utheris wappynnis invasive'. Tacks, or leases, were set by the earls of Argyll for military service, such as that in 1564 to sir Colin Campbell of Boquhan, who had the keeping of Skipnish castle and who agreed to provide a galley of twenty oars as and when required. Bonds of manrent often highlighted forms of military support, for example, that granted to the sixth earl of Argyll by the Macalastairs in 1576 promised to serve the earl on fifteen days warning. In the 1594 Glenlivet campaign, the seventh earl of Argyll fielded an army of at least 6,000 foot, of whom 1,500 were armed with hagbuts, the remainder with bows and two-handed swords. It was with good reason that Elizabeth I wrote to Argyll that 'we are of opinion that no subject he [James VI] hathe is of greater commandement then yourselfe'. The Islay revolt of 1615 was put down by Argyll's men buttressed by ships and troops paid for by the king, and it was Argyll who was instructed to finish the job with 'his privat meanes'. In 1625, the mobilisation of the Campbells involved the muster of thousands of men, the fitting out of galleys and the organisation of a sophisticated watch system, all done under the auspices of the crown, but under the command of lord Lorne, who would prove to be one of the major military entrepreneurs of the covenanting wars.[20]

The regal union with England in 1603 and the ending of rebellion in Ireland in conjunction with the campaign against feuding struck a blow at Highland military lordship, reducing the need for professional retainers and making the clans vulnerable to crown policing. This series of linked changes created tension between lords and men as the former sought to negotiate new leases that placed greater emphasis on payment in cash or produce rather than service. In 1624 the Clanchattan began a campaign of intimi- dation against the third earl of Moray because he had removed them from kindly, or customary, tenancies their families had possessed for generations in return for small rents but 'faithfull service', replacing them with 'febill persones unabill to serve the Erll thair maister, as thay could have done'. This process should not be exaggerated, and the real drive towards com- mercial estate management in the Highlands did not occur until after 1660. When in 1627 chancellor Dupplin was trying to enlist the support of sir Duncan Campbell of Glenorchy in raising men for a regiment to serve in Denmark, he remarked that those who survived the experience would be 'the abler heirefter to live and to do you service', an interesting insight into how this former soldier viewed the ongoing necessity of nobles raising armed and trained men from their own estates. The opening up of alterna- tive employment for soldiers on the continent ensured that when domestic warfare again broke out in 1638 Highland lords were able to intervene dramatically in both Scottish and British politics.[21]

The willingness of lords to switch their priorities in times of peace does not mean that nobles lost sight of the need to remain alert to potential military requirements. On the extensive frontier between the grain growing northeast and the Highlands, noblemen remained sensitive to the dangers of leaving themselves undefended. Sir Robert Gordon of Gordonstoun advised the thirteenth earl of Sutherland in the 1620s, 'In tyme of peace prepare your countreymen for warre' by keeping up military exercises and musters and by continuing to lease land in return for military service. The young earl was advised to 'lead fourth your countreymen your selfe in persone; so shall they obey the more willingly, and fight with better courage'. In 1633, Gordonstoun's nephew entered into an agreement with the first lord Reay, granting him the lands of Durness on condition that the latter and his heirs not only served and accompanied the earls of Sutherland at parliaments and conventions, but that they would attend wapenschaws within Sutherland under the earl's banner and colours. A similar continuity in preserving a military dimension to lordship persisted on the neighbour- ing Fraser estates. During the 1630s, the seventh lord Lovat followed in the traditions of his house by encouraging men throughout his domain to practise archery and shooting, ensuring that they were equipped with guns, bows and arrows for domestic defence should it be required and for overseas service.[22]

Evidence of a martial ethos in noble society survives in other forms. Noble residences provide some insight into their desire to dominate the landscape by projecting wealth and a degree of military might. Baronial architecture never lost sight of the importance of defence, even if many of the martial embellishments of houses were militarily impractical, for example, crenellations, machiolations and turrets were ineffective against gunpowder, while gunloops often served no military purpose. Houses did act as power centres, however, and architectural styles were intended primarily to convey a political message about noble identity and political dominance. In 1636, the English traveller, sir William Brereton, expressed surprise to find that lesser nobles were living in 'houses all built castle-wise'.[23] Nevertheless, while conspicuous consumption accounted for much of the phenomenal building boom of the period from the 1540s to the 1630s, that massive investment in castles and tower houses was a product of political conditions, especially in the sixteenth century. Parliament encouraged the trend with the legislation of 1535 requiring all landlords with land valued at £100 new extent to build a defensive dwelling. Clearly, the international threat from England continued to influence the planning of castles in the south of the kingdom, but few private buildings of the period were designed to keep an army at bay, and the more immediate concern was with the threat posed by civil war, rebellion and feuding. On the island of Skye alone there were seven castles with two more on neighbouring Raasay. In some cases the investment and effort in creating or sustaining a private military defence-work was enormous, as the second earl of Orkney discovered in maintaining his castle at Kirkwall, which was described in 1615 as 'one of the strongest houssis in Breitane'. On the Borders, sir Robert Ker of Ancram remodelled one of his houses in the mid-1630s, insisting that its defensive nature should not be weakened for 'the world may change agayn', a cautious view that proved well-founded. Undeniably, Ancram favoured a martial appearance for display reasons, and was critical of a neighbour who dismantled his battlements, 'for that is the grace of the house and makes it looke lyk a castle, and hence so nobleste, as the other would make it lyke a peele [= peel tower]'. The first earl of Nithsdale's remodelling of the internal courtyard at Carlaverock on the former western marches provides a salutary lesson of a castle redesigned at great expense in the 1630s only to be sacked by the covenanters in 1640.[24] Scotland remained a country dotted with castles that still had as one of their primary functions the defence of their inhabitants.

The increasing effectiveness of guns made most castles vulnerable, and while the nobility had the men and the small arms in greater quantity than the crown, the latter had larger ordinance that proved decisive in any trial of force between the king and his rebels. When the first earl of Mar took possession of the arsenal at Edinburgh castle in March 1567, its stock of weaponry, including a collection of artillery, far exceeded the firepower to be found in most noble castles. Of course, some of the great noble houses were well stocked with arms, and the crown expected them to act as regional power centres even though it was known that these weapons could be used in rebellion or feud. At the battle of Glenlivet in 1594, the sixth earl of Huntly and his allies brought to the field 'foure peces of great ordonance' that were deployed in the defeat of the king's lieutenant. Nevertheless, in general it was the effectiveness of artillery in reducing castles that differentiated the military capacity of the crown from individual nobles. Hence, in 1581 the friends of the imprisoned fourth earl of Morton concluded that they lacked the powder, armour and appropriate weapons necessary to launch a coup.[25]

Such military hardware made the castles of the nobility increasingly vulnerable. Dunure castle, the principal residence of the fourth earl of Cassillis, was described in the mid-1560s as 'A fare castell, not stronge nor worth fortifying', and even Edinburgh castle, situated on one of the most formidable sites in Europe, proved unable to withstand English bombardments in 1560 and 1573. The major problem facing the crown was transporting its train of artillery to the locality where it was required: once in place, defenders saw little point in further resistance. In 1559, the fourth earl of Bothwell chose to abandon Crichton castle to the Protestant lords rather than defend it, while the laird of Whitelaw surrendered Dunbar castle to the regent Moray in October 1567 immediately artillery arrived from Edinburgh. In 1570, Hamilton castle and its garrison of fifty soldiers withstood an initial bombardment by English field artillery, but surrendered when heavy ordinance arrived from Stirling. One chronicler of the royal campaign against the Hamiltons in 1579 recorded that this same castle 'wes nocht abill to abyd the force of the cannone quhilk wes brocht frome Stirling and Dumbarttane'. In May 1588, the Maxwell garrison in Lochmaben castle refused to surrender to royal troops, but capitulation was inevitable following the arrival of borrowed English artillery from Berwick. By the early seventeenth century the need for heavy expenditure on ordinance declined. The collection of 'great gunnis and feeld pieces' in the arsenal at Dunrobin castle was repaired in 1618, but when Gordonstoun was ordered to stamp out the fifth earl of Caithness's rebellion five years later, he required artillery from Edinburgh.[26]

Early modern nobles and their followers carried weapons and were instructed by professional masters of arms in all aspects of combat to humiliate, maim or kill an opponent.[27] Scotland's nobles displayed the ambivalence towards private violence that was typical of the age. In March 1579, the noble dominated privy council pronounced that it was unacceptable for lords and their men to turn up in great numbers at Stirling to see the king armed 'specialie with daggis, pistolettis, jakis, and secreitis of plait'. Yet those same nobles shared a view that armed protection was necessary both for defence and to project status. In April 1588, the sixth earl of Glencairn and his kinsmen argued that they were unable to appear before the privy council in Edinburgh 'without the assembly of all their friends armed for battle'. At issue in this on-going debate was not the wearing of swords by nobles, since James VI conceded that rapiers and daggers were 'knightly and honourable', but the widespread wearing of concealed armour and guns, especially by the ranks of followers in noble trains.[28] This universal presence of arms was unsurprising. From the outbreak of war with England in 1542 through to the ending of the civil war in 1573 there was a high demand for military equipment, stimulating a steady growth of the gun-making industry, while shipments of arms poured into the kingdom from elsewhere. That trade in arms continued in peacetime. The second earl of Orkney was thought to own the greatest store of weapons of any private subject in the kingdom as a consequence of his systematic purchasing of arms, piracy and the recovery of guns from a Spanish ship that had sunk in 1588. In 1589, the fifth earl of Bothwell made a claim against the English government for the loss of a ship and its cargo, including a large quantity of guns, shot and armour. These magnates were seeking to create large private caches of arms, and it is no accident that both were involved in treasonable activities.[29]

In a feuding society in which military power was dispersed and competitive, and in which it was difficult to enforce royal authority, the effect of the universal carrying of weapons was predictable. In 1585, a terrified English agent reported that 'When every man carries a pistol at his girdle, as they do in Scotland, it is an easy matter to kill a man through a window or door, and not be able to discover who did it'. Casual and explosive violence surfaced from the spontaneous shooting of chancellor Glamis at Stirling in 1578, to the pitched battles at Dryfe Sands in December 1593 between the Maxwells and Johnstones; at Lochgruingart in 1598 between sir James MacDonald and sir Lauchlin MacLean of Duart when the latter was slain along with hundreds of casualties; and at Ayr in December 1601 between rival branches of the Kennedies when scores of well-armed men took part.[30] In spite of the crack-down on feuding, displays of private violence continued into the seventeenth century in towns and in the countryside. During the sitting of the July 1606 parliament at Perth, there was a street brawl between rival families that was blamed on 'sum rascall servandis'. A few months after this incident, the locality of Nithsdale was polarised over a land dispute in which one side mobilised 'to the nowmer of twa hundreth personis on horse and fute, all bodin in feir of weir, come with sound of drum and pype to the place appointed'. Only after the first decade of the seventeenth century did private violence decline appreciably in the context of prolonged peace, greater political stability, a campaign against feuding by church and crown and a shift in attitudes within noble society.[31]

Early modern governments struggled with the tension between the need to encourage nobles to retain a local military capacity and a desire to control the use of weapons. Although the Scottish crown made some impact in controlling the wearing and use of weapons, especially handguns that had a levelling impact that concerned many nobles, noble society remained wedded to the idea that weapons were a legitimate extension of a nobleman's identity. Furthermore, significant parts of the kingdom ignored the government's efforts to restrict the wearing and bearing of arms, especially in Border and Highland localities. In 1619, the privy council reissued its proclamation against the wearing of armour in the middle shires (the former Border marches), while in 1626 the commissioners of the peace for Dumfriesshire reported that in the upland parishes there were many men who 'beiris pestolatis in thair pocattis and behind thair bakis'. Sir Robert Gordon of Lochinvar admitted that in Kirkcudbright it was impossible to supply the council with a list of men who broke the law regarding the wearing of guns since 'almost everie man caries pistoletts'.[32] In the Highlands, the 1609 statutes of Iona and subsequent legislation sought to discourage military retaining, seeking to drive a wedge between clan chiefs and those military retainers contemptuously dismissed as 'idill belleis'. The chiefs were permitted to carry arms and ordinary clansmen were encouraged to be armed if they were in crown service, a definition that proved to be flexible. The problem spilled over into neighbouring shires where fear of raiding remained acute, and in 1616 the privy council issued special commissions like that to lord Gordon in Aberdeen, Banff, Elgin and Forres to try and contain the gun problem.[33] Consequently, while there was an undercapacity in military equipment available to the crown when civil war again broke out in 1638–9 many nobles had access to private caches of arms and armour. That reservoir of arms was inadequate for the purposes of foreign war, hence, the covenanter government's need to import arms, but it was sufficient to exercise local military superiority. When sir Colin Campbell of Glenorchy mustered his men at the behest of the house of Argyll to defend the National Covenant, the armed readiness of his following amounted to a regiment of light infantry. Glenorchy had arms and armour for three mounted men, ten hagbuts, twenty muskets, three small field pieces and an assortment of shot, armour and other hand weapons. Among his twenty-three domestic servants only eight had guns and three had no weapons at all, but a further 112 men were mustered from his lands of whom twenty-two carried hagbuts, the remainder being armed with swords and shields with some carrying bows.[34] This was a modest but adequate armoury for a Highland baron that was multiplied many times over throughout Scotland. Furthermore, the laird of Glenorchy alone was able to mobilise more men than Charles I had under his direct command in the whole of Scotland.

Military Enterprise

Sixteenth-century European governments increasingly made use of mercenaries in the pursuit of diplomatic and military objectives, creating a buoyant international market for contractors who could supply professional soldiers. Initially dominated by the Germans and Swiss, the Scots soon saw the opportunities to operate in a lucrative business for which they had the available manpower, skills and enthusiasm.[35] Although military recruiting for service in continental armies took place throughout Britain and Ireland,

Scottish nobles were especially effective in persuading their men to enlist, allowing them to maintain a military ethos on their estates and providing a reservoir of military forces when they were required; as they were in 1638–9 when a covenanter army was created from a blend of estate levies and returning professionals. In 1580, an English observer noted 'the Scottish nation is at this day stronger in feats of arms than it was afore-time, by reason of their exercise in civil wars and their being in the Low Countries'. The Scottish professional soldier, or mercenary, was to become a familiar figure in the following decades, and the nobility played a key role in facilitating that business as military entrepreneurs, negotiating with their own and other governments, and as serving officers. Among the peerage, military service rose from 39 per cent in 1610 to 61 per cent by 1635, a development encouraged by financial necessity, notions of honour and a literature determined to promote the idea of a militant, Protestant nobility.[36] Scots served in Sweden's war with Muscovy in the 1550s, and by the time of the Thirty Years' War Sweden was by far the biggest recruiter of Scottish soldiers, while neighbouring Denmark also recruited heavily in Scotland. Over 3,000 men enlisted in Dutch service between 1573 and 1579, and in 1609 4,100 Scots were enlisted in a Dutch army that totalled 29,000 men. Highland troops served on both sides throughout Tyrone's rebellion in Ulster and had a significant impact on the course of the campaigns. Scots soldiers were found in Poland from the 1570s and were present in Russia where Alexander Leslie pursued a successful career during the Smolensk War of 1632–4. Scots were involved from the earliest engagements of what became the Thirty Years' War, with the first recruits arriving in Moravia in 1619 and they took part in the Bohemian campaign in the following year. Throughout the conflict at least 50,000 men were mobilised to fight in a war that is estimated to have engaged up to 20 cent of the adult male population of Scotland. Hence, in his 1652 book, *The jewel*, sir Thomas Urquhart of Cromarty related that the Scots 'have been of late so ingaged in all the wars of Christendome, espousing in a manner the interest of all the princes thereof'.[37]

The motives that persuaded lords and men to pursue a military career were multiple and complex. Often the military campaigns in which Scottish soldiers participated were in the service of princes who were allies of the crown and their involvement amounted to a legitimate expression of Stewart foreign policy. This was true of service to the Danish house of Oldenburg, the family of queen Anne, or to Frederick of Bohemia, son-in-law of James VI and I. Interventionist crown policy alongside a shared ideology and religion resulted in a huge increase in Scottish soldiers enlisting in Danish and Swedish service during the early seventeenth century. Between 1625 and 1629 over 300 Scottish officers found service under Christian IV of Denmark, and among these men was the cash-strapped first earl of Niths-dale who was appointed to the rank of general. Sweden offered particularly good opportunities and Scots participated in all of Sweden's wars from the 1550s. Among the many officers who enlisted under the Swedish crown were Andrew Keith, nephew of the fourth earl Marishcal, who was created a baron in 1574, and John Stewart who was ennobled in 1585. During the Thirty Years' War the number of lesser nobles and their kinsmen enlisting in Swedish service grew, and in 1629 alone some 208 officers accepted a Swedish commission, including James Spens of Wormiston, Alexander Leslie, James King and Patrick Ruthven, alongside 25,000 men. Between 1629 and 1637 thirty-three Scottish officers were appointed as military governors on Sweden's frontiers, and up to a quarter of the entire Swedish military was under Scottish command. Among the most successful of the Scots in Swedish service was Robert Munro, who epitomised the professional soldier whose career was driven both by financial reward and by a real commitment to the Swedish crown, his Protestant faith – Munro's *Expedition* (1637) contained his religious meditations – and a belief that 'The world hath nothing so glorious as vertue'. Significantly, the overwhelming majority of Scottish mercenaries served Protestant employers. Combining religious beliefs and financial interests was not impossible, and accounts for some of the success the covenanters had in attracting many of the best professionals to enlist in their armies in 1638–9.[38]

Not surprisingly, the crown saw dangers in professional forces being deployed in domestic politics, while recognising the potential in acquiring management over military contracting as a means of exercising diplomatic influence. As early as 1571 the privy council began to exert control over the flow of soldiers leaving the country through the issuing of licences. By the seventeenth century this was an established practice. In January 1602, an impressive array of nobles with lands in the Highlands were commanded to provide 2,700 men for service against Elizabeth I's rebels in Ireland. This force was raised by military contractors like the second duke of Lennox, the first marquis of Huntly, the earls of Argyll, Atholl, Caithness and Sutherland, lord Lovat and a string of barons and chiefs. A decade later, the privy council was concerned at the unlicensed raising of troops for service with the king of Sweden, and the forceful impressment of men by the captains of these companies. But from 1625 licences were issued more frequently. Sir Robert McLellan of Bombie had a contract to raise a troop of fifty horse and a company of 100 men to serve in Ireland. In the spring of 1626, 2,000 men were raised by sir Donald McKay of Farr under commission from the crown for service in Germany. The third marquis of Hamilton was authorised in March 1631 to raise 6,000 men for service under the Swedish king in Germany, in June the first lord Reay had a warrant to raise another 2,000 men for that same campaign, and in 1636, the first lord Almond was contracted to raise 300 men for service in the Low Countries. These contracts were not simply private arrangements between military entrepreneurs and their paymasters, but were an extension of Scottish foreign policy.[39] Where military contracting was in opposition to crown policy, as occurred in 1627 when the seventh earl of Argyll raised troops for service in Flanders under Habsburg command, official disapproval forced him to chose between loyalty to Spain or to Charles I. In fact, large numbers of Catholics were attracted to French service and some 10,400 men enlisted in the armies of the king of France between 1624 and 1642. Although it was different from other forms of military service, the appointment of lord Gordon as captain of the *Garde d'Ecosse* in 1632 and his taking a company into the king of France's service continued a much older tradition of Franco-Scottish cooperation.[40]

For some soldiers the attraction of foreign military service was a combination of money and personal advancement, and for these individuals loyalties could be fluid. Writing in 1631 about his plans to take up service under Gustav Adolf, the king of Sweden, the third marquis of Hamilton admitted that this was an enterprise 'wherein both my fortoun and honour ar so deiplie ingadged'. In the summer of 1627, an exasperated first lord Reay grumbled that he might transfer from Danish to Spanish service on the grounds that Philip III was 'ane true man and ane good payer'. Reay is unlikely to have been serious, but the option to change employer was one that professional soldiers did consider and some did take. Nevertheless, for the majority of officers, the profits of military service were not great, although especially for younger sons soldiering represented an honourable lifestyle. The recruitment of between twenty and fifty officers per annum by Sweden throughout the 1620s offered a welcome opportunity to pursue what had for long been a popular career. When colonel Henry Lindsay of Ballinscho made his will in 1639 he left 34,000 merks to his kinsmen and friends, the proceeds largely of his military service in Sweden. And for some men a military career continued to offer the traditional route to noble status. John Cunningham of Gjerdrup and Andrew Sinclair of Ravenscraig were raised into the Danish and Swedish nobility, respectively.[41] But there were also financial risks. The sixth earl of Morton's son-in-law informed him that he had arranged with William Dick to raise credit for the payment of his officers, but that unless there was employment for his troops 'it is to no purpose to ware money on them'. Others failed to make their fortune. Captain James Halkerston, a distant cousin of James VI with an impressive military record and a man who made a career in the murky underworld of court politics as an enforcer, ended his days penniless in London.[42]

This willingness to hire themselves for pay made professional soldiers unpopular. In the autumn of 1559, at the height of the Reformation struggle, the waged soldiers in the employment of the Protestant lords mutinied when their pay was late, issuing a proclamation that 'they would serve anie man'. Such individuals stood outside the normal bonds of lordship and in the same incident the soldiers mocked those nobles who tried to pacify them. Similarly, in 1571 there was suspicion of the professional captains on both sides of the conflict because 'if the warres ceased, they would get no more wages'. It is not surprising to find, therefore, that following the end of the civil war in the summer of 1573, 4,000 men were recruited by the prince of Orange and 1,000 men by the king of Sweden.[43] Here was the easiest means of disposing of unwanted and dangerous soldiers unfit to dwell in civil society. Hence, the hostility David Calderwood expressed towards former soldiers like captain James Stewart (chancellor Arran) and colonel William Stewart (lord Pittenweem), 'upstart soldiours, trained up in slaughter, not fitt to be counsellers to intertaine peace in a commoun weale'.[44]

The role of the professional soldier or mercenary was most established in the Highlands. Along the western seaboard the gallowglass accounted for at least 6,000 semi-professional soldiers, formed principally from the younger sons of the clan elite, the *fine*. They fought for tribute in Ireland, especially from the 1540s, and when at home provided protection for the clan, taking part in raids in return for quarter within its territory. One of the most successful warlords, Sorley Boy MacDonnell, carved out a territorial foothold in Antrim in the face of opposition from the Tudor government. Naturally, the number and reputation of these men added to the status of their chief. In 1595, Lauchlan Maclean of Duart lobbied the English government to get employment against the Irish rebels, although both he and his chief, the seventh earl of Argyll, were prepared to sell men to either side. When Duart mobilised his men that summer he had at his command 100 men in mail coats with iron helmets and two-handed swords, 100 armed with guns and 100 bowmen.[45] The ending of the rebellion in Ireland closed off these opportunities, but the outbreak of large-scale warfare on the continent from 1618 created a new demand. In the early 1620s, the exiled seventh earl of Argyll recruited men for service under his command in the Spanish army, while the first lord Reay led 3,000 men into Germany in 1627 at a time when Lowland lords were experiencing resistance to recruiting. Between 1626 and 1634, 105 gentlemen volunteers, those men in the bottom ranks of noble society, joined Reay's regiment.[46]

Yet this was not a business confined to the Highlands. The involvement of Scottish mercenaries in the Dutch struggle with Spain was almost as long as the wars, earning the Scots a fierce reputation. Patrick Gray, master of Gray, tried to establish himself as a mercenary contractor to the earl of Leicester's army in the Netherlands in 1586, and in 1590 the fifth earl of Bothwell opened negotiations with England to fit out privateers to prey on Spanish shipping under letters of *marque*.[47] Possibly Border lords were more forward in contracting their men, especially after 1603 when military service in that region became less useful to them. The first lord Buccleuch fought for the Dutch between 1604 and the peace of 1609, having the rank of colonel and command of his own regiment of 200 men. His son, the first earl of Buccleuch, continued the military tradition of his family, serving in

Flanders between 1627 and 1633, receiving a commission from the States General appointing him a colonel in 1629. Another Border lord, the first earl of Nithsdale, was commissioned by Christian IV of Denmark in February 1627 to raise a regiment of 3,000 men for service in Germany.[48]

By the early seventeenth century, some families had established strong military traditions. In 1629, the fourteenth earl of Crawford raised a regiment of 300 men and took service under the king of Sweden in which he was joined by his brothers and four of his cousins. Crawford and three of his kinsmen, all colonels, were killed in Germany.[49] An equally martial family was that of Forbes. All five legitimate sons and one illegitimate son of the tenth lord Forbes went into military service, while lord Forbes engaged 800 men under the command of his eldest son, Alexander, for service with the first lord Reay in Denmark in 1626. Alexander Forbes led his men into the service of Gustav Adolf in 1630, was captured at Lützen in 1632, and remained a prisoner of the emperor for almost two years. Three of his brothers and his illegitimate half-brother were killed in Germany.[50] Many other noble families could attest to involvement in European warfare at a level that was more intense than anything experienced since the fourteenth-century wars with England, and Scots noble blood was shed on the fields of all the great battles of the era, such as at Nördlingen in 1634 where a younger brother of the thirteenth earl of Sutherland was killed. This on-going martial tradition allowed the nobility to respond militarily in defence of the National Covenant against a de-militarised crown. Sir William Ker took service with the duke of Buckingham on his ill-fated expedition to the Île de Ré in 1627, he was with the British fleet that attempted to relieve La Rochelle the following year, and in 1629 saw service with the Dutch in their war with Spain. Sir William retired to Scotland where he acquired the earldom of Lothian and later put his military experience at the service of the covenanters.[51]

Defending the Kingdom

In spite of its military tradition, Scotland was an insignificant military power, the diplomatic pretensions of James IV and James V having been abandoned in the wake of a series of catastrophic military defeats. The kingdom lacked a professional army, an effective navy and the financial means to pay for defending itself.[52] Scotland endured intense, if interrupted, international warfare from 1542 to 1560 with large and destructive English and French armies active on its soil.[53] The Reformation initiated an intermittent civil warfare that lasted from 1559 to 1573, amounting to a series of localised campaigns between rival nobles with further English intervention in 1570 and 1573.[54] The legacy was a stockpile of arms, a generation of men bred for war, and for another three decades nobles continued to conduct national politics and local bloodfeuds as private war.[55] Noble followings were mobilised and kept in a state of semi-permanent war readiness. In the 1568 Langside campaign the various forces raised by the regent Moray, the Hamiltons, the Gordons and Campbells were each estimated at between 3,000 and 5,000 followers, while nine earls and twelve lords of parliament were present at the battle.[56] This conflict was conducted in sporadic but savage outbursts of violence that brutalised the political community for a generation. The hanging in 1570 of the entire garrison of Brechin, some 150 men, or the burning of the castle of Towie with its lady and twenty-six others indicates an escalation of violence such that by 1572 it was reported that 'thair is nothing but hanging on eather syde'.[57] For the generation of lords who lived through these decades war was as much their natural business as it had ever been for men of their rank.

After 1573, Scotland experienced no international or large-scale civil war until the Bishop's Wars of 1639–40, and therefore it did not undergo even the modest level of militarisation that occurred in England during the last quarter of the sixteenth century. The campaign of 1547 was the last occasion on which the Scottish host was fully mobilised in defence of the nation, but its limitations were embarrassingly demonstrated in a crushing defeat by the English at the battle of Pinkie.[58] There was no royal army, thus denying the nobility the professional training and military experience enjoyed by French nobles (apart from those who trained on the continent), while preventing the formation of any formal relationship between lords and the crown's military infrastructure. Of course, even France did not employ a standing army before the 1630s, and most princes employed a mixture of options in raising armies in which nobles were expected to play a major part in creating and in leading military forces. Scotland did not even have a local militia with established military offices to provide a means by which local elites were bound into the service of the prince as occurred, for example, in Tuscany or England where the idea of the Roman *campus martius* was popular.[59] Instead, the political community continued to place its faith in the notional idea of the host, an outdated body of noble retinues and burgh bands to which might be attached a small number of professional soldiers such as gunners. In domestic campaigns these forces could be highly effective, and the point has been made previously that few rebellions succeeded. In May 1568, the regent Moray led a military expedition through the southwest consisting of 4,000 armoured horsemen, 1,000 infantry armed with harquebus or halberds, 4,000 carriage horses with victual and 3,000 non-combatants to attend the soldiers and horses. It was sufficiently powerful to meet no significant opposition except at Hoddam castle, which withstood a siege for a few days before surrendering. Twelve castles or towers were handed over to the regent, three of which were destroyed.[60]

In practice, the terrible defeat inflicted by England in 1547 and the subsequent military occupation of much of Lowland Scotland led to the collapse of the kingdom's military organisation, which was not repaired or addressed over the following quarter of a century. Wapenschaws, designed to maintain local defence, were revived in 1575 in an effort to implement the over-ambitious act of 1540 requiring that they be held twice a year. Another attempt was made to place them on a regular footing in 1584, and summons were issued in 1587 and 1588 in the context of the perceived threat from Spain, which was the reason for a further summons in 1595. In addition, there were more geographically restricted levies summoned to deal with rebellions or law and order problems, particularly on the Borders. Consequently, local military mobilisation of a sort was scheduled to take place on a regular basis with general or local wapenschaws being summoned each year from 1578 to 1585 and again from 1592 to 1598.[61]

Nevertheless, wapenschaws were badly attended, and the privy council's erratic and unsuccessful efforts at persuading people to take them seriously fell on deaf ears, especially outside the larger burghs. Between 1591 and 1639 the only occasion a wapenschaw was held within the jurisdiction of Monimail regality court was on 20 November 1616.[62] Sheriffs proved to be unwilling and ineffective at coordinating local defence, and the absence of the equivalent of French military governors, or English lords lieutenants, meant that there was no intermediate step between noble affinities and a national army. Furthermore, the military preparedness of the men who did attend only drew attention to their military shortcomings. When a wapenschaw was held by the sheriff of Moray in February 1596, around 900 men turned out, a not unreasonable response. John Grant of Freuchie presented his entire following of 500 men, of whom 300 men were suitably armed for local defence but only 80 men were equipped for service under the king. This was a significant turnout by a Highland chief who probably had his reasons for wanting to impress on the local community his military prowess. Few other nobles were so eager to display their power and two-fifths of those men present were unarmed, while under a quarter of them were equipped adequately to serve on a military campaign.[63]

The entire system, therefore, was heavily dependent upon the willingness of nobles to respond to appeals from the crown. Hence, letters like that from Mary to William Douglas of Lochleven in July 1566 asking him to accompany her on a Border raid 'with youre houshaldis and substanciouse freindis bodin in weirlik maner'. Consequently, it was essential for the crown that nobles had recourse to an armed following for war and to suppress the king's domestic enemies. The kingdom would have been defenceless if lords had been prevented from exercising military power, and it was crucial that men like the sixth lord Erskine had the authority to order his tenants on the lands of Over and Nether Nisbet to be ready to join him at short notice.[64] At the local level, it was up to those lords to maintain a military preparedness and some did take it seriously. In 1586, Calder barony court in west Lothian imposed fines of £5 on those men who failed to follow the baron or his officers in pursuing an affray, and £10 on men who failed to turn up at military musters on Calder Hill properly equipped with their own weaponry. The court listed 106 men of the barony with the value of their horses and the weapons they were expected to possess. Obviously some localities were likely to take their military responsibilities more seriously than others. The Anglo-Scottish marches had long been a region of high military activity, the southeastern localities having the reputation for being 'mair expert in ordiring a battell [= infantry formation] than vtheris', while the men of Dumfries 'ar ay in radines, and al ar hors men'. Yet the crown had only a tenuous control over these lords, and the later sixteenth century saw a progressive decline in the military responsibilities of the wardens, the one office that reported directly to the king.[65] The problem for the crown was in mobilising this fragmentary, decentralised and inharmonious power network, particularly as the external threat to the kingdom from England receded.

The crown's dependence on noble military power was more apparent in dealing with rebellion and domestic disorder. In the summer of 1585, James VI wanted to lead an expedition against the rebellious eighth lord Maxwell, but the English ambassador correctly predicted failure:

> for though the custom of the country is that men shall serve on their own charges, yet they dislike it much, and will hardly be kept together unless they receive pay, which the king, at this time, cannot give them for lack of money.

In theory the king could 'send his hired men out day or night; they will intercept the enemy, and go through the force of the greatest earl in Scotland'.[66] But James VI could not afford these professional forces, certainly not in the numbers necessary to overawe his more powerful nobles, and he struggled even to maintain a small royal guard. Any suggestion of creating royal forces was regarded with suspicion, chiefly on the grounds of cost. In the midst of yet another emergency in the summer of 1592, James VI asked the barons of Fife to maintain a guard of 100 horsemen for his protection, but this was denied since it would establish an unwelcome precedent. While the crown did have an advantage in heavy guns that could be used to good effect in siege warfare, they were less effective in open battle, and at Langside in May 1568, Aberdeen in November 1571 and Glenlivet in October 1594 guns proved to be either indecisive or less effective than the bowmen and cavalry levied by the nobility.[67]

This absence of money was crippling, but that was not the end of the king's difficulties. The point was made during the 1589 rebellion that nobles and their followers were reluctant to be involved in the King's political disputes because of the risks of becoming entangled in long bloodfeuds. The network of bonds and marriages along with the inter-connected feuds cut across political loyalties, forcing the king into a series of negotiations and concessions in order to rally support. The privy council issued the usual general summons to serve the king 'weill bodin in weirlike maner with speiris and hacquebutis' for an indeterminate period, but when James VI did march north against the Catholic rebels in the spring of 1589, Thomas Fowler noted that 'The most strengthe of this army is of the lardes', while many earls and lords 'neyther cum nor send to the Kinge, notwithstondinge all his procklemacyons'. Of course, in the end the nobles did their deals, the king did have an adequate army, and when faced by James VI in the field the rebels backed down. But the king's dependence on the military strength of his nobles was striking.[68] Even the less contentious issue of addressing disorder on the Borders was sufficiently unpopular for the crown to find itself scrabbling around for enough nobles to cooperate with its plans. In February 1597, a royal raid on the west march was proclaimed, but the turnout was poor, especially among the lower ranks of landowners. At a further raid in November of that year the privy council complained that in spite of the king being in Dumfries awaiting men to answer his summons for a major judicial raid on the west march, 'verie few hes yit convenit, bot still remanis and abyds at hame'. The privy council had to remind those who did bother to turn up not to carry guns or to engage in feuding with one another.[69] Major royal campaigns planned for the western isles in 1596 and 1598 were undermined by the usual absence of enthusiasm from those expected to contribute, the messy inter-clan politics of the region and the wily behaviour of the chiefs. In the case of the former the crown scaled down its plans within two weeks of the initial proclamation in response to protests, and there was nervousness around the predictable news that the seventh earl of Argyll was displeased that the lieutenancy had been granted to colonel William Stewart of Pittenweem when 'his ancestors have long enjoyed that office'.[70]

This veto on the king's freedom to wage war, or even to put down rebellion, enhanced the political power of the nobles who were presiding over an antiquated, amateur and ineffective military infrastructure that compared unfavourably with either the English trained bands or the Dutch army.[71] There is some evidence that from the mid-1590s efforts were being made to recalibrate the military organisation of the kingdom, but this is easy to exaggerate. When it was intimated that troops were to be levied for service in the western isles in 1596, each shire was ordered to send twenty horsemen and thirty foot, or the equivalent cash value, suggesting a move in the direction of a military tax. At the same time, the church urged a parish-based militia for defence against the perceived threat from Catholic Spain.[72] It was acknowledged that while there was an excess of weapons in private hands, there was a lack of up-to-date arms required to wage war. This was not a new problem. In 1541, parliament recognised that the kingdom lacked adequate, modern weapons, and the estates legislated to force nobles to acquire arms and merchants to import them. So concerned was James VI that he would be unable to field an army in pursuit of the English succession that in 1598 he entered into negotiations with sir Michael Balfour of Burleigh to import arms to equip his nobles. In the summer of 1599 a convention of estates established a commission headed by the second earl of Mar and staffed by a mixture of nobles and military professionals to overhaul the military preparedness of the kingdom. The chief problem, it was believed, was that Scotland had been defeated repeatedly due to a lack of military discipline and an over-reliance on 'an unskilful and unarmed multitude'. It was conceded, however, that 'the poverty of the crown and country is not able to sustain waged men under commandment'. The convention of estates approved Burleigh's role in importing within the year armour for 2,000 horsemen and 8,000 infantry. At a further meeting in December 1599, a convention of estates set out the expectation for men to purchase this armour according to their rank. Earls were required to possess a minimum of twenty stands of armour, lords must own at least ten stands of armour and every baron should have at least one stand of armour for each measure of victual or rent. In other words, the crown had no option but to insist that the nobility stock weapons and arm their followers in readiness to serve the king when summoned. Individuals like John Lennox of Cally did purchase the requisite amount of equipment, but on the whole the privy council's directives were treated with indifference. In the following year a convention of estates at Falkland set up a standing committee of nobles to investigate how to improve the unsatisfactory defences of the kingdom, and in 1600 James entered into a contract with leading nobles who agreed to provide money to help finance his pursuit of the English crown.[73] The near comic efforts of James VI to mobilise a war-making capacity in 1599 in pursuit of his claim to the English throne highlights the king's feeble military power.

The regal union altered the military balance between the king and the nobility as the Borders were demilitarised, rebellion in Ireland ended in 1604, English naval power became available for action in the western isles and the king appeared to be invulnerable to armed rebellion.[74] Yet the crown's underlying dependence on nobles to deal with local problems that required a military solution did not alter. In 1607, the privy council issued a proclamation, pointing out that no wapenschaws had been held for years due to the negligence of local officers of the crown.[75] When in 1608 the third lord Ochiltree was appointed lieutenant of the western isles and summoned the lieges, he was met by wholesale indifference, and it was in spite of the shambolic organisation of his force that he succeed in overawing some of the island chiefs.[76] That year there was trouble in Orkney, and the privy council reminded the king that 'Your majestie knowis that we haif no forceis to send to Orknay, to mak the said erll conformable bot your majesteis awne gairdis, who, in respect of your heynes awne service, may not be weill spairit'. When Orkney finally was reduced to submission in 1614, it was done by the fifth earl of Caithness, Orkney's bitter enemy, with the help of artillery sent up from Edinburgh.[77] Similarly, when in August 1615 the seventh earl of Argyll was given charge of suppressing the rebellion on Islay, he levied 500 men in the king's name and although their equipment was provided at the crown's charge, the operation was conducted by his own private forces. Argyll's commission as lieutenant spells out the fact that he was selected for the role because of 'his awne freindschip power, and auctoritie' in the region. At the same time, a rebellion on Lewis was entrusted to a commission of Mackenzies, appointed by the crown but in effect acting for the young second lord Kintail.[78]

In its lack of modern military organisation, early seventeenth-century Scotland was less developed than James VI and I's kingdom of England where local capacity was organised from the centre and supplemented by private enterprise.[79] The contrast was far greater with continental neighbours where a more professional military was forced on crown and nobility by the needs of sustained and large-scale warfare.[80] The regal union of 1603 removed the likelihood of Anglo-Scottish war, while James VI and I's pacific foreign policy kept Britain formally out of European conflicts for the remainder of his reign, although it did not prevent Scots being involved in proxy wars on the continent that served the king's complex foreign policy interests. The involvement of Scottish soldiers in foreign service sustained a significant military capacity, in effect a military reserve, which increased rapidly from the outbreak of war in Bohemia. Between 1620 and 1625, 25,000 men enlisted either with the Dutch or in the German war theatre, for example, in 1624–5 some 4,000 of count Mansfield's 13,000-strong army were Scots.[81]

Charles I favoured a more aggressive foreign policy than his father, and in the 1620s his court became aligned with chivalric values and martial qualities. Unfortunately, his policies and behaviour between 1625 and 1640 resulted in him presiding over the abject failure of English military power, first, in Europe and then its collapse within Britain and Ireland.[82] From early in his reign, therefore, he attempted to alter the crown's capacity to wage war, and Scotland was dragged into war with Spain from 1625 to 1630 and with France from 1626 to 1629. On instruction from the king, a convention of estates in October 1625 tentatively agreed to finance a force of 2,000 men and some shipping for three years, and it summoned a general wapenschaw for December. The privy council stepped up military preparations, but it quickly became apparent that Scotland was woefully unprepared to fight a modern war as nobles were called upon to provide the organisational basis of the kingdom's military capacity. In December 1625, with war against Spain looming, sir Patrick Hume of Polwarth complained of the military unpreparedness of the country, writing that he 'never saw this kingdom in worse equippage both for hors and armes', and 'thare is not a craftisman to make a steal bonnet in al the land'. There was such a shortage of gunpowder that the privy council had to request its importation from England.[83]

A council of war was established in July 1626, presided over by the fourth earl of Montrose and including five peers (lord Gordon was heir to the first marquis of Huntly), the remaining eleven members being a mixture of crown officers, barons and soldiers. The council of war quickly uncovered the scale of the problem facing the government, and a further general muster was scheduled for the spring of 1627. The privy council was forced to recognise that preceding musters had been characterised by widespread evasion of the legislation with men turning up unarmed, or not at all, and officials failing to maintain any record so that there was 'no certane knowledge of the strenth of this kingdom'. An attempt was made to establish greater central control over the administrative record-keeping, and a second general wapenschaw was ordered to take place in November 1627. Little appears to have changed, and when the barons and gentlemen of Kincardine held their wapenschaw they were concerned to discover how few men possessed arms. They were even more worried about being obliged to purchase arms from a crown-appointed supplier, and they held a specially convened meeting to put in place their own requirements for military preparedness, hoping that this might head off any additional burden. In 1628, the eighth lord Yester was unlikely to have been alone in receiving details of the 1598 regulations for mustering the heritors of his locality, an indication that there had been no progress made on devising a more effective method of raising troops.[84]

The only innovation was the attempt to deploy the relatively new commissioners of the peace who, in consultation with parish ministers, were required to exercise a role in the organisation of local defence militias after it was found that men had become 'ignorant of the millitarie exerceis and discipline'. Unfortunately, these local officers made little impact, and even in the sheriffdom of Edinburgh the privy council discovered that the men charged with this responsibility 'hes slighted and neglected the same to the great hinder and disappointing of his Majesteis service'. Instead, the crown had to turn to the traditional representatives of local power like the sixth earl of Cassillis, hereditary baillie of Carrick, who was asked to hold wapenschaws in preparation for the defence of the kingdom against invasion.[85] Dumbarton castle, one of the kingdom's major fortresses, is symbolic of the appalling condition of Scotland's military preparedness. In December 1627, it was discovered that sir John Stewart of Methven had abandoned his post as keeper and gone off to Ireland leaving this castle that guarded the approaches to the river Clyde in a state of disrepair and with a garrison of only four men. The privy council investigated the situation, but was unable to act without seeking the formal approval of the absentee fifteen-year-old fourth duke of Lennox who had heritable possession of this royal stronghold.[86]

The problem was not only one of organisation. The war was unpopular and was damaging to Scotland's traditional Danish ally, which was facing the threat posed by imperial armies by diverting troops elsewhere.[87]

Consequently, the privy council again had to cajole men to purchase arms and armour while resorting to scouring the highways and prisons in a desperate search for men. As the covenanters discovered in 1638–9, widespread evasion of the requirement to purchase arms meant that they had to enter the overseas market for weapons. The poor condition of the recruits forced the crown to appeal to nobles to do what they could to raise and furnish 2,000 men for Buckingham's expedition to La Rochelle in 1627. Command of this force was handed to the sixth earl of Morton because of 'the multitude of his kinsmen, allyes and friends', and it was to Morton that William Douglas dedicated his 1627 pamphlet, 'Encouragements for the Warres of France to excitate etc, Noble men, Gentlemen and courageous Scottes'. In August 1627, Charles I wrote to the young third marquis of Hamilton asking him to demonstrate his loyalty 'by speedie furnishing of the greatest nomber of men able for warlike servive that you can provide by your meanes and frends well knawn unto us'. Sir Duncan Campbell of Glenorchy offered his men £40 for clothing and equipment to volunteer for service in the war against France, the money being raised by a local tax on his tenants. In return for their help in raising men, the nobility assumed control of all the major military offices. The second lord Spynie was appointed general muster-master and colonel of the militia for the entire kingdom, the second earl of Kinghorn and the first marquis of Huntly had responsibility for the construction of fortifications and the creation of early warning systems, and the sixth earl Marischal was contracted to provide naval transport on condition that he was granted a licence to engage in privateering. Hamilton and his partners were commissioned to fit out and man up to five privateers for a period of five years, the lion's share of the profits being assigned to the marquis and his associates.[88] It was the nobles who controlled the entire process of raising, arming and paying for troops, leading to rumours that noblemen were increasing the number of their retainers under the guise of recruiting for military service in Europe. The government's own efforts in contributing to the war effort between 1626–9 were not insubstantial as a facilitator and organiser, but the end product was scarcely worth the energy expended and the ill-feeling generated. Subsequent efforts to create a national militia during the mid-1630s foundered when the privy council baulked at introducing it by stealth.[89]

The war was so unpopular that even the nobility had difficulties in meeting the crown's expectations. John Innes of Coxton complained that the efforts of the second lord Spynie's recruiters 'wil tend to the undoing of the tennents quha yet skarslie entrit to thair harvest and consequentlie wil do me gryt skaith throw not winning of thair cornis quhilk most of my land duity'. The correspondence received by the first earl of Nithsdale from his subordinates about the problems in recruiting a few thousand men for service in Denmark in the summer of 1627 suggests a country stripped bare of available fighting men. It is possible that men were unenthusiastic about the terms of service, especially when continental armies offered better opportunities. Sir William Ker could not find officers or raise a company of soldiers for service under the duke of Buckingham, complaining to his father 'how hard men are to be leavied in this country'.[90] Morton's efforts to raise and find employment for a regiment was a source of continual vexation, and even lord Lorne, his son-in-law and head of the massive Argyll affinity, was unable to arouse enthusiasm. By September 1627, he reported that he had cobbled together a company of only 100 men, sixty of these being from his own estates. Spynie told Morton in May 1627 that it would be impossible to raise the men 'onless ther be a press'.[91] In 1628, desertions among the recruits destined for colonel Mackay's regiment, decimated by high losses in Denmark, threatened its viability as a fighting unit, and the crown had to turn to the first earl of Seaforth, lord Gordon and the sixth lord Lovat to round up the missing soldiers and to punish their resetters. In 1631, the third marquis of Hamilton wrote to other magnates like the thirteenth earl of Sutherland asking for their help in raising troops for service in Germany, but again found recruiting difficult. The issue, however, was not the lack of adequate men since many thousands of men were raised by military contractors to engage in foreign service, but the unwillingness of nobles to raise those men on behalf of Charles I either because of the terms on offer or due to wider dissatisfaction with the king's policies. Chancellor Dupplin expressed irritation with sir Duncan Campbell of Glenorchy in *c.* 1629 because of his apparent inability to raise troops, sarcastically pointing out that 'above all the people of the worlde yours ar onwilling to go out of thair awin glens, muche les to go to the warres for riches or honour in forrayne pairtes'. In December 1630, Dupplin wrote to Morton about the latter's difficulties in raising troops for service in France, suggesting that the lesser nobility, from whose ranks the chancellor had risen, had depended in the past on lords like Morton from whom they held land and offices in return for protection. These men

> fought and ministered under thes noble mens baners, accompanie them to court and publike assemblies and if the noblemen had neid of men or anyething els, which thair owne proper lands culd not furniss, thai wer thairin supplied by thess gentlmen.

No doubt with the revocation in mind, Dupplin pointed out that the nobility were annoyed since the king 'intendeth that the gentrie shall have thair role and immediat dependencie upon himselff, it is reason they beare a pairt of all services'.[92] In other words, if Charles I did not want lords to exercise lordship in times of peace, he could not expect them to reactivate that same lordship when it suited him.

Conclusion

Evidence for the falling away of military attributes among European nobilities suggests that it was a long, drawn-out process and that the important changes occurred in the later seventeenth and eighteenth centuries.[93] The embedding of chivalrous ideas and the associated martial ethos that was so integral to medieval ideas of nobility did not disappear in early modern Scotland. Enthusiasm for a military identity remained at the core of noble society, and even the enhanced adoption of learning as a mark of nobility did not exclude a thirst for knowledge about war and the instruments of war. As in so many other aspects of societal change, nobles rose to the occasion, embracing new ideas and new practices. By the end of the 1630s, nobles had ceased to think of themselves as armoured knights, but they did not lose the belief in their right to lead in war, the requirement to be trained in arms and their self-perception as warriors descended from a warrior lineage. Warfare discouraged reactionary attitudes, and even as armchair enthusiasts the nobility embraced the new so that when they were mobilised for war in 1638 they accepted the advice of those kinsmen, friends and dependants who returned home as seasoned professional officers, fitting into an organisation that was to become an up-to-date European army. Clearly, those serving professionals were continuing in a long tradition of nobles and their men who went elsewhere when there were few opportunities at home, but these were not mercenary exiles cut off from Scottish society. These soldiers were rooted in their local communities with which they remained in close contact, exchanging information, seeking out recruits and to which many returned to settle down. Noble society was host to a generous leavening of martial experiences that kept the business of war and the projection of military values close to the surface of that community. From the third marquis of Hamilton down to the impoverished Highland tacksmen who followed their chiefs into foreign service, every noble family had it soldiers.

The thesis that early modern states were a product of war appears increasingly unsustainable when exposed to empirical evidence, and the strains placed on seventeenth-century governments to sustain warfare probably undermined any state-formation process. Arguably, Charles I's efforts to wage war wrecked his ability to govern England in 1625–9 and again in 1639–40.[94] There is certainly no significant evidence to suggest that a fiscal–military state was emerging in early seventeenth-century Scotland. The crown lacked any military power beyond a few defensive strongholds and a greater concentration of artillery than individual nobles, but the political relationships between crown, nobles and burghs needed to create the bureaucratic, fiscal and military infrastructure that would free government from reliance on noble power was absent. Therefore, when political revolution broke out from the summer of 1637 it was not the crown apparatus that mattered in terms of mobilising force. Military power remained in the hands of nobles who had been trained to lead, who were linked by kinship, lordship and other forms of obligation to networks of professional soldiers, and who commanded within their localities strongholds, weapons arsenals and manpower. In April 1638, Robert Baillie wrote of his fears for the country caught in the midst of political paralysis for months. He was concerned about the possibility of civil strife arising from a royalist reaction, but it was the actions of the royalist nobility he feared, not the king. He highlighted the fact that 'our Highlands are making ready their arms', while in the Lowlands those nobles sympathetic to the king 'are openly arming among us' and were stockpiling weapons in their houses and castles.[95]

Except in a handful of larger burghs, when war did break out in 1639 and 1640 it was to the nobility that both sides turned for military leadership in conjunction with returning professionals. In Stirlingshire, for example, it was the third earl of Mar who was entrusted with organising the defence of the locality, raising 184 men in Strathdon to serve under his command, and this experience was repeated in locality after locality.[96] Of the fifty-seven regiments known to have been raised in the name of the National Covenant in 1638–9, only three regiments were not commanded by noblemen who recruited largely from their own estates. In the west the eighth earl of Argyll raised a number of Campbell regiments that secured the region from a possible royalist invasion from England. In Ayrshire, the sixth earl of Cassillis and the sixth earl of Eglinton shared responsibility for the region's defence. To meet the threat from royalists in the northeast, regiments were raised by a number of nobles from among their tenants and dependants. The Earl Marischal's Foot was commanded by the seventh earl Marischal who raised a force of around 1,000–1,200 men from his Kincardine estates and which played a crucial role in securing Aberdeen and the northeast for the covenanters between March and June 1639. It was the noble-dominated covenanter government that established a greater level of central control over the military infrastructure than previous royal governments had been able to achieve.[97]

CHAPTER 6

Governors

In December 1591 a tired and frustrated James VI complained to his clerk register that he could find no officials, that instructions were not acted upon, meetings were unattended and 'what is spoken late tonight is forgotten in the morning'. Foreign observers, too, were unimpressed by the effective authority of the Scottish crown. Even in June 1600, at a time when James VI could draw some satisfaction from international recognition, growing domestic stability and relative economic prosperity, the English agent in Edinburgh cited as evidence of the crown's weakness the murder of sir John Carmichael of that Ilk, warden of the west march, the shambolic mismanagement of a convention of estates that refused adequate taxes and the factious nature of the court. He commented that James VI presided over a 'strange government that all things should be thus cast loose'.[1] A few weeks later the Gowrie conspiracy rocked the kingdom; had it succeeded, Scotland would have been plunged into another divisive minority. Years earlier, in 1589, it was observed that the young King's power to take direct military action against rebel lords was restrained by the understandable caution of lesser nobles 'afraid of a feud hereafter if they touch any great man'. This informal restraint led sir James Melville of Halhill to observe that the crown was 'mair nor a monarque' yet 'les than electywe'. Similarly, that archetypal Tudor royal servant, lord Burghley, argued that James VI's authority was less than that of English monarchs, for 'the nobiliti ther ar not acqueynted with absolut government of ther King but rather ar them selves in a sort absolut'.[2] This description was inaccurate, but the Englishman's puzzlement is understandable, and he was correct to identify the relationship between king and nobles as crucial in defining the political parameters of royal government. In serving the king, nobles were not only filling an office, they were also expressing the quality of an affective bond, a personal relationship that went beyond working for an abstract political idea.[3] In the small, decentralised Scottish kingdom the emphasis on that bond between king and nobles was more important than institutional agencies. Hence, the observation by an English agent from the early 1580s that the nobility:

> are all born councillors to the state ... in making public laws and orders, league, war, officers, determining in high justice and other matters of state,

their authority is joint with the prince's and more than can stand in a just monarchy.[4]

Again, this is an inaccurate understanding of the locus of political authority, but it is not entirely mistaken in explaining how things in fact worked. Early modern royal government was reliant on that dynamic between kings and nobles, less so on powerful ideologies of imperial monarchy or administrative structures. It was the success of that network of relationships between the king and individual nobles that permitted royal authority to expand in the early seventeenth century, just as it was the erosion of those bonds under Charles I that led to the exposure of the insubstantial infrastructure of that government and the collapse of royal power.

The Ideal of Service

In 1586, the imprisoned queen Mary scribbled a note on the question of whether a king ought to govern with the advice of his nobility, writing: 'so far as it is not corrupt, but discreet and well bred'. The virtues that qualified nobles for service were ancestry, education and the fact that they had 'more honour and goods to lose than others'. But Mary recognised that a hereditary system could not guarantee those attributes. What did kings do about the heir of a noble house who 'has learnt nothing but to play the great man and to take his ease and to command, and to disdain the king and all laws'?[5] The issue the imprisoned queen addressed was not that of an over-powerful nobility, but of lazy, incompetent or irresponsible nobles. James VI was given more time to learn how to manage his nobles than his mother, but in September 1594 he admitted to being 'utterlie wearied and ashamed of the misgovernement of the cuntrey for lakke of concurrence of noblemen on the ane pairt, and of my extreame wante on the other pairt'. In return for aid, the king was 'resolvid to follow constantlie thaire counsaill, bake thaire conclusions, and thankefullie (quhen evir occasion sall serve) requyte thaire traivellis'. The counsel the king wanted from his nobles was that 'ye will use als mekill of my advyce, suppose I waire not a King, as of any other friends'. He spelled out his ideas in *Basilikon doron* in 1598, insisting that royal government was enhanced by the participation of the nobility since 'they must be the armes and executers of your lawes'. The king's desire that the nobility must serve him and live within the law did not detract from the fundamental reliance of the crown on their cooperation. This was not mere theory for from an early stage in his reign this king insisted that the peace and quiet of the realm required 'the gude avyse and concurrence of our nobilitie'. It was a view he retained in his mature years, instructing his privy council on 31 March 1604 to admit to their membership the master of Montrose as 'it is expedient that men of his rank and qualitie sould in thair

youth be trayned up in imployment in our affairis, that, being of rype age,
thay may be the mair capable'.[6]

The Aristotelian concept of government having as its true end the
common good was well established by the mid-fifteenth century, while the
chivalric code had long been interpreted in terms of public service and civic
responsibilities.[7] By the later sixteenth century these Renaissance values
were commonplace. In a 1569 letter of advice, the regent Moray was
reminded that the purpose of government was by:

> persuasion or constraint to induce the haill multitude and everie member
> thairof in particular, to rander his just dewtie to God and to man, to the effect
> the same haill multitude, yea and everie member thairof, may enjoy ane godlie
> honest and blissit lyfe.[8]

Moray had precisely the educational background that predisposed him to
share this view of government, and enforcing law and order was a priority
on his agenda as a royal counsellor and as regent. A generation later, the first
earl of Dunfermline, James VI's longest serving chancellor, was described
as 'a good justiciar, courteous and humane both to strangers and to his
owne countrie people'. Both men were products of a noble society that had
imbued an ideology of civil government that held out the best hope for a
well-ordered and just commonweal.[9]

The extent to which European nobles needed royal service varied con-
siderably, with the level of dependency perhaps being greatest in Poland
and Russia where something like a hereditary service nobility evolved.[10]
Scotland lay at the other end of the spectrum, with crown office being
desirable but unnecessary to the maintenance of a noble house, hence, the
relative absence of competitive bidding for office. The implied threat to
nobles as royal officers lay in a concern that virtuous men might not easily
be found within their ranks, forcing kings to turn to the growing cadre of
educated administrative officials who might challenge traditional concepts
of nobility.[11] Yet nobles were educated from an early age to expect to give
service to the king, embracing new educational opportunities and honing
their collective skills to meet the demands of royal service, even if nobles
largely saw service in terms of advancing the interests of their house, its
kinsmen and friends. Halhill recognised the dangers in this ambition
and encouraged James VI to take the view that 'na man ... be placit nor
preferrit about your maiestie, be favour of surname, kin, frend or allia, bot
for sufficiency, vertu, and loyalte'. Nevertheless, kings had to be careful of
ignoring the nobility or dismissing their demands. An accusation against the
unpopular government of the first duke of Lennox and the earl of Arran in
1581–2 was that 'maters of estat were not governed by advice of nobilitie'.
Similarly, when the king returned from Denmark in 1590, it was believed
that 'the wholl nobilitie shalbe prejudiced in their auncient priveledges for
their free accesse to the King's person, and vote in Counsell and matters of

estate'. This allegation was made by one group of nobles aggrieved at the behaviour of another court faction in seeking to monopolise power and led to a withdrawal of cooperation in the court, parliament and privy council that quickly brought the king to his senses.[12] But the self-interested behaviour of nobles in royal office remained a problem that kings were unable to address. A generation later, the first lord Napier advised Charles I that he was not well served either by great men with extensive clienteles or by men whose first priority was enriching themselves.[13]

Consequently, the rise and fall of nobles was accompanied by changes in crown personnel that reflected altered patterns of political patronage. Hence, networks of Setons, Murrays, Melvilles and Stewarts spread throughout the court and council after the fourth earl of Morton's fall in 1580. John Maitland of Thirlestane's introduction of his Seton cousins to the privy council and his acquisition of the office of secretary for his nephew, Richard Cockburn of Clerkington, had little to do with changing the nature of royal administration and much to do with strengthening Thirlestane's power base and rewarding his family.[14] In c. 1630, sir John Stewart of Traquair wrote to his patron, the sixth earl of Morton, about the vacancy in the office of lord president of the court of session, emphasising 'how much it may concerne your Lordship that it be sean your freind is preferred'.[15] James VI was aware of the problems created by noble clientage networks, warning against those who recommended their friends and kinsmen for royal offices 'more for serving in effect, their friends that put them in, then their master that admitted them'.[16] There was nothing he could do to prevent it.

While the apparent public spiritedness of the Venetian patriciate was beyond what Scottish kings might expect of their nobles, the latter were not lacking in a sense of public duty. Napier suggested that in the world of the 1630s it made sense for a wise man 'to fix his private ends on the center of the publik good' such that 'the circle of his travels may compas the publik good, and easilie in it his own'.[17] But good service was not new. In October 1589, before James VI departed for Norway, he personally selected those nobles who would govern in his absence 'quhilk wes done with gritt quyetnes and peace'.[18] Naturally, those men who served their prince expected rewards for as the justice clerk, John Cockburn of Ormiston, told the king in a letter in 1615, royal gifts encourage men 'to indevore thamselves by all service on thair pairt to acquyre ane impressioun in thair princes heartis of thair dewtyfull caryage'.[19] Service earned less immediately tangible means of applying leverage on the crown. A memorial compiled for the second earl of Mar c. 1625 details how his family's good service to the kings of Scotland since 1366 might be deployed to escape the worst implications of the revocation.[20] Besides, to turn away from royal service could be risky as powerful men suddenly became vulnerable. When in 1629 the elderly Mar called a council of his kinsmen and friends to discuss relinquishing the office of lord treasurer and retiring, his clients argued against it, recognising that 'how soone so evir he gave over the quhyt staf he micht resolve to leave at home in Allowa [= Alloa], for no man wald regard him thereafter'.[21] Mar was a powerful and rich man, but without office he would be damaged in his private actions, and under pressure from his kinsmen, friends and dependants he soldiered on for a few more years. In 1594, the clergy lobbied the seventh earl of Argyll to take up the office of lieutenant in the campaign against the Catholic earls as this 'wald be a thing acceptable unto God, profitable for the commonweill, and honorable for himself'.[22] Public duty, private interests and even religious calling all demanded of nobles that they take their place on the public stage.

Persuading nobles to fulfil the role of a royal servant was difficult because they were busy with their own affairs and were uninterested in the routine of government. Halhill argued in 1590 that the crown had no choice other than to make the nobility 'partakers of honours and offices', but he recognised their problem:

> For the nobilite being sa many, be lang evell custom, they esteam them selves to be borne consellours; and yet will not remain at court, nor upon the consaill, without [= unless] it be at conventions, or for some particulaire proffit.[23]

In his opening speech to parliament in July 1593, James VI complained about the number of nobles and councillors who deserted the court so that he was 'slenderly accompanied' and unable to conduct business. At the beginning of 1600, apathy among the nobility was such that 'noblemen forbear Court and Council, unless for their own particulars, when their occasions force them'. A few months later, a delegation of Border barons did not bother to turn up in Edinburgh for a meeting with the king.[24] Unfortunately, the king's penury before 1603 ensured that there was little to attract nobles to court. Why should a nobleman bother with the hard work, not to mention the financial and personal risks, of royal service? This was a question the regent Morton attempted to answer shortly before surrendering office in March 1578: 'for ambicioun surely we think nane can justlie accuse us, for in our privat estait we culd and can leif as weill contented as ony of our degre in Scotland, without further aspiring'. While Morton was being disingenuous, he made a pertinent point. When chancellor Dunfermline died in June 1622, neither secretary Melrose nor treasurer Mar wanted the office, which went by default to sir George Hay of Kinfauns.[25] Moreover, most royal service was mundane, like the commission undertaken by a number of nobles in 1606 to investigate the threat posed to the burgh of Dumbarton by flooding.[26] This was the nitty-gritty of government and it is difficult to see its attractions to all but a minority of men who enjoyed administration, men like Mar who took up the office of treasurer in

1616 and was given a five-page briefing paper on his new duties. Besides, there were other responsibilities that did not disappear on assuming royal office. Sir James Campbell of Ardkinglass resigned from his office of comptroller of the household in July 1585 because he needed to spend time on the business of his chief, the young seventh earl of Argyll. Such pressures were even greater on lords who had huge estates to run and complex local affairs to oversee.[27] As the first earl of Melrose told Mar in 1622, royal office was 'a casuell imployment of no assured continouance', and the treasurer could at any time retire 'to your old assumption which is the honorable estate God wes pleased to allote to you at our birth where your lo[rdship] may exspect more secure contentment in a day, nor in this charge in a yeir'.[28]

The experience of early modern European nobilities was that strong, expansionist government provided opportunities for employment, advancement and enrichment.[29] While Scotland did not experience any marked change in the scale of royal government, other than in acquiring access to the English court after 1603, for some families the emphasis on service was especially strong. In 1621, the first viscount Lauderdale solicited support for a vacancy on prince Charles's council because he desired 'to succeid to my forebears, who, to the fourth generatione, hes had the honour to be employed in particular services be his Hyenes most noble ancestors'. For the Maitlands this record of royal service was due to a combination of geographic proximity to Edinburgh and family patronage. The Elphinstones also had a good royal service history, reinforced by insider connections, and by 1605 there were four members of the family on the privy council. The Elphinstones were raised to the peerage in 1509, while the Maitlands had to wait until 1590, but both these noble houses enjoyed a long and close relationship to the crown.[30] In discussing his own service to the king, Halhill proudly described himself as James VI's 'humble servant, as his domestik, first in the office of gentilman of his chamber, and syn of his consall'. Even the king's own cousin, the second duke of Lennox, was described by the privy council in May 1604 as the king's 'owne creature', a formulation of words intended as complimentary.[31] For a handful of nobles service did approximate to servility. The first earl of Dunbar was one of James VI's most faithful household servants, having begun his career as a boy in the royal household, and he owed everything to his master. In November 1606, he wrote to Mar about colleagues who lacked his own apparachnik enthusiasm, threatening that 'gew thay will nocht do thar honeste dewtteyis his Majeste will be servitt with otheris, for that is honeste men anewe that will strewe to do his Majestie serves'. Dunbar was of relatively humble origins, as was another household boy made good, David Murray, first lord Scone, whose only response to a question about his role in persecuting presbyterian ministers was 'I must serve the king'. It was certainly easier for the king to discipline those nobles of less exalted rank and less independent means, men like the first lord Balfour of Burleigh whose opposition to the king's tax demands and to his choice of lords of the articles in the 1612 parliament resulted in his removal from the privy council.[32]

On the whole James VI agreed with Halhill that he should 'hear a chosen nomber of honest consellouris raisoun upon his affaires', rather than concurring with chancellor Arran who told the young king that this would prove 'a faschious busynes to be encombrit with many contrary oppinions'.[33] In early 1626, the elderly second earl of Mar lectured Charles I on this point, telling him that 'a hundrith tyms your worthie father hes sentt doun directions unto us quhilk we have stayed, and he hes givin us thanks for itt quhen we have informed him of the trewth'. In spite of his long years as a courtier, the first earl of Roxburghe expressed approval of a fellow nobleman who was determined 'to hold to that libertie which ane frie mynd requireth, to think as ye say, and to say as ye think'. Like many nobles who shared the same educational background and cultural values, Roxburghe thought a man should act according to his virtue and that 'reasone should be his directer, according to the good or evill that may follow either in the mater, or in the man himself'. Such honest counsel was more likely to be forthcoming from the higher nobility who spoke with the confidence derived from a life-time of exercising power over their own domains, who enjoyed the wealth to ensure that they could survive without crown employment, and who possessed the education that encouraged independent thought. Those nobles who were dependent on royal patronage were understandably more cautious, but even within the inner circles of James VI's government there was disagreement over this issue. When in the course of a debate within the privy council in June 1611, archbishop Spottiswoode told sir Thomas Hamilton of Drumcairn that 'it wes frie to Counsallours to expres thair opiniones', the latter replied that 'my office wes ane warrand to me to meanteane his Majesties prerogative'. Chancellor Dunfermline recognised limitations to his obedience over the king's liturgical policy, and when challenged by Drumcairn, now promoted to earl of Melrose, 'Will ye reasoun, whether his Majestie must be obeyed or not?', Dunfermline replied, 'We may reason, whether we sall be the bishops' hangmen or not'.[34] Dunfermline's successor, sir George Hay of Kinfauns, told Charles I during a debate on the revocation that 'quhatever counsalor be he that gives his Majestie nocht trew counsall both against his knawledge and law, that is nott aine loyall subjectt'. Charles I, however, remodelled his privy council to remove the independently-minded men tolerated by his father, and was immune to advice once his mind was made up. Nor did he like the frankness with which Scots nobles offered their opinion, a 'sturdy style of address', that was observed with distaste by the English courtier, Edward Hyde. The failure to allow criticism from within the privy council contributed to the unravelling of royal government in 1637–8 when faced with deter-mined opposition.[35] Mar, Roxburghe, Dunfermline and Kinnoul's attitude approximated more closely to the Renaissance nobleman's idea of a good counsellor than the knee-jerk subservience of Dunbar, Scone and Melrose.

Parliament

The early modern period saw an erosion of the powers of representative assemblies throughout Europe. The purpose of such bodies was to meet the needs of rulers rather than to engage in constitutional deliberation, and if rulers could acquire their objectives by other means the reason to summon assemblies was reduced. The relative decline of assemblies, therefore, was largely a consequence of pragmatic decisions, not ideological differences within the political community.[36] By the early fourteenth century, the Scottish parliament had acquired a central role in ideas about sovereignty and in the consciousness of the political elite, but over the course of the following two and a half centuries its power vis-à-vis the crown waxed and waned with the life cycle of individual kings. While parliament's claim to be the fount of political legitimacy was established, it was at risk of being ignored in the early years of the sixteenth century during the reign of James IV. The repetitive dynastic crisis that befell the Stewart monarchy produced further minorities, however, and by the 1550s there were indications that parliament's importance to the commonweal had been rediscovered.[37] That centrality of the estates to the commonweal was evident in the summer of 1560 when parliament sat to resolve the political fall-out after the overthrow of the French-backed Guise regime and the Roman Catholic church.[38]

In the unstable politics of the period from the Reformation parliament in 1560 to the end of the civil war in 1573, there were fifteen parliaments and twelve conventions of the estates or the nobility. The only year in which either parliament or a convention did not sit was 1562, while in the summer of 1571 rival parliaments loyal to the King's Party and the Queen's Party sat at Edinburgh. From the end of the civil war to the regal union in 1603 there were twelve parliaments, and the king also consulted through conventions of the estates or conventions of the nobility, bodies with less formal authority than parliament, but which offered a quick route for the king to consult a selected range of opinion. The use of conventions grew in the later sixteenth century, and between 1573 and 1603 forty-eight conventions have been identified to date so that the only years in which the political community was not summoned were 1574, 1576, 1577, 1580 and 1589. Consultation of the individual estates, especially the nobility, occurred in preparatory meetings, such as when James VI summoned nobles to a meeting on 20 April 1592 to discuss issues to be resolved at a parliament set for the following month. Parliaments and conventions, alongside the privy council and the court generally, ensured that, at least until 1603, the nobility was in regular contact with the king and that royal government was consultative. After 1603 the king drew on a narrower range of counsel at court. From 1609, there was an increasing number of years in which no representative body sat, and neither a parliament nor convention was held in 1610–11, 1613–16, 1618–20, 1622–4, 1626–9, 1631–2 and 1634–9. There was a reduction to nine parliaments and eight conventions in the period to 1633, following which there was no meeting of the estates until the revolutionary parliament of 1639–40.[39]

Scottish society was not divided into three recognisable estates in spite of this being the conceptual framework within which sir David Lindsay's *Ane satyre of the thrie estatis* (1552) directs its devastating critique. The late medieval commonweal's legacy of parliament as an assembly organised around the interests of three estates, the clergy, the nobility and the burghs, continued to influence how representation was conceived, but questions were asked about the role of the church, the influence of the king and the responsibilities of the lesser nobility.[40] Consequently, the latter half of the sixteenth century and the early decades of the seventeenth century saw changes in the composition of parliament that significantly increased the representation of the landed nobility. The second estate of nobles had evolved since the thirteenth century to embrace a titled peerage on which was conferred the privilege of an individual summons to parliament 'to have plaice, voit, ranke and dignitie among the noblemen of the kingdome'. In 1560, the number of peers stood at fifty and rose to fifty-eight by 1600 with most of the increase taking place in the 1580s. Thereafter there was a more dramatic expansion to seventy-four peers by 1610, eighty-one by 1620, ninety-six by 1630 and there were 106 peers in 1637.[41] Part of this increase in numbers was fuelled by the secularisation of the temporal estates of the church, a process that saw the gradual replacement of the twenty-seven heads of religious houses by hereditary lords of parliament, which was formalised in the creation of the lords of erection in 1606. Opposition within the church to any form of representation was only partially overcome in 1606 with the formal re-establishment by parliament of an episcopal estate of two archbishops and eleven bishops appointed by the king.[42] The third estate of burgh commissioners grew in number from thirty-five royal burghs in 1560 to fifty-six in 1633, attendance by burgh commissioners became more regular, the growing importance of taxation raised the political influence of the burghs and the convention of royal burghs ensured their cohesion and effectiveness in parliament, although the burgh commissioners never represented a threat to the nobility.[43]

Confusion over the role of the lesser nobility has led to some misunderstanding of the significance that should be attached to the emergence of what amounted to a fourth estate.[44] Barons or lairds had always attended parliament, although that attendance was unpredictable; they appeared in strength at the 1556 parliament, while none was present at the 1558 parliament.[45] The desire to attend parliament depended on the issues under discussion, taxation being high on the agenda in 1556, and while individual barons acted on their initiative, many lesser nobles were kinsmen and dependants of powerful lords and attended at their behest. When summoned to parliament, the greater nobles believed they had the right to be 'honestlie accompaneit with our freindis according to our estait'. In an undated letter, the eighth lord Maxwell informed John Maxwell of Pollok that he would be attending parliament, and he wanted Pollok to ensure that he had an adequate entourage befitting 'the honour of our house ... as uthers houses of the realme at sic tymis usis'. At the 1560 parliament, the duke of Chatelherault was accompanied by eleven kinsmen and dependants, the fourth earl Marischal by a similar number and the fourth earl of Glencairn by at least nine followers. The Reformation parliament saw a successful packing of parliament with at least ninety-nine barons, mostly Protestants, who exploited the ambiguity surrounding baronial attendance.[46] It was in this revolutionary context that those barons, encouraged no doubt by their lords, petitioned for the formal regularisation of their right to attend. These lesser nobles claimed 'we aucht to be hard to ressoune and vote in all caussis concerning the commoune wele alsweill in counsallis as in parliamentis', and they were rewarded by an ad hoc arrangement that legitimised the unusually high attendance.[47]

Thereafter the pattern of irregular attendance resumed. The few surviving sederunts for the following decades indicate that a handful of barons sat in the conventions of 1561 and 1566, mostly as officers of the crown. No barons were present at the April 1567 parliament, but 'diverse barons' were in attendance at the August 1567 convention, another highly-charged political occasion when the revolutionary regency government needed a demonstration of public support. The petition for representation by the barons in December 1567 followed, and the estates agreed that 'of law and reason, the barons of this realm ought to have vote in parliament as a part of the nobility'.[48] Perhaps this recognition encouraged 'a great number of ancient barons' to turn up at a well-attended convention at Perth in July 1569, while the November 1572 convention lists the names of twenty-eight barons 'with many others' under 'those who assisted'. Thereafter, with the ending of the civil war, apart from a handful of crown officers, the barons disappear from surviving sederunts.[49]

The question of baronial attendance remained unresolved, but it became more pertinent as James VI reached adulthood and the extent of the crown's poverty became increasingly pressing. At the December 1585 parliament, a petition was presented to the king suggesting that baronial representation would assist the king and parliament 'to be truly informed of the needs and causes pertaining to his loving subjects in all estates, especially the commons of the realm'. It requested that he consider the issue and drew attention to the abortive legislation of James I's reign that sought to establish a form of shire representation. The petition was presented by sir John Maitland of

Thirlestane and sir William Douglas of Glenbervie, and since the former was secretary of state it is likely that the initiative had crown backing.[50] It was not until after the king attained his full majority that parliament addressed the problem in the summer of 1587. The new legislation was modelled on the 1428 act, determining that freeholders who met the property qualification of 40 shillings of old extent valuation would annually elect two commissioners for each shire (Clackmannan and Kinross had one commissioner each) to attend parliament if summoned. The principle of personal attendance by all tenants-in-chief of the crown, which the lesser barons had been avoiding for centuries, was abandoned since the election of shire commissioners 'shall relieve the whole remaining small barons and freeholders of the shires of their suits and presence owing in the said parliaments'. The 1587 legislation regularised baronial responsibilities, investing in the two shire commissioners rights of *plena potestas*, but restricting their independence by allocating only one vote between them. The barons were required to pay £40,000 in taxation for this new privilege, indicating that the crown's primary concern was to bring the lesser nobility into regular discussions about royal finances.[51]

The 1587 act broadened contact between the crown and the localities, while removing the possibility of parliament being flooded with a potentially unmanageable number of lairds as occurred in 1560. The most significant consequence of the act in terms of political power within the estates was to increase the regular representation of the landed nobility. There was no tension between the new shire commissioners and the peerage, all of whom were drawn from the same noble society with shared values and assumptions. Those barons responsible for supervising shire elections in 1589 were drawn from the wealthier and more powerful of the untitled baronial houses, and the heads of a little over a quarter of these houses entered the peerage over the next four decades.[52] The barons paid the £40,000, but if James VI expected them to be more compliant over taxation he miscalculated seriously as it was the shire commissioners who provided the most vociferous opposition to tax demands throughout the 1590s.[53]

Parliamentary politics were not determined by mere head counting, although the above evidence indicates a significant growth in the numerical strength of the nobility – peerage and barons – at the expense of the church with the burghs just holding their own. A full attendance in 1563 would have been fifty-three clerics, fifty-one peers, forty-four burgh commissioners and an indeterminate number of barons. Actual attendance was normally lower: at a parliament in April 1566 there were eighteen clerics, twenty-six peers and the commissioners of seven burghs present, while at a parliament in May 1584 there were sixteen clergy (eleven were lay commendators), twenty-five nobles and the commissioners of twenty-three burghs present. These parliaments were reasonably well-attended, whereas a convention in December 1583 was attended by four clergy, nineteen peers, three barons and five officers of state, while a convention in September 1594 was attended by two clergy, seven peers, twelve barons, a number of whom were there as officers of state, and the commissioners of four burghs. By 1633 the potential membership of parliament had increased to 248 (thirteen clergy, 106 peers, sixty-four shire commissioners, fifty-seven burgh commissioners and up to eight officers of state), and the turn-out was the largest to date. The assembly included twelve clergy, sixty-six peers (including nineteen proxies), forty-five shire commissioners (representing twenty-seven shires), fifty-one burgh commissioners and eight officers of state, a total of 182 members.[54] Whatever the numbers in attendance, these unicameral assemblies, where voting was by head and not by estate, the nobility casting their votes first, were dominated by the nobility, particularly the more powerful magnate houses. In a political culture shaped by lordship and clientage, bishops, commendators, officers of state and burgh commissioners often were kinsmen, friends and dependants of lords. For example, at a convention of estates in Perth in July 1569 the regent Moray presided over a body that ostensibly contained twenty-eight peers or their heirs and twenty-nine others. But of the five bishops, four were kinsmen or clients of peers, and five of the burgh delegations were led by baronial provosts who were clients of peers.[55]

Some caution must be exercised in assigning to nobles too great an eagerness to attend parliament and the fines were levied to encourage attendance.[56] Lord Hamilton refused to attend the 1587 parliament, which introduced fines on absentees, because of a private feud and the same parliament saw the sixth lord Hume remain in his lodgings and offering to fight a duel with the sixth lord Fleming over an issue of precedence. For many peers the most important issues were resolving who had the right to bear the crown, whether the hereditary marshal or constable had superior jurisdiction during the sitting of parliament, or who had precedence in the order of voting. James VI was 'much offended' and frustrated by nobles who did not frequent either parliament or conventions, such as in March 1597 when the earls of Argyll, Crawford, Marischal and Glencairn stayed away from a thinly attended convention at Perth. The crown continued to pressurise peers to attend parliament or conventions after 1603, for example, in seeking to ensure a good attendance at the 1609 parliament the earl of Dunbar wrote to the fifth earl Marischal pleading with him 'not to frustrate his Majesties occasions by your absence, nor the noblemen that will looke to have your assistance'. Kings did become more sympathetic to the use of proxy votes, however, particularly if they were given to officers of state.[57]

The commissioners for the barons proved equally unwilling to leave their localities, and the issue of expenses proved to be sensitive, leaving many commissioners regretful of their experience.[58] The organisation of elections was devolved to local men, such as in May 1589 when sir John Maxwell of Pollok and John Shaw of Greenock were instructed to convene a meeting of

Renfrewshire barons to choose commissioners for parliament. At the 1592 parliament at least twelve barons were in attendance from a possible total of thirty-five, and they had equal representation on the lords of the articles with the other three estates. Early modern society was often uncomfortable with elections as they represented division within the community and it was not uncommon for names to emerge by consensus. How much competition took place within shires is unknown, but the earliest record of an election occurred on 31 January 1596 in Aberdeenshire when sir John Leslie of Balquhane and sir Alexander Fraser of Philorth were elected.[59] Parliamentary representation acquired unwanted associations with royal fiscal expedients as the crown sought to enlist the help of shire commissioners as collectors of taxation. When in 1588 the barons of Ayrshire gathered to elect a collector of the taxation, a decision had to be postponed because of the low turn-out. Many freeholders were more concerned at finding ways to avoid paying the tax than to claim any rights to vote.[60] The new system slowly gained acceptance, however, and in Fife the commission of 30 September 1593 authorising sir John Wemyss of Tullybreck and sir John Melville of Carnbee to represent the barons of the shire in parliament was signed by only twelve barons.[61]

In the changing political climate of the early seventeenth century, the crown tried to manipulate shire elections to acquire greater influence over parliament. In 1612, royal letters were issued recommending the lairds of Kilsyth and Dundas as commissioners for Linlithgow and the crown tightened up its record-keeping of commissioners throughout the kingdom.[62] The barons remained apathetic and elections of shire commissioners failed to meet the expectations of crown officials. Preparations for the parliament that met in 1633 began in 1627 and it was prorogued eight times. During that period the crown put much effort into managing the shire and burgh elections. In 1629, Charles I issued instructions that sheriffs, a growing number of whom were royal nominees, and other influential nobles should ensure the election of 'such able and sufficient men as you kno to be weall affected to our service and the publick good'. Yet there was persistent opposition to crown interference. In August 1628, the electors of Midlothian were summoned by the privy council to explain their conduct; in 1629 the electors of Ayrshire were charged with taking 'a direct contrarie course' in their choice of commissioners; and in the autumn of 1632 it was revealed that thirty sheriffdoms had not carried out annual elections. At the 1633 parliament only forty-five of the possible sixty-four shire commissioners attended, nine shires sending only one of their two commissioners and six not sending any representation. This level of disengagement was in spite of heavy-handed interference by the privy council in the elections in Bute, Perth, Dumbarton, Renfrew and Stirling where there had been abuses or irregularities. Fife did not bother to elect any commissioners on the excuse that the sheriff had been at court, but the real reason was political lethargy.[63] The electoral system was prone to misunderstanding and bungling. In 1629, Dumbarton elected commissioners who lacked the necessary property qualifications, while in Roxburgh the barons chose Andrew Riddell of that Ilk, 'a man of great age, being now neere fourescore yeeres and very infirme in his persoun and his judgement not so rype and quicke as formerlie it hes beene'.[64] Disenchantment with Charles I's policies accounts for much of the dissent, but the crown's desire to operate through lesser nobles backfired because political power remained in the hands of the great lords whose willingness to co-operate was problematic. When in 1627 Charles I wanted to secure the election of sir William Stewart of Minto and sir James Lockhart of Castlehill as commissioners for Lanarkshire it was to the third marquis of Hamilton that he turned for help. Two years later in Ayrshire it was another hereditary sheriff, the second lord Loudon, who organised the elections. In Argyll, magnate influence was even more blatant, and in April 1633 Archibald Campbell, lord Lorne, simply summoned his friends to choose baronial commissioners to the forthcoming parliament.[65]

The eagerness among nobles to address private matters is reflected in the fact that there were more private than public acts in most parliaments, but the desire to acquire ratifications of titles offered the crown a useful political lever. In April 1567, a desperate queen Mary held a parliament that conducted little public business of note, but it passed eighteen ratifications and eight reductions of forfeitures. On this occasion the manipulation of patronage failed to produce the desired political support. On other occasions parliament was used to recognise new regimes, as in 1581 when parliament rewarded those men who had connived in the fall of the fourth earl of Morton while forfeiting the friends of the former regent.[66] James VI observed that parliament was prone to 'being abused to men's particulars' with legislation being passed by the estates without fully understanding who was likely to be hurt by it. Certainly, individual nobles behaved without thought to the public good. When at the July 1593 parliament, lord Hamilton failed to get Arbroath abbey erected into a temporal lordship, he stormed out of the chamber. Prior to the sitting of the Perth parliament in the summer of 1606, the fifth earl of Cassillis wrote to his friend, John Vaus of Barnbarroch, asking the latter to accompany him because the earl had important business to transact, not because there were significant public issues to discuss. Similarly, Gordonstoun's only comment on the controversial 1617 parliament was that he 'wes verie carefull least anie thing should then passe at that convention in prejudice of the Earle of Southerland'.[67]

A report prepared for the English government in 1580 observed that 'the Prince's authority is so limited that he has not so much as a negative, but must ratify that which is agreed on by the suffrage of the greater part of the nobility and commons in their Parliaments'.[68] There always had been a tension between kings and the estates over the management of parliamentary business and the desire for a free parliament, but it was not only kings who sought to exercise political control. In spite of an assurance that all might attend the 1560 parliament 'without fear or force done to them by any person', the Protestant lords ruthlessly set out to achieve their objectives, casting doubt on John Knox's claim that this assembly was 'more lawful and more free than any other parliament that they are able to produce this hundred years before it, or yet any that hath ensued since it was'. Nevertheless, there was within the political community an idea of the freedom of parliament to offer counsel. In May 1571, the fourth earl of Morton argued that 'it has always been the ancient custom that the noblemen convening in parliament should resist all unlawful and unreasonable proceedings by good reason and probabill argumentis' in full parliament and in the lords of the articles. When in July 1578 at the height of the crisis that accompanied the end of Morton's regency, a parliament was held within the threatening confines of Stirling castle, the sixth lord Lindsay protested that it was not a free parliament, prompting the young king and the gathered estates to issue a formal statement that this was 'a free and public parliament'.[69]

The adult James VI was less comfortable with the idea that a free parliament might facilitate criticism of himself and opposition to his policies. Following the Ruthven raid, a convention of the estates sat in October 1582 and approved the actions of the new government, but in December of 1583, following the king's escape, another convention of estates condemned the actions of the Ruthven lords and had the declaration of the previous convention deleted. Meetings of the estates were unpredictable and continued to be subject to changing political pressures. The 1584 parliament showed a surprising appetite for authoritarian government; in 1585 the Ruthven lords were restored; the 1587 parliament proved to be highly co-operative and marked the king's formal majority with a substantial legislative programme; the 1592 parliament saw the king desperately trying to establish his authority against a background of deteriorating confidence in his policies and judgement.[70] At a convention of the nobility held in January 1593 the king was angered when large numbers of barons tried to persuade him into taking a hard line with the Catholic earls, and he 'allegeit that he fand thayme never sa obedient to conveyne at his command, nather in tyme nor nomber'.[71] Richard Douglas poured scorn on James VI's falling popularity, pointing out that 'the King by his own negligence and the fault of his officers is in a miserable estate', and that such was the mutual contempt between king and nobility that hardly anyone had attended the recent convention on 28 October 1598. That year the king tried to tighten his control over attendance at conventions and in the drawing up of agendas for discussion, but the nobles used their influence on the privy council and their muscle on the streets of Edinburgh to dash the proposals. The second earl of Mar led the opposition, making a scathing attack on those nobles prepared to leave all to the king's pleasure, saying 'it was not well that they should not freely give their advice as Councillors'.[72] Publicly the king conceded the point, and James VI was capable of using similar language. In 1604 when parliamentary union with England was discussed, the king let it be known that his 'inclinatioun is to haif it led with a sein contentement of all thame quha ar fitte to juge quhat is thair best'. But the public rhetoric disguised an increasing impatience with parliament, an impatience magnified by parliament's obstructive derailing of the king's union project.[73]

It is understandable that some historians are led to see parliament as an administrative arm of royal government, since that was how kings wished it to be understood. James VI insisted in *The trew law of free monarchie* (1598) that parliament was 'nothing but the head Court of the king and his vassals', a denial of parliament's role as the pre-eminent seat of sovereign authority in the kingdom.[74] Yet in spite of counselling against the holding of frequent parliaments, until his departure for London the king summoned the estates at least once a year, often with disappointing consequences, particularly in relation to much-needed taxes. Even in the more stable political conditions of the later 1590s the estates remained beyond royal control as the meeting of the June 1600 convention demonstrates. The king wrote to prominent barons and held pre-meetings between privy councillors and leading parliamentary commissioners 'for advising, resoning and conferring', but the convention of the estates denied the king's tax demands, provoking James to threaten to remove the barons from parliament because of the numbers of lesser nobles voting against his proposals.[75]

The regal union of 1603 dramatically altered the king's relationship with parliament, and James VI and I now had two other parliaments to consider in London and Dublin.[76] The king was no longer present in person, and James VI attended parliament again only in 1617, while Charles I made his only pre-revolution appearance in 1633. Instead, the king was represented by a new officer, the king's commissioner, a high-ranking nobleman, the first of whom in 1604 was the third earl of Montrose. The cooperation of nobles of this rank was essential for parliament to function effectively as a forum in which a range of negotiations took place informed by court politics, conciliar disagreements, local and personal loyalties and feuds. In the spring of 1609 it was the earl of Dunbar and the previously critical Mar who were entrusted with managing the king's business through parliament, and with keeping a record of those who supported or opposed royal policies. For the potentially explosive 1621 parliament James VI turned to the second marquis of Hamilton to manage affairs. In 1633, it was Hamilton's son, the third marquis, who was urged by the sixth earl of Morton 'to mak thingis in parliament the easier and to the end that you may have your awin thankis I pray you wret to your freindis that they may give thar hartie concurrance to the advancement of our Masters just ends'.[77] But the king's political position was strengthened because he was no longer vulnerable to direct noble pressure, he was less dependent on parliamentary taxes and he had greater patronage resources at his disposal. In addition to the eight officers of state who sat in parliament, one form of patronage that gave the king a useful core of loyalists was the restoration of the clerical estate in the form of the crown-appointed episcopate. This restoration had faced noble opposition, and the king's determination to raise the status of the two archbishops led in 1609 to 'great derisioun and detestatioun' from among the nobility.[78]

Central to the crown's increased control of parliamentary procedure was the role of the committee of the lords of the articles. This preparatory committee screened and redrafted proposed legislation along with agreeing parliamentary business. Members were elected by estate in elections free from overt royal control and the committee debated relatively freely, although political management could intrude on its conduct, as occurred in 1560 and 1584. From 1606 the crown's control over the election process tightened, but even within the privy council there was unease, particularly from nobles concerned at the increasing use of bishops. After 1612 the crown's control grew such that by 1621 all the members of the committee of the articles were crown nominees.[79]

By a series of unplanned stages over succeeding parliaments the royalist core of officers of state, privy councillors and bishops armed with patronage set about reducing the possibilities of defeating the crown's agenda. Even by the 1606 parliament there was an improvement in the management of business, for example, the creation of the lords of erection bought compliance from a number of powerful noble families. Yet the combination of provocative ecclesiastical policies, increasing demands for taxation and the inevitable division into court families who benefited from royal patronage and those who were disappointed brought into being a pool of dissent that found a voice at parliament. At the 1612 parliament, the crown reduced its tax demands and retreated from the king's plans to increase the power of bishops in determining the composition of the committee of the lords of the articles, a point which the 'noble men debated ... verie preciselie'. With chancellor Dunfermline threatening to resign in defence of noble privileges, it was only the intervention of the second marquis of Hamilton and the effective organisational skills of Drumcairn, the lord clerk register, that rescued the crown from further embarrassment.[80] Noble concerns were expressed publicly, and James VI was irritated by rumours that 'theye begin to talke in Scotland of ancient nobiletye and there previledges must not be brokin'. Viscount Fenton warned the second earl of Mar, as argumentative as ever, that 'you have ever lyked too mutche to dispute in publike and at suche tymes'. Yet Mar was a hard-working privy councillor, and even Fenton, a close intimate of the bedchamber, disliked the king's increasingly intolerant attitude, being 'nevir soe angrye in my lyfe as I was at that conference with his Majestie, quher we had a great dispute'.[81]

Crown officers learned from the experience of managing the 1612 parliament, but those men who had opposed the king also absorbed lessons.

At the 1617 convention of estates the nobility sabotaged the king's agenda, focusing on the role of officers of state and privy councillors within conventions, arguing that if they were allowed to vote, the king could swamp assemblies with his servants. Secretary Binning commented that 'none appeired so bent in the mater as the small barrons'.[82] In 1621, in the context of looming war and the king's problems with the English parliament, a hand-picked convention of estates proved to be reluctant to vote a tax. The king summoned a parliament at which peers and barons who opposed the taxation and the liturgical policy met to discuss their grievances and came close to wrecking the crown's programme. A carefully selected and closely managed committee of the lords of the articles, and the effective deployment of royal patronage won the day, but between forty-eight and fifty-one individuals voted against the crown, which carried its legislative programme with a majority of only twenty-seven votes. Among the nobility, twenty-eight peers and the baronial commissioners of nine shires voted in favour of the king's legislative programme, while twenty-two peers and the baronial commissioners representing thirteen shires abstained or voted against it. That disloyalty was not forgotten and when Mar sought assurances over his lawsuit against the fourth lord Elphinstone, the king told him not to worry for 'he remembers of my Lord Elphinstones cariage and his sones bothe in tyme of the Parliament'.[83]

Opposition continued under Charles I. The conventions of the estates held in 1625 and 1630 were relatively generous with regard to taxation, hence, the continued usefulness of parliament to the king. Nevertheless, these conventions refused to be cowed by the crown. At the 1625 convention of estates the barons petitioned on a number of issues, including against royal interference in the court of session, while at the 1630 convention of the estates the select committees established to review economic policies were used to express dissenting views and to form networks among the discontented.[84] By the time parliament met in 1633, the revocation, the teind commission, the role of bishops, liturgical reform, Roman Catholics at court and concern at diminishing Scottish influence on the anglicised monarchy made a meeting of the estates risky for the crown. Huge efforts were put into managing elections and attendance and into controlling parliamentary procedures. Less than a quarter of the 182 members of parliament had attended the previous meeting in 1621, and this included twenty men (six peers, two shire commissioners and eight burgh commissioners) who had voted against the five articles of Perth. The sixth earl of Rothes, the second lord Loudon and the second lord Balmerino emerged as leaders of a nascent opposition, and Balmerino's role in preparing a supplication protesting against crown policies and practices resulted in 1635 in his trial and conviction for treason, although the death sentence was not carried out. Meanwhile, the crown agenda, including further unpopular taxes, was ruthlessly forced through parliament by the court. The crown's victory in

1633 and the subsequent victimisation of Balmerino for an offence that included criticism of the conduct of the parliament, could not conceal the complete break-down of trust between the king and a wide range of the political community, most significantly the nobility.[85]

Privy Councillors, Officers of State and Judges

The Lords of the Congregation claimed in 1559 that 'God hath made us counsellers, by birth, of this realme', and half a century later Alexander Gardyne, the Aberdeen poet and advocate, praised the members of the privy council and court of session as the 'Most powerfull peers, cheef pillers of th'Empire,/ Strong Pedestals, whereon the State does stay'.[86] Privy councillors were the king's servants, swearing an oath of allegiance before admission to office, but most councillors were nobles, hence, the description by the privy council of the fifth earl of Bothwell as 'a borne and chosin counsellour'.[87] Privy councillors had access to the king, influence over royal policies, a route to patronage and wealth, and they were positioned to promote or protect private interests. The value in having friends on the privy council and in the law courts was not lost on Gordonstoun, who advised his nephew 'to have some of the ringleaders both in counsell and session to be your assured friends'. Such connections were useful as when in January 1600 the second duke of Lennox raised before his fellow councillors the problem his tenants were facing from Campbell raids.[88] Furthermore, the privy council offered a route to advancement, and some spectacular success stories emerged from that body, although the royal court, military command, diplomatic service, regional offices and the court of session were all equally desirable, and kings did not regard privy council service as more important than other forms of service.[89]

The privy council was a new body formed during the reign of Mary, and over the reign of James VI its competence widened and the volume of its business expanded fourfold.[90] Formally the privy council was a large body but its size varied. For the king, the challenge in terms of composition lay in finding a balance that reflected political opinion, while having the cohesion and expertise to operate effectively. Until the 1590s James VI did not enjoy complete freedom over the appointment of his councillors and his nominations required confirmation by parliament. The membership of the privy council was debated at the 1560 parliament and in 1592 the estates asserted their right to confirm nominations. That year one observer noted the disadvantages of drawing on too small a circle of councillors, pointing out that 'the courtiers cannot sustain the burden of the government of this broken estate without the assistance of more of the nobility, and the advice of wise and well affected persons of the barons, Kirk and burghs'.[91] A series of experiments took place from 1579 in an effort to regulate the size of the council and to agree a working quorum that fell to as low as five in 1587. In 1593, the privy council was opened up to peers who happened to be at court, but the December 1598 convention of the estates reduced it in size to thirty-one members of whom a minimum of sixteen should be peers. The privy council itself recognised in 1607 that in Scotland 'thair is mo[re] counsellouris nor in England, France, Italie and Spayne'. Yet the 1610 reconstitution raised the membership to thirty-five councillors with a quorum of seven, and of the thirty-four appointed there were eighteen peers (including one heir), thirteen lairds (eleven of whom were knights), the two archbishops and one bishop. A half-hearted effort was made to enforce attendance by threatening to deprive councillors who were absent from four consecutive sittings without licence.[92]

Following the accession of Charles I in 1625, the privy council recommended that the quorum for council meetings be established at the officers of state along with five instead of eight ordinary members because of the difficulty in getting sufficient councillors to attend. When the king named his new council, he increased its size to forty-seven individuals: six archbishops and bishops, twenty-nine peers, or the eldest sons and heirs of peers, nine barons or lairds and three Englishmen for whom this was a nominal honour. Once again attendance was poor, and a rota system was devised alongside other efforts to persuade councillors to turn up. The 1631 reconstitution maintained a nominal majority of peers: there were twenty-eight peers and four eldest sons of peers, eight barons and eight members of the episcopate. The nobility retained a numeric dominance on the privy council, but continued to vote with their feet, and in April 1636 archbishop Spottiswoode bemoaned the unwillingness of lay councillors to attend to the king's business.[93] One further development after 1603 was the number of Scots appointed to the English privy council in an effort initially to promote a greater level of union, but increasingly to provide some level of coordination between the two kingdoms. Around one in five members of the English privy council were Scots under James VI and Charles I, a mixture of court grandees like the heads of the houses of Lennox and Hamilton, officers of state and household servants.[94]

That reluctance to attend the privy council regularly offers an indication of the importance nobles attached to council business in relation to attending the royal court, parliament or remaining in their own localities. James VI was irregular in his attendance, averaging only ten occasions per annum between 1585 and 1592 after which his attendance increased threefold.[95] Of course, there were episodes of intense competition to gain access to the council as well as times when rivalries between privy councillors threatened the cohesion of its business. Queen Mary's privy council was riven by bloody factionalism; the overthrow of the regent Morton in 1578 and his execution in 1581 was determined by conciliar politics; and in the decade after the 1585 raid on Stirling the bitter rivalry between the two leading officers of state, sir John Maitland of Thirlestane and sir Thomas Lyon, master of Glamis, was one of the fixed elements of politics. After 1603 the rivalries within the privy council were less dangerous, but just as significant: chancellor Dunfermline was a focal point for conservatives determined to block less cautious courtiers, and in the later 1620s Charles I's privy council was divided between his father's old advisers and a new breed of aggressive councillors. In the following decade the cracks within the privy council grew until over the course of 1637–8 the majority of councillors sided with the covenanters against the king.[96]

The pre-eminence of noble families on the privy council gave this royal policy forum the appearance of a council of the great magnate families, hence, the second marquis of Hamilton was admitted to the privy council on 14 January 1613 because of his 'hereditarie vertewis'.[97] The problem facing kings and nobles was that the administrative side of the council's business required legal expertise, while its growing business was making unacceptable demands on men's time. Between 1590 and 1603, a period for which there are 1,099 recorded sederunts of the privy council, 154 different men sat as councillors. Of these men, sixty-five (42 per cent) were hereditary peers, but few peers were regular in their attendance.[98] An examination of the attendance records of the heads of noble houses reveals that a combination of minorities, lack of interest, political dissent and invalidity or old age meant that the privy council was often deprived of expertise and authority. The greatest territorial magnate house, that of the earls of Argyll, was absent from the central organ of crown administration throughout most of the twenty years before 1603. Did this matter to the power of the house of Argyll within its own territories, or was it the king who was deprived of the single most important figure required to make a Highland policy work? The involvement of the leading Douglas houses of Angus and Morton, crucially important in the government of the Lowlands and Borders over this quarter century, was erratic, depending on dramatically changing political fortunes and personal circumstances.[99]

Closer analysis of privy council composition by sampling attendance at five-year intervals indicates that the upper ranks of the nobility remained in a comfortable majority prior to 1590, but there was a fall in the percentage of peers attending the council in the 1590s and 1600s (Table 6.1). Thereafter, the promotion to the peerage of royal servants drawn from the baronial ranks raised the predominance of peers to the point where by the 1630s they exceeded their share of council seats in the 1570s. A more nuanced measurement of attendance indicates that few councillors attended more than two-thirds of recorded meetings, and a large share of councillors did not attend even one in three meetings (Table 6.2).

If the non-working councillors are discarded, that is those attending less than a third of recorded sederunts, peers constituted a majority of the working councillors in 1580, but fell to under a third for most of the next

Table 6.1 Composition of the privy council (by attendance)[100]

	Councillors	Peers	Non-peers
1575	38	24 (63.2%)	14 (36.8%)
1580	30	17 (56.7%)	13 (43.3%)
1585	38	15 (39.5%)	23 (60.5%)
1590	38	13 (34.2%)	25 (65.8%)
1595	46	20 (43.5%)	26 (56.5%)
1600	46	17 (37%)	29 (63%)
1605	63	33 (52.4%)	30 (47.6%)
1610	56	28 (50%)	28 (50%)
1615	37	16 (43.2%)	21 (56.8%)
1620	44	23 (52.3%)	21 (47.7%)
1625	44	22 (50%)	22 (50%)
1630	38	27 (71.1%)	11 (28.9%)
1635	35	24 (68.6%)	11 (31.4%)

Table 6.2 Privy council attendance

	Seder-unts	Coun-cillors	Peers $>\frac{2}{3}$	Peers $>\frac{1}{3}$	Peers $>\frac{1}{3}$	Others $>\frac{2}{3}$	Others $>\frac{1}{3}$	Others $>\frac{1}{3}$
1575	20	38	1 (2.6%)	5 (13.2%)	18 (47.4%)	4 (10.5%)	1 (2.6%)	9 (23.7%)
1580	54	30	2 (6.7%)	7 (23.3%)	8 (26.7%)	4 (13.3%)	4 (13.3%)	5 (16.7%)
1585	50	38	1 (2.6%)	2 (5.3%)	12 (31.6%)	3 (7.9%)	4 (10.5%)	16 (42.1%)
1590	42	38	0 (0%)	3 (7.9%)	10 (26.3%)	1 (2.6%)	5 (13.2%)	19 (50%)
1595	32	46	2 (4.3%)	2 (4.3%)	16 (34.8%)	4 (8.7%)	5 (10.9%)	17 (37%)
1600	78	46	4 (8.7%)	1 (2.2%)	12 (26.1%)	5 (10.9%)	7 (15.2%)	7 (15.2%)
1605	39	63	3 (4.8%)	6 (9.5%)	24 (38.1%)	5 (7.9%)	14 (22.2%)	11 (17.5%)
1610	93	56	1 (1.8%)	5 (8.9%)	22 (39.3%)	5 (8.9%)	6 (10.7%)	17 (30.4%)
1615	83	37	2 (5.4%)	3 (8.1%)	11 (29.8%)	9 (24.3%)	4 (10.8%)	8 (21.6%)
1620	72	44	5 (11.4%)	4 (9.1%)	14 (31.8%)	7 (15.9%)	6 (13.6%)	8 (18.2%)
1625	48	44	2 (4.5%)	9 (20.5%)	11 (25%)	6 (13.6%)	7 (15.9%)	9 (20.5%)
1630	80	38	6 (15.8%)	6 (15.8%)	15 (39.5%)	4 (10.5%)	3 (7.9%)	4 (10.5%)
1635	86	35	1 (2.8%)	12 (34.3%)	11 (31.4%)	3 (8.6%)	5 (14.3%)	3 (8.6%)

four decades before promotions again raised their profile in the 1620s and 1630s, when they represented some two-thirds of the active councillors in the latter decade. The sustained business of the privy council, therefore, was carried on by a relatively small number of dedicated nobles who staffed a range of council committees, like the 1610 exchequer commission, the 1618 commission to negotiate fishing rights with the Dutch, or the 1623 commissions to discuss the wool trade with the English and to oversee the encouragement of manufacture. High-profile committees like the commission of grievances appointed in 1623, or the council of war set up in 1626, were even more top heavy with nobles. The teind commission that was established in November 1627 was made up of sixty-eight men, forty-six of whom were nobles, twenty-two peers and twenty-four barons.[101]

At the beginning of James VI's reign there was a revolution and civil war when the kingdom's traditional leaders were at the fore of government. By the 1590s there was an adult king and the nobility retreated from regular administration, leaving it to lesser men to carry on with mundane business, men like David Carnegy of Colluthie, the younger son of a baronial family, who was employed by the king for his financial abilities and legal training.[102] But James VI did not displace noblemen on the privy council in spite of Halhill's allegation that in 1590 Thirlestane planned to reform that body, 'the nobilitie to be debarred therfra'. There was no 'new nobility of service' or *noblesse de robe*.[103] Unlike in France where certain offices conferred nobility (thus ensuring the king was served by men of rank if not always of birth), in Scotland the king largely chose his servants from the nobility. Of fifty-six middle-ranking privy councillors who served James VI between 1580 and 1603, fifty-three were crown freeholders. Sir Robert Melville of Murdocairny, James Elphinstone, a younger son of the third lord Elphinstone, and John Lindsay of Menmuir, the second son of the ninth earl of Crawford, were recruited from inside noble society.[104] Those few councillors whose origins lay outside or on the fringes of noble society were few. Alexander Hay entered crown service as a clerk in the early 1560s, and was clerk register from 1579 until his death in 1594, having secured his position on the bottom ranks of the nobility in 1583 by purchasing the crown freehold of Easter Kennet. These men were sensitive of their modest origins, for example, the earl of Dunbar declined the office of commissioner at the 1609 parliament, being 'farre inferiour' to older established peers, and the first earl of Haddington stated with exaggerated modesty that he was 'but a gentill man of meine Birthe'.[105]

When in 1603 the king departed for England the privy council contained experienced and reliable nobles at ease governing in his absence. It was James VI's relationship with these nobles, not the bureaucratic structures of government, that allowed him to make the exaggerated boast to the English parliament in 1607 that 'here I sit and governe it [Scotland] with my pen, I write and it is done, and by a clerke of the councell I governe Scotland now, which others could not do by the sword'. The king knew he must ensure that powerful nobles remain engaged in government, but there is some evidence that the growing emphasis within government on royal authority created tensions among privy councillors. In February 1606, a decision to pre-empt a judicial decision in a case of violent possession of a house by a lesser noble-man was challenged by the marquis of Huntly, the tenth earl of Angus and the second earl of Mar who failed to make the case that the privy council was acting against law and custom. Here the more aggressive of the king's servants won the day. A month later, the lord advocate, sir Thomas Hamilton of Drumcairn, charged the sixth lord Herries to exhibit a rebel who had been in his house without Herries' permission, but the first lord Balmerino, president of the court of session and the younger son of a peer, argued that this was 'ane over rigorous strait to nobill men'. In spite of such views among his noble councillors, James VI never risked excluding his most powerful subjects from the privy council even when in 1621 an inner executive committee of privy councillors was established.[106] Charles I, however, resented the entrenched power of his father's old councillors, and challenged the critical role played by the privy council, which was increasingly filled by less independently-minded men. The king challenged the conciliar government that had evolved during his father's reign, and while some change in personnel was necessary, Charles's intervention destabilised the status quo without any corresponding improvements in government. When in January 1626, the unscrupulous first earl of Nithsdale made allegations of corruption against the second earl of Mar who was proving uncooperative over the revocation, the dignified old man told the king:

> I had the honor to be sworn Counsallor to his worthie father thir seivin and fourtie yeiris past; I had bein his fathers Tresurar and his awin thir ten yeirs past, and gif my lyf war devyded in twentie parts thaer is nyntein and a half of thaem past, and now to be acoused in the few days I have to leive as aine that shall swett for my actions, quhat can I say, Sir?[107]

At the same time, in offending men like Mar, the king risked creating a gulf between his government and the localities, a development observed by the first earl of Haddington as early as April 1629.[108] The disengagement of men with power and influence in the localities from the privy council reduced its ability over the following years to ensure that the king's policies would be understood, accepted and enforced.[109]

The most important of the king's councillors in terms of formal responsibilities were the offices of state, the origins of which were believed to lie in the early eleventh century.[110] The later sixteenth century saw an enhancement of these offices of which there were between six and eight, although the individual office-holder remained more important than the office itself, hence, the earl of Dunbar's domination of the privy council between 1603 and 1611 while holding the office of treasurer.[111] Offices of state carried additional responsibility and brought with them patronage and political power, but their greatest value lay in the public advertisement of royal favour. When in 1627 the office of lord privy seal fell vacant, lord Erskine petitioned the sixth earl of Morton, pointing out that he did 'nott value the thing so much as thatt I sall tak itt as a mark of my maisters favor'.[112] Royal offices were surprisingly secure against loss, there being no recognised system of competitive bidding for office that would have provided the crown with additional income. Once conferred for life, office was regarded as a form of property, and it was common for nobles to bargain over places while the king watched passively from the sidelines. When in 1599 the third earl of Montrose was appointed chancellor he purchased the great seal for 1,000 crowns from the second duke of Lennox who had acquired it on

Thirlestane's death. A year later, the first marquis of Huntly unsuccessfully tried to buy the office from Montrose for the same sum. In 1600, James found he could not sack treasurer Blantyre, but was obliged to negotiate his retirement. Two decades later, the sixth earl of Morton entered into negotiations to purchase the reversion of the treasurership from the second earl of Mar, who in April 1630 resigned the office into Morton's hands.[113] Charles I had little option other than to renew for life the offices of his father's principal officers of state, and he expressed frustration at the absence of distinction between 'ane hereditarie right of a private estate, and of the guift of a domestick office in our service, where the benefite should accompanie the imployment, which doth depend upon our trust'.[114] So entrenched were these rights that particular families formed attachments to certain crown offices, and even the chancellorship became the object of proprietary claims.[115] Of course, certain royal offices were hereditary, the constable and marshall being in the hands of the earls of Errol and Marischal, respectively. The office of justice general remained with the earls of Argyll until it was resigned to the crown in 1628 when the king granted it on an annual basis to the seventh earl of Menteith until his disgrace in 1633.[116]

A number of the offices of state held no attraction to the higher ranks of nobles. For example, the clerk register was a long-established office that was developing in scope and in authority, but that required a combination of record-keeping and legal expertise.[117] The second duke of Lennox guarded jealously the lord chamberlain's office, a position that was not an office of state but was located in the king's household. By contrast, when in 1592 the possibility arose of the chancellorship becoming available, he dismissed it because 'that office should "imbase" the perception of his estate and person'. This view of the chancellor as a sophisticated clerk was encouraged by James VI, who commented in 1596 that 'he would no more use Chancellor or other great men in those his causes but such as he might convict and were hangable'. James wrote *Basilikon doron* during the four-year hiatus when he was dithering over what to do about the chancellorship, indicating his preference for easily disposable men in high office. Such low-ranking individuals, he wrote, 'wer so haitted, by being raissed from a mean estaite to overtope all men, that every one held it a pretty recreation to have them often turnid oute'. A concern was that placing major offices in the hands of a magnate might be risky since 'being a great man and Chancellor and withal a courtier as of necessity he must be better attended upon than the King himself'. But there were disadvantages in appointing a man of lesser rank, for 'to make a mean man Chancellor the King thinks will ever maintain one faction or other to make himself strong', exactly the problem encountered during Thirlestane's tenure of office between 1587 and 1595. Having emphasised the need to find virtuous, talented men who would not fail to speak the truth, James VI concluded that a king should 'delight to be served with men of the noblest blood that may bee had: for besides that their service shall breed you great good-will and least envie, contrarie to that of start-ups: ye shall oft finde vertue follow noble races'. Finally, in January 1599, he appointed to the chancellorship the third earl of Montrose, believing that his gravity and status enhanced the office and the king he served. Unfortunately, neither the king nor Montrose was comfortable with the bargain. As sir Patrick Hume of Polwarth later commented: 'Quho wes thocht a wyser nobleman, at least a griter politician then the auld Earle of Montrose? but quhen he wes made Canceller, his scant of clergie bewrayed him'. Montrose lacked adequate legal expertise, and his successor, the first earl of Dunfermline was a nobleman and a brilliant lawyer.[118]

Thomas Craig of Riccarton was proud of Scots law, claiming that 'the forms we use in Scotland are better than those in any country I know of'. Riccarton's patriotic pride is understandable, but English common lawyers disagreed, their contempt for Scots law being one of the stumbling blocks to legal and parliamentary union after 1603. In 1580, a source compiled for English intelligence reported on the scarcity of lawyers, most of whom were employed at the court of session, whereas 'in the shires all matters are ordered after the great men's pleasures'. A generation later, in his 1617 satire of Scotland, sir Anthony Weldon claimed that 'thair be fewe lawieris, and those nott ritche'. Another Englishman abroad in 1636 was favourably impressed with the workings of Scottish justice, but was appalled by the court of session where he 'observed the greatest rudeness, disorder, and confusion, that ever I saw in any court of justice'.[119] In fact, by the 1550s Scotland had a cadre of professional lawyers whose social and political role was not prominent, but who were useful to the king and the nobility. The legal profession evolved rapidly from the establishment of the court of session in 1532, and Lethington claimed that this powerful civil court with its increasingly professional judges, of whom he was one, was crucial in preventing a decline into anarchy. Initially, the senators of the new college of justice comprised fourteen ordinary lords of session, but by the 1560s these had been augmented by an additional four extraordinary lords selected from within the privy council. Throughout the period 1560–1637, when the normal number of judges remained at around eighteen, some 140 individuals sat as lords of session.[120]

The process of appointing court of session judges was reformed by parliament in 1579, but occasional struggles erupted between the king and the court over the filling of vacant offices. James VI believed that kings should operate within a legal framework, but that the law was created by the king alone: 'the kings were the authors and makers of the Lawes, and not the Lawes of the kings'. While this view did not lead to the intensive clashes with the legal establishment that he encountered with English common lawyers, largely because the king did not press the point, there were tensions. When lawyers questioned royal authority, as a number did in the Hartsyde case of 1608, James VI condemned them as 'those pettyfoggeris', ordering

that all who had signed the protest be warded.[121] The king packed the court
of session with loyal servants, by-passing regulations in order to appoint
his men, and often allowing political considerations to weigh more heavily
than professionalism.[122] The development of the office of lord advocate was
important in seeking to overawe the judges and in initiating prosecutions
according to a political agenda. In 1609, when sir Thomas Hamilton of
Drumcairn prosecuted the first lord Balmerino for treason, he expressed
concern that the defendant was 'ane man of learning and great experience'
who was likely to get the best advocates in the country to take up his case,
and so he recommended packing the jury.[123] The relationship between the
privy council and the court of session was sensitive, there being a significant
overlap in personnel between the two bodies. Of the 140 court of session
judges in the period 1560–1637 seventy-nine (56 per cent) served as privy
councillors, thirty-eight of these men being appointed to the bench from
their place on the privy council and forty-one of them being appointed to
the privy council from their positions as lords of session. Extraordinary
lords predominated among the former, indicating their more political
function, and ordinary lords among the latter, reflecting career advancement
by successful judges.[124] In 1625–6, Charles I broke up this close arrangement, believing that his political objectives might be better served in having
a court of session with less politically powerful members. Nevertheless, he
was unable to achieve his objective of judges appointed *ad beneplacitum*
instead of for life.[125]

The law was one among a number of career choices open to nobles
throughout Europe, and even in France where the division between so-
called traditional nobles and a *noblesse de robe* is most pronounced the
cultural division has been exaggerated.[126] In Scotland the lines between
professionally trained judges and noble magistrates was especially blurred.
The picture of the regent Moray as a magistrate who 'sat daylie amangis the
lordis of Sessioun and causit gret iustice to be done in the sessioun daylie to
the puire' was intended to inspire admiration. But when on 2 March 1578
the regent Morton boasted to his cousin, William Douglas of Lochleven,
that 'We have done justice, and schewen our selff thairin, and in things
promissed indifferent to all', he was fooling no one. As a client, Lochleven
would have been disappointed if what Morton wrote was true, and one of
the purposes of the 1579 legislation was to address corruption. When in
1583 John Grant of Freuchie wrote to sir Alexander Hay of Easter Kennet,
lord clerk register and court of session judge, asking for 'your lordschipis
guid will and fortherance, in this my honest caus', he had a good expectation
of being helped. Chancellor Thirlestane stuffed the court of session with
family and friends between 1587 and 1592, and the first earl of Haddington
was disappointed at Charles I's separation of the personnel of the court
of session from that of the privy council because it reduced the opportunity
to exercise political patronage, telling a friend that it was now more diffi-

cult to lobby the judges. Of course, that was exactly what the king intended by re-establishing his own control of court of session patronage, and in particular reducing opposition to the revocation.[127]

Essentially, the legal profession was a service branch of the nobility, staffed overwhelmingly by men drawn from noble society, and it was the growing volume of litigation over heritable title to land that was the single most important factor in developing the court of session's jurisdiction. Parliament demanded that court of session judges be men of substantial means, the 1592 act requiring an income of 1,000 merks per annum, making the office beyond the reach of most men who lacked an estate, and these men moved easily from central to local courts to informal arbitration. Legally trained officials like sir John Skene of Curriehill and Riccarton discussed the language of lordship without antipathy, and the latter was enthusiastic about the mutual obligations that bound lords and men together. The correspondence of sir Patrick Waus of Barnbarroch, a court of session judge, reveals a man rooted in his own Wigtonshire locality and its values.[128] Only one in ten of the court of session judges belonged by birth to peerage families, men like the fifth earl of Huntly or Alexander Seton, a younger son of the fourth lord Seton, but a further 57 per cent were drawn from among the lesser nobility. Furthermore, analysis of social background at the time of their appointment to the court of session indicates that nine out of ten judges had already attained the status of landed nobility with 20 per cent being peers.[129]

By *c.* 1600 there were well-established dynasties on the bench, most obviously the Bellendens, Maitlands and a branch of the Hamiltons, baronial houses determined to enhance their landed possessions by securing a grip on the most lucrative legal offices. By 1608, sir Thomas Hamilton of Priestfield and three of his sons filled almost a quarter of the places in the court of session. Such developments were aided by the occasional privilege of resigning in favour of kinsmen, for example, in February 1601 sir Robert Melville of Murdocairny resigned in favour of his son and in 1612 Curriehill did likewise. In both cases the sons were qualified to fill their offices, and it is unsurprising that nobles were well placed to acquire the necessary education for a legal career. Even among the advocates, the greatest recruitment to the profession in the seventeenth century was from the lower nobility or lairds. At the same time, one of the principal drivers in the growth in the legal profession was the business generated by nobles who were the single most important source of patronage for lawyers.[130] Nevertheless, up to a third of court of session judges originated outside the nobility, men like David Borthwick, burgess of Haddington, who was elected an ordinary lord of session in 1573, and the law even offered a route for a few individuals to enter the bottom ranks of the nobility. John Shairp was the son of a wealthy Edinburgh merchant who trained for a church career but switched to the law in 1562, practised as an advocate, establishing a successful legal business that allowed him to acquire the estate and barony of Houston.[131] Men like Shairp were not perceived as a threat to the nobility, but as additions to their lower ranks.

There was no obstacle to nobles becoming lawyers. Denmilne believed that noblemen could plead in court without dishonouring themselves, and might practise as advocates because they defended the poor and the innocent, but he drew the line at notaries. The number of court of session judges recognised as advocates was a little under a quarter, and while twenty-four of the ninety-one men who held office (26 per cent) between 1560 and 1600 were advocates, only nine of the forty-nine men in office (18 per cent) between 1600 and 1637 were qualified advocates. Professional lawyers were being squeezed out by nobles with a generalist humanist education, and of the forty men appointed to the bench between 1580 and 1610, seventeen (43 per cent) are known to have received some formal legal training and eighteen (45 per cent) are known to have received none (the remaining five cases cannot be traced accurately). Over the following decade only two of the eleven new judges had a formal legal training.[132] Among the high-flyers in James VI's government who studied law, only Edward Bruce, commendator of Kinloss, practised law to earn a living, the others, John Lindsay, Alexander Seton and James Elphinstone, were younger sons of nobles for whom the study of law was an acceptable route to maintaining their social status. Like those English gentry or Norman magistrates who practised law in order to secure a second income, these men did not set out to become professional lawyers, nor did they betray their roots in noble society. Political sensitivity and social awareness ensured there was none of the reaction seen in Germany by nobles against the lawyers who were filling up administrative positions over the course of the sixteenth century.[133]

Royal justice in any period expanded not only because strong kings willed it, but because the landed elite of that society allowed it to expand.[134] Yet there were limits to what nobles would tolerate. The most influential jurists of the period, sir James Balfour of Pittendreich, Riccarton, Curriehill and Craighall, were drawn from the lower ranks of the nobility, but while these men all held crown office they did not share James VI's view of the law as subject to the king. Riccarton and John Russell argued for restraints on the king's freedom to act, restraints that James VI recognised in practice even if he baulked at the implication behind George Buchanan's argument that the Scots 'have no laws but their acts of parliament'. This belief in the primacy of statute law meant that the courts and the judges could be obstructive, as in 1598 when the court of session took a tough stance against the king over the treatment of the dissident minister, Robert Bruce. The president of the court of session, Alexander Seton, lord Fyvie, told the king that while the judges were bound to obey the king in all matters affecting their lives, lands and gear, 'they would do as their consciences led them' unless the king ordered it, in which case they would abstain. Treasurer Blantyre even advised the defence counsel, an action that cost him his office.[135] In 1634, in spite of increased royal control over the appointment of judges, Alexander Gibson of Durie wrote a tract attacking the extension of the power of bishops and later joined the covenanters, as did the king's most senior law officer, the lord advocate, sir Thomas Hope of Craighall.[136] Lawyers defended particular noble behaviours in the face of crown prosecution. In 1592, the rebel fifth earl of Bothwell set about reducing his forfeiture 'with skill of men expert in the lawis'. In January 1611, the king lambasted the privy council over its toleration of lawyers who defended the right of William Douglas, younger of Drumlanrig, to kill a man who was at the horn, and who argued that private imprisonment was not a criminal offence, warning that such innovations in legal argument would be punished in future. On 28 February 1617, George Gordon of Gight was brought to trial for the judicial murder in Aberdeen of Francis Hay. Gight had the backing of the first marquis of Huntly who had kept the case out of court for two years. The Gordon lawyers further delayed the proceedings with technicalities, provoking an outraged lord Binning to order the clerk 'to deleit furth of thair boukes all that was writtin upon that subject'.[137] Binning overawed the court, but the Gordon lawyers had unsettled the privy council and an out-of-court settlement was agreed.

Conclusion

Nobles provided kings with a pool of born counsellors, men with the virtue and skills necessary in the art of government. Among the higher ranks of the nobility that duty and that right to give counsel was heritable as was recognised by parliament in the personal summons issued to peers. Mary, James VI and Charles I each recognised this relationship with their nobles, and while they called on the services of different men none of these rulers entirely ignored the counsel of the nobility or recruited significant numbers of advisers and servants to government from outside noble society. Previous kings had failed to take adequate account of the nobility in governing the kingdom, most notably James I and James III who paid for the mistake with their lives. Mary in the 1560s failed to placate a powerful noble party or faction that believed she was failing to take sufficient account of their interests, but Mary was not attempting to rule without noble counsel. Charles I, however, did upset the relationship between king and nobility. His failing was not that of refusing to employ nobles in government, it was his refusal to listen to the broad counsel that his nobles might offer that created a chasm between himself and his most powerful subjects. By contrast, James VI understood the need to listen to a range of opinion, he constantly sought to draw the nobles into the business of governing the kingdom, and mostly he selected his advisers on the basis of their talent.

Yet the problem of governance had its origins in James VI's reign. The

later sixteenth century saw a remarkable enhancement of the role of parliament, which alongside conventions of the estates met regularly, legislated at
an increasing rate and assumed greater political significance. The decline of
the clerical estate and the weakness of the crown allowed parliament to be
dominated by the nobility, and the creation in 1587 of shire commissioners
drawn from the untitled barons or lairds created a second noble estate. While
the parliaments of the 1560s, 1570s and early 1580s were subject to the
fortunes of hostile factions, from the fall of the Arran regime in 1585 until
the regal union in 1603 parliament was as close to a free assembly as might
reasonably be expected. James VI had little control over parliament either
through procedural powers or the application of patronage, and even the
more manageable conventions of estates proved to be unmanageable. That
all changed with the regal union. Parliament increased in membership with
the nobility seeing their numeric advantage grow fastest as the number of
peers multiplied and as the election of shire commissioners became more
routine. But parliament sat less frequently, the number of conventions
decreased dramatically and the crown tightened its grip over the management of parliament's business. By 1621 the political initiative lay with the
king in an assembly where dissent was still tolerated, but the 1633 parliament made clear to the nobility that their counsel was no longer required,
only their presence and their assent to the king's wishes. When parliament
next sat, in 1639, the nobles set about restoring those lost freedoms.

One key factor that made the covenanting revolution of 1637–8 so
successful was the total collapse of royal government. Apart from the
bishops and a handful of nobles, like the first earl of Traquair, who
attempted to maintain the fiction of royal authority, the privy councillors,
officers of state and judges either stood aside or defected to the covenanters.
This is unsurprising given the extent of discontent throughout the kingdom
and the level of dissent within noble society from which kings recruited their
servants. It is easy to be misled by the names of office-holders and government records into a misunderstanding of who exercised power.[138] In spite of
the commonplace rhetoric levelled by critics at various royal officers and
advisers as being low-born creatures, Mary, James VI and Charles I were
dependent on noble families to supply them with privy councillors, officers
of state and judges. But the crown was unable to insulate these men from
that society. At the level that mattered, government was not staffed by a
cadre of professional administrators wholly dependent on the king, but by
nobles whose educational experiences and values were unlikely to differ
greatly from those nobles not engaged in royal government, and whose
estates, kinsmen and friends drew them back into their local communities.
The point has been made elsewhere in Europe that this period saw an
improvement in the coordinating functions of government without any
significant or durable increase in its autocratic power. Those many criticisms
levelled at notions of absolutism among the more powerful European states

have even greater resonance in the case of Scotland.[139] Even the limited advance that royal government made in Scotland was achieved by careful negotiation with local nobles whose participation in parliament, in the privy council and in the law courts was essential in progressing that process. Ultimately, it was personal relationships between the king and his nobles, and between them and their clients, that made government work effectively, not bureaucratic structures and administrative measures.

CHAPTER 7

Courtiers

The early modern royal court was the most powerful and influential institution in European kingdoms, and while not every aspect of politics and political culture was necessarily embraced within the life of the court, it was more than the royal household and the entertainments that took place in the king's presence.[1] Unfortunately, the Stewart court of the later sixteenth century suffers in contrast to that of England and France, but also in contrast to the glittering courts of James IV and James V when the majesty and wealth of the dynasty attained its heights.[2] Mary's court shone brightly for a few brief years in the 1560s before disappearing with the collapse of her government in 1567. Civil war and a long minority was followed by James VI's struggle to establish his court against a background of political instability and severe financial difficulties. Yet while James VI was constantly short of money, and while his court could not compete with the greatest royal courts of Europe, his achievement should not be overlooked, and it was not so different from the Swedish court and in terms of scale, if not wealth, was similar to the ducal court of Bavaria.[3]

Under Mary and James VI the Stewart royal court continued to be a major arena in which high-level politics was conducted, being the principal point of contact between nobles who were attracted there in search of office, patronage and power. The royal court was the major cultural driver in the kingdom, and was a centre of international intrigue. No noble household was able to compete by itself with the royal court in terms of scale, or as a source of patronage. In 1603, the arrival of a new Scottish dynasty, royal officers and nobles in London dramatically changed the composition, structure and style of the stuffy Tudor court that had for so long revolved around the ageing Elizabeth I. The impact James VI and I and his Scottish nobles had on the English court was significant, arguably creating a new imperial British royal court and shifting the ground of English politics. The regal union had an even more dramatic impact on the Scots, who now had to engage with a court physically located hundreds of miles to the south in a larger and wealthier foreign kingdom. Consequently, the relationship between the king and the nobility was altered immediately. The removal of the king and his court from Scotland created a marked and unbridgeable gulf in wealth and power between the king and individual nobles, and it made the king more secure from direct political pressure. London residence brought about some differentiation within the nobility between those who had access to the king on a regular basis and those nobles who became dependent on courtiers, imposing a division that had never been a significant feature of politics before 1603. Finally, Scottish nobles now mingled and competed with the wealthier English nobles of England, resulting in a limited degree of integration and some modest anglicisation. But while the regal union did alter the role of the court as a meeting place between the king and his nobles, it is unhelpful to exaggerate the influence of a royal court in refashioning behaviours. Even in the glittering Habsburg and Bourbon monarchies of the seventeenth century, royal courts were not agents of an irresistible transformative power bearing down on passive and acquiescent nobles.[4]

Structures and Offices

Royal courts of the later sixteenth century and early seventeenth century drew European nobles into a lifestyle in which the roles envisaged by Castiglione in *The courtier* (1528) were embraced and cultivated, and where they had to acquire a new range of skills in order to capture the attention of kings and to impress one another with the sophistication and taste now required as marks of nobility.[5] The specialist courtier, however, was not much in evidence in Scottish political culture before 1603; even during the reigns of James IV and James V the court was neither set apart from local society nor did it impose values on the nobility. Furthermore, at a time when European royal courts were becoming more centralised and establishing geographical roots, the Stewart court remained peripatetic, shifting around from Holyrood palace in Edinburgh, Linlithgow palace in west Lothian and Falkland palace in Fife, all within half a day's ride of one another, while Edinburgh or Stirling castles served as bases for the court as did some of the houses of the nobility, such as Dalkeith palace.[6] Nevertheless, by the sixteenth century Edinburgh had emerged as the Scottish capital, being the largest and richest town with a population of around 12,000 in 1560 rising to around 21,000 in greater Edinburgh by 1600, the site of the principal law courts, the preferred meeting place of parliament, and most royal administration was carried on in the burgh which subsidised the royal court. For the nobility, attendance at court meant following James VI around the country since 'the king lies not long at any place', but also living in or close to Edinburgh. Consequently, many of the higher nobility had castles and houses within a short distance of the city, or they were forced to buy or rent accommodation in Edinburgh. Hence, sir Robert Gordon of Gordonstoun's advice to 'buy some resting place' in the Edinburgh vicinity.[7]

Although a high degree of fluidity shaped court life, structure was created by court offices. The size of the royal household grew from around

125 people in 1580 to an estimated 800 individuals by 1603, many of whom were relatively lowly, and only a handful of the most sought after household places were filled by men of noble rank. As was the case with offices elsewhere in the royal administration, court offices were a form of property that an individual held throughout his lifetime, and nobles made every effort to retain court offices within the family, commonly making resignations *in favorem*. In 1580, sir William Murray of Tullibardine, fearing that he was going to lose the comptroller's office amid a factional struggle, surrendered it to the king who granted it to Tullibardine's eldest son. Similarly, in July 1606, the first earl of Lothian demitted his office of master of requests in favour of his eldest son, while in November 1613 sir Robert Ker of Ancram was succeeded as captain of the guard by sir Andrew Ker of Oxenham.[8] But, of course, the formal household was only part of the royal court. In addition, nobles, their wives, kinsmen and dependants came and went, while privy councillors, foreign ambassadors or agents were in residence from time to time, specialist advisers such as soldiers, travellers, merchants, clergy and lawyers might be summoned, entertainers and artists were employed, and petitioners turned up hoping to see the king or catch the attention of someone with access to the king.

The court of queen Mary, like that of her mother, Mary of Guise, was fundamentally French in character and even in personnel. Those closest to the queen were not the great lords, but her illegitimate half-brothers, French servants and women, while nobles who established a foothold in Mary's court generally had some relationship within this inner circle. The fifth earl of Argyll was married to Mary's illegitimate half-sister, Jean Stewart, and the collapse of their marriage had significant political repercussions, while the fifth lord Seton, master of the queen's household, the fourth lord Fleming and the sixth lord Livingston had sisters who were friends and ladies-in-waiting to the queen. Unlike Argyll, these men remained loyal to the queen. Mary's political difficulty lay in the fact that her privy council was dominated by nobles with whom she had little sympathy, while many of the friends with which she surrounded herself at court aroused suspicion on account of their suspected Catholicism. Only briefly in 1565–6 was the queen able to impose herself on her Protestant nobles.[9]

During James VI's minority there was no need for a court, and the regents who governed in the king's name operated with expanded versions of their own households. From 1566, the infant prince along with his small household resided at Stirling castle in the custody of the family of the first earl of Mar. Here the king was accompanied by young nobles, some of whom remained lifelong companions, men like Walter Stewart, the future first lord Blantyre, Thomas Erskine, the future first earl of Kellie, and his cousin, John Erskine, second earl of Mar, who had been 'nurcist and brocht up with his hienes in his company', and who in turn became responsible for the keeping of prince Henry.[10] Even with the end of the regency government in

1578 the privy council thought the twelve-year-old king too young to need a formal household establishment. The arrival at court of Esmé Stewart from France in September 1579 and the king's ceremonial entry to Edinburgh a month later altered the situation. A handful of nobles and their kinsmen began to take up household offices, and in the autumn of 1580 a bed-chamber was formed in a conscious effort to create an alternative centre of power to a privy council that was still dominated by the ex-regent Morton. The new institution was French in style, consciously based on James V's court, and was staffed by a compliment of twenty-four young nobles, all subject to the authority of a lord chamberlain and first gentleman of the chamber. The lord chamberlain possessed a powerful office both in terms of his control over the gentlemen of the bedchamber, and arising from his personal access to the king. When the bedchamber was created on 15 October 1580, Esmé Stewart, now first earl of Lennox, was appointed lord chamberlain with sir Alexander Erskine, master of Mar, as the vice-chamberlain, and it was the former who chose the other gentlemen and officers who were 'all dependers on Lennox'. These young nobles, sons of peers and barons, were on duty for three months at a time and four of them were always required to be at court. Further changes followed in August 1580 when Lennox took charge of the king's wardrobe, while his client, sir John Seton, was appointed master of the stables. From this strong base in the household, Lennox was able to strike out and destroy Morton.[11]

The creation of a tight-knit bedchamber generated new problems. The royal court was where the nobility expected to encounter the king, open access to the king's bedchamber being a privilege for at least the titled peerage. A recurrent theme of late medieval minorities was resentment generated by any restrictions to that access as occurred following the palace coup of December 1580 that led to Morton's arrest when a guard of waged soldiers was placed around Holyrood palace. Lennox's own removal from court following the Ruthven raid in August 1582, and his death shortly afterwards, resulted in the focus of power shifting from the bedchamber to those nobles who exercised power through the privy council on which the king was forced to accept men not of his own choosing in 1582–3 and again in 1585–9. Yet the bedchamber remained the centre of intrigue against the anglophile and more radically Protestant faction that dominated the privy council, hence, the frantic concerns of the English government as to its composition. In 1589, an English agent believed that the king's servants in the bedchamber and in the stables were predominantly supporters and friends of the Catholic sixth earl of Huntly. Those suspicions appeared to be borne out when Huntly used his position as captain of the guard to launch an unsuccessful coup against the rival faction, and chiefly against the chancellor, sir John Maitland of Thirlestane, that ended in rebellion, defeat and a loss of his court offices.[12]

Ongoing factional power struggles continued with the bedchamber men conspiring to have 'the maist part of the consaill at ther devotion, or els chengit and others mair frendly for them placit in ther rowmes'. This contest came to a head in 1589–90 when James VI went to Denmark and the bedchamber faction exploited the opportunity to persuade the king to impose a new regime of restricted access. Critics represented this development as an attempt to undermine the nobility since 'hall, chamber, and all durris wer sa straitly and indiscretly keped, that they culd get na entre; therfor many of them returnit malcontent to ther houses'. Nobles reacted by boycotting the court, a tactic that proved to be effective since business ground to a halt. As sir James Melville of Halhill observed, 'sindre necessary refourmations wer intendit, bot nathing perfourmed', and a convention of estates in June 1590 was poorly attended since 'very few obeyed the said wretingis, or wald com neir the court'. The fifth earl of Bothwell was among those nobles 'muche discontented' at being prevented from gaining entry to the king, while lord Hamilton departed in a rage after being held at the door, exclaiming that 'this newe order wold offend all men and might not be used'. In November 1590 those councillors still smarting from the enhanced influence of the chamber, supported treasurer Glamis in putting down a motion that 'the mynyons in the King's chamber might be holden so straite within their lymittes, as they should not have powre to inriche them selves above measure, nor to alter the resolucions of the Counsaill at their pleasure'.[13]

The issue was exacerbated by the use of the royal guards to control access to the king. Mary maintained a small guard, but in October 1582 a convention of estates agreed to the raising of a much larger royal guard. Without adequate funds to pay it the king struggled to maintain sufficient numbers to be militarily effective and only English subsidies kept it going. In 1590, numbers temporarily swelled to around 100 horsemen and 100 foot, causing some outrage that 'the wholl nobilitie shalbe prejudiced in their auncient priveledges for their free accesse to the king's person, and vote in counsell and matters of estate'. Thereafter the apparent threat from this highly unreliable body disappeared and by the later 1590s the king dispensed with paid soldiers, although the occasional use of 'domestics in warlike manner' to control access continued to irritate other nobles.[14] One further structural development that emerged from the king's marriage in 1590 was the creation of a small, separate queen's household that James VI could ill-afford. Nevertheless, Anne of Denmark succeeded in situating herself at the centre of an effective power network, offering noble women some influence in a male-dominated court, but it also created a new set of rivalries that reached its greatest intensity after 1594 in the struggle for control of the infant prince Henry.[15]

By the mid-1590s the division between a court faction that was stronger on the privy council and a rival faction located chiefly within the bedchamber was no longer so important. Individual courtiers continued to rise and fall in favour, which was measured out in privileges such as sleeping in the king's chamber or dining rights. George Hume's rise from household servant to spectacular fortune as earl of Dunbar had its origins in his eclipse of sir William Keith, the master of the wardrobe, who offended the king at the royal wedding in Denmark by upstaging his costume. Yet the king learned from the misjudged enthusiasm for Danish practices in 1590, even suggesting in *Basilikon doron* (1599) that an open access policy at court, allowing barons and gentlemen to deal directly with the king, would break the power of those magnates who acted as court brokers. But James VI never adopted such a policy, being torn between his preference for surrounding himself with a tight-knit group of loyal noble friends and servants and allowing relatively free and even casual access. Where the king did maintain some distinction was in his use of close friends and household servants to provide informal, private counsel and companionship. This behaviour was noted by the English agent in Edinburgh in 1599, who commented that James VI was 'so inclinable to his chamber and his favourites' advices and for their desires to do anything now inconvenient soever' that others, including privy councillors, were discouraged from attending court. This observation is exaggerated, but the point is that while James VI remained accessible and allowed his privy council to get on with administering the kingdom, he retreated into a semi-private place with those noble companions upon whose advice he most relied. The king made clear his preference to be surrounded by young men of unblemished noble lineage since:

> it is most certaine, that vertue or vice will oftentimes, with the heritage, be transferred from the parents to the posteritie, and runne on a blood (as the Proverbe is) the sicknesse of the minde becomming as kindly to some races, as these sicknesses of the body, that infect in the seede.

Here was a king who wanted his court to be filled with his friends and enhanced by the attendance of great nobles. In 1601, it was decreed that no one should have entry to the presence chamber, the outer chamber preceding the bedchamber, other than members of the peerage, their eldest sons or heirs and privy councillors.[16]

The prominent role of the nobility was evident in court ritual, especially at the key moments in the history of the Stewart dynasty. Mary's royal entry to Edinburgh in August 1561 was a lacklustre event that failed to impress anyone. By contrast, the baptism of prince James at Stirling in December 1566 was the high-point of Mary's reign when the key roles assigned to politically conservative and Roman Catholic nobles was intended to convey nuanced political messages. James VI's royal entry to Edinburgh on 19 October 1579 was the culmination of a series of staged events that announced the young king's intention to rule. The theatricality of the occasion was followed by a parliament that forfeited the once powerful Hamilton family. Anne of Denmark's entry to Edinburgh and coronation on

17 May 1590 was a politically crucial demonstration of James VI's international pretensions and his domestic authority. It was of crucial importance
to the king that his nobility were in attendance, and key roles in the coronation ceremonial were found for the first duke of Lennox, lord Hamilton and
the ninth earl of Angus. Hamilton, the fifth earl of Bothwell and a host of
other noblemen subsequently accompanied the new queen on a progress.
The participation of these men, and their wives, enhanced the legitimacy
and the profound nature of the event. Similarly, the annoyance felt by some
nobles that they were not appropriately involved in the proceedings was
not mere pique but had real political implications evident in a subsequent
boycott of the court and a convention of estates. Clearly, these royal
occasions did not always have the desired effect. In spite of the sophistication and cost of the baptism of prince Henry on 30 August 1594, the event
failed to impress visiting diplomats, or to engage the nobility, an indication
of the king's extreme political weakness at the time and of the broad level of
dissatisfaction among the nobles.[17]

The later early modern period witnessed a remarkable expansion of
European royal courts with a migration of nobles to the court from where
they were able to dominate crown offices.[18] For the Scottish nobility that
experience was played out in the context of the English royal court, since
James VI's succession to the English throne in the spring of 1603 brought to
an end a distinct Stewart royal court located in Scotland. There was a rush
to revive moribund places and privileges in 1617 and in 1633 when James VI
and Charles I made brief progresses of the kingdom.[19] But apart from these
exceptions, the court was located in London where occasional royal events
attracted the attendance of relatively large numbers of nobles south, such as
to prince Henry's funeral in 1612 or James VI's funeral in 1625 when 'the
most pairt of the nobility of both his kingdoms' accompanied the dead king's
procession. More commonly, Scots were few in number so that when
Charles I awaited the arrival of his new queen, Henrietta-Maria, in June
1625 the only Scot in the company of twenty-eight peers was the third
marquis of Hamilton.[20] Those nobles who attended court participated
in entertainments and cultural life as they had done before 1603; some
individuals like the second duke of Lennox, the first earl of Carlisle, the first
earl of Holdernesse and the third marquis of Hamilton were significant
cultural patrons. Others like the first earl of Stirling and the first earl of
Roxburghe promoted the idea of British imperial monarchy, but the number
of nobles engaged at this level was low. Consequently, the political messages
embedded by artists like Ben Johnson, Inigo Jones and Peter Paul Rubens in
the various mediums of the court had little penetration into noble society.
Instead, those Scots most associated with the court risked losing touch with
their native country. A handful of nobles embraced their new identity, it
being said of sir Robert Ker, first earl of Somerset, that he was 'naturally
more addicted to the English than to the Scots', while sir James Hay, earl of

Carlisle, established 'greater affection and esteem with the whole English nation than any other of that country by choosing their friendships and conversations, and really preferring it to any of his own'. But overwhelmingly the nobility maintained strong links with kinsmen and friends at home, with their own estates and tenants and with Scottish political issues.[21]

The crucial role of the court in England as a point of contact among the political elite increased under the Tudors, but while Elizabeth I mastered public display, she was never accessible in the manner of Scottish monarchs, and in spite of James VI and I's modifications to English court culture, aspects of the Tudor model of restrictive accessibility persisted.[22] But much of the ethos of the Stewart court was carried south with the king. Initially, the Scottish presence in the newly imported bedchamber to which the king continued to retreat with his most intimate servants was overwhelming, and because of its importance in the king's style of government that dominance was important to court politics. Scottish nobles, however, found that it was not only distance that separated them from the king, but that the scale and organisation of the court acted as a barrier in a manner that had been impossible to sustain before 1603. In 1614, the first lord Binning, the secretary of state, had to ask his friend John Murray of Lochmaben, a groom of the bedchamber, for help in furthering the cause of a client for 'Your help to his accesse, and his majesties heiring, will be his chief desyre'. On the other hand, Scots did well in acquiring around two-fifths of the higher court offices. The offices of first lord of the bedchamber, groom of the stool and keeper of the privy purse were held by Scots throughout the reign, along with ten of the fifteen gentlemen of the bedchamber appointed by James VI and I (there were between five and seven at any one time). These favoured household men included among their number the most spectacularly successful courtiers of the period: the second duke of Lennox; the second marquis of Hamilton; the first earls of Dunbar, Somerset, Kellie, Carlisle, Holdernesse and Annandale. There was only one Englishman in the bedchamber until 1615 when sir George Villiers, the future duke of Buckingham, gained entry. Even he was never able to disregard the influence of the bedchamber Scots, and it was only in the last year of James's reign that the English gained parity in numbers. Among the grooms of the bedchamber, an office with almost as great a potential for exploitative brokerage and royal favour, twelve of the fifteen appointed by James VI and I were Scots, with no Englishman being appointed before 1617. Eight of the eleven grooms in office in 1625 were Scots.[23]

The innovation of the Scottish bedchamber in London resulted in the downgrading of the previously important English privy chamber, although some of its officers, like the gentlemen ushers, were significant court brokers. James VI and I established equal numbers of Scots and English gentlemen, twenty-four each, although the share of the former fell as the

total number increased over succeeding years.[24] In the outer court, the earl
of Dunbar held the lucrative offices of master of the great wardrobe and
gentleman of the robes, combining these offices with the privy purse,
making him the principal financial officer of the household (he was also
treasurer in Scotland) and one of the most powerful figures at court. These
two offices were later held by another bedchamber Scot, the spendthrift first
earl of Carlisle. Sir Thomas Erskine of Gogar, later earl of Kellie, was
captain of the yeoman of the guard from 1603 to 1617, a sensitive office that
from 1605 he combined with the groom of the stool, giving him crucial
influence over access to the king. The second duke of Lennox was appointed
to the revived office of lord steward of the household in 1616 after a hiatus
of almost thirty years, and on his death in 1624 was succeeded by the second
marquis of Hamilton, another powerful court broker, prompting even an
enemy to remark 'I am glaide a Scotsman hes it'.[25]

At Charles I's court the Scottish household presence continued, although
the number of Scots steadily decreased. In spite of fears by old servants
of the dead king that Charles I was 'resolved as yet not to have anye of his
father's bedchamber cume to his', all James VI and I's servants retained
their places in the bedchamber and privy chamber. Most of these men were
reduced to the role of supernumeraries, but Carlisle became groom of the
stool in 1631, Annandale retained his political influence, while younger men
like sir Patrick Maule of Panmure and James Maxwell of Innerwick were
promoted. Prior to 1625, Charles's own household, like that of prince Henry
before his death in 1612, was staffed by Scots in key positions.[26] Most of
these men were transferred to the king's household on Charles's accession.
Sir James Fullerton, sir Robert Ker of Ancram and sir Robert Douglas of
Mains carried on their respective offices of groom of the stool, keeper of the
privy purse and master of the king's household. Sir William Alexander of
Menstrie and William Murray, the king's one-time whipping boy, became
gentlemen of the bedchamber, while sir Robert Gordon of Gordonstoun,
formerly of the prince's bedchamber, was appointed to the king's privy
chamber. Charles I continued to give due recognition to the houses of
Lennox and Hamilton, appointing both the fourth duke of Lennox and the
third marquis of Hamilton to his bedchamber. It was reported of Lennox
that he 'used to discourse with his majesty in his bedchamber rather than
at the Council-board', and such influence in terms of patronage and
policy should not be underestimated. Hamilton was elevated in 1628 to the
important office of master of the horse in succession to Buckingham,
making Hamilton the most influential Scot at court over the following
decade. The captaincy of the guard returned to Scottish hands in 1632
when the chancellor's son, sir George Hay of Kinfauns, was appointed, and
three years later he was succeeded by his father-in-law, the sixth earl of
Morton.[27]

One point of continuity between the pre-1603 court and the post-union court were diplomatic offices. These were among the most prestigious court positions and were dominated by the nobility with the rank of the leader of a mission depending on the importance attached to it or on the status of the host prince. For example, in October 1583, the fifth lord Seton was appointed ambassador to Henry III of France; the high level embassy of 1589 to Denmark was entrusted to the wealthy fifth earl Marischal because the king hoped he would defray at least some of the expenses; and the second earl of Mar conducted a highly successful embassy to London in the spring of 1601. In that same year the French-born second duke of Lennox headed a major embassy to Henry IV's court, and Lennox was employed in negotiating with France after 1603.[28] Following James VI's accession to the English throne, Scottish nobles and their sons continued to be prominent in establishing a foreign policy with a strong commitment to the house of Stewart's new British priorities. That policy was at times at odds with English interests, and Scottish nobles were at the fore in promoting the ambitions of the monarchy, for example, in relations with the Danish house of Oldenburg. Sir Andrew Sinclair of Ravenscraig and sir Robert Anstruther served as ambassadors at the Danish court, while sir James Spens and sir Andrew Keith held ambassadorial positions at the Swedish court. Diplomats and courtiers, like the experienced first earl of Carlisle, took a leading role in pursuing James VI and I's ambivalent policy towards the Palatinate in the early years of that crisis; the first earl of Nithsdale was involved in peace negotiations with cardinal Richelieu between 1628 and 1630; William Murray (later first earl of Dysart) was engaged in a mission to Flanders in 1632; and sir George Douglas, son of the laird of Mordington served in the army of Gustav Adolph and was ambassador at the Polish court from 1633–6 when he assisted in negotiating peace between Poland and Sweden.[29]

Court Clientage

James VI counselled that a king should 'make your Court and companie to bee a patterne of godlinesse and all honest vertues to all the rest of the people', recommending, unrealistically, that courtiers should be discouraged from helping their own kinsmen and friends for 'since ye must be of no surname nor kinne, but equall to all honest men; it becommeth you not to bee followed with partiall or factious servants'. The contrast between James VI's ideals and the reality of his court was stark; both in Scotland and later in England James VI's court was characterised by corruption, extravagance and vicious faction, behaviour that was not unusual among the royal courts of early modern Europe. In trying to make sense of this world historians have focused increasingly on relational networks that examine the impact of the court within the broader polity of the kingdom. Among the most politically important relationships in the early modern court was that defined by patron–client roles, including the increasingly dominant role of the king as patron.[30]

Court brokerage fell within the traditional responsibility of lordship, and the greater nobles had always acted as mediators between kings and their own dependants, especially in the pursuit of patronage. Nobles knew that while the local base of their power was essential, they needed court influence to feed the demands of their followers and to protect their interests from the predatory behaviour of rivals. When in May 1583 the first earl of Gowrie wrote to John Wemyss, apparent of that Ilk, promising to support him and his father in a quarrel, he did so against a background of political manoeuvring that was to cost Gowrie his life. Gowrie wrote, 'As for freynd-schip in court, ye ma assuir yourself that all the moyane and crydite I hef salbe extendit in the Lairdis favour and yowris', and in doing so he was shoring up his own power, not merely doing a favour for a friend. Halhill described the court in 1590 as a place where 'Officers and servandis ar not chosen for ther qualites, bot at the instance of this or that frend or courteour', alleging that an excessive number of servants were appointed 'wheras twa ar anew in every office'. Adopting the critical tone of the period that saw court life as inherently immoral, he implied that the court was awash with dishonest, greedy and highly competitive men. When in 1598 sir David Lindsay of Edzell asked his brother, John, lord Menmuir, to find places at court for a couple of clients, the latter was not optimistic since 'planting of men about the king is noth esie as ye belive, specialie if sik quhais competitors is alredie plantit'.[31]

In this environment nobles promoted favoured candidates demanding office, pensions, gifts and favours, and even the officers of state were attached to individual noble clientages. In 1600, both the secretary, James Elphinstone, and his elder brother, the master of Elphinstone, the treasurer, were described as clients of the first marquis of Huntly. Although the court was relatively accessible to lesser barons, it fell to the magnates like Huntly to act on behalf of their dependants. Sir Duncan Campbell of Glenorchy could attend court, but his interests were better represented by his lord, the seventh earl of Argyll, and it would have been a relief to receive a letter from court in *c.* 1603 telling him that 'Your cheif the erle of argyile hes caried him self heir with muche credit and to the k[ing's] contentment and nevir depairted being in so goode graice'.[32] A lord who failed as a courtier was likely to see the dissolution of his clientage, which in turn might under-mine his local lordship. Hence, after his political restoration in 1585 it was essential that lord Hamilton stuck close to the king if he was to rebuild the shattered Hamilton affinity. By 1587 the master of Gray was suing to become Hamilton's client; following the eighth lord Maxwell's death in 1593 that house grew increasingly dependent; and sir Rory Macdonald looked to Hamilton to help him out against the Campbells in 1594.[33] In contrast to Hamilton, the first duke of Lennox had no secure local base, being a Frenchman who was granted the Lennox estates and titles by default in 1580. He wrote to men like the laird of Buchanan pointing out that in the past the Buchanans had been 'tender friends of that our house', thus seeking to recreate a clientage based on those historic relationships. The appeal to history was desperate, but others recognised Lennox's usefulness as a powerful courtier with access to royal patronage. Hence, the Kers and Humes sought his maintenance in their efforts to oppose Douglas influence on the east and central marches. Another source of clientage for Lennox was the bedchamber in which he was appointed lord chamberlain with the right to nominate the other officers and gentlemen, while former Marians like Robert Melville and John Maitland who suffered during the Morton ascendancy sought out his patronage.[34]

A common figure of noble resentment at the renaissance court was the allegedly low-born favourite. History has its share of men who had been dispatched by supposedly virtuous lords acting in the interests of the commonweal: thus, Thomas Cochrane in the reign of James III and sir James Hamilton of Finnart in the reign of James V were brought down and killed because of the influence they were believed to wield. Similarly, Mary's private secretary, David Rizzio, 'occupied hir Majesteis ear of tymes in presens of the nobilite and when ther was greatest conventions of the estatis; quhilk maid hym to be so invyed and hated ... that some of the nobilitie wald glowm upon him, and some of them wald schulder him and schut him by'. On 9 March 1566, Rizzio was brutally stabbed to death in front of the queen in her chambers at Holyrood palace.[35] In his early years, James VI showed favour to a string of court favourites, although none of these were low-born. Walter Stewart, prior of Blantyre, described in the early 1580s as 'ane of the Kingis cheife mynonis', a term borrowed from France, was a childhood companion. Others were recruited from among the younger sons of the peerage. James Stewart of Bothwellhaugh, a younger son of the second lord Ochiltree, used his position in the king's guard to gain the juvenile king's confidence, rising to become earl of Arran and chancellor in 1584. Alexander Lindsay, the younger son of the tenth earl of Crawford, seemed likely to become a great courtier but by 1590 was undermined by more powerful nobles who dominated the court throughout the remainder of the decade. Efforts by dissident nobles to portray the first lord Thirlestane as a similar type failed because it was so obviously untrue, but the choice of propaganda is significant.[36]

The case for the centralisation of political patronage in early modern courts and its political use to rulers in extending their control over localities is often exaggerated, but the pattern of patronage relationships was increasingly focused on princely courts.[37] After 1603 a successful court career offered the fastest and most rewarding rise to wealth and status. The king's household consumed around 40 per cent of his enormous English revenue, and with somewhere between £250,000 and £400,000 sterling available in

fees and gratuities the competition was worthwhile entering. Sir Patrick
Murray was a gentleman usher in the privy chamber where he received
an annual pension of £300 sterling and gifts to the value of at least £3,000
sterling, a huge sum by Scottish standards. It was little wonder that in 1622
the first earl of Kellie advised the second earl of Mar to spend between £800
and £900 sterling to secure his son a place in the privy chamber. Even
modest offices were pursued with great energy. In October 1615, an excited
Robert Douglas wrote to his father, James Douglas, commendator of
Melrose, that 'I am now will agreid for ane place of ane sirgant giv it will ples
my Lord and your to consent onto it for it is the hei way to my gret advancement and preferment'. Similarly, sir Thomas Hope of Craighall was
delighted when in December 1634 his son, Alexander, was appointed an
extraordinary carver to the king, and two years later this young man was
promoted to ordinary carver after paying off a rival. Here men were
presented with opportunities to rise in the world that would have been
unthinkable before 1603. Patrick Maule of Panmure arrived in London in
1603 as a groom of the bedchamber, inherited a heavily indebted estate three
years later, and was able to relieve that debt piece by piece with the proceeds
of his court career, becoming a wealthy earl. Panmure recognised that
'except he had favour in court, his house had ended'. Especially in the early
years of the regal union the Scots received massive rewards from the king,
amounting by 1610 to £10,614 sterling in pensions, £88,280 sterling in cash,
£133,100 sterling in old debts and £11,093 sterling in annuities. The second
duke of Lennox and his brother, d'Aubigny, the earl of Dunbar, the second
earl of Mar and sir James Hay exploited practices such as selling pensions,
collecting old debts, manipulating indirect grants and skimming revenue
from commercial activities in which the crown had a stake. By the reign of
Charles I, Scots no longer enjoyed such disproportionate rewards, but the
court continued to be a source of significant financial benefits.[38]

Much of this wealth was squandered in an extravagant world of conspicuous consumption, and a handful of courtiers established themselves
with estates in England and Ireland, acquiring alongside their new lands
English wives and honours. One or two families became established as
English noble houses increasingly disconnected from Scotland, the dukes
of Lennox, the earls of Somerset and the Bruce house of Kinloss being
the most prominent, but the overwhelming majority of noble families,
including the house of Hamilton, remained rooted in their own localities,
investing in their Scottish estates.[39] Of course, there was a huge financial risk
involved in establishing a presence in London. Even the greatest of nobles
had to be careful about remaining at court for long without support from the
king's largesse, hence, the concerted campaign in 1625-7 by Charles I to
persuade the third marquis of Hamilton to come to court. Hamilton wisely
held out until he had sufficient guarantees that the king would meet his
costs. Consequently, the court nobility was placed in a client relationship

with the king, but this did not mean that they were politically neutralised since they enjoyed political influence as the king's most immediate advisers.[40]

That huge growth in royal patronage in the early seventeenth century altered the relationship between crown and nobility. In a speech to a convention of estates in March 1617, secretary Binning arguing that the king could not be denied taxation by men who had been so 'honored with dignities and inriched ... as had almost over throwne both the Churche and the Crowne'. Few men would have disagreed that the royal bounty had been bestowed on many nobles, and economic clientage was a fact of life, as it was in France where debts to the crown and pensions were exploited by the king to exert greater influence over the nobility.[41] In practice this development placed power in the hands of courtiers and much of the factional intrigue at court was a struggle to control resources. The need to maintain the flow of patronage came at a price, as William Drummond of Hawthornden observed in his 1635 'Apologetical letter' where he criticised 'the Avarice of the Officers of and Favourites of Princes; who are brought foolishly to believe that by tearing of the skins of the flock they shall turn the Shepherd rich'. The popular attitude to crown patronage was expressed in 1615 by John Cockburn of Ormiston, the justice clerk, in a letter to the king requesting the ward and non-entry of his grandson, the ninth lord Sinclair. He asked for this gift as evidence 'that I am still in your Majesties gratious favour (sence it hathe bein customeable to those in publick places and employed in daylie service to be ever respected in this kynd'. Kings understood the need to meet this expectation, knowing that good service was primed by incentives. When in 1629 the first earl of Carrick's pension of £500 sterling remained unpaid for four years, Charles I wrote to his treasurer pointing out that the hold-up was not only to Carrick's 'great loss and prejudice', but that the earl was 'much dishabled for our service'. Unsurprisingly, therefore, in asking for favours, the most skilful courtiers were careful to phrase their requests in a manner that suggested it was the king who would benefit from his own generosity.[42] Yet while pensions gave the crown leverage over the nobility, it is noticeable that most of the great lords remained regional magnates whether or not they held high office or were able to draw on a royal pension. The houses of Argyll and Huntly did relatively poorly from royal patronage in the early seventeenth century, yet it was these two great interests that emerged as among the handful of leading power brokers of the 1640s solely on the strength of their inherited power.

Nevertheless, after 1603 the court's expensive and distant location, access to which was controlled through the necessity of acquiring a travel licence, alongside a more centralised political culture, resulted in an enhanced role for court brokers.[43] That role continued to be filled by the great magnates like the heads of the houses of Lennox and Hamilton, and by royal servants with ready access to the king and without the physical vulnerability that such men risked before 1603. When in 1611 one of the second duke of Lennox's dependants urged him to return to Scotland to fill the power vacuum created by the earl of Dunbar's death, the duke replied 'I must confess that I am loathe to leave my personall attendance on his Majestie'. Lennox was dim and lazy, he hated administration and he enjoyed the comforts of London, but the king's cousin knew that he could best serve his own interests and those of his clients by remaining at court.[44] Any absence from the court brought the risk of being forgotten or undermined. In October 1611, while in Scotland, sir Robert Ker of Ancram, a gentleman of prince Henry's chamber, wrote a concerned letter to Adam Newton, the prince's secretary, asking 'that ze will be ane instrument to keep me in my maister's favour ... especially thatt no detractor have power to begett an ill opinion of me for descharge of this service the King has been pleased to putt in my hands'.[45] Similarly, in 1615, the twelfth earl of Sutherland wrote to his brother, Gordonstoun, lamenting that he was home in Scotland when there was important business to be conducted at court, but concluded that they should be thankful since 'God hath cassin yow in thais pairtis not onlie for your selff, bot also for the weall of our hous, for what moyen wald we haif at court if ye wer not thair'. Gordonstoun's better access to the king, and his London connections (in a fifteen-month spell throughout 1611–12, he made six trips back and forth between London and Sutherland), helped to ensure that his family got the better of the rival fifth earl of Caithness. Gordonstoun took with him young kinsmen 'to remark the court, therby to serve the earle of Southerland, when it should please him to imploy them agane'.[46] Even the second earl of Mar, the king's lifelong friend and the lord treasurer, worried over his courtier friends' ability to influence the king. Mar disliked London and asked Kellie to suggest 'the choice of a man to lie at court for him', but while Mar was fortunate to have his cousin close to the king it was no substitute for his own presence. In 1622, Mar wrote to Kellie, his 'Good Gossup', about various lawsuits with the fourth lord Elphinstone, fearing that defeat would be doubly damaging since 'the warld will think that my Lord Elphinstoun has mor favor of my master than I haive, quhilk will doo me mor herm than all the land is worth'.[47] Absences from court could be disastrous. Some of the explanation for the decline in power of the first marquis of Huntly lay in his increasing difficulties after 1603 in gaining access to the court, and when the sixth earl of Morton was lobbying for the order of the garter in 1634, the earl of Pembroke told him that his rival's case was lost only because he had returned prematurely to Scotland.[48]

Dame Julian Ker, the extravagant and ambitious third wife of the first earl of Haddington, nursed the hope that if her eldest son by a previous marriage took her advice and cultivated his patron, he 'wolbe ane gret courteour'. In pursuit of that ambition courtiers were subjected to constant lobbying, especially as James VI and I used his favourites and courtiers to channel suitors away from himself. The first lord Napier reported that 'The King's consent once being got, every man who had power putt in for his friend, without respect of his sufficiency or ability: Bot no man could bee proposed against whom his Majestie did not take some exception'. In May 1613, John Livingston wrote from Whitehall to his lord and chief, the first earl of Linlithgow to remind him that he would be 'ever redy to call his Majestie to memory of your Lordship's meritt at all occasiounes' Here Linlithgow was in danger of being beholden to a minor dependant. Chancellor Dunfermline's relationship with John Murray of Lochmaben, a gentleman of the bedchamber, was one in which the former had the greater status, wealth and official authority, but the latter's court influence and proximity to the king could not be disregarded. In writing to Lochmaben in the spring of 1615, Dunfermline assured him that 'friends and kinsmen as wie are man daylie be doand to otheris all guid offices thay can, everie ane in his vocatioun, place and calling'. Similarly, rank appeared to be reversed when Patrick Maule of Panmure wrote to the sixth earl of Morton in November 1630 that he had spoken to the king on his behalf, assuring Charles I that Morton was 'ane honest and real servant'. And not all patrons were Scots. Alexander Innes revealed his high hopes of receiving the duke of Buckingham's favour in an excited letter to his father, telling him that 'Nixt unto almightie God they depend upon my lorde Deuke by whoes favour befor many dayes I hope to obtaine a part of my desyres'.[49] It was these courtiers that sir Thomas Urquhart of Cromarty had in mind when he mocked the vanity of those who 'having no higher qualification, then to sweep the privie rooms, or at most to make the king's bed, were short while after so bedaubed with honours'.[50]

It is easy to be cynical about the sincerity of the language used in letters between court brokers and their clients, but the expressions of fidelity were precisely gauged to achieve a social and political purpose in a world where words carried weight. The exercise of court patronage and the values underlying it is revealed in the correspondence between the sixth earl of Morton and the third marquis of Hamilton, or between the second earl of Mar and his cousin, the first earl of Kellie. Sir Robert Ker of Ancram's place in the bedchamber ensured that he was the recipient of numerous begging letters from family, friends and would-be clients. In 1621, the first viscount Lauderdale wrote to Ancram asking for his support in getting a place on prince Charles's council; the archbishop of St Andrews sought preferment for his sons in February 1622; and sir John Stewart of Traquair tried to enlist his help in getting a title in 1625. Even when Ancram proved to be unable to move a client's interests forward, as in the case of sir Thomas Hope of Craighall in 1625, he expected that because he had done his best, then 'I desyre and expect the continowance of your good will'.[51]

The cultivation of these relationships with courtiers required subtlety and persistence, and for the client the greatest worry was to be neglected by their patron. A frustrated and deeply worried suitor wrote to the sixth earl of Morton, 'I could never have thoct that I suld have bin absolutlay forgot'. By contrast, in the spring of 1629 Ancram sent a message to James Johnstone of that Ilk, assuring him that 'howsoever I do not wryte often, yet I do forget no cause of kyndnes that is between you and me, eyther by blood or allyance or kyndnes with your worthy father, which I shall never forgett above all other obligations'.[52] For the likes of Johnstone, kicking his heels in the southwest of Scotland and waiting for an opportunity to serve the king, this news from a well-connected courtier would have been received with enormous relief. Clients, therefore, had to ensure that their court patrons were reminded from time to time of their existence. Sir William Livingston of Kilsyth's regular intelligence from Scotland to the second duke of Lennox when in France *c.* 1605 served the dual purpose of allowing Kilsyth to influence the duke's opinions while ensuring that Kilsyth continued to command his attention. On his return, Lennox thanked Kilsyth, promising 'I shall not willinglei oversee any occation whairby I may be effects schow my thankfullness'.[53] Writing in *c.* 1620, Gordonstoun, an experienced former courtier, advised his nephew to 'insinuat your self in favour with some favourit as is in greatest credit at court for the tyme'.

> Trouble him not for triffles. Complement with him as often as you can find occasion. Present him with many yet small gifts and of lytle charge; and if you have cause to bestowe any great gratuitie on him, let it be no kist commoditie or obscure thing, but such a present as may be daylie in sight, the better to be remembred. Being thus carefull to have good freinds at court, your prince shall be alwayes rightly enformed of any bussines which doth concerne you or your freinds.[54]

Clients repeatedly reminded patrons of their usefulness by drawing attention to their willingness to serve. In the 1620s sir John Stewart of Traquair felt no embarrassment in describing himself in letters to the sixth earl of Morton as the latter's servant. Another Morton client, sir John Wemyss of Wemyss, having been created a lord of parliament on 1 April 1628, wrote to thank the earl for supporting his cause, promising that he was 'ever boithe redie and glaid to be commandit be your L[ordship] to ventour my lyf and all I have in the woirld in your L[ordship's] service'. When in June 1629 sir William Seton of Kylesmuir ran into Ancram in Edinburgh he seized the opportunity to remind the influential courtier of 'the old love betuixt his father and me', and 'wold to his deathe honour me as ane father; wissing I sould mak tryell of him, and if I fand not his actiouns ansuer to his words, let never man give him trust'. Warmed by the compliments and promises of kindness Ancram went on his way 'glaid'. Kylesmuir had achieved his aim of placing himself at the centre of Ancram's thoughts.[55]

Men placed great value on these cultivated relationships, some of which endured over decades. In December 1613, John Murray of Lochmaben, a gentleman of the bedchamber, wrote to Thomas Hamilton of Drumcairn, a privy councillor, the secretary of state and recently created lord Binning, assuring him that:

> As for your lordschippis favour to me in all my turnes, I will never doubt off it and, as the warld goethe, naither yee nor I can promees for mor nor our selffis, and in one thinge that may concerne youe, ather in credit or honour, yee shall be confident that I will not change.[56]

This friendship endured throughout both men's successful careers. Similarly, the second marquis of Hamilton's message to the sixth earl of Morton that 'he [Hamilton] is as much yours as he is any mans, as he for his part is as confidant of your lordships affection to him as of any frends', articulated a set of values that recognised the value of stable friendships between men, especially in dealings at court.[57] These lasting friendships mattered. When chancellor Hay's political career was in danger of being broken over his opposition to the revocation in 1626, one observer predicted, rightly, that he would survive 'for hei hes manie freindis'.[58] Such fixed relationships were hugely important in a court where competition for place and factional politics had a corrosive impact on trust. In 1634, Craighall advised the first earl of Nithsdale not to fall out with Annandale over a property transaction because 'nather of you hes samony freindis in this old world that ye haif reasoun to suffer any dissolution of that true friendship quhilk hes bene so long betuix you'.[59] In a similar vein, the first earl of Stirling warned one of his allies that they must be careful not to fall out with their friends for 'there are some who wold not greeve to see everie one of us ruine another, and others in our place'.[60] Consequently, much effort was put into resolving disputes. When in 1623 a quarrel between the second marquis of Hamilton and the second earl of Mar was mediated by friends, the latter wrote to Hamilton that 'in the auld Scotts fassion lett thir bypast foleis of ours bee all buried with you as thay ar and still shalbe with me, and latt thaim go to the devill quha hes cassin thaim in amongst us'.[61]

Court Faction

Court faction should not be divorced from wider political debates in the country, and rival factions often represented ideological positions, but factional competitiveness took place between courtiers who shared a common view of broader issues such as religion or foreign policy.[62] The remarkably long and successful court career of the second duke of Lennox was attributed by one writer to the fact that he was above faction, meaning he followed the king in everything. In large measure this was true, but most courtiers found it impossible to avoid being drawn into factional intrigue and competition for patronage, hence, the near neurotic obsession with favour as a measure of political virility.[63] In 1623, the first earl of Roxburghe optimistically told sir Robert Ker of Ancram that he should not be concerned over a loss of royal favour since 'fortune may eclipse for ane tyme bot it can not overthraw vertew and honestie and boithe curage and knowledge is well deservit in strong suffering'.[64] In this case Roxburghe was right and Ancram was restored to favour, but few courtiers believed that virtue would triumph of its own accord. Over half a century earlier, sir Richard Maitland of Lethington provided his son with advice on how to be a model courtier in a poem warning him of the transience of fortune. Modest circumspection and obedience to the prince were the qualities he believed to be essential for survival in the dangerous environment of the court. Another writer conveyed this sense of the insubstantial nature of good fortune since 'all thais that puttis maist confidence in the court of a Prence, be at sumtyme happelie exaltit, and at uther tymes miserablie dejectit'. Such was the pessimism of this anonymous writer that when commenting on the first duke of Lennox's acquisition of the office of great chamberlain, he wrote that the duke 'considderit litill that the mair men of honor be promovit, ather be thair awin procurement, or be intysement of thair counsallors, thay are the mair neir to a great fall'.[65]

In Halhill's *Memoirs* reflecting on the court before 1603, and in the letters of the first earl of Kellie from the London court, there is a prevalent sense of uncertainty and mutability, of the caprices of fortune, the fickleness of friends and the unpredictability of kings and of God who might raise men up or throw them down at any moment and without any apparent reason. The first lord Napier made this point about the London court where open factions rarely did any serious damage, but 'it is the subtle practizes and secreat aspersions of supposed frends that ar the noysum vapours which breede a perpetual plague and mortalitie to our fortunes and reputation'.[66] Nobles, therefore, exhibited great psychological insecurity on account of inhabiting a dynamic and unstable political universe in which the only fixed points were those provided by the lineage. In the aftermath of James VI's death in 1625 and the fall-out over the revocation, when both Kellie and his cousin, the second earl of Mar, suddenly became yesterday's men, the latter sought to impress Charles I with a documented record of his family's loyal service since the fourteenth century. Fortune and age were no longer on Mar's side, but by appealing to history he sought to retain royal favour for his family in the future. This sense of the transience of royal favour was further enhanced by a belief that the court was overwhelmingly the preserve of ambitious young men. While older courtiers like Halhill or Mar might retain influence because of past service, or because the monarch was grow-ing old, those who hoped to rise had to be young and as men inevitably aged they lived with the constant dread of falling.[67]

The focus of all courtiers was the king, and success or failure often rested on the personal nature of the relationship with the monarch. The affection of a king for particular courtiers cut across the calculations of the best political commentators, and most royal courts had a dominant favourite who played a particular political role as an intermediary between the king and other courtiers. This was the case with James VI from Esmé Stewart, who captured the admiration of the young king in the autumn of 1579, through to the duke of Buckingham, who was the king's closest confidante during the last years of his life. As early as 1581, observers noted the appearance at James VI's court of 'Cabinet Councillors' who wielded considerable influence, while the king's persistent favour towards the sixth earl of Huntly in the later 1580s and into the early 1590s perplexed the Protestant Anglophile party and Elizabeth I who warned the king that 'eache faction seeketh, eyther by force or practise, to possesse himself either of his favour or person, that under the cullour of his aucthoritie they maie prosecute their particuler revenges by charginge the contrarie partie with disloyaltie'. Of course, the Tudor court was no less riven by faction, and Elizabeth I's objection was to the political implications of Huntly's influence at court, not to the system of favourites and factions.[68]

Intense factionalism was rife at the court and the dizzying change in friendships and enmities reflected the fact that political loyalties were more fluid than in the localities where kinship and lordship defined relatively stable relationships. One seasoned courtier recalled 'how necessary it is to have gud frendis besyd the prince, and how hurtfull and dangerous, when sic as have the prince ear ar ennemys. Otherwayes what soever he be that reposes upon his gud service, is commonly cowped [= overturned] and wraked.' Indeed, as Halhill observed in 1583, the many sudden and partial changes in office-holding, inspired by jealousy and taking the form of un-justified accusations, had bred 'sa furious a faction' that civil war loomed.[69] In this environment there thrived, at least temporarily, men like the fifth earl of Bothwell, 'an undertaking man' of no fixed loyalties, 'feared of both sides, trusted of neither'. In the context of the court, friendship was unstable even if nobles went out of their way to demonstrate public integrity. In September 1580, when the eighth earl of Angus was pressed to enter into friendship with the eighth earl of Lennox, he avoided the issue, saying 'he was his friend already', while the second earl of Mar left court rather than acquiesce in the king's efforts to bring him into alliance with Lennox.[70] Such matters appear of little consequence, but behind them was the serious issue of gauging support for Lennox if and when he moved against the fourth earl of Morton. Angus's evasion and Mar's actions signalled their desire to distance themselves from Lennox and in time they made their enmity public.

The cynical and nostalgic view of court politics that is expressed in Lethington's poem, 'Na kyndnes at court without siller', offers an insight into the allegedly corrupt values of Mary's court where no relationship could be sustained without financial inducements and favours.[71] Examples of weak political bonds in this environment are not difficult to identify. Commenting on the fall of the fourth earl of Morton in 1580, Halhill observed that the former regent had been careless in attending to his clientele. His sudden collapse of fortune

> was thocht strange, in respect of his many freindis that wer in court for the tym, wha wer then found to be bot frendis of his fortoun; for he was lovit be nane, and envyed and hatted be many, sa that they all luked throw ther fingers to se his fall.

Here the crucial ingredients were the appearance at court of Esmé Stewart who was pushed into the role of royal favourite, a powerful combination of discontented nobles at court and in the localities, and the exploitation of royal revenues by treasurer Gowrie to fund Morton's enemies.[72] Of course, detachment from the evils of the court, the inevitable disappointment of public life, and reflection on a former golden age, were common refrains in a culture exposed to neo-stoic concepts of virtue. Half a century after Lethington penned his verses, Gordonstoun expressed the view that the royal court was full of untrustworthy and ambitious men whose loyalties were so inconstant that none could be trusted. His own kinsman, the sixth earl of Huntly, had experience of the transience of court friendships in the 1590s. The extent to which Huntly's faction at court was built on family connections, religion or simple hatred of chancellor Thirlestane, remains debateable, but at the time of the Brig o' Dee conspiracy in 1589 its fragility was exposed. Further evidence of that weakness surfaced in February 1592 in the face of the public outrage that greeted the murder of the second earl of Moray when 'Few of Huntly's great friends in Court are found to stick by him'. This weakness at court was in contrast to the loyalty Huntly enjoyed in the northeast, or even on account of his nominal leadership of the kingdom's Catholic community. Therefore, it was difficult for men to use their court influence to create a significant power base in the localities.[73] For example, none of the dominant court politicians of the 1580s and 1590s were able to make inroads into the east march in spite of repeated efforts, and power continued to be exercised by local nobles. In the end it was more advantageous to the king to reach out to the locality and draw to court men like sir George Hume of Spott, who carved out a successful career as a courtier and in time was able to represent the king on the east march.[74]

These factions were particularly dangerous in the years between the end of the Morton regency in 1578 and the mid-1590s when the adult James VI finally assumed leadership over his own court. Robert Bowes' report in 1580 related that:

> The strife in the nobility and others about the King at present is raised and nourished by the inordinate desire occupying each several party and faction to attain and hold the ear and nearness of the King, which they would turn to their own advantage and for their private respects, according to their several and secret intentions, agreeable to their plots devised, and for the gaining wherof all, in manner, who serve for it, wholly neglect the public causes.[75]

At times in the later 1580s the reports of the inexperienced young English agent, William Asheby, convey an impression of utter confusion and constant conflict. To cite one example, the incompetent shambles over the captaincy of the guard in 1588, when the master of Glamis, Alexander Lindsay and the sixth earl of Huntly all competed for the office, is indicative of the vicious in-fighting that characterised the period. Another English diplomat commented in May 1593 that 'This Court and all therein are so rent and divided, and so little credit is given to any promises that some of the best affected are resolved to leave it'. As the French ambassador observed in 1587, factionalism was to some extent a product of deliberate royal policy by which James VI sought:

> To nourish them in pike on with an other; thinkinge, he shall beste maintaine him self in suretie with them, by this meanes, rather than by their union, which he hathe hindered as much as bene in him to do.

Such a policy was consistent with James VI's behaviour and it might have been necessary as a means to enhance his own power, but the reputational cost was high and the impact on noble behaviour in a feuding society was predictable. The Gowrie conspiracy, which resulted in the killing of the third earl of Gowrie and his brother by the king's servants at Perth in August 1600, was in part a consequence of a bitter factional struggle within the court.[76]

The glue that held court clientage relationships together, linking the court to the localities in a currency of exchanged favours, was patronage and the alleged corruption that often accompanied it.[77] Scottish kings had extensive forms of patronage, mostly relating to local office and resources that were the primary interest of nobles, but the squabble over the few worthwhile court offices and the modest pensions and gifts could be equally intense. The court was among the most vigorously contested public spheres, and success or failure was a significant measure of noble power, affecting a lord's ability to control his own locality and reward his own kinsmen, dependants and friends. Hence, the antagonistic rhetoric, often focused on allegations of corruption, that surrounded issues of patronage. In March 1578, for example, the regent Morton defended himself from critics who said he was greedy by suggesting that they were jealous, pointing out that 'It lyis not in us sa liberally to deale the Kingis geare as to satisffie all cravers'. It was to stem corruption and the dangers of factional influence in government that from that year there were repeated and futile efforts by privy councillors to tighten up the procedures by which documents passed through the seals. Yet dealing in the king's wealth was exactly what was expected of those who held office and influence at court, not least to cope with the heavy expense of remaining in the king's presence. Indeed, financing the court was a constant problem, and from 1586 the king was himself a client of Elizabeth I, the pension he received being distributed among courtiers such that 'what he gettes from Ingland, if it were a myllion, they wold get it from him, so careless is he of any welth if he may enjoy his pleasure in huntynge'. Similarly, it was alleged of the bedchamber in 1590 that its members were responsible for 'causing his Maieste subscryve sindre hurtfull signatours and commissions; and gat past for them selves and ther frendis, the best and maist proffitable casualties'.[78] But James VI was not being careless; he understood the importance of lubricating political life with patronage if he was to retain the support of his nobles. In turn, those nobles, like nobles elsewhere, knew that a presence at court was essential if they were to control access to royal patronage and to frustrate the ambitions of their rivals. Consequently, even with his English pension, the king remained short of cash and was liberal in the use of his privy seal. A succession of financial expedients were tried and discarded, and the formation in 1596 of a reform administration staffed largely by the queen's financial officers – the Octavians – enjoyed a measure of success. Unfortunately, that success included savage spending cuts that aroused the resentment of courtiers and impacted on the king's ability to satisfy his nobles so that the Octavians had to abandon their plans even if most of them continued in royal service. Nevertheless, the widespread support James VI enjoyed from his nobles throughout what proved to be the last few years of the king's residence in Scotland, alongside the less dangerous nature of court politics during that period, indicates that the balance between the deployment of patronage and the exercise of royal oversight over court faction had attained an acceptable, if fragile, level of political stability.[79]

The skills needed to survive in the new British court after 1603 were not new to nobles who travelled throughout Europe, nor were they absent from James VI's Scottish court, but in London it was important to understand the rules of conduct for what was a new and different environment. Here an apparent superficiality and rootless loyalty often concealed real talent in the art of being a successful courtier, along with sharp political instincts and even genuine commitment on a range of issues among men like the earl of Somerset and the duke of Buckingham, or the third marquis of Hamilton and the earl of Holland.[80] Unsurprisingly, factionalism did not end, and for nobles the mores of court politics were complicated by the need to maintain a presence in London while seeking to exercise influence in Scotland. In the 1630s, for example, the third marquis of Hamilton was able to live at court only because he had useful friends like the first earl of Traquair holding powerful offices in Edinburgh.[81] Those nobles who based themselves at court did not lose sight of their local interests, and the issue of a divergence between court and country is problematic. Court nobles did not immediately lose touch with their localities because they were in London, and many nobles moved in and out of the court depending on a variety of circumstances such as age, health, finance or political connections. Hamilton and the second earl of Antrim combined a court presence alongside maintaining active interests in their affairs in Scotland and Ireland. The picture of the second duke of Lennox, Hamilton and the first earl of Kellie sitting in the king's bedroom at Whitehall striking a bargain that would allow Hamilton to acquire the second earl of Mar's teinds of the kirk at Lanark suggests that little escaped the notice of court grandees.[82] The issue of the extent to which Caroline court culture was divorced from the kingdoms ruled by Charles I is no longer so clear-cut, and something like a distinct Scottish court culture did endure beyond 1603. As far as Scottish nobles are concerned the evidence for a cultural divergence between a handful of politically influential courtiers and the rest of the nobility is thin. These courtiers may have demonstrated greater loyalty to the king when his government collapsed over the summer of 1637, but they were not divorced from Scottish society and politics.[83]

While court faction had a less immediate impact on Scottish politics after 1603, the rise and fall of courtiers still had repercussions. In the early years, the earl of Dunbar was the dominant courtier in London, acting as a powerful link between the king and the privy council in Edinburgh until his unexpected death in January 1611 suddenly altered the political landscape.[84] The remarkable career of sir Robert Ker, earl of Somerset, was based entirely on his relationship with the king and, from 1612, with the increasingly powerful Howard family whose pro-Spanish and conciliatory stance towards Roman Catholics he supported. From 1606 he rose steadily in favour and Dunbar's death, followed by that of the earl of Salisbury in 1612, allowed Somerset to consolidate his position as the pre-eminent broker in Scottish business at court. Changes in the personnel of the Edinburgh administration reflected Somerset's influence: his maternal uncle, sir Gideon Murray of Elibank, became treasurer depute; his cousin, sir Robert Ker of Ancram replaced sir William Cranstoun as captain of the border guard; his brother-in-law, sir Thomas Hamilton of Drumcairn was clerk register before being promoted to secretary of state in 1612; and Somerset became lord treasurer in 1613. He remained the king's favourite for another two years and his dramatic fall in 1616 came when he was accused and subsequently convicted of a murder for which he was imprisoned. Somerset's fate had repercussions for his friends and there were risks in being identified too closely with a great courtier.[85] Buckingham was the greatest court patron of the age, acquiring influence that extended into most fields of crown policy, and even among the highest ranking nobles Buckingham's patronage was important, but after his assassination in 1628 some of his clients were swept away. The first earl of Nithsdale attached himself to Buckingham, marrying his cousin, but after the duke's death, he rapidly lost favour and was exposed on account of his Catholicism and heavy debts.[86]

When James VI died in 1625, the first lord Napier recounted, 'Then was there nothing but factions, and factious consultations, of the one, to hold that place and power they possess before, of the other, to wrest it out of their hands, and to invest themselves'. Napier recalled a court in which it was the king's manner:

> to give way to strong opposition, or his favourites intreaties, yet never to give
> over his purpose, but at another tyme to worke it by the meanes of a contrary
> faction, to free and discharge himselfe of the others discontentment upon the
> faction.

In other words, James encouraged faction within his court. The extent of these bitter disputes could be farcical. In the autumn of 1630, treasurer Mar protested that Napier, his depute, was making separate preparations of his own for the visit of the king to Scotland. Neither man was prepared to co-operate, just as they had made the administration of the king's financial affairs a matter of personal vindictiveness between them after Napier's appointment as Mar's depute in 1622.[87] And while blood was no longer spilled, there continued to be casualties. The fall of the seventh earl of Menteith in 1633 is significant chiefly as a demonstration of the devastating effect of cleverly controlled factional politics.[88] What is less clear is the extent to which court faction was integral to political debate. The factionalism that spilled over from the court into the English parliament in the 1620s does not appear to have followed a similar process in Scotland, although individual Scots were identified with Spanish and French factions at court. In 1617, the Spanish ambassador sought to recruit support from, among others, chancellor Dunfermline and the seventh earl of Argyll whom he believed to be sympathetic to the Spanish cause, and there was a Scottish contingent sympathetic to the proposed Spanish match. On the other hand, the second duke of Lennox and the second marquis of Hamilton were key players in rejecting the Spanish treaties in 1624. Hamilton was a close friend of Charles I, who was described as an individual 'with the greatest power over the affection of the king of any man at that time' and he was a strong advocate of a pro-French foreign policy in the 1630s.[89]

There is a sense in which, for all their divisions, Scottish courtiers were seen by the English as akin to a faction. Such thinking formed a background to the gunpowder plot in 1605 and to much of the discussion surrounding the management of James VI and I's finances.[90] The first indication that the geographic location of the court had a political impact occurred for many nobles and royal servants who accompanied James VI south in the spring of 1603 when they were denied a place. Consequently, most lower rank servants were sent home, and in an effort to prevent Whitehall being flooded by Scots, from February 1604 a licence was required to attend court. Even with 193 offices available for nobles and gentlemen, the king did not have adequate places to satisfy demand, and he risked alienating the English by treating his Scottish servants over-generously. Yet that is exactly what James VI and I did, and one Englishman complained as early as November 1603 that 'the respect at court of the Scots by all the attendant officers is so partiall, as the English find themselves muche disgraced. The meanest of that countrie may enter your presence without controlment; but the English [are] verie unreasonablie putt backe'. The king's refusal to be separated from his long-favoured servants and friends, combined with his irritation at English intransigence over his British union project, ensured that Scots dominated the inner court circles for a decade and continued to hold a disproportionate share of court offices. Throughout James VI and I's reign, the Scots captured 43 per cent of the higher court offices, concentrated largely in the king's bedchamber, privy chamber, the queen's household and the households of the two princes. Some 149 Scots were successful in acquiring court office, and sir John Holles's claim that the king 'filled every corner of the court with theis beggarly blew caps' is understandable. Scots dominated the households of queen Anne and of prince Henry. In 1611, the king gave in to English pressure to halt the influx of Scots to London and the court where their success and swagger exacerbated tensions between members of the two nations, prompting the Scottish privy council to denounce unlicensed suitors. But it was not until the second decade of union that large-scale attendance by Scots at court declined. In 1617, one young gentleman gave up trying to get a position because of the 'envy of the Englishe crue'. Leaving London for Italy, he grumbled that 'our Scottish-men are in verie lyttle regaird among the Englishe and I think more hated now than befoir the King com in England'. In December 1635, the sixth earl of Eglinton was advised that if he wished to get a place for his younger son in prince Charles's bedchamber he must work hard, soliciting the king personally and engaging the aid of his friends 'for many great mens sonnes heer are ayming at this mark, the place being great and honorable'. In fact, the prince of Wales's household was dominated by Englishmen, the highest ranking Scot in 1638 being Archibald Primrose, one of the gentlemen ushers.[91] The days of the Scots strutting through a court they dominated was long over.

By the 1630s a large number of nobles with enhanced status and expec-tations were chasing a restricted number of places in which insider families operated closed patronage networks. Few men who were not already court insiders were able to break into this privileged ring of courtier families, chiefly Stewarts, Hamiltons, Erskines, Murrays and Douglases, and by 1633 the average age of the twenty leading Scottish courtiers was a greying forty-six. In spite of mixed marriages, court offices and English estates this small, select group of courtiers was not anglicised, but as the older generation of independently-minded courtiers died or lost influence they were replaced by courtiers who worked out how to please Charles I by telling him what he wanted to hear. This latter point was evident from the beginning of the reign in the devising of the revocation among a small group of courtiers in London, men like the first earl of Nithsdale whose corrosive influence on a range of policies was highly damaging, while the privy council in Edinburgh was deliberately kept uninformed. Increasingly, courtiers like sir Alexander Strachan of Thornton or sir William Alexander of Menstrie sought to justify policy by asserting the king's prerogative powers. By the later 1630s the men surrounding the king were not so much out-of-touch with opinion in Scotland as determined to ignore it, since they understood that their careers depended on delivering what the king demanded. Meanwhile, at court they were exposed to an insulated court culture with its emphasis on sacral kingship and the absolute authority of the monarch.[92]

With only a modicum of exaggeration Edward Hyde, earl of Clarendon, pointed out that among English courtiers 'there was so little in the Court or the country to know anything of Scotland, or what was done there'. Far more damaging was his claim that Scottish courtiers before the outbreak of revolution 'had the least influence in their own country', and that the vast sums lavished on them brought the crown little by way of sustained loyalty.[93] It is true that the sixteen peers who held, or who had held, court office on the eve of the signing of the National Covenant in February 1638, along with another twelve peers who had a strong court presence, proved ineffective in the king's cause. A few of these men were too anglicised to have any impact on Scotland. The fourth duke of Lennox had a French father, an English mother, he was educated at court and the university of Oxford, he held English titles, offices and estates, his wife was English and his only visit to Scotland was for the coronation parliament in 1633. But this is an extreme example. Other nobles like the third marquis of Hamilton, the sixth earl of Morton, the first earls of Stirling, Ancram, Kellie, Annandale, Roxburghe, Traquair and Nithsdale all maintained strong bonds with their Scottish kinsmen, friends and estates. It was not because they were rootless courtiers that they failed to prevent unpopular policies or to defend the king's interests adequately. Instead, Charles I failed to listen to his courtiers or to deploy them in time or with attainable objectives. Lennox, Roxburghe, Traquair, Nithsdale and Panmure were in Scotland in the summer of 1637, but their advice was ignored. On the other hand, there is no doubt that the staunchest covenanters had only the most tenuous of connections with the court.[94]

Conclusion

The royal court of the later sixteenth century suffers from unfavourable comparisons with that of James IV and James V and with its close contemporaries in England or France, while the early seventeenth-century court is often overlooked as English and of little relevance to Scotland.[95] Compared to the courts of James IV and James V those of Mary and James VI were poor, but the point is often overstated, while comparisons with contemporaries like Denmark are more relevant. Because the crown was relatively impoverished it does not mean that the court was politically irrelevant.

Nobles chased office, wealth and influence at court, and much of the politics of the period focused on court power struggles that were enmeshed in the turbulent politics of the localities. The political and cultural significance of the post-1603 court cannot be dismissed and the long-term detrimental impact on Scotland requires a more sophisticated interpretation.[96]

Most European early modern courts proved to be settings within which the power of the nobility was preserved and enhanced, particularly the power of the higher nobility.[97] Court offices, the wealth of the court and the relational networks that operated there were largely the preserve of the nobility, especially the higher ranks of nobles and their immediate kinsmen. It was not until the 1630s that bishops began to exercise a collective influence at court, while rich burgesses appear only in the shadows of court life, advancing money to the king and his needy courtiers. There were no rivals to noble power at court, but how important was the court to sustaining noble power? In some respects it could appear optional since a great many nobles of all ranks showed little interest in court office, clientage or faction. Successive earls Marischal, for example, preserved their great wealth in the northeast of Scotland over the eight decades between the Reformation and the outbreak of revolution with only minimal regard to the court. The overwhelming majority of untitled barons may have attended court only once or twice in a lifetime, especially after 1603. These men held on to their estates and their local offices and they maintained their position in noble society without incurring the cost and the political risk of court life. But most nobles, whatever their status, were connected to the court. Every earl and lord could attend court and gain access to the king if necessary and every baron knew someone who could plead his case at court. The regal union dramatically altered the dynamic, giving the king a stronger hand, but in fact placing increasing influence and power in the hands of a diminishing number of court brokers. These men were not anglicised, but when confronted by a king determined to use them to serve his interests they ceased to offer counsel that reflected the interests of the wider noble society from which they were drawn. In the context of the National Covenant and a set of popular grievances against the London-based crown, however, it became understandable to think of courtiers as divorced from Scottish interests. Even after the collapse of Charles I's power, the court held a grip on the popular imagination as a place of great power. In June 1641, Robert Baillie expressed disappointment that the covenanting sixth earl of Rothes was 'lyke to be the greatest courteour either of Scotts or English' and be offered a coveted place in the bedchamber. He also commented that this could result in Rothes becoming 'little more Scottish man'.[98]

CHAPTER 8

Noble Power and Politics, 1603–37

Throughout medieval and early modern European history cases can be uncovered in every century of individual noble houses falling into decline, or being extinguished, and of individual kings gaining particular political advances over their most powerful subjects. The longer perspective, however, reveals that, at least until the end of the eighteenth century, many noble houses that underwent episodes of eclipse recovered their fortunes, that those families who disappeared were replaced quickly, and that powerful kings were followed by weak kings. The history of early modern European nobilities is not one of gradual and inevitable decline, and increasingly the question exercising historians is the remarkable success and durability of nobilities.[1] Tudor monarchs, for example, remained dependent on their nobility in war and in the governing of their localities, maintaining a mutual partnership that ensured the preservation of noble power whatever misfortune befell individuals such as the dukes of Northumberland or Norfolk. Even at the outbreak of civil war in 1642 noble power was immense.[2] The French nobility of the late mediaeval period suffered decline in relation to the rural peasantry, only to recover their dominance in the early modern era. Spanish rule in Naples led to an increase in noble power over the rest of the population. In Denmark, in the period from 1536 to 1660 the nobility successfully expanded their power, while at the same time becoming an exclusive and closed caste. Even in Holland where social and economic changes far outpaced those in Scotland, the nobility continued to enjoy remarkable success.[3] Discussion of the shifting relationship between crown and nobility in Scotland tends to exaggerate the latter's power in the late medieval period and underestimates it thereafter. The destruction of, for example, the house of Comyn in the early fourteenth century or the Black Douglases in the fifteenth century has little more significance for the nobility generally than does the fate of the fifth earl of Bothwell or the second earl of Orkney during the reign of James VI.[4]

Those 'absolutist' monarchs of seventeenth-century Europe understood that their ability to rule rested on the cooperation of their nobilities; hence, cardinal Richelieu's dictum that strong nobilities were the foundation of the authority of princes. For their part, most nobles knew that the advancement of their own interests and those of their houses lay in cooperation with the crown. This was as true in Scotland as any other early modern kingdom.[5] Nevertheless, noble society was not impervious to change, and the durability of noble political power was grounded in the successful adaptation to social, economic, religious and cultural developments.[6] From the mid-1590s, the growing influence of a competent, adult king saw a perceptible shift take place in crown–noble relations that recalibrated the equilibrium established by previous Stewart kings. The peaceful succession of an adult king in 1625, the first since 1390, reinforced the recovery of royal power, but it was the regal union that threatened to tip the balance of political authority towards the crown in a more pronounced manner by altering the relationship between the king and his subjects. It was that massive disruption to the checks and balances that secured the kingdom's political stability that in due course led to a noble-led revolution against Charles I's increasingly arbitrary power.[7] From 1603 an increasingly self-confident crown sought to go further than previous Stewart kings in cultivating a culture of obedience among the nobility, placing greater restraints on unacceptable noble behaviour and extending the king's practical authority over religious beliefs and practices. Noble cooperation was secured by the combination of the crown's enhanced wealth and patronage alongside the kingdom's greater prosperity, allowing this more authoritarian agenda to develop, creating the impression that beneath the surface there was taking place a fundamental shift in power towards the king. Yet evidence for a sustained diminution in the nature and degree of noble power is slight. As previous chapters have indicated, the roots of the nobility's political power lay in the continued vitality of kinship and lordship, their dominance of local office, military power, government and the royal court. Below the surface of public life and behind the overblown rhetoric of royalist propaganda the nobility continued to exercise immense power that could be mobilised against the king if they were sufficiently provoked.[8]

Cultivating Obedience

In 1604, the first marquis of Huntly told James VI in a letter that he was 'halelie disposit never to be ane contradictour, bot altogidder ane folwar of your most excellent majestis will', adding the incredible phrase, 'as I have ever beine heirtofor'.[9] The irony of this comment from one of the king's most persistent rebels of the previous decade would not have escaped James VI, but this rhetoric of obedience was what the king liked to hear. After 1585 the Protestant nobility's retreat from a predisposition to resistance followed from the mid-1590s by the distancing of the Catholic nobles from Counter Reformation. The form of royalism that was embraced by the nobility was to endure over the following five decades, ranged from the instinctively conservative to the pragmatic, owing less to ideas about absolutism than to a desire to avoid a repetition of civil war and to promote peace and stability. Furthermore, even before the regal union of 1603, nobles were anticipating the potential rewards awaiting them in England. In 1599, a bond signed by the second duke of Lennox, ten earls and sixteen lords and barons bound them to support the king in pursuit of his claim to the English throne, beginning with a statement of unimpeachable royalist ideology.[10] James VI understood clearly the conservative reflexes of his nobles, hence, the appeal of his argument in *Trew law* (1598) that:

> if it be not lawfull to any particular Lordes tenants or vassals, upon whatso-
> ever pretext, to controll and displace their Master, and over-lord (as is clearer
> nor the Sunne by all Lawes of the world) how much lesse may the subjects and
> vassals of the great over-lord the King controll or displace him?[11]

Here was one of the key arguments of the queen's party in the civil war over a quarter of a century earlier, a view propagated by men like the fifth lord Seton, head of an impeccably loyal and conservative family, who erected above the entrance to his house at Seton a stone carving on which was engraved his political philosophy, *Un dieu, une foy, un roy, une loy*.[12]

A generation later, William Drummond of Hawthornden made much the same point as James VI, and in 1638 when the political order was already crumbling around him, he argued that those 'who do Falshood to their Superiors, teach Falsehood to their Inferiors'. Elsewhere Hawthornden reflected on the benefits of an orderly society. In his *History of the five Jameses*, he has James I (a victim of tyrannicide) argue that:

> To think Virtue and Civility true Nobility; that to be accounted Noblest which
> is Best, and that a Man's own Worth begets true Glory. By these, and the
> Obedience to their Princes your Ancestors acquired what ye now enjoy; There
> is no stronger means to keep the Goods acquired from a Prince, than the same
> by which they were first purchased, which is still Obeying.[13]

Robert Gordon of Gordonstoun, a successful courtier, emphasised the importance of loyalty to the king in his family history, holding up as exemplars men like the fourteenth-century seventh earl of Sutherland who 'advanced the service of his prince and cuntrey'.[14] When in the 1630s the eleventh earl of Angus came to edit for publication David Hume of Godscroft's *History of the house of Douglas*, he was so unhappy at being associated with dissident ideas that he toned down the original text which presented his ancestors as men who stood up to tyrannical kings.[15] The first lord Napier, a man who was deeply involved in the policies of Charles I's government, held to a more extreme view that while kings were subject to God's law, to reason and to natural equity, they were not subject to the civil law of their own dominions since 'Civil lawes ar reules for the subjects to live by; but the Soverane is exempt from them, because they ar his own commands'.[16] Unsurprisingly, the crown's own rhetoric reflected the greater emphasis on obedience, for example, in the language deployed by the privy council, and the meaning of obedience narrowed from obeying the law to conforming to the king's will. Charles I wrote to the convention of estates in October 1625 that 'you will give testimony of your due obedience to us and of your love to your native country' by supporting the agenda proposed by his officers.[17]

Nevertheless, mainstream royalism continued to be balanced by a belief that kings ought to listen to the counsel of their nobility. An arch conservative like sir James Melville of Halhill told the king in 1583 that if he was to avoid further troubles he must 'convene the maist ancien of your nobility, and barrons of best reputation' to seek their counsel.[18] It is unclear if Halhill was thinking of parliament, or merely the seeking out of advice from individual lords, but that strand of thinking remained a key to James VI's success as a ruler. Indeed, when in January 1594 parliament reconstituted the privy council, it recorded that the king 'promises to use and follow their counsel', a principle that has about it the ring of constitutionalism.[19] A generation later the desirability of good counsel continued to be advocated by Hawthornden, who insisted on the king governing with the 'ancient nobility' while advocating that he should select councillors on the basis of wisdom rather than only birth and rank. Hawthornden thought that, along with their privileges, the nobility had a responsibility to be critical of bad government, quoting approvingly George Buchanan in the context of discussing good counsel, and suggesting that the king should inspire obedience through love rather than fear. Of course, such honesty required a king willing to listen, and Charles I proved to be incapable of hearing loyal criticism. The purpose of good counsel, Hawthornden believed, was to save the king from making mistakes that might ignite rebellion, a concept that receded further and further from men's minds as one peaceful decade was followed by another. Indeed, in his history of the late medieval Stewart dynasty, Hawthornden made the point that 'the love of subjects is such towards their natural Kings, that except they be first deceived by some pretence and notable sophism, they will not arise together in arms and rebel'.[20] In thinking about this issue, Gordonstoun agonised over an imaginary situation in which his nephew might have to take sides in a civil conflict, for example, over a disputed succession. Mixing a desperate concern to obey legitimate authority with pragmatism, he told the young thirteenth earl of Sutherland to give allegiance to whoever, in his opinion, had the best claim, regardless of the interests of friends, kinsmen and dependants, and 'whose tytle soever you shall sie once setled by a parliament, defend him with all your might'.[21] In line with previous practice, counsel was formalised within parliament, a body whose independence James VI and Charles I increasingly undermined by heavy-handed political management. When revolution and civil war broke out in 1637–8, Gordonstoun and his nephew found themselves opposing Charles I, the old courtier's royalism having been eroded by frustration and disillusionment.

Other nobles retained a more active interest in notions of resistance, veiling their thoughts beneath the surface of public expressions of royalist conformity, and while Buchanan's resistance theories may have become unfashionable, this was in some measure due to there being no need for resistance to a king whose policies were broadly acceptable. But subversive ideas remained in the public consciousness, ready to be deployed when required. The first earl of Buccleuch had in his library both Jean Bodin's *Les six livres de la république* (1576) and George Buchanan's *Rerum Scoticarum historia* (1582), and while there is no evidence to suggest he had any enthusiasm for either of these opposing ideologies, both were within reach.[22] An earlier generation of nobles like the regent Moray had been familiar with Ramist ideas, and the Ramism prevalent at the universities of Glasgow, St Andrews, Edinburgh and Marischal college was associated with dissent so that young nobles were likely to be exposed to the diet of classical republican traditions so admired by Buchanan. The royal court, too, saw a growing interest in republican ideas among English nobles during the 1620s that fed through into the revolutionary actions of the 1640s.[23]

The political ideas of those nobles who emerged as the leaders of the covenanter movement have not been explored adequately, but a handful of insights into their early thinking can be uncovered. Prominent among them was the sixth earl of Rothes, who as a young man vigorously opposed the five articles of Perth at the 1621 parliament. On 14 April 1625, within three weeks of James VI's death, Rothes penned a letter to sir Robert Ker of Ancram indicating the need for political reform. He included among his complaints changes in the way the privy council operated, innovations in the church and 'the impairing of the libertys of the Nobility both in Counsell and Parliament'. Rothes continued to campaign against royal policies, taking part in a delegation to London in 1626 to protest against the revocation and playing a role behind the scenes in encouraging dissent at the 1633 parliament. By 1637–8 Rothes was one of the leading figures among the covenanters, assisting Archibald Johnston of Wariston in redrafting the National Covenant and along with Wariston was the co-author of *A short relation of proceedings concerning the affairs of Scotland from August 1637 to July 1638*.[24] Like Rothes, John Elphinstone, second lord Balmerino, was a Fife noble with a long record of dissent, opposing the five articles of Perth at the 1621 parliament and being involved in trying to organise opposition to the king at the 1633 parliament. The latter involved him having some editorial role in William Haig's petition of grievances, an action that resulted in him being found guilty of treason and condemned to death. Balmerino was pardoned, but continued to support dissenting ministers and contributed towards the text of the National Covenant.[25] Exactly when the courtier first earl of Ancram's son, the third earl of Lothian, wrote down his maxims is unknown, but they reflect this covenanter's desire to return to good government by removing bad counsel and making considered reforms. He argued that:

> When kingdomes and estates are in disorder and neede reformation they that
> goe about to order and reforme them should take tyme to do it ... For if there
> be any thing in the affaires of the world that requires tyme and good advice, it
> is the reformation of Estates.[26]

Archibald Campbell, lord Lorne, one of the most prominent of the covenanter lords, drew on a tradition that was at odds with the high-blown
rhetoric of Stewart kingship. Argyll was not an original thinker, but he saw
himself standing at the end of a Scottish and Gaelic tradition, infused with
Calvinist and Althusian ideology, that regarded it as the duty of the greater
magistrates of the kingdom to constrain a prince who acted illegally.[27] Ideas
about resistance, therefore, were not far below the surface of noble society,
and it was understandable that the clerk of Aberdeen burgh council, understood the National Covenant of 1638 to be 'the nobility's covenant'.[28]

Yet in the years following 1603 as Stewart power waxed and gained a
new British empire, the nobility had little reason to consider resistance and
individual nobles were well aware of the shift in their relationship with the
crown. Gordonstoun warned c. 1620 that:

> our king will do what he can to courb the nobilitie of Scotland, and diminishe
> ther powar, therby to conforme them to the custome of England. It is not now
> with our noblemen as when our king was resident in Scotland. Hardlie then
> could the kings majestie punishe any of our greatest nobilitie when they hade
> offended, by reason of ther great dependencies and freindship. But now he
> being absolute king of all Great Britain, the caise is altered.[29]

It is difficult to disagree with Gordonstoun's analysis and there is evidence
of the crown treating individual nobles in a more high-handed manner after
1603. Even those nobles who loyally served the king were more disposable.
In 1608, the first lord Balmerino, the secretary of state, was obliged to sacri-
fice himself to save James VI's embarrassment by confessing to conducting
secret correspondence with Pope Clement VIII in 1599 without the king's
knowledge. Balmerino was condemned to a traitor's death, and while not
executed, he was confined to Falkland and received no pardon.[30] Similarly,
the disgrace and ruin of the seventh earl of Menteith in 1632–3 after his
genealogical research led him to stray into making unguarded comments
regarding his own family's proximity to the royal succession was a dramatic
lesson to anyone who served Charles I.[31]

Those nobles who repeatedly defied the king faced severe consequences
compared with the fate of those who engaged in far more provocative
behaviour before James VI's migration to England. The charges against the
second earl of Orkney in 1610 amounted to sustained oppression and a
disregard for crown authority, but the decision by parliament to annex his
earldom to the crown in October 1613 was prompted by a combination of
local rivalry and a desire to extend crown authority over the northern isles.

Even after a futile rebellion by his son and followers in 1614 it was believed that this cousin of James VI would escape execution if he came into the king's will. Unfortunately, his delay in taking this route resulted in the case going to assize where Orkney was convicted and subsequently beheaded. Nevertheless, the king's actions aroused discomfort, and the 'wiser and elder sort of the nobilitie withdrew themselfis from his assise'.[32] Similarly, when in June 1609 processes of treason were moved against the ninth lord Maxwell, who had committed a disgraceful murder under trust, the lords of the articles were 'more scrupulous and precise in sindrie poyntis of that proces, nor we did forsie or suspect', but the king had his way, bullying parliament to proceed. Maxwell was captured four years later and the king insisted on his execution against the advice of a divided privy council.[33]

Charles I showed a similar willingness to deal with individual nobles on a case-by-case basis. In 1631, the obnoxious fourth lord Ochiltree was tried for sedition, and while the court failed to prove that he had invented treasonable allegations against the third marquis of Hamilton, he was imprisoned in Blackness castle, remaining there until 1652 when English troops freed him.[34] The trial of the second lord Balmerino, however, was of pivotal political importance in provoking many nobles into opposing the king in 1637–8. Balmerino was a long-standing critic of royal policies and had a shadowy role in redrafting a petition drawn up by William Haig, an influential lawyer acting for a group of dissident lords during the 1633 parliament. The petition, which the king refused to receive when the sixth earl of Rothes tried to present it, attacked the crown's taxation plans, the failure of the 1625 and 1630 conventions to address grievances, the manipulation of the committee of the lords of the articles, the direction of ecclesiastical policy, the king's bullying behaviour at the parliament and the five articles of Perth. John Spottiswoode, archbishop of St Andrews, brought the issue to the attention of the king, initiating the process that led to formal charges against Balmerino who refused to submit to the king's will, forcing a show trial in the spring of 1635. Balmerino conducted an effective defence against the flimsy charges, which amounted to knowing about and not reporting a treasonable document, and he received widespread sympathy from other nobles. He was condemned of leasing-making by the assize, but only on the casting vote of the first earl of Traquair, and was sentenced to death. Such was the public outcry and so weak was the case against Balmerino that the king did not dare execute him. Julian Ker, countess of Haddington, was scathing of those whose 'malece and develisch plots' had brought Balmerino to trial, and Hawthornden wrote his 'Apologetical letter' satirising rulers who censored political debate. 'Wise princes', he wrote, 'have never troubled themselves much about talkers; weak spirits cannot suffer the liberty of judgements, nor the indiscretion of tongues.' After a period of house arrest, Balmerino was pardoned and restored in November 1636, but played a prominent role in the subsequent revolution. The episode undermined confidence in the king and his advisers, especially the bishops who were portrayed as waging a vindictive campaign against a nobleman, while serving to publicise the criticisms contained in the previously unnoticed petition.[35]

While individual nobles were handled robustly by early seventeenth-century kings, the behaviour of these monarchs was not unusual by late medieval Stewart standards. Furthermore, there was no general attack on the nobility – the revocation was interpreted by some as such but that was not its intent – nor was there any attempt to destroy an entire lineage. On the whole kings were patient and forgiving in dealing with noble criminals, only occasionally carrying out executions as occurred from time to time in France. The English crown's elimination of the power of the Catholic earls in Ireland after 1607 and the harsh treatment of the Bohemian nobility by Emperor Ferdinand II after 1620 were exceptions. In Scotland those families who were punished did not suffer irreparable damage. The heirs of the first lord Balmerino, ninth lord Maxwell and second earl of Orkney were all well-treated and either restored to their lands and titles, or in the Orkney case granted alternative income and honours.[36] Similarly, when in 1619 the house of Argyll was threatened with destruction on account of the seventh earl of Argyll's recusancy and massive debts, the king responded positively to a petition requesting that 'wee might be pleased not to extende our juste displeasour conceaved against the earle of Argyle, to the overthrow of that ancient and noble house'.[37] There was no long-term advantage to the crown in destabilising local communities, and while conditions were imposed as the price of not enforcing the law to its limits, the crown was less of an obstacle to the restoration of disgraced nobles than were other nobles who had profited at the fall of one of their number.[38]

Refashioning Behaviour

James VI reserved some of his most damning criticism of the nobility for their involvement in bloodfeuds, urging his son in *Basilikon doron* that 'yee roote out these barbarous feides'. In particular, he cited the carrying of guns as conducive to feuding, regarding all who wore and used them as 'brigands and cut-throates'. Naturally, James VI and his servants assumed for the king sole credit in uprooting feuds, and it is tempting to see in this crown propaganda a correlation between the decline of feuding and the formation of a crown monopoly of violence, which may in turn be viewed as a pre-condition of state formation.[39] Yet explanations as to why feuding disappeared at different times across medieval and early modern Europe remain highly particular, defying easy categorisation. What is clear is that the process is not related to a simple model of state-building. In Scotland the campaign to eradicate violence involved a broad alliance of the king, the church and the greater part of noble society who recognised that there were better ways to provide justice. As in France, the nobility concurred in allowing the crown to claim and to exercise greater political power in order to better promote an orderly society. Although this process signalled a recognition that normally the crown had the sole right to exercise legitimate violence, it did not signify a *de facto* monopolisation of violence by the crown. The decline in feuding was a consequence of a change in attitudes and behaviours within noble society such that vengeance was less likely to be accepted as civilised or Christian.[40] In September 1592, the tenth earl of Angus prodded sir James Johnstone of that Ilk to avoid seeking revenge for the slaughter of a follower, arguing that:

> In suspending your wreithe and leiffin off all violent reveng, I doubt nocht bot it salbe ane beginning of ane gretter quyett boytht to your freindis and self, and it will move his majestie to be the mor favourable unto you.

Those views expressed by Angus were becoming more common and were expressed more publicly. Four decades later, Gordonstoun advised 'If you be given to choller, stryve to overcome that passion, for it doth not become a nobleman'.[41] That change in cultural attitudes permitted James VI to pursue policies from the later 1590s that attacked feuding on the grounds that the prevalence of private violence represented a challenge to his own authority. Crucially, the regal union altered the parameters within which politics were conducted. Deprived of a royal court that could be influenced by violence, nobles understood that military lordship was irrelevant and expensive and so they turned to more commercial estate management and to litigation. Under pressure from a critique emerging within noble society that redirected ideas about honour, vengeance and violence, a religious awakening that questioned the appropriateness of private violence in a Christian society, and the sensitive actions of royal government that was keen to promote the perception of the king as an effective peacemaker and ruler, and in the context of a changing political and economic environment, violent feuding, as distinct from feud as a means of restoring peace, withered away from the second decade of the seventeenth century.[42] But there was no guarantee that the demise of feuding would be permanent.

Over the course of the sixteenth century, European intellectuals renewed criticisms about the values and behaviour of the nobility and their followers, particularly in relation to violence.[43] That debate was conducted in Scotland, too, where John Mair and David Lindsay were the most significant critics of a martial nobility during the first half of the sixteenth century.[44] Even in the midst of the Marian civil war writers raised questions about the assumptions underlying the honour culture that appeared to glorify bloodshed:

Think ye that honnour consistis in vain weidis,
Or noblenes in outward braggis and bruitis?
Gentilnes is kythed be noble deidis,
As kyndly trees ar knawen be ther fruitis.

This alternative version of virtue was promoted within noble society in the glorification of ancestors, and a classical understanding of virtue underpinned noble education, cultural tastes and philosophical influences. Architecture and landscape were deployed by the first earl of Dunfermline to indicate that nobility was not only measured in martial behaviour. His country house at Pinkie issued a clear challenge to those assumptions, and an inscription placed on a garden wall boldly stated 'There is nothing here to do with warfare, not even a ditch or rampart to repel enemies'.[45] The poets of the early seventeenth century drove home the point that true nobility did not rest on martial deeds, or even on lineage without evidence of virtue. Sir David Murray of Gothry was scathing of those nobles who looked only to their ancestry for evidence of nobility:

Ah foolish they that bragge so much in vaine,
Onelie by blood nobilitate to be,
While in their bosomes they do scarce retaine,
The smallest sparke of magnanimity!

William Drummond of Hawthornden, was equally critical, and praised the greater peace and prosperity of a kingdom in which quite different attributes of nobility were celebrated.[46]

When James VI asked the elderly Hugh Rose of Kilravock how he could live among such unruly neighbours, Kilravock replied that 'they were the best neighbours he could have, for they made him thrice a-day to pray to God upon his knees, when, perhaps, otherwayes he would not have gone once'. Such Christian stoicism was at odds with an evangelical agenda that believed in engineering social change in an era when the church's traditional peacemaking role was infused by a new urgency. In part, the motives of the clergy were driven by concern for social justice in a world where nobles enforced their own version of justice by force of arms, but also by the more immediate impact on their own lives in the form of feuding over church seating or outbreaks of violence against ministers.[47]

Denunciations of noble behaviour and of feuding grew steadily from the 1576 general assembly, which highlighted the problem, through the following decade until in the 1590s when James VI agreed to address the issue. The 1576 general assembly enabled ministers to engage in local peacemaking, and by the 1590s the crown was working in partnership with ministers, for example, in 1597 the king turned to the clergy in his efforts to pacify the feuds of the nobility in the northeast. Although powerful lords were beyond the reach of church discipline, over time church courts had some success in

putting pressure on the lesser nobility, as in August 1614 when the
presbytery of Glasgow decreed that sir James Kincaid of that Ilk should
make public repentance at Campsie church following a quarrel after the
church service in which weapons were drawn and a man was slain. The
crown's efforts from 1609 to establish a more formal role for bishops in
peacemaking through the commissioners of the peace had mixed fortunes,
and it was left to a few determined individuals like John Spottiswoode,
archbishop of Glasgow, and Andrew Knox, bishop of the Isles, to promote
better law and order on the Borders and Highlands, respectively.[48]

The church's principal role in undermining feuding, at least in the
Lowlands, lay more in the ideological assault it made on the values of a
feuding society than in any formal administrative assault on noble power.
Ministers attacked the presumption that private individuals had the right
to extract vengeance when this was a duty entrusted by God to kings and
magistrates. James Melville condemned 'all revenge as devillrie'; Robert
Rollock expressed a desire that 'our bloody men, whether they be noblemen,
lords, earls, barons, or others, had been beheaded long since'; Robert Bruce
preached 'let no community of name, ally, proximity of blood, or whatsoever
it be, move you to pervert justice'; and John Davidson demanded that
'the conversioun of great men long inbred with evill doing, is not straight
credited, without notable signes of repentance'. The outpouring of condemnation and the persistent campaign to clean up Scotland's appallingly
violent reputation hit home. Increasingly, nobles came to accept that the
values that underlay the bloodfeud were inconsistent with godliness.[49] When
in the summer of 1627 James Campbell, lord Kintyre, occupied the castle
of Kintyre he showed commendable restraint, assuring his father-in-law
that 'I shall do nothing unworthie of a christian and a nobill man'. Similarly,
when in 1635 James Melville of Halhill and his cousin, John Melville of
Raith, became rivals to succeed the second lord Melville, the latter was
worried that the quarrel 'was lyk to bring ane slander upon the gospell'.[50]

The shift in attitudes towards honour and vengeance within noble society
combined with a changed political context and a more determined approach
from the king and his councillors to address law and order issues from the
later 1590s. The 1598 act anent feuding was the centrepiece of a legislative
assault that brought about a marked decrease in feuding and attendant forms
of violence, most significantly in the Lowlands. After 1603 the royal court
was no longer vulnerable to pressure from nobles with their large followings
of armed men; the Borders ceased to be a frontier and were subject to heavy-
handed government from England and Scotland; and the western seaboard
of the Highlands ceased to be a frontier region supplying troops into
Ireland. Meanwhile, the crown's engagement in dealing one by one with
high profile feuds slowly and painfully brought peace to locality after
locality, creating a context in which nobles looked increasingly to their
lawyers to resolve differences. This was a process in which crown and

nobility worked together in drafting laws for parliament, in determining policy and making judgements in the privy council, and in enforcement in local courts and through the personal authority of local lordship. The level of success was considerable and compares favourably with the French crown's difficulties in reducing the incidence of duelling.[51]

A number of dramatic exemplars aroused concern within some quarters of noble society, but the cases, all between 1612 and 1615, were so notorious that few really believed that the fates of these men signalled a threat to nobles generally. The hanging of the rootless and quarrelsome sixth lord Sanquhar on 29 June 1612 took place in London following his conviction for a murder carried out on his instructions in that city and was intended to placate English public opinion. The wayward ninth lord Maxwell went to his death on 21 May 1613, having been convicted four years earlier of the dishonourable murder under trust of sir James Johnstone of that Ilk. The second earl of Orkney was beheaded for treason on 6 February 1615 following the rebellion staged by his son and followers, but Orkney, who had been a prisoner since 1611, had a sustained record of oppression and a long list of debts.[52] It is difficult to read anything more into these executions than that the king exploited the broader campaign of discouraging feuding and violence to get rid of persistent troublemakers. Other nobles who engaged in, or were connected to, private violence, for example, the killers of the first lord Spynie in 1607, or the murderers of the first lord Torthorwald in July 1608, were not treated so severely and the privy council nudged the two sides towards reconciliations in 1616 and 1613, respectively.[53]

The key to changing noble behaviour lay in the blend of rhetorical claims made on behalf of the crown, which were often exaggerated, and a pragmatic approach to dealing with individual nobles. By 1616, James VI was urging that all criminal acts must be punished, and from the London court he lectured his councillors that:

> wee rigne not *precario* bot a frie and absolute king, so we will nather suffer the reconciliatioun of pairties amongst thame selffis to interrupt the dew course of justice in the punishment of crymes whairin wee have interesse, nor that the lauchfull instance of pairties interested against suche malefactoris to be punished by the hand of our Justice salbe ane occasioun of discorde amongst the freindis of suche pairties therefter.[54]

Yet James VI was realistic enough to recognise that the existence of laws did not guarantee conformity to those laws, hence, parliament's repetition of legislation, while the extent of noble power and the limits of his own power required the king to overlook incidents of law-breaking and to promote peace by private negotiation. Royal indulgence continued to be claimed and granted by noblemen who fought duels, as in 1620 when the king forgave Francis Sinclair, an illegitimate son of the fifth earl of Caithness, when he severely wounded sir William Sinclair of Moy in a combat at Leith. In 1611, the king recommended that a feud between Robert Sinclair of Longformacus and John Spottiswoode of that Ilk (in which the former's brother had been killed) should be settled by assythment (= a mutually agreed level of compensation), while in 1616 the bloody quarrel between the first marquis of Huntly and the tenth lord Forbes was settled by arbitration.[55] But a negotiated settlement was not necessarily a soft option. Lawrence Bruce of Cultmalundie remained in exile for eighteen years following his killing of David Tosheoch of Monzievaird in 1618, being unable to persuade the latter's family to accept the assythment that would allow him to receive a remission. Finally, in February 1636 a decreet arbitral was delivered by a committee of the privy council that required Cultmalundie to make a humiliating public confession and submission to Andrew Tosheoch of Monzievaird to whom he was required to make a crippling payment in compensation.[56]

Yet while feuding and other forms of noble disorder declined dramatically, the structural and behavioural shift can be exaggerated. In spite of legislative initiatives against violence in the uplifting of teinds, and in the face of repeated intervention of the privy council, incidents continued into the 1630s.[57] Casual violence between nobles remained an occurrence, although this rarely escalated beyond brawling in public. On 2 July 1607, the business of the privy council was interrupted by a punch-up between sir William Cranstoun, captain of the border guard, and sir John Hume of North Berwick. A similar clash occurred in February 1627, when sir David Livingston of Dunipace and James Crichton of Benshiels turned up at Edinburgh tollbooth to discuss their differences in the presence of the second earl of Linlithgow, a privy councillor.[58] Consequently, councillors and magistrates, especially in towns, remained sensitive to the explosive potential such incidents had for becoming more serious. In March 1609 sir David Lindsay of Edzell was hunted through the streets of Edinburgh by the twelfth earl of Crawford and a party of armed men. Edzell had good reason to be afraid since Crawford had murdered his brother in 1605, while in 1607 Edzell's son tried to murder Crawford on those same streets, killing the first lord Spynie by mistake. Nobles in Edinburgh continued to be accompanied by armed retinues, one such being described by Alexander Lindsay, bishop of Dunkeld, in the summer of 1611 as 'ane greitt convocation of our soveraine Lordis leidges and be no frendlie forme'. In the summer of 1629 the privy council took steps to ensure that there was not a serious incident in Edinburgh when the sixth earl of Cassillis and the second earl of Wigton along with their followers took part in a series of 'tumultous convocatiouns and unseemelie backings'.[59] Other towns experienced the lingering remnants of a feuding society. James VI was furious in 1606 when the Cunningham–Montgomery feud spilled on to the streets of Perth during the sitting of parliament, seeing in the incident the potential 'in bringing money of the nobilitie, then present in towne, to haif enterit in bloode with otheris, and thairby to haif revived that new mortifeit monster of deidlie feud'. The magistrates of Aberdeen were under no illusion that noble violence was still an issue, especially at times of the year when people congregated in the burgh. The problem was that nobles came to Aberdeen

> accompanied by such large numbers of their friends and dependents armed as ready for offence as defence, that often great trouble has arisen in the burgh when those at feud with others have met, and the burgh has been forced to take up arms for 'redding' of them, during which some of the inhabitants have been hurt, mutilated and slain.[60]

This complaint was made in 1631.

Although feuding had been widespread throughout Scotland, it was more common and more vicious in some regions than in others, and that regional pattern continued to be noticeable in the period during which those rivalries came to be expressed in less violent forms. By the second quarter of the seventeenth century much of the central Lowlands was largely free of blood-feuds, but violence remained close to the surface of local politics in parts of the Borders, much of the northeast and throughout the Highlands. From the mid-1590s better Anglo-Scottish relations reduced cross-Border incidents, and after 1603 the activities of the Border commission had a marked effect on lawlessness, although the government was premature in thinking that by 1621 the region was normalised. In 1622, the first earl of Nithsdale sought to enforce his claims to Kirkconnell tower by sending his younger brother with some forty armed men to besiege it, a reminder that the potential for military display remained below the surface of civil society. The long feud between the Elliots and the house of Buccleuch rumbled on into the seventeenth century, and in the course of 1624 a disgruntled Elliot laird plotted unsuccessfully to assassinate the first earl of Buccleuch. In August 1626, Charles I wrote to the privy council about the threat to civil peace of convocations after a number of powerful individuals attended the commission of grievances with excessive numbers of friends and servants. Official vigilance was urged if 'rude and barbarous' practices were not to gain acceptability again, but within the year the sheriff-clerk of Dumfries, John Young, was slain. The notorious Maxwell–Johnstone feud ended in 1623, but their supporters were still shedding one another's blood in 1629, and in 1636 the first lord Johnstone acquired a renewal of the old exception from the ordinary jurisdiction of the Maxwell chief. Significantly, the two families took opposite sides when civil conflict broke out in 1637–8.[61]

In the northeast the crown's campaign to uproot feuding was undermined by its efforts to weaken the power of the persistently Catholic first marquis of Huntly. Incidents such as when James Ogilvy of Podula was killed in a fight with sir George Ogilvy of Banff in 1628, or when later that year John Grant of Carron was slain along with a number of other men in a clash with John Grant, apparent of Ballindalloch, continued to occur. The feud between James Crichton of Frendraught and William Gordon of Rothiemay erupted into widespread local warfare in 1630 in the course of which Huntly's son, John Gordon, viscount Aboyne, and his party were burned to death at Frendraucht tower. Huntly suffered more family loss in 1633 when his nephew was murdered by Highland bandits in a separate case and the Gordons took a heavy vengeance in terms of spoil and destruction as well as the execution of a number of lesser individuals. He was warded for a few months in 1635–6, and there was some suspicion that he had encouraged the dispute, but government failed to offer an alternative to Gordon power to pacify the region.[62]

In the Highlands the case has been made for a significant encroachment of effective crown authority, but it is unpersuasive. Privy council promulgations and the compliance of clan chiefs in accepting greater accountability for the actions of their men does not constitute either societal change or an administrative revolution. An alternative view suggests that crown policy may have been responsible for the on-going instability of the region, as a reaction to internal colonialism, interference in local politics and efforts to recruit men for military service overseas.[63]

The long-term decline in inter-personal violence between the late medieval and late modern periods is often discussed in terms of a trend directly related to changes in manners, religion and crown power. Empirical case studies are less supportive of theorising on the civilising process, emphasising instead the immediate political, social and economic context in which violence occurred. In France, fundamental changes in noble attitudes towards private violence and in behaviour did not begin until the latter half of the seventeenth century. In the absence of noble cooperation, early modern governments lacked the military power to enforce their authority and the inherent instability of society was likely to surface as soon as that cooperation was compromised.[64] Unsurprisingly, when confronted by the realities of local politics, Gordonstoun's neo-stoical and classical education was superseded by the need to practice cynical power politics and violence in a manner that was little different from the later sixteenth century.[65] Given the pervasive reach of the nobility into local courts and royal government, the residual respect for ideas about honour that connected to a world of private violence, and the continued access to the men and the weaponry through which force was exercised, it is unsurprising that an increasingly unpopular king risked driving the nobility back into a recourse to violence in the pursuit of private and public aims. As crown authority degenerated in the 1630s, the veneer of order was stripped away. In the course of 1635 the followers of the sixth earl of Cassillis, baillie of Carrick, and sir Patrick Agnew of Lochnaw, sheriff of Galloway, engaged in acts of petty violence; a feud broke out in the north between Alexander Brodie of Letham and Alexander Dunbar of Grange; the second lord Spynie ordered his officers to gather their men and drive the tenants of Robert Fletcher of Ballinsho from

a disputed peat moss; and the burgesses of Peebles and John Scott of
Hundislop clashed in a series of incidents in which property was destroyed,
weapons were brandished and men were wounded.[66] The rivalries between
noble families continued to be the stuff of local politics, and while ideas of
civility and godliness had gained the upper hand in a context of domestic
peace, relative economic prosperity and a sound partnership in governing
between crown and nobility, no one could be certain that the world of the
bloodfeud would not be resurrected by civil strife as it had been in the mid-
sixteenth century. As the political crisis unfolded from the summer of 1637
old battle lines emerged: Maxwells against Johnstones in the southwest;
Gordons against Forbes in the northeast; MacDonalds against Campbells in
the west. It would require quite different political regimes to complete the
task of refashioning noble behaviour.[67]

Religion and Revolution

Seventeenth-century Europe continued to experience revolts and civil wars
inspired by the religious divisions initiated by the Reformation. Yet by the
1600s Scotland appeared to have resolved the major confessional issues and
nobles largely left the clergy to debate the finer points of theology. During a
meeting at London in 1606 to discuss controversies between the crown and
a number of ministers, Andrew Melville rounded on those privy councillors
present to proclaim 'they were degenerated from the ancient nobilitie of
Scotland, who were wount to give their lives and their lands for the freedome
of their countrie and the Gospell'. Yet it would be mistaken to assume that
the nobility of the early seventeenth century were any less religious than the
previous generation, and in terms of personal piety and Protestant doctrinal
understanding the opposite may have been the case.[68] Melville's anger arose
from the nobles' unwillingness to back the kind of radical politics he and his
colleagues espoused. Indeed, one of James VI's most profound successes
in the years after 1585 was in distancing the nobility from Melville and his
presbyterian colleagues. Following the failed Edinburgh insurrection of
1596 the more outspoken ministers were isolated and a *modus operandi* of
church government evolved that preserved the best features of presbyterian
polity with a level of crown influence that satisfied the king. There is no
persuasive evidence that James VI was aiming at the full restoration of
diocesan episcopacy before 1603, or that he could have achieved it.[69]
The regal union of 1603 had a profound effect on the church and on its
government, increasing the power of the crown, and depriving the general
assembly of the ability to place the absentee king under direct pressure.
James VI's preference for erastian bishops in England became apparent at
the January 1604 Hampton court conference, and exposure to and support
from a grateful English episcopate followed. Since it was no secret that the

king's union plans included his desire for a convergence of the English and
Scottish churches it was always likely that the model of the former would
prevail. There was considerable sensitivity towards any threat to the dis-
tinctiveness of the church, and when the question of parliamentary union
with England was debated at the 1604 parliament, it was the elderly fifth
earl of Morton who led a protest, resulting in an act to ensure that the
commission entrusted with negotiating union could not prejudice the rights
of the church. Nevertheless, it is mistaken to underestimate the degree of
opposition in lay and clerical circles to bishops, and the control, repression
and censorship of dissidents did not suddenly appear following public disquiet at the five articles of Perth.[70]

Among those nobles for whom the politics of religion remained im-
mensely important were Roman Catholics who endured increasing levels
of harassment with a consequent impact on their power. Against the background of a successful European Counter Reformation and some Catholic
missionary activity in Scotland, the Catholic nobility experienced greater
interference by church courts, reflecting the unease of an embattled Protestantism. Their treatment was relatively mild, and persistent recusants like
sir John Ogilvy of Craig were disciplined from time to time, but he still
succeeded in defying the crown and the church over his religious practices
from the 1590s until the 1640s. The singular execution of John Ogilvie, the
eldest son of a Banffshire laird, was primarily on account of his treasonable
actions not because of his beliefs.[71] In spite of the activity by jesuit and other
missions from the 1590s, Catholics concentrated on survival, retreating into
a localised and quietist seigneurial phenomenon that offered no threat to the
crown or the church. By the early seventeenth century, many nobles who had
been Catholics in their youth conformed, taking an easier and more self-
preserving route in later life. This is not to deny the faith of men like the first
earl of Dunfermline who was educated in Rome and Bologna, and was
considered to be 'an excellent Catholic although he still seeks to inculcate
the belief that he is indifferent'. Yet Dunfermline's faith was that of a
depoliticised Catholicism in which service to a Protestant king did not
conflict with his inner beliefs, allowing him to hold the office of chancellor
from 1604 until his death in 1622. He had no time for those Catholic lords
who tried to avoid outward conformity, and after the first marquis of Huntly
was sent home from England in the spring of 1605, Dunfermline commented in a letter to the earl of Salisbury that the incident 'will make the
courses of all our great hidalgos the more temperate'.[72]

The reference to Spanish nobles may not have been incidental for since
the Reformation Protestants had sought to portray Catholics as unpatriotic
creatures of Rome, France or Spain. Catholic nobles often maintained their
continental relationships, and even in the early seventeenth century a number of nobles were involved with Habsburg agents and their conspiracies.
The exiled fifth earl of Bothwell was a pensioner at the Spanish court, from

where he attempted to find backers for his unlikely schemes until ordered to leave Spain in 1609. Throughout 1622–5 the seventh earl of Argyll intrigued on behalf of Spain, and it was only the outbreak of war in 1625 that forced him to chose Charles I over Philip IV. But those Scots like colonel William Semple who continued in the Spanish camp were a dwindling and marginalised irrelevance. More commonly, Catholics like the first earl of Nithsdale, sir Andrew Gray and sir Robert Hepburn were prepared to act as recruiters and military commanders for Protestant armies.[73]

In some respects it was becoming less politically important that individual nobles clung to their Catholicism as the spread of Protestantism among the general population weakened the bonds between lords and men who did not share confessional allegiances. The behaviour of the Campbell clan in response to the seventh earl of Argyll's conversion to Catholicism in 1618, effectively disowning him, is a demonstration of the limits of lordship in the face of the collective views of the kindred.[74] Nevertheless, pressure to conform did come from a king determined to demonstrate his Protestant credentials. In September 1606, James VI wrote to his privy council to complain about the number of papists in the country, and in particular about 'entire families of recusants' who were encouraged by jesuits and other priests who were often 'interteyned in noblemenis houses and companyis'. A series of anti-Catholic measures were passed by parliament between 1604 and 1609, many directed against nobles, and the harassment of individuals and their families was enthusiastically adopted by bishops desperate to demonstrate that they were not soft on Catholics. Among the rank and file of Protestant nobles such a hard-line policy was relatively popular, and the long list of nobles granted commissions to suppress Catholic activities in 1629 is an indicator of those men the crown trusted in the localities to implement a policy that was spearheaded by the bishops.[75]

The oppression of Catholic nobles was no respecter of rank. The house of Huntly remained the most prominent Catholic family in the kingdom, protecting recusants for decades. While the first marquis never fully recovered from his failed rebellions in the first half of the 1590s, he remained the foremost target of ambitious Protestant clergy like John Spottiswoode, archbishop of Glasgow, determined to enforce conformity or break his regional power. Huntly experienced sustained persecution, including a spell of imprisonment in Stirling castle in 1608–10, and Spottiswoode hounded him throughout the next three decades. Not only did Huntly lose the influence and office he had enjoyed at court in the 1580s, but in 1629 he was forced to surrender his sheriffdoms of Aberdeen and Inverness. The old marquis was returning home from his latest incarceration in Edinburgh castle in 1636 when he died, Catholic to the last, but undoubtedly politically weaker. Yet a less powerful house of Huntly did not mean a stronger crown, and the disorderly Frendraucht affair of 1630 underlined the crown's on-going dependence on Gordon power in the northeast. Even this humbling of the greatest Catholic noble in the kingdom brought little reassurance to Protestants, who continued to worry, needlessly, over events on the continent and the apparent growth in Catholic influence centred on the queen at court.[76]

The overwhelming majority of early seventeenth-century nobles were Protestant and shared a Protestant world view with the clergy, working at a local level as lord and minister to ensure social order and cohesion. The kirk session of the parish of Linlithgow in 1611 included the first earl of Linlithgow (even though his wife was a Catholic), a number of local barons and the provost and baillies of the burgh of Linlithgow. In Fife the overlapping bonds between nobles and ministers was particularly strong. The second lord Balmerino was appointed to a commission of the synod of Fife on 5 September 1615, while among the ruling elders for the presbytery of Cupar in 1619 was the first lord Melville and a number of local barons. It was this foothold within the church courts that the nobility used so effectively in 1638 to ensure that the general assembly had the lay backbone to oppose Charles I.[77] The crown even promoted the involvement of nobles in church courts, most obviously in the two courts of high commission created in February 1610 as part of the reconstruction of diocesan episcopacy.[78]

One important difference between the pre- and post-Reformation church was the absence of nobles in church offices. The secularisation of the abbeys and the downgrading of the role of bishops provided a generation of younger sons with heritable estates, while depriving a relatively poor church of offices sufficiently attractive to men of high rank. Only a handful of younger children of lesser nobles became parish ministers, men like Alexander Hume, the second son of the laird of Polwarth, who turned away from a legal career to become minister of Logie in 1598. Other kinship relationships were formed between ministers and the lower ranks of the nobility, for example, Robert Rollock, the son of a Stirlingshire laird, and Patrick Simson were married to daughters of James Baron of Kinnaird.[79] Even if few family members were placed in church livings, nobles exercised patronage over large numbers of parish churches, and especially from 1587 this was a cause of frequent clashes with the ecclesiastical authorities. Often compromises could be negotiated, as at Newlands parish in 1592 when the fifth earl of Morton clashed with the presbytery over the collation of his nominee. On other occasions, the church could be robust in warding off unwelcome interference. In 1592, the presbytery of Glasgow utilised the sworn statements of the fifth earl of Eglinton's own tenants in their capacity as elders of Eaglesham parish church, blocking the master of Eglinton's efforts to overturn the appointment of Andrew Boyd as minister. From the second decade of the seventeenth century, the restored bishops found themselves engaged in confrontations with nobles over patronage rights which were part ideological and part local power struggles. In the summer of 1627, the second earl of Linlithgow tried to secure a parish for John Livingston, but was informed by archbishop Spottiswoode that his nominee was an undesirable who 'wold not submit him self to the orders of the church'. In 1630, the sixth earl Marischal succeeded in having his nominee, James Guthrie, confirmed to the vacant parsonage and vicarage of Duffus in the face of opposition from the bishop of Moray and the archbishop of St Andrews. Marischal had his way because he persuaded the privy council to employ its powers under the 1612 act to enforce a presentation where the candidate was a qualified minister and the patron had observed the correct forms.[80]

Nevertheless, while nobles continued to demonstrate high levels of religious conviction and maintained on-going engagement with the church, the more radical clergy were disappointed that they showed little enthusiasm for participating in their controversies with the king. Among many clergy there was a sullen acquiescence in the direction of royal policy, and even if most parish ministers lacked the courage or conviction to oppose the king, neither did they give up their Calvinist theology, or the subversive political ideas of the Melvillian generation that continued to be nursed within clerical dynasties and at parish level.[81] For the nobility, the royal supremacy established in 1584 was not unreasonable and the form of church government was largely a matter of indifference, but not all nobles were comfortable with the king's emerging agenda after 1603 to establish accountable leadership of the church under royal direction. The dissident ministers made their stand at Aberdeen in July 1605 where they convened an illegal general assembly. Even within the privy council there was disquiet at the direction of royal policy, and it was left to the ruthless earl of Dunbar to bully a nervous chancellor Dunfermline, a closet Catholic, into taking action. A select committee of privy councillors was handpicked to arraign the dissident ministers, but the assize chosen to try the case proved to be uncooperative and six barons voted to absolve the accused clergy, while the influential second earl of Mar, formerly a fellow exile with Andrew Melville, was among those who voiced opposition to convicting the ministers. Again it was Dunbar who secured the desired result. Following the trial and conviction of the ministers a petition was presented to parliament in July 1606 appealing to the nobility not to abandon their role as protectors of the church. They were enjoined to remember 'that God hath sett you to be nurish fathers of his kirk, craving at your hands, that yee should foster, mainteane, and advance by your authoritie the kirk'. The appeal fell on deaf ears, especially as the king had the law on his side, but there was sympathy for the ministers' plight. Among the friends and supporters of the imprisoned John Welsh was Lilias Graham, wife of the sixth lord Fleming and daughter of the third earl of Montrose, president of the privy council.[82]

For the present, the king and his bishops had their way, and while support from the nobility was unenthusiastic, there were those who sensed an opportunity to profit. At the July 1606 parliament the crown succeeded in securing the re-establishment of the bishops' estate, noble support being more forthcoming as a result of the creation of the lordships of erection formed from former ecclesiastical lands.[83] Individuals like sir David Carnegie of Kinnaird proved to be enthusiastic supporters of the king, and select nobles were recruited to overawe the general assembly, while those laymen appointed as assessors and commissioners to the general assemblies of 1608, 1609 and 1610 were in agreement with court policy.[84]

At a local level the role of cooperative nobles was vital. In 1607, the first lord Scone, a bedchamber servant, was appointed a special commissioner for the synod of Perth with a remit to ensure that local presbyteries complied with the king's ecclesiastical policy. Scone tried to overawe the synod, raging and threatening the assembled ministers to little avail, but he stuck doggedly to his task and brought the power of the privy council down on the heads of the more difficult clergy. In other presbyteries the lay commissioners appointed by the privy council were generally barons in sympathy with the direction of crown policy, men like sir William Livingston of Kilsyth, a privy councillor, and John Murray of Polmaise, provost of Stirling. The only peers appointed other than Scone were the fifth earl of Caithness, the eighth lord Saltoun and the tenth lord Forbes in various northern presbyteries, while the third lord Ochiltree was appointed commissioner for the presbytery of Ayr. Each of these men had significant debts and were easily manipulated by the crown. In fact, not all commissioners proved to be acceptable to the king and a number of uncooperative barons were denounced. But the practice of crown interference continued, and in August 1607 the synod of Clydesdale was browbeaten into accepting archbishop Spottiswoode as its moderator by the first earl of Abercorn on instruction from the king, while elsewhere courtiers like the first lord Roxburghe and sir Robert Ker of Ancram put pressure on the presbyteries of Melrose and Jedburgh.[85]

The restoration of a diocesan episcopate subject to the king's authority was complete by 1610 and was achieved with noble cooperation. The direction of crown policy towards the church provided an ideology and an administrative framework that supported the king's aspirations, but the limited impact of the bishops within the secular sphere ensured that for the remainder of James VI's reign there was little controversy over their role. The argument within the church over its form of government was largely of interest to the clergy, but the laity was subject to church courts, and tensions arose where nobles had to submit to the authority of ministers or bishops. This might be relatively mundane, such as in 1605 when sir Robert Douglas of Glenbervie was required to acquire a testimonial from the local minister and kirk session stating that he was ill at the time of an affray. Yet even this bureaucratic intrusion might annoy powerful laymen. Bishops pursued conventional if irritating policies of pressuring nobles to fund adequately parish ministers, such as when in April 1617 archbishop Spottiswoode wrote to sir John Murray of Lochmaben about the church at Gretna. There was an increasingly fussy intervention by ministers in what many nobles regarded as their private affairs; for example, by 1616 ministers were expected to make visitations of the houses of nobles, gentlemen and burgesses to ensure that prayers for the king were said after every meal. Finally, the activity of kirk sessions, presbyteries and synods impacted directly on nobles where they, their families or their servants were cited to appear before the church on disciplinary matters.[86] On the whole, however, these incidents were more annoying than controversial, or at most amounted to little more than the mundane stuff of local politics. Even the restoration of the two courts of high commission in 1610, while being sufficiently resented by the laity for archbishop Spottiswoode to concede that they created 'great discontent of those that ruled the estates', did not translate into meaningful confrontation.[87]

Discontent with episcopal authority became more significant under Charles I, who was determined to make greater use of bishops in implementing royal policies. By the later 1620s the unpopularity of bishops as agents of the crown, especially in relation to the activities of the teind commission, was widespread. By the middle of the following decade hostility towards the bishops was commonplace. Within the localities this hostility extended to the bishops' role as exploitative landlords, for example, in imposing entry fines with attendant legal costs each time a new bishop took office. Talk among the Campbell lairds was that 'the church men rewlis all for the present', and when in 1636 lord Lorne flexed his muscles to protect Alexander Gordon of Earlston from the court of high commission, the issue for him and other lay privy councillors was the growing power of the bishops. Aggrieved nobles looked forward to the day when gentlemen would 'no more be prey to the avarice of these base borne fellowes'. By January 1637 Robert Baillie was of the opinion that the nobility overwhelmingly opposed the further enhancement of the church through projected developments like the restoration of abbots.[88] The first lord Napier, treasurer depute, recorded that 'histories witnes what trubles hath been raysed to Kings, what tragedies among subjects, in all places wher churchmen were great'. The sixth earl of Rothes, a man ideologically opposed to Napier, shared his views on this topic, writing in 1638 that the gradual reintroduction of bishops had been intended 'to overthrow the truth of religione and liberties of subjects'. Here was the rediscovered voice of a Calvinist nobility realigning itself with presbyterian principles.[89]

Since the Reformation there had been a strong critique of the nobility's wealth, their greed in seizing ecclesiastical assets and their unwillingness to fund the church adequately. In March 1600, however, an English agent commented on the ecclesiastical lands formerly held by the bishops that 'the nobility having their livings will never be brought to return them', and all hope the clergy may have had of there ever being a renegotiation of the *de facto* settlement appears to have been abandoned.[90] James VI recognised this point, but Charles I was determined to address the issue of renegotiating the distribution of former church lands between the crown, the episcopate and the nobility in a way that could only mean losses for the nobility. This was the purpose of the revocation, aptly described by sir James Balfour of Denmilne as 'the ground stone of all mischief that followed'. Charles I's total misunderstanding of local government and land-holding, about which he did not seek appropriate advice, led in the first few months of his reign to a hurried, misconceived and unworkable plan to exploit a reform of the possession of former ecclesiastical lands to break the link between the nobles and their dependants. The king's objective, which included some worthwhile public benefits, was to require the surrender of superiorities, the abolition of heritable jurisdictions, teind redistribution and the provision of income streams for the clergy and the crown, a programme that unravelled when confronted by the complexities of land-holding rights, the law, the absence of suitable compensation and massive political opposition. Some two-fifths of all land was affected, alienating a broad cross-section of the landed community, including lesser nobles who were the intended beneficiaries of the scheme, and a quarter of the privy council who were affected by the proposals. Little was achieved beyond ill-feeling and the alienation of the greater part of the nobility. The establishment of the teind commission and its parish sub-commissions merely drove discontent deeper into local communities where the nobility withdrew their cooperation, forcing the king to rely on increasingly unpopular bishops. Even the parish ministers, whose stipends were rising steadily during this period, opposed the work of the teind commission and colluded with landowners in undermining its efforts. The teind commission was universally unpopular, for example, the Renfrew commission rarely met, attendance was 'verie evill keeped', and when local commissions did convene they galvanised communities into bonding together against the crown, using the lines of communication developed by royal government to frustrate its own intentions. In May 1627, the barons and gentlemen of Ayrshire met to elect representatives to the teind commission, but the meeting was marred by 'ane greitt confusioune', angry argument and a walk-out by the barons of Carrick before a thinly attended election took place. The king ploughed on, exacerbating the situation by seeking to promote the financial condition of bishops and extending their rights of patronage. This attempt to reorganise local government in the 1620s and 1630s increased the possibility of local men meeting to discuss their grievances in the way that quarter sessions and assizes did in England.[91]

The revocation threatened to alter the relationship between crown and nobility, and individual nobles were sensitive to the weight of crown authority behind the scheme. In February 1634, the third earl of Winton advised his brother, the sixth earl of Eglinton, to hurry up in processing the valuation of his kirks of erection in order to get the best deal, and not to risk seeking ways to circumvent royal policy. The impression is of men who knew they were dealing with a determined king. But most nobles were less easily intimidated, and resorted to the usual device of putting the blame on evil counsel, particularly the bishops. Even royal councillors, many of whom held former ecclesiastical estates, warned that the revocation 'may bring ruine to ane infinite number of families of all qualities in everie regioun of this land', and they tried unsuccessfully to reassure worried nobles on the security of their titles. Small landlords who were expected to benefit from becoming tenants of the crown were horrified. The laird of Glenkindie wrote in 1632 to his former superior to intimate unease at no longer having an earl of Mar to protect him from the vagaries of royal justice. The third earl of Lothian found the revocation costly, while the sixth earl of Rothes and the first lord Balmerino, were damaged by the findings of the subsequent teind commission.[92] All three of these lords became prominent covenanters.

European royal courts often established the expectations of religious conduct and belief throughout noble society.[93] Yet there was a risk that rapid change at the court could create clashes with provincial society as occurred in Scotland over the liturgy. James VI's growing sympathy for the forms of worship found in the Church of England, his continued determination to draw the English and Scottish churches closer together and the desire of the king and his increasingly assertive bishops to enforce conformity, set him on a damaging course to reform the church's liturgy that threatened the stability he had engineered. That reform introduced rituals and practices that the majority of clergy and many laity, especially in the more assertively Protestant regions, regarded as crypto-Catholic. Kneeling at communion in particular was regarded with suspicion and distaste. Even prominent courtiers and councillors, like the second marquis of Hamilton and the second earl of Mar, refused to take communion in the Anglican manner in March 1617, and it was soon evident that the liturgical innovations had the potential to arouse many nobles to engage in dissent. That dissent was not entirely an expression of religious faith, and David Calderwood conceded that at the June 1617 parliament some nobles made a populist connection between ecclesiastical policy and 'a prejudice to their estate', chiefly in relation to the security of their possession of former ecclesiastical lands and teinds. Those nobles who gave public support to the king's policy during James VI's visit to Scotland in the summer of 1617 were taking sides in an unfolding ideological division that proved to be more dangerous than that over the form of church government.[94]

The fault lines within the political community paralleled those created by the revocation and the work of the tend commission. While a number of nobles identified closely with the enforcement of royal policy, and the great majority conformed, the king's determination to implement the five articles rejuvenated the presbyterian underground, encouraged the spread of conventicling throughout much of the Lowlands and drew prominent nobles into contact with dissident clergy. That contact had never been broken. Robert Bruce continued to be patronised by the second earl of Mar in spite of being in disfavour with the king, while in 1605 Archibald Simpson was protected by the fifth earl of Morton. Following David Calderwood's banishment in 1617, he was aided by the first lord Cranstoun, his wife and their sons. Calderwood had been appointed to the church at Crailing in 1604 under the patronage of Cranstoun's father, and while lord Cranstoun's career was based on loyalty to the king, he was persistent in his efforts to get Calderwood's sentence altered to confinement to his own parish. Lady Cranstoun concealed Calderwood at Jedburgh for two years, and continued to provide protection when he returned from exile. Other dissenting ministers continued to receive protection from nobles. Archibald Simpson dedicated the 1618 manuscript 'Life' of his radical brother, Patrick Simpson, minister of Dalkeith, to Jean Hamilton, wife of the second lord Melville, who gave encouragement and help to dissident ministers. In Ayrshire, David Dickson was protected by the sixth earl of Eglinton in the 1630s.[95] What emerged was a growing network of support for dissident ministers that ranged from privy councillors and court of session judges to burgh magistrates and ordinary parishioners. When kneeling communion at was introduced to Edinburgh at Easter 1619, crown servants led the way in conforming, but sir George Erskine, lord Innerteill and sir James Skene of Curriehill, court of session judges, absented themselves. A popular, subversive literature was circulating, reflecting no doubt the table-talk of households throughout the kingdom, and the connection was being explicitly made between James VI's increasingly 'defective' knowledge of Scotland and the 'neglect of parliaments, conventions of the estates and of free assemblies of the kirk'.[96]

James VI's determination to give the five articles the status of parliamentary statute further raised the political temperature and offered a platform for critics of other royal actions to focus on the liturgical issue. The 1621 parliament was a highly charged affair, doubly so on account of the crown's request for the largest taxation to date alongside approval of the five articles of Perth. Dissenting clergy directed propaganda at the nobility, appealing to their self-image as defenders of the kirk and of the liberties of the people, and asking them 'to remember the labours and sufferings of their honourable predecessors'. Noble dissent at the parliament was substantial in spite of heavy management by the crown. Sir John Hamilton of Preston ignored pressure from crown ministers and the bishops, insisting on publicly recording his dissent from the five articles of Perth in the committee of the lords of the articles. Secretary Melrose was in no doubt that behind Preston was his 'instructour', John Ker, minister of Salt Preston, and he sought to humiliate Preston by making him ride among the meaner of the barons in the procession. Some nobles, like the sixth earl of Morton, the sixth earl of Buchan and the first viscount Lauderdale, avoided voting on the ecclesiastical issues before the parliament, but their dissatisfaction was well known. Close analysis of parliament's membership and behaviour demonstrates that in spite of management by crown officers there was across central Scotland a coterie of nobles and burghs bitterly opposed to royal policies on religion and taxation. Furthermore, while familial, local and personal factors continued to determine loyalties, the divisions exposed in 1621 introduced something approaching a party element to politics that would continue to develop over the next two decades. In Fife, opposition to royal policy was particularly strong, with two out of every five parish ministers publicly indicating their opposition to the five articles, while eleven burghs voted against them along with the sixth earl of Rothes, the second lord Balmerino and the second lord Burleigh. These noble found themselves at the head of a body of opinion that spanned rural and urban communities, and that embraced a determined and vociferous number of ministers.[97]

Having bullied parliament, the king exacerbated the deteriorating situation by insisting on enforcement. James VI instructed his privy councillors and bishops that no one should be permitted to hold office at any level in his service unless they conformed to the five articles of Perth. Individual nobles like the old fifth earl Marischal, a staunch Calvinist, received the privy council order of 10 October 1621 insisting on conformity, a development that is likely to have been interpreted as highly provocative. The struggle over the five articles of Perth demonstrated the limitations of James VI's government along with the king's growing isolation from public opinion, breaking the habit of obedience he had built up over the previous quarter century. Whether it was among the local networks of nobles, merchants and ministers of Fife, the magistrates and burgesses of Edinburgh or the nationwide bonds of kinship between the great noble houses, the five articles had generated a culture of dissent.[98]

Charles I took a harder line on enforcing the five articles of Perth, encouraging more radical innovations of the liturgy, and promoting a growing unease at the direction of crown policy.[99] Those nobles who had hoped for a reversal in autocratic government were quickly disappointed. On 14 April 1625, the young sixth earl of Rothes wrote to the first earl of Ancram following the king's death to suggest that there was now an opportunity to ensure that Charles I restore the 'libertys of the Nobility' and would discontinue his father's 'Novations imposed on the kirk'. That link would grow in the minds of Rothes and his fellow nobles over the succeeding twelve years as Charles I continued to disappoint their expectations. In 1628, Patrick Campbell of Edinample, a younger son of sir Duncan Campbell of Glenorchy, wrote to his father about changes in his local kirk session, commenting that 'the best of the houss is thocht to be cassin'. Criticism grew bolder, for example, in 1630 a petition requesting a return to a form of worship 'free of pomp and ceremonies' was signed by the sixth earl of Rothes, the first earl of Seaforth, the sixth earl of Cassillis, the second lord Balmerino, the first lord Loudon, the eighth lord Yester, the sixth lord Ross and the second lord Melville. Of these men, Rothes, Balmerino, Loudon, Yester and Ross had voted against the five articles in 1621. During Charles I's visit to Scotland in 1633, Melville upset the king at a meeting of the privy council during a debate on the liturgical policy by bluntly announcing that 'I have sworn with your father and the whole kingdom to the confession of faith, in which the innovations intended by these articles were solemnly abjured.' His cousin and successor as third lord Melville also voiced criticisms of the crown in public and had a younger brother, Thomas, who was a minister along with a sister, Elizabeth, who was married to another minister. Elizabeth Melville, his cousin, was the author of *Ane godlie dreame* (1603), an influential meditative work, and played an active role in the conventicling underground. Here was a Fife noble family with a long record of loyal service to James VI, but with strong clerical connections and deep religious convictions, increasingly at odds with Charles I. By the mid-1630s, men like Rothes were running out of patience, and he warned the courtier sixth earl of Morton that the privy council would be unwise to investigate men's attitudes to the proposed prayer book. Rothes pleaded with Morton 'to keip bak such an unfound piece of work', suggesting that 'ther be things in itt, your Lo[rdship] wold be unwilling to heir or practise'. In 1634, the dying first viscount Kenmure condemned the liturgical innovations in the church as 'superstitious, idolatrous, and antichristian, and come from hell'. But, showing pessimism that would prove to be unfounded, he prayed for forgiveness for the nobility 'for they are either key-cold, or ready to welcome Popery, whereas they should resist'. All this was taking place against a background of growing episcopal power and rumours of a popish plot at court in the context of the adverse military situation on the continent.[100]

Noblewomen took a prominent role in encouraging dissent. Anna Cunningham, mother of the second marquis of Hamilton, actively encouraged conventicles, while Jane Campbell, lady Kenmure, Margaret Livingston, countess of Wigton, Christian Hamilton, lady Boyd, Catherine Erskine, lady Binning and Anna Erskine, countess of Rothes, all gave encouragement and support to ministers. Marie Stewart, the ageing countess of Mar, wife of the lord treasurer and mother of lady Binning and the countess of Rothes, maintained close contact with dissenting ministers into the 1630s, attempting to lure Alexander Henderson to Stirling in 1631. In April 1633, Samuel Rutherford wrote to lady Kenmure, sister of lord Lorne, asking her to 'stir up your husband' in preparation for the upcoming parliament. Julian Ker, countess of Haddington, worked behind the scenes, while her husband, the lord privy seal, was preparing for the parliament. In a letter of May 1633 she wrote to her son, George Hume of Belshiel, about a minister friend, warning him to burn any correspondence on the matter, and a little over a year later she commented on the treatment of the second lord Balmerino, asking that 'the lord in his gret merce to preserve and delyver him from al thar malece and develisch plots'. She continued her involvement with dissidents, participating in a conventicle in Edinburgh until her death in March 1637.[101]

The royalist John Spalding criticised those nobles who joined the petitioning movement in 1637–8, alleging that 'They begin at religion as the ground of their quarrel ... whereas their intention is only bended against the king's majesty and royal prerogative.'[102] Yet the contact between lay and clerical dissenters was in place long before April 1637. It is true that for many nobles the presbyterian underground with its covert publications and its illegal conventicles still represented dangerously subversive behaviour. Nervous nobles were informed by more recent evidence, such as when on 9 March 1630 Joseph Lowrie, minister of Stirling, was charged with 'mis-behaviour and unreverend speeches dispersit be him againes the Erle of Mar'. Few nobles wanted a return to the outspoken sermons of the later sixteenth century.[103] Nevertheless, by the 1630s anger against the liturgical changes brought together the various strands of dissent throughout the kingdom. Even if religion was not the only issue that angered the nobility, it was the issue that most united opposition to the king, and in August 1637 the second lord Burleigh made exactly this point to the sixth earl of Morton, telling him that a great many people had been angered by the innovations in the church.[104]

Furthermore, the clergy knew they needed the nobility and actively wooed them. Andrew Cant, minister of Pitsligo, urged the nobles to act, reminding them that they were 'the natural mountains of this kingdom' whose houses had long been the defenders of 'kirk and commonwealth', but who were now overshadowed by the bishops, 'these artificial and shooted mountains'. Samuel Rutherford wrote to the second lord Loudon on 9 March 1637 saying that while he did not favour 'tumults or arms' as the means to achieve their religious aims, he desired that 'the zeal of God were in the nobles to do their part for Christ', and he urged Loudon to encourage Lorne to act. Similarly, on 7 September 1637 as the protest against the king's liturgical innovations gathered momentum, he warned the first earl of Lindsay that 'it is now time, my worthy and noble Lord, for you who are the little nurse-fathers, under our sovereign prince, to put on courage for the Lord Jesus, and to take up a fallen orphan'. In October 1637, the first earl of Annandale received a letter from Gavin Young, minister of Ruthwell, who was supportive of the petitioning movement taking place in the country and who wrote to Annandale as someone likely to be sympathetic to the cause. As the revolution unfolded and royal government collapsed, Rutherford picked up the same language employed by John Knox over eighty years earlier, reminding the nobles that 'God hath set you [nobles] as stars in the firmament of honour; upon your influence depends the whole course of the inferior world'. But as with that previous generation, Rutherford would later observe that such pre-eminence was not acquired by antiquity or pedigree, but 'in that adoption by which you are made the sons of God, children of the King of kings, and brethren of the eternal Son of God'.[105]

Conclusion

It is not difficult to be influenced by the growing volume and assertive rhetoric of early seventeenth-century crown records into thinking that a significant shift was taking place in the relationship between crown and nobility. In the later 1590s James VI began to make progress in resolving the three key areas in which noble power impacted most on the exercise of royal authority: noble resistance; noble disorder; and noble support for religious movements. The failure of the 1596 Edinburgh insurrection marked the end of noble toleration of Protestant radicalism, James VI's confident pronouncements on divine right monarchy in *The trew law of free monarchies* (1598) announced a political philosophy that was passively accepted by the nobility, and the 1598 act anent feuding demonstrated that the nobility was prepared to work with the king to address the law and order issue. While the 1600 Gowrie conspiracy was a warning as to how easily the kingdom might be tipped back into political crisis, by 1603 James VI was able to leave Scotland confident that rebellion was unlikely, feuding was declining and the radical clergy no longer had the support of noble patrons. But this achievement was won with the cooperation of the nobility, not their eclipse. Noble power was still very much intact, and while the acquisition of the Tudor inheritance in England, Wales and Ireland along with the physical move of the king to London altered the context within which the relationship between the monarch and his most powerful subjects was acted out, the regal union had little impact on the structural or ideological basis of that power within Scotland.

The underlying weakness of British imperial monarchy in Scotland is well understood. Stewart kings increasingly inhabited a court in which the illusion of power masked its fragility. That is not to say that after 1603 James VI did not find himself in a stronger position in relation to his nobles than he had enjoyed before the union, or even in relation to all previous Scottish kings. Distance, English resources and greatly enhanced patronage gave the king advantages that James VI, on the whole, exploited effectively. By contrast, Charles I was politically incompetent and the cracks in the imperial monarchy that had become apparent in the latter years of his father's reign widened. At that point the reality of where real power lay was exposed as the crown struggled to impose its agenda. Under the surface of conforming to a form of royalist absolutism many nobles continued to adhere to a view of good counsel that was able to make a relatively easy transition to resistance. The intellectual apparatus was readily available, and in 1637–8 the nobility had no difficulty in adapting it to their present purpose. Although feuding declined dramatically, the world of kinship, lordship, martial ideas and embedded local power had not been dismantled, and in the 1630s there is significant evidence that feuding and attendant law and order issues were recurring on the Borders, the Highlands and much of the northeast region. The extent to which it would spread would be determined by the nature of the conflicts of the 1640s. Finally, and fatally for Charles I, the reconnection of radical Protestantism and the nobility over the expansion of episcopal authority and the imposition of an anglicised liturgy allowed nobles to take up a popular cause. Defending the Protestant faith from a crypto-Catholic threat was combined with other grievances against the imperial monarchy, and, of course, with asserting the rights and privileges of the nobility. Confronted by noble power with its interconnectedness throughout every corner of society and government, the crown's authority collapsed and Scotland succumbed to revolution.

Conclusion

At the heart of this book lies a question about the continuity of noble power in an early modern society. It is not long since historians saw the sixteenth and seventeenth centuries collectively as a period in which so-called traditional nobilities were pitched into crisis by a combination of demographic change that loosened their social control, economic developments that undermined their financial stability, religious and cultural shifts that challenged their security, technological innovations that eroded their military prowess, and the emergence of dynastic state systems that tamed their political independence. The final collapse of the power of European aristocracies in the half century after 1914 coincided with this historical fashion being at its height.[1] Mid-twentieth-century historians can be forgiven for seeing in early modern society a reflection of the decaying grandeur of country-house culture around them and the emergence of a meritocratic civil service and managerial class they educated. But this was a thesis driven more by contemporary influences and political theory than by sustained empirical research. Ideas about the state and about class required that the nobility be airbrushed out of the picture, and the earlier and more completely this could be achieved the sooner the early modern nation-state could be distinguished from its late medieval predecessor. Those kingdoms, like Scotland, that appeared to remain for longer in the grip of over-mighty baronial families remained stuck on a lower level of evolutionary development. Playing catch-up with the precocious Dutch or English encouraged some Scottish historians, trapped within this paradigm, to privilege evidence of a Stewart monarchical state and of the supposedly more commercially-minded men who served it, while subscribing to the thesis of a declining nobility.

At the heart of the rebirth of interest in the history of early modern nobilities was a desire to explain this perceived crisis.[2] But instead of disappearing gracefully, European nobilities made a stunning historiographical comeback for complex reasons that range from the rethinking of theoretical perspectives to publication trends and external influences on historians themselves. Consequently, since the middle of the twentieth century there has been a remarkable growth in interest in the history of European nobilities, so much so that it has inspired questions about the historiographical meaning of this trend.[3] For early modern historians, one awkward problem is in explaining the apparent decline of the nobility in the face of strong evidence for the survival of noble power well into the modern era. Meanwhile, medievalists have demonstrated time and again how in previous ages nobilities made effective adaptations in order to preserve their power in the face of significant societal change. What the growing body of research into national, regional and local nobilities across early modern Europe delivered was a growing awareness of the persistence of noble power. The period from roughly the middle decades of the sixteenth century to the middle decades of the eighteenth century saw the consolidation of noble power across Europe, fuelled by the acquisition of significant amounts of new land, changes in family and inheritance patterns, the availability of opportunities for reward and advancement through an expanded state and the stratification of the nobility from which emerged an aristocratic elite. Nobilities, and there was no one pan-European nobility, changed and adapted, but they endured, supported on a socio-economic structure and a culture characterised by continuity rather than crisis, their political potency intact. There is more that is recognisably the same than different about the structures and ideas that sustained the power of late medieval lords and their early modern descendants. For European nobilities the early modern era increasingly looks like an age of modest transition rather than one of crisis, one in which hereditary power may even have been reinforced.[4]

In posing a question about noble power, this book primarily investigates aspects of political power. Obviously, there are other forms of power; economic, social and cultural power all operated alongside overtly political power, but those forms of power have been discussed in a previous study of noble society in Scotland. There it was concluded that by recalibrating their behaviours, becoming more entrepreneurial, adapting family structures and embracing new educational opportunities, nobles positioned themselves to retain a dominant position in the overall society.[5] In this regard, Scottish nobles conformed to the European norm of ensuring continuity through energetic adaptation. Given the success of noble society in ensuring the structural and cultural foundations of noble power, it is unsurprising that the nobility was well-positioned to protect and even enhance their political power.

In discussing the turbulent politics of later sixteenth-century Scottish politics three key issues impinge on noble power: resistance to royal authority; engagement in politicised religion; and involvement in disorder. This lethal concoction was not unique to Scotland and France was equally destabilised by the same issues over the same period.[6] Scottish nobles overthrew the Guise regency in 1560, enforced the abdication of queen Mary in 1567, engaged in a series of rebellions and coups over the following three decades and indulged in an orgy of feuding. This was a society under extreme stress, in which war, revolution and religious division exacerbated

the worst aspects of bloodfeud, creating conflict in every corner of the kingdom. A measure of political stability emerged following the failed Catholic
rebellion of 1594 and the failed Protestant insurrection of 1596, which
marked the end of violent religious movements. The 1598 legislation to
control feuding signalled intent to address domestic disorder, leading to a
significant decline in feuding by the second decade of the seventeenth
century. This process towards a more peaceful form of politics did not mean
that nobles necessarily became less powerful, however, because noble power
was not measured by equating it with the freedom to engage in rebellions
and feuds. Nor did the shift towards a more peaceful kingdom occur because
the crown found hidden resources to overawe the nobility. Instead, from the
mid-1590s the nobles abandoned using force (apart from the perplexing
Gowrie plot of 1600) against an adult king whose personality, policies and
choice of counsel were broadly acceptable. In effect, ideas of resistance were
stored away for another day. At much the same time, nobles distanced themselves from the radical wing of the Protestant clergy and from the Counter
Reformation politics of the jesuits, joining with the king in pursuing a
moderate form of church government more susceptible to royal control
and less critical of king and nobles alike. The nobility also addressed the
most vehement of those criticisms which was directed against feuding
and violence generally, working with the king, parliament and the church
to restore peace to fractured communities. None of the above could be
regarded as permanent as the sixteenth century drew to a close, and only
the king's life stood between this fragile peace and the previous decades of
instability and strife. At that point, the regal union with England in 1603
changed the political landscape.

The power of the nobility at a local level was exercised through the inter-
connected roles nobles acted out as chiefs of kindreds and clans, as lords
of their affinities and as magistrates in local courts. Kinship was an extraordinarily strong bond in early modern Scotland, centred on the agnatic
lineage but able to draw in affinal allies, rooted in territorial possession and
providing the core measure of a nobleman's power. It defined many of the
political conflicts of the period, while providing a means of softening the
harshness of political conduct. But while the worst attributes of behaviour
associated with the blind defence of kinsmen came under attack during this
period, there is little evidence from the early seventeenth century of nobles
altering their attitude to the importance of kinship. Government even
encouraged nobles in their roles as chiefs to continue to exercise authority
over their kinsmen. Kinship, therefore, remained an essential building block
of noble power.

Similarly, there is little evidence to suggest that ideas about lordship,
or the exercise of lordship, fundamentally changed. No one was writing in
the early seventeenth century about lordship as something different from
previous generations, even if a few scattered literary texts harked back to

better times, and a handful of disgruntled men had bad things to say about particular lords. Local residence on the estate, the physical symbolism of the castle or country house, the importance of hospitality and peacemaking and the protection of kinsmen, tenants and dependants all remained features of how nobles reinforced their position as lords. Meanwhile, men continued to serve nobles much as they had always done, attending on their lord, defending his causes and offering counsel. It is true that men stopped giving lords their bonds of manrent, primarily because in the more peaceful conditions of the early seventeenth century lesser nobles did not see the need to seek the protection of more powerful men. But at the outset of the troubles in 1637–8 noble affinities were still the most potent means of applying pressure quickly and effectively on local communities.

Those local communities continued to be governed by nobles much as they had been for centuries. There was a problem with local justice in the latter half of the sixteenth century as the impact of war, feuding and weak oversight from the crown allowed its provision to become so entangled in local politics. Yet ideas about justice did not require much revision. Nobles knew perfectly well what was expected of good lords in exercising the powers of magistracy, but there was a tension between justice and the fierce determination of nobles to protect their own men and their own judicial privileges. The court system, which was overwhelmingly the private domain of the nobility, worked reasonably effectively in less strained times, and as civil strife and feuding declined the worst attributes of partial behaviour by magistrates was addressed by the privy council. Meanwhile, the court of session played an increasing role in civil disputes without arousing much controversy. The desire by kings and some of their advisers, chiefly bishops and lawyers, to address the more fundamental issue of hereditary jurisdictions proved impossible to reform as James VI recognised, while Charles I's more aggressive approach failed and may even have contributed to an increase in disorder. The creation of crown-appointed commissioners of the peace in a parallel administration to the existing court system delivered little, and the lesser nobles who largely filled the commissions were themselves in possession of baronial courts whose privileges they had no desire to undermine. Local government remained noble government even when it was carried out in the king's name.

One of the most important responsibilities of local magistrates in linking them to the crown was in the organisation of military forces to suppress disorder, confront rebellion or defend the kingdom from external threats. Here was the role that lay closest to the heart of noble identity. The political instability of the later sixteenth century ensured that nobles maintained significant private military resources, drawing on their armed kinsmen and followers to project what might be described as hard power, which they deployed in the pursuit of private quarrels as well as in public affairs. The cessation of rebellions, the decline in feuding and the demilitarisation of the frontiers following regal union and peace in Ireland resulted in nobles placing less and less emphasis on expensive military hardware and force. Yet large numbers of nobles and their followers continued to follow professional military careers by engaging in warfare elsewhere, serving in continental armies in campaigns that were mostly aligned with Stewart foreign policy. The scale of this military force by the 1620s and 1630s was huge, and it was largely controlled by networks of nobles and their kinsmen, providing a reservoir of military power that the covenanting nobility mobilised in 1638–40 to defeat Charles I in the Bishops' Wars. By contrast, the crown's military capacity was insignificant, consisting of the summoning of nobles and their followers in times of war and the reliance on nobles to use their local jurisdictions as the basis for training men in wapenschaws. The former was redundant and the latter were haphazard, being dependent largely on the enthusiasm of individual nobles to bother. In the absence of money this left the crown to rely on persuading individual nobles to support them against rebels, while the muddled, ineffective attempts to place Scotland on some kind of war footing in 1625–30 exposed the extent of the problem without leading to any attempt to address it. The Scottish crown was militarily naked in the face of whatever military resources the nobility could assemble.

A nobleman's education placed great emphasis on service and public duty to the king and commonweal, which was reinforced by the self-interest of individual nobles, their kinsmen and their clients who saw benefits in exercising government at the highest levels. Great lords, however, had more than enough to occupy their time, and there was a limit to how much interest they might show in parliamentary scrutiny or how much effort they would apply to royal administration. Even attendance at parliament, the fount of sovereign authority in the kingdom, was avoided by peers who received individual summons, while most barons never bothered attending before 1587 and showed a marked reluctance to be elected as shire commissioners after that date. But parliament was important and nobles enhanced their position among the estates at the expense of the church and in proportion to the burghs, ensuring that the later sixteenth-century parliament was a reasonably independent representative assembly that repeatedly frustrated James VI. After 1603, however, the crown deployed its greater patronage to manage the now infrequent parliaments, creating a source of growing resentment that found expression in the parliamentary constitution imposed on Charles I in 1641. Meanwhile, those nobles who served the king as officers of state and privy councillors accounted for only a very small number of men, the more attentive of whom were unusual in their appetite for administration. What is certain is that monarchs wanted nobles in these important royal offices, but had difficulty persuading the more powerful magnates to attend privy council on a regular basis. Increasingly, in the early seventeenth century it was lesser nobles who staffed the regular work of the privy council, seeing this as a route to higher rank and wealth. Many of these men had some legal training, but these career officials and judges were only rarely drawn from outside noble society, most being younger sons of peers or heads of baronial houses for whom the law was a respectable means to maintain their status. Both the privy council and the bench was subjected to greater political control by the king after 1603, especially under Charles I, thus resulting in poorer policy advice, unsure administration and in 1637 the implosion of a royal government that remained ultimately dependent on the nobility to make it work.

The Stewart royal court of the later sixteenth century was only modestly impressive, but it was still the centre of royal power, political intrigue and the disposal of patronage. Nobles, especially the greater nobles, were not in awe of what they encountered on attending the king at his palaces at Linlithgow or Holyrood, but they did not neglect to put in appearances. Attempts to limit noble rights of access to the king were resented and swiftly resolved, while nobles dominated important court offices and rituals. After 1603 the royal court was dramatically changed. Scottish nobles continued to enjoy more access than their English counterparts thought fair, but with each passing decade their numbers and influence at court diminished leaving a smaller and smaller number of courtiers to fill the role of brokers. The nature of court faction altered from one in which the politics of court and locality were separated by osmotic boundaries to one in which the London court became increasingly remote from Scotland. What remained relatively constant in the refined and yet vicious world of the Stewart court before and after 1603 was the struggle to gain royal attention and favour, to outdo rivals and to appease the clamour from friends and clients for a share of the spoils, all of which remained the domain of the nobility whose birth and education made them the natural companions of the king.

In an undated letter to a friend in which he dwelt on the game of chess as a metaphor for the affairs of the kingdom, William Drummond of Hawthornden made the point that 'there is no danger in the state a king should so much fear as the revolt of his nobles'.[7] This book begins and concludes with revolution, and while it is not shaped by an attempt to explain the outworking of the Reformation or the origins of the National Covenant, both were events in which noble power overthrew royal authority by aligning with broader popular and national movements. Here were the occasions when rulers learned, as kings had discovered before and would again, that they required the consent of the nobility to go on ruling. James VI learned enough from the fate of his mother and the experiences of his childhood and youth to understand this point, but Charles I made the mistake of underestimating the capacity of the Scottish nobles to mobilise kinsmen and dependants, paralyse local government, command effective armed forces, seize control of parliament and council and nullify the efforts of the court to stop them. This is not to argue that the covenanting revolution was only a baronial revolt any more than the English revolution or the Fronde were only baronial revolts, but it was noble-led and it was the nobles who controlled the dismantling of Charles I's monarchy between 1637 and 1641.

Noble power was likely to be contested from two directions: from below by the commons and from above by the king. This book says little about those people who were subject to the consequences of nobles exercising their power, but that is because the Scots had no tradition of anti-noble sentiment. Late medieval and early modern Scotland did not experience popular revolts or protest directed at noble society. It was not until the eighteenth century that ecclesiastical patronage and political reform caused some modest criticism of social structures. This level of popular passivity was not universal throughout early modern Europe, and in France, for example, there was a strong tradition of popular opposition to nobles. The working hypothesis for explaining Scotland's strong social cohesion remains that of a society in which noble power was securely entrenched and yet so finely calibrated with the means to relieve pressure that it was not challenged from below. The combination of kinship, paternalistic lordship, the generally fair exercise of judicial authority, the rootedness of elites in the locality and shared religious beliefs created strong vertical relationships that did not break when placed under strain.

Throughout much of Europe the replacing of customary ideas of nobility with a statutory definition assisted in separating out an upper rank of court nobility from an impoverished local nobility. The division between a higher and lower nobility acquired explicit political significance in some countries such as in Poland–Lithuania where there was a struggle between the great magnates and the lesser nobility to prevent the former imposing oligarchic rule.[8] Scotland, however, does not appear to fit into this pattern, certainly not in the period covered by this book, and even in the eighteenth century court aristocrats and local lairds continued to inhabit a shared world. A different version of this split within the nobility pits a 'traditional' nobility against a 'new' nobility which was harnessed to the interests of the crown, but while it is clear that such divisions occurred from time to time as nobilities underwent renewal, there is little evidence of behavioural differences between such groups. Even the division between nobles of the sword and the robe in France has disappeared under the impact of close scrutiny.[9] In Scotland, too, the evidence for the existence of such distinctions with regard to economic behaviour, family strategies or cultural values is sparse.[10] The problem with such an argument is that in almost every period individual rulers patronised lesser nobles in order to create a clientele distinct from those of the great lords of the day. David Hume of Godscroft, writing in the early decades of the seventeenth century, discussed the politics of James II's minority in these terms, making the point that certain men turned the king against the Douglases and other nobles 'as indeed sik new men gois about to perswade princes, that noble men are enemies to them, and barres to their greatnes'.[11]

Of course, some families rose while others fell for all sorts of reasons, but there was no wholesale transformation of the personnel at the top of noble society which continued to look much as it had throughout the late medieval period and would continue well into the eighteenth century. At the apex of the 1,500–2,000 heads of noble houses were the 50 peers in 1560 rising to 106 by 1637, and these still represented the wealthiest, most influential and most powerful noble families in Scotland.[12] As in 1560 so in 1637 the houses of Hamilton, Angus, Huntly and Argyll remained the greatest in the kingdom. Most lesser noble houses, like the Boyles of Kelburn in north Ayrshire, served their communities and the king at a local level while keeping their heads down and avoiding controversy. This avoidance of the court and high politics was precisely what many noble families cultivated in an effort to preserve their local dominance whether this was the Lacger family in Languedoc or the Carracciolo in Naples.[13] Men at this level did have aspirations to increase their estates, win royal favour and acquire higher rank, but no one wanted to undermine the power structures of noble society. Apart, perhaps, from Charles I who wished to 'frie the gentrie of this kingdome from all those bandis whiche may force them to depend upoun any other than upoun his Majestie'.[14] Instead, nobles of every rank held together against the king's intrusive and incompetent meddling, the cohesion of noble society being an essential factor in ensuring the success of the revolution.

There is no need here to rehearse the arguments about early modern European absolutism, suffice it to say that even its proponents now offer a nuanced version in which the limits of the state to act, and even its multiple and conflicting agencies, are recognised. The old presumption of competition between crown and nobility in an early modern Europe in which state-building took place at the expense of noble power, even in Louis XIV's France, is no longer persuasive. Instead, nobles colluded in and prospered under what appears to have been the limited growth in state power, and it is mistaken to conflate the changes affecting the French nobility with the development of the French state.[15] In this historiographical context, and in the face of the above evidence concerning noble power, it is difficult to agree that there were any significant developments in a Scottish state. What is important to recognise is the fundamental role of the power networks that infused life into institutional agencies and bureaucratic processes. In pre-covenanter Scotland the business of governing is best understood by examining a relational network of noble families who inhabited the public and private spaces where power was exercised.

The persistence of noble power in Scotland was a consequence of the right combination of things staying the same and deft adaptation where it was necessary. The political context within which this process occurred in early modern Scotland was unique in its detail, but easily recognisable elsewhere in Europe. None of this should be surprising given what we know about this society. Only the legacy of crisis that once dominated thinking about early modern nobilities, alongside a misreading of the connections between state power and noble power, might suggest otherwise. In some respects the Scottish case study simply adds to the accumulation of data, underlining the argument for the continuity of noble power, and since most historians work by painstakingly adding to the findings of others in a highly collective process of discovery that is no bad thing. Perhaps those historians who think widely about European nobilities might also find in this study some reason to turn their attention away from what is thought of as the European core to take some account of the rich variety that can be found on the neglected peripheries.

Notes

Chapter 1: Noble Power and Politics, 1560–1603

1. Brown, *Noble Society*.
2. There is a vast literature on this topic, but the best starting point is Scott (ed.), *European Nobilities*, i–ii; Asch, *Nobilities in Transition*.
3. *CSP Scotland*, xii, 106.
4. Brown, 'Taming the magnates?'; Wormald, *Lords and Men*; Grant, *Independence and Nationhood*, 120–46, 171–99; Brown, *Black Douglases*; Brown, 'Scotland tamed?'; and see the essays in Boardman and Ross (eds), *Exercise of Power*.
5. Donaldson, *James V to James VII*, 63–106; Merriman, *Rough Wooings*; Ritchie, *Mary of Guise*; Brown, 'Reformation parliament'.
6. Donaldson, *Scotland. James V to James VII*; Wormald, *Court, Kirk and Community*; Goodare and Lynch (eds), *Reign of James VI*.
7. Brown, *Noble Society*, 228–50.
8. Holt, 'Putting religion back', and see Heller, 'A reply to Mack P. Holt'.
9. Brown, *James I*, 194–9; Brown, 'I have thus slain a tyrant'; MacDougall, *James III*, 235–68; MacDougall, *James IV*, 59.
10. Burns, *True Law*, 54–92; Mason, 'Kingship, nobility and Anglo-Scottish union', 97–205; and on legitimacy, Goodare, *Government*, 22–41.
11. Hume, *General History*, 378; Mason, 'Kingship, tyranny and the right to resist'; Burns, *True Law*, 19–121; Brown, 'Scotland tamed?'; Tanner, *Scottish Parliament*; Tanner, 'I arrest you sir'; Brown and Tanner (eds), *Parliament and Politics in Scotland 1235–1560*; Macdougall, *James III*.
12. *CSP Scotland*, viii, 492–3.
13. Buchanan, *Vernacular Writings*, 17–36; Donaldson, *Queen's Men*; Lee, *Moray*, 212–75; Cowan, 'Marian civil war'; Brown, *Bloodfeud*, 109–11; Dawson, *Politics of Religion*; *CSP Scotland*, iii, 74–7, 116; vi, 85–6; Melville, *Memoirs*, 243.
14. Henneman, 'Military class'; Knecht, *French Wars*; Salmon, *Society in Crisis*, 117–308; Harding, *Anatomy of a Power Elite*, 71–80; Carroll, *Noble Power*; Carroll, 'Peace in the feud'; Major, 'Crown and aristocracy', 643; Dewald, *Provincial Nobility*.
15. Murray, 'Huntly's rebellion'; *CSP Scotland*, iii, 590; Melville, *Memoirs*, 305, 383–5. There was no question of the nobility favouring a Polish form of constitution, Kaminski, 'The *szlachta* of the Polish-Lithuanian Commonwealth'.
16. The Spanish blanks were documents signed by leading Catholic nobles and discovered in the possession of an agent on his way to Spain, *CSP Scotland*, v, 562–5; x, 14, 52; xi, 98, 164; xiii, pt 2, 621; Brown, 'The price of friendship'; Lee, 'Fall of the regent Morton'; Goodare and Lynch, 'James VI', 1–3.
17. Knox, *Works*, i, 272–4, 326–7, 330, 344–5, 382, 387–8, 411, 443; iv. 469–538; Calderwood, *History*, i, 540–5; Herries, *Memoirs*, 60; *First Book*, 62–7; Ryrie, *Origins of the Scottish Reformation*, 161–8; Burns, *True Law*, 122–84; Mason, 'Covenant and commonweal', 98–9; Mason, 'Knox, resistance and the moral imperative'; Mason, *Kingship and Commonweal*, 139–64; Mason (ed.), *John Knox. On Rebellion*; Mason,

'Resistance and the royal supremacy'; Dawson, 'Trumpeting resistance'.

18. Wormald, *Mary Queen of Scots*, 106–66; Donaldson, *Queen's Men*, 31–82; Lee, *Moray*, 88–211; Dawson, *Politics of Religion*, 86–169; Goodare, 'Queen Mary's Catholic interlude'; Herries, *Memoirs*, 69; Calderwood, *History*, ii, 314; *Honorum de Morton* I, 22, 24.

19. Bonney, *European Dynastic States*, 169; Kingdom, 'Calvinism and resistance theory'; Trevor-Roper, 'George Buchanan'; McFarlane, *Buchanan*, 385–7, 394–6, 409–10; Mason, '*Rex Stoicus*', 9–33; Mason, 'People power?'; Hume, *De Unione*, 1–9; Kidd, *Subverting Scotland's Past*, 166; Brown and Mann (eds), 'Introduction', 17.

20. *RPC*, first ser., iii, 508–9; *RPS*, A1582/10/2; *Historie*, 188–93; Moysie, *Memoirs*, 38–43; Melville, *Diary*, 95–6, 276–83; Calderwood, *History*, ii, 391–2.

21. *RPC*, first ser., iv, 30–1; *CSP Scotland*, v, 316; vi, 144, 151–2, 165, 173; vii, 63–5, 97–103, 692; viii, 141–5; Calderwood, *History*, iii, 419–22, 637–40, 651–65; iv, 26–31, 250, 360–1, 383–93; *Historie*, 215; Melville, *Memoirs*, 350–1; Lee, *Maitland of Thirlestane*, 44–76. On Arran's tyrannical reputation, Hume, *General History*, 378; Calderwood, *History*, iv, 22–5, Melville, *Memoirs*, 324. Critics of the Ruthven faction accused them of evil counsel, *CSP Scotland*, vi, 177.

22. Calderwood, *History*, iv, 466, 471–2, 478–80; Hume, *House of Douglas*, ii, 350ff; Hume, *House of Angus*, 375–92; Hume, *General History*, 221–31, 414–28; Williamson, 'Patriotic nobility?'; Hume, *De Unione*, 19–23; Lee, *Maitland of Thirlestane*, 77–86; MacDonald, *Jacobean Kirk*, 30–5.

23. Moysie, *Memoirs*, 75; Grant, 'Brig o' Dee affair'; Brown, *Bloodfeud*, 148–52; Lee, *Maitland of Thirlestane*, 176–92; *CSP Scotland*, x, 28.

24. On Cochrane, Macdougall, 'Is it I?'; *CSP Scotland*, x, 300, 306, 355, 433; Melville, *Memoirs*, 376–7. In England, the Pilgrimage of Grace made similar allegations against Thomas Cromwell, Starkey, 'Court and council', 197; as did the earl of Essex in his criticism of sir Robert Cecil, McCoy, 'Old English honour', 138.

25. Lee, *Maitland of Thirlestane*, 216ff; Cowan, 'Darker vision', 134; Brown, *Bloodfeud*, 156–62; MacDonald, 'Parliament of 1592'; *CSP Scotland*, xi, 61–4, 429–30, 825–8; Melville, *Memoirs*, 414–15; *RPC*, first ser., v. 310–11.

26. Brown, *Noble Society*, 19–21 and for examples see *House of Seytoun*, xii–xiii; Fraser, *Sutherland*, ii, 337; Allan, 'Ane ornament'; Gordon, *Sutherland*, ii, 13, 78, 178–9; Hume, *House of Douglas*, i, lxiii–lxiv, 27–8, 31; ii, 300–1; Hume, *General History*, 215.

27. For Chatelherault, *CSP Scotland*, i, 568; for Orkney, Anderson, *Orkney*, 79–81, 112–17; and see Mar, *HMC Mar and Kellie*, i. 32–4.

28. For Huntly, *CSP Scotland*, i, 650–62; Calderwood, *History*, ii, 196–9, 487–8; Herries, *Memoirs*, 65; Donaldson, *Queen's Men*, 53; White, 'Queen Mary's northern province', 55–64. For Hamilton, Hewitt, *Scotland under Morton*, 64–71; *CSP Scotland*, v, 336–7; Moysie, *Memoirs*, 21–2; Spottiswoode, *History*, ii, 264. For Angus, *RPC*, first ser., iii, 368. For Argyll, Dawson, *Politics of Religion*.

29. Lee, 'Sir Richard Maitland', 34; Mason, 'Kingship, tyranny and the right to resist', Mason, 'Covenant and commonweal'; Donaldson, *Queen's Men*.

30. *House of Seytoun*, ix–x; Maitland, *Poems*, 20; Bannatyne, *Memorials*, 5–13, 126–7; *CSP Scotland*, iv, 224; Calderwood, *History*, iii, 103; Blake, *Lethington*. For charges of tyranny against the regents Moray, Morton and chancellor Arran, *Historie*, 40–3, 45, 146–51, 209.

31. *CSP Scotland*, i, 240; Herries, *Memoirs*, 71, 115; Donaldson, *Queen's Men*, 70–6, 102–3; Lee, *Moray*, 135–52. On the relationship between nobles and popular support in rebellion see Bernard, 'Tudor nobility in perspective' and Carroll, 'Guise affinity'.

32. *Historie*, 52 and see Lee, 'Sir Richard Maitland', 31–3. This was the experience of the nobility in France, Bohannan, *Crown and Nobility*, 27–31.

33. Melville, *Memoirs*, 39–52, 89, 271; Burns, *True Law*, 222–54.

34. *CSP Scotland*, vii, 55–6, 58; x, 42–9; Calderwood, *History*, v, 55, 141–2.

35. Wormald, *Lords and Men*, 70.

36. *Historie*, 279.

37. Cuttler, *Law of Treason*; Bellamy, *Law of Treason*; Bellamy *Tudor Law of Treason*;

NOTES TO CHAPTER I

Nicholls, 'Treason's reward'; Barron, 'Penalties of treason'; Kesserling, *Northern Rebellion*, 91–143.

38. *RPS*, 1314/1, 1424/3, 1424/4, 1540/12/27, 1579/10/50, A1579/8/2, 1584/5/17, 1587/43–4, 1593/4/20; Knox, *Works*, ii, 327; Hope, *Major Practicks*, i, 13; Edington, *Court and Culture*, 39.

39. *Political Writings*, 22; *CSP Scotland*, x, 137. Although Henry VIII used execution selectively and could be surprisingly forgiving, Ellis, 'Henry VIII'; Carey, *Surviving the Tudors*, 40–96.

40. *Historie*, 237; Brown, 'Making of a *politique*'.

41. Pitcairn, *Criminal Trials*, i, pt. 2, 172–82; Brown, *Bloodfeud*, 144–82; Grant, 'Brig o' Dee affair'.

42. The Catholic earls and Bothwell were the subject of much consideration by parliament in 1593–4, *CSP Scotland*, xi, 118, 121–4, 127; Pitcairn, *Criminal Trials*, i, pt, 2, 310–17; *RPS*, 1593/4/4, 1593/4/9, 1593/4/4, 1593/4/19, 1593/4/21–4, A1593/4/1, A1593/4/5, A1593/4/10, A1593/4/13, A1593/4/18, A1593/4/20, 1594/4/4, 1594/4/7, 1594/4/11–12, *Historie*, 330; Calderwood, *History*, v, 330–2; Spottiswoode, *History*, ii. 454–5. The king faced similar obstruction in his efforts to forfeit the master of Gray in 1587, Spottiswoode, *History*, ii, 373; *RPC*, first ser., iv, 164–9.

43. *CSP Scotland*, xii, 45; Spottiswoode, *History*, ii, 113; Melville, *Memoirs*, 319–24; Lander, 'Attainder and forfeiture'; Bush, *Noble Privilege*, 1–2.

44. *RPS*, 1585/12/31. For the eighth earl of Angus's failure to get adequate restoration in 1582, see *CSP Scotland*, vi, 169, 182.

45. Hope, *Major Practicks*, i, 60–1, 272–82; Fraser, *Sutherland*, i, 120–1; *RPS*, 1567/4/28–9; Gordon, *Sutherland*, 124–5. In 1584, forfeitures were passed by parliament on the first earl of Gowrie, the eighth earl of Angus, the second earl of Mar, the master of Glamis and twenty-nine other individuals, Pitcairn, *Criminal Trials*, i, pt. 2, 116–29; *RPS*, 1584/5/60, 1584/5/71–2, most of whom were restored.

46. Calderwood, *History*, vi, 28–100; vii, 392, 563; Hope, *Major Practicks*, i, 58–9; Lee, 'Gowrie conspiracy revisited'.

47. Melville, *Memoirs*, 385; *CSP Scotland*, x, 55; xi, 520.

48. Spottiswoode, *History*, ii, 23; Knox, *Works*, ii, 526–7.

49. Morton probably was guilty of the charge for which he was executed, Pitcairn, *Criminal Trials*, i, pt. 2, 114–16, 142–54; Hume, *General History*, 349; *CSP Scotland*, v, 662–3; vi, 18; Moysie, *Memoirs*, 33–4; *Historie*, 182; Calderwood, *History*, iii, 556–76; Hewitt, *Morton*, 199–202; Lee, 'Fall of the regent Morton'.

50. Knox, *Works*, ii, 380–1; *RPC*, first ser., vi, 145; Balfour, *Works*, i, 408; *Early Travellers*, 142; *CSP Scotland*, xiii, pt. 2, 737; Pitcairn, *Criminal Trials*, ii, 148ff, 167–8 for the sentence.

51. James, 'English politics and the concept of honour', 370–4; Sharpe, 'Last dying speeches'; Smith, 'English treason trials'; *Bannatyne Miscellany*, i, 91–105; *CSP Scotland*, vii, 103–7, 157–9; Calderwood, *History*, iv, 35–7, 41–2. Neither the condemned lairds of Drumquhassill nor Mains admitted to conspiring against the king in the winter of 1584–5. By contrast, the laird of Duntreath, whose confession secured their conviction, was allowed to live, Moysie, *Memoirs*, 52; Calderwood, *History*, iv, 363.

52. Heal, *Reformation*, 353–67; Kellar, *Scotland, England, and the Reformation*, 177–208; Donaldson, *Scottish Reformation*; Cowan, *Scottish Reformation*, 89–138; Cowan, *Regional Aspects*; Ryrie, *Origins*, 161–205; Wormald, '"Princes" and the regions'; Lynch, 'Calvinism in Scotland', 241–7; Cameron, 'Faith and faction'; Brown, 'Reformation parliament'.

53. For example, see that of 1570, *CSP Scotland*, iii, 458–9; *Estimate*; for jesuits, *CSP Scotland*, xii, 106.

54. Knox, *Works*, iv, 494–6; *First Book*, 62–7, 85–6; Calvin, *Institutes*, ii, 654; Wormald, *Court, Kirk and Community*, 138.

55. *Second Book*, 64–5, 168, 213–16. For England, Collinson, 'Magistracy and ministry'.

56. Ryrie, *Origins*, 164–80; Kellar, *Scotland, England, and the Reformation*, 184–219;

Donaldson, *Queen's Men*; Wormald, '"Princes" and the regions', 67; Cowan, 'Marian civil war'; Brown, 'Reformation parliament'; Lee, *Moray*; Dawson, *Politics of Religion*. For French case studies that emphasise religious faith, Wolfe, 'Piety and political allegiance'; Davies, 'Neither politique nor patriot?'; Holt, *Duke of Anjou*.

57. NAS GD 112/39/4/19; Dawson, *Politics of Religion*, 124–7.

58. Knox, *Works*, i, 267–8, 273–4; *CSP Scotland*, i, 362.

59. Knox, *Works*, i, 340; ii, 348–50; Fraser, *Eglinton*, ii, 192–3; Sanderson, *Ayrshire*; McNeill and McQueen eds, *Atlas*, 129. For another local study see Bardgett, *Scotland Reformed*. Neither Catholic nor Protestant nobles became associated with the leagues and confraternities that were a feature of the French religious wars, Harding, *Anatomy*, 46–67.

60. *CSP Scotland*, i, 467; Brown, 'Reformation parliament'; *RPS*, A1560/8/1.

61. Knox, *Works*, ii, 167–8.

62. *BUK*, i, 58, 265; Calderwood, *History*, ii, 159, 247, 287; Knox, *Works*, ii, 484, 539–41. On the transformation of society see Cowan, *Scottish Reformation*, 159–81; Todd, *Culture of Protestantism*; Lynch, 'A nation born again?', 82–91.

63. *Second Book*, 169–72, 213–16; Calderwood, *History*, iii, 415–16, 427, 433; iv, 507.

64. For Moray, *BUK*, i, 120; Calderwood, *History*, ii, 513–15, 525–6, 546; iv, 514; Spottiswoode, *History*, ii; Lindsay, *Historie*, ii, 223; *CSP Scotland*, i, 510; *Historie*, 47; Lee, *Moray*, 279–80. For Argyll, see *CSP Scotland*, i, 469; Reid, 'Earls of Argyll'; Dawson, *Politics of Religion*. For Glamis, see Melville, *Diary*, 43, 47; Calderwood, *History*, iii, 397. For Dun, see Knox, *Works*, i, 317; Spottiswoode, *History*, ii, 412. Other Protestant exemplars are Arran, see Durkan, 'James, third earl of Arran', 166. Morton, see Calderwood, *History*, iii, 393–4, 395–6, 483, 573; Melville, *Diary*, 47–8; *CSP Scotland*, v, 17; Hewitt, *Scotland under Morton*: Gowrie, *Bannatyne Miscellany*, i/I, 124; Calderwood, *History*, iv, 117, 164. Ochiltree, see Calderwood, *History*, ii, 50, 164, 201–2, 293–4, 382, 416, 426, 543; Spottiswoode, *History*, ii, 27.

65. Calderwood, *History*, ii, 147; Knox, *Works*, ii, 421–3; Donaldson, *Scottish Reformation*, 140–1; Cowan, 'Church and society', 186–8.

66. Finnie, 'House of Hamilton'; Brown, *Noble Society*, 238–44; Kirk, 'Royal and lay patronage'; Kirk, *Patterns of Reform*, 368–425; Heal, *Reformation*, 408–11; *First Book*, 10–14, 62; Knox, *Works*, ii, 311; Calderwood, *History*, ii, 50; and the issue continued to be divisive, *Second Book*, 64–5, 213–16.

67. Knox, *Works*, ii, 388; Calderwood, *History*, ii, 220–1; iii, 301–2, 309–28, 395–6; Leslie, *Historie*, ii, 463.

68. Knox, *Works*, i, 272; *Second Book*, 163–72, 213–16; *CSP Scotland*, vii, 216–17; Calderwood, *History*, iv, 525, 541–2; on Adamson see Mullan, *Episcopacy*, 54–73.

69. *BUK*, i, 5; Calderwood, *History*, v, 140; Kirk, *Patterns of Reform*, 232–79.

70. Calderwood, *History*, iii, 646–7, 676–9; iv, 114; *RPS*, A1582/10/2; Donaldson, *All the Queen's Men*, 141; MacDonald, *Jacobean Kirk*, 6–29; MacDonald, 'Subscription crisis'; Heal, *Reformation*, 367–72.

71. *Scots Peerage*, I, 194–6; Calderwood, *History*, iv, 465, 680; Spottiswoode, *History*, ii, 389–90; Hume, *History*, 399, 410–13, 423, 428–30; Melville, *Diary*, 211; Brown, 'Price of friendship'. Angus bears comparison with English Protestant lords, Cross, *Puritan Earl*; Adams, 'A godly peer?', 225–32.

72. Donaldson, 'Scottish presbyterian exiles'; *CSP Scotland*, vi, 228; Melville, *Diary*, 169; Calderwood, *History*, iv, 478–9; vi, 93–5; Hume, *General History*, 423, 428–30; HMC *Mar and Kellie*, i, 46.

73. For Bothwell, see *CSP Scotland*, xi, 192–3, 225, 310–14, 327–8, 454–5, 536, 543; *Historie*, 306–10; Calderwood, *History*, v, 295. For Thirlestane, see Melville, *Diary*, 221; Calderwood, *History*, v, 382 offers a more cynical view. For letters from Thirlestane to Robert Bruce see Calderwood, *History*, v, 83–6, 92–3; vi, 93–5, and see Lee, *Maitland of Thirlestane*, 156, 293–5.

74. MacDonald, *Jacobean Kirk*, 30–73; Graham, *Uses of Reform*, 259–79; Calderwood, *History*, v, 42–5.

75. Calderwood, *History*, v, 187, 191, 216, 221.

76. Mason, 'George Buchanan, James VI and the presbyterians'; Calderwood, *History*, v, 215–18.
77. Calderwood, *History*, v, 161, 339, 395; Bruce, *Sermons*, 313–14; Brown, *Bloodfeud*, 184–214; MacDonald, 'Parliament of 1592', 68–73.
78. *RPC*, first ser., v, 359; *CSP Scotland*, xii, pt 1, 259–60, 393–410, 425, 427, 471; Calderwood, *History*, v, 512–16, 534–5; xii, 557; Spottiswoode, *History*, iii, 28, 34–5; Moysie, *Memoirs*, 130–1; Goodare, 'Attempted coup of 1596'; MacDonald, 'James VI and the general assembly', 171–6; MacDonald, *Jacobean Kirk*, 74–100.
79. *CSP Scotland*, xiii, pt. 2, 852; Calderwood, *History*, vi, 94–5, 130–5, 137–8, 146; Lee, 'Gowrie conspiracy', 113–14.
80. Dewald, *European Nobility*, 178–80; Carroll, *Noble Power*; *Scots Brigade*; *Honorum de Morton*, i, 143 and see 160–2.
81. Brown, 'Reformation parliament'; Calderwood, *History*, ii, 37; Spottiswoode, *History*, i, 327.
82. Leith, *Narratives*; *Memoirs*, 1–185; Sanderson, 'Catholic recusancy'; Lynch, *Edinburgh*, 187–99; Cowan, *Reformation*, 159–81; Hanlon, *Confession and Community* on co-existence; Spottiswoode, *History*, iii, 208; *RPC*, first ser., ix, 160.
83. *CSP Scotland*, i, 555; Spottiswoode, *History*, ii, 8; Goodare, 'Queen Mary's Catholic interlude'; Donaldson, *All the Queen's Men*, 52–3; Wormald, '"Princes" and the regions', 76–7; White, 'Queen Mary's northern province'. Contrast Gordon uncertainty with the Guise family in France, Carroll, *Noble Power*.
84. Wormald, '"Princes" and the regions', 67–8; Sanderson, 'Catholic recusancy'; Sanderson, *Ayrshire*; Knox, *Works*, ii, 533.
85. Knox, *Works*, i, 362–3; *CSP Scotland*, vi, 197, 306–7, 321; vii, 4, 14, 18; x, 784.
86. Calderwood, *History*, iii, 468, 477, 480, 583–5, 594–5, 642; *RPC*, first ser., iii, 431–3, 492. See the 1588 petition to enforce existing laws against papists, *CSP Scotland*, ix, 560–1.
87. Grant, 'Making of the Anglo-Scottish alliance'; Elder, *Spanish Influences*, 77–108; McCoog, 'Pray to the lord of the harvest'; Grant, 'Brig o' Dee affair', 95–6; *CSP Scotland*, viii, 220, 261.
88. *CSP Scotland*, vi, 685–6; Grant, 'Brig o' Dee affair', 95–8.
89. *CSP* Scotland, viii, 81–2, 239, 364; *Historie*, 223–4; Brown, 'Making of a politique'.
90. Elder, *Spanish Influences*, 181–231; Shearman, 'Spanish blanks'; *CSP Scotland*, xi, 18–19; Durkan, 'Two jesuits'. Grant, 'Brig o' Dee affair' argues that Huntly was pushed into Counter Reformation activity by Protestant provocation.
91. Donaldson, 'Scotland's conservative north'; Grant, 'Brig o' Dee affair'; *RPC*, first ser., iv, 376–80.
92. Lynch, *Edinburgh*, 187–99; *Chronicle of the Kings of Scotland*, 15; *CSP Scotland*, xiii, pt. 2, 754; *Chronicle of Perth*, 10.
93. Brown, *Bloodfeud*, 157–62, and see the outraged letter by Robert Rollock, NRA(S) 237/F/488–9.
94. Calderwood, *History*, v, 261–8; *CSP Scotland*, , ix, 682–98; x, 829; xi, 21, 70–1, 119; *Historie*, 284–6; *HMC*, xi, 64–5; Shearman, 'Spanish blanks'.
95. *CSP Scotland*, xi, 197–8, 277, 349–55, 435–6; Brown, *Bloodfeud*, 162–8.
96. *Honorum de Morton*, i, 166; *Historie*, 339; *CSP Scotland*, ix, 699–701; xiii, pt. 1, 128, 131–2; *Letters and State Papers*, 29; Brown, *Bloodfeud*, 169–70. Tyrone's rebellion in Ireland provides some indication of the military power required to crush a revolt that had popular religious support, Morgan, *Tyrone's Rebellion*; McGettigan, *Red Hugh O'Donnell*.
97. *House of Gordon*, i, p. xxxii; *CSP Scotland*, xii, 134; xiii, pt. 1, 489; Calderwood, *History*, v, 462.
98. *Letters and State Papers*, 16; *Historie*, 325–7, 333; Calderwood, *History*, v, 330–1.
99. *CSP Scotland*, ix, 641; Lee, 'King James's popish Chancellor'; Brown, 'Making of a politique'; and for comparison, Haigh, 'Continuity of Catholicism'.
100. Worthington, *Scots In Habsburg Service*; 29–33; Elder, *Spanish Influences*, 232–92; Yellowlees, 'Father William Crichton's estimate'; *CSP Scotland*, xii, 104–11.

101. Knox, *Works*, i, 332.
102. Calderwood, *History*, iii, 644–5; iv, 26–7; v, 233–5, 773–5; Knox, *History*, ii, 347–50; Melville, *Diary*, 240–3
103. *Honorum de Morton*, i, 15; Fraser, *Douglas*, iv, 176; NLS MS 75/76; *HMC Mar and Kellie*, ii, 220.
104. Wormald, 'Bloodfeud'; Boardman, 'Politics and the feud'; Brown, *Bloodfeud*.
105. *Political Writings*, 28; *CSP Spanish*, iii, 95; xi, 663.
106. For the early modern feud see Netterstrom, 'Study of feud', in Netterstrom and Poulsen (eds), *Feud*; Carroll, 'Introduction'; Lansing, *Florentine Magnates*, 164–91; Kaminsky, 'Noble feud'; Muir, *Mad Blood Stirring*; Ruggiero, *Violence in Early Modern Venice*; Wright, 'Venetian law and order'; Brunner, *Land and Lordship*, 14–35, 90–4; Zmora, *State and Nobility*; Zmora, 'Princely state making'; Volckart, 'Economics of feuding'; Carroll, 'Peace in the feud'; Harding, *Anatomy*, 71–80; Ruff, 'Rural feuds'; Greenshields, *Economy of Violence*; Hanlon, 'Rituels de l'aggression'; Hoyle, 'Faction, feud and reconciliation'; Cust, 'Honour, rhetoric and political culture; Manning, *Hunters and Poachers*; Manning, *Swordsmen*, 141–92; Edwards, 'Escalation of violence'.
107. Gluckman, 'Peace in the feud' presents the classic case that influenced Wormald, 'Bloodfeud, kindred and government'. For some cautionary observations, White, 'Feuding and peace-making', Netterstrom, 'Introduction', and Brown, *Bloodfeud*; and on the reporting of violence, Ruff, *Violence*, 1–43.
108. Brown, *Bloodfeud*; and see Carroll, *Blood and Violence*, 264–84.
109. Gordon, *Sutherland*, 150.
110. *RPC*, first ser., ii, 531; Moysie, *Memoirs*, 4; Brown, *Bloodfeud*, chs 1, 3, 4–6; *CSP Scotland*, x, 573–5.
111. Brown, *Bloodfeud*, 30–3; and for violent feud in France and Ireland see Carroll, *Blood and Violence*, 83–159 and Edwards, 'Escalation of violence'. By contrast the German feud existed in more stable conditions, Brunner, *Land and Lordship*, 36–90; Zmora, *State and Nobility*.
112. *Political Writings*, 28; Melville, *Memoirs*, 385; Leslie, *Historie*, i, 103. For Eglinton and Glencairn see Brown, *Bloodfeud*, 95–6 and the quote is from *Historie*, 238. For Huntly and Moray see Brown, *Bloodfeud*, 156–8 and the quote is from *CSP Scotland*, x, 431.
113. Brown, *Bloodfeud*, 4–8, 276–8.
114. Fraser, *Chiefs of Grant*, i. 125–54.
115. Gordon, *Sutherland*, 188–9, 329 and for earlier settlements of the feud in 1589, 1591 and 1612 detailing the catalogue of violence see Fraser, *Sutherland*, iii, 157–67, 183–7; for the Borders, Leslie, *Historie* i, 101; for France see Greenshields, *Economy of Violence*.
116. Brown, *Bloodfeud*, 6–7, 277; Brown, 'Burghs, lords and feuds'; Lindsay, *Historie*, ii, 201; *CSP Scotland*, x, 437; *Historie*, 345–6. For a number of incidents in Perth, see *RPC*, first ser., v, 6–8, 80–1; *Chronicle of Perth*.
117. Brown, *Bloodfeud*, 85–106, 144–82; Cowan, 'Angus–Campbells'; Brown, 'House divided'; Brown, 'Making of a *politique*'; McLean, 'MacLean–MacDonald feud'. Also, for the eastern march see Meikle, *British Frontier?*, 72–82.
118. Brown, *Bloodfeud*, 26–32; and for similar acts Carroll, *Blood and Violence*, 160–81.
119. Leslie, *Historie*, i, 92–3; Bartlett, *'Mortal enmities'*; Davies, *God's Playground*, i, 352; and see Carroll, *Blood and Violence*, 16–20.
120. *Letters and State Papers*, 95, 97; Brown, *Bloodfeud*, 85–106.
121. Fraser, *Sutherland*, ii, 347–8.
122. *CSP Scotland* xii, 360; Pitcairn, *Criminal Trials*, iii, 66; *RPC*, first ser., viii, 128, 144, 153, 543; x, 1, 45; *Melrose Papers*, i, 104, 51–2 for the first report to the king on this 'unhappy accident'; Spottiswoode, *History* iii, 40. For other instances of long feuds see Brown, *Bloodfeud*, 27–8.
123. NLS MS 20,793; Wormald, *Lords and Men*, 115–36; Brown, *Bloodfeud*, 6, 277.
124. Brown, *Bloodfeud*, 65–72; Brown, *Noble Society*, 25–48; Maitland, *Poems*, 101–4.
125. For example, *Family of Kilravock*, 235–6, 269; NAS GD 24/5/57/10; NAS GD 19/39; NAS GD 112/13/1; NLS MS 21,183/7–16; NAS GD 38/2/1/17.

126. Brown, *Bloodfeud*, 67–8; Brown, *Noble Society*, 27–8, 43–4; NRA(S) 2312/107/1/93; *RPC*, first ser., ii, 273–4; iv, 99–101. For other cases see *ibid*, ii, 291–3; 411–12; iii, 35; iv, 18–20; *HMC*, xii, 103–4; NAS GD 38/2/1/1.
127. Macinnes, 'Crown, clans and *fine*', 31–3. On the idea that the crown caused violence in the Highlands, Macinnes, *Clanship*, 30–55. For Argyll, Dawson, 'Two kingdoms or three?'; Cowan, 'Angus–Campbells'; Cowan, 'Clanship'; Macinnes, 'Crown, clans and *fine*', 34–7; Lee, *Government by Pen*, 138–44.
128. *CSP Scotland*, vii, 330, 334; ix, 636; x, 9.
129. *House of Gordon*, i. 21–98; *RPC.*, first ser., vii, 509; viii, 271; Pitcairn, *Criminal Trials*, ii, 532.
130. This had long been a problem, Duby, *Chivalrous Society*, 115; Brown, *Bloodfeud*, 20–1. On Maxwell, *RPC*, first ser., vii, 425, 539, and for other cases of fathers unable to control their violent sons see *RPC*, first ser., vii, 60 and Pitcairn, *Criminal Trials*, iii, 61–5; and *RPC*, first ser., ix, 1, 4, 16, 40–2, 574–6, 578.
131. Brown, *Bloodfeud*, 108–43.
132. Donaldson, *Queen's Men*; Knox, *Works*, ii, 361; Calderwood, *History*, iii, 58–9, 284–5.
133. Morton's fall was also a consequence of his own failure to pay attention to the feuds of his supporters, see Calderwood, *History*, iii, 479–80 for the desertion of lord Ruthven, and Hewitt, *Scotland under Morton*, 43–4 for the Argyll–Atholl feud.
134. NAS GD 75/563; *CSP Scotland*, x, 68.
135. *CSP Scotland*, xi, 102.
136. Hale, 'Sixteenth-century explanations'; Eurich, *Economics of Power*, 19–29, 99. The view that early modern people were more predisposed to violent behaviour is unconvincing, see Stone, *Crisis of the Aristocracy*, 223–34; Stone, 'Homicide and violence'; Wrightson, *English Society*, 55, 62–5; Sharpe, 'Domestic homicide'.
137. Brown, *Bloodfeud*, 184–214; Graham, 'Conflict and sacred space'; *BUK*, iii, 874–5; Calderwood, *History*, v, 410. For the views of Calderwood himself and archbishop Spottiswoode, Calderwood, *History*, v, 359; Spottiswoode, *History*, ii, 465.
138. Brown, *Bloodfeud*, 239–65; *Melrose Papers*, i, 273; *RPS*, 1598/6/2.
139. Hume, *House of Douglas* ii, 445–7.
140. Dewald, *Aristocratic Experience*, 15–44; *Historie*, 52–3.
141. *Chronicles of the Frasers*, 156; and see *CSP Scotland*, vi, 86; for an English example, Gunn, 'Henry Bourchier'.
142. *CSP Scotland*, vii, 271.
143. Melville, *Memoirs*, 291; *Historie*, 229. For earlier efforts to express unity in the form of bonds in 1583–4, Calderwood, *History*, iii, 700–2; vii. 20–1.
144. *CSP Scotland*, xii, 415.
145. Lee, *Maitland of Thirlestane*, 251, 284, 297. The Tudor monarchy's dealings with individual nobles in England and Ireland is no longer seen as part of any greater scheme, Hoyle, 'Henry Percy'; McCormick, *Earldom of Desmond*; Carey, *Surviving the Tudors*. The significance of the 1601 Essex revolt as the last fling of an outmoded form of noble politics appears as such only long after the event, James, 'The Essex revolt, 1601'.

Chapter 2: Chiefs

1. Fox, *Kinship and Marriage*; Holy, *Anthropological Perspectives*; Schneider, *Critique*.
2. Bouchard, *Those of My Blood*; Crouch, *Birth of Nobility*, 124–55; Duby, 'Lineage'; Herlihy, 'Making of the medieval family'; Barton, *Aristocracy*, 38–46; Moore, 'Anglo-Norman family' argues the case for a nuclear family; for a useful summary of recent literature, Drell, *Kinship and Conquest*, 5–11. For Scotland, Duncan, *Making of the Kingdom*, 108–10; Barrow, *Anglo-Norman Era*; MacQueen, 'Kin of Kennedy'.
3. Stone, *Crisis of the Aristocracy*, 589–93, 669–71; Laslett, *World We Have Lost*, 84–112; Houlebrooke, *English Family*, 39–62; Wrightson, *English Society*, 66–88; Macfarlane,

Origins; Cressy, 'Kinship and kin interaction'. Kettering, 'Patronage and kinship', sees obligations to kinsmen as less important than clientage relationships in early modern France.

4. Fox, *Kinship and Marriage*; Keesing, *Kin Groups*; Hareven, 'History of the family'; Flandrin, *Families*, 4–10; Goody, *Development of the Family and Marriage*, 231–2, 262–78; Cressy, 'Kinship and kin interaction'; Plakans, *Kinship in the Past*, esp. 25–50 and 217–40; Anderson, *Approaches*, 4–24; Mitterauer and Sieder, *European Family*, 24–47; Hurwich, 'Lineage and kin', 33–40. For a case study that demonstrates English kinship did extend beyond the nuclear family, Mitson, 'Kinship networks'.

5. Schneider, *Critique*; and for a historical application, see Tadmor, *Family and Friends*, esp. 1–17.

6. Bloch, *Etymologies and Geneaologies*, 64–91; Barrow, *Anglo-Norman Era*; Grant, *Independence and Nationhood*, 203–6, 211–14; Brown, *Black Douglases*, 156–82; Wormald, *Lords and Men*, 76–90; Brown, *Bloodfeud*, 15–17; Rae, *Administration*, 5–11; Dodgshon, *Chiefs to Landlords*, 31–54; Macinnes, *Clanship*, 1–29; Murdoch, *Network North*, 13–48.

7. Brown, *Noble Society*, 113–80.

8. Fraser, *Maxwells of Pollok*, ii, 154–5, No. 152. The same interest in paternal ancestry was common in England, Stone, *Crisis of the Aristocracy*, 22–3.

9. *Regiam Majestatem*, 139–40, 144, 160; Gardener, 'Origin and nature'; Pomata, 'Blood ties and semen ties'.

10. Fraser, *Sutherland*, i, 184; Gordon, *Sutherland*, 232; Brown, *Noble Society*, 32–9; Meikle, *British Frontier?*, 27–8; for a ratification, *RPS*, 1592/4/143.

11. NAS GD 75/563; for spelling variants of Mackay see Mackay, *Book of Mackay*, 4–6; and for another example, see Arnot, *House of Arnot*, 4–5; for Douglas, Hume, *House of Douglas*, i, 11; for Frasers, *Estimate*, 27; for Ruthvens, *RPS*, 1600/11/11; *RPC*, first ser., vi, 510–11.

12. Fraser, *Melvilles*, i, 23–4.

13. *Estimate*, 10; Brown, 'House divided'; *Scots Peerage*, ii, 468–75.

14. *Scots Peerage*, ii, 231–3; Fraser, *Buccleuch*, i–ii.

15. Patterson, *Cattle, Lords and Clansmen*, 207–87; Nicholls, *Gaelic and Gaelicized Ireland*, 8–12; Sellar, 'Origin and ancestry'; Macinnes, *Clanship*, 1–29; Dodgshon, *Chiefs to Landlords*, 31–54; Cathcart, *Kinship and Clientage*, 13–26.

16. Goody, *Development of Family and Marriage*, 222–37. The Scottish kindred does not equate to the French *lignage*, which has less emphasis on agnatic relations, Flandrin, *Families*, 15–19; on Germany see Hurwich, 'Lineage and kin', 48–61.

17. Geary, *Phantoms of Remembrance*, 48–80; Fentress and Wickham, *Social Memory*; Molho, Barducci, Battista and Donnini, 'Genealogy and marriage alliance'. On memory as a tool with a high cultural value, Caruthers, *Book of Memory*.

18. Aurell, 'Western nobility', 265–7; Drell, *Kinship and Conquest*, 130–46 provides these categories; Astarita, *Continuity of Feudal Power*, 21–2, 160–6; Banac and Bushkovitch, 'Nobility', 5.

19. Tayler, *Book of the Duffs*, i, 1–2; Murray, *Chronicles*, i, 1; Campbell, *Clan Campbell*, i, 1–19; Sellar, 'Earliest Campbells'; McLeod, *Divided Gaels*, 118–26. For other examples, *Estimate*, 7–28; Boyd, *Pedigree of the House of Boyd*; Innes, 1–3; Livingston, *Livingstons*, 1–5; Arnot, *House of Arnot*, 8–39. For the Mackintoshes and Grants see Cathcart, *Kinship and Clientage*, 13–20; Spiegel, 'Genealogy'; Maclagan, 'Geneaology and heraldry'; Allan, 'What's in a name?'; Macgregor, 'Genealogical histories'.

20. Klapisch-Zuber, 'Genesis of the family tree'; Nisbet, *System of Heraldry*, ii, appendix; Brown, *Noble Society*, 265–70; Howard, *Scottish Architecture*, 86–90; Bath, 'Painted ceilings'; Apted, *Painted Ceilings*; Bath, *Renaissance Decorative Painting*, 151–6.

21. For Hamiltons, Durkan, 'James, third earl of Arran', 155; for Maitlands, *House of Seytoun*, 15; for Sinclairs, NLS Adv. MS 15.2.31; for Cunninghams, *Sheriffdoms of Lanark and Renfrew*, 21 and see Allan, 'What's in a name?', 149.

22. NLS MS 21,187A/6–14; NLS Adv. MS 17.2.4; NLS Adv. MS 33.2.28/1–8. The greater part of the Leslie history, 'A breviat of the genealogie of the honourable surname of the

Lesleyes', appears to have been written later in the seventeenth century, but was begun by Denmilne.

23. Urquhart, *Works*, 151–75; Tayler, *Family of Urquhart*, 3–4, 7.

24. Reid, 'Hume of Godscroft's 'The origine and descent''; Hume, *House of Douglas*, i, 12. See his emphasis on male succession in passing on a hereditary 'nobilitie of their blud', 21.

25. Sellar, 'Origin and ancestry', 111–12; Sellar, 'Earliest Campbells'; Boardman, 'Medieval origin legend'; Gillies, 'Invention of tradition'; Gillies, '"British" genealogy'; McLeod, *Divided Gaels*, 118–26; Dawson, *Politics of Religion*, 59, 76–7; Campbell, *Clan Campbell*, i, 1–19; MacLean-Bristol, *Warriors and Priests*, 1–8, 158–73.

26. Tayler, *Family of Urquhart*, 2; *Estimate*, 12; Fraser, *Douglas*, iv, 302; NAS GD 406/1/9325. See also NAS GD 24/1/823 for the Drummond connection with Portugal, and also Murdoch, *Network North*, 20–5.

27. Ellis, 'Genealogy'; Gordon, *Sutherland*; Allan, 'Ane ornament', 37–8; Mackay, *Book of Mackay*, 6–20; Hume, *House of Douglas*, i, 27–9; *Scots Peerage*, i, 232, 250–1.

28. Mitterauer and Sieder, *European Family*, 10–11; Rosenthal, *Patriarchy and Families*, 23–101.

29. Arbuthnot, *Memories*, 30–3; Hume, *House of Douglas*, i, 14–17, 68–127; Brown, *Black Douglases*, 9–31.

30. *Estimate*, 7–9, 14; Livingston, *Livingstons*, 24; *Scots Peerage*, i, 106–8.

31. Macinnes, *Clanship*, 3–4; Munro, 'Clan system'; Cathcart, *Kinship and Clientage*, 59–98.

32. For Bothwell, *CBP*, i, 408; for Dunlop, Pont, *Topographical Account*, 16; for Stirling, Rogers, *Memorials*, 32–204; for Gordonstoun, Fraser, *Sutherland*, ii, 358.

33. Duncan, *Making of the Kingdom*, 48–9; Goody, *Development of the Family*, 222–7.

34. *House of Seytoun*, 24–5, 29–31; *House of Gordon*, ii, 111–52.

35. Brown, *Noble Society*, 113–36; Meikle, *British Frontier?*, 31–2; Davies, 'Politics of the marriage bed'; Kalas, 'Marriage', 370–7. For a similar conclusion based on evidence from Germany see Hurwich, 'Lineage and kin', 43–8.

36. *Abbotsford Miscellany*, 207; *RPC*, first ser., x, 542–3, 841–2; xi, 269–70.

37. Knox, *Works*, ii, 480; Lindsay, *Historie*, i, 407; Ulpian is quoted in Pomata, 'Blood ties and semen ties', 48.

38. *House of Seytoun*, 31, 69–70, 102, and *RPS*, 1581/10/65 and for another example see *RPS*, 1581/10/65, 1587/7/145. The Scots did not adopt double-barrelled surnames, a practice found in England, since this advertised the break in continuity, Innes, *Scots Heraldry*, 127; and for England, Stone and Stone, *An Open Elite?*, 129–35.

39. Dawson, 'Fifth earl of Argyle', 13–17; Cathcart, *Kinship and Clientage*, 99–112; Fraser, *Chiefs of Grant*, iii, 145–7; Fraser, *Sutherland*, ii, 344.

40. NAS GD 112/39/9/5, 112/39/32/9; *Estimate*, 25; Klapische-Zuber, 'Genesis of the family tree'; Innes, *Scots Heraldry*, 136–54; Brown, *Noble Society*, 258–64; NAS GD 112/39/54/10.

41. Brown, *Bloodfeud*, 43–64; Hope, *Practicks*, ii, 299–301; *Innes*, 161–3.

42. *RPC*, second ser., iv, 378.

43. Fraser, *Douglas*, iv, 247; Fraser, *Elphinstone*, ii. 264; Brown, *Noble Society*, 173. Ignoring this convention led to conflict, Brown, 'House divided', 170–1; Brown, *Bloodfeud*, 89–102; there are countless examples of cautions in the volumes of the register of the privy council, *RPC* first and second ser.

44. Enright, 'Lady with a mead cup'; Ward, 'Noblewomen' emphasises the contraction of women's roles; Klapisch-Zuber, 'Family trees'; Brown, *Noble Society*, 38, 72–9, 115–33 137–66, 169–71.

45. Heal and Holmes, *Gentry*, 94–5; Kettering, 'Patronage and kinship', 420–9; Chojnacki, 'Kinship ties'.

46. *House of Forbes*, 164–5; *HMC Various V*, 114–15; Fraser, *Annandale*, ii, 30.

47. Fraser, *Sutherland*, ii, 344; Brown, *Bloodfeud*, 58, 170–1.

48. NRA(S)237/C/158; Lander, *Crown and Nobility*, 94–126; Rheubottom, *Age, Marriage and Politics*, 102–31; Davies, 'Politics of the marriage bed', 91; Wormald, *Lords and Men*, 79–80; Wormald, 'Bloodfeud', 67.

49. For the evolution of feudalism as an alternative social organisation see Bloch, *Feudal Society*, 134–42; Duby, *Chivalrous Society*, 134–48; Sabean, 'Aspects of kinship behaviour and property'; Dewald, *Aristocratic Experience*, 70.

50. Hume, *General History*, 363; Gordon, *Sutherland*, 187; Napier, *Plaine Discovery*, 106; *Chronicles of the Frasers*, 254; NLS 79/15; Fraser, *Sutherland*, ii, 358.

51. Wilson, *House of Airlie*, 12–13; Flandrin, *Families*, 11–14; *House of Seytoun*, 16; Gordon, *Sutherland*, 25; NLS Adv. MS 33.2.28/9–24.

52. Rae, *Administration*, 5–9; Meikle, *British Frontier?*, 13–15.

53. Dodgshon, *Chiefs to Landlords*, 13–14, 31–54; Macinnes, *Clanship*, 5–6; for a detailed case study see Cathcart, *Kinship and Clientage*, 129–36, 145–57. On Argyll, Pitcairn, *Criminal Trials*, iii, 21, and on the wider context, Stevenson, *Alasdair MacColla*, 22–49; Cowan, 'Clanship'.

54. 'Military report', in *AWAA*, iv, 17, 19–20; *Estimate*; *Historie*, 128; Gordon, *Sutherland*, 83.

55. *RPC*, first ser., iv, 283; Wormald, *Lords and Men*, 81–2; NLS MS 80/37.

56. Wormald, *Lords and Men*, 83–4; Murray, *Chronicles*, i, 20–1; *HMC*, iv, 533–4.

57. *RPC*, first ser., iii, 261; Cowan, 'Clanship', 144–5; Ohlmeyer, *Civil War and Restoration*, 42–8.

58. *Estimate*, 7–28; NRA(S) 217/3/14; *HMC Laing*, i, 83–4.

59. *CSP Scotland*, i, 335.

60. Wormald, 'Bloodfeud', 71; Wormald, *Lords and Men*; Dodgshon, *Chiefs to Landlords*, 55–83. On England, James, *Family, Lineage and Civil Society*; Watts, *Border to Middle Shire*; Robson, *English Highland Clans*, 111–215; Ellis, *Tudor Frontiers*. On France, Flandrin, *Families*; Mentzer, *Blood and Belief*, 142–61; Heers, *Family Clans*.

61. For longitudinal case studies, Brown, *Black Douglases*; Boardman, *Campbells*.

62. *Honorum de Morton* i, 65–8; Wormald, *Lords and Men*, 83; *RPC*, first ser., iii, 166–80, 183–4, 187–8; Macinnes, *Charles I*, 5.

63. *HMC*, xv, pt. 9, 27.

64. Drell, *Kinship and Conquest*, 127; Meikle, *British Frontier?*, 32–45; *RPC*, first ser., viii, 253; and for a closer analysis, Brown, *Bloodfeud*, 85–105.

65. Wormald, *Lords and Men*, 78; NRA(S) 2171/581; Fraser, *Annandale*, i, p. lxxvii; and for the Maxwells, Fraser, *Carlaverock*, i, 228.

66. Wormald, *Lords and Men*, 76; for Hume, *HMC*, xii, 170; for Ogilvy, *HMC*, iii, 404; *HMC Various V*, 113. Some bonds were used to strengthen kinship with contractual obligations in relation to land and service, see Fraser, *Chiefs of Grant*, i, 209; iii, 135–6, 165–6, 209–13. On fictive kinship, Murdoch, *Network North*, 27–38.

67. Fraser, *Sutherland*, ii, 346, 354. For some discussion of Sidney Painter's question, 'Did a man feel he had family obligations towards his second cousin?', see Holt, 'Feudal society and the family'; Murdoch, *Network North*, 38–48 provides some answers. Kettering, 'Patronage and kinship', sees kinship as a subsidiary of clientage with the responsibilities imposed by the former as voluntary and the latter as obligatory.

68. Arbuthnot, *Memories*, 46–7; Searle, *Predatory Kinship*, especially chs 14 and 22; Boardman, 'Politics and the feud'; Brown, *Bloodfeud*..

69. Brown, *Bloodfeud*, 85–105; for a late example, Tayler, *Family of Urquhart*, 33–4; *RPC* first ser., xiii, 173–4, 177–8, 182.

70. Brown, *Bloodfeud*, 43–64; NRA(S) 237/F/506–7.

71. Crumney, *Aristocrats and Servitors*, 82–106. There is conflicting evidence from England and France, Lander, 'Family, "friends" and politics'; Warwicke, 'Family and kinship'; Cust, 'Honour, rhetoric and political culture'; Neuschel, *Word of Honor*, 78–93; Kettering, 'Patronage and kinship'.

72. Brown, *Bloodfeud*, 107–82; Wormald, *Lords and Men*, 77; NAS GD 406/1/61.

73. Hume, *General History*, 391–2; NAS GD 38/2/1/69. Although the two men had been at feud with one another shortly before this date.

74. *RPC*, first ser., iii, 232–3, 658; Donaldson, *Queen's Men*, 134; NAS GD 112/39/301.

75. *House of Gordon*, i, 7–10, 21–98. But see Stevenson, 'English devil' for effect of the second marquis of Huntly's neglect of his responsibilities to his kindred.

76. Fraser, *Eglinton*, ii, 209–10; Wormald, *Lords and Men*, 85–6.

77. Fraser, *Annandale*, i, p. lxxvii; *HMC Laing*, i, 33; NAS GD 38/1/73a, and for another bond of 1595, 38/1/85a; NAS GD 124/7/21; and for others Fraser, *Carlaverock*, i, 228; Murray, *Atholl and Tullibardine*, 18–19.

78. Carroll, *Blood and Violence*, 29–37; on Ireland, Edwards, *Ormond Lordship*, 108–19 which discusses the division of the Butlers following the death of the tenth earl in 1614.

79. NAS GD 17/239; Craig, *Jus Feudale*, i, 592–3; Fraser, *Sutherland*, ii, 354; Gordon, *Sutherland*, 164.

80. *Chronicles of the Frasers*, 176–8, 183; Fraser, *Buccleuch*, ii, 237–41.

81. Brown, *Bloodfeud*; Lindsay, *Lives*, i, 385–91; *Innes*, 34–40, 133–40, 145–7; for Campbells, Cowan, 'Clanship'; Hill, 'Rift within clan Ian Mor'; *CSP Scotland*, x, 430, 562; Spottiswoode, *History*, ii, 411; for Kennedies, Brown, 'House divided'.

82. Hicks, 'Cement or solvent?'; Loyn, 'Kinship'; Davies, 'Survival of the bloodfeud'; Patterson, 'Patrilineal kinship'; Skinner, *Family Power*. Among the earliest theses that pinned the blame on migration is Philpotts, *Kindred and Clan*, 275–65.

83. Maitland, *Poems*, 62, 89–92; Sanderson, *Rural Society* ; Brown, *Noble Society*, 25–70; Fraser, *Sutherland*, ii, 154–5; Fraser, *Carlaverock*, ii, 114; James, 'Concept of order', 276.

84. *CSP Scotland*, i, 421, 467; vii, 427.

85. Bossy, 'Blood and baptism', 136; Wormald, '"Princes" and the regions'; Knox, *History*, ii, 38; Calderwood, *History*, viii, 248; Bruce, *Sermons*, 355; Rollock, *Works*, i, 52; ii, 107; Brown, *Bloodfeud*, 201–2; Williamson, 'Patriot nobility?'.

86. Craig, *Jus Feudale*, i, 2. On discussions of citizenship, which largely has its roots in Cicero, see Burns, *True Law*, 196–7.

87. *Melrose Papers*, i, 10–12; Scally, 'Hamilton'.

88. Rae, *Administration*, 116–18; *RPS*, 1587/7/70, 1594/4/48, 1594/11/2; *RPC*, first ser., iv, 356; Brown, *Bloodfeud*, 252; Goodare, *State and Society*, 258–61, 268–9; Spalding, *Memorial*, 60.

89. For individual families see Slater, *Family Life* and Larminie, *Wealth, Kinship and Culture*; for local society, Fletcher, *County Community*, especially 44–57; Everitt, *Landscape and Community*, 309–20; and for the war, Durston, *Family in the English Revolution*; Farr, 'Kin, cash, Catholics and cavaliers'; Tadmor, *Family and Friends*; and for the Lacger, Mentzer, *Blood and Belief*.

90. Allan, 'What's in a name?'; MacGregor, 'Genealogical histories'.

91. This is most obvious in the Highlands, see Stevenson, *Alastair MacColla*; Macinnes, *Clanship*, 88–121. It was also a key factor in the northeast where Gordons were pitted against their old Forbes rivals, or the southwest where Maxwells and Johnstones found themselves in opposition to one another.

92. Gordon, *Short Abridgement*, 18–19; and see Gordon, *Scots Affairs*, ii, 206 for similar kin-based politics.

Chapter 3: Lords

1. Neville, *Native Lordship*; Boardman, *Campbells*; Brown, *Black Douglases*; Boardman and Ross (eds), *Exercise of Power*; Wormald, *Lords and Men*. On England, see Macfarlane, *Nobility of Late Medieval England*; Davies, *Lords and Lordship*; Hudson, *Land, Law and Lordship*; Given-Wilson, *English Nobility*. On Ireland see Frame, *English Lordship in Ireland*; Doran and Lyttleton (eds), *Lordship in Medieval Ireland*; and for Wales, Davies, *Lordship and Society*.

2. Scott, 'Early modern European nobility'; Brown, *Noble Society*, 25–70.

3. Fraser, *Chiefs of Grant*, iii, 157–8.

4. Neuschel, *Word of Honor*, 9–11; Smith, *Culture of Merit*, 18–32

5. *House of Seytoun*, ix–x.

6. Melville, *Memoirs*, 178; *Historie*, 151; Calderwood, *History*, vii, 595; also see *HMC Buccleuch*, i, 27–8.

7. Hume, *General History*, 399; Spalding, *Memorial*, 73; Fraser, *Sutherland*, i, 167; *Chronicles of the Frasers*, 254–5; Fraser, *Sutherland*, ii, 346, 354.

8. Anderson, *Orkney*, 77; NRA(S) 217/3/226–9, 217/3/232, 217/3/236–7, 217/3/255.

9. Brown, 'Scottish aristocracy'; NAS GD 39/2/1, 39/2/4–30. For other examples, NAS GD 150/3441/10; Fraser, *Douglas*, iii, 296–7.

10. McKean, *Scottish Chateaux*, 59–78, 107–12, 141–58; Howard, *Architectural History*, 48–107; Glendinning, Macinnes and MacKechnie, *Scottish Architecture*, 40–50; Samson, 'Tower houses'; Maxwell-Irving, *Border Towers*; and see Oram and Stell (eds), *Lordship and Architecture*, chs 10–13.

11. NAS GD 112/39/53/14; NAS GD 150/3437/11, 150/3442/13, 150/3442/12; Fraser, *Sutherland*, ii, 347, 363.

12. Davis, *Gift*; Heal, 'Idea of hospitality'; *Early Travellers*, 88; *Kilravock*, 91; Dodgshon, *Chiefs to Landlords*, 8, 14–15, 55–92.

13. Gluckman, 'Peace in the feud'; Wormald, 'Bloodfeud'; Brown, *Bloodfeud*, 43–64; Fraser, *Eglinton*, i, 196–7.

14. Wormald, *Lords and Men*, 173, appendix A, Ailsa, No.15; *HMC Laing*, i, 27–8; *Abbotsford Miscellany*, 44–7; Fraser, *Eglinton*, ii, 216–19; NRA(S) 234/523/86.

15. NAS GD 112/39/8/19, 112/39/8/22, 112/39/9/1, 112/39/9/13–14, 112/39/9/24; Fraser, *Eglinton*, ii, 207; NRA(S) 237/F/489–93 and NRA(S) 237/C/178–9, 237/C/181–2. Also see the first earl of Roxburghe, NAS GD 40/2/12/50; and the laird of Kilravock, *Kilravock*, 289–92.

16. NLS MS 3416/65–6; NLS MS 21,174/70.

17. NRA(S) 217/3/245; *HMC Mar and Kellie*, i, 45, 49–50, 173; ii, 252.

18. Fraser, *Douglas*, iv, 243; for other examples, Fraser, *Chiefs of Grant*, ii, 51; iii, 285; Fraser, *Wemyss*, iii, 73–5.

19. *Regiam Majestatem*, 105–11; and on arbitration see Godfrey, *Civil Justice*, 355–440; Godfrey, 'Arbitration and dispute resolution'; Brown, *Bloodfeud*, 43–64; Wormald, 'Bloodfeud', 56, 72–8, 96. For England see Rawcliffe, 'Great lord as peace-keeper'; Rowney, 'Arbitration'; Powell, 'Arbitration'; Hindle, 'Keeping of the public peace'.

20. Fraser, *Annandale*, ii, 274–5 and see *Black Book*, 236–7.

21. For Wemyss–Glenorchy, *HMC*, vi, 697, 708; Johnstone–Graham, Fraser, *Annandale*, i, p. lxxiii; Gordon–Forbes, *RPC*, first ser., iii, 261, 279–80; see NAS GD 39/1/118 and *RPC*, first ser., iv, 195–6, 221, 503, 536. Townsmen, too, were helped by the arbitration of nobles, see NRA(S) 2312 107/1/110–11; *HMC*, vi, 717.

22. Wormald, *Lords and Men*, 66; Fraser, *Douglas*, iii, 278–9; Fraser, *Annandale*, i, pp. lxxxiii–lxxxiv.

23. NAS GD 8/167; *HMC*, xiv, 32–3; and see *Abbotsford Miscellany*, 378 and NRA(S) 217/1/407.

24. *CSP Scotland*, x, 48, 196; Fraser, *Sutherland*, ii, 356.

25. NAS GD 150/3439/5; *Historie*, 297–9; Fraser, *Annandale*, i, pp. cxlvii–cliv; Brown, 'Making of a *politique*', 172–3; NRA(S) 237/F/514–17; 237/G/527–8; NRA(S) 237/D/250–2; Gordon, *Sutherland*, 295.

26. Wormald, *Lords and Men*, 129–31; Brown, *Bloodfeud*, 241–6; *Chronicles of the Frasers*, 187–90; *RPC*, first ser., ix, 35; xi, 54–5, 178; xiii, 112–14, 444–50; *RPC*, second ser., iii, 553–4; NAS GD 124/6/71; NAS GD 38/1/121; *Selected Justiciary Cases*, i, 239–41.

27. Fraser, *Maxwells of Pollok*, ii, 132–6.

28. For Drummond, *RPC*, first ser., iii, 60–1; Mar, NAS GD 24/5/57/9; *HMC*, iii, 419.

29. Waus, *Correspondence*, i, 228–9; ii, 380; *Ayrshire and Wigton*, v, 118–19; and see Pollok, Fraser, *Maxwells of Pollok*, ii, 165–7; Craig, *Jus Feudale*, i, 583–610; Wormald, *Lords and Men*, 24–6.

30. Fraser, *Sutherland*, ii, 359–60, and see, Gordon, *Sutherland*, 350–1; Macinnes, *Clanship*, 2–8.

31. For Boyd, *Abbotsford Miscellany*, 19–20; for Johnstone, *HMC*, xv, 25 and see 29–30; and also, *CSP Scotland*, xii, 509–10.

32. For Argyll, *Kilravock*, 230; NAS GD 112/39/2/10; and for Cassillis, *Kennedy*, 21; also, see *CSP Scotland*, x, 452.
33. Fraser, *Annandale*, ii, 274.
34. For Gight, *House of Gordon*, i, 199; *CSP Scotland*, xiii, pt. 2, 864; *RPC*, first ser., vi, 295–6, 298–9, 336; and Maxwell, *RPC*, first ser., v, 74.
35. *Political Writings*, 28. Similar complaints were directed against the French nobility, Major, 'Crown and aristocracy', 638.
36. *CSP Scotland*, x, 11, 274, 453; Melville, *Memoirs*, 383; and on violence see Brown, *Bloodfeud*, 12–42.
37. For Dunfermline, Fraser, *Menteith*, ii, 73–4; Annandale and Buccleuch, Fraser, *Buccleuch*, ii, 346–9; *Melrose Papers*, ii, 578–82; *RPC*, first ser., xiii, 475–6, 486–7, 572–3, 614, 651–2; Galloway, *RPC*, first ser., iii, 557–8; Womet, *RPC*, second ser., v, 278.
38. Maitland, *Poems*, 24, 61–2.
39. Lithgow, 'Scotland's Welcome to Her Native Sone', in Lithgow, *Poetical Remains*.
40. NAS GD 112/39/25/14; Fraser, *Sutherland*, i, 167.
41. For Argyll, NAS GD 112/39/2/7–8, 112/39/2/20–1, 112/39/9/21, 112/39/9/25; Angus, Hume, *General History*, 411; Mar, *HMC Mar and Kellie*, i, 33–4; Rothes, NRA(S) 237/F/4789, 237/F/481–2 and Lindsay, *Lives*, ii, appendix xxxiii/iv; and for Morton, NAS GD 150/5.
42. Scott, 'Early modern European nobility'; for a persuasive case study see Astarita, *Continuity of Feudal Power*.
43. Craig, *Jus Feudale*, i, p. xi; Wormald, *Lords and Men*, 67–70. For examples from the Highlands and the Lowlands, *Abbotsford Miscellany*, 31–3; Fraser, *Eglinton*, ii, 216–17; *Black Book*, 236; Fraser, *Sutherland*, 142.
44. *HMC Various*, 201. See the letters from the fifth earl of Atholl in 1597, NAS GD 38/2/1/9–10; and the first marquis of Huntly's letter of February 1617, *Innes*, 205–6; and also Fraser, *Maxwells of Pollok*, 73; Waus, *Correspondence*, i, 94. This form of service did not decline immediately in the early seventeenth century, see Fraser, *Pollok*, ii, 25–6, 73.
45. *Kilravock*, 230; Fraser, *Douglas*, iv, 244–5; NAS GD 150/2694; NAS GD 112/39/54/12.
46. Dawson, *Politics of Religion*, 64–8; Cathcart, *Kinship and Clanship*, 66–75 where elected lordship is dismissed. For a late medieval example see, Brown, *Black Douglases*, 157–65; and also Rawcliffe, 'Baronial councils'. For early modern examples, see James, 'Tudor magnate', 50; Mertes, *English Noble Household*, 126–31; Carroll, 'Guise affinity', 128–9. Dependants were expected to listen to the counsel of their lords, Wormald, *Lords and Men*, 191, appendix A, Argyll, No. 61.
47. Fraser, *Sutherland*, ii, 354–5; *Kilravock*, 249–50, 253, 256–7. For Crawford, NRA(S) 237/C/172–5; NLS MS 6406/7. For examples of such letters to clients see those from the second earl of Mar in 1579, *Honorum de Morton*, i, 120; and William Douglas of Glenbervie in 1589, Fraser, *Douglas*, iv, 239.
48. *CBP*, ii, 775–6; NAS GD 24/5/57/7, 24/5/57/9–14.
49. *HMC Mar and Kellie*, i, 158–9.
50. For Hume, *CSP Scotland*, iii, 68; Morton, Spottiswoode, *History*, ii, 208; Angus, Fraser, *Douglas*, iii, 315–16; iv, 188–9; Johnstone, Fraser, *Annandale*, ii, 288–90.
51. Wormald, *Lords and Men*, 28–9; Cowan, 'Clanship', 142; NAS GD 112/39/40/29.
52. Dewald, *European Nobility*, 42; Brown, *Noble Society*, 84–5; NRA(S) 237/E/392–3; Fraser, *Sutherland*, ii, 355; NAS GD 10/648. For other household lawyers see NRA(S) 237/F/472–5; *Honorum de Morton*, i, 117; NAS GD 39/2/7, 39/2/29; NAS GD 86/345; Fraser, *Carlaverock*, ii, 63; *Melrose Papers*, ii, 428; *House of Forbes*, 165–8. Political lawyers like the earl of Melrose were feared in the courts, Fraser, *Carlaverock*, ii, 65–6.
53. *Miscellany of the Scottish History Society*, i, 85–105; Hope, *Diary*, 10. Craighall was much sought after by noble clients, NAS GD 150/2288.

54. NAS GD 38/2/1/34, 38/2/1/25; Fraser, *Chiefs of Grant*, iii, 332; Fraser, *Sutherland*, ii, 359–60.
55. *CSP Scotland*, iv, 561; Gordon, *Sutherland*, 267; Hume, *History*, 344; NAS GD 112/39/2/4, and see Fraser, *Elphinstone*, ii, 264. Loyalty to lords might be considered patriotic, Williamson, *Scottish National Consciousness*, 133. For its medieval origins, Crouch, *Birth of Nobility*, 56–62.
56. NAS GD 124/1/650; Wormald, *Lords and Men*, 64.
57. Major, 'Crown and the aristocracy'; Greengrass, 'Noble affinities'; Holt, 'Patterns of *clientelé*'; Harding, *Anatomy*; Neuschel, *Word of Honor*; Kettering, *Patrons, Brokers and Clients*; Major, 'Vertical ties'; Kalas, 'Marriage, clientage, office-holding', 368–70.
58. For Boyd, *Abbotsford Miscellany*, 19–47; Angus, Fraser, *Douglas*, iii, 266–8, 272–4; and Huntly, Wormald, *Lords and Men*, 278–98, appendix A, 'Gordon'; Brown, *Bloodfeud*, 144–82; for the Clan Chattan, see Cathcart, *Kinship and Clientage*, 112–28, and for John Grant of Freuchie in the 1580s and 1590s, Fraser, *Chiefs of Grant*, iii, 165, 170–6, 189–205.
59. Heal and Holmes, *Gentry*, 192; Wormald, *Lords and Men*, 87–8; Harding, *Anatomy*, 36–7 argues that loyalty was more reliable where the social and economic distance between men was greatest.
60. Fraser, *Eglinton*, ii, 216–17; *CSP Scotland*, iv, 299; *RPC*, first ser., xiv, 365–7.
61. *CSP Scotland*, xii, 36; Brown, 'A house divided'.
62. Fraser, *Sutherland*, i, 129–30, 156–61; Fraser, *Chiefs of Grant*, iii, 180–1; Cathcart, *Kinship and Clanship*, 168–79, 190–200; Cathcart, 'Crisis of identity'.
63. Calderwood, *History*, ii, 511; Major, *Renaissance Monarchy*, 65–6; Motley, *Becoming a French Aristocrat*, 62–4; Kettering, 'Gift-giving and patronage', 132–42; James, 'Tudor magnate', 52–4; Stone, *Crisis of the Aristocracy*, 34–5, 747–50; Fletcher, *Gender, Sex and Subordination*, 212–22; Manning, 'Aristocracy', 40–1; *Early Travellers*, 102.
64. Fraser, *Sutherland*, ii, 356–7; Stevenson, 'English devil'.
65. Fraser, *Sutherland*, ii, 127; NLS MS 3724/81; NAS GD 39/2/28; and see *RPC*, second ser., iv, 288–9; v, 160–1, 173–4.
66. *RPC*, first ser., vii, 185–6, 736–7. See the case of second earl of Lothian in 1611, *RPC*, first ser., ix, 159, 164–5, 174, 180, 606–7, 609–10, 672–3, 675, 681; and the fifth earl of Caithness in 1618, *RPC*, first ser., xi, 490–1.
67. *RPC*, second ser., v, 491–2. For another case from 1619, *RPC*, first ser., xi, 512–15.
68. Wormald, *Lords and Men*, 90; Macinnes, *Clanship*, 8–14; Rentet, 'Network mapping'.
69. Crouch, *Birth of Nobility*, 185–6; Cooper, 'Retainers'; Adams, 'Dudley clientele'; Coward, *Stanleys*, 84–126; Coward, 'A 'crisis of the aristocracy''; Holt, 'Patterns of *clientelé*'; Carroll, *Noble Power*, 53–88; Carroll, 'Guise affinity'. The nature of affinities can be misunderstood by over-reliance on particular sources, Neuschel, *Word of Honor* and see Kettering, 'Patronage in early modern France'.
70. Anderson, *Orkney*, 137, 165–86, and see the affinity of the second earl of Orkney, Anderson, *Black Patie*, 158–60.
71. Boardman, *Campbells*; Dawson, 'Fifth earl of Argyll', 3–20; Dawson, *Politics of Religion*, 48–85; Wormald, *Lords and Men*, 108–14; Cowan, 'Clanship', 132–57.
72. Wilson, *House of Airlie*, i, 163; Fraser, *Sutherland*, ii, 348–51.
73. Wormald, *Lords and Men*, 91–3; *Estimate*, 16; HMC, xi, 43.
74. Fraser, *Annandale*, i, pp. xcvii–c. In a respite granted to Johnstone in 1594 there are listed 160 of his friends and dependants, Fraser, *Annandale*, i, p. cxxix. For the Borders see Meikle, *British Frontier?*, 9–52.
75. Lindsay, *Lives*, ii, 12; Gordon, *Sutherland*, 278–9; Fraser, *Elphinstone*, i, 148.
76. Mertes, *English Noble Household*, 52–74; Holt, 'Patterns of *clientelé*', demonstrates that households fluctuated in size; Calderwood, *History*, iii, 561; NAS GD 124/17/2. For character references, Fraser, *Eglinton*, i, 182; HMC Various, 141; Lindsay, *Lives*, ii, appendix xxxiii–viii.
77. *RPS*, 1621/6/33; and see Fraser, *Eglinton*, i, 199, 215; NRA(S) 237/F/426–8.
78. For Glenorchy, NAS GD 112/39/20/9, 112/39/20/11–12, 112/39/32/15, 112/39/

21/4, 112/39/21/8, 112/23/10/17. For Traquhair, Fraser, *Eglinton*, i, 45; Pitcairn, *Criminal Trials*, i, pt. 2, 60–2; *RPC*, second ser., v, 438–9; *Selected Justiciary Cases*, i, 290–4.

79. Neuschel, 'Noble households'; Mertes, *English Noble Household*, 17–51; James, 'Tudor magnate', 51.

80. *Kennedy*, 26; *RPC*, first ser., v, 272; NAS GD 150/3442/1; Hume, *General History*, 370.

81. Eurich, *Economics of Power*, 101–22; James, 'Tudor magnate', 54–5. Fees in the household of the first earl of Buccleuch in the early 1630s ranged from his chamberlain who was paid £340 per annum to £20 for a footman, NAS GD 224/930/38/9. For comparison, see the first earl of Kinghorn's household, NRA(S) 885/161.

82. Fraser, *Sutherland*, ii, 341; and see Dodgshon, 'West Highland chiefdoms'. For examples of a lord making gifts on land, NAS GD 86/230 and NAS GD 26/5/577; clothes, Lindsay, *Lives*, i, 374; trees, NAS GD 38/1/159; and using a will to try and guarantee employment after his own death, Fraser, *Elphinstone*, ii. 266. For a generous reward granted by the dying first earl of Home see *HMC*, xii, 106–7.

83. Ellis, *Tudor Frontiers*; Wormald underestimates the importance of land, *Lords and Men*, 23–4, 26–7, 47–75. In a society where cash was scarce the making of new grants of land had some connection with lord–man relationships, Grant, 'Service and tenure'; Brown, *Noble Society*, 25–70. In France, too, land remained crucial to lordship, Major, *Renaissance Monarchy*, 61–8; Eurich, *Economics of Power*, 78–80; Neuschel, *Word of Honor*, 132–85.

84. Brown, 'Rejoice'; Gordon, *Sutherland*.

85. Craig, *Jus Feudale*, ii, 804, 949, 1019–53; Hume, *General History*, 311; *CSP Scotland*, ix, 666–7; xiii, pt. 1, 59; *Estimate*; Gordon, *Sutherland*, 12; Fraser, *Sutherland*, ii, 354.

86. Cash payments occurred within the Albret affinity during the French wars of religion, Eurich, *Economics of Power*, 78–123; and see Neuschel, *Word of Honor*, 69–78, 93–102, 132–85.

87. For a cash payment from 1584, NRA(S) 237/C/176–7; for Boyd, *Abbotsford Miscellany*, 31–6, 38–40, but also for cash payments on either side of the civil war, 17–18, 48–9; for Eglinton, Fraser, *Eglinton*, ii, 199–200, 211–13, 216–17; for Moray, Donaldson, *All the Queen's Men*, 72–3 and *RPC*, first ser., x, 141.

88. NAS GD 112/39/2/20; Dawson, *Politics of Religion*, 71–2.

89. NAS GD 65/18, 65/20, 65/22; *Spalding Miscellany*, iv, 241–2; NRA(S) 234/1633.

90. *CSP Scotland*, ix, 667 and Fraser, *Douglas*, iv, 241.

91. Wormald, *Lords and Men*, 137–43; Lynch, 'Introduction', 20–2; for France, Harding, *Anatomy*, 88, 98, 202 and Carroll, 'Guise affinity'; and for an English example, Coward, *Stanleys*, 127–41.

92. Howard, *Architectural History*, 118; Anderson, *Orkney*, 72; *RPC*, first ser., ii, 15–16, 18–19; for the 1569 convention, *RPC*, first ser., ii, 3.

93. NRA(S) 217/9/22; *CSP Scotland*, v, 564; vi, 622; vii, 577; for Renfrew, Wormald, *Lords and Men*, 191, appendix A, Argyll, No. 60. Also, see Jedburgh in 1581, NAS GD 40/2/10/42.

94. Verschur, 'Merchants and craftsmen'; Knox, *Works*, i, 337, note 1; Spottiswoode, *History*, iii, 87; *RPC*, first ser., iv, 115–16; vi, 159–160.

95. Brown, 'Burghs, lords and feuds', 105–6; Wormald, *Lords and Men*, 340, appendix A, Maxwell, No. 34; Spottiswoode, *History*, ii, 325; *RPC*, first ser., iv, 349; vi, 478–9; viii, 36–7, 85–6; *Melrose Papers*, ii, 433.

96. For Kirriemuir, Fraser, *Douglas*, iv, 248–9; and for Musselburgh, NAS GD 28/1393, 1412; for Edinburgh, NAS GD 406/1/18, 406/1/286. In 1627, Lothian landlords sought the patronage of the sixth earl of Morton to counter the encroachments of Edinburgh and its powerful court broker, NLS MS 79/72, 84/50. The earl of Mar's longstanding involvement in Stirling continued, see, for example, *RPC*, ix, 63–4, 137–8, 581. Nobles forged contacts with individuals in the burgh, NAS GD 137/37; and became burgesses, for example, lord Elphinstone and Stirling in 1632, Fraser, *Elphinstone*, i, 195, and the earl of Glencairn and Banff in 1637, NAS GD 39/1/272.

97. For Forres, *RPC*, first ser., ii, 314–17, 353–4; and Ayr, *RPC*, first ser., iii, 44–5; iv, 224–5; and see the case of Pittenweem in 1598, *RPC*, first ser., v, 488.

98. Wormald, *Lords and Men*, 138–43; White, 'Menzies era'; White, 'Religion, politics and society', 304–5, 310–16; Brown, 'Burghs, lords and feuds', 106–8; Lynch, 'Introduction', 22; *RPC*, first ser., iii, 481–4; iv, 533–4; v, 51; Wormald, *Lords and Men*, 140–3, 292–3, appendix A, Nos 71–2; *CSP Scotland*, x, 784; xi, 380–1, 385–6, 391; Fraser, *Douglas*, iv, 374–5; *Historie*, 332.

99. *RPC*, first ser., vii, 292, 302–4, 735–7.

100. NAS GD 39/1/235–9, 39/1/242–4, 39/2/13. See Hawick's problems with sir James Douglas of Drumlangrig in 1612, *RPC*, first ser., ix, 311–13.

101. *RPC*, first ser., xiv, 386–7. For the barons allied to and dependent on the house of Mar in the 1570s see NAS GD 124/10/40; *RPC*, first ser., ii, 690–1. Occasionally, peers gave their manrent as in 1598 when the sixth lord Lovat gave his bond of manrent to the sixth earl of Huntly, Wormald, *Lords and Men*, 285, 296, appendix A, 'Gordon', Nos 35, 87. For similar conditions in fifteenth-century England, Carpenter, 'Beauchamp affinity', 515.

102. *RPC*, iv, 572; *RPS*, 1584/5/23; Brown, *Bloodfeud*, 251.

103. *Chronicles of the Frasers*, 148; *CSP Scotland*, xi, 523; xiii, pt. 1, 134.

104. Fraser, *Chiefs of Grant*, iii, 137–8; *RPC*, first ser., vi, 284–5.

105. Wormald, *Lords and Men*, 101–2 and for the bonds 218–49. Highland chiefs extended their clienteles by admitting outsiders to the clan, Cathcart, *Kinship and Clanship*, 63.

106. Mackay, *Book of Mackay*, 423–4.

107. *Political Writings*, 28. Given-Wilson, *English Nobility*, 172 describes a similar partnership.

108. *CSP Scotland*, v, 370, 564; xiii, pt. 2, 1118; x. 46; Melville, *Memoirs*, 383–4.

109. *RPC.*, iv, 825; *CSP Scotland*, x, 469, 719. For the relationship between Huntly and the Mackintoshes and Grants see Cathcart, *Kinship and Clanship*, 159–208. For similar complaints about English nobles, James, 'Change and continuity', 97; and James, 'Concept of order', 292.

110. *CSP Scotland*, vii, 334, 452; ix, 668; x, 24, 534ff, 558–9, 687; *RPC*, first ser., v, 91–3; Calderwood, *History*, v, 141–2, 148–9. Conde and his followers confronted similar problems in the 1550s and 1560s, Neuschel, *Word of Honor*, 38–58.

111. NAS GD 112/39/15/10; *Campbell Letters*, 133; Dewald, *Aristocratic Experience*, 104–17; Smith, *Culture of Merit*, 31; Kettering, 'Friendship and clientage'; Hume, *General History*, 391; *CSP Scotland*, xi, 45.

112. Spalding, *Memorial*, i, 28.

113. Knox, *Works*, i, 273–4, 344–5, 471; ii, 61–4; Wormald, *Lords and Men*, 143–56, 405–7, appendix C, Nos 14, 15, 20.

114. Wormald, *Lords and Men*, 153, 161, appendix B, Nos 55–107, appendix C, Nos 405–10; *HMC Mar and Kellie*, i, 31; *RPC*, first ser., v, 189; and for a copy of the 1599 bond NAS GD 38/1/85b.

115. Bean, *Lord to Patron*, 235–6.

116. Barrow, *Anglo-Norman Era*; Neville, *Native Lordship*.

117. Wormald, *Lords and Men*; Grant, 'Scottish peerage', Grant, 'Service and tenure'. On the 'bastard feudalism' debate see the essays by Coss, Couch and Carpenter, 'Bastard feudalism revised'; also, Bean, *Lord to Patron*.

118. Major, 'Revolt of 1620'; Major, 'Vertical ties'.

119. Bean, *Lord to Patron*; Adams, 'Baronial contexts?'; Dewald, *Pont-St-Pierre*; Kettering, 'Decline of great noble clientage'.

120. Brown, *Bloodfeud*, chs 7–9.

121. Knox, *Works*, ii, 323; Brown, *Noble Society*, chs 1–4.

122. Wormald, *Lords and Men*, 44–6, 65, 161; *HMC*, iv, 482–3, No. 176. Stray bonds did turn up into the 1620s, Wormald, *Lords and Men*, appendix A, No. 171, Ailsa, No. 7; 193, Argyll, No. 71; 246, Breadalbane, No. 171; 252, Campbell of Barrichbyan, No. 13; 259, Campbell of Cawdor, No. 30; and see Mackay, *Book of Mackay*, 432. Written pledges

between French nobles survived into the mid-seventeenth century, Major, *Renaissance Monarchy*, 307–8.

123. Macinness, *Charles I*, 49–76.

Chapter 4: Magistrates

1. Bush, *Noble Privilege*, 157–63; Dewald, *Formation*, 165–8; van Nierop, *Nobility of Holland*, 141–7; Bernard (ed.), *Tudor Nobility*, 180; Coward, 'A "crisis of the aristocracy"'; Benadusi, *Provincial Elite*; Astarita, *Continuity of Feudal Power*, 20, note 2.

2. McQueen, *Common Law*; Godfrey, *Civil Justice*; Finlay, *Men of Law*.

3. Harding, *Anatomy*, 122, 132–4, 179–90. Benadusi, 'Rethinking the state'; Subtelny, *Domination*, 13–52.

4. *Political Writings*, 27–8.

5. Maitland, *Poems*, 25–6, 99–101.

6. *Political Writings*, 22, 28; *RPC*, first ser., vii, 465.

7. Sanderson, *Mary Stewart's People*, 64; *Historie*, 245; Hume, *General History*, 331; Fraser, *Sutherland*, ii, 340.

8. Wormald, *Lords and Men*, 1–13, 126–7; Wormald, 'Bloodfeud, kindred and government', 72.

9. *RPC*, first ser., iv, 63–4; viii, 545; *Melrose Papers*, i, 30–1; *HMC, Laing*, i, 83; *Letters and State Papers*, 94.

10. NRA(S) 237/F/497–8; *RPC*, first ser., viii, 105; ix, 217; xiv, 406.

11. *RPC*, first ser., iii, 22–2; iv, 681–2; second ser., v, 151–2.

12. Spottiswoode, *History*, ii, 279; *RPC*, first ser., ii, 282–3; Hewitt, *Morton*, 130–6, 140–3.

13. *Chronicles of the Frasers*, 163–4. For Glenorchy, *Black Book*, 22–3; *Honorum de Morton*, i, 178–9; *RPC*, second ser., v, 175–6.

14. *CSP Scotland*, i, 593, 637–8; v, 34; Calderwood, *History*, ii, 182–3, 388; iv, 605; Gordon, *Sutherland*, 346. Moray's wife was an equally severe law enforcer, *Kilravock*, 251–5, 257–8, 263–4, 267, 272.

15. For Bothwell, *Historie*, 1–2; Calderwood, *History*, ii, 325. For Maxwell, Brown, 'Making of a *politique*', 173. For Carmichael, *RPC*, first ser., vi, 117–18, 127–8; For Westfield, *RPC*, first ser., ix, 621–2. For a case from 1631, *RPC*, second ser., iv. 343–6.

16. *RPC*, first ser., ii, 613, 618; vi, 843–6.

17. *RPC*, first ser., iii, 73–86; Spottiswoode, *History*, ii, 260–2; and see *HMC Hamilton Supplementary*, 7–8. Local men often had a better grasp of legal technicalities, *RPC*, first ser., iv, 585–6.

18. Gordon, *Sutherland*, 192; NAS GD 10/681; *Ancram and Lothian*, i, 43; Goodare, *Government*, 70–86.

19. *RPC* first ser., ii, 37–40, 57–9, 188–90, 360–1; iv, 771–2; second ser., ii, 219; v, 283–4. For the deforcement of messengers, see *RPC*, first ser., ii, 29, 663–4; iii, 18–19, 210–11; iv, 657. Similar problems exercised the French crown in the 1560s, Carroll, 'Peace in the feud', 81; Carroll, *Blood and Violence*, 185–91.

20. *CSP Scotland*, ii, 319–20; *Diurnal*, 107–8; Melville, *Memoirs*, 174; Calderwood, *History*, ii, 348–50; v, 56–7, 117, 253–4; *RPC*, first ser., iv, 254–6.

21. *CSP Scotland*, x, 453, 523–4; NAS GD 406/1/10430; Leslie, *Historie*, i, 96.

22. For Herries, *RPC*, iv, 349, and in 1628 the Herries family was still using bully-boy tactics in the burgh, *RPC*, second ser., iii,12–14; and the Hay case, *RPC*, first ser., x, 496–502, 575–7, 604–5; Pitcairn, *Criminal Trials*, iii, 401–2, 418–22 For other cases of alleged judicial abuse through to the 1630s, *RPC*, first ser., iv, 283–4; vi, 481; viii. 445–6; second ser., iv, 296–7; v, 623; NAS GD 150/3443/4.

23. *CSP Scotland*, xii, 52. This issue was debated at the 1598 convention of estates, *CSP Scotland*, xiii, pt. 1, 229. For the Maxwells, [*Melrose Papers*], ii, 509–11; Fraser, *Carlaverock*, i, 3–4, 46–7; ii, 52–3. For other examples, see *RPC*, first ser., ii, 515–17; iii, 303–4, 570–1; viii, 463–5; xiii, 261–2; NRA(S) 885/125.

24. NRA(S) 237/F/497–8; *Selected Justiciary Cases*, i, 171–6.
25. For Eglinton, Calderwood, *History*, iii, 68–70; *Bannatyne Memorials*, 63–70; *RPC*, ii, 124–7. For Orkney, *Oppressions*, 1–11; Anderson, *Orkney*, 82–94; Anderson, *Black Patie*, 53. For Caithness, Gordon, *Sutherland*, 177–80.
26. Brown, *Bloodfeud*, 20; Macinnes, *Clanship*, 32–7; Macinnes, 'Crown, clans and *fine*', 31; Fraser, *Chiefs of Grant*, i, 226–36. For similar networks elsewhere, Hobsbawm, *Bandits*; Ruff, *Violence*, 217–39; Weisser, 'Crime and punishment in early modern Spain', 82–3; Wright, 'Venetian law and order', 193; James, 'Change and continuity'; Williams, 'Welsh borderland'.
27. For Renfrew, *RPC*, first ser., iv, 34–5; Lauder, *CSP Scotland*, xiii, pt. 1, 207, 214; Forfar and Dundee, *RPC*, first ser., viii, 610–11.
28. Bush, *Noble Privilege*, 66–71; *RPC*, first ser., viii, 602, 610; ix, 566; x, 44; Pitcairn, *Criminal Trials*, iii, 50–2, 74–6, 260–5, 267–9; Brown, 'Laird'; Brown, 'House divided'.
29. For example, Fraser, *Annandale*, ii, 293–4; on the costs see Brown, *Noble Society*, 84–5; and for similar developments in England and Spain see Sharpe, 'Such disagreement betwyx neighbours'; Muldrew, 'Culture of reconciliation'; Kagan, 'Golden age'.
30. *House of Forbes*, 155–7; Brown, *Bloodfeud*, 110–12.
31. Gordon, *Sutherland*, 248; *Ancram and Lothian*, i, 60.
32. Macinnes, *Charles I*, 49–101.
33. This was true of the medieval Highlands, Boardman, 'Campbells and charter lordship'. For Herries, Fraser, *Haddington*, ii. 70–1; also see Fraser, *Douglas*, iv, 377. For an attempt to destroy the Sutherland archive see Gordon, *Sutherland*, 151–2; Hope, *Major Practicks*, i, 238–43.
34. *RPS*, 1617/5/30; NAS GD 39/1/255–65. See Robert Swinton of that Ilk's efforts to recover lands lost under James III, NAS GD 12/152.
35. Fraser, *Elphinstone*, i, 153–8, 194–5. For the charters NAS GD 124/1/227–31; retours as heir of the earldom of Mar NAS GD 234/1/234, 234/1/260 and 234/1/263. NAS GD 124/1/5 and 224/1/254–5 for extract copies of parliament's confirmations; for the legal papers, NAS GD 124/6/61 and reductions, 124/1. For the arbitration agreement, NAS GD 124/1/307–18. Reductions of other landowners continued throughout the 1630s, NAS GD 124/1/325, 124/1/333, 124/1/340–2. For litigation arising from the revocation, NAS GD 124/5/7, 124/5/14/2–4, 124/14/5/6, 124/5/14/15, 124/5/14/26. Mar did compromise on ecclesiastical superiorities, NAS GD 124/1/1019, 124/1/1022.
36. *Sheriff Court Book of Fife*, pp. xvi–xvii; Hope, *Major Practicks*, ii, 32–7; Goodare, *Government*, 175–81. For an example of a sheriff's and depute's commission, NAS GD 12/176, 19/400, and for the formal ceremony infefting a new sheriff in office, *HMC*, xii, 111–12.
37. *Sheriff Court of Aberdeenshire*, i, pp. xiii–xvi; ii, pp. xxi–xxx; iii, pp. xi–xix; *Sheriff Court Book of Fife*, 344–6.
38. NAS SC 47/1/1–2.
39. NAS SC 67/1/1.
40. Harding, *Anatomy*; Noonskester, 'Dissolution'; Craig, *Jus Feudale*, i, 212; *RPC*, first ser., iii, 87; *HMC*, xii, 111–12; NAS GD SC67//1/1. The sheriffdom of Aberdeenshire was sold in 1510 and 1541, while the earls of Huntly lost Aberdeenshire in 1563 and 1594, but regained it in 1567 and 1597, *Sheriff Court of Aberdeenshire*, i, 419–26, 429.
41. For an initially successful challenge see Linlithgowshire in 1571, *RPC*, ii, 94–5, 105–6; *Sheriff Court Book of Aberdeenshire*, i, 230, 322–3.
42. For Caprington and a range of other examples, *Barony of Urie*, pp. viii–ix, xiv; NAS GD 86/339; Gordon, *Sutherland*, 362; NAS GD 26/2/1; *Kilravock*, 246–7, 251–3; NAS GD 77/173. Lords granted local commissions to enforce decreets of the court, see NAS GD 38/1/93 for letters of fire and sword granted in 1606 by the second earl of Atholl.
43. *RPC*, first ser., v, 229–30, 262; *Sheriff Court Book of Aberdeenshire*, i, 470–5; NAS SC 1/1/3.
44. *RPC*, first ser., iii, 12–14; vi, 79–80; Fraser, *Douglas*, iii, 301–8; *Historie*, 263. For some

indication of the workload, Fraser, *Douglas*, iv, 199–233. For a general discharge of lieutenancies in December 1590 see *RPC*, first ser., iv, 552.

45. Rae, *Administration*, 104–11, appendix 4.

46. For Huntly, *RPC*, first ser., iv, 51, 725; Angus, v, 19–20, 93–4; the Argyll, Atholl, Forbes commissions, v, 157; Lennox, v, 187, 192–3, 207–8, 309, 480, 483; vi, 8–10, 255–6, 837; Argyll, vi, 215–16, 507; vii, 426–7; x, 744–5; Scone, vii, 115–17; Ochiltree, viii, 113–14, 173–5; Caithness, x, 702–5, 715; Cawdor, x, 720–2; and Moray, xiii, 609–10.

47. For the late medieval inheritance see Goodman, 'Anglo-Scottish marches'; and on the early modern era, Rae, *Administration*; Goodare and Lynch, 'Scottish state and border-lands'; for the eastern march see Meikle, *British Frontier?*; for the western march see Rule, 'Anglo-Scottish western borders' and Brown, 'Making of a *politique*'; and for an English perspective, Robson, *English Highland Clans*, 203–28.

48. Rae, *Administration*, 74–89, 241–3, appendix 2; *RPC*, first ser., i, 282–3; xii, 149–51; *CSP Scotland*, vi, 374; xii, 97; Meikle, *British Frontier?*, 2–4, 9–10, 53–5, 62–3; Goodare and Lynch, 'Scottish state and borderlands', 189, 195–7, 201–7.

49. *RPC*, first ser., iii, 500–1, 504, 510; iv, 300–2; *CSP Scotland*, ix, 629–34; Melville, *Memoirs*, 375; Goodare, *Government*, 199–200 . The powers conferred and the objective of the commission varied greatly, for example, suppressing the Magregors, *RPC*, first ser., iv, 453–6; ix, 166–8, 178–80; subjugating Lewis, *RPC*, first ser., ix, 13–15; tackling theft, Fraser, *Douglas*, iii, 319–21. For Menteith, Fraser, *Menteith*, ii, 318–20; *HMC*, iii.,399, No. 38; Fraser, *Annandale*, ii, 30; Wormald, *Court, Kirk and Community*, 18–19. For examples of lesser offices see *Chronicles of the Frasers*, 179; *HMC*, xi, 30.

50. Although the system was less dynamic than that of Normandy, Dewald, *Formation*, 167–75.

51. NAS GD 124/1/931; and *Sheriffdoms of Lanark and Renfrew*, 72 for the repeated sale of Renfrew. Heritable jurisdictions were subject to the feudal law of wardship, for example see *RPC*, first ser., iv, 446.

52. *Sheriffdoms of Lanark and Renfrew*, 1–63. For a contemporary description of Cunning-hame, Pont, *Topographical Account*, 7; and for the eastern march where Berwickshire alone contained twenty-six baronies and one regality, ten of which were possessed by non-residents, see Meikle, *British Frontier?*, 53–63.

53. Fletcher, 'Honour, reputation and local officeholding'; Cust, 'Honour, rhetoric and political culture'.

54. NAS SC 47/1/1–2. For other disputes, see *RPC*, first ser., v, 282–4; NRA(S) 2312/107/2/8.

55. NRA(S) 237/C/169–71, 237/C/176–8.

56. *RPC*, first ser., xiv, 431–2.

57. Melville, *Memoirs*, 405.

58. Lindsay, *Historie*, ii, 181, note 1, 184, 189; NAS GD 150/455; *HMC*, iv, 501, Nos. 74–80.

59. Spalding, *Memorial*, i, 5, 9–10; Gordon, *Sutherland*, 413.

60. *RPC*, first ser., i, 459; iii, 357–60, 541–1; *RPS*, 1584/5/98; Fraser, *Sutherland*, i, 132, 137, 177.

61. *RPC*, ii, 161–2.

62. *RPC*, ii, 357–8. For another challenge to his authority, NAS GD 10/446–7, 644, and see *RPC*, first ser., v, 88–9, 338–40; *Historie*, 297–9. For examples on the other marches, *RPC*, first ser., iii, 562–3, 622–3.

63. For a lord and his vassal in 1613, *RPC*, first ser., ix, 372–4; the sheriff of Linlithgow and his depute in 1571, *RPC*, first ser., ii, 94–5, 105–6, 257–8; over coronerships *RPC*, first ser., iii, 491, v, 378–9. See the case of John Stewart, younger of Arntullie who was bailie of the bishopric of Dunkeld and of the regality of Atholl, NAS GD 38/2/1/4, unnum-bered letter dated 4 October 1593, in box, 38/2/1/5.

64. For the third earl of Eglinton and the burgh of Irvine in 1573, *Muniments*, i, 57–9; ii, 15–20; and for the first earl of Linlithgow and the burgh of Stirling in 1603, *RPC*, first ser., vi, 563–4.

65. NAS GD 112/39/21/19.

66. *RPC*, second ser., ii, 30–1.

67. For Angus, Fraser, *Douglas*, iii, 311–14. For Bothwell, *RPS*, 1585/12/64. For Argyll, Dawson, *Politics of Religion*, 56–9; Dawson, 'Fifth earl of Argyle', 10–11; *CSP Scotland*, xiii, pt. 2, 833; *HMC*, iv, 486, No. 264. For Broughton, Scott, *Staggering State*, 104. A similar relationship between jurisdiction, landed wealth and political dominance occurred elsewhere, for example in Brittany, Collins, *Classes, Estates and Order*, 114–18.

68. *Barony of Carnwath*, 'Introduction'; *Regality of Melrose*, pp. xlvi–xlviii; NAS GD 11/75. For an example, see the lairds of Grant building up of the barony of Freuchie, Fraser, *Chiefs of Grant*, i, pp. xxxv–xxxix.

69. Grant, 'Scottish peerage', 5; *Barony of Urie*, pp. v–vii, xix, xxii.

70. McQueen, *Common Law*, 33–73; Godfrey, *Civil Justice*, 192–6; *Barony of Urie*; *Regality of Melrose*, i, p. xii; Dalrymple, *Institutions*, 386–7; Sanderson, *Scottish Rural Society*, 18–19.

71. Fraser, *Sutherland*, i, 1623; *RPC*, first ser., xi, 212; second ser., iii, 171.

72. *Historie*, 265–6; Spottiswoode, *History*, ii, 413–14; Prest, 'Judicial corruption', 74–81.

73. *Barony of Urie*, p. xvi; Hope, *Major Practicks*, i, 5; ii, 41–5; NAS RH 11/68/1–2; Sanderson, *Mary Stewart's People*, 65–6; NAS GD 112/21/202.

74. Davies, 'The court and the Scottish legal system'; Sanderson, *Scottish Rural Society*, 12–14; Whyte, *Agriculture*, 45–6; *Regality of Melrose*, p. xix; 'Barons of Alloway', 20; NAS GD 10/450; NAS GD 26/2/1; *Barony of Urie*, 24, 51, 53, 72; NAS B 6/28/2ff.7b.

75. *Regality of Melrose*, pp. xiii–xv.

76. Fraser, *Douglas*, iv, 236.

77. *Honorum de Morton*, i, 174–5.

78. *RPC*, first ser., xiii, 367–8, 505–6. Mostly lords repledged from one another's courts, NAS GD 122/17/1/8.

79. Hanlon, 'Justice'; *Black Book*, 368–90; NAS GD 26/2/1, see, for example, the entries at 13 July 1600 and 11 August 1610. For the contrasting experiences of the Spanish kingdoms see Thompson, 'Nobility in Spain', 211–14.

80. *Barony of Urie*, 3–11, 45–6, 72–4.

81. Dalrymple, *Institutions*, 387; *RPC*, first ser., iv, 590; v, 124–6; *Barony of Urie*, 9–10; NAS GD 28/1331, 28/1403.

82. *RPS*, 1540/12/13–2 for a number of reforms regarding judicial process; *Sheriff Court Book of Fife*, pp. xciv–lxxxviii.

83. Sanderson, *Scottish Rural Society*, 11, 14–19; *Barony of Urie*, p. viii–ix and for court procedures pp. x–xv. For example, see Raith barony court on 27 May 1628, NAS GD 26/2/2; and Calder barony court, NLS MS 3724/23–5.

84. NLS MS 3724.

85. *Black Book*, 352–67.

86. NRA(S) 2312/113/88, 2312/113/220. She had to nudge Pollok again in 1632 and 1634, 2312/113/225, 2312/113/94.

87. Goodare *Government*, 83–6; *CSP Scotland*, ix, 640; also see xiii, pt. 2, 1116. In fact, Bothwell was warded.

88. *Regality of Melrose*, pp. xiii, xiv–xv; Thompson, 'Nobility in Spain', 210–15; Dewald, *Formation*, 165–8.

89. *RPS*, 1455/8/5, 1617/5/26; Hope, *Major Practicks*, ii, 38.

90. Hope, *Major Practicks*, ii, 38. The dukes of Lennox were bailies of the regality of Glasgow, while in 1631 the second earl of Dunfermline granted the burgh of Dunfermline the offices of bailies in hereditary, *RPC*, first ser., ii, 697–8; NAS GD 28/1393. After the Reformation, ecclesiastical regalities were incrementally secularised. For example, lord Somerville acquired the office of bailie of the regality of Glasgow for nineteen years in 1584, NAS GD 124/1/4/458, while the lairds of Dairsie had their office as stewards of the regality of St Andrews repeatedly confirmed after the Reformation, GD 20/1/138, 20/1/140–1, 20/1/147–8.

91. NAS RH 11/46/1; NAS RH 11/54/1.

92. NAS GD 26/2/1; NAS GD 20/1/150–78.
93. *Regality of Melrose*, 1–82, 8–9, 65; NAS GD 26/2/1; *Barony and Regality of Falkirk and Callendar*.
94. *Registrum de Panmure*, i, p. xcvi; and on their origin see Grant, 'Thane and thanages'.
95. *Political Writings*, 29.
96. *RPS*, 1567/12/33; 1617/5/38; *RPC*, first ser., xi, 196, note.
97. *RPS*, A1567/12/8, 1609/4/17; Hope, *Major Practicks*, ii, 4; *RPC*, second ser., iii, 247–8, 317–20; iv, 68; vi, 23; Lee, *Road to Revolution*, 62–6; on the Catholic nobility, Brown, *Noble Society*, 244–9.
98. *RPS*, 1587/7/18.
99. *RPS*, 1605/6/124–5, 1605/6/130–1.
100. *RPS*, 1633/6/28; Hope, *Major Praticks*, ii, 39–40, 86.
101. For Mar, *RPS*, 1567/4/7 and *HMC Mar and Kellie*, ii, 20–1; for Thirlestane, *RPS*, 1587/7/116; for Dunbar, *RPS*, 1605/6/49; for Argyll, *RPS*, 1633/6/91. The king continued to make grants that the privy council found unacceptable, *RPC*, first ser., ix, 616–17, 619–20.
102. *RPS*, 1587/7/67, 1598/6/2, 1598/6/6; Brown, *Bloodfeud*, 239–65. Justice ayres were largely redundant by the end of the sixteenth century, Goodare, *Government*, 197–8. At the head of the justices sat the earls of Argyll as heritable lord justice general.
103. *RPC*, first ser., v, 420–1; vi, 23, 56–8, 68. For complaints, see the cases against the sheriffs of Elgin and Forres in 1574, *RPS*, first ser., ii, 353–4, 409; Ayr in 1575, *RPS*, first ser., ii, 464–5; Peebles throughout 1586, *RPS*, first ser., iv, 24–5, 67–8, 70, 80–1; Dumfries in 1599, *RPS*, first ser., vi, 49–50; Moray in 1602, *RPS*, first ser., vi, 397–401, 404, 422–3, 432–7.
104. *RPS*, 1621/6/14; *RPC*, second ser., i, 84–5; ii, 582–3; iv, 550; v, 378, 424; *HMC Laing*, i, 88.
105. Lee, *Government by Pen*, 123–5; *HMC Mar and Kellie*, i, 48. For Renfrew sheriffs from 1613 see *RPC*, first ser., x, 20–1, 30, 43, 215, 275, 389; xi, 7, 418, 462; xii, 40, 335, 775; xiii, 333, 592; second ser., i, 120, 386; ii, 52, 451; iii, 274; iv, 24, 322, 535; v, 132, 359.
106. For a rare case in 1529 see Godfrey, *Civil Justice*, 226–7. Murchill continued to be reappointed at least until 1626, *RPC*, first ser., x, 608–9; xii, 174, 307–8, 313; xiii, 24–6; second ser., i, 258; *Historie*, 391; Gordon, *Sutherland*, 338–9.
107. Fraser, *Haddington*, ii, 119–20; *Melrose Papers*, i, 257, 295; *RPC*, first ser., xi, 586–7; xii. 289–90; *HMC*, vii, 731. For Selkirk sheriffs 1620–37, *RPC*, first ser., xii, 322, 575; xiii, 43, 333, 592; second ser., i, 120, 386; ii, 56, 451; iii, 273–4; iv, 27, 336, 533; v, 125, 359; vi, 138, 523.
108. Appointments can be tracked in the volumes of *RPC* first and second series.
109. *RPC*, first ser., iv, 177, 189; v, 364–5, 377, 459–60; vi, 222–3, 296–7, 499–500; *Sheriff Court of Aberdeenshire*, i, 370, 428–9, 443–4; ii, 533.
110. Braddick, 'Administrative performance'; Stater, *Noble Government*, 8–31; Noonskester, 'Dissolution'; *Melrose Papers*, i, 107–8, 172; ii, 429–30, 466–7; *RPC*, first ser., xii, 615–16, 624–6; xiii, 186. Local government broke down in Caithness by 1629 due to the appointment of a man lacking the status and means to exercise authority, *RPC*, second ser., iii, 191.
111. *RPC*, second ser., iii, 317–20; iv, 68; vi, 23; Spalding, *Memorial*, i, 9–10, 21, 55ff; Spalding, *Memorial*, 13–20, 24–5, 42, 45–51, 54–66, 71. The destabilising effect of crown intervention on regional government occurred elsewhere, Ellis, *Tudor Frontiers*.
112. *HMC Mar and Kellie*, i, 60–1; *Melrose Papers*, i, 268, 282–3, 332. Although deputes were appointed who were clients of the sheriff, see the case of Forfar in 1632, *Registrum de Panmure*, ii, 319–20.
113. *RPC*, second ser., ii, 52–3.
114. *RPS*, first ser., vii, 141–2; Fraser, *Sutherland*, ii, 350.
115. Lee, *Maitland of Thirlestane*, 139; *Honorum de Morton*, i, 191; *RPC*, first ser., vii, 734.
116. *Melrose Papers*, ii, 539–40, 542; *RPC*, first ser., xiii, 367–8.

117. Macinnes, *British Revolutions*, 86–93; Macinnes, *Charles I*, 59; Fraser, *Menteith*, ii, 8–9, 14; and for further negotiations with sir Hugh Wallace of Craigie, NAS GD 406/1/289, 406/1/292, 406/1/299. There is scattered evidence that by the 1630s a few lords were consulting the privy council on difficult cases, *RPC*, second ser., iv, 202; v, 253; NAS GD 25/9/32 bundle dated 1600–1688.

118. *RPS*, A1630/7/2; NAS GD 28/1353; Fraser, *Sutherland*, i, 175–6, 218–19; Gordon, *Sutherland*, 451; Macinnes, *Charles I*, 57, 67–8. For fruitless negotiations involving the third marquis of Hamilton, *RPC*, second ser., iii, 364–6; Hugh Wallace of Craigie, *RPC*, second ser., iii, 366–9; NAS GD 406/1/289, 406/1/292, 406/1/299; Balfour, *Works*, 136; the fifth lord Sempill, Fraser, *Eglinton*, i, 174; and the third earl of Mar, *HMC Mar and Kellie*, i, 195.

119. *RPS*, 1587/7/67, 1609/4/26, 1617/5/22; *RPC*, first ser., ix, 75–80, 220–6, 409–11; Fraser, *Chiefs of Grant*, ii, 11–12; Wormald, *Court, Kirk and Community*, 162–3; Lee, *Government by Pen*, 125–8; Meikle. 'Invisible divide', 79–80; Mitchison, *Lordship to Patronage*, 15; Goodare, *Government*, 8–31; Wells, 'Constitutional conflict', 91; *Political Writings*, 221. For the replacement of the convener of the Renfrew commissioners, Fraser, *Pollok*, ii, 72.

120. Ellis, *Tudor Frontiers*, 258–9; Wormald, *Lords and Men*, 164; Goodare, 'The nobility and the absolutist state', 176.

121. Calderwood, *History*, vii, 178, but he cites the case wrongly as the individuals were the fifth earl of Cassillis and George Corrie of Kelwood, see *RPC*, first ser., x, 25, 40, 60, 111, 140.

122. *RPC*, first ser., ix, 496–7, 544–5, 714–15; xiv, 570–1, 621–2; NAS JP 35/4/1.

123. *Minutes of the Justices of the Peace for Lanarkshire*, p. xix; Macinnes, *Charles I*, 10; *RPS*, A1630/7/20, 1633/6/4; *RPC*, second ser., v, 173; vi, 175–6, 228.

124. Fraser, *Pollok*, ii, 74–9, 82–3, 86; NRA(S) 2312/108/2/3, 2312/108/2/6–13, 2312/109/9–13; NAS JP 35/4/1; *RPC*, first ser., xii, 307–8, second ser., vi, 496–7.

125. *RPC*, first ser., xiv, 569. The commissioners lobbied for an increase in their powers in 1630, *RPS*, A1630/7/20. For local tensions, *RPC*, ix, 206, 460–1, 496, 518–19; and for similar issues in early seventeenth-century England, Cust, 'Honour, rhetoric and political culture'.

126. *RPC*, first ser., ix, 446–7, 686–7; xii, 769–80; second ser., i, 653–4; iii, 77–8, 196; v, 378–89; vi, 71; Macinnes, *Charles I*, 94–6.

127. Rae, *Administration*, 115–33; as an example of Angus's activity see *RPC*, first ser., vi, 28, 31.

128. Lee, *Government by Pen*, 45–6, 72–4, 207–9; Newton, *Making of the Jacobean Regime*, 99–102; *RPC*, first ser., vii, 728–9; viii, 30, 200, 814, 205; ix, 194–6, 208; x, 72; xi, 345; xii, 149–51, 670–1, 673–9, 694–6; xiii, 155–7, 482, 681–2; second ser., i, 193; ii, 98–9; iii, 147–8; iv, 308, 388–9; v, 496–9; vi, 161–5; Fraser, *Carlaverock*, ii, 3, 35–8, 108–10.

129. Dawson, 'Origin'; Goodare and Lynch, 'Scottish state and its borderlands', 186–95, 197–201, 205–7.

130. For a similar model see Bohannan, *Crown and Nobility*. Macinnes, 'Crown, clans and *fine*', 32; Goodare, *Government*, 220–45; Lynch, 'James VI and the highland problem'; *RPS*, 1587/7/70, 1594/4/48, 1597/11/40; *RPC*, first ser., iv, 787–9, 796–7, vi, 441–2, 447. See the various excuses made by the second earl of Orkney in 1598, *RPC* first ser., v, 436–7; the fifth earl of Morton in 1608, *RPC*, first ser., viii, 55, 67–8, 646; and sir John Grant of Freuchie in 1629, Fraser, *Chiefs of Grant*, iii, 441–2, 448–9. Some lords demanded assurances from their men, Fraser, *Chiefs of Grant*, iii, 185–6. In September 1635 the government reaffirmed its faith in the general band as the principal means of maintaining order in the localities, *RPC*, second ser., vi, 106.

131. *RPC*, first ser., x, 113–15; Cathcart, 'Crisis of identity?'. See the case of Huntly and Alan Cameron of Lochiel in 1621, *RPC*, first ser., xii, 402–4, 427–8, 454, 539–43, 744–5. A similar process of negotiation and renegotiation occurred in Ireland where central authority was much stronger, Ellis, *Tudor Frontiers*, 260–1; Gillespie, 'Negotiating order'.

132. Spottiswoode, *History*, iii, 192; Gordon, *Sutherland*, 248. For Hamilton, *RPC*, first

ser., xi, 19. For Argyll, *RPC*, first ser., x, 736; second ser., i, 20–4, 109–10; Macinnes, *Clanship*, 59–76. Fraser, *Haddington*, ii, 167–8; *RPC*, second ser., v, 441–2. On Highland policy generally, Lee, *Government by Pen*, 75–82; Lee, *Road to Revolution*, 97–8; Lynch, 'James VI and the highland problem'; Magregor, 'Civilising Gaelic Scotland'.

133. Lynch, 'The crown and the burghs', 56–8; MacDonald, *Burghs and Parliament*, 37–41; *CSP Scotland*, x, 416; Balfour, *Works*, ii, 28–9; Calderwood, *History*, iii, 731; *RPC*, first ser., vi, 34; *RPS* 1609/4/27; GD 45/12/319. For Lennox and Glasgow, *RPC*, first ser., iii, 325; vii, 141–2, 230–1, 234–5, 240–7, 249–50; *HMC Various, V*, 111; Baillie, *Letters and Journals*, i, 22.

134. Lynch, 'The crown and the burghs', 63–6; *RPC*, first ser., xii, 120–1, 130–1, 142–3, 152–3; second ser., ii, 212–14, 233–6, 280, 326; NAS GD 406/1/984; Fraser, *Chiefs of Grant*, iii, 449–50.

135. Goodare, *Government*, 192–219.

136. Adams, 'James VI and the politics of south-west of Scotland'.

137. Beik, *Absolutism and Society*, 179–97, 303–28; also see Bohannan, *Crown and Nobility*, 30–1.

138. Coss, 'Formation of the English gentry'; Cogswell, *Home Divisions*, 302–4, 314–15.

139. Benadusi, *Provincial Elite*.

Chapter 5: Soldiers

1. Keen, *Chivalry*, 243, 247, 249; Bouchard, *Strong of Body*, 103–44; Schalk, *Valor to Pedigree*, 3–20; Asch, *Nobilities in Transition*, 126–33; Bitton, *French Nobility*, 27–41; Motley, *Becoming a French Aristocrat*, 48–50; Hale, 'Military education'; 'Adamson, 'Baronial context', 93; Jespersen, 'Rise and fall of the Danish nobility', 43–4; Trim (ed.), *Chivalric Ethos*.

2. Neville, *Violence, Custom and Law*; MacDonald, *Border Bloodshed*; Brown, *Black Douglases*; Stevenson, *Chivalry and Knighthood*; Edington, 'Paragons and patriots'.

3. Phillips, *Anglo-Scots Wars*; Merriman, *Rough Wooings*; Fissel, *English Warfare*, 21–34, 114–23, 135–6; Donaldson, *Queen's Men*.

4. Mair, *History*, 30–1, 190, 199–201, 217–19, 358–9, 383–5; Edington, *Court and Culture*, 84–8. Mason, 'Chivalry and citizenship' is premature in relegating the martial myth from the heart of Scottish identity; Brown, *Bloodfeud*, 184–214 places the critique towards the end of the sixteenth century.

5. Douglas, *Palice*; Hume, *House of Douglas*, i, 68–127, 209–36; Donagan, 'Halcyon days'; Kellie, *Pallas Armata*; Smith, *Culture of Merit*, 37–9.

6. Smith, *Culture of Merit*, 42–9; Anglin, 'Schools of defence'; Manning, *Swordsmen*, 103–38; Dewald, *Aristocratic Experience*, 57. A truly professional military career did not emerge until the later seventeenth century, Trim, 'Introduction', 14–23; Roy, 'Profession of arms'; Brown, 'Scottish lords to British officers'.

7. Stevenson, *Chivalry and Knighthood*, 17–25; Brown, *Noble Society*, 196–201.

8. Vale, *War and Chivalry*, 147–74; Parker, 'Military revolution'; Parker, 'In defence'; Storrs and Scott, 'Military revolution'; Rogers (ed.), *Military Revolution Debate*; Phillips, 'Of nimble service'; Feld, 'Middle class society'; Trim, 'Army, society and military professionalism'.

9. Durkan, 'James, third earl of Arran', 160; Ryrie, *Origins*, 161–95; Calderwood, *History*, iii, 99–101, 213; *Historie*, 26; Knox, *Works*, ii, 355–7; Murdoch, 'James VI and the foundation of a Scottish–British military identity', 5–11; Brown, *Bloodfeud*; *CSP Scotland*, xiii, pt. 2, 982.

10. Stevenson, *Chivalry and Knighthood*, 63–102; Edington, 'Tournament'; Ferguson, *Chivalric Tradition*; Young, *Tudor and Jacobean Tournaments*.

11. Schalk, *Valor to Pedigree*, 3–36; Neuschel, *Word of Honor*, 38–68; Wood, *Nobility of Bayeux*, 81–95; Tucker, 'Eminence over efficacy'; Major, *Renaissance Monarchy*, 97; Dewald, *Aristocratic Experience*, 45–58; Bitton, *French Nobility*, 27–41.

12. Stone, *Crisis of the Aristocracy*, 266; Ferguson, *Chivalric Tradition*, 101–5; Bernard, 'Tudor nobility in perspective', 8–9; Manning, *Swordsmen*, 17–50; Adamson, 'Chivalry'. In Italy a declining martial culture survived under Spanish discipline, Hanlon, *Twilight*.

13. Manning, *Swordsmen*, 18, 24–5; *Kilravock*, 238.

14. Calderwood, *History*, ii, 512–13; *CSP Scotland*, iii, 83, 587–8; *RPC*, first ser., ii, 219–20. In 1567 the rebel lords levied 500 waged soldiers, Lindsay, *Historie*, ii, 195. See Carroll, *Noble Power*, 69–76 for the military following the house of Guise at this time.

15. Calderwood, *History*, iv, 695; v, 57; Spottiswoode, *History*, ii, 385; *CSP Scotland*, x, 27; Gavin, 'Two letters', 110. Bothwell was remarkably good at raising troops, *CSP Scotland*, x, 707–10. The fourth lord Ruthven paid for waged soldiers in June 1572, *RPC*, first ser., iv, 336. In 1593, the eighth lord Maxwell 'waygeit bayth horsemen and futemen' for his campaign against the laird of Johnstone, *Historie*, 299.

16. Craig, *Jus Feudale*, i, 257; Grant, 'Service and tenure', 149–51; *Honorum de Morton*, i, 57; NAS GD 96/78; *CSP Scotland*, vi, 325–6; NAS GD 12/138; *HMC*, iii, 412; Gordon, *Sutherland*, 198; Fraser, *Sutherland*, iii, 154–5.

17. Wormald, *Lords and Men*, 68, 161. To date there is insufficient analysis of the documentary evidence to indicate the trends in the lord–tenant relationship. For the decline in the military tenure in northern England, James, 'Cumberland', 153–7.

18. Macinnes, *Clanship*, 57–9; Duffy (ed.), *World of the Galloglass*; Hill, *Fire and Sword*; MacCoinnich, 'His spirit was only given to warre'; Cathcart, *Kinship and Clientage*, 93–8; McLeod, *Divided Gaels*, 47. On Ireland see Edwards, 'Escalation of violence'; Carey, *Surviving the Tudors*, 78–96.

19. *CSP Scotland*, xi, 253–4; Macinnes, *Clanship*, 57–9.

20. Dawson, *Politics of Religion*, 51–6; Dawson, 'Fifth earl of Argyle', 3–7; Dawson, 'Two kingdoms or three?', 120–31; *RPC*, first ser., iii, 94–5; *HMC*, iv, 477, No. 60; Wormald, *Lords and Men*, 189, appendix A, Argyll, No. 53; *Historie*, 338; *HMC*, vi, 610, 631; *Melrose Papers*, i, 241–4. For the French comparison, Major, 'Crown and aristocracy', 638–9; Carroll, *Noble Power*.

21. *RPC* first ser., xiii, 558, 590–1, 609–10; NAS GD 112/39/37/3; Macinnes, *Clanship*, chs 2–5; Spalding, *Memorials*, 1–8.

22. Fraser, *Sutherland*, i, 221; ii, 358–9; *Chronicles of the Frasers*, 150, 184, 250, 257.

23. Samson, 'Tower houses'; Samson, 'Rise and fall'; Slade, 'Gordons and the north-east'; Oram and Stell (eds), *Lordship and Architecture*; chs 10–13; Glendinning, MacInnes and Mackenzie, *History of Scottish Architecture*, 40; Howard, *Architectural History*, 48–107; McKean, *Scottish Chateaux*, 17–19, 39–58; *Early Travellers*, 148. The contrast with England is often exaggerated, Stone, *Crisis of the Aristocracy*, 217–18; Bernard, 'Tudor nobility in perspective', 30–4.

24. *RPS*, 1535/31; Miket and Roberts, *Mediaeval Castles*; *Melrose Papers*, i, 176; *Ancram and Lothian*, i, 63, 64, 65, 66.

25. Ruff, *Violence*, 45–52; McIvor, 'Artillery'; *Historie*, 340; *CSP Scotland*, v, 697; *HMC Mar and Kellie*, ii, 21–6.

26. For Dunure, 'Military report', *AWAA*, iv, 17–25; for Crichton, Calderwood, *History*, i, 549; for Dunbar, *Historie*, 20; for Hamilton, Calderwood, *History*, ii, 564; *Chronicle of the Kings of Scotland*, 133; *Historie*, 175–6; for Lochmaben, *Historie*, 236; for Dunrobin, *RPC*, first ser., xiii, 332–3. Caithness had his own guns, *RPC*, first ser., xiii, 394.

27. Stone, *Crisis of the Aristocracy*, 219–220; Anglo, *Martial Arts*, 271–82; Anglin, 'Schools of defence'.

28. *RPC*, first ser., iii, 105; NAS GD 39/5/68; *Political Writings*, 53.

29. Caldwell, 'Royal patronage', 82; a shipment of arms was brought over from France in 1571, *Historie*, 75. For Orkney, Anderson, *Black Patie*, 45; *Historie*, 387; and for Bothwell, *CSP Scotland*, x, 217.

30. *CSP Scotland*, viii, 109. Thomas Randolph was shot at through his window during his 1581 embassy. On feuds see Brown, *Bloodfeud*; Brown, 'Making of a *politique*'; Brown, 'House divided'; and for Loch Gruinart, *Chronicles of the Frasers*, 232–3.

31. *Melrose Papers*, i, 17–18; *RPC*, first ser., vii, 428–30; Brown, *Bloodfeud*, chs 7–9, 270–2.

32. Ruff, *Violence*, 49–52; Brown, *Bloodfeud*, 246–50; *RPC*, first ser., xi, 546–7; second ser., i, 675–6, 678.

33. *RPC*, first ser., ix, 27–8; x, 445–6, 474–5; Macinnes, 'Crown, clans and *fine*', 39.

34. *Black Book*, 398–402. For Glenorchy's personal weaponry, NAS GD 112/20/5/5. On the general dearth of weapons fit for waging war, Edwards, 'Arming and equipping', 244–7.

35. Redlich, *German Military Enterpriser*; Mallett, *Mercenaries*; Potter, 'International mercenary market'.

36. *CSP Scotland*, v, 504; Manning, *Apprenticeship in Arms*, 18, 24, 41–93; Bartlett, 'Scottish mercenaries'; Miller, *Swords for Hire*, 10.

37. Grosjean, *Unofficial Alliance*, 14–24; Grosjean, 'Century of Scottish governorship', 77; Glozier, 'Scots in the French and Dutch armies', 126; Morgan, *Tyrone's Rebellion*, 35–9, 44, 49, 74; Frost, 'Scottish soldiers'; Dukes, 'First Scottish soldiers in Russia'; Dukes, 'New perspectives'; Polisensky, 'Scottish soldiers in the Bohemian war'; Murdoch, 'Introduction', 9–14, 19–20; Williamson, 'Foreward'; Urquhart, *Jewel*, 98 and for the names 92–9.

38. Murdoch, 'Introduction', 3–4, 15–18; Murdoch and Mackillop, 'Introduction', xxx–xxxii; Murdoch, 'House of Stuart', 43–8; Murdoch, 'Scotsmen on the Danish–Norwegian frontier', 10–17; Dunthorne, 'Scots in the wars'; Grosjean, *Unofficial Alliance*, 14–24; Grosjean, 'Century of Scottish governorship'; Grosjean, Scotland: Sweden's closest ally?'; Brockington, 'Munro', 225; Trim, 'Calvinist internationalism'; Brockington (ed.), *Munro, His Expedition*.

39. *RPC*, ii, 235–6, 237–8, 256–7; vi, 343–4; ix, 432–7; second ser., i, 196–7, 244–5, 247–8, 315–16; iv, 193–4, 219; vi, 225–6; Manning, *Apprenticeship in Arms*, 79–80. Reay's activities as a military entrepreneur can be followed in NAS GD 84/2/149–91, and for Hamilton see Scally, 'Political career'.

40. For lord Gordon, Spalding, *Memorial*, i, 32; Glozier, 'Scots in the French and Dutch armies', 118–24; and for Argyll, Worthington, *Scots in Habsburg Service*, 57–73, 87–91.

41. Bartlett, 'Scottish mercenaries'; Grosjean, *Unofficial Alliance*, 41–73; Fraser, *Sutherland*, ii, 38; NRA(S) 237/C/164; Murdoch, 'Scotsmen on the Danish–Norwegian frontier', 4. On the medieval antecedents, MacDonald, 'Profits, politics and personality'.

42. NLS MS 82/97 and for a list of the regiment see 84/4–6; Lyall, 'Kinship, kingship and Latiny'.

43. Calderwood, *History*, i, 547–8; iii, 166; Lindsay, *Historie*, ii, 306; Dow, *Ruthven's Army*.

44. Calderwood, *History*, iv, 47. Professional soldiers or mercenaries were associated with more absolutist forms of government, see Kiernan, 'Foreign mercenaries'.

45. Hayes-McCoy, *Scots Mercenary Forces*; Macinnes, 'Crown, clans and *fine*', 33–4, 40–1; Hill, *Fire and Sword*; McLeod, *Divided Gael*, 49–54; *CSP Scotland*, xi, 467, 591–2, 581, 628–9, 651–2, 668 and *infra* in this and succeeding volumes. See *CSP Scotland* , xii, 201–11 for a description of the fighting qualities of the island clans.

46. For Argyll, *RPC*, first ser., xii, 730–1; NAS GD 112/39/32/19; NLS 79/13–14; for Reay, Beller, 'Military expedition'; Manning, *Apprenticeship in Arms*, 70–1; Gordon, *Sutherland*, 401–2, 406. The elderly sir Duncan Campbell of Glenorchy avidly followed the course of Gustav Adolf's victories in Germany, NAS GD 112/39/45/7, 112/39/45/24, 112/39/46/12.

47. Dunthorne, 'Scots in the wars of the Low Countries'; *Scots Brigade*, i, 396–405; Glozier, 'Scots in the French and Dutch armies'; *CSP Scotland*, viii, 308, 410, 418–19, 494, 589; x, 263.

48. Fraser, *Buccleuch*, i, 235, 253–9; NAS GD 224/889/3; Fraser, *Carlaverock*, ii, 6, 12.

49. For Crawford, *RPC*, second ser., iii, 313; Lindsay, *Lives*, ii, 53–7.

50. *House of Forbes*, 168–9, 178; *HMC Second Report*, ii, 195. For another military kindred see Dukes, 'Leslie family'.

51. Gordon, *Sutherland*, 471; *Ancram and Lothian*, i, pp. xlix–li.

52. For a useful discussion of this topic see Goodare, *State and Society*, 133–71; and see Cooper, *Scottish Renaissance Armies*.

53. Phillips, *Anglo-Scots Wars*; Merriman, *Rough Wooings*.

54. Cowan, 'Marian civil war'; Donaldson, *Queen's Men*.
55. Brown, *Bloodfeud*, chs 1–6.
56. Knox, *Works*, ii, 6–13; Melville, *Memoirs*, 200–2; Calderwood, *History*, ii, 414–16; Spottiswoode, *History*, ii. 88.
57. *Historie*, 59, 97; Lindsay, *Historie*, ii; Bannatyne, *Memorials*, 232; Spottiswoode, *History*, ii, 169–70; *CSP Scotland*, iv, 258. From 1572 Morton allegedly executed prisoners in the hope of ending the war more quickly, Spottiswoode, *History*, ii, 174.
58. Caldwell, 'Battle of Pinkie'. On the relative merits of the English army in the first half of the sixteenth century, Miller, *Henry VIII*, 133–61; Phillips, 'Army of Henry VIII'. It was certainly more effective than the Scottish army, and the gap widened by the end of the sixteenth century, Nolan, 'Militarisation'.
59. Dewald, *Aristocratic Experience*, 45–68; Bitton, *French Nobility in Crisis*, 27–41; Harding, *Anatomy*, 22–7; Corvisier, *Armies and Societies*, 25–37, 87–105; Benadusi, *Provincial Elite*, 163–75.
60. *Bannatyne Miscellany*, i, 23–9.
61. *RPS*, 1540/12/28–34 for a raft of legislation in 1540 on military matters; *RPC*, first ser., ii, 463; iii, 676–7; iv, 196, 301, 307–8, 314; v, 235–6.
62. NAS GD 26/2/1.
63. *RPC*, first ser., xiv, 376–80. Of those who obeyed the summons, 5 per cent were horsemen, 18 per cent were armed foot, 34 per cent were unarmed or lightly armed foot, and 42 per cent were non-combatants, Goodare, *State and Society*, 138.
64. *Honorum de Morton*, i, 16; also see, for example, *RPC*, first ser., iv, 28; for lord Erskine, NAS GD 124/17/677.
65. For Calder, NLS MS 3724/34, 3724/37; and the Borders, Rae, *Administration*, 43–7; Leslie, *Historie*, i, 10, 12; Fraser, *Buccleuch*, i, 180–227.
66. *CSP Scotland*, viii, 120; x, 46–7.
67. *CSP Scotland*, x, 747; Spottiswoode, *History*, ii, 86–8; Calderwood, *History*, iii, 153–5. On the royal guard, Goodare, *State and Society*, 145–50.
68. *RPC*, first ser., iv, 371–2; *CSP Scotland*, x, 46–7; Grant, 'Brig o' Dee affair'; Brown, *Bloodfeud*, 148–9; Lee, *Thirlestane*, 176–92.
69. *RPC*, v, 366, 373, 417–18, 421; Rae, *Administration*, 133–41.
70. *RPS*, A1596/5/3, A1598/6/2; *RPC*, first ser., v, 296–7, 306–10, 324, 475; *CSP Scotland*, xii, 281–2, 290–1, 295, 311, 343; xii, pt. 1, 259–63.
71. Nolan, 'Militarisation', 399–403.
72. Spottiswoode, *History*, iii, 5–6.
73. *RPS*, 1540/12/65–6, 1599/7/14, 1599/7/15, 1599/7/17, 1599/12/2; *RPC* first ser., iv, 168–9, 190–1; *CSP Scotland*, xiii, pt. 1, 583–4; NAS GD 10/675; *HMC*, iii, 396, No. 199. The amount and type of weaponry varied with rank. The tension between the desire to limit the use of arms and the need to maintain an armed nobility was common throughout Europe, Ruff, *Violence*, 49–52.
74. Lee, *Government by Pen*.
75. *RPC*, first ser., vii, 407; and for another in 1608, viii, 78.
76. *RPC*, first ser., viii, 113–14, 173–5, 521–6, 533–4, 739–41.
77. *Melrose Papers*, i, 55, 143–58, 174–7; Anderson, *Black Patie*, 108–24.
78. *RPC*, first ser., x, 346–7, 738–42, 746–66. For Lewis, *RPC*, first ser., x, 609–11, 692, 697.
79. Nolan, 'Militarisation'; Fissel, *English Warfare*, 1–47; and for an older interpretation that emphasises the corrupt and inefficient nature of the system, Cruickshank, *Elizabeth's Army*; Boynton, *Elizabethan Militia*.
80. Hale, *War and Society*; Oman, *War*; Roberts, 'Military revolution'; Parker, 'Military revolution?'; Barker, 'Armed services and nobility'; Baxter, *Servants of the Sword*; Black, *European Warfare*.
81. Murdoch, 'James VI', 15–24; Murdoch, *Britain, Denmark–Norway and the House of Stuart*, 44–63; Murdoch (ed.), *Scotland and the Thirty Years' War*; Grosjean, 'Scotland: Sweden's closest ally?'; Grosjean, *Unofficial Alliance*, 41–103.
82. Adamson, 'Chivalry'; for the Caroline military record see Fissel, *English Warfare*, 255–81.

83. *RPS* A1625/10/23, A1625/10/30–1; *RPC*, second ser., i, 180–1, 185–6, 191–2, 197–8, 213–15; *Ancram and Lothian*, i, 482. Quarrels between nobles continued to disrupt the process, *RPC*, second ser., i, 213–15; ii, 30–1.

84. *RPC*, second ser., i, 337–8, 378–9, 418–20, 502–5; ii, 88–90, 559–60, 571; NLS MS 14,480/70.

85. *RPC*, second ser., ii, 62, 93–5, 114–15, 168–71. A similar report was received for the sheriffdom of Forfar. NRA(S) 2312/108/2/11–13, 2312/109/13 for Renfrewshire; NAS GD 25/9/45.

86. *RPC*, second ser., ii, 150–3, 156–8.

87. Murdoch, 'Scottish ambassadors', 33–5; Murdoch, 'James VI', 22–4.

88. Edwards, 'Arming and equipping'; *Ancram and Lothian*, i, 1; *RPC*, second ser., i, 158–9, 293–4, 418–20, 580–1, 604–5, 613; ii, 37–9, 50–1, 53–4, 63; NAS GD 406/1/79; *Black Book*, 385–6; *Scots Peerage*, vi, 376. Sir John Grant of Freuchie was a recognised military contractor, Fraser, *Chiefs of Grant*, ii, 7, 13–14. On privateering, *RPC*, second ser., i, 324–5, 531–2, 539–40, 550–2, 579–80, 585 and see Murdoch, *Terror of the Seas*. On Morton's military preparations see NLS MS 82; for Hamilton see Scally, 'Political career'.

89. Lee, *Road to Revolution*, 79–87; Macinnes, *Charles I*, 51, 141.

90. Fraser, *Carlaverock*, ii, 79–105; *Ancram and Lothian*, i, 45. Similar problems were faced by the government in England, Stearns, 'Conscription'.

91. *Innes*, 215; NLS MS 84/4–10, 82/12/75 contains lists of the soldiers and details of Morton's preparations and MS 83/82 is a letter in February 1629 indicating that the estates general were interested in his services; for Lorne, NLS MS 79/22–3, 79/25; and for letters from other nobles complaining about the shortage of men, NLS MS 79/74, 79/91, 80/28, 81/5, 81/32.

92. *RPC*, second ser., ii, 296–7; Fraser, *Sutherland*, ii, 38; Fraser, *Pollok*, ii, 82–3 ; NAS GD 112/39/39/4; NLS MS 82/10/45. See too MacCoinnich, 'His spirit was given only to warre', 154–5.

93. Storrs and Scott, 'Military revolution'; Trim (ed.), *Chivalric Ethos*; Hanlon, *Twilight*, encapsulates the main arguments.

94. Parrott, *Richelieu's Army*; Glete, *War and the State*; Sharpe, *Personal Rule*, 9–62, 792–824, 885–95.

95. Baillie, *Letters*, i, 65.

96. *HMC Mar and Kellie*, i, 197–8.

97. Furgol, *Covenanting Armies*, 16–39; Furgol, 'Scotland turned Sweden'. For example, see Baillie's comments on the second marquis of Huntly, Baillie, *Letters*, i, 65.

Chapter 6: Governors

1. Simpson, 'Personal letters', 141; *CSP Scotland*, xiii, pt. 2, 664. For insight into the workings of government see Goodare, *Government*; Donaldson, *James V to James VII*, 276–91.

2. *CSP Scotland*, x, 14, 46 and see v, 370; Melville, *Memoirs*, 384.

3. For France, see Beik, *Absolutism and Society*, 223–44; Smith, *Culture of Merit*, 32–7; and for a case study, Sturdy, *D'Aligres de la Rivière*.

4. *CSP*, xiii, pt. 2, 1118.

5. *CSP*, viii, 492–3.

6. *HMC Mar and Kellie*, i, 37, 43; *Political Writings*, 29 and see 23–4, 35–6; *HMC*, vi, 611; *RPC*, first ser., vi, 605.

7. Mason, 'Chivalry and citizenship', 57–60; Mason, 'Kingship, tyranny and the right to resist'.

8. *HMC*, vi, 645.

9. Calderwood, *History*, vii, 549.

10. Crumney, *Aristocrats and Servitors*; Kivelson, *Autocracy*, 7–8; Frost, 'Nobility', 287–90.
11. Dewald, *European Nobility*, 36–40; Smith, *Culture of Merit*, 93–123; MacHardy, 'Cultural capital'. In England, office-holding rarely breached established social structures, Aylmer, *King's Servants*, 322–36.
12. Brown, *Noble Society*, 181–202; *CSP Scotland*, v, 564; x, 285; xiii, pt. 1, 228; Melville, *Memoirs*, 304, 385–6, 391.
13. *Memorials of Montrose*, i, 25.
14. Zulager, 'Middle-rank administrators', 150–3; Donaldson, *All the Queen's Men*; and for the Hamiltons see Fraser, *Haddington*, i, 23–9, 184–7.
15. NAS GD 150/3438/3, dated 23 November 16...
16. *Political Writings*, 36. Henry IV's introduction of the *paulette* in 1604 made venal offices hereditary in return for an annual payment, thus raising revenue and reducing the likelihood of royal office being colonised by great noble houses, Major, 'Crown and aristocracy', 641.
17. Queller, *Venetian Patriciate* for the Venetian concept of a selfless, patriotic patriciate; *Memorials of Montrose*, i, 74–5.
18. *Chronicle of the Kings of Scotland*, 142; *RPC*, first ser., 423–7, 429–30.
19. Zulager, 'Middle-rank administrators', 137.
20. *HMC Mar and Kellie*, ii, 240–3, and see 246.
21. NAS GD 150/3438/3.
22. *Historie*, 338.
23. Melville, *Memoirs*, 385–6.
24. *CSP Scotland*, xi, 696; xiii, pt. 2, 618; *RPC*, first ser., vi, 136–7. For similar issues in Holland, see van Nierop, *Nobility*, 148–66.
25. *Honorum de Morton*, i, 90–1; *Melrose Papers*, ii, 455–6, 462; *HMC Mar and Kellie*, ii, 122–7.
26. *RPC*, first ser., vii, 431, 497, 538–9; second ser., ii, 625–7.
27. NAS GD 124/10/117; *RPC*, first ser., iii, 753–4.
28. Lee, 'Unpublished letter', 178.
29. Bonney, *European Dynastic States*, 336; Dewald, *European Nobility*, 140–7; Bush, *Noble Privilege*, 79–120; Scott and Storrs, 'Consolidation', 34–42; Giesey, 'Rules of inheritance'; Kalas, 'Marriage, clientage, office-holding'. For a more unusual pattern, see the urban, patrician nature of Italian state bureaucracies, Litchfield, *Emergence of a Bureaucracy*.
30. *Ancram and Lothian*, i, 26–7; Fraser, *Elphinstone*, ii, 171–3.
31. Fraser, *Elphinstone*, ii, 171–3; Melville, *Memoirs*, 300–1; and see NLS MS 80/67.
32. *HMC Mar and Kellie*, ii, 38–9; Calderwood, *History*, vi, 167–8; *RPC*, first ser., ix, 505.
33. Melville, *Memoirs*, 293–5.
34. *HMC Mar and Kellie*, i, 144, 146; *RPC*, xiv, 621–2; NAS GD 40/9/8/2; Calderwood, *History*, vii, 450.
35. Lee, 'Charles I'; *Mar and Kellie*, i, 132–3; Hyde, *History*, i, 172; Donald, *Uncounselled King*; Stewart, *Urban Politics*, 309–12.
36. Myers, *Parliaments and Estates*; Graves, *Parliaments*; Rogister, 'Some new directions'; Young, 'Scottish parliament' offers a comparative insight.
37. See the essays in Brown and Tanner (eds), *Parliament and Politics in Scotland 1235–1560* and Brown and MacDonald (eds), *Parliament in Context*; Tanner, *Late Medieval Scottish Parliament*; Goodare, *State and Society*; Goodare, *Government*, 37–86. For less positive views of parliament see Terry, *Scottish Parliament*; Rait, *Scottish Parliament*; Rait, *Parliaments of Scotland*. On a representative assembly as an instrument of state see Elton, 'Parliament'.
38. Brown, 'Reformation parliament'.
39. The precise number of meetings of conventions remains uncertain, *RPS*; Goodare, *Government*, 47–9; for noble pre-meetings see Fraser, *Wemyss*, iii, 29–30 and NLS MS 20,774/31.

40. Lindsay, *Ane Satyre*. See the essays on the estates in Brown and MacDonald (eds), *Parliament in Context*.
41. Fraser, *Wemyss*, ii, 222; Brown, 'Second estate'. The numbers are based on Paul (ed.), *Scots Peerage*.
42. McAlister and Tanner, 'First estate'; Lee, 'James VI and the revival of episcopacy'; MacDonald, 'Ecclesiastical representation'.
43. MacDonald, *Burghs and Parliament*; MacDonald, 'Third estate'.
44. Lee, *Maitland of Thirlstane*, 145–51; Goodare, 'Nobility', 180; Wormald, *Court, Kirk and Community*, 119, 157; Goodare, 'Estates'.
45. Tanner, *Parliament*, 30–4; Ritchie, 'Marie de Guise and the three estates', 194–5; *RPS*, 1558/11/2.
46. Fraser, *Douglas*, iv, 245; and see NAS GD 112/39/14/7; NRA(S) 2312/107/5/2NRA(S) 2312/113/910; Brown, 'Reformation parliament', 214–15, 224. For patronage networks in the English parliament, Adams, 'Dudley clientele and the house of commons'.
47. Brown, 'Reformation parliament'; *RPS*, A1560/8/2.
48. *RPS*, 1561/12/1, 1566/10/1, 1567/4/5, 1567/8/1, 1567/12/2, 1567/12/4, 1567/12/12, 1567/12/28–9, 1567/12/43, 1567/12/45.
49. *RPS*, A1569/7/1, A1572/11/1, 1587/7/143; Rait, *Parliaments*, 203–8.
50. *RPS*, 1585/12/93–4.
51. *RPS*, 1587/7/143; *RPC*, first ser., iv, 251, 440–1; Calderwood, *History*, iv, 640; Brown and Mann, 'Introduction', 19–22.
52. *RPC*, first ser., iv, 384–5; Brown and Mann, 'Introduction', 19–22; and for similar practices in Brittany see, Collins, *Classes, Estates and Orders*, 160–4.
53. Goodare, 'Admission of lairds'; Goodare, 'Estates', 17–20; Goodare, 'Parliamentary taxation', 23–52; Rait, *Parliaments*, 208–10.
54. Goodare, 'Scottish political community', 375; *RPS*, 1567/4/2, A1583/12/1, 1584/5/6, A1594/4/1, 1633/6/14; Young, 'Charles I and the 1633 parliament', 117–19.
55. *RPC*, first ser., ii, 2–3. The extent of noble influence over burgh members was less than in England and only 7.5 per cent of burgh commissioners in the period 1560–1651 were nobles, MacDonald, *Burghs and Parliament*, 17–18, 45–6.
56. *RPS*, 1587/7/26; Hope, *Major Practicks*, i, 11, 13–14.
57. *CSP Scotland*, ix, 453; xii, 482–3; Hope, *Major Practicks*, i, 16–17; *RPC*, first ser., vii, 221, 424; xii, 548; *HMC*, iii, 412. For an example of a proxy, see the third lord Kinloss's letter to the sixth earl of Morton in May 1633, NAS GD 150/3443/3. Calderwood infers that at the 1621 parliament some noblemen preferred to obtain licences to be absent rather than oppose the king, Calderwood, *History*, vii, 470.
58. *RPC*, second ser., v, 58–9, 66–7, 269–70, 345–6. Taxes were levied in Renfrewshire in 1604 and 1609 to pay the commissioners, NRA(S) 2312/108/2/1–2.
59. NRA(S) 2312/108/1/2; MacDonald, 'Parliament of 1592', 65; *Sheriff Court of Aberdeenshire*, i, 372–3. For the debate over competitive elections in England see Hirst, *Representatives of the People?* and Kishlansky, *Parliamentary Selection*.
60. *RPC*, first ser., iv, 296–7, 303–4, 312–13, 353, 361–2.
61. Fraser, *Wemyss*, ii, 219. That of 1598 was signed by seven men, Fraser, *Wemyss*, 220–1.
62. NAS GD 75/604. In 1616 the privy council requested that commissioners for the small barons annually send chancery the names of those who had been elected, *RPC*, first ser., x, 502–3.
63. Young, 'Charles I and the 1633 parliament', 104–14; *RPC*, second ser., v, 45, 48, 54, 100.
64. Macinnes, *Charles I*, 82, 86; Fraser, *Wemyss*, ii, 16; *RPC*, second ser., iii, 43–4, 54, 104–5.
65. For Hamilton, NAS GD 406/1/80 and see 406/1/583 for 1628; for Loudon, *RPC*, second ser., iii, 104–5 and see 43–4 and 54; for Argyll, NAS GD 112/39/48/5; lord Yester was required to return acceptable commissioners, NLS 7102/3.
66. *RPS*, 1567/4/7–10, 1567/4/13–34; 1581/10/60, 1581/10/62–72, 1581/10/76–86, 1581/10/88–118, 1581/10/120–32.

67. *Political Writings*, 21–2; *CSP Scotland*, xi, 128; *Ayrshire and Wigton*, v, 16; Gordon, *Sutherland*, 343. Gordon confused the parliament with the convention held in March of that year.

68. *CSP Scotland*, v, 562; and see Burns, 'Political ideas and parliament'.

69. Brown, 'Reformation parliament', 210; Knox, *History*, i, 343; *CSP Scotland*, iii, 573; Calderwood, *History*, iii, 413–14; *RPS*, 1578/7/1.

70. *RPS*, 1582/10/2; A1583/12/2; Lee, *Maitland of Thirlestane*, 120–55; MacDonald, 'Parliament of 1592'.

71. *Historie*, 261. There is no formal record of this convention meeting before the April parliament.

72. *CSP Scotland*, xiii, pt. 1, 331, 353, 356; Fraser, *Elphinstone*, ii, 170–1.

73. Brown and Mann, 'Introduction', 26–7.

74. He softened this in *Basilikon doron* by describing parliament as 'the honourablest and highest judgement in the land', *Political Writings*, 21–2, 74. This royalist view is reflected in Lee, *Maitland of Thirlestane*, 120–54 and Goodare, *State and Society*, 16, 45–7, 73, 88, 97, 100.

75. *CSP Scotland*, xiii, pt. 2, 632–4, 663, 670; Fraser, *Wemyss*, iii, 37–9. On taxes, Goodare and Lynch, 'James VI', 9–10; Goodare, 'Parliamentary taxation'; Goodare, 'Scottish politics', 42–3; Goodare, 'Thomas Foulis'; Brown and Mann, 'Introduction', 24–6; MacDonald, *Burghs and Parliament*, 103–6 highlights the difficulties faced by the crown in controlling burgh commissioners.

76. On the political context see Lee, *Government by Pen*; Brown, *Kingdom or Province?*, 86–99; Brown and Mann, 'Introduction', 27–32. The English literature is vast and a useful starting point is Smith, *Stuart Parliaments*.

77. *Mar and Kellie*, i, 63–4; Calderwood, *History*, vii, 469; NLS MS 78/20.

78. Lee, 'James VI and the revival of episcopacy', 88–98; MacDonald, 'Ecclesiastical representation'; Wells, 'Constitutional conflict', 84.

79. Rait, 'Parliamentary representation'; Tanner, 'Lords of the articles'; MacDonald, 'Deliberative processes'; Wells, 'Constitutional conflict', 84–90; Brown and Mann, 'Introduction', 29–30.

80. Wells, 'Constitutional conflict', 82–94.

81. *HMC Mar and Kellie*, ii, 45, 55.

82. Wells, 'Constitutional conflict', 94–100; *Melrose Papers*, i, 270–8; Calderwood, *History*, vi, 250.

83. *Melrose Papers*, ii, 423–4; *RPC*, first ser., xii, 404–5; Goodare, 'Scottish parliament of 1621'; *HMC Mar and Kellie*, ii, 117.

84. *RPC*, second ser., i, 173; Lee, *Road to Revolution*, 13–14, 99–100; Macinnes, *Charles I*, 107–8; Macinnes, *British Revolution*, 84. See, too, Collins, *Classes, Estates and Orders*, 154–8; and Thompson, 'Crown and *cortes* in Castile'.

85. Lee, *Road to Revolution*, 131–3; Macinnes, *Charles I*, 86–9; Young, 'Charles I and the 1633 parliament', 114–35; Scally, 'Constitutional revolution', 55–9. For a useful model of an emergent opposition see Hexter, 'Power struggle', 27; and on the relationship between infrequency and management see Major, 'Loss of royal initiative'.

86. Calderwood, *History*, i, 531; Gardyne, *Garden*, poem entitled 'To the most noble lords of his most excellent majestie his most honorable privie councel'.

87. *RPC*, first ser., iv, 331–2; xiii. 435; Fraser, *Buccleuch*, ii, 262–3.

88. Fraser, *Sutherland*, ii, 355; *RPC*, first ser., vi, 69–70.

89. Miller, *Henry VIII*, 118; Wormald, *Court, Kirk and Community*, 151.

90. Goodare, *Government*, 128–72.

91. Goodare, *Government*, 147; Brown, 'Reformation parliament', 205, 226–7; MacDonald, 'Parliament of 1592', 72; *CSP Scotland*, x, 774.

92. *RPS*, 1579/10/49, 1587/7/29, 1592/4/63, 1593/4/65; *RPC*, first ser., v, 116–17, 499–500; vii, 530; viii, 515–16, 815; *CSP Scotland*, x, 371–4, 387, 416; *Chronicle of the Kings of Scotland*, 179.

93. For 1625–6, *RPC*, second ser., i, 183–5, 249, 297, 348–9, and for the ongoing debate,

RPC, i, 435–6, 439, 483, 487–8; for 1631, iv, 188–90; *HMC*, ix, 256.

94. For further details see Brown, 'Scottish aristocracy', 556.

95. Goodare and Lynch, 'James VI', 3–4. Figures are based on surviving sederunts.

96. The best discussion of the politics of the privy council is found in Lee, *Maitland of Thirlestane*; Lee, *Government by Pen*; Lee, *Road to Revolution*. The editorial introductions to *RPC* first and second series are also useful.

97. *RPC*, first ser., ix, 530. Resignation in favour of sons was permitted, for examples, *RPC*, first ser., iii, 356, 548–9. For comparison, Bonney, *European Dynastic States*, 336.

98. Zulager, 'Middle-rank administrators', 12–13, 16–19.

99. Zulager, 'Middle-rank administrators', appendix I, 204–5.

100. The numbers indicate councillors who attended at least one meeting in that year. In 1600 the master of Elphinstone is included as a peer, having been placed in charge of all his father's affairs almost twenty-five years earlier.

101. *RPC*, first ser., ix, 85; xi, 462–3; xiii, 172; and see the commission for manufacturing, *RPC*, first ser., xiii, 290–1, 299–302; for the commission of grievances, *RPC*, first ser., xiii. 219–23; and see Balfour's scathing remarks, *Works*, ii, 131. For the council of war, *RPC*, second ser., i, 337–8, 378–81; Macinnes, *Charles I*, 58.

102. Zulager, 'Middle-rank administrators', 125–8; and see Murray, 'Sir John Skene' for an individual career.

103. Melville, *Memoirs*, 373. On which see, Lee, *Maitland of Thirlestane*, 153; Lee, 'James VI's government'; Mitchison, *Lordship to Patronage*, 10–11; Wormald, *Court, Kirk and Community*, 153; Wormald, *Lords and Men*, 162; Goodare, 'Nobility', 166; Meikle, 'Invisible divide', 83. The division is no longer accepted by some French historians, Mettam, 'French nobility', 127–33. For the situation in England, Bernard, 'Tudor nobility', 22–3; Stone and Stone, *An Open Elite?*, 256–8.

104. Zulager, 'Middle-rank administrators', 26–57, 75, 79–131; Meikle, 'Invisible divide', 74–6; Bonney, *European Dynastic States*, 340–5.

105. Zulager, 'Middle-rank administrators', 30–1, 44–7; *Chronicle of the Kings of Scotland*, 170; Calderwood, *History*, vii, 38; Fraser, *Haddington*, i, 10–20; ii, 287; *Honorum de Morton*, i, 181; NAS GD 112/39/36/1.

106. Lee, 'The "inevitable" union', 3; Lee, *Government by Pen*; Newton, *Making of the Jacobean Regime*, 20–3; *Political Writings*, 173; *RPC*, first ser., vii, 178, 188; xii, 604, 701–2. The executive committee consisted of men drawn from four old peerage houses, two powerful baronial families promoted to the peerage, four lesser baronial houses and an archbishop.

107. Lee, 'Charles I'; *HMC Mar and Kellie*, i, 138.

108. Fraser, *Menteith*, ii, 84–7.

109. See the inability of the government to repair the roads in 1633 without local noble cooperation, *RPC*, second ser., v, 63–4.

110. Spottiswoode, *History*, i, 57.

111. Goodare, *Government*, 138–41; Meikle, 'Invisible divide', 85; Lee, *Maitland of Thirlstane*, 143; Lee, *Government by Pen*, 8; Lee, 'James VI's government'.

112. NLS MS 79/68–9.

113. For Montrose, *CSP Scotland*, xiii, pt. 1, 369–70, 373, 375, 381–2, 386, 388, 399, 404; xiii, pt. 2, 721; Blantyre, *CSP Scotland*, xiii, pt. 1, 434–5; and Morton, NLS MS 78/28; on competitive bidding see Aylmer, *King's Servants*, 449–52.

114. Fraser, *Haddington*, ii, 88–90.

115. By the house of Glamis, Calderwood, *History*, v, 394; *CSP Scotland*, xi, 609, 682; xii, 163; and more speculatively the house of Huntly, Gordon, *Sutherland*, 143.

116. Fraser, *Menteith*, i, 334, 338.

117. Murray, 'Lord clerk register'. The office of justice clerk was held by men of knightly rank, Hannay, 'Office of the justice clerk'.

118. Meikle, 'Invisible divide', 85; *CSP Scotland*, x, 777; xii, 43, 117; *Political Writings*, 37; *Ancram and Lothian*, i, 42. On the appropriateness of nobles holding important financial offices see Melville, *Memoirs*, 380; *Memorials of Montrose*, i, 20.

119. Craig, *Jus Feudale*, i, p. ix; CSP *Scotland*, v, 564; *Abbotsford Miscellany*, 300; *Early Travellers*, 137; on legal union see Levack, *Formation of the British State*, 76–97.

120. Godfrey, *Civil Justice*; Finlay, *Men of Law*; Maitland, *Poems*, 49–52; Brunton and Haig, *Historical Account*.

121. Cooper, 'King versus the court'; *RPS*, 1579/10/55; *Political Writings*, 72–5; Hart, *Rule of Law*, 5–17, 56–7, 62–6, 67–70, 115–57; *RPC*, first ser., viii, 79–80, 516.

122. Zulager, 'Middle-rank administrators', 100–4.

123. Finlay, 'James Henryson'; Goodare, *Government*, 163–5; Fraser, *Haddington*, ii, 216–19; Pitcairn, *Criminal Trials*, ii, 568–604.

124. Analysis based on *ODNB*; *RPC* first and second series; Brunton and Haig, *Historical Account*; Grant, *Faculty of Advocates*.

125. Lee, *Road to Revolution*, 17–24; McNeill, 'Independence', 135–44. In Spain royal supervision of the judiciary slipped away in the face of rising professional standards, Bonney, *European Dynastic States*, 339–40.

126. Benadusi, *A Provincial Elite*, 97–112; Dewald, *Provincial Nobility*, 15–68, 307; Dewald, *Aristocratic Experience*, 22; Major, *Renaissance Monarchy*, 321–6; Bohannan, *Old and New Nobility*.

127. Donaldson, 'Legal profession'; Wormald, *Court, Kirk and Community*, 154, 162; Meikle, 'Invisible divide', 85; Goodare, *Government*, 55–7; Lee, *Maitland of Thirlstane*, 153–4; *RPS*, 1579/10/55; NLS Adv. MS 25.2.2/133–4; Lindsay, *Historie*, ii, 202; *Honorum de Morton*, ii, 87–9; Fraser, *Chiefs of Grant*, ii, 36; Calderwood, *History*, v, 290–1; Lindsay, *Lives*, i, 488–9; HMC *Laing*, i, 189; Lee, *Road to Revolution*, 18–24.

128. Godfrey, 'Assumption of jurisdiction'; *RPS*, 1592/4/72; Godfrey, 'Arbitration'; Cairns, 'Legal humanism'; Brown, *Kingdom or Province?*, 55–9; Wormald, *Lords and Men*, 133–4; Waus, *Correspondence*, i, and ii.

129. Analysis based on *ODNB*; *RPC*, first and second ser.; Brunton and Haig, *Historical Account*; Grant, *Faculty of Advocates*.

130. Donaldson, 'Legal profession', 9–13; Brown, *Noble Society*, 181–202; Goodare, 'Hamilton, Thomas'.

131. Finlay, 'Borthwick, David'; Sanderson, *Mary Stewart's People*, 22–33.

132. NLS Adv. MS 15.2.14/70–1. The analysis is based on *ODNB*; *RPC* first and second ser.; Brunton and Haig, *Historical Account*; Grant, *Faculty of Advocates*.

133. Zulager, 'Middle-rank administrators', 73; Zulager, 'Bruce, Edward'; MacDonald, 'Lindsay, John'; Lee, 'Seton, Alexander'; Zulager, 'Elphinstone, James'; Goodare, 'Hamilton, Thomas'; Heal and Holmes, *Gentry*, 133–5; Dewald, *Formation*, 113–220; Bonney, *European Dynastic States*, 337–8.

134. Frame, *Political Development*, 84–5 makes this point for twelfth-century England.

135. Walker, *Scottish Jurists*, 33–105; Levack, 'Law, sovereignty and the union'; Cooper, 'King versus the court'; Goodare, *Government*, 73–82; CSP *Scotland*, xiii, pt. 1, 426–8.

136. Wells, 'Origins', 291–2; Stevenson, 'Hope, Thomas'.

137. *Historie*, 278; *RPC*, first ser., ix, 731; *Melrose Papers*, i, 281; Pitcairn, *Criminal Trials*, iii, 418–28.

138. This was also true of late medieval Scotland, Brown, 'Scottish "establishment"'.

139. MacHardy, *War, Religion and Court Patronage*, 22–5; Henshall, *Myth of Absolutism*; Beik, *Absolutism and Society*, 335–9; Kivelson, *Autocracy*.

Chapter 7: Courtiers

1. See the essays in Adamson, *Princely Courts*; Asch, 'Introduction', 11–24.

2. Macdougall, *James IV*; Cameron, *James V*, 255–85; Thomas, *Princelie Majestie*; Edington, *Court and Culture*. For cultural issues see Robinson, *Court Politics*, and the various essays in Williams (ed.), *Stewart Style* and Mapstone and Wood (eds), *Rose and the Thistle*.

3. Thomas, *Princelie Majetie*, 33–7; Juhala, 'Household and court'; Persson, *Servant of*

Fortune, 19–20; Adamson, 'Making of the *ancien-régime* court'; Duindam, 'Bourbon and Austrian Habsburg courts'.

4. Elias, *Court Society*; and see the essays in Adamson (ed.), *Princely Courts* for a more nuanced interpretation.

5. Dewald, *European Nobility*, 122–33; Burke, *Fortunes of the Courtier*.

6. Dunbar, *Scottish Royal Palaces*; Howard, *Scottish Architecture*, 16–47; McKean, *Scottish Chateaux*, 159–212; Juhala, 'Household and court', 121–46.

7. *CSP Scotland*, xiii, pt. 1, 983; Juhala, 'Advantageous alliance'; Lynch, *Edinburgh and the Reformation*; Stewart, *Urban Politics*; Brown, *Noble Society*, 8; Fraser, *Elphinstone*, i, 150–1; Sanderson, *Mary Stewart's People*, 71; Fraser, *Haddington*, i, 130; Fraser, *Sutherland*, ii, 347.

8. Juhala, 'Advantageous alliance', 343; *CSP Scotland*, v, 498, 503; *HMC Various, V*, 104; *RPC*, first ser., vii, 226; *Ancram and Lothian*, i, p. xi; Balfour, *Works*, ii, 44; *HMC Mar and Kellie*, ii, 130. For greater detail on the household see Juhala, 'Household and court'. On the broader European context, Adamson, 'Making of the *ancien-régime* court', 16.

9. Donaldson, *All the Queen's Men*, 56–69; Dawson, *Politics of Religion*, 27–35; Goodare, 'Queen Mary's Catholic interlude'; see also, Sanderson, *Mary Stewart's People*.

10. Juhala, 'Household and court', 19–28; *RPC*, first ser., iii, 112–14, 281–2; Hewitt, *Morton*, 36–8; NAS GD 124/10/37; *Mar and Kellie*, i, 16–23, 39–44.

11. Juhala, 'Household and court', 28–39; *RPC*, first ser., ii, 694; iii, 316, 322–3, 416; *CSP Scotland*, v, 511, 519; vi, 560.

12. Calderwood, *History*, iii, 487; *CSP Scotland*, x, 17; Grant, 'Brig o' Dee affair'; and for English concerns see Brown, 'Price of friendship'. Juhala, 'Household and court', 44–5 indicates only a handful of household personnel were replaced following political change.

13. Melville, *Memoirs*, 375–7; *RPS*, A1590/6/1; *CSP Scotland*, x, 285, 297–9.

14. *CSP Scotland*, x, 285, xiii, pt. 1, 352–3; Juhala, 'Household and court', 45–7; Goodare, *State and Society*, 145–9.

15. Meikle, 'Anna of Denmark's coronation'; Meikle, 'Meddlesome princess'; Juhala, 'Household and court', 47–64, 77–83; Brown, *Bloodfeud*, 130–2; and see Mears, 'Courts, courtiers and culture' on the role of women in court networks.

16. Juhala, 'Household and court', 65–6; *CSP Scotland*, x, 276, 299, 306, 371; xiii, pt. 1, 369, 446–7; *Political Writings*, 28, 35; *RPC*, first ser., vi, 208.

17. Gray, 'Royal entry'; MacDonald, 'Mary Stewart's entry to Edinburgh'; Lynch, 'Queen Mary's triumph'; Lynch, 'Court ceremonial and ritual'; Meikle, 'Anna of Denmark's coronation'; Stevenson, *Scotland's Last Royal Wedding*, 57–62, 100–19; Juhala, 'Household and court', 193–234 discusses a range of royal events.

18. Hernandez, '"Refeudalisation" in Castile', 256–62, and for more emphasis on the political process see Casalilla, 'Castilian aristocracy', 277–300.

19. McNeill and McNeill, 'Scottish royal progress'; *Melrose Papers*, i, 289–90. On offices in 1617, NLS MS 20,777/39; and in 1633, *RPC*, second ser., v, 49–50, 58–60, 102, 107–8, 298–300, 607–8, 611–12; NAS GD 112/39/48/5.

20. Parry, *Golden Age*, 86–91; Balfour, *Historical Works*, ii, 116–17; Nichols (ed), *Progresses*, ii, 493–504; BL Add MSS 12,496/41.

21. Brown, 'Scottish aristocracy', 546–52; *Secret History*, i, 376; Hyde, *History*, i, 77. On court culture see Akrigg, *Jacobean Pageant* and Parry, *Golden Age*; and for the careers of Scottish courtiers see Schreiber, *First Carlisle* and Seddon, 'Robert Carr'.

22. Elton, 'Tudor government'; Loades, *Tudor Court*; Adams, 'Eliza enthroned?'; Cuddy, 'King's chambers'; Cuddy, 'Revival of the entourage' and Sharpe, 'Image of virtue' both Starkey (ed.), *English Court*, 173–225, 226–60; Cuddy, 'Reinventing a monarchy'; Stone, *Crisis of the Aristocracy*, 464–70; Adamson, 'Tudor and Stuart courts'; Mears, 'Courts, courtiers and culture'.

23. Lee, *Great Britain's Solomon*, 129–63; *Melrose Papers*, i, 190; Cuddy, 'King's chambers'; Cuddy, 'Revival of the entourage', 188–90; Cuddy, 'Reinventing a monarchy'; Seddon, 'Patronage and officers', 155–72, 293–310; Brown, 'Scottish aristocracy', 553–4 contains a full list of bedchamber Scots.

24. Seddon, 'Patronage and officers', 155–72, appendix 3; Carlisle, *Enquiry*; Brown, 'Scottish aristocracy', 553–4 contains a full list of privy chamber Scots.

25. Seddon, 'Patronage and offices', 155–72, appendix 3; *HMC Mar and Kellie*, ii, 130, 193.

26. In prince Charles's household Scots held the offices of groom of the stool, keeper of the privy purse, treasurer, master of the household, both secretaries, five gentlemen of the bedchamber and eight of the grooms, Seddon, 'Patronage and officers', 164–6, 308–9; Aylmer, *King's Servants*, 26–32.

27. *HMC Mar and Kellie*, ii, 227; Hyde, *History*, i, 207; Brown, 'Scottish aristocracy', 555–6; Brown, 'Courtiers and cavaliers'.

28. *RPC*, first ser., iii, 604, iv, 389–91, 536–7; v, 458; *CSP Scotland*, xiii, pt. 2, 765ff, 833–4ff.

29. Murdoch, *Britain, Denmark–Norway and the House of Stuart*, 17–20, 36–42; Murdoch, 'Diplomacy in transition'; Murdoch, 'Scottish ambassadors', 28–31; Grosjean, *Unofficial Alliance*; Worthington, 'Alternative diplomacy?'; Fraser, *Carlaverock*, ii, 111–13, 118, 121–7; *Ancram and Lothian*, p. xxvii.

30. *Political Writings*, 37–8; Mears, 'Courts, courtiers and culture'; Peck, *Court Patronage and Corruption*; Kettering, *Patrons, Brokers and Clients*; Kettering, 'Friendship and clientage'; Kalas, 'Marriage, clientage, office-holding'.

31. Harding, *Anatomy of a Power Elite*, 15; Kettering, 'Patronage in early modern France'; Schalk, 'Court as "civilizer"'; Fraser, *Wemyss*, iii, 79–80; Melville, *Memoirs*, 380–1; NRA(S) 237/F/495–6.

32. *CSP Scotland*, xiii, pt. 2, 721; NAS GD 112/39/19/7.

33. NAS GD 406/1/39, 406/158, 406/1/61, 406/1/8390.

34. *CSP Scotland*, v, 430–1, 503, 511, 513.

35. MacDougall, 'It is I, the earle of Mar'; McKean, 'Sir James Hamilton of Finnart', Melville, *Memoirs*, 132; and see Adams, 'Favourites and factions'.

36. Moysie, *Memoirs*, 40 ; for Arran and Thirlestane see Chapter 1, above.

37. Adamson (ed.), *Princely Courts*; Kettering, *Patrons, Brokers and Clients*; Neuschel, *Word of Honor*, 1–25; Powis, *Aristocracy*, 51–7.

38. Brown, 'Scottish aristocracy', 557–8; *Mar and Kellie*, ii, 127; NAS GD 150/3437/18; Hope, *Diary*, 16, 47–8; *Registrum de Panmure*, i, pp. xxxviii–ix; and for the broader context see Peck, *Court, Patronage and Corruption*.

39. Brown, 'Scottish aristocracy', 559–76.

40. Brown, *Noble Society*, 87–9; Stone, *Crisis of the Aristocracy*, 398–403; NAS GD 406/1/8229, 406/1/85, 406/1/90, 406/1/150, 406/1/8177; Brown, 'Courtiers and cavaliers'; Scally, 'Political career'; Donald, *Uncounselled King*.

41. *Melrose Papers*, i, 274; Stone, *Crisis of the Aristocracy*, 478–81; see the case of the Albret family in France, Eurich, *Economics of Power*, 44–77.

42. Drummond, *History*, 244; Zulager, 'Middle-rank administrators', 137; Fraser, *Menteith*, i, 15–16; *Letters and State Papers*, 125–7. Peck, '"For a king not to be bountifull were a fault"', 36–7.

43. *RPC*, vi, 602.

44. *HMC Laing*, i, 123–4.

45. *Ancram and Lothian*, ii, pp. ix–x.

46. Fraser, *Sutherland*, ii, 113.

47. *HMC Mar and Kellie*, ii, 41; Brown, 'Scottish aristocracy', 544–5.

48. Gordon, *Sutherland*, 318, 320; Lee, *Government by Pen*, 42, 158; NLS MS 78/77.

49. *Memorials of Montrose*, i, 7–10; *Mar and Kellie*, ii, 127; *HMC*, xiv, 108; *HMC Laing*, i, 128–9; *Melrose Papers*, i, 199–200; Fraser, *Haddington*, ii, 131; NLS MS 84/19, and also NAS GD 45/14/2, 45/14/7 for correspondence from other suitors; *Innes*, 213.

50. Urquhart, *Works*, 388.

51. Herman, 'Language of fidelity'; for Morton, NLS MS 78/20, 82/10, 83/56 and 83/57; for Hamilton, Fraser, *Melvilles*, ii, 84, see his manoeuvring in 1616 to ensure that Mar got the treasurer's staff, *HMC Mar and Kellie*, i–ii; see also, *Ancram and Lothian*, i, 20–1, 26–9, 39–41; Fraser, *Elphinstone*, ii, 181.

52. NLS MS 83/62 and also 83/63; *Ancram and Lothian*, ii, 281.

53. *HMC Various*, V, 111.

54. Fraser, *Sutherland*, ii, 355.

55. NLS MS 81/70; NLS MS 81/111; Fraser, *Eglinton*, i, 220. For examples, see the letter from the third earl of Gowrie from Padua to the king in 1595, *Bannatyne Miscellany*, 351–2; Denmilne to Stirling in 1631, NLS Adv. MS 33.7.26/1b–2b; Craighall to Menteith in 1631, Fraser, *Menteith*, ii, 130, 132–7, 140–1, 47–9. On the role of gifts see Kettering, 'Gift-giving and patronage'.

56. Fraser, *Haddington*, ii, 127 and *Melrose Papers*, i, 106.

57. NLS MS 83/89.

58. *HMC Laing*, i, 173.

59. Fraser, *Carlaverock*, ii, 129.

60. NAS GD 150/3438/4, Stirling to Morton, 3 March 16...

61. *HMC Mar and Kellie*, ii, 159, 164, 183.

62. Asch, 'Introduction', 2; Adams, 'Favourites and factions'; Adams, 'Faction, clientage and party', 13–14; MacHardy, *War, Religion and Court Patronage*, 151–207 demonstrates the connection between faction and confessional allegiance.

63. Gordon, *Sutherland*, 125.

64. NAS GD 40/9/8/1.

65. Maitland, *Poems*, 19–22; *Historie*, 187, 252–3.

66. *Memorials of Montrose*, i. 75–6.

67. Dewald, *Aristocratic Experience*, 15–44; *HMC Mar and Kellie*, ii, 240–3.

68. Lee, *Great Britain's Solomon*, 233–41; Adams, 'Favourites and factions'; Adamson, 'Making of the *ancien-régime* court', 19–20; *CSP Scotland*, v, 641; x, 3–4; Fraser, *Douglas*, iv, 29.

69. Melville, *Memoirs*, 304–5, 404.

70. *CSP Scotland*, v, 508; ix, 677; Hewitt, *Scotland Under Morton*, 19–82.

71. Maitland, *Poems*, 45–6.

72. Melville, *Memoirs*, 263, 266; Lee, 'Fall of the regent Morton'; Lynch, Court ceremonial and ritual', 74–81; Hewitt, *Scotland Under Morton*, 35–8.

73. Gordon, *Sutherland*, 385–6; *CSP Scotland*, x, 653; Allan, *Philosophy and Politics*, 46–133; Grant, 'Brig o' Dee', 98–101; Brown, *Bloodfeud*, 156–62.

74. Meikle, *British Frontier?*, 61–2, 67–82.

75. *CSP Scotland*, v, 516.

76. *CSP Scotland*, ix, 635–6 638, 647, 655; xi, 94; quote in Grant, 'Brig o' Dee', 100; Brown, *Bloodfeud*, 108–43; Juhala, 'Household and court', 66–8; Lee, 'Gowrie conspiracy revisited'; see also, Starkey, 'Court, council and nobility', 203.

77. The concept of corruption is difficult to verify, Hurstfield, 'Political corruption'; Harding, 'Corruption'; Peck, *Court Patronage and Corruption*.

78. *Honorum de Morton*, i, 91, 108–10; *CSP Scotland*, ix, 650; Melville, *Memoirs*, 375.

79. Brown, *Noble Society*, 64–8, 87–9; Goodare, 'James VI's English subsidy'; Dewald, *Aristocratic Experience*, 15–46; Rodriguez-Sagado, 'Court of Philip II', 228–36 ; Zmora, 'Princely state-making'.

80. Seddon, 'Robert Carr'; Lockyer, *Buckingham*; Scally, 'Political career'; Donagan, 'Courtier's progress'.

81. NAS GD 406/1/998; and see Lee, *Government by Pen* and Lee, *Road to Revolution* for a broader contextualisation of these relationships.

82. Schalk, 'Court as "civilizer"'; Brown, 'Scottish aristocracy'; Scally, 'Political career'; Ohlmeyer, *Civil War and Restoration*; *Mar and Kellie*, ii, 148–50.

83. Pittock, 'Edinburgh to London'; Smuts, *Court Culture*; Sharpe (ed.), *Criticism and Compliment*; Sharpe, *Personal Rule*; Brown, 'Courtiers and cavaliers'.

84. Lee, *Great Britain's Solomon*, 241–57; Lee, *Government by Pen*, 61–111; Croft, *King James*, 69–70.

85. Seddon, 'Robert Carr'; Bellany, 'Somerset'; Spottiswoode, *History*, iii, 214–15.

86. Lockyer, *Buckingham*; *Memorials of Montrose*, i, 52.

87. *Memorials of Montrose*, i, 22–4; *HMC Mar and Kellie*, i, 174–5.

88. Lee, *Road to Revolution*, 120–6.
89. Russell, *Parliaments and English Politics*; Worthington, *Scots in Habsburg Service*, for example, 50–1, 73–9; Adams, 'Foreign policy', 144, 156; Sharpe, *Personal Rule*, 166–7, 518; Scally, 'Political career'.
90. Wormald, 'Gunpowder, treason and Scots'; Cramsie, *Kingship and Crown Finance*, 115, 120–1, 124–5, 214, 216; Clucas, 'Cotton's *A Short View*, 179–80.
91. *RPC* first ser., vi, 602; ix, 173–4; Calderwood, *History*, vi, 238; *HMC*, ii, 194; Fraser, *Eglinton*, i, 237; BL Harl. 7623/9; Seddon, 'Patronage and officers', 169–70, 293–310; Murdoch, *Britain, Denmark–Norway and the House of Stuart*, 3–4; Strong, *Henry, Prince of Wales*, 220–5; Adamson, 'Tudor and Stuart court'.
92. Brown, 'Courtiers and cavaliers'; Donald, *Uncounselled King*, 15–42. For another process of differentiation elsewhere see Asch, 'Introduction', 24–35; Adamson, 'Making of the *ancien-régime* court', 27–33; Melton, 'Prussian Junkers', 126–30; Jespersen, 'Rise and fall of the Danish nobility', 52–3; Upton, 'Swedish nobility', 16–17.
93. Hyde, *History*, i, 108, 145–6.
94. Brown, 'Courtiers and cavaliers'.
95. For example, see Stevenson, *Scottish Revolution*, 324.
96. Brown, 'Vanishing emperor'.
97. Adamson, 'Making of the *ancien-régime* court', 15.
98. Baillie, *Letters and Journals*, i, 354.

Chapter 8: Noble Power and Politics, 1603–37

1. Dewald, *European Nobility*, 1–14; Scott (ed.), *European Nobilities*, i–ii; Asch, *Nobilities in Transition*; Weary, 'House of la Tremouille'.
2. Bernard, 'Tudor nobility', 4; Bernard, *Power of the Tudor Nobility*, 197–208; Stone, *Crisis of the Aristocracy*, 250–7; Heal and Holmes, *Gentry*, 195–8; Coward, 'A "crisis of the aristocracy"'; Adamson, *Noble Revolt*.
3. Major, *Renaissance Monarchy*, 59 ff; Astarita, *Continuity of Feudal Power*, 202–32; Jespersen, 'Rise and fall of the Danish nobility', 44–6; van Nierop, *Nobility*, 221.
4. Young, *Robert the Bruce's Rivals*; Brown, *Black Douglases*; Macpherson, 'Francis Stewart'; Anderson, *Black Patie*.
5. Dewald, *European Nobility*, 140; Bush, *Noble Privilege*, 12–13; Wormald, *Lords and Men*, 158.
6. Asch, *Nobilities in Transition*; Brown, *Noble Society*.
7. Brown, *Kingdom or Province?*; Lee, *Government by Pen*; Lee, *Road to Revolution*; Macinnes, *Charles I*; but see also, Wormald, 'Happier marriage partner'.
8. For a critique of the argument that noble power was undermined by state formation see Lachmann, 'Elite conflict and state formation'.
9. *Letters and State Papers*, 60.
10. Wormald, *Lords and Men*, 410, appendix C, No. 33.
11. *Political Writings*, 76.
12. Seton, *Family of Seton*, i, 165.
13. Rae, 'Historical writing', 39; Smart, 'Monarchy and toleration'.
14. Gordon, *Sutherland*, 34.
15. Hume, *House of Douglas*, pp. xi–xiv.
16. *Memorials of Montrose*, i, 77–8; Stevenson, 'Letter'.
17. *RPS*, A1625/10/7.
18. Melville, *Memoirs*, 305.
19. *RPS*, A1594/1/17/5.
20. Rae, 'Political attitudes'; Smart, 'Monarchy and toleration; Drummond, *History*, 111.
21. Fraser, *Sutherland*, ii, 358.
22. NAS GD 224/935/22.

23. Durkan, 'Beginnings of humanism', 259–79; Reiss, 'The idea of meaning and practice of method'; Kearney, *Scholars and Gentlemen*, 46–70; Bushnell, *Culture of Teaching*, 183; Mackie, *University of Glasgow*, 78–90; Twigg, *University of Cambridge*, 11–41; Brockliss, *French Higher Education*, 4; McCoy, 'Old English honour'; and see Adamson 'Baronial context'.

24. Wells, 'Leslie, John'.

25. Coffey, 'Elphinstone, John'.

26. *Ancram and Lothian*, 35–8; NLS MS 5787/5.

27. Cowan, 'Political ideas'.

28. *Aberdeen Council Register*, i, 487–8.

29. Fraser, *Sutherland*, ii, 357.

30. Calderwood, *History*, vi, 789–819; vii, 10–18; Pitcairn, *Criminal Trials*, ii, 568–604.

31. Fraser, *Menteith*, i, 366–78, 342–78; ii, 47, 49, 50–8, 150–5; *RPC*, second ser., v, 139–41; Pearce, 'John Spottiswoode', 159–64.

32. Anderson, *Black Patie*, chs 6–9; Calderwood, *History*, vi, 195; *RPS*, 1609/10/22; *RPC*, first ser., viii, 584, 587; ix, 181, 185–7; Pitcairn, *Criminal Trials*, iii, 272–327.

33. *RPC*, vi, 121, 356; vii, 539; viii, 19–20, 24, 28–9, 33, 36–7, 83, 487–8, 765–6, 769–73, 805–7; ix, 359–60, 362–3, 378, 461–2, 603–4, 608, 639–40, 744; x, 29, 44–5; Fraser, *Annandale*, i, p. cxliii; Fraser, *Carlaverock*, i, 300–24; Spottiswoode, *History*, iii, 191–2; Calderwood, *History*, vi, 704; *RPS*, 1609/4/2, 1609/4/7, 1609/4/13; *Melrose Papers*, i, 67–8, 108–9; Pitcairn, *Criminal Trials*, iii, 32–53. For the crown's tough dealing with the fifth earl of Caithness in 1622, see *RPC*, first ser., xiii, 124–8, 133, 150–1, 157, 168–9, 183, 280–4, 332–3, 351, 391–2, 433; Gordon, *Sutherland*, 330–40, 375–82; Fraser, *Haddington*, ii, 84–5, 134–5.

34. *Selected Justiciary Cases*, i, 176–97; *RPC*, second ser., iv, 352–3, 358; Gordon, *Sutherland*, 452–8; *HMC Mar*, i, 181–92; Lee, *Road to Revolution*, 88–9.

35. *RPC*, second ser., v, 409–10; vi, 43–4, 47, 334–5; Stirling, *Register*, ii, 734–5, 773–4, 823, 838–9; *HMC*, xiv, 108; Row, *History*, 376–89; Balfour, *Works*, ii, 216–20; Drummond, *History*, 244; Macinnes, *Charles I*, 138–41; Lee, *Road to Revolution*, 157–62.

36. Dunn, *Politics*, 179–83; Carroll, *Blood and Violence*, 191–213; Bohannan, *Crown and Nobility*, 46–58; McGettigan, *Red Hugh O'Donnell*, 118–20; Fraser, *Haddington*, ii, 74–5; Fraser, *Carlaverock*, i, 325–9, 334; *HMC*, ix, 244.

37. *HMC Mar and Kellie*, i, 84–5.

38. See the Bothwell inheritance, Fraser, *Haddington*, ii, 150; Fraser, *Buccleuch*, ii, 361–7, 435–42; *RPC*, first ser., x, 217, 518–19; second ser., iv, 328–9, 341, 358–9, 373–4, 447–8, 451–2, 459–60, 476–9, 494–5, 499, 504, 506–7, 510–13, 536–7, 554–5, 561, 565–9; NAS GD 224/906/35, 224/906/68/5. See also the correspondence between 1623 and 1632 at GD 224/175/5/17–19, and the extensive material in 906/71/8, 906/72, 906/74.

39. *Political Writings*, 28–9; Donaldson, *James V to James VII*, 212–37; Goodare, *State and Society*, 310–11; Goodare, *Government*, 117–18.

40. Wormald, 'Bloodfeud'; Brown, *Bloodfeud*, 183–265. For France, Collins, *Classes, Estates and Order*, 13–17; Carroll, *Blood and Violence*, 285–329.

41. Fraser, *Annandale*, ii, 27; Fraser, *Sutherland*, ii, 356.

42. Brown, *Bloodfeud*, 183–274.

43. Netterstrom, 'Introduction'; Dewald, *European Nobility*, 33–6; Neuschel, *Word of Honor*, 186–208; Carroll, *Blood and Violence*, 5–15, 307–11; James, 'English politics', 316–25; Bernard, *Early Tudor Nobility*, 185–93; Ferguson, *Chivalric Tradition*, 107–25.

44. Stevenson, *Chivalry and Knighthood*, 131–69; Mair, *History*, 30–1, 190, 199–201, 217–19, 358–9, 383–5; Edington, *Court and Culture*, 84–8.

45. Melville, *Memoirs*, 272; Hume, *House of Douglas*, i, 35, 37, 47, 49; Brown, *Noble Society*, chs 8–10; Allan, *Philosophy and Politics*, chs 1–3; McKean, *Scottish Chateaux*, 183–212.

46. Murray, *Poems*, unpaginated; Drummond, *Poems*, 129–42, 170, 219.

47. *Kilravock*, 79–80. For church seating see the cases at Largo, *RPC*, first ser., viii, 83, 106, 145, 153–4, 194, 196, 248, 350–1; Duns, *RPC*, first ser., ix, 100–2; Fettercairn, *RPC*, first ser., x, 208; Peterhead, *RPC*, first ser., xii, 652–5, 667–8, 699–700, 710–11, 724–7, 733,

735–6, 738; xiii, 69, 71, 76–7, 86–90; Carnbee, *RPC*, second ser., ii, 361–2; and see also GD 124/15/97 for the 1633 letter from Patrick Falconer of Newton to the second earl of Mar regarding church seating. For the medieval church and peacemaking see Bossy, 'Blood and baptism'; Bossy, 'Holiness and society', 130–5; and for parallel disputes in Catholic France, Carroll, *Blood and Violence*, 65–73.

48. Spottiswoode, *History*, iii, 62; Pearce, 'John Spottiswoode', 95–101; Brown, *Bloodfeud*, 184–6; Brown, *Noble Society*, 235–8 .

49. Melville, *Diary*, 16; Rollock, *Works*, i, 505; Bruce, *Sermons*, 335; Calderwood, *History*, v, 338; Todd, *Culture of Protestantism*, 249–61; Wormald, 'Bloodfeud', 93–5; Brown, *Bloodfeud*, 186–214.

50. NLS MS 79/19; *Melrose Papers*, ii, 617; *Maitland Miscellany*, i, pt. 2, 422; NAS GD 26/13/319.

51. Brown, *Bloodfeud*, chs 8–9 discusses this process in detail; for France, Carroll, *Blood and Violence*, 258–9, 285–305; Ranum, 'Courtesy', 428.

52. For Sanquhar, Calderwood, *History*, vii, 165. For Maxwell and Orkney, see above, 213–14.

53. NRA 237/i/D/6 November 1616; *RPC*, first ser., viii, 129; x, 45; Balfour, *Works*, ii, 42.

54. *RPC*, first ser., x, 595.

55. Gordon, *Sutherland*, 363; *RPC*, first ser., ix, 602–3, 622–3; for the Gordon–Forbes settlement, NAS GD 52/466–7; and see Brown, *Bloodfeud*, 243–5.

56. *RPC*, second ser., vi, 139, 143, 193–7, 238–40, 255–6.

57. Whyte, *Agriculture*, 97–8; *RPC*, second ser., v, 324–5; *RPS*, 1617/5/23; *HMC Laing*, i, 122–3. For disputes in the early seventeenth century, *RPC*, second ser., ii, 66–7; iv, 543–4; ix, 253; Fraser, *Sutherland*, ii, 126–7; Fraser, *Haddington*, ii, 129–30; NAS GD 86/368; NAS GD 124/8/102; *HMC Mar and Kellie*, i, 171–2; *Honorum de Morton*, i, 188.

58. *RPC*, first ser., vii, 402, 406; second ser., i, 526–7.

59. For Edzell, *RPC*, first ser., vii, 143, 161, 343, 383, 439, 448; Lindsay, *Lives*, i, 387–90; and for the other cases, NAS GD 38/2/1/34; *RPC*, second ser., iii, 224–5.

60. For Perth, *RPC*, first ser., vii, 222–6, 498; for Aberdeen, *RPC*, second ser., iv, 661–2.

61. For Nithsdale, *RPC*, first ser., xii, 644–5; for Buccleuch, Fraser, *Buccleuch*, ii, 266–8; for the Maxwell–Johnstone dispute, Fraser, *Annandale*, i, pp. clxxiii–clxxiv; *HMC*, xv, 41–2; NRA(S) 2312/113/198 ; and for other examples, *RPC*, first ser., xiii, 550–2, 564–6, 573–4, 675–7, 703–4, 722; second ser., i, 401–2; ii, 166.

62. *RPC*, second ser., ii, 484–6, 490–3, 533–5, 600; iii–vi, *passim*; Stirling, *Register*, ii, 762, 809 Spalding, *Memorial*, i, 13–14, 19, 43, appendix, No 1; Gordon, *Sutherland*, 412, 416–21, 461, 467–8, 474–9; Fraser, *Chiefs of Grant*, iii, 447–8; Lee, *Road to Revolution*, 172–5.

63. Goodare, *Government*, 220–4; Goodare, 'Statutes of Iona'; Macinnes, *Clanship*, 30–87; MacCoinnich, 'His spirit was given only to warre'.

64. Goodare, *Government*, 276–97. For a sceptical view of the civilising theory, chiefly in relation to France, Carroll, 'Introduction'; Carroll, *Blood and Violence*, 311–18; Nassiet, 'Vengeance'; Collins, *Classes, Estates and Order*, 28–9.

65. For some insights on his historical writing see Allan, 'Ane ornament', 39–44.

66. *RPC*, second ser., v, 487–8, 509–10; vi, 51–3, 60–1, 85.

67. Similar local disputes informed the early stages of civil war in England, Smith, *Country and Court*; Cogswell, *Home Divisions*; Beaver, 'Bragging and daring words'.

68. Asch, *Nobilities in Transition*, 103–12; Calderwood, *History*, vi, 582; Brown, *Noble Society*, 228–50; and for the wider context of an increasingly Protestant society see Graham, *Uses of Reform*; Todd, *Culture of Protestantism*.

69. MacDonald, *Jacobean Kirk*, 74–100; for an older view, Lee, 'James VI and the revival of episcopacy'.

70. MacDonald, *Jacobean Kirk*, 101–70; MacDonald, 'British ecclesiastical convergence'; Calderwood, *History*, vi, 263; Wells, 'Origins', 217–78.

71. Wormald, '"Princes" and the regions', 70–1; *Irish Franciscan Mission*; Macinnes,

'Catholic recusancy'; Brown, *Noble Society*, 244–9; Dewald, *European Nobility*, 181; Pearce, 'John Spottiswoode', 172–84; Wilson, *House of Airlie*, i, 151–5; Durkan, 'William Murdoch'.

72. Roberts, 'Popery'; *CSP Scotland*, xiii, 107; Lee, 'King James's popish chancellor', 171–2; quote from Lee, *Government by Pen*, 42; for other examples see Brown, *Noble Society*, 245–6. The treatment of Huntly was less severe than was meted out to loyal Catholic families in Ireland, see Edwards, *Ormond Lordship*, 263–5.

73. Elder, *Spanish Influences*, 312–15; Worthington, *Scots in Habsburg Service*, 73–9, 80–115; Murdoch, 'Introduction', 17.

74. Dawson, 'Clan, kin and kirk', 217–18.

75. *RPC*, first ser., vii, 500–1; second ser., iii, 237–42, 252–3, 321–5; *RPS*, 1607/3/13, A1609/1/3–5, 1609/4/16–19; Macinnes, 'Catholic recusancy'; Pearce, 'John Spottiswoode', 151–225.

76. Pearce, 'John Spottiswoode', 195–215; Roberts, 'Popery'; Spalding, *Memorial*, 66–71; *RPC*, second ser., vi, 9–11, 16; Hibbard, *Charles I and the Popish Plot*.

77. *Synod of Fife*, 24, 68–9, 116–19; Muir, 'Covenanters in Fife', 55–94.

78. For the commissions of 1610, 1615 and 1634, see Calderwood, *History*, vii, 58–9, 206, 384–5; Baillie, *Letters and Journals*, i, 424–5; McMahon, 'Scottish courts of high commission'; MacDonald, *Jacobean Kirk*, 152–5.

79. Hume, *Hymns*; Mullan, *Scottish Puritanism*, 20.

80. Kirk, 'Royal and lay patronage', 145; *HMC Various*, V, 127; *RPC*, second ser., iii, 500–1; *Maitland Miscellany*, i, 60–1, 64.

81. See the contrasting views of the so-called Jacobean compromise in Foster, *Church before the Covenants*; Mullan, *Scottish Puritanism*; MacDonald, *Jacobean Kirk*, 101–88; Wells, 'Origins', 17–59; Stewart, 'Brothers in truth'.

82. *RPC*, first ser., vii, 478–80; Pitcairn, *Criminal Trials*, ii, 494–504; Calderwood, *History*, vi, 286, 374, 388, 486; Melville, *Diary*, 575; NLS MS 20,772/1–2; MacDonald, 'James VI and the general assembly', 178–82; Pearce, 'John Spottiswoode', 61–8; Lee, *Government by Pen*, 62–70.

83. *RPS*, 1605/6/98–9, 1605/6/101, 1605/6/105, 1605/6/110, 1605/6/124–5, 1605/6/130–1.

84. *HMC*, vii, 722–3; Calderwood, *History*, vi, 757, 769; vii, 27, 104, 107.

85. *RPC*, first ser., vii, 347–8, 376–7, 385–91, 401, 413; Calderwood, *History*, vi, 649–53; Balfour, *Works*, ii, 22; McDonald, *Jacobean Kirk*, 124–47.

86. *HMC Laing*, i, 102–3; Calderwood, *History*, vii, 225; NAS GD 8/246–7, 287, 289; Pearce, 'John Spottiswoode', 91; Brown, *Noble Society*, 229–38.

87. Pearce, 'John Spottiswoode', 106–9; McMahon, 'Scottish courts of high commission';

88. NAS GD 26/10/8; NAS GD 112/39/53/11; Macinnes, *Charles I*, 155; Baillie, *Letters and Journals*, i, 7; Lee, *Road to Revolution*, 49–51, 57.

89. *Memorials of Montrose*, i, 70; Leslie, *Relation*, 1–2.

90. *Second Book*, 122–4; Mullan, *Scottish Puritanism*, 118–20, 281–4; *CSP Scotland*, xiii, 629–30.

91. Fraser, *Haddington*, ii, 154–5; Fraser, *Pollok*, 79–81, 85, 87; Balfour, *Works*, ii, 128; *Mar and Kellie*, ii, 140; Macinnes, *Charles I*, 57–72; Macinnes, *British Revolutions*, 86–93; Lee, *Road to Revolution*, 24–9, 34–6, 43–78, 91–2, 163–8, 202. See the advice given to friends by chancellor Dunfermline and chancellor Hay, *Innes*, 206; NAS GD 112/39/35/3, 112/39/35/12.

92. Fraser, *Eglinton*, i, 233; *HMC Mar and Kellie*, i, 139–40, 151–3; Fraser, *Haddington*, ii, 148, 150–1; NAS GD 124/15/92/2; *HMC Mar and Kellie*, i, 160–2; *Ancram and Lothian*, i, 80; Lee, *Road to Revolution*, 50–2, 61; Macinnes, *Charles I*, 54, 60–6. In 1635 the first earl of Haddington wrote detailed papers on the subject of the financial losses incurred by the lords of erection due to the revocation, NAS GD 406/1/315.

93. Adamson, 'Making of the *ancien-régime* court', 24–7.

94. Fraser, *Wemyss*, iii, 44; Calderwood, *History*, vii, 223, 246–7, 284, 304, 322–3, 391;

viii, 250; MacDonald, *Jacobean Kirk*, 148–70; MacDonald, 'James VI and the general assembly', 182–4; Pearce, 'John Spottiswoode', 28–2; MacKay, 'Reception'; Stewart, 'Brothers in truth'.

95. Mullan, *Scottish Puritanism*, 280; Calderwood, *History*, vii, 273–82; Wells, 'Origins', 63–4. Manuscript copies of the 'Life and death of that reverend father Maister Patrick Symsone' and 'Ane apologetike against ane false pretendit palmod of Mr Archibald Symsone' survive in the Leven and Melville archive, NAS GD 26/10/5. Lord Melville also had in his possession John Forbes's narrative concerning Catholic activities in 1607, and the bishops' 1631 objections to the direction of the commission of surrenders and teinds, GD 26/10/3 and 26/10/7.

96. Wells, 'Origins', 60–98; *RPC*, first ser., xi, 595–6, 598–600; Calderwood, *History*, vii, 359, 383; Stevenson, 'Conventicles'; Stewart, 'Brothers in truth', 167.

97. Calderwood, *History*, vii, 475–500; Goodare, 'Scottish parliament of 1621'; Muir, 'Covenanters in Fife', 55–94.

98. Spottiswoode, *History*, iii, 262–3; NLS MS 21,174/64; Lee, *Government by Pen*, 188–9; Muir, 'Covenanters in Fife', 57–72; Stewart, *Urban Politics*, 172–8, 195–7.

99. Lee, *Government by Pen*, 191–208; Stewart, *Urban Politics*, 198–222; Macinnes, *Charles I*, 141–7.

100. *Ancram and Lothian*, i, 35–8; NAS GD 112/39/38/7; Fraser, *Melvilles*, i, 130; *Select Biographies*, i, 397; NLS MS 81/14; Macinnes, *Charles I*, 128–32; Wells, 'Origins', 269–70, 272–3.

101. For Mar, NLS MS 5070/10; MS 5155/5, and also see 5070/31–1; for Haddington, NAS GD 158/2697/6, 158/2597/9, 158/2597/10, 158/2597/13; Wells, 'Origins', 99–133.

102. Spalding, *Memorials*, i, 79–80.

103. *HMC Mar and Kellie*, i, 172, 175.

104. NLS MS 79/56.

105. Mullan, *Scottish Puritanism*, 305–6; Rutherford, *Letters*, 236, 257, 457, 459, 520; *HMC Laing*, i, 198–9; *Select Biographies*, i, 381–2; Coffey, *Politics*, 41–2, 46–7, 233–5.

Conclusion

1. Scott, 'Early modern European nobility'.
2. Most importantly see Stone, *Crisis of the Aristocracy*; and for another example, see Bitton, *French Nobility in Crisis*.
3. Reuter, 'Medieval nobility'; Scott, 'Early modern European nobility'.
4. The broad thrust of this argument is supported by Scott, *Nobilities*, i–ii; Asch, *Nobilities in Transition*; Dewald, *European Nobility*; Scott 'Acts of time and power'. For sample case studies from Spain and France see Jago, 'Crisis of the aristocracy' and Wood, 'Decline of the nobility'; for a longitudinal study, Weary, 'House of la Tremouille'.
5. Brown, *Noble Society*.
6. Carroll, *Blood and Violence*.
7. Drummond, *History*, 262.
8. Asch, *Nobilities in Transition*, 9–29; Kaminski, 'The *szlachta*'.
9. Dewald, *Formation of a Provincial Nobility*; Bohannan, *Old and New Nobility*.
10. Brown, *Noble Society*.
11. Hume, *House of Douglas*, ii, 399.
12. Brown, *Noble Society*, 1–21 for the definition of nobility and their number.
13. Boyle, *Boyles of Kelburne*, 9–12; Mentzer, *Blood and Belief*; Astarita, *Continuity of Noble Power*.
14. *RPC*, second ser., i, 227–32.
15. Beik, *Absolutism and Society*; Collins, *Classes, Estates and Orders*; Neuschel, *Word of Honor*, 4–5.

Bibliography

(i) Manuscript Sources

National Archive of Scotland (NAS)

B	6/28	Burgh of Ayr
GD	8	Boyd Papers
GD	10	Broughton and Cally Muniments
GD	11	Bruce of Kennet Charters
GD	12	Swinton Charters
GD	17	Carnock and Plean Writs
GD	19	Kirkpatrick of Closeburn
GD	20	Crawford Priory Collection
GD	19	Closeburn Writs
GD	24	Abercairny Muniments
GD	25	Ailsa Muniments
GD	26	Leven and Melville Muniments
GD	28	Calendar of Yester Writs
GD	38	Dalguise Muniments
GD	39	Glencairn Muniments
GD	40	Lothian Muniments
GD	45	Dalhousie Muniments
GD	52	Lord Forbes Collection
GD	65	Inventory of Carlops and Abotskerse Muniments
GD	75	Inventory of Dundas of Dundas Papers
GD	77	Fergusson of Craigdarroch MSS
GD	84	Mackay Family, Lords Reay
GD	86	Fraser Charters
GD	96	Inventory of Mey Papers
GD	112	Breadalbane Muniments
GD	122	Little Gilmour of Craigmiller and Liberton
GD	124	Mar and Kellie Muniments
GD	137	Scrymgeour Wedderburn of Wedderburn Earl of Dundee
GD	150	Morton Papers
GD	158	Hume of Marchmont
GD	224	Buccleuch Muniments
GD	234/1	William Murray of Touchadam
GD	406	Hamilton Muniments (Correspondence)
JP	35/4/1	Justices of Peace of the City of Edinburgh, Record of Cases, 1613–1663
RH	11/46	Local Courts in Scotland, Stewartry of Kircudbright, 1625–1686
RH	11/54	Local Courts in Scotland, Stewartry of Menteith, 1629–1733
RH	11/68	Local Courts in Scotland, Regality of Torphichen, 1470–1830
SC	1	Aberdeen Sheriff Court
SC	47/1	Forfar Sheriff Court
SC	67/1	Stirling Sheriff Court

National Register of Archives (Scotland) (NRA(S))
217   Moray MSS
237   Inventory of the Scottish Muniments at Haigh
885   Charters and Documents From Glamis Dated 1329–1668
2312   Stirling-Maxwell of Pollok

National Library of Scotland (NLS)
MS 75, 78–84, 86	Morton Chartulary and Papers, vols 3, 6–12
MS 3,416	Mure of Rowallan
MS 3,724	Court Book of the Barony of Calder
MS 5,070, 5,155	Erskine Murray Papers
MS 6,406	Pitfarrane Papers
MS 5787	Newbattle Collection
MS 7,102, 14,480	Yester Papers
MS 20,772, 20,777, 20,793	Fleming of Wigton
MS 21,174, 21,187A,	
21,183	Murray of Auchertyre
MS 15.2.14, 15.2.18,	
15.2.31, 17.2.4,	
25.2.2, 33.7.26,	
32.6.8, 33.2.28,	
33.2.38, 33.7.5,	
33.7.26, 34.4.16	Advocates Library

British Library (BL)
Add MSS 12,496/41
Hl 7623/9

(ii) Printed Sources

Abbreviations for Historical Associations, Clubs and Societies (publication)
AC   Abbotsford Club (Edinburgh)
AWAA   Ayrshire and Wigtonshire Archaeological Association (Edinburgh)
BC   Bannatyne Club (Edinburgh)
GC   Grampian Club (London)
MC   Maitland Club (Glasgow)
SC   Spalding Club (Aberdeen)
SHS   Scottish History Society (Edinburgh)
SpS   Spottiswoode Society (Edinburgh)
StS   Stair Society (Edinburgh)
STS   Scottish Text Society (Edinburgh)
WS   Wodrow Society (Edinburgh)

[*Abbotsford Miscellany*] *Miscellany of the Abbotsford Club* (ed.) J. Maidment (AC 11, 1837).

[*Aberdeen Council Register*] *Extracts from the Council Register of the Burgh of Aberdeen 1625–1642* (ed.) J. Stuart (Edinburgh, 1871).

[*Ancram and Lothian*] *Correspondence of Sir Robert Kerr, first Earl of Ancram, and his son, William, third Earl of Lothian* (ed.) D. Laing, 2 vols (BC, 125, 1875).

[Baillie, *Letters and Journals*] *Letters and Journals of Robert Baillie*, R. Baillie (ed.) D. Laing, 3 vols (BC, 73, 1841–2).

[Balfour, *Works*] *Historical Works of Sir James Balfour*, J. Balfour (ed.) J. Haig, 4 vols (Edinburgh, 1825).

[Bannatyne, *Memorials*] *Memorials of Transactions in Scotland. AD MDLXIX–MDLXXIII*, R. Bannatyne (ed.) R. Pitcairn (BC, 51, 1836).

Bannatyne Miscellany, 3 vols (BC, 19, 1827, 1836, 1855).

['Barons of Alloway'] 'The barons of Alloway, 1324–1754' (ed.) A. Hendry, *Ayrshire Archaeological and Natural History Society. Ayrshire Monograph* 10 (Ayr, 1882).

[*Barony of Carnwath*] *Court Book of the Barony of Carnwath, 1523–1542* (ed.) W. C. Dickinson (SHS, third series, 29, 1837).

[*Barony and Regality of Falkirk and Callendar*], *Court Book of the Barony and Regality of Falkirk and Callendar, Vol. 1:1638–1656* (ed.) D. M. Hunter (StS, 38, 1991).

[*Barony of Urie*] *Court Book of the Barony of Urie in Kincardineshire 1604–1747* (ed.) D. G. Barron (SHS, first series, 12, 1892).

Black Book of Taymouth (ed.) C. Innes (Edinburgh, 1855).

Brockington, W. S. (ed.), *Munro, His Expedition with the Worthy Scots Regiment Called Mac-keys* (London, 1999).

[Bruce, *Sermons*], *Sermons by the Rev. Robert Bruce* (ed.) W. Cunningham (WS, 6, 1843).

[Buchanan, *Vernacular Writings*], *Vernacular Writings of George Buchanan* (STS OS, 26, 1892).

[*BUK*] *Booke of the Universall Kirk of Scotland: Acts and Proceedings of the General Assemblies of the Kirk of Scotland from the Year MDLX* (ed.) T. Thomson, 4 vols (BC, 81 and MC, 49, 1894–6).

[Calderwood, *History*] *History of the Kirk of Scotland*, D. Calderwood, 8 vols (WS, 7, 1842–9).

[*CBP*], *Calendar of Letters and Papers, Relating to the Affairs of the Borders of England and Scotland* (ed.) J. Bain, 2 vols (Edinburgh, 1894–6).

[*CSP Scotland*] *Calendar of State Papers Relating to Scotland and Mary, Queen of Scots, 1547–1603* (ed.) J. Bain *et al.*, 13 vols (Edinburgh, 1898–1969).

[*CSP Spanish*], *Calendar of Letters and State Papers, Spanish, Elizabeth* (eds) M. A. S. Hume *et al.*, 10 vols (London, 1892–1954).

Calvin, *Institutes of the Christian Religion*, trans. H. Beveridge, 2 vols (Edinburgh, 1849).

[Carlisle, *Enquiry*] *An Enquiry into the Place and Quality of the Privy Chamber*, N. Carlisle (London, 1929).

Chronicle of Perth. A Register of Remarkable Occurrences, Chiefly Connected with that City, from the Year 1210 to 1668 (MC, 10, 1831).

Chronicles of the Frasers, J. Fraser (SHS, first series, 47, 1905).

Chronicle of the Kings of Scotland, from Fergus the First to James the Sixth (MC 8, 1830).

Clan Campbell Letters, 1559–1583 (ed.) J. E. A. Dawson (SHS, fifth series, 10, 1997).

[Craig, *Jus Feudale*] *Jus Feudale*, T. Craig, trans. J. A. Clyde, 2 vols (Edinburgh, 1934).

[Dalrymple, *Institutions*] *Institutions of the Law of Scotland*, J. Dalrymple (ed.) D. M. Walker (Edinburgh and Glasgow, 1981).

Diurnal of Remarkable Occurrents (ed.) T. Thomson (MC, 46, 1833).

[Douglas, *Palice*] *Palice of Honour. By Gawyn Douglas, Bishop of Dunkeld*, G. Douglas (ed.) J. G. Kinnear (BC, 17, 1827).

Drummond, W., *The History of Scotland. From the Year 1423 until the Year 1542* (London, 1655).

[Drummond, *Poems*] *Poems of William Drummond of Hawthornden*, W. Drummond (ed.) T. Maitland (MC, 18, 1832).

[*Early Travellers*] *Early Travellers in Scotland* (ed.) P. H. Brown (Edinburgh, reprinted, 1973).

[*Estimate*] *Estimate of the Scottish Nobility during the Minority of James VI* (ed.) C. Rogers (GC, 6, 1873).

[*First Book*] *First Book of Discipline* (ed.) J. K. Cameron (Edinburgh, 1972).

[Fraser, *Annandale*] *Annandale Family Book of Johnstones*, W. Fraser, 2 vols (Edinburgh, 1894).

[Fraser, *Buccleuch*] *Scotts of Buccleuch*, W. Fraser, 2 vols (Edinburgh, 1878).

[Fraser, *Carlaverock*] *Book of Carlaverock*, W. Fraser, 2 vols (Edinburgh, 1873).

[Fraser, *Chiefs of Grant*] *Chiefs of Grant*, W. Fraser, 3 vols (Edinburgh, 1883).

[Fraser, *Douglas*] *Douglas Book. Memoirs of the House of Douglas and Angus*, W. Fraser, 4 vols (Edinburgh, 1885).

[Fraser, *Eglinton*] *Memorials of the Montgomeries of Eglinton*, W. Fraser, 2 vols (Edinburgh, 1859).

[Fraser, *Elphinstone*] *Elphinstone Family Book*, W. Fraser, 2 vols (Edinburgh, 1897).

[Fraser, *Haddington*] *Memorials of the Earls of Haddington*, W. Fraser, 2 vols (Edinburgh, 1889).

[Fraser, *Maxwells of Pollok*] *Memoirs of the Maxwells of Pollok*, W. Fraser (Edinburgh, 1875).

[Fraser, *Melvilles*] *Melvilles Earls of Melville and the Leslies Earls of Leven*, W. Fraser, 3 vols (Edinburgh, 1890).

[Fraser, *Menteith*] *Red Book of Menteith*, W. Fraser, 2 vols (Edinburgh, 1880).

[Fraser, *Sutherland*] *Sutherland Book*, W. Fraser, 3 vols (Edinburgh, 1892).

[Fraser, *Wemyss*] *Memorial of the Family of Wemyss*, W. Fraser, 3 vols (Edinburgh, 1888).

[Gardyne, *Garden*] *Garden of Grave and Godlie Flowers, by Alexander Gardyne* (ed.) W. B. D. D. Turnbull (AC, 36, 1845).

[Gordon, *Scots Affairs*] Gordon, J., *A History of Scots Affairs from MDCXXXVII to MDCXLI* (eds) J. Robertson and G. Grub, 3 vols (SC, 1841).

[Gordon, *Short Abridgement of Britane's Distemper*] *Short Abridgement of Britane's Distemper from the Year of God MDCXXXIX to MDXLIX*, P. Gordon (SC, 10, 1844).

[Gordon, *Sutherland*] *Genealogical History of the Earldom of Sutherland*, R. Gordon (Edinburgh, 1813).

[*HMC Hamilton Supplementary*] *Historical Manuscripts Commission. Supplementary Report of the Manuscripts of the Duke of Hamilton* (London, 1932).

[Herries, *Memoirs*] *Historical Memoirs of the Reign of Mary Queen of Scots and a Portion of the Reign of King James the Sixth* (ed.) R. Pitcairn (AC, 6, 1836).

[*Historie*] *Historie and Life of King James the Sext* (ed.) T. Thomson (BC, 14, 1825).

[*HMC*] *Historical Manuscripts Commission*, 15 vols (London, 1871–97).

[*HMC Buccleuch*] *Historical Manuscript Commission. Buccleuch*, 3 vols (London, 1899, 1903, 1926).

[*HMC Various*] *Historical Manuscripts Commission. Various Collections, V* (London, 1909).

[*HMC Laing*] *Historical Manuscripts Commission. Report on the Laing Manuscripts*, i (London, 1914).

[*HMC Mar and Kellie*] *Historical Manuscripts Commission: Mar and Kellie*, 2 vols (London, 1904, 1930).

[*Honorum de Morton*] *Registrum Honorum de Morton* (ed.) T. Thomson, 2 vols (BC, 94, 1853).

[Hope, *Diary*] *Diary of the Public Correspondence of Sir Thomas Hope of Craighall, bart., 1633–1645*, T. Hope (ed.) T. Thomson (BC, 76, 1843).

[Hope, *Major Practicks*] *Hope's Major Practicks, 1608–33*, T. Hope (ed.) J. A. Clyde, 2 vols (StS, 3–4, 1937–8).

House of Forbes (eds) A. Tayler and H. Tayler (Third SC, 8, 1937).

House of Gordon (ed.) J. M. Bulloch, 2 vols (New SC, 1903, 1907).

[*House of Seytoun*] *History of the House of Seytoun to the Year MDLIX. By Sir Richard Maitland of Lethington, Knight. With the Continuation, by Alexander Viscount Kingston, to MDCLXXXVII*, R. Maitland (ed.) J. Fullarton (MC, 1, 1829).

[Hume, *De Unione*] *The British Union. A Critical Edition and Translation of David Hume of Godscroft's De Unione Insulae Britaniae* (eds) P. J. McGinnis and A. H. Williamson (Aldershot, 2002).

[Hume, *General History*] *General History of Scotland from the Year 767 to the Death of King James*, D. Hume (London, 1657).

[Hume, *House of Douglas*] *David Hume of Godscroft's The History of the House of Douglas*, D. Hume (ed.) D. Reid, 2 vols (STS, fourth series, 25–6, Edinburgh, 1996).

[Hume, *House of Angus*] *David Hume of Godscroft's The History of the House of Angus*, 2 vols (STS, fifth series, 4–5, Edinburgh, 2005).

[Hume, *Hymns*] *Hymns and Sacred Songs*, A. Hume, presented by J. G. Kinnear (BC 41, 1832).

[Hyde, *History*] *History of the Rebellion*, E. Hyde, 7 vols (Oxford, 1849).

[*Innes*] *Account of the Familie of Innes, compiled by Duncan Forbes of Culloden, 1698* (ed.) C. Innes (SC, 34, 1864).

Irish Franciscan Mission to Scotland, 1619–46 (ed.) C. Giblin (Dublin, 1964).

John Knox. On Rebellion (ed.) R. Mason (Cambridge, 1994).

[Kellie, *Pallas Armata*] *Pallas Armata or Military Instructions for the Learned*, T. Kellie (Edinburgh, 1627).

[*Kennedy*] *Historical Account of the Principal Families of Kennedy* (ed.) R. Pitcairn (Edinburgh, 1830).

[*Kilravock*] *Genealogical Deduction of the Family of Rose of Kilravock* (ed.) C. Innes (SC, 1848).

[Knox, *History*] *John Knox's History of the Reformation* (ed.) W. C. Dickinson, 2 vols (Edinburgh, 1949).

[Knox, *Works*] *Works of John Knox*, J. Knox, ed. D. Laing, 6 vols (WS, 12, 1846–52).

Leith, W. F. (ed.), *Narratives of Scottish Catholics under Mary Stuart and James VI* (Edinburgh, 1885).

[Leslie, *Historie*] *Historie of Scotland*, J. Leslie (ed.) E. J. Cody, 2 vols (STS, 1888–95).

[Leslie, *Relation*] *A Relation of Proceedings Concerning the Affairs of the Kirk of Scotland from August 1637 to July 1638*, J. Leslie, earl of Rothes (ed.) D. Laing (BC, 40, 1830).

Letters and State Papers during the Reign of King James the Sixth (ed.) J. Maidment (AC 13, 1838).

Lindsay, R., *Ane Satyre of the Thrie Estaits*, introduced by R. Lyall (Edinburgh, 1989).

[Lindsay, *Historie*] *Historie and Chronicles of Scotland*, R. Lindsay (ed.) A. J. G. Mackay, 3 vols (STS, 1899–1911).

[Lithgow, *Poetical Remains*] *Poetical Remains of William Lithgow*, W. Lithgow (ed.) J. Maidment (Edinburgh, 1863).

[*Maitland Miscellany*] *Miscellany of the Maitland Club* (eds) J. Dennistoun and A. Macdonald, 4 vols (vol. i in two parts) (MC, 25–6, 53, 59, 69, 1840–7).

[Maitland, *Poems*] *Poems of Sir Richard Maitland*, R. Maitland (ed.) J. Bain (MC, 4, 1830).

[Mair, *History*] Mair, J., *A History of Greater Britain as well England as Scotland* (ed.) A. Constable (SHS, 10, 1892).

[*Melrose Papers*] *State Papers and Miscellaneous Correspondence of Thomas, Earl of Melrose* (ed.) J. Maidment, 2 vols (AC, 9, 1837).

[Melville, *Diary*] *Diary of Mr James Melvill, 1556–1601*, J. Melville (ed.) J. R. Kinloch (BC, 34, 1829).

[Melville, *Memoirs*] *Memoirs of His Own Life, 1549–93*, J. Melville (ed.) T. Thomson (BC, 18, 1827).

Memorials of Montrose and his Times (ed.) M. Napier, 2 vols (MC, 66, 1848–50)

Memorials of the Earl of Stirling and the House of Alexander (ed.) C. Rogers, 2 vols (Edinburgh, 1877).

'Military report on the districts of Carrick, Kyle and Cunningham. Prepared by an English official between the years 1563 and 1566' (ed.) R. B. Armstrong (*AWAA* 4, 1884), iv, 1–25.

Minutes of the Justices of the Peace for Lanarkshire 1707–1723 (ed.) C. A. Malcolm (SHR, third series, 17, 1931).

Miscellany of the Scottish History Society: Vol. I (SHS, first series, 15, 1893).

[Moysie, *Memoirs*] *Memoirs of the Affairs of Scotland from 1577 to 1603*, D. Moysie (ed.) J. Dennistoun (BC, 39, 1830).

Muniments of the Royal Burgh of Irvine, 2 vols (AWAA, 1890–1).

[Murray, *Poems*] *Poems of Sir David Murray of Gothry*, D. Murray, presented by T. Kinnear (BC, 22, 1823).

[Napier, *Plaine Discovery*] *Plaine Discovery of the Whole Revelation*, J. Napier (Edinburgh, 1593).

[Nichols, *Progresses*], J. Nichols (ed.), *The Progresses of James the First*, 4 vols (London, 1828).

[Nisbet, *System of Heraldry*] *System of Heraldry, Speculative and Practical*, A. Nisbet, 2 vols (Edinburgh, 1984 [1722]).

Oppressions of the Sixteenth Century in the Islands of Orkney and Zetland (ed.) D. Balfour (AC, 31, 1859).

[Pitcairn, *Criminal Trials*] *Criminal Trials in Scotland from 1488 to 1624* (ed.) R. Pitcairn, 3 vols (Edinburgh, 1833).

[*Political Writings*] *King James VI and I Political Writings*, J. Stewart (ed.) J. P. Sommerville (Cambridge, 1994).

[Pont, *Topographical Account*] *Topographical Account of the District of Cunningham, Ayrshire. Compiled about the Year 1600, by Mr Timothy Pont*, T. Pont (MC, 76, 1858).

[*RPS*] *Records of the Parliaments of Scotland to 1707* (eds) K. M. Brown *et al.* (St Andrews, 2007–9), see http://www.rps.ac.uk.

[*Regality of Melrose*] *Selections from the Records of the Regality of Melrose, 1605–1661* (ed.) C. S. Romanes, 3 vols (SHS, second series, 6–7, 13, 1914–15, 1917).

Regiam Majestatem and Quoniam Attachiamenta (ed.) T. M. Cooper (StS, 11, 1947).

Registrum de Panmure, J. Stuart, 2 vols (Edinburgh, 1874).

[*RPC*] *Register of the Privy Council of Scotland*, first series (eds) J. H. Burton *et al.*, 14 vols (Edinburgh, 1877–98).

[*RPC*] *Register of the Privy Council of Scotland*, second series (eds) D. Masson and P. H. Brown, 8 vols (Edinburgh, 1899–1908).

[Rollock, *Works*] *Select Works*, R. Rollock (ed.) W. Gunn, 2 vols (WS, 1844–9).

[Row, *History*] *History of the Kirk of Scotland*, J. Row (ed.) D. Laing (WS, 4, 1842).

Rutherford, S., *Letters of Samuel Rutherford* (ed.) A. A. Bonar (Edinburgh, 1891).

[*Scots Brigade*], *Papers Illustrating the History of the Scots Brigade in the Services of the United Netherlands* (ed.) J. Ferguson, 3 vols (SHS, first series, 32, 35, 38, 1899, 1901).

[Scott, *Staggering State*] *Staggering State of Scottish Statesmen from 1550–1650*, J. Scott (ed.) C. Rogers (Edinburgh, 1872).

Secret History of the Court of James the First (ed.) W. Scott, 2 vols (Edinburgh, 1811).

[*Second Book*] *Second Book of Discipline* (ed.) J. Kirk (Edinburgh, 1980).

Select Biographies (ed.) W. K. Tweedie, 2 vols (WS, 9, 1845–7).

Selected Justiciary Cases, 1624–1650 (eds) A. Gillon and J. I. Brown, 3 vols (StS, 16, 27–8, 1953, 1972, 1974).

[*Sheriff Court of Aberdeenshire*] *Record of the Sheriff Court of Aberdeenshire*, 3 vols (NSC, 1904–6).

Sheriff Court Book of Fife, 1515–1522 (ed.) W. C. Dickinson (SHS, third series, 12, 1928).

[*Sheriffdoms of Lanark and Renfrew*] *Descriptions of the Sheriffdoms of Lanark and Renfrew Compiled about MDCCX* (ed.) J. Maidment (MC, 12, 1831).

[Spalding, *Memorial*] *Memorial of the Troubles in Scotland and in England. AD 1624–AD 1645. By John Spalding*, J. Spalding (ed.) J. Stuart, 2 vols (SC, 21, 23, 1850–1).

[*Spalding Miscellany*] *Miscellany of the Spalding Club* (ed.) J. Stuart, 5 vols (SC, 3, 6, 16, 20, 24, 1841–52).

[Spottiswoode, *History*] *History of the Church of Scotland*, J. Spottiswoode (eds) M. Napier and M. Russell, 3 vols (SpS, 6, 1847–51).

[Stirling, *Register*] *The Earl of Stirling's Register of Royal Letters, Relative to the Affairs of Scotland and Nova Scotia from 1615 to 1635* (ed.) C. Rogers, 2 vols (Edinburgh, 1885).

[*Synod of Fife*] *Ecclesiastical Records. Selections from the Minutes of the Synod of Fife, MDCXI–MDCLXXXVII* (ed.) G. R. Kinloch (AC, 8, 1837).

[Urquhart, *Jewel*] *The Jewel*, T. Urquhart (eds) R. D. S. Jack and R. J. Lyall (Edinburgh, 1983).

[Urquhart, *Works*] *Works of Sir Thomas Urquhart of Cromarty*, T. Urquhart (ed.) T. Maitland (MC 30, 1834).

[Waus, *Correspondence*] *Correspondence of Sir Patrick Waus* (ed.) R. Vans Agnew, 2 vols (Edinburgh, 1887).

(iii) Secondary Works: Books

Adams, S. (ed.), *Leicester and the Court. Essays on Elizabethan Politics* (Manchester, 2002).

Adamson, J. (ed.), *The Princely Courts of Europe: Ritual, Politics and Culture under the Ancien Régime 1500–1750* (London, 1999).

Adamson, J., *The Noble Revolt. The Overthrow of Charles I* (London, 2007).

Akrigg, G. P. V., *Jacobean Pageant or the Court of King James I* (London, 1962).

Allan, D., *Philosophy and Politics in Later Stuart Scotland: Neo-Stoicism, Culture and Ideology in an Age of Crisis, 1540–1690* (East Linton, 2000).

Anderson, M., *Approaches to the History of the Western Family* (Cambridge, 1995).

Anderson, P. D., *Robert Stewart Earl of Orkney Lord Of Shetland 1533–1593* (Edinburgh, 1983).

Anderson, P. D., *Black Patie. The Life and Times of Patrick Stewart Earl of Orkney, Lord of Shetland* (Edinburgh, 1992).

Anglo, S., *The Martial Arts of Renaissance Europe* (New Haven, CT, 2000).

Apted, M. R., *The Painted Ceilings of Scotland, 1550–1650* (Edinburgh, 1966).

Arbuthnot, P. S., *Memories of the Arbuthnots of Kincardineshire* (London, 1920).

Arnot, S., *The House of Arnot and Some of its Branches* (Edinburgh, 1918).

Asch, R. G. and A. M. Birke (eds), *Princes, Patronage and the Nobility* (Oxford, 1991).

Asch, R. G., *Nobilities in Transition 1550–1700. Courtiers and Rebels in Britain and Europe* (London, 2003).

Astarita, T., *The Continuity of Feudal Power: the Caracciolo di Brienza in Spanish Naples* (Cambridge, 1992).

Aylmer, G. E., *The King's Servants. The Civil Service of Charles I, 1625–1642* (London, 1974).

Aylmer, G. E. and J. Morrill (eds), *Land, Men and Beliefs. Studies in Early-Modern History* (London, 1983).

Banac, I. and P. Bushkovitch (eds), *Nobility in Russia and Eastern Europe* (Columbus, OH, 1983)

Bardgett, F., *Scotland Reformed. The Reformation in Angus and the Mearns* (Edinburgh, 1989).

Barrow, G. W. S., *Anglo-Norman Era in Scottish History* (Oxford, 1980).

Bartlett, R., *'Mortal Enmities': the Legal Aspects of Hostility in the Middle Ages* (Aberystweth, 1998).

Barton, S., *The Aristocracy in Twelfth-Century Leon and Castile* (Cambridge, 1997).

Bath, M., *Renaissance Decorative Painting in Scotland* (Edinburgh, 2003).

Baxter, D. C., *Servants of the Sword: French Intendants of the Army, 1630–70* (Urbana, DC, 1976).

Bean, J. M. W., *From Lord to Patron: Lordship in Late Medieval England* (Manchester, 1989).

Beik, W., *Absolutism and Society in Seventeenth-Century France: State Power and Provincial Aristocracy in Languedoc* (Cambridge, 1988).

Bellamy, J., *The Law of Treason in England in the Late Middle Ages* (Cambridge, 1970).

Bellamy, J., *The Tudor Law of Treason in England in the Late Middle Ages* (London, 1979).

Benadusi, G., *A Provincial Elite in Early Modern Tuscany. Family and Power in the Creation of the State* (Baltimore, MD and London, 1996).

Bernard, G. W., *The Power of the Early Tudor Nobility. A Study of the Fourth and Fifth Earls of Shrewsbury* (Brighton, 1985).

Bernard, G. W. (ed.), *The Tudor Nobility* (Manchester, 1992).

Bitton, D., *The French Nobility in Crisis 1560–1640* (Stanford, CA, 1969).

Black, J., *European Warfare 1494–1660* (London, 2002).

Blake, W., *William Maitland of Lethington 1528–1573. A Study of the Policy of Moderation in the Scottish Reformation* (New York, 1970).

Bloch, M., *Feudal Society* (London, 1978).

Bloch, R. H., *Etymologies and Geneaologies. A Literary Anthropology of the French Middle Ages* (Chicago, IL, 1983).

Boardman, S., *The Campbells, 1250–1513* (Edinburgh, 2006).

Bohannan, D., *Old and New Nobility in Aix-en-Provence 1600–1675* (Baton Rouge, LA, 1992).

Bohannan, D., *Crown and Nobility in Early Modern France* (Basingstoke, 2001).

Bonney, R., *The European Dynastic States 1494–1660* (Oxford, 1992).

Bossy, J. (ed.), *Disputes and Settlements: Law and Human Relations in the West* (Cambridge, 1983).

Bouchard, C. B., *Strong of Body, Brave and Noble: Chivalry and Society in Medieval France* (Ithaca, NY, 1998).

Bouchard, C. B., *Those of My Blood: Constructing Noble Families in Medieval Francia* (Philadelphia, PA, 2001).

Boyd, *Pedigree of the House of Boyd* (1904), private printing by the Boyd family.

Boyle, R., *Genealogical Account of the Boyles of Kelburne Earls of Glasgow* (Glasgow, 1904).

Boynton, *The Elizabethan Militia 1558–1638* (London, 1967).

Braddick, M. J. and J. Walter (eds), *Negotiating Power. Order, Hierarchy and Subordination in Britain and Ireland* (Cambridge, 2001).

Brockliss, L. W. B., *French Higher Education in the Seventeenth and Eighteenth Centuries* (Oxford, 1987)

Brown, K. M., *Bloodfeud in Scotland, 1573–1625: Violence, Justice and Politics in an Early Modern Society* (Edinburgh, 1986).

Brown, K. M., *Kingdom or Province? Scotland and the Regal Union 1603–1715* (Basingstoke, 1992).

Brown, K. M., *Noble Society in Scotland. Wealth, Family and Culture from the Reformation to the Revolution* (Edinburgh, 2000).

Brown, K. M. and R. J. Tanner (eds), *The History of the Scottish Parliament, Vol. 1: Parliament and Politics in Scotland 1235–1560* (Edinburgh, 2004)

Brown, K. M. and A. J. Mann (eds), *The History of the Scottish Parliament, Vol. 2: Parliament and Politics in Scotland 1567–1707* (Edinburgh, 2005).

Brown, K. M. and A. R. MacDonald (eds), *The History of the Scottish Parliament, Vol. 3: Parliament in Context, 1235–1707* (Edinburgh, 2011).

Brown, M., *James I* (East Linton, 1994).

Brown, M., *The Black Douglases* (East Linton, 1998).

Brunner, O., *Land and Lordship: Structures of Goverance in Medieval Austria*, trans. H. Kaminsky and J. Van Horn Melton (Philadelphia, PA, 1992).

Brunton, G. and D. Haig, *An Historical Account of the Senators of the College of Justice* (Edinburgh, 1836).

Burke, P., *The Fortunes of the Courtier: the European Reception of Castiglione's Cortegiano* (University Park, PA, 1996).

Burns, J. H., *The True Law of Kingship. Concepts of Monarchy in Early Modern Scotland* (Oxford, 1996).

Bush, M. L., *The European Nobility Vol. 1: Noble Privilege* (Manchester, 1983).

Bushnell, R. W., *A Culture of Teaching. Early Modern Humanism in Theory and Practice* (Ithaca, NY and London, 1996).

Caldwell, D. H. (ed.), *Scottish Weapons and Fortifications 1100–1800* (Edinburgh, 1981).

Cameron, J., *James V. The Personal Rule 1528–1542* (East Linton, 1998).

Campbell, A., *A History of the Clan Campbell*, 2 vols (Edinburgh, 2000, 2002).

Carey, V. P., *Surviving the Tudors. The 'Wizard' Earl of Kildare and English Rule in Ireland, 1537–1586* (Dublin, 2002).

Carroll, S., *Noble Power During the French Wars of Religion. The Guise Affinity and the Catholic Cause in Normandy* (Cambridge, 1998).

Carroll, S., *Blood and Violence in Early Modern France* (Oxford, 2006).

Carroll, S. (ed.), *Cultures of Violence. Interpersonal Violence in Historical Perspective* (Basingstoke, 2007).

Caruthers, M., *The Book of Memory. A Study of Memory in Medieval Culture* (Cambridge, 1990).

Cathcart, A., *Kinship and Clientage. Highland Clanship 1451–1609* (Leiden, 2006).

Coffey, J., *Politics, Religion and the British Revolutions. The Mind of Samuel Rutherford* (Cambridge, 1997).

Cogswell, T., *Home Divisions. Aristocracy, the State and Provincial Conflict* (Manchester, 1998).

Collins, J., *Classes, Estates and Order in Early Modern Brittany* (Cambridge, 1994).

Cooper, J., *Scottish Renaissance Armies 1513–1550* (Oxford, 2008).

Corvisier, A., *Armies and Societies in Europe, 1494–1789*, trans. A. T. Siddall (Bloomington, IN, 1979).

Cowan, I. B., *Regional Aspects of the Scottish Reformation* (Historical Association, 1978).

Cowan, I. B., *The Scottish Reformation. Church and Society in Sixteenth-Century Scotland* (London, 1982).

Cowan, I. B. and D. Shaw (eds), *The Renaissance and Reformation in Scotland* (Edinburgh, 1983).

Coward, B., *The Stanleys. Lords Stanley and Earls of Derby 1385–1672. The Origins, Wealth and Power of a Landowning Family*, Chetham Society, third series, xxx (Manchester, 1983).

Cramsie, J., *Kingship and Crown Finance under James VI and I, 1603–1625* (Woodbridge, 2002).

Croft, P., *King James* (Basingstoke, 2003).

Cross, C., *The Puritan Earl. The Life of Henry Hastings, Third Earl of Huntingdon, 1536–1595* (London, 1966).

Crouch, D., *The Birth of Nobility. Constructing Aristocracy in England and France 900–1300* (Harlow, 2005).

Cruickshank, C. G., *Elizabeth's Army* (Oxford, 1966).

Crumney, R. O., *Aristocrats and Servitors. The Boyar Elite in Russia, 1613–1689* (Princeton, NJ, 1983).

Cuttler, S. H., *The True Law of Treason and Treason Trials in Later Medieval France* (Cambridge, 1981).

Davies, N., *God's Playground. A History of Poland*, 2 vols (Oxford, 1981).

Davies, R. R., *Lordship and Society in the March of Wales, 1282–1400* (Oxford, 1978).

Davies, R. R., *Lords and Lordship in Late Medieval Society* (Oxford 2009).

Davis, N., *The Gift in Sixteenth-Century France* (Oxford, 2000).

Dawson, J. E. A., *The Politics of Religion in the Age of Mary, Queen of Scots. The Earl of Argyll and the Struggle for Britain and Ireland* (Cambridge, 2002).

Dewald, J., *The Formation of a Provincial Nobility: the Magistrates of the Parlement of Rouen, 1499–1610* (Princeton, NJ, 1980).

Dewald, J., *Pont-St-Pierre, 1398–1789: Lordship, Community and Capitalism in Early Modern France* (Berkeley, CA, 1987).

Dewald, J., *Aristocratic Experience and the Origins of Modern Culture. France, 1570–1715* (Berkeley, CA, 1993).

Dewald, J., *The European Nobility 1400–1800* (Cambridge, 1996).

Dodgshon, R. A., *From Chiefs to Landlords. Social and Economic Change in the Western Highlands and Islands, c. 1493–1820* (Edinburgh, 1998).

Donald, P., *An Uncounselled King. Charles I and the Scottish Troubles 1637–1641* (Cambridge, 1990).

Donaldson, G., *The Scottish Reformation* (Cambridge, 1960).

Donaldson, G., *Scotland. James V to James VII* (Edinburgh, 1965).

Donaldson, G., *All The Queen's Men. Power and Politics in Mary Stewart's Scotland* (London, 1983).

Doran, L. and J. Lyttleton (eds), *Lordship in Medieval Ireland: Image and Reality* (Dublin, 2007).

Dow, J., *Ruthven's Army in Sweden and Estonia* (Stockholm, 1965).

Drell, J. H., *Kinship and Conquest. Family Structures in the Principality of Salerno During the Norman Period, 1077–1194* (Ithaca, NY, 2002).

Duby, G., *The Chivalrous Society* (London, 1977).

Duffy, S. (ed.), *The World of the Gallowglass. Kings, Warlords and Warriors in Ireland and Scotland, 1200–1600* (Dublin, 2007).

Duggan, A. J. (ed.), *Nobles and Nobility in Medieval Europe. Concepts, Origins and Transformations* (Woodbridge, 2000).

Dunbar, J. C., *Scottish Royal Palaces. The Architecture of Royal Residences during the Late Medieval and Early Renaissance Periods* (East Linton, 1999).

Duncan, A. A. M., *Scotland. The Making of the Kingdom* (Edinburgh, 1975).

Dunn, A., *The Politics of Magnate Power, England and Wales 1389–1413* (Oxford, 2003).

Durston, C., *The Family in the English Revolution* (Oxford, 1989).

Edington, C., *Court and Culture in Renaissance Scotland. Sir David Lindsay of the Mount* (East Linton, 1994).

Edwards, D., *The Ormond Lordship in County Kilkenny 1515–1642. The Rise and Fall of Butler Feudal Power* (Dublin, 2003).

Elder, J. R., *Spanish Influences in Scottish History* (Glasgow, 1920).

Elias, N., *The Court Society*, trans. E. Jephcott (New York, 1983).

Ellis, S., *Tudor Frontiers and Noble Power. The Making of the British State* (Oxford, 1995).

Eurich, S. A., *The Economics of Power: the Private finances of the House of Foix-Navarre-Albret during the Religious Wars* (Sixteenth Century Essays and Studies 24, 1994).

Everitt, A., *Landscape and Community in England* (London, 1995).

Fentress, J. and C. Wickham, *Social Memory* (Oxford, 1992).

Ferguson, A. B., *The Chivalric Tradition in Renaissance England* (Cranbury, NJ, 1986).

Finlay, J., *Men of Law in Pre-Reformation Scotland* (East Linton, 2000).

Fissel, M. C., *English Warfare 1511–1642* (London, 2001).

Flandrin, J. L., *Families in Former Times: Kinship, Household and Sexuality* (Cambridge, 1979).

Fletcher, A., *A County Community in Peace and War. Sussex 1600–1660* (London, 1975).

Fletcher, A., *Gender, Sex and Subordination in England 1500–1800* (New Haven, CT and London, 1995).

Foster, W. R., *The Church before the Covenants – the Church of Scotland 1596–1638* (Edinburgh, 1975).

Fox, R., *Kinship and Marriage. An Anthropological Perspective* (Cambridge, 1967).

Frame, R., *English Lordship in Ireland, 1318–1361* (Oxford, 1982).

Frame, R., *The Political Development of the British Isles 1100–1400* (Oxford, 1995).

Furgol, E. M., *A Regimental History of the Covenanting Armies 1639–1651* (Edinburgh, 1990).

Gatrell, V., B. Lenman and G. Parker (eds), *Crime and the Law: the Social History of Crime in Western Europe since 1500* (London, 1980).

Geary, P. J., *Phantoms of Remembrance. Memory and Oblivion at the End of the First Millennium* (Princeton, NJ, 1994).

Given-Wilson, C., *The English Nobility in the Late Middle Ages: The Fourteenth-Century Political Community* (London, 1987).

Glendinning, M., R. MacInnes and A. MacKechnie (eds), *A History of Scottish Architecture. From the Renaissance to the Present Day* (Edinburgh, 1996).

Glete, J., *War and the State in Early Modern Europe. Spain, the Dutch Republic and Sweden as Fiscal–Military States, 1500–1660* (London, 2002).

Godfrey, A. M., *Civil Justice in Renaissance Scotland. The Origins of the Central Court* (Leiden, 2009).

Goodare, J., *State and Society in Early Modern Scotland* (Oxford, 1999).

Goodare, J., *The Government of Scotland 1560–1625* (Oxford, 2004).

Goodare, J. and M. Lynch (eds), *The Reign of James VI* (East Linton, 2000).

Goodare, J. and A. A. MacDonald (eds), *Sixteenth-Century Scotland. Essays in Honour of Michael Lynch* (Leiden, 2008).

Goody, J., *The Development of the Family and Marriage in Europe* (Cambridge, 1983).

Goody, J., J. Thirsk and E. P. Thompson (eds), *Family and Inheritance. Rural Society in Western Europe 1200–1800* (Cambridge, 1976).

Graham, M. F., *The Uses of Reform. 'Godly Discipline' and Popular Behaviour in Scotland and Beyond, 1560–1610* (Leiden, 1996).

Grant, A., *Independence and Nationhood. Scotland 1306–1469* (London, 1984).

Grant, F. J., *The Faculty of Advocates in Scotland 1532–1943, with Genealogical Notes* (SRS, 165, 1944).

Graves, M. A. R., *The Parliaments of Early Modern Europe* (Harlow, 2001).

Greenshields, M., *An Economy of Violence in Early Modern France. Crime and Justice in the Haute Auverge 1587–1664* (University Park, PA, 1994).

Grosjean, A., *An Unofficial Alliance. Scotland and Sweden 1569–1654* (London, 2003).

Hale, J. R., *War and Society in Renaissance Europe, 1450–1620* (London and Baltimore, MD, 1985).

Hanlon, G., *Confession and Community in Seventeenth-Century France. Catholic and Protestant Co-existence in Acquitaine* (Philadelphia, PA, 1993).

Hanlon, G., *The Twilight of a Military Tradition. Italian Aristocrats and European Conflicts, 1560–1800* (London, 1997).

Harding, R. H., *Anatomy of a Power Elite. The Provincial Governors of Early Modern France* (London and Yale, CT, 1978).

Hart, J. S., *The Rule of Law 1603–1660* (Harlow, 2003).

Hayes-McCoy, G. A., *Scots Mercenary Forces in Ireland* (Dublin and London, 1937).

Heal, F. and C. Holmes, *The Gentry in England and Wales 1500–1700* (Basingstoke, 1994).

Heal, F., *Reformation in Britain and Ireland* (Oxford, 2003).

Heers, J., *Family Clans in the Middle Ages. A Study of Political and Social Structures in Urban Areas* (Amsterdam, 1977).

Henshall, N., *The Myth of Absolutism: Change and Continuity in Early Modern European Monarchy* (London, 1992).

Hewitt, G., *Scotland under Morton, 1572–80* (Edinburgh, 1982).

Hibbard, C., *Charles I and the Popish Plot* (Chapel Hill, NC, 1983).

Hill, J. M., *Fire and Sword. Sorley Boy MacDonnell and the Rise of Clan Ian Mor 1538–90* (London, 1993).

Hirst, D., *The Representatives of the People? Voters and Voting in England under the Early Stuarts* (Cambridge, 1975).

Hobsbawm, E., *Bandits* (London, 1969).

Holt, M. P., *The Duke of Anjou and the Politique Struggle during the Wars of Religion* (Cambridge, 1986).

Holy, L., *Anthropological Perspectives on Kinship* (London, 1966).

Houlebrooke, R. A., *The English Family, 1450–1700* (London, 1984).

Howard, D., *The Architectural History of Scotland. Scottish Architecture from the Reformation to the Restoration, 1560–1666* (Edinburgh, 1995).

Hudson, J., *Land, Law and Lordship in Anglo-Norman England* (Oxford, 1994).

Innes, T., *Scots Heraldry* (Edinburgh, 1956).

James, M. E., *Family, Lineage and Civil Society* (Oxford, 1974).

James, M. E. (ed.), *Society, Politics and Culture. Studies in Early Modern England* (Cambridge, 1988).

Jones, C. (ed.), *The Scots and Parliament* (Edinburgh, 1996).

Jones, M. (ed.), *Gentry and Lesser Nobility in Late Medieval Europe* (Gloucester, 1986).

Kearney, H., *Scholars and Gentlemen. Universities and Society in Pre-Industrial Britain, 1500–1700* (London, 1970).

Keen, M., *Chivalry* (New Haven, CT and London, 1984).

Keesing, R. M., *Kin Groups and Social Structure* (New York, 1975).

Kellar, C., *Scotland, England, and the Reformation 1534–1561* (Oxford, 2003).

Kesserling, K. J., *The Northern Rebellion of 1569. Faith, Politics, and Protest in Elizabethan England* (Basingstoke, 2007).

Kettering, S., *Patrons, Brokers and Clients in Seventeenth-Century France* (Oxford, 1986).

Kirk, J., *Patterns of Reform. Continuity and Change in the Reformation Kirk* (Edinburgh, 1989).

Kidd, C., *Subverting Scotland's Past. Scottish Whig Historians and the Creation of an Anglo-British Identity, 1689–c.1830* (Cambridge, 1993).

Kishlansky, M., *Parliamentary Selection: Social and Political Choice in Early Modern England* (Cambridge, 1986).

Kivelson, V., *Autocracy in the Provinces. The Muscovite Gentry and Political Culture in the Seventeenth Century* (Stanford, CA, 1997).

Knecht, R. J., *The French Wars of Religion, 1559–1598* (London, 1989).

Lansing, C., *The Florentine Magnates:Lineage and Faction in a Medieval Commune* (Princeton, NJ, 1991).

Larminie, V., *Wealth, Kinship and Culture. The 17th-Century Newdigates of Avbury and Their World* (Woodbridge, 1995).

Laslett, P. *The World We Have Lost* (London, 1976).

Lee, M., *James Stewart, Earl of Moray* (New York, 1953).

Lee, M., *John Maitland of Thirlestane and the Foundation of the Stewart Despotism* (Princeton, NJ, 1959).

Lee, M., *Government by Pen. Scotland under James VI and I* (Urbana, DC, 1980).

Lee, M., *The Road to Revolution. Scotland under Charles I* (Urbana, DC, 1985).

Lee, M., *Great Britain's Solomon: James VI and I in His Three Kingdoms* (Urbana, DC, 1990).

Lee, M., *The 'Inevitable' Union and other Essays on Early Modern Scotland* (East Linton, 2003).

Levack, B. P., *The Formation of the British State. England, Scotland, and the Union 1603–1707* (Oxford, 1987).

Lindsay, A., *Lives of the Lindsays*, 2nd edn, 3 vols (London, 1849).

Litchfield, R. B., *The Emergence of a Bureaucracy: the Florentine Patricians 1530–1790* (Princeton, NJ, 1986).

Livingston, E. B., *The Livingstons of Callendar and Their Principal Cadets* (Edinburgh, 1920).

Loades, D., *The Tudor Court* (London, 1986).

Lockyer, R., *Buckingham. The Life and Political Career of George Villiers, First Duke of Buckingham 1592–1628* (London, 1981).

Lynch, M., *Edinburgh and the Reformation* (Edinburgh, 1981).

Lynch, M. (ed.), *The Early Modern Town in Scotland* (London, 1987).

MacDonald, A. J., *Border Bloodshed: Scotland and England at War, 1369–1403* (East Linton, 2000).

MacDonald, A. R., *The Jacobean Kirk, 1567–1625. Sovereignty, Polity and Liturgy* (Aldershot, 1998).

MacDonald, A. R., *The Burghs and Parliament in Scotland, c. 1550–1651* (Aldershot, 2007).

Macdougall, N., *James III* (Edinburgh, 1982).

Macdougall, N. (ed.), *Church, Politics and Society in Scotland 1408–1929* (Edinburgh, 1983).

Macdougall, N., *James IV* (Edinburgh, 1989).

Macdougall, N. (ed.), *Scotland and War AD 79–1918* (Edinburgh, 1991).

Macfarlane, A., *The Origins of English Individualism* (Oxford, 1978).

Macfarlane, K. B., *The Nobility of Later Medieval England* (Oxford, 1973).

MacHardy, K. J., *War, Religion and Court Patronage in Habsburg Austria. The Social and Cultural Dimensions of Political Interaction, 1521–1622* (Basingstoke, 2003).

Mackie, J. D., *The University of Glasgow, 1451–1951: a Short History* (Glasgow, 1954).

Mackillop, A. and S. Murdoch (eds), *Military Governors and Imperial Frontiers c. 1600–1800* (Leiden, 2003).

MacLean-Bristol, N., *Warriors and Priests: the History of the Clan MacLean, 1300–1570* (East Linton, 1995).

Macinnes, A. I., *Charles I and the Making of the Covenanting Movement 1625–1641* (Edinburgh, 1991).

Macinnes, A. I., *Clanship, Commerce and the House of Stuart, 1603–1788* (East Linton, 1996).

Macinnes, A. I., *The British Revolutions 1629–1660* (Basingstoke, 2005).

Macinnes, A. I., T. Riis and F. G. Pederson (eds), *Ships, Guns and Bibles in the North Sea and the Baltic States c. 1350–c. 1700* (East Linton, 2000).

Mackay, A., *The Book of Mackay* (Edinburgh, 1906).

Major, J. R., *From Renaissance Monarchy to Absolute Monarchy. French Kings, Nobles and Estates* (Baltimore, MD and London, 1994).

Mallett, E. W., *Mercenaries and their Masters: Warfare in Renaissance Italy* (London, 1974).

Manning, R. B., *Hunters and Poachers: a Cultural and Social History of Unlawful Hunting in England, 1485–1640* (Oxford, 1993).

Manning, R. B., *Swordsmen. The Martial Ethos in the Three Kingdoms* (Oxford, 2003).

Manning, R. B., *An Apprenticeship in Arms. The Origins of the British Army 1585–1702* (Oxford, 2006).

Mason, R. A. (ed.), *Scotland and England 1286–1815* (Edinburgh, 1987).

Mason, R. A. and N. A. T. Macdougall (eds), *People and Power in Scotland. Essays in Honour of T. C. Smout* (Edinburgh, 1990).

Mason, R. A. (ed.), *Scots and Britons. Scottish Political Thought and the Union of 1603* (Cambridge, 1994).

Mason, R. A., *Kingship and Commonweal. Political Thought in Renaissance Scotland* (East Linton, 1998).

Mason, R. A. (ed.), *John Knox and the British Reformations* (Aldershot, 1998).

Maxwell-Irving, A. M. T., *The Border Towers of Scotland: Their History and Architecture* (Stirling, 2000).

Maynes, M. J., A. Waltner, B. Soland and U. Strasser (eds), *Gender, Kinship, Power. A Comparative Interdisciplinary History* (New York, 1996), 43–64.

McCormick, A. M., *The Earldom of Desmond 1463–1583. The Decline and Crisis of a Feudal Lordship* (Dublin, 2005).

McFarlane, I. D., *Buchanan* (London, 1981).

McGettigan, *Red Hugh O'Donnell and the Nine Years' War* (Dublin, 2005).

McKean, C., *The Scottish Chateaux. The Country House of Renaissance Scotland* (Stroud, 2004).

McLeod, W., *Divided Gaels. Gaelic Cultural Identities in Scotland and Ireland c. 1200–c. 1650* (Oxford, 2004).

McNeill, P. G. B. and H. L. McQueen (eds), *Atlas of Scottish History to 1707* (Scottish Medievalists, 1996).

McQueen, H. L., *Common Law and Feudal Society in Medieval Scotland* (Edinburgh, 1993).

Meikle, M. M., *A British Frontier?Lairds and Gentlemen in the Eastern Borders, 1540–1603* (East Linton, 2004).

Mentzer, R. A., *Blood and Belief. Family Survival and Confessional Identity among the Provincial Huguenot Nobility* (West Lafayette, IN, 1994).

Merriman, M., *The Rough Wooings. Mary Queen of Scots 1542–1551* (East Linton, 2000).

Mertes, K., *The English Noble Household 1250–1600* (Oxford, 1988).

Miket, R. and Roberts, D. L., *The Medieval Castles of Skye and Lochalsh* (Portree, 1990).

Miller, H., *Henry VIII and the English Nobility* (Oxford, 1989).

Miller, J., *Swords for Hire. The Scottish Mercenary* (Edinburgh, 2007).

Mitchison, R., *Lordship to Patronage. Scotland 1603–1745* (London, 1983).

Mitterauer, M. and R. Sieder, *The European Family. Patriarchy to Partnership from the Middle Ages to the Present* (Chicago, IL, 1982).

Morgan, H., *Tyrone's Rebellion* (Woodbridge, 1993).

Morrill, J. (ed.), *The Scottish National Covenant in its National Context* (Edinburgh, 1990).

Motley, M., *Becoming a French Aristocrat: the Education of the Court Nobility, 1580–1715* (Princeton, NJ, 1990).

Muir, E., *Mad Blood Stirring. Vendetta and Factions in Friuli during the Renaissance* (Baltimore, MD, 1993).

Mullan, D. G., *Episcopacy in Scotland: the History of an Idea* (Edinburgh, 1986).

Mullan, D., *Scottish Puritanism 1590–1638* (Oxford, 2000).

Murdoch, S. (ed.), *Scotland and the Thirty Years' War, 1618–48* (Leiden, 2001).

Murdoch, S., *Britain, Denmark–Norway and the House of Stuart, 1603–1660. A Diplomatic and Military Analysis* (East Linton, 2003).

Murdoch, S., *Network North. Scottish Kin, Commonweal and Covert Association in Northern Europe, 1603–1746* (Leiden, 2006).

Murdoch, S., *The Terror of the Seas? Scottish Maritime Warfare, 1513–1713* (Leiden, 2010).

Murdoch, S. and A. Mackillop (eds), *Fighting for Identity. Scottish Military Experience c. 1550–1900* (Leiden, 2002).

Murray, J., *Chronicles of the Atholl and Tullibardine Families*, 5 vols (Edinburgh, 1908).

Myers, A. R., *Parliaments and Estates in Europe to 1789* (London, 1975).

Netterstrom, J. P. and B. Poulsen (eds), *Feud in Medieval and Early Modern Europe* (Aarhus, 2007).

Neuschel, K. B., *Word of Honor: Interpreting Noble Culture in Sixteenth-Century France* (New York, 1989).

Neville, C., *Violence, Custom and Law. The Anglo-Scottish Border Lands in the Late Middle Ages* (Edinburgh, 1998).

Neville, C., *Native Lordship in Medieval Scotland. The Earldom of Strathearn and Lennox, c. 1140–1365* (Dublin, 2005).

Newton, D., *The Making of the Jacobean Regime. James VI and I and the Government of England 1603–1605* (Woodbridge, 2005).

Nicholls, K., *Gaelic and Gaelicized Ireland* (Dublin, 1972).

Ohlmeyer, J. H., *Civil War and Restoration in the Three Stuart Kingdoms. The Career of Randal MacDonnell, Marquis of Antrim, 1609–1683* (Cambridge, 1993).

Oman, C. *A History of War in the Sixteenth Century* (London, 1937).

Oram, R. and G. Stell (eds), *Lordship and Architecture in Medieval and Renaissance Scotland* (Edinburgh, 2005).

Oxford Dictionary of National Biography (*ODNB*), Oxford University Press, 2004, at: http://www.oxforddnb.com 2010.

Parrott, D., *Richelieu's Army. War, Government and Society in France, 1624–1642* (Cambridge, 2001).

Parry, G., *The Golden Age Restored. The Culture of the Stuart Court, 1603–42* (Manchester, 1981).

Patterson, N., *Cattle, Lords and Clansmen. The Social Structures of Early Ireland* (London, 1994).

Peck, L. L., *Court Patronage and Corruption in Early Stuart England* (London, 1990).

Persson, F., *Servant of Fortune. The Swedish Court between 1598 and 1721* (Lund, 1999).

Phillips, G., *The Anglo-Scots Wars 1513–1550* (Woodbridge, 1999).

Philpotts, B. S., *Kindred and Clan in the Middle Ages and After* (New York, 1974).

Plakans, A., *Kinship in the Past. An Anthology of European Family Life 1500–1900* (Oxford, 1984).

Powis, J., *Aristocracy* (Oxford, 1984).

Queller, D. E., *The Venetian Patriciate. Reality Versus Myth* (Chicago, IL, 1986).

Rae, T. I., *The Administration of the Scottish Frontier 1513–1603* (Edinburgh, 1966).

Rait, R. S., *The Scottish Parliaments before the Union of the Crowns* (London, 1901).

Rait, R. S., *The Parliaments of Scotland* (Glasgow, 1924).

Redlich, F., *The German Military Enterpriser and his Workforce*, 2 vols (Wiesbaden, 1964–5).

Rheubottom, D., *Age, Marriage and Politics in Fifteenth-Century Ragusa* (Oxford, 2000).

Ritchie, P., *Mary of Guise in Scotland, 1548–1560* (East Linton, 2002).

Robinson, J., *Court Politics, Culture and Literature in Scotland and England 1500–1540* (Aldershot, 2008).

Robson, R., *The Rise and Fall of the English Highland Clans: Tudor Responses to a Mediaeval Problem* (Edinburgh, 1989).

Rogers, C. J. (ed.), *The Military Revolution Debate. Readings on the Military Transformation of Early Modern Europe* (Oxford, 1995).

Rosenthal, J. T., *Patriarchy and Families of Privilege in Fifteenth-Century England* (Philadelphia, PA, 1991).

Ruff, J. R., *Violence in Early Modern Europe 1500–1800* (Cambridge, 2001).

Ruggiero, G., *Violence in early Renaissance Venice* (New Brunswick, 1980).

Russell, C., *Parliaments and English Politics, 1621–1629* (Oxford, 1979).

Ryrie, A., *The Origins of the Scottish Reformation* (Manchester, 2006).

Salmon, J. H., *Society in Crisis. France in the Sixteenth Century* (London, 1975).

Sanderson, M. B. H., *Scottish Rural Society in the 16th Century* (Edinburgh, 1982).

Sanderson, M. B. H., *Mary Stewart's People. Life in Mary Stewart's Scotland* (Edinburgh, 1987).

Sanderson, M. B. H., *Ayrshire and the Reformation. People and Change 1490–1600* (East Linton, 1997).

Schalk. E., *From Valor to Pedigree: Ideas of Nobility in France in the Sixteenth and Seventeenth Centuries* (Princeton, NJ, 1986).

Schneider, D. M., *A Critique of the Study of Kinship* (Ann Arbor, MI, 1984).

Schreiber, R. E., *The First Carlisle. Sir James Hay, First Earl of Carlisle as Courtier, Diplomat and Entrepreneur, 1580–1636* (Transactions of the American Philosophical Society, 74, part 7, 1984).

Scots Peerage (ed.) J. B. Paul, 9 vols (Edinburgh, 1904–14).

Scott, H. M. (ed.), *The European Nobilities in the Seventeenth and Eighteenth Centuries*, 2 vols (Basingstoke, 2007).

Searle, E., *Predatory Kinship and the Creation of Norman Power, 840–1066* (Berkeley, CA, 1988).

Seton, G., *A History of the Family of Seton*, 2 vols (Edinburgh, 1896).

Sharpe, K. (ed.), *Criticism and Compliment: the Politics of Literature in the England of Charles I* (London, 1986).

Sharpe, K., *The Personal Rule of Charles I* (New Haven, CT and London, 1992)

Skinner, P., *Family Power in Southern Italy. The Duchy of Gaeta and its Neighbours, 850–1139* (Cambridge, 1995).

Slater, M., *Family Life in the Seventeenth Century. The Verneys of Claydon House* (London, 1984).

Smith, A. H., *Country and Court: Government and Politics in Norfolk 1558–1603* (Oxford, 1974).

Smith, D. L., *The Stuart Parliaments 1603–1689* (London, 1999).

Smith, J. M., *The Culture of Merit. Nobility, Royal Service and the Making of Absolute Monarchy in France, 1600–1789* (Ann Arbor, MI, 1996).

Smuts, R. M., *Court Culture and the Origins of a Royalist Tradition in Early Stuart England* (University Park, PA, 1987).

Starkey, D. (ed.), *The English Court from the Wars of the Roses to the Civil War* (Harlow, 1987).

Stater, V. L., *Noble Government: the Stuart Lord Lieutenancy and the Transformation of English Politics* (Athens, GA, 1994).

Stevenson, D., *The Scottish Revolution, 1637–44* (Newton Abbot, 1975).

Stevenson, D., *Alasdair MacColla and the Highland Problem in the Seventeenth Century* (Edinburgh, 1980).

Stevenson, D., *Scotland's Last Royal Wedding. The Marriage of James VI and Anne of Denmark* (East Linton, 1997).

Stevenson, K., *Chivalry and Knighthood in Scotland, 1424–1513* (Woodbridge, 2006).

Stewart, L. A. M., *Urban Politics and the British Civil Wars. Edinburgh, 1617–53* (Leiden, 2006).

Stone, L., *The Crisis of the Aristocracy, 1558–1641* (Oxford, 1965).

Stone, L. and J. C. F. Stone, *An Open Elite? England 1540–1880* (Oxford, 1984).

Strong, R., *Henry, Prince of Wales and England's Lost Renaissance* (London, 1986).

Sturdy, D. J., *The D'Aligres de la Rivière. Servants of the Bourbon State in the Seventeenth Century* (London, 1986).

Subtelny, O., *The Domination of Eastern Europe. Foreign Absolutism and Native Nobilities* (Montreal, 1986).

Tadmor, N., *Family and Friends in Eighteenth-Century England. Household, Kinship and Patronage* (Cambridge, 2001).

Tanner, R., *The Late Medieval Scottish Parliament. Politics and the Three Estates, 1424–1488* (East Linton, 2001).

Tayler, H., *The Book of the Duffs*, 2 vols (Edinburgh, 1914).

Tayler, H., *History of the Family of Urquhart* (Aberdeen, 1946).

Terry, C. S., *The Scottish Parliament: its Constitution and Procedure* (Glasgow, 1905).

Thomas, A., *Princelie Majestie. The Court of James V of Scotland, 1528–1548* (Edinburgh, 2005).

Thompson, I. A. A. and B. Y. Casalilla (eds), *The Castillian Crisis of the Seventeenth Century* (Cambridge, 1994).

Todd, M., *The Culture of Protestantism in Early Modern Scotland* (New Haven, CT, 2002).

Trim, D. J. B. (ed.), *The Chivalric Ethos and the Development of Military Prtofessionalism* (Leiden, 2003).

Twigg, J., *The University of Cambridge and the English Revolution 1635–1688* (Cambridge, 1990).

Vale, M. G. A., *War and Chivalry: Warfare and Aristocratic Culture in England, France and Burgundy at the End of the Middle Ages* (London, 1981).

Van Nierop, H. F. K., *The Nobility of Holland. From Knights to Regents, 1500–1650* (Cambridge, 1984).

Walker, D. M., *The Scottish Jurists* (Edinburgh, 1985).

Watts, S. J., *From Border to Middle Shire: Northumberland 1586–1625* (Leicester, 1975).

Whyte, I. D., *Agriculture and Society in Seventeenth-Century Scotland* (Edinburgh, 1979).

Williams, J. H. (ed.), *Stewart Style 1513–1542. Essays on the Court of James V* (East Linton, 1996).

Williamson, A. H., *Scottish National Consciousness in the Age of James VI* (Edinburgh, 1979).

Wilson, W., *The House of Airlie*, 2 vols (London, 1924).

Wood, J. B, *The Nobility of the Election of Bayeux, 1463–1666* (Princeton, NJ, 1980).

Wormald, J., *Court, Kirk and Community. Scotland 1470–1625* (London, 1981).

Wormald, J., *Lords and Men: Bonds of Manrent 1442–1603* (Edinburgh, 1985).

Wormald, J., *Mary Queen of Scots. A Study in Failure* (London, 1988).

Worthington, D., *Scots in Habsburg Service, 1618–1648* (Leiden, 2004).

Wrightson, K., *English Society 1580–1680* (London, 1982).

Young, A., *Tudor and Jacobean Tournaments* (London, 1987).

Young, A., *Robert the Bruce's Rivals: the Comyns, 1212–1314* (East Linton, 1997).

Zmora, H., *State and Nobility in Early Modern Germany. The Knightly Feud in Franconia, 1440–1567* (Cambridge, 1997).

(iv) Secondary Works: Articles and Essays

Abbreviations

AHCAW	*Archaeological and Historical Collections Relating to the Counties of Ayr and Wigton*
AHR	*American Historical Review*
ARH	*Archive for Reformation History*
BIHR	*Bulletin of the Institute of Historical Research*
CC	*Continuity and Change*
CH	*Church History*
CJH	*Canadian Journal of History*
CSSH	*Comparative Studies in Society and History*
EcHR	*Economic History Review*
EHR	*English Historical Review*
EHQ	*European History Quarterly*
Emblematica	*Emblematica: an Inderdisciplinary Journal for Emblem Studies*
FHS	*French Historical Studies*
FS	*French History*
HJ	*Historical Journal*
HR	*Historical Research*
IR	*Innes Review*
JBS	*Journal of British Studies*
JEH	*Journal of Ecclesiastical History*
JFH	*Journal of Family History*
JGH	*Journal of Garden History*
JHI	*Journal of the History of Ideas*
JIH	*Journal of Interdisciplinary History*
JMH	*Journal of Modern History*
JR	*Juridical Review*
JSH	*Journal of Social History*
LQR	*Law Quarterly Review*
NS	*Northern Scotland*
PP	*Past and Present*
PSAS	*Proceedings of the Society of Antiquaries of Scotland*
RSCHS	*Records of the Scottish Church History Society*
RQ	*Renaissance Quarterly*
SC	*Scottish Studies*
SCJ	*Sixteenth-Century Journal*
SH	*Social History*
SHR	*Scottish Historical Review*
SLJ	*Scottish Literary Journal*
SSL	*Studies in Scottish Literature*
ST	*Scottish Tradition*
TGSI	*Transactions of the Gaelic Society of Inverness*
TRHS	*Transactions of the Royal Historical Society*

Adams, S., 'James VI and the politics of south-west Scotland', in Goodare and Lynch (eds), *Reign of James VI*, 228–40.

Adams, S., 'Foreign policy and the parliaments of 1621 and 1624', in K. Sharpe (ed.), *Faction and Parliament. Essays on early Stuart History* (Oxford, 1985), 139–72.

Adams, S., 'The Dudley clientele, 1553–1563', in Bernard (ed.), *Tudor Nobility*, 241–65.

Adams, S., 'Favourites and factions at the Elizabethan court', in Asch and Birke (eds), *Princes, Patronage and the Nobility*, 265–87.

Adams, S., 'Faction, clientage and party: English politics, 1550–1603', in Adams (ed.), *Leicester and the Court*, 13–23.

Adams, S., 'Eliza enthroned? The court and politics', in Adams (ed.), *Leicester and the Court*, 24–45.

Adams, S., 'Favourites and factions at the Elizabethan court', in Adams, *Leicester and the Court*, 46–67.

Adams, S., 'The Dudley clientele and the House of Commons', in Adams, *Leicester and the Court*, 196–224.

Adams, S., 'A godly peer? Leicester and the puritans', in Adams (ed.), *Leicester and the Court*, 225–32.

Adams, S., 'Baronial contexts? Continuity and change in the noble affinity 1400–1600', in Adams (ed.), *Leicester and the Court*, 374–410.

Adamson, J. S. A., 'The baronial context of the English civil war', *TRHS* 5th series, 40 (1990), 93–120.

Adamson, J. S. A., 'Chivalry and political culture in Caroline England', in K. Sharpe and G. Lake (eds), *Culture and Politics in Early Stuart England* (Basingstoke, 1993), 161–98.

Adamson, J. S. A., 'The making of the *ancien-régime* court 1500–1700', in Adamson (ed.), *Princely Courts*, 7–42.

Adamson, J. S. A., 'The Tudor and Stuart courts 1509–1714', in Adamson (ed.), *Princely Courts*, 95–118.

Allan, D., 'What's in a name? Pedigree and propaganda in seventeenth-century Scotland', in E. J. Cowan and R. J. Finlay (eds), *Scottish History: the Power of the Past* (Edinburgh, 2002), 147–67.

Allan, D., 'Ane ornament to you and your famelie: Sir Robert Gordon of Gordonstoun and the *Genealogical History of the earldom of Sutherland*', *SHR* 80 (2001), 24–44.

Anglin, J. P., 'The schools of defence in Elizabethan London', *RQ* 37 (1984), 393–410.

Asch, R. G., 'Introduction: Court and household from the fifteenth to the seventeenth centuries', in Asch and Birke (eds), *Princes, Patronage and the Nobility*, 1–40.

Aurell, M., 'The western nobility in the late middle ages: a survey of the historiography and some prospects for new research', in Duggan (ed.), *Nobles and Nobility*, 263–73.

Banac, I. and P. Bushkovitch, 'The nobility in the history of Russia and eastern Europe', in Banac and Bushkovitch (eds), *Nobility in Russia and Eastern Europe*, 1–16.

Barker, T. M., 'Armed services and nobility: general features', in T. M. Barker (ed.), *Army, Aristocracy and Nobility: Essays on War, Society and Government in Austria, 1618–1780* (New York, 1982), 22–36.

Barron, W. R. J., 'The penalties of treason in medieval life and literature', *Journal of Medieval History*, 7 (1981), 187–202.

Bartlett, I. R., 'Scottish mercenaries in Europe, 1570–1640: a study in attitudes and policies', *Scottish Tradition* 13 (1984–5), 15–23.

Bath, M., 'Painted ceilings, 1550–1650: applied emblematics in Scotland', *Emblematica* 7 (1993), 259–305.

Beaver, D., '"Bragging and daring words": honour, property and the symbolism of the hunt in Howe, 1590–1642', in Braddick and Walters (eds), *Negotiating Power*, 149–65.

Bellany, A., 'Carr , Robert, earl of Somerset (1585/6?–1645)', *ODNB*.

Beller, E. A., 'The military expedition of Sir Charles Morgan to Germany, 1627–9', *HER* 43 (1928), 528–39.

Benadusi, G., 'Rethinking the state: family strategies and state formation in early modern Tuscany', *SH* 20 (1995), 157–78.

Bernard, G. W., 'The Tudor nobility in perspective', in Bernard (ed.), *Tudor Nobility*, 1–48.

Boardman, S., 'The medieval origin legend of the Clan Campbell', *Journal of the Campbell Society UK* 27 (2000), 5–7.

Boardman, S., 'The Campbells and charter lordship in medieval Argyll', in S. Boardman and A. Ross (eds), *The Exercise of Power in Late Medieval Scotland c. 1200–1500* (Dublin, 2003), 95–117.

Bossy, J., 'Blood and baptism: kinship, community and Christianity in Western Europe from the fifteenth to the seventeenth centuries', in D. Baker (ed.), *Sanctity and Secularity: the Church and the World*, Ecclesiastical History Society 10 (Oxford, 1973), 129–43.

Bossy, 'Holiness and society', *PP* 75 (1977), 119–37.

Braddick, M. J., 'Administrative performance: the representation of political authority in early modern England', in Braddick and Walters (eds), *Negotiating Power*, 166–87.

Brockington, W. S., 'Robert Monro: professional soldier, military historian and scotsman', in Murdoch (ed.), *Scotland and the Thirty Years' War*, 215–41.

Brown, A. L., 'The Scottish "Establishment" in the later fifteenth century', *Juridical Review*, new series, 23 (1978), 89–105.

Brown, J. M., 'Taming the magnates?' in G. Menzies (ed.), *The Scottish Nation* (London, 1972), 46–59.

Brown, K. M., 'Burghs, lords and feuds in Jacobean Scotland', in Lynch (ed.), *Early Modern Town*, 102–24.

Brown, K. M., 'The price of friendship: the "well affected" and English economic clientage in Scotland before 1603', in R. A. Mason (ed.), *Scotland and England 1286–1815* (Edinburgh, 1987), 139–62.

Brown, K. M., 'The making of a *politique*: the Counter Reformation and the regional politics of John Eighth Lord Maxwell', *SHR* 66 (1987), 152–75.

Brown, K. M., 'From Scottish lords to British officers: state building, elite integration, and the army in the seventeenth century', in Macdougall (ed.), *Scotland and War*, 133–69.

Brown, K. M., 'The laird, his daughter, her husband and the minister: unravelling a popular ballad', in Mason and Macdougall (eds), *People and Power*, 104–25.

Brown, K. M., 'Courtiers and cavaliers: service, Anglicization and loyalty among the royalist nobility', in Morrill (ed.), *Scottish National Covenant in its National Context*, 155–92.

Brown, K. M., 'The Scottish aristocracy, anglicization and the court, 1603–38', *HJ* 36 (1993), 543–76.

Brown, K. M., 'The vanishing emperor: British kingship and its decline 1603–1707', in Mason (ed.), *Scots and Britons*, 58–90.

Brown, K. M., 'A house divided: family and feud in Carrick under John Kennedy, fifth earl of Cassillis', *SHR* 75 (1996), 168–96.

Brown, K. M., 'The Reformation parliament', in K. M. Brown and R. J. Tanner (eds), *Parliament and Politics in Scotland, 1235–1560* (Edinburgh, 2004), 203–32.

Brown, K. M., 'The second estate: parliament and the nobility', in Brown and MacDonald (eds), *Parliament in Context*, 67–94.

Brown, K. M. and A. J. Mann, 'Introduction: parliament and politics in Scotland, 1567–1707', in Brown and Mann (eds), *Parliament and Politics in Scotland, 1567–1707*, 203–32.

Brown, M., 'Scotland tamed? Kings and magnates in late medieval Scotland: a review of recent work', *IR* 45 (1994), 120–46.

Brown, M., '"I have thus slain a tyrant": *The dethe of the kynge of Scotis* and the right to resist in early fifteenth-century Scotland', *IR* 47 (1996), 24–44.

Brown, M., '"Rejoice to hear of Douglas": the House of Douglas and the presentation of magnate power in late medieval Scotland', *SHR* 76 (1997), 161–84.

Burns, J. H., 'Political ideas and parliament', in Brown and MacDonald (eds), *Parliament in Context*, 216–43.

Cairns, J. W., 'Legal humanism and the history of Scots law: John Skene and Thomas Craig', in MacQueen (ed.), *Humanism in Renaissance Scotland* (Edinburgh, 1990), 48–74.

Caldwell, D., 'Royal patronage of arms and armour making in fifteenth and sixteenth-century Scotland', in D. Caldwell (ed.), *Scottish Weapons and Fortifications, 1100–1800* (Edinburgh, 1981), 73–93.

Caldwell, D., 'The battle of Pinkie', in Macdougall (ed.), *Scotland at War*, 61–94.

Cameron, J. K., 'Faith, faction and conflicting loyalties in the Scottish Reformation', in M. Hurst (ed.), *States, Countries and Provinces* (London, 1986), 72–90.

Carpenter, C., 'The Beauchamp affinity: a study of bastard feudalism at work', *EHR* 45 (1980), 514–32.

Carroll, S., 'The Guise affinity and popular protest during the French Wars of Religion', *FH* 9 (1995), 125–51.

Carroll, S., 'The peace in the feud in sixteenth and seventeenth-century France', *PP* 17 (2003), 74–115.

Carroll, S., 'Introduction', in Carroll (ed.), *Cultures of Violence*, 1–43.

Casalilla, B. Y., 'The Castilian aristocracy in the seventeenth century: crisis, refeudalisation or political offensive', in Thompson and Casalilla (eds), *Castilian Crisis*, 277–300.

Cathcart, A., 'Crisis of identity? Clan Chattan's response to government policy in the Scottish Highlands c. 1580–1609', in Murdoch and Mackillop (eds), *Fighting for Identity*, 163–84.

Chojnacki, S., 'Kinship ties and young patricians in fifteenth-century Venice', *Renaissance Quarterly* 38 (1985), 240–70.

Clucas, S., 'Robert Cotton's *A Short View of the Life of Henry the Third* and its presentation in 1614', in S. Clucas and R. Davies (eds), *The Crisis of 1614 and the Addled Parliament* (Aldershot, 2003).

Coffey, J., 'Elphinstone, John, second lord Balmerino (d. 1649)', *ODNB*.

Collinson, P., 'Magistracy and ministry: a Suffolk miniature', in R. B. Knox (ed.), *Refor-mation, Conformity and Dissent: Essays in Honour of Geoffrey Nuttall* (London, 1977), 70–91.

Cooper, J. P., 'Retainers in Tudor England', in G. E. Aylmer and J. S. Morrill (eds), *Land, Men and Beliefs: Studies in Early Modern History* (London, 1983), 78–96.

Cooper, T. M., 'The king versus the court of session', *JR* 58 (1946), 83–92.

Coss, P. R., 'Bastard feudalism revised', *PP* 125 (1989), 27–64.

Coss, P. R., 'The formation of the English gentry', *PP* 147 (1995), 38–64.

Cowan, E. J., 'Clanship, kinship and the Campbell acquisition of Argyll', *SHR* 58 (1979), 132–57.

Cowan, E. J., 'The darker vision of the Scottish Renaissance: the devil and Francis Stewart', in Cowan and Shaw (eds), *Renaissance and Reformation*, 125–40.

Cowan, E. J., 'The Angus–Campbells and the origins of the Campbell–Ogilvie feud', *Journal of the School of Scottish Studies, University of Edinburgh* 25 (1981), 25–38.

Cowan, E. J., 'The political ideas of a covenanting leader. Archibald Campbell, marquis of Argyll', in Mason (ed.), *Scots and Britons*, 241–61.

Cowan, I. B., 'Church and society in post-Reformation society', *RSCHS* 17 (1971), 185–201.

Cowan, I. B., 'The Marian civil war, 1567–1573', in Macdougall (ed.), *Scotland and War*, 95–112.

Coward, B., 'A "crisis of the aristocracy" in the sixteenth and seventeenth centuries? The case of the Stanleys, earls of Derby, 1504–1642', *NH* 18 (1982), 54–77.

Cressy, D., 'Kinship and kin interaction in early modern England', *PP* 113 (1986), 38–69.

Cuddy, N., 'The revival of the entourage: the bedchamber of James I', in D. Starkey (ed.), *The English Court from the Wars of the Roses to the Civil War* (Harlow, 1987), 173–225.

Cuddy, N., 'Reinventing a monarchy: the changing structure and political function of the Stuart court, 1603–88', in Cruickshanks (ed.), *Stuart Courts*, 59–85.

Cust, R., 'Honour, rhetoric and political culture: the earl of Huntingdon and his enemies', in S. Amussen and M. Kishlansky (eds), *Political Culture and Cultural Studies in Early Modern England* (Manchester, 1995), 84–111.

Davies, J. M., 'Neither politique nor patriot? Henri duc de Montmorency and Philip II, 1582–89', *HJ* 34 (1991), 539–66.

Davies, J. M., 'The politics of the marriage bed: matrimony and the Montmorency family, 1527–1612', *FH* 6 (1992), 63–95.

Davies, R. R., 'The survival of the bloodfeud in medieval Wales', *History* 54 (1969), 538–57.

Davies, S. J., 'The court and the Scottish legal system 1600–1747: the case of Stirlingshire', in Gatrell, Lenman and Parker (eds), *Crime and the Law*, 120–54.

Dawson, J. E. A., 'Two kingdoms or three? Ireland in Anglo-Scottish relations in the middle of the sixteenth century', in Mason (ed.), *Scotland and England*, 113–38.

Dawson, J. E. A., 'The fifth earl of Argyle, Gaelic lordship and political power in sixteenth-century Scotland', *SHR* 183 (1988), 1–27.

Dawson, J. E. A., 'The origin of the "road to the isles": trade, communications and Campbell power in early modern Scotland', in Mason and Macdougall (eds), *People and Power*, 4–103.

Dawson, J. E. A., 'Clan, kin and kirk: the Campbells and the Scottish Reformation', in N. S. Amos, A. Pettegree and H. van Nierop (eds), *The Education of a Christian Society. Humanism and the Reformation in Britain and the Netherlands* (Aldershot, 1999), 211–42.

Dawson, J. E. A., 'Trumpeting resistance: Christopher Goodman and John Knox', in Mason (ed.), *John Knox and the British Reformations*, 131–53.

Dodgshon, R. A., 'West highland chiefdoms, 1500–1745: a study in redistributive exchange', in R. Mitchison and P. Roebuck (eds), *Economy and Society in Scotland and Ireland 1500–1939* (Edinburgh, 1988), 27–37.

Donagan, B., 'A courtier's progress: greed and consistency in the life of the earl of Holland', *HJ* 19 (1976), 317–53.

Donagan, B., 'Halcyon days and the literature of war: England's military education before 1642', *PP* 147 (1995), 65–100.

Donaldson, G., 'Scottish presbyterian exiles in England 1584–8', in Donaldson (ed.), *Scottish Church History*, 178–90.

Donaldson, G., 'Scotland's conservative north in the sixteenth and seventeenth centuries', *TRHS* fifth series 16 (1966), 65–79.

Donaldson, G., 'The legal profession in Scottish society in the sixteenth and seventeenth centuries', *JR* 31 (1976), 1–19.

Duby, G., 'Lineage, nobility and chivalry in the region of Macon during the twelfth century', in R. Foster and O. Ranun (eds), *Family and Society. Selections from the Annales. Economies, Societies, Civilizations* (Baltimore, MD, 1976), 16–40.

Duindam, J., 'The Bourbon and Austrian Habsburgs courts. Numbers, ordinances, ceremony – and nobles', in Asche (ed.), *Europaische Adel*, 182–206.

Dukes, P., 'The Leslie family in the Swedish period (1630–5) of the Thirty Years' War', *European Studies Review* 12 (1982), 401–19.

Dukes, P., 'The first Scottish soldiers in Russia', in G. Simpson (ed.), *The Scottish Soldier Abroad 1247–1967* (Edinburgh, 1992), 47–54.

Dukes, P., 'New perspectives: Alexander Leslie and the Smolensk war, 1632–4', in Murdoch (ed.), *Scotland and the Thirty Years' War*, 174–89.

Dunthorne, H., 'Scots in the wars of the Low Countries 1572–1648', in G. G. Simpson (ed.), *Scotland and the Low Countries, 1124–1994* (East Linton, 1996), 101–21.

Durkan, J., 'The beginnings of humanism in Scotland', *IR* 4 (1953), 5–24.

Durkan, J., 'Two jesuits: Patrick Anderson and John Ogilvie', *IR* 21 (1970), 157–61.

Durkan, J., 'William Murdoch and the early Jesuit mission in Scotland', *IR* 35 (1984), 3–11.

Durkan, J., 'James, third earl of Arran: the hidden years', *SHR* 65 (1986), 154–66.

Edington, C., 'Paragons and patriots: national identity and the chivalric ideal in late medieval Scotland', in D. Broun, R. J. Finlay and M. Lynch (eds), *Image and Identity: the Making and Re-Making of Scotland through the Ages* (Edinburgh, 1988), 69–81.

Edington, C., 'The tournament in medieval Scotland', in M. Strickland (ed.), *Armies, Chivalry and Warfare in Medieval Britain and France: Proceedings of the 1995 Harlaxton Symposium* (Stanford, CA, 1998), 46–62.

Edwards, D., 'The escalation of violence in sixteenth-century Ireland', in D. Edwards, P. Lenihan and C. Tait (eds), *Age of Atrocity. Violence and Political Conflict in Early Modern Ireland* (Dublin, 2007), 34–78.

Edwards, P., 'Arming and equipping the covenanting armies, 1638–1652', in Murdoch and Mackillop (eds), *Fighting for Identity*, 239–64.

Ellis, H. A., 'Genealogy, history and aristocratic reaction in early eighteenth-century France: the case of Henri de Boulainvilliers', *AHR* 58 (1986), 414–51.

Ellis, S., 'Henry VIII, rebellion and the rule of law', *HJ* 24 (1981), 513–31.

Elton, G., 'Tudor government: the point of contact III. The court', *TRHS* 26 (1976), 211–28.

Elton, G. R., 'Parliament in the sixteenth century: functions and fortunes', *HJ* 22 (1979), 255–78.

Enright, M. J., 'Lady with a mead cup: ritual, group cohesion and hierarchy in the Germanic warband', *Frühmittelalterliche Studien* 22 (1988), 170–203.

Farr, D., 'Kin, cash, Catholics and cavaliers: the role of kinship in the financial management of major-general John Lambert', *HR* 74 (2001), 44–62.

Feld, M. D., 'Middle class society and the rise of military professionalism: the Dutch army, 1589–1609', *Armed Forces and Society* 1 (1975), 419–42.

Finlay, J., 'James Henryson and the origins of the office of the king's advocate', *SHR* 79 (2000), 17–38.

Finlay, J., 'Borthwick, David (*d.* 1581)', *ODNB*.

Finnie, A., 'The house of Hamilton: patronage, politics and the church in the Reformation period', *IR* 36 (1985), 3–28.

Fletcher, A., 'Honour, reputation and local office-holding in Elizabethan and Stuart England', in A. Fletcher and J. Stevenson (eds), *Order and Disorder in Early Modern England* (Cambridge, 1985), 92–115.

Frost, R. I., 'The nobility of Poland–Lithuania, 1569–1795', in Scott (ed.), *European Nobilities*, ii, 266–310.

Frost, R. I., 'Scottish soldiers, Poland–Lithuania and the Thirty Years' War', in Murdoch (ed.), *Scotland and the Thirty Years' War*, 192–213.

Furgol, E. M., 'Scotland turned Sweden: the Scottish covenanters and the military revolution, 1638–1651', in Morrill (ed.), *Scottish National Covenant in its National Context*, 134–54.

Gardener, J. C., 'The origin and nature of the legal rights of spouses and children in the Scottish law of succession', *JR* 39 (1927), 209–16.

Giesey, R. E., 'Rules of inheritance and strategies of mobility in prerevolutionary France', *AHR* 82 (1977), 271–89.

Gillespie, N., 'Negotiating order in seventeenth-century Ireland', in Braddick and Walters (eds), *Negotiating Power*, 188–205.

Gillies, W., 'The invention of tradition, Highland style', in A. MacDonald, M. Lynch and I. Cowan (eds), *The Renaissance in Scotland* (Leiden, 1994), 82–95.

Gillies, W., 'The "British" genealogy of the Campbells', *Celtica* 23 (1999), 82–95.

Glozier, M., 'Scots in the French and Dutch armies during the Thirty Years' War', in Murdoch (ed.), *Scotland and the Thirty Years' War*, 117–41.

Gluckman, M., 'The peace in the feud', in M. Gluckman (ed.), *Custom and Conflict in Africa* (Oxford, 1963), 1–26.

Godfrey, A. M., 'The assumption of jurisdiction: parliament, the king's council and the college of justice in sixteenth-century Scotland', *Journal of Legal History* 22 (2001), 21–36.

Godfrey, A. M., 'Arbitration and dispute resolution in sixteenth-century Scotland', *Tijdschrift voor Rechtgerschiedenis* 70 (2002), 109–35.

Goodare, J., 'Queen Mary's Catholic interlude', in M. Lynch (ed.), *Mary Stewart. Queen in Three Kingdoms* (Oxford, 1988), 154–70.

Goodare, J., 'Parliamentary taxation in Scotland, 1560–1603', *SHR* 68 (1989), 23–52.

Goodare, J., 'The nobility and the absolutist state in Scotland, 1584–1638', *History* 78 (1993), 161–82.

Goodare, J., 'The Scottish parliament of 1621', *HJ* 38 (1995), 29–51.

Goodare, J., 'The estates in the Scottish Parliament', in Jones (ed.), *Scots and Parliament*, 11–32.

Goodare, J., 'The statutes of Iona in context', *SHR* 77 (1998), 31–57.

Goodare, J., 'Thomas Foulis and the Scottish fiscal crisis of the 1590s', in W. M. Ormrod, M. Bonney and R. Bonney (eds), *Crises, Revolutions and Self-Sustained Growth: Essays in European Fiscal History, 1130–1830* (Stamford, CA, 1999), 170–97.

Goodare, J., 'Scottish politics in the reign of James VI', in Goodare and Lynch (eds), *Reign of James VI*, 32–54.

Goodare, J., 'James VI's English subsidy', in Goodare and Lynch (eds), *Reign of James VI*, 110–25.

Goodare, J. and Lynch, M., 'James VI: a universal king?', in Goodare and Lynch (eds), *Reign of James VI*, 1–31.

Goodare, J. and Lynch, M., 'The Scottish state and its borderlands', in Goodare and Lynch (eds), *Reign of James VI*, 186–207.

Goodare, J., 'The admission of lairds to the Scottish parliament', *EHR* 116 (2001), 1101–33.

Goodare, J., 'The Scottish political community and the parliament of 1563', *Albion* 35 (2003), 373–97.

Goodare, J., 'Hamilton, Thomas, earl of Melrose and first earl of Haddington (1563–1637)', *ODNB*.

Goodare, J., 'The first parliament of Mary Queen of Scots', *SCJ* 36 (2005), 55–75.

Goodare, J., 'The attempted Scottish coup of 1596', in Goodare and MacDonald (eds), *Sixteenth Century Scotland*, 311–36.

Goodare, J., 'Parliament and politics', in Brown and MacDonald (eds), *Parliament in Context*, 244–74.

Goodman, A. E., 'The Anglo-Scottish marches in the fifteenth century: a frontier society', in Mason (ed.), *Scotland and England*, 18–33.

Graham, M. F., 'Conflict and sacred space in Reformation-era Scotland', *Albion* 33 (2001), 371–87.

Grant, A., 'The development of the Scottish peerage', *SHR* 57 (1997), 37–62.

Grant, A., 'Service and tenure in late medieval Scotland, 1314–1475', in A. Curry and E. Matthew (eds), *Concepts and Patterns of Service in the Later Middle Ages* (Woodbridge, 2000), 145–79.

Grant, A., 'Thanes and thanages from the eleventh to the fourteenth centuries', in A. Grant and K. Stringer (eds), *Medieval Scotland. Crown, Lordship and Community* (Edinburgh, 1993), 39–81.

Grant, R., 'The Brig o' Dee affair, the sixth earl of Huntlyand the politics of the Counter Reformation', in Goodare and Lynch (eds), *Reign of James VI*, 93–109.

Grant, R., 'The making of the Anglo-Scottish alliance of 1586', in Goodare and MacDonald (eds), *Sixteenth-Century Scotland*, 211–36.

Gray, D., 'The royal entry in sixteenth-century Scotland', in S. L. Mapstone and J. Wood (eds), *The Rose and the Thistle: Essays on the Culture of Late Medieval and Renaissance Scotland* (East Linton, 1998), 10–37.

Greengrass, M., 'Noble affinities in early modern France: the case of Henri I de Montmorency, constable of France', *European History Quarterly* 16 (1986), 275–311.

Grosjean, A., 'A century of Scottish governorship in the Swedish empire, 1574–1700', in Mackillop and Murdoch (eds), *Military Governors and Imperial Frontiers*, 53–78.

Grosjean, A., 'Scotland: Sweden's closest ally?', in Murdoch (ed.), *Scotland and the Thirty Years' War*, 143–71.

Gunn, S. J., 'Henry Bourchier, earl of Essex (1472–1540), in Bernard (ed.), *Tudor Nobility*, 134–79.

Haigh, C., 'The continuity of Catholicism in Elizabethan England', in Haigh (ed.), *The English Reformation Revised* (Cambridge, 1992), 176–208.

Hale, J. R., 'Sixteenth-century explanations of war and violence', *PP* 50 (1971), 3–26.

Hale, J. R., 'The military education of the officer class in early modern Europe', in C. H. Cough (ed.), *Cultural Aspects of the Italian Renaissance* (Manchester, 1976), 440–61.

Hanlon, G., 'Les rituals de l'aggression en Acquitaine au XVIIc siecle', *Annales* 40 (1985), 244–68.

Hanlon, G., 'Justice in the age of lordship: a feudal court in Tuscany during the Medici era', *SCJ* 35 (2004), 1005–33.

Hannay, R. K., 'The office of the justice clerk', *JR* 47 (1935), 311–29.

Harding, R., 'Corruption and the moral boundaries of patronage in the Renaissance', in G. F. Lytle and S. Orgel (eds), *Patronage in the Renaissance* (Princeton, NJ, 1981), 47–64.

Hareven, T. K., 'The history of the family and the complexity of social change', *AHR* 96 (1991), 95–124.

Heal, F., 'The idea of hospitality in early modern England', *PP* 102 (1984), 66–93.

Henneman, J. B., 'The military class and the French monarchy in the late middle ages', *AHR* 83 (1978), 946–65.

Heller, H., 'Putting history back into the religious wars: a reply to Mark P. Holt', *FHS* 19 (1996), 853–73.

Herlihy, D., 'The making of the medieval family: symmetry, structure and sentiment', *Journal of Family History* 8 (1983), 116–30

Herman, A. L., 'The language of fidelity in early modern France', *JMH* 67 (1995), 1–24.

Hernandez, A. I., '"Refeudalisation" in Castile during the seventeenth century: a cliche?', in I. A. A. Thompson and B. Y. Casalilla (eds), *The Castilian Crisis of the Seventeenth Century* (London, 1994), 249–76.

Hexter, J. H., 'Power struggle, parliament and liberty in early Stuart England', *JMH* (1978), 1–50.

Hicks, M., 'Cement or solvent? Kinship and politics in late medieval England: the case of the Nevilles', *History* 83 (1998), 31–46.

Hill, J. M. 'The rift within Clan Ian Mor: the Antrim and Dunyveg MacDonnells, 1590–1603', *SCJ* 24 (1993), 865–79.

Hindle, S., 'The keeping of the public peace', in P. Griffiths, A. Fox and S. Hindle (eds), *The Experience of Authority in Early Modern England* (Basingstoke, 1996), 213–48.

Holt, J. C., 'Feudal society and the family in early medieval England: III Patronage and politics', *TRHS* fifth ser., 34 (1984), 1–27.

Holt, M. P., 'Patterns of *clientelé* and economic opportunity at court during the wars of religion: the household of François duke of Anjou', *FHS* 13 (1984), 305–22.

Holt, M. P., 'Putting religion back into the Wars of Religion', *FHS* 18 (1993), 524–51.

Hoyle, R. W., 'Henry Percy, sixth earl of Northumberland and the fall of the house of Percy, 1527–1537', in Bernard (ed.), *Tudor Nobility*, 180–211.

Hoyle, R. W., 'Faction, feud and reconciliation amongs the Northern English nobility, 1525–1569', *History* 84 (1999), 590–613.

Hurstfield, J., 'Political corruption: the historian's problem', in J. Hurstfield (ed.), *Freedom, Corruption and Government in Elizabethan England* (London, 1973), 127–62.

Hurwich, J. J., 'Lineage and kin in the sixteenth-century aristocracy: some comparitive evidence on England and Germany', in A. L. Beir, D. Cannadine and J. M. Rosenheim (eds), *The First Modern Society. Essays in English History in Honour of Lawrence Stone* (Cambridge, 1989), 33–64.

Jago, C., 'The 'crisis of the aristocracy' in seventeenth-century Castile', *PP* 84 (1979), 60–90.

James, M. E., 'English politics and the concept of honour, 1485–1642', in James (ed.), *Society, Politics and Culture*, 308–415.

James, M. E., 'A Tudor magnate and the Tudor state: Henry fifth earl of Northumberland', in James (ed.), *Society, Politics and Culture*, 48–90.

James, M. E., Change and continuity in the Tudor north: Thomas first Lord Wharton', in James (ed), *Society, Politics and Culture*, 91–147.

James, M. E., 'The first earl of Cumberland (1493–1542) and the decline of northern feudalism', in James (ed.), *Society, Politics and Culture*, 148–75.

James, M. E., 'The concept of order and the Northern rising', in James (ed.), *Society, Politics and Culture*, 270–307.

James, M. E., 'At a crossroads of the political culture: the Essex revolt, 1601', in James (ed.), *Society, Politics and Culture*, 416–66.

Jespersen, K. J. V., 'The rise and fall of the Danish nobility, 1600–1800', in Scott (ed.), *European Nobilities*, ii, 43–73.

Juhala, A. L., 'An advantageous alliance: Edinburgh and the court of James VI', in Goodare and MacDonald (eds), *Sixteenth Century Scotland*, 337–63.

Kagan, R. L., 'A golden age of litigation: Castile, 1500–1700', in Bossy (ed.), *Disputes and Settlements*, 145–66.

Kalas, R. J., 'Marriage, clientage, office-holding and the advancement of the early modern French nobility – the Noailles family of Limousin', *SCJ* 27 (1996), 365–83.

Kaminski, A., 'The *szlachta* of the Polish–Lithuanian Commonwealth and their government', in Banac and Bushkovitch (eds), *Nobility in Russia and Eastern Europe*, 17–45.

Kaminsky, H., 'The noble feud in the later middle ages', *PP* 177 (2002), 55–83.

Kettering, S., 'Gift-giving and patronage in early modern France', *FH* 2 (1988), 131–51.

Kettering, S., 'Patronage and kinship in early modern France', *FHS* 16 (1989), 408–35.

Kettering, S., 'The decline of great noble clientage during the reign of Louis XIV', *Canadian Journal of History* 24 (1989), 157–77.

Kettering, S., 'Friendship and clientage in early modern France', *FH* 6 (1992), 139–58.

Kettering, S., 'Patronage in early modern France', *FHS* 17 (1992), 839–62.

Kiernan, V., 'Foreign mercenaries and absolute monarchy', *PP* 11 (1957), 66–86.

Kingdom, R. A., 'Calvinism and resistance theory, 1550–1580', in J. H. Burns and M. Goldie (eds), *The Cambridge History of Political Thought 1450–1700* (Cambridge, 1991), 193–218.

Kirk, J., 'Royal and lay patronage', in Macdougall (ed.), *Church, Politics and Society*, 127–50.

Klapisch-Zuber, C., 'The genesis of the family tree', *I Tatti Studies* 4 (1991), 105–29.

Klapisch-Zuber, C., 'Family trees and the construction of kinship in Renaissance Italy', in Maynes *et al.* (eds), *Gender, Kinship, Power*, 101–13.

Lachmann, R., 'Elite conflict and state formation in 16th and 17th century England and France', *American Sociological Review* 54 (1989), 141–62.

Lander, J. R., 'Attainder and forfeiture, 1453–1509', in J. R. Lander (ed.), *Crown and Nobility 1450–1509* (London, 1976), 127–58.

Lander, J. R., 'Family, "friends" and politics in fifteenth-century England', in R. A. Griffiths and J. Sherborne (eds), *Kings and Nobles in the Later Middle Ages* (Gloucester, 1986), 27–40.

Lee, M., 'James VI's government of Scotland after 1603', *SHR* 55 (1976), 41–53.

Lee, M., 'An unpublished letter of Thomas Hamilton, earl of Melrose', *SHR* 58 (1979), 175–8.

Lee, M., 'King James's popish chancellor', in Cowan and Shaw (eds), *Renaissance and Reformation*, 170–82.

Lee, M., 'The "inevitable' union"', in Lee (ed.), *'Inevitable' Union*, 1–24.

Lee, M., 'Sir Richard Maitland of Lethington: a Christian laird in the age of Reformation (1969)', in Lee (ed.), *'Inevitable' Union*, 25–39.

Lee, M., 'The fall of the regent Morton: a problem in satellite diplomacy', in Lee (ed.), *'Inevitable' Union*, 59–80.

Lee, M., 'James VI and the revival of episcopacy in Scotland, 1596–1600', in Lee (ed.), *'Inevitable' Union*, 81–98.

Lee, M., 'The Gowrie conspiracy revisited', in Lee (ed.), *'Inevitable' Union*, 99–115.

Lee, M. (ed.), 'Charles I and the end of conciliar government in Scotland (1980)', in Lee (ed.), *'Inevitable' Union*, 169–88.

Lee, M., 'Seton, Alexander, first earl of Dunfermline (1556–1622)', *ODNB*.

Lee, M., 'Hume, George, earl of Dunbar (d. 1611)', *ODNB*.

Levack, B. P., 'Law, sovereignty and the union', in Mason (ed.), *Scots and Britons*, 213–37.

Loyn, H. R., 'Kinship in Anglo-Saxon England', *Anglo-Saxon England* 3 (1974), 197–209.

Lyall, R., 'Kinship, kingship and Latiny', in Goodare and MacDonald (eds), *Sixteenth-Century Scotland*, 237–55.

Lynch, M., 'Calvinism in Scotland, 1559–1638', in M. Prestwich (ed.), *International Calvinism 1541–1715* (Oxford, 1985), 225–55.

Lynch, M., 'Introduction', in Lynch (ed.), *Early Modern Town*, 1–35.

Lynch, M., 'The crown and the burghs', in Lynch (ed.), *Early Modern Town*, 55–80.

Lynch, M., 'Queen Mary's triumph: the baptismal celebrations at Stirling in December 1566', *SHR* 66 (1990), 1–21.

Lynch, M., 'A nation born again? Scottish identity in the sixteenth and seventeenth centuries', in D. Broun, R. J. Finlay and M. Lynch (eds), *Image and Identity. The Making and Re-Making of Scotland Through the Ages* (Edinburgh, 1998), 82–104.

Lynch, M., 'Court ceremonial and ritual during the personal reign of James VI', in Goodare and Lynch (eds), *Reign of James VI*, 71–92.

Lynch, M., 'James VI and the highland problem', in Goodare and Lynch (eds), *Reign of James VI*, 208–27.

MacCoinnich, A., '"His spirit was given only to warre": conflict and identity in the Scottish Gaidhealtachd c. 1580–c. 1630', in Murdoch and Mackillop (eds), *Fighting for Identity*, 133–61.

MacDonald, A. A., 'Mary Stewart's entry to Edinburgh: an ambiguous triumph', *IR* 43 (1991), 101–10.

MacDonald, A. J., 'Profits, politics and personality: war and the later medieval Scottish nobility', in D. Ditchburn and T. Brotherstone (eds), *Freedom and Authority: Scotland c. 1050–c. 1650; Historical and Historiographical Essays Presented to Grant G. Simpson* (East Linton, 2000), 118–30.

MacDonald, A. R, 'The subscription crisis and church and state relations, 1584–1586', *RSCHS* 25 (1994), 222–55.

MacDonald, A. R., 'Ecclesiastical representation in parliament in post-Reformation Scotland: the two kingdom theory in practice', *JEH* 50 (1999), 38–61.

MacDonald, A. R., 'James VI and the general assembly, 1586–1618', in Goodare and Lynch (eds), *Reign of James VI*, 170–85.

MacDonald, A. R., 'Deliberative processes in the Scottish parliament before 1639: multi-cameralism and the lords of the articles', *SHR* 89 (2002), 23–51.

MacDonald, A. R., 'The parliament of 1592: a crisis averted?', in Brown and Mann (eds), *Parliament and Politics in Scotland 1567–1707*, 57–81.

MacDonald, A. R., 'Lindsay, John, of Balcarres, Lord Menmuir (1552–1598)', *ODNB*.

MacDonald, A. R., 'James VI and I, the church of Scotland, and British ecclesiastical convergence', *HJ* 48 (2005), 885–903.

MacDonald, A. R., 'The third estate: parliament and the burghs', in Brown and MacDonald (eds), *Parliament in Context*, 95–121.

Macdougall, N., '"It is I, the earle of Mar": in search of Thomas Cochrane', in Mason and Macdougall (eds), *People and Power*, 28–49.

Macgregor, M., 'The genealogical histories of Gaelic Scotland', in A. Fox and D. Woolf (eds), *The Spoken Word: Oral Culture in Britain 1500–1850* (Manchester, 2002), 196–239.

MacHardy, K. J., 'Cultural capital, family strategies and noble identity in early modern Habsburg Austria, 1579–1620', *PP* 163 (1999), 36–76.

Macinnes, A. I., 'Catholic recusancy and the penal laws, 1603–1707', *RSCHS* 23 (1987), 27–63.

Macinnes, A. I., 'Crown, clans and *fine*: the "civilising" of Scottish Gaeldom, 1587–1638', *NS* 13 (1993), 31–55.

MacKay, P. H. R., 'The reception given to the five articles of Perth', *RSCHS* 19 (1975–7), 185–201.

Maclagan, M., 'Genealogy and heraldry in the sixteenth and seventeenth centuries', in Fox (ed.), *English Historical Scholarship*, 31–48.

MacQueen, H., 'The kin of Kennedy, "kenkynd" and the common law', in A. Grant and K. J. Stringer (eds), *Medieval Scotland. Crown, Lordship and Community* (Edinburgh, 1993), 274–96.

Magregor, M., 'Civilising Gaelic Scotland: the Scottish isles and the Stewart empire', in M. O. Siochru and E. O. Ciardha (eds), *The Plantation of Ulster, 1609–2009: a Laboratory for Empire?* (Manchester, forthcoming).

Major, J. R., 'The crown and the aristocracy in Renaissance France', *AHR* 69 (1963–4), 631–45.

Major, J. R., 'The revolt of 1620: a study of ties of fidelity', *FHS* 14 (1986), 391–408.

Major, J. R., 'The loss of the royal initiative and the decay of the estates general in France, 1421–1615', in J. R. Major (ed.), *The Monarchy, the Estates and the Aristocracy in Renaissance France* (London, 1988), VIII.

Major, J. R., 'Vertical ties through time', *FHS* 17 (1992), 863–71.

Manning, B., 'The aristocracy and the downfall of Charles I', in B. Manning (ed.), *Politics, Religion and the English Civil War* (London, 1973), 37–82.

Mason, R. A., '*Rex stoicus*. George Buchanan, James VI and the Scottish polity', in Dwyer, Mason and Murdoch (eds), *New Perspectives*, 9–33.

Mason, R. A., 'Covenant and commonweal: the language of politics in Reformation Scotland', in Macdougall (ed.), *Church, Politics and Society*, 97–126.

Mason, R. A., 'Kingship, tyranny and the right to resist in fifteenth-century Scotland', *SHR*, 66 (1987), 125–51.

Mason, R. A., 'Chivalry and citizenship: aspects of national identity in Renaissance Scotland', in Mason and Macdougall (eds), *People and Power*, 50–73.

Mason, R. A., 'Kingship, nobility and Anglo-Scottish union: John Mair's *History of Greater Britain* (1521)', *IR* 41 (1992), 182–222.

Mason, R. A., 'George Buchanan, James VI and the presbyterians', in Mason (ed.), *Scots and Britons*, 112–37.

Mason, R. A., 'Knox, resistance and the royal supremacy', in Mason (ed.), *John Knox and the British Reformations*, 154–75.

Mason, R. A., 'People power? George Buchanan on resistance and the common man', in R. von Friedberg (ed.), *Widerstandsrecht in der Fruhen Neuzeit … Forschung im Deutschritischen Vergleich, 1488–1688* (Berlin, 2001), 163–81.

McAlister, K. and R. J. Tanner, 'The first estate: parliament and the church', in Brown and MacDonald (eds), *Parliament in Context*, 31–66.

McCoog, T. M., '"Pray to the lord of the harvest": Jesuit missions to Scotland in the sixteenth century', *IR* 53 (2002), 127–88.

McCoy, R., 'Old English honour in an evil time: aristocratic principle in the 1620s', in R. M. Smuts (ed.), *The Stuart Court and Europe. Essays in Politics and Political Culture* (Cambridge, 1996), 133–55.

McIvor, I., 'Artillery and major places of strength in the Lothians and the east Border', in Caldwell (ed.), *Scottish Weapons and Fortifications*, 94–152.

McKean, C., 'Sir James Hamilton of Finnart: a renaissance courtier-architect', *Architectural History* 42 (1999), 141–72.

McLean, W. K., 'The Maclean–MacDonald feud: disputed landholding in Islay in the sixteenth century', *Transactions of the Gaelic Society of Inverness* 56 (1991), 223–43.

McMahon, G. I. R., 'The Scottish courts of high commission, 1610–38', *RSCHS* 15 (1965), 193–209.

McNeill, P. G. B., 'The independence of the Scottish judiciary', *JR* NS 3 (1958), 134–47.

McNeill, W. A. and P. G. B. McNeill, 'The Scottish royal progress of James VI, 1617', *SHR* 75 (1996), 38–51.

Mears, N., 'Courts, courtiers and culture in Tudor England', *Historical Journal* 46 (2003), 703–22.

Meikle, M. M., 'The invisible divide: the greater lairds and the nobility of Jacobean Scotland', *SHR* 71 (1992), 70–87.

Meikle, M. M., 'A meddlesome princess: Anna of Denmark and Scottish court politics, 1589–1603', in Goodare and Lynch (eds), *Reign of James VI*, 126–40.

Meikle, M. M., 'Anna of Denmark's coronation and entry into Edinburgh, 1590: cultural, religious and diplomatic perspectives', in Goodare and MacDonald (eds), *Sixteenth-Century Scotland*, 277–94.

Melton, E., 'The Junkers of Brandenburg-Prussia, 1600–1806', in Scott (ed.), *European Nobilities*, ii, 118–70.

Mettam, R., 'The French nobility, 1610–1715', in Scott (ed.), *European Nobilities*, i, 127–55.

Mitson, A., 'The significance of kinship networks in the seventeenth century: south-west Nottinghamshire', in C. Phythian-Adams (ed.), *Societies, Cultures and Kinship 1580–1850. Cultural Provinces and English Local History* (Leicester, 1993), 24–76.

Molho, A., R. Barduccie, G. Battista and F. Donnini, 'Genealogy and marriage alliance: memories of power in late medieval Florence', in S. K. Cohn and S. A. Epstein (eds), *Portraits of Medieval and Renaissance Living: Essays in Memory of David Herlihy* (Ann Arbor, MI, 1996), 39–70.

Moore, J. S., 'The Anglo-Norman family: size and structure', *Anglo-Norman Studies* 14 (1991), 153–96.

Muldrew, C., 'The culture of reconciliation: community and the settlement of economic disputes in early modern England', *Historical Journal* 39 (1996), 915–42.

Munro, R. W., 'The clan system – fact or fiction?', in L. MacLean (ed.), *The Middle Ages in the Highlands* (Inverness Field Club, 1989), 117–29.

Murdoch, S., 'The house of Stuart and the Scottish professional soldier 1613–1640: a conflict of nationality and identities', in B. Taithe and T. Thornton (eds), *War and Identities in Conflict 1300–1640* (Stroud, 1998), 37–56.

Murdoch, S., 'Diplomacy in transition. Stuart-British diplomacy in northern Europe, 1603–1618', in Macinnes, Riis and Pederson (eds), *Ships, Guns and Bibles*, 93–114.

Murdoch, S., 'Scotsmen on the Danish–Norwegian frontiers', in Mackillop and Murdoch (eds), *Military Governors and Imperial Frontiers*, 1–28.

Murdoch, S., 'James VI and the formation of a Scottish–British military identity', in Murdoch and Mackillop (eds), *Fighting for Identity*, 1–31.

Murdoch, S., 'Introduction', in Murdoch (ed.), *Scotland and the Thirty Years' War*, 1–20.

Murdoch, S., 'Scottish ambassadors and British diplomacy 1618–1635', in Murdoch (ed.), *Scotland and the Thirty Years' War*, 27–50.

Murdoch, S. and A. Mackillop (eds), 'Introduction. Military identity and multiple identities', in Murdoch and Mackillop (eds), *Fighting for Identity*, xxiii–xliii.

Murray, A. L., 'Sir John Skene and the exchequer, 1596–1612', *StS Miscellany* (1971), i, 125–55.

Murray, A. L., 'The lord clerk register', *SHR* 53 (1974), 124–56.

Murray, A. L., 'Huntly's rebellion and the administration of justice in north-east Scotland 1570–1573', *NS* 4 (1981), 1–6.

Nassiet, M., 'Vengeance in sixteenth- and seventeenth-century France', in Carroll (ed.), *Cultures of Violence*, 117–28.

Netterstrom, J. P., 'Introduction', in Netterstrom and Poulsen (eds), *Feud in Medieval and Early Modern Europe*, 9–68.

Netterstrom, J. P. 'The study of feud in medieval and early modern history', in Netterstrom and Poulsen (eds), *Feud in Medieval and Early Modern Europe*, 9–68.

Neuschel, K., 'Noble households in the sixteenth century: material and human communities', *FHS* 15 (1988), 595–622.

Nicholls, M., 'Treason's reward: the punishment of conspirators in the Bye plot of 1603', *HJ* 38 (1995), 821–42.

Nolan, J. S., 'The militarization of the Elizabethan state', *Journal of Military History* 58 (1994), 391–420.

Noonskester, M. C., 'Dissolution of the monasteries and the decline of the sheriff', *SCJ* 23 (1992), 677–98.

Parker, G., 'The military revolution, 1560–1660 – a myth?', *JMH* 47 (1976), 195–214.

Parker, G., 'In defence of the military revolution', in Roger (ed.), *Military Revolution Debate*, 337–66.

Patterson, N. W., 'Parilineal kinship in early Irish society: the evidence from the Irish law texts', *Bulletin of the Board of Celtic Studies* 37 (1990), 133–65.

Peck, L. L., '"For a king not to be bountifull were a fault": perspectives on court patronage in early Stuart England', *JBS* 25 (1986), 31–61.

Phillips, G., 'The army of Henry VIII: a reassessment', *Journal of the Society for Army Historical Research* 75 (1997), 8–22.

Phillips, G., '"Of nimble service": technology, equestrianism and the cavalry of early modern European armies', *War and Society* 20 (2002), 1–21.

Pittock, M., 'From Edinburgh to London. Scottish court writing and 1603', in Cruickshanks (ed.), *Stuart Courts*, 13–28.

Polisensky, J. V., 'A note on Scottish soldiers in the Bohemian war 1619–1622', in Murdoch (ed.), *Scotland and the Thirty Years' War*, 109–15.

Pomata, G., 'Blood ties and semen ties: consanguinity and agnation in Roman law', in Maynes et al. (eds), *Gender, Kinship, Power*, 43–64.

Potter, D., 'The international mercenary market in the sixteenth century: Anglo–French competition in Germany, 1540–50', *WHR* 111 (1996), 24–58.

Powell, E., 'Arbitration and the law in England in the late middle ages', *TRHS* 23 (1982), 49–67.

Prest, W. R., 'Judicial corruption in early modern England', *Past and Present* 133 (1991), 67–95.

Rae, T. I., 'The political attitudes of William Drummond of Hawthornden', in G. W. S. Barrow (ed.), *The Scottish Tradition. Essays in Honour of Ronald Cant* (Edinburgh, 1974), 132–46.

Rae, T. I., 'The historical writing of Drummond of Hawthornden', *SHR* 54 (1975), 22–62.

Rait, R. S., 'Parliamentary representation in Scotland: V the lords of the articles', *SHR* 13 (1915), 68–83.

Ranum, O., 'Courtesy, absolutism, and the rise of the French state', *JMH* 52 (1980), 426–51.

Rawcliffe, C., 'Baronial councils in the later middle ages', in C. D. Ross (ed.), *Patronage, Pedigree and Power in Later Medieval England* (Gloucester, 1979), 87–108.

Rawcliffe, C., 'The great lord as peacekeeper: arbitration by English noblemen and their councils in the later middle ages', in J. A. Guy and H. G. Beale (eds), *Law and Social Change in British History* (Royal Historical Society, 1984), 34–54.

Reid, D., 'Hume of Godscroft's "The origine and descent of the most noble and Illustre familie and name of Douglas" as humanist historiography', *SLJ* 22 (1995), 35–45.

Reid, W. S., 'The earls of Argyll and the Reformation', *Scottish Tradition* 17 (1992), 1–50.

Reiss, T. J., 'The idea of meaning and practice of method in Peter Ramus, Henri Estienne, and others', in P. Desan (ed.), *Humanism in Crisis. The Decline of the French Renaissance* (Ann Arbor, MI, 1991), 125–51.

Rentet, T., 'Network mapping: ties of fidelity and dependency among the major domestic officers of Anne de Montmorency', *FR* 17 (2003), 109–206.

Reuter, T., 'The medieval nobility in twentieth-century historiography', in M. Bentley (ed.), *Companion to Historiography* (London, 1997), 177–202.

Ritchie, P. E., 'Marie de Guise and the three estates, 1554–1558', in Brown and Tanner (eds), *Parliament and Politics in Scotland 1235–1560*, 179–202.

Roberts, A., 'Popery in Buchan and Strathbogie in the early seventeenth century', *RSCHS* 27 (1997), 127–55.

Roberts, M., 'The military revolution, 1560–1660', in M. Roberts (ed.), *Essays in Swedish History* (London, 1967), 195–225.

Rodriguez-Salgado, M. J., 'The court of Philip II of Spain', in Asch and Birke (eds), *Princes, Patronage and the Nobility*, 205–44.

Rogister, J., 'Some new directions in the historiography of state assemblies and parliaments in early and late modern Europe', *PER* 16 (1996), 1–16.

Rowney, I., 'Arbitration in gentry disputes of the later middle ages', *History* 67 (1982), 367–76.

Roy, I., 'The profession of arms', in W. Prest (ed.), *The Professions in Early Modern England* (London, 1987), 181–219.

Ruff, J., 'Rural feuds and the control of conflict in the Guyenne, 1696–1789', *Proceedings of the Western Society for French History* 14 (1987).

Sabean, D., 'Aspects of kinship behaviour and property in rural western Europe before 1800', in Goody, Thirsk and Thomson (eds), *Family and Inheritance*, 96–111.

Samson, R., 'The rise and fall of tower houses in post-Reformation Scotland', in R. Samson (ed.), *The Social Archaeology of Houses* (Edinburgh, 1990), 197–243.

Samson, R., 'Tower houses in the sixteenth century', in S. Foster, A. Macinnes and R. MacInnes (eds), *Scottish Power Centres from the Early Middle Ages to the Twentieth Century* (Glasgow, 1998), 132–46.

Sanderson, M. H. B., 'Catholic recusancy in Scotland in the sixteenth century', *IR* 31 (1970), 87–107.

Scally, J., 'Constitutional revolution, party and faction in the Scottish parliament of Charles I', in Jones (ed.), *Scots and Parliament*, 54–73.

Scally, J., 'Hamilton, James, first duke of Hamilton (1606–1649)', *ODNB*.

Schalk, E., 'The court as "civilizer" of the nobility: noble attitudes and the court of France in the late sixteenth and early seventeenth centuries', in Asch and Birke (eds), *Princes, Patronage and the Nobility*, 245–64.

Scott, H. M., '"Acts of time and power": the consolidation of aristocracy in seventeenth-century Europe, c. 1580–1720', *Bulletin of the German Historical Institute London* 30 (2008), 3–37.

Scott, H. M., 'The early modern European nobility and its contested historiographies, c. 1950–1980', in C. Lipp and M. Romaniello (eds), *New Essays on the Early Modern Nobility* (forthcoming).

Scott, H. M. and C. Storrs, 'The consolidation of noble power in Europe, c. 1600–1800', in Scott (ed.), *European Nobilities*, i, 1–60.

Seddon, P. R., 'Robert Carr, earl of Somerset', *Renaissance and Modern Studies* 14 (1970), 48–68.

Sellar, D., 'The origin and ancestry of Somerled', *SHR* 45 (1966), 123–42

Sellar, D., 'The earliest Campbells: Norman Britons or Gael?', *Scottish Studies* 17 (1973), 109–25.

Sharpe, J. A., 'Domestic homicide in early modern England', in *HJ* 24 (1981), 29–48.

Sharpe, J. A., '"Such disagreement betwyx neighbours": litigation and human relations in early modern England', in Bossy (ed.), *Disputes and Settlements*, 167–87.

Sharpe, J. A., '"Last dying speeches": religion, ideology and public execution in seventeenth-century England', *PP* 107 (1985), 144–67.

Sharpe, K., 'The image of virtue: the court and household of Charles I, 1625–1642', in Starkey (ed.), *English Court*, 226–60.

Shearman, F., 'The Spanish blanks', *IR* 3 (1952), 81–103.

Simpson, G. G., 'The personal letters of James VI: a short commentary', in Goodare and Lynch (eds), *Reign of James VI*, 141–53.

Slade, H. G., 'The Gordons and the north-east, 1452–1640', in Oram and Stell (eds), *Lordship and Architecture*, 251–72.

Smart, I. M., 'Monarchy and toleration in Drummond of Hawthornden's works', *Scotia* 4 (1980), 44–50.

Smith, L. B., 'English treason trials and confessions in the sixteenth century', *JHI* 15 (1954), 471–98.

Spiegel, G. M., 'Genealogy: form and function in medieval historical narrative', *History and Theory* 22 (1983), 43–53.

Starkey, D., 'Court, council and nobility in Tudor England', in Asch and Birke (eds), *Princes, Patronage and the Nobility*, 175–204.

Stearns, S. J., 'Conscription and English society in the 1620s', *JBS* 11 (1972), 1–23.

Stevenson, D., 'Conventicles in the kirk, 1619–37: the emergence of a radical party', *RSCHS* 18 (1972–4), 99–114.

Stevenson, D., 'The "Letter on sovereign power" and the influence of Jean Bodin on political thought in Scotland', *SHR* 61 (1982), 25–43.

Stevenson, D., 'The burghs and the Scottish revolution', in Lynch (ed.), *Early Modern Scottish Town*, 167–91.

Stevenson, D., 'The English devil of keeping state: elite manners and the downfall of Charles I in Scotland', in Mason and Macdougall (eds), *People and Power*, 126–44.

Stevenson, D., 'Hope, Sir Thomas, of Craighall, first baronet (1573–1646)', *ODNB*.

Stewart, L. A. M., '"Brothers in truth": propaganda, public opinion and the Perth articles debate in Scotland', in R. Houlbrooke (ed.), *James VI and I: Ideas, Authority and Government* (Aldershot, 2006), 151–68.

Stone, L., 'Homicide and violence', in L. Stone (ed.), *the Past and the Present Revisited* (New York, 1987), 295–310.

Storrs, C. and H. M. Scott, 'The military revolution and the European nobility, *c.* 1600–1800', *War and History* 3 (1996), 1–41.

Tanner, R. J., '"I arrest you sir, in the name of the three estaittes in parliament": the Scottish parliament and resistance to the crown in the fifteenth century', in T. Thornton (ed.), *Social Attitudes and Political Structures in the Fifteenth Century* (Stroud, 2000), 101–17.

Tanner, R. J., 'The lords of the articles before 1540: a reassessment', *SHR* 79 (2000), 189–212.

Thompson, I. A. A., 'Crown and *cortes* in Castile, 1590–1665', *PER* 2 (1982), 29–45.

Thompson, I. A. A., 'The nobility in Spain, 1600–1800', in Scott (ed.), *European Nobilities*, i, 191–255.

Trevor-Roper, H., 'George Buchanan and the ancient Scottish constitution', *EHR* Supplement 3 (1966).

Trim, D. J. B., 'Introduction', in Trim (ed.), *Chivalric Ethos*, 1–38.

Trim, D. J. B., 'Army, society and the development of military professionalism in the Netherlands during the eighty years' war', in Trim (ed.), *Chivalric Ethos*, 269–89.

Trim, D. J. B., 'Calvinist internationalism and the English officer corps, 1562–1642', *History Compass* 4 (2006), 1024–48.

Tucker, T. J., 'Eminence over efficacy: social status and cavalry service in sixteenth-century France', *SCJ* 32 (2001), 1057–95.

Upton, A. F., 'The Swedish nobility, 1600–1772', in Scott (ed.), *European Nobilities*, ii, 13–42.

Volckart, O., 'The economics of feuding in late medieval Germany', *Explorations in Economic History* 41 (2004), 282–99.

Verschur, M., 'Merchants and craftsmen in sixteenth-century Perth', in Lynch (ed.), *Early Modern Town*, 36–54.

Ward, J. C., 'Noblewomen, family and identity in later medieval Europe', in Duggan (ed.), *Nobles and Nobility*, 245–62.

Warwicke, R. M., 'Family and kinship relations at the Henrician court: the Bolyns and Howards', in D. Hoak (ed.), *Tudor Political Culture* (Cambridge, 1995), 31–53.

Weary, W. A., 'The house of la Tremouille, fifteenth through eighteenth centuries: change and adaptation in a French noble family', *JMH* 49 (1977), 1001–38.

Weisser, M., 'Crime and punishment in early modern Spain', in Gatrell, Lenman and Parker (eds), *Crime and the Law*, 76–96.

Wells, V. T., 'Constitutional conflict after the union of the crowns: contention and continuity in the parliaments of 1612 and 1621', in Brown and Mann (eds), *Parliament and Politics 1567–1707*, 82–100.

Wells, V. T., 'Leslie, John, sixth earl of Rothes (c. 1600–1641)', *ODNB*.

White, A., 'Queen Mary's northern province', in Lynch (ed.), *Mary Stewart*, 53–70.

White, A., 'The Menzies era: sixteenth-century politics', in E. P. Denistoun *et al.* (eds), *Aberdeen before 1800: a New History* (East Linton, 2002), 224–37.

White, S., 'Feuding and peace-making in the Tourraine around the year 1000', *Traditio* 42 (1986), 195–263.

Williams, P., 'The Welsh borderland under Queen Elizabeth', *Welsh Historical Review* 1 (1960), 19–36.

Williamson, A. H., A patriot nobility?', *SHR* 72 (1993), 1–21.

Williamson, A., 'Foreward. The problematics of patriotism: conflict, identity and British mission', in Murdoch and Mackillop (eds), *Fighting for Identity*, xiii–xx.

Wolfe, M., 'Piety and political allegiance: the duc de Nevers and the protestant Henry IV, 1589–93', *FH* 2 (1988), 1–21.

Wood, J. B., 'The decline of the nobility in sixteenth- and early seventeenth-century France: myth or reality?', *JMH* 38 (1976), 1–29.

Wormald, J. M., 'Bloodfeud, kindred and government in early modern Scotland', *PP* 87 (1980), 54–97.

Wormald, J. M., '"Princes" and the regions in the Scottish Reformation', in Macdougall (ed.), *Church, Politics and Society*, 65–84.

Wormald, J., 'Gunpowder, treason and Scots', *JBS* 24 (1985), 141–65.

Wormald, J., 'The happier marriage partner: the impact of the union of the crowns on Scotland', in G. Burgess (ed.), *The Accession of James I. Historical and Cultural Consequences* (Basingstoke, 2006), 69–87.

Worthington, D., 'Alternative diplomacy? Scottish exiles at the court of the Habsburgs and their allies, 1618–1648', in Murdoch (ed.), *Scotland and the Thirty Years' War*, 51–75.

Wright, A. D., 'Venetian law and order: a myth?', *BIHR* 53 (1980), 192–202.

Yellowlees, M. J., 'Father William Crichton's estimate of the Scottish nobility, 1595', in Goodare and MacDonald (eds), *Sixteenth-Century Scotland*, 295–310.

Young, J. R., 'The Scottish parliament in the seventeenth century: European perspectives', in Macinnes, Riis and Pederson (eds), *Ships, Guns and Bibles*, 139–72.

Young, J. R., 'Charles I and the 1633 parliament', in Brown and Mann (eds), *Parliament and Politics 1567–1707*, 101–37.

Zmora, H., 'Princely state-making and the "crisis of the aristocracy" in late medieval Germany', *PP* 153 (1996), 37–63.

Zulager, R. R., 'Bruce, Edward, first Lord Kinloss and first Baron Bruce of Kinloss (1548/9–1611)', *ODNB*.

Zulager, R. R., 'Elphinstone, James, first Lord Balmerino (1557–1612)', *ODNB*.

(v) Unpublished Theses

Boardman, S. I., 'Politics and the feud in late medieval Scotland', Ph.D., University of St Andrews, 1989.

Cuddy, N., 'The king's chambers. The bedchamber of James I in administration and politics 1603–1625', D.Phil., University of Oxford, 1987.

Juhala, A. L., 'The household and court of king James VI of Scotland', Ph.D., University of Edinburgh, 2000.

Macpherson, R., 'Francis Stewart, 5th earl of Bothwell, c. 1562–1612: Lordship and politics in Jacobean Scotland', Ph.D., University of Edinburgh, 1999.

Muir, A. G., 'The Covenanters in Fife, c. 1610–1689: religious dissent in the local community', Ph.D., University of St Andrews, 2001.

Pearce, A. S. W., 'John Spottiswoode, Jacobean administrator and statesman', Ph.D., University of Stirling, 1998.

Rule, J. S., 'The Anglo-Scottish western borders, 1557–1573', D.Phil., University of Oxford, 2001.

Scally, J., 'The political career of James, Third Marquis and First Duke of Hamilton (1606–1649) to 1643', Ph.D., University of Cambridge, 1992.

Seddon, P. R., 'Patronage and officers in the reign of James I', Ph.D., University of Manchester, 1967.

Wells, V. T., 'The origins of covenanting thought and resistance c. 1580–1638', Ph.D., University of Stirling, 1998.

Zulager, R. R., 'A study of the middle-rank administrators in the government of King James VI of Scotland, 1580–1603', Ph.D., University of Aberdeen, 1991.

Index